EVOLUTIONARY ECONOMICS

Volume I   FOUNDATIONS OF
INSTITUTIONAL THOUGHT

EVOLUTIONARY ECONOMICS

Volume I FOUNDATIONS OF INSTITUTIONAL THOUGHT

Edited by Marc R. Tool

M. E. SHARPE, INC.
ARMONK, NEW YORK
LONDON, ENGLAND

Published in the United States by M. E. Sharpe, Inc., 80 Business Park Drive, Armonk, New York 10504

Available in the United Kingdom and Europe from M. E. Sharpe, Publishers, 3 Henrietta Street, London WC2E 8LU.

Library of Congress Cataloging-in-Publication Data

Evolutionary economics.

   Essays originally published in the Sept. and Dec. 1987 issues of the Journal of economic issues.

   Bibliography: p.
   1. Institutional economics. I. Tool, Marc R. II. Association for Evolutionary Economics.
HB99.5.E96   1988   330   88-4502
ISBN 0-87332-483-8 (set)
ISBN 0-87332-481-1 (v. 1)
ISBN 0-87332-482-X (v. 2)

Printed in the United States of America

Dedicated to Recipients
of the Veblen-Commons Award
presented annually by the
Association for Evolutionary Economics

CONTENTS

EVOLUTIONARY ECONOMICS I: FOUNDATIONS OF INSTITUTIONAL THOUGHT

| Introduction | MARC R. TOOL | 1 |

Part I

| The Beginnings of Institutionalism | ANNE MAYHEW | 21 |

Part II

The Philosophical Basis of Institutional Economics	PHILIP MIROWSKI	51
The Theory of Human Nature	HANS E. JENSEN	89
Theory of Institutional Change	PAUL D. BUSH	125
Instrumental Valuation	STEVEN R. HICKERSON	167

Part III

The Concept of Technology Within the Institutionalist Perspective	MILTON D. LOWER	197
Institutions	WALTER C. NEALE	227
Human Resource Development and the Formulation of National Economic Policy	VERNON M. BRIGGS JR.	257
Resources Are Not; They Become: an Institutional Theory	THOMAS R. DEGREGORI	291
The Institutionalist Theory of Capital Formation	BALDWIN RANSON	315
Evolution of Time Constructs and Their Impact on Socioeconomic Planning	F. GREGORY HAYDEN	329

Information: An Emerging Dimension
 of Institutional Analysis WILLIAM H. MELODY 361

Power and Economic Performance:
 The Institutionalist View PHILIP A. KLEIN 389

The Neoinstrumental Theory
 of Democracy RICK TILMAN 427

About the Authors 451

INTRODUCTION

This collection of solicited papers is the first of a two-volume work bearing the general title of *Evolutionary Economics*. Volume I is addressed to the *Foundations of Institutional Thought* in essays that identify the origins of insitutional analysis, set forth the social philosophy undergirding institutional economics, and explore fundamental constructs that are primary tools of inquiry in the development of institutional analysis. Volume II extends the presentation through consideration of *Institutional Theory and Policy*. It will include papers on basic economic processes, aggregate stabilizing and planning institutions and operations, institutional power and accountability, and institutions and global interdependence. These two volumes are intended to provide a comprehensive, contemporary formulation of institutional political economy as a viable alternative perspective to the prevailing neoclassical orthodoxy.

The Needed Shift in Perspective

Mark Blaug has said that "it takes a new theory, and not just the destructive exposure of assumptions or the collection of new facts, to beat an old theory." [Blaug 1978, p. 713] And Clarence Ayres once observed that "whatever the defects of the classical design, it remains the only overall design we have, and will remain until another conception of the meaning of the economy has taken form" [Ayres 1944, p. 21]. The contributors to these volumes demonstrate that "another conception of the meaning of the economy" is now within reach; it is a demonstration to which Ayres himself contributed significantly. These two volumes on *Evolutionary Economics* are, in combination, an extended effort to show how and why the institutionalist approach is essentially different from the orthodox neoclassical approach.

1

Some perceive change in fundamental perspective as an incremental and evolutionary development. Others see such change as a matter of extensive and explosive shifts after a long period of comparative quiescence. Fortunately, we are not compelled here to choose between these two perceptions. It is enough to observe that modes of inquiry do change and that whether or not they continue is a consequence ultimately of overt discretionary actions, reflecting an emerging and cumulative sense of their relevance and worth. Whether such changes occur with glacial slowness or are pressed with revolutionary fervor is, however, of special interest to institutionalists. Indeed, in any period, those not persuaded by the dominant view will ask "what is required to effect a change?" The institutionalists' answer is to help erode the hegemony of orthodoxy and to assist with a comprehensive shift to a more productive and pertinent mode of inquiry in political economy.

Even so, the *primary* focus of these two volumes is *not* the development of yet another pervasive critique of orthodoxy, an attack on "the old theory." In these essays the main concern is the positive formulation of the institutionalist alternative. Authors of these essays pursue appraisals of the neoclassical positions only where it is essential, through comparing and contrasting, to present and clarify the institutionalist view. And in so doing they challenge the dominion of orthodoxy and its exclusive claims to superior analysis and policy relevance.

The Genesis of These Papers

Discussions among institutionalists over the last three years, in correspondence and at conferences, have increasingly converged on a recognition that a more comprehensive treatment of the basic institutional approach to inquiry in political economy would be a valuable addition to the institutionalist literature. Where, for example, do you send a colleague or graduate student who stumbles over an orthodox anomaly or by chance or design is intrigued by a reading of Thorstein Veblen, Clarence Ayres, or William Kapp, and wishes access to a general presentation of the institutionalist approach? Where may one look for a comprehensive statement of the institutionalist alternative to methodological individualism or dialectical materialism? These two volumes offer that statement. Moreover, institutionalist scholars who are often widely dispersed geographically, who work in academic environments that are sometimes non-supportive, who pursue their specialized inquiry in comparative isolation, have also expressed the need for a more comprehensive work in institutional thought that provides a cogent underpinning for their own work. We intend this collection to provide that underpinning.

At meetings of the Association for Institutional Thought, in San Diego in 1984, the editor, in response to these conversations and concerns, convened and chaired an ad hoc Advisory Committee on this project. Its members were Paul Dale Bush (California State University, Fresno), David B. Hamilton (University of New Mexico), F. Gregory Hayden, (University of Nebraska, Lincoln), Philip A. Klein (Pennsylvania State University), Anne Mayhew and Walter C. Neale (University of Tennessee), and Harry H. Trebing (Michigan State University). The Committee's task was to explore the feasibility of designing a framework and soliciting papers for a comprehensive symposium on evolutionary economics as it is currently perceived by institutional economists. Suggestions of topics to be included and recommendations of scholars to be invited to contribute papers were requested formally and informally from some fifty institutionalists in the United States and abroad. Over the next year the Advisory Committee decided upon the subject areas to be included and a roster of corresponding potential contributors to be contacted. In all cases, scholars with special competencies in the specific areas addressed were recruited. The response from invited participants was enthusiastic. Tentative outlines were submitted and approved by the editor, sometimes in consultation with members of the Advisory Committee. The project was carried to completion through a collegial and supportive process of writing and review. Each paper reflects the author's own formulation and synthesis of the topics addressed. Accordingly, readers will observe differences in perception and analysis among the several contributors; these differences derive from divergent backgrounds, notions of pertinence, and analytical styles and techniques. The quest, then, was not for a homogenized symposium. The concern, rather, was that these moderately divergent essays be provocative and compelling enough to set inquiry in political economy more vigorously in motion. The desire was to provide as definitive a treatment as constraints would allow. Even so, we all recognize that open inquiry will generate differences as well as agreements. We believe that the latter overwhelmingly exceed the former and that the papers as a set are mutually reinforcing and present an integrated institutionalist theory of political economy.

The Contents of Volume I

The fourteen essays comprising Volume I of *Evolutionary Economics*

are arranged under three main headings: The single essay in Part I
opens the volume with an exploration of the emergence and century-
long development of institutionalism as a predominently American
contribution to economic thought. Part II, consisting of four lengthy
papers, examines in considerable detail the philosophical underpinnings of institutionalism with special reference to epistemology and
methodology, views of human nature, determinants of social change,
and criteria of social value. These essays in particular clearly indicate
the differences between the philosophical roots of orthodoxy and institutionalism.

Part III is comprised of nine essays, each of which examines in depth
a central analytical construct of critical importance for the institutionalist perspective. The two leading essays in this part address the core
concepts of technology and institutions. Three essays explore the meaning and character of resources on which any economy depends—
persons with creativity and skills, technologically defined material
resources, and discretionary financial means. Two essays root the institutionalist perspective in the post-Newtonian and post-Darwinian
world of processural reality and inquiry by rendering a critical consideration of the concepts of time and information. The final two essays
of the volume reinforce the political-economy character of the institutionalist position by demonstrating the need for economists to consider
the nature and use of authority and power in the economic system.
They also reveal the central role played by the theory of democracy in
the institutionalist analysis of policy formation. As the Volume I subtitle suggests, these fourteen papers characterize the philosophical and
analytical foundations of institutional thought.

A Review of the Papers

Anne Mayhew's paper, "The Beginnings of Institutionalism," places
the origins of the institutionalist perspective in the context of the economic and intellectual history of nineteenth century America. The accelerating urbanization, corporate industrialization, and more activist
government reflected a profound change in the character of the economy, and marked the "end of laissez faire." Concurrently a new social
science appeared in which attention was focused on four critical ideas:
evolution, culture, cultural relativity, and instrumental valuing, all of
which became prominent in the writings of the early institutionalists,
ThorsteinVeblen and John R. Commons. Mayhew does not see the
emergence of institutionalism primarily as a by-product of the social
reform movements of that period, nor as an articulation of the frontier

experience, nor as a transplantation of the German Historical School's canons to American shores. It is, rather, a creative replacement of prevailing social and economic doctrine by a post-Darwinian revamping of social inquiry. The essay identifies the "fork in the road" of social inquiry, where institutional heterodoxy emerges as a fundamental departure from neoclassical orthodoxy in quest of a more theoretically adequate and policy-oriented approach.

Philip Mirowski, in his "Philosophic Bases of Institutional Economics," contends that "institutional economics was the offspring of an entirely distinct philosophical tradition from that which gave rise to neoclassical economics." Using a "vortex model of the sociology of science" as an analytical construct, Mirowski explains the origins of discrete economic doctrines as deriving from a cultural and ideational interplay of conceptions of the natural and social worlds, on the one hand, and of mastery and control and an ideal of order, on the other. In this setting, he then distinguishes between the Cartesian tradition in philosophy and the corollary tenets of neoclassicism that contrast so starkly with the Peirceian tradition in philosophy and the corollary tenets of institutionalism. Point by point comparisons are provided. His hermeneutical mode of assessment, a process of interpretation by a self-identified community of inquiry, leads him to an extensive consideration of the Peirceian tradition. That tradition, for example, perceives inquiry as encompassing not only deductive and inductive inference, but also *abductive* reflection, the process of formulating explanatory hypotheses. In canvassing the methodologies of institutionalists from Veblen to the present, Mirowski finds in nearly all an incomplete reflection of the Peirceian legacy. He sees, then, the need for continuing inquiry into the nature of inquiry. In addition, he sees recent developments in philosophy as further repudiation of the Cartesian philosophy of science. Accordingly, contemporary neoclassicists' claims to scientific standing, rooted as they are in the Cartesian legacy, are even more suspect.

Hans Jensen continues the philosophical discussion by addressing "The Theory of Human Nature" in the institutionalist perspective. Perhaps nowhere in these two volumes is the difference between the institutionalist and orthodox methodologies more sharply delineated than it is in this discussion of human nature. From the beginning, Veblen took his cues on human nature from evolutionary biology (following Darwin) and not, as did neoclassicists, from Newtonian physics. As Jensen shows, institutionalists have developed the concept of persons as those whose natures are not fixed, final, and given as utility maximizers. Rather their natures evolve; they are products of interaction with culture. Habits of mind and habits of behavior are acquired in a cultural context. Intellects guide conduct; choices are judged by reference to the consequences invoked. People are economic agents who choose and judge.

These attributes are traced by Jensen through Veblen's theory of instincts (basic impulses to workmanship or predation, but guided by intellect); John Dewey's theory of habits (behavior modes acquired in interaction with culture and modified by education); Commons's theory of institutional conditioning (major collective structures, through sanctions, require compliance and conformity, but human will is the final arbiter); Ayres's theory of socio-cultural determination (technological and ceremonial behavior are dichotomized); and finally, through extensions and refinements among Ayres's students. That these characterizations have virtually nothing in common with the orthodox concept of "economic man," or a rational maximizer of utility, will surprise few. For the one-dimensional man of orthodoxy, institutionalists (as Jensen demonstrates) offer the socio-cultural person whose motivations are multiple and complex, whose behavior is conditioned, but whose intellect can and does modify the conditioning process.

Paul Dale Bush, in the next article, moves to the heartland of evolutionary institutional economics with his treatment of "The Theory of Institutional Change." Reflecting the institutionalist methodology derived from Peirce and Dewey, and incorporating Jensen's view of people as emergent, acculturated, and discretionary agents, Bush explains the evolution of the theory of institutional change from its origins with Veblen at the turn of the century to its most recent characterizations.

Bush defines an institution as "a set of socially prescribed patterns of behavior" and contends that virtually all behavior is institutionally prescribed. Such prescriptions are internalized as habits, consciously and unconsciously. Behavioral patterns are purposeful and are correlated through the use of values as standards of conduct. He then offers a definitive analysis of the ceremonial-instrumental dichotomy as a normative accounting of two pervasive and different kinds of prescriptive behavior patterns. He finds the continuing inducement or stimulus for social and economic change in the dynamic continuum of the growth of knowledge and its incorporation in technology. His direct consideration of regressive economic change is rooted in his construct of the "ceremonial encapsulation" of knowledge. Such ceremonial encapsulation may be "past-binding," "future binding," or of the Lysenko type. These impediments to change are well illustrated through reference to monographs on particular problem areas in the institutionalist literature.

His concept of progressive economic change rests on the displacement of ceremonial patterns of behavior with instrumental patterns of behavior. The fund of knowledge defines what change is feasible; the character and extent of "ceremonial dominance" delimits what can be changed. Fundamental to Bush's analysis is the demonstration that institutional change is continuously necessary, discretionary, and normative. This being the case, institutional change is a vital consideration in the planning and assessment of social policy.

Steven Hickerson's paper on "Instrumental Valuation: The Normative Compass of Institutional Economics," addresses what is perhaps the most important philosophical concept in the philosophical foundations of institutional economics—the instrumental value principle.

Taking as his point of departure Gunnar Myrdal's recurring insistence that "valuation is always with us," Hickerson dismantles the value-neutral pretentions of orthodoxy through a penetrating critique of Kurt Klappholz's defense of *wertfrei* methodology. "Value impregnation [of inquiry] is, in fact, inevitable," concludes Hickerson. Reaffirming an argument introduced by Mirowski, Hickerson finds in the Cartesian tradition, as absorbed by neoclassical economics, a dichotomization of reason and experience, in which reason is ranked as "a far more reliable source of knowledge" than is experience. Deductive inferences predominate; matters of goals, ends, or "oughts" have no place in a science based on Cartesian rules.

Hickerson refutes the Cartesian contentions and argues that institutionalists cannot accept the normative-positive dichotomy. In a means-determines-ends context, ends are not antecedently given and are not separate and discrete from means. Because they serve as subsequent means, they are a necessary part of inquiry. Logically, then, economists cannot be "entirely neutral between ends." The normative-positive dichotomy cannot be sustained on logical and empirical grounds. Recourse to a warranted principle of valuing is absolutely essential in inquiry.

Hickerson concludes the paper by tracing the evolutionary development of the instrumental value principle through the institutionalist tradition of Veblen, Dewey, Ayres, J. Fagg Foster, and Foster's students. The principle reflects a cultural origin and a processual character. Building on Bush and others, he distinguishes between ceremonial and instrumental modes of valuation. Finally, Hickerson provides an exploratory and illustrative application of instrumental valuation in the area of environmental protection and waste disposal.

Milton Lower addresses "The Concept of Technology" in institutional economics. Lower says that the "concept of technology, in all of the uses for which institutionalists employ it, refers to an aspect of culture." He contends that the "distinctive contribution of institutionalism" resides in "its discovery of the *general* theoretical significance of technology as the foundation for a unified theory of cultural evolution." Lower explores this contribution through consideration of "technology and cultural evolution," "technological progress," and "technology and instrumental valuation." His approach is processual and non-mechanistic. Using evolutionary analogues from biology, he seeks a "genetic accounting of the cumulative causation at work" in particular cultural circumstances.

Thus technological change, broadly conceived, "plays a dynamic role in cultural evolution." It is an activist, change-inducing facet of culture. Technology derives from the growth of knowledge itself, and from trans-cultural borrowing. But cultural patterns dictate the extent and character of absorption and determine the nature of the cumulative transformation of the culture. Technological progress, in Lower's view, derives from the process of combining tools and ideas—in Ayres's terms, "the tool-combination principle"—in which tools and knowledge are, and must be, interdependent. Progress results from the cumulative development of ideas, tools, and skills and their cultural employment. "This functional continuum, a cumulative and accelerating process of tool-combination," runs through all history and imparts direction to cultural change. Cultural progress and economic growth are not, as the neoclassicists suggest, the consequences of saving and capital formation; nor are they the result of the enleashing of the competitive entrepreneurial spirit.

Finally, Lower adds significant normative insights to those provided by Bush and Hickerson by exploring the theoretical connections between technology and instrumental valuing as it emerges from the writings of the classical institutionalists—Veblen, Dewey and Ayres. He considers among other matters, ceremonial impediments to the growth of knowledge and technology. Lower further demonstrates that the method of instrumental valuing is the *same* as the method of scientific knowing. The quest for the truth and for the good are identical in Lower's view of institutional political economy.

Walter Neale brings to the discussion of "institutions" distinctively anthropological concepts and merges them with relevant institutionalist counterparts. His special concern is to contribute to the clarification of the meaning of this "root-word" that characterizes evolutionary economics as "institutionalist."

Neale's core idea is that *"most* of what people do is *governed* by the *institutions* of their society." "Governed" means the definition of what is permissible and forbidden, right and wrong. Institutions govern by stipulating both opportunities and restraints; they create *and* limit choices. "Institutions give meaning and continuity to actions." The array of institutions that govern provisioning of real income is the object of inquiry for institutionalists.

In the fuller search for an operational definition of institutions, Neale concludes that three characteristics identify an "institution": a number of *people doing* things; *"rules* giving the activities repetition, stability, and predictable order"; and *folkways* that "explain or justify the activities and the rules." Answers elicited by the question "why?" are folkviews; answers to questions of "how?" and "why?" are the rules that govern. "Folkviews indicate which activities belong within which institutions," and "delimit the groups of situations or activities that call forth and constitute the institution."

Neale reinforces his operational definition with a survey of analytical benefits derived from the consistent use of his construct. He then illustrates the significance of these benefits with a brief exploration of John Munkirs's account of "centralized private sector economic planning." He concludes his paper with an analysis of how actions prompted by motives are structured by institutional rules but do not themselves determine either the structure or the action, and with a discussion of origins of institutions and of functional relationships among institutions. In addition, he salvages the term "institutions" from a naive and exclusive identification with what is ceremonial or invidious. He intends his operational definition of "institutions" to facilitate analysis, to help inquirers escape their own cultural preconceptions, and to avoid fruitless concern with motives and generalized social functions.

Vernon Briggs, Jr. opens his essay on "Human Resources" with a chronicle of the pre-World War II historic indifference to concerns over human resource development, both in formal orthodox analysis and in actual industrial development. Except by Veblen, Marx, and Commons, labor was viewed largely as a homogeneous, low-skill, quantitative factor of production, a commodity to be bought and manipulated by owner-managers, not a resource to be developed. That human resource development could be the key to sustained growth was largely unrecognized.

After World War II, interest in the human resource area expanded rapidly: Theodore Schultz (evidently prompted by a visit to the Soviet Union and observations there of worker education and training) and his Chicago colleagues began the development of "human capital" theory as an only slightly differentiated product of mainstream neoclassicism. Briggs rejects this analysis with a persuasive critique. A second acceleration of interest resulted from the historical analysis of Edward Denison, who demonstrated that nearly three-fourths of the U.S. long-term growth resulted from human resource development (including the growth of knowledge). The Denison contribution is compatible with institutional analysis.

A third elevation of interest arose from contributions of labor economists with institutionalist leanings who demonstrated that the structure of employment over the last half-century had changed dramatically because of technological advances, scientific innovations, foreign rivalry, population growth, and changes in the gender and race composition of the labor force. Working in this institutionalist tradition, Briggs recommends "prescribed interventionist human resource policies" to facilitate the labor adjustment-to-change process in the areas of training, education, information, job creation, and the like. "The human resource approach seeks specific remedies for specific individual circumstances." The "menu" of policy options generated in the pre-Reagan decades was generally successful, claims to the contrary notwithstanding.

Briggs then considers three "dimensions" of human resource development at some length: (1) With regard to available aggregate resources, he considers issues of immigration, full employment, and underutilization. (2) With regard to qualitative opportunities available, he explores issues of ideological inhibitions, manpower training, minority qualification, salvage of unemployables, and long-run education. (3) With regard to "artificial barriers imposed on the labor market," he examines issues involving neoclassical apologia, civil rights legislation and other anti-discrimination measures. In sum, Briggs's institutional analysis of human resource development is an excellent, cogent, and normative assessment of applicable theory and experience-grounded policy-making.

In his "Resources Are Not, They Become," Thomas De Gregori argues that the "creative process of fashioning the material and non-material stuff of our environment in a form usable and serviceable to human beings is determined by science and technology." Following in the tradition of Erich Zimmerman and Clarence Ayres, De Gregori affirms that: "It is the sum total of human knowledge and capability that is the prime resource and the one that defines all others." Accordingly, all references to "natural resources," "resource endowments," "given resources," and "fixed and finite resources," in the neoclassicist literature are outmoded.

De Gregori continues: "Resources, then, are not stuff or materials; they are a set of capabilities. These capabilities use the stuff of the material and non-material universe in a life-sustaining manner. These capabilities define a functional relationship that we call resources." Given the prior existence of humans and materials, it is people as active, discretionary agents employing ideas who create resources.

The process of resource creation is one of "dynamic interaction and reinforcing feedback mechanisms" reflected in the "human generation of ideas, their embodiment in the process of technology, and in the creation of resources." The interdependence of idea and tool combinations, explored above by Lower, is here extended to include resources. The cumulative and evolutionary growth in understanding of these idea-tool-resource connections undergird all discretionary expansion of real income.

De Gregori refines meanings, generates examples, critiques alternate views, and demonstrates the cogency and credibility of this theory of resource creation. Consideration is given to resource dependency, entropy-based pessimisms, and resource renewability. Two extended applications of this theory of the technological determination of resources are the world-wide availability of minerals and the provision of food stuffs.

He concludes the essay with the suggestion that technology as ideas and as the creator of resources is "liberating" in several respects: it opens new and optimistic avenues for consideration of the sustainability of human life; it offers some intellectual escape from the heavy orthodox dependency on the construct of scarcity; it provides a process of choosing that actually expands the range of choices. The process of resource creation is one of "emergent evolution." It requires that people must choose their future. This essay suggests implicitly, as the earlier essays by Bush and Hickerson state explicitly, that instrumental valuing is the credible way of determining the character of that future.

Baldwin Ranson's paper, "The Institutionalist Theory of Capital Formation," concludes this section on resource creation. As a community has substantial discretion over its human resource complement and its technologically defined resource base, so also does it have substantial control over its capital formation. Ranson begins with a brief review of the evolution of meanings of the term "capital." He finds a continuing thread among otherwise diverse concepts: "each referent has been a human-created object thought indispensable . . . to the continuity of production." Historical use identifies "man-made agents thought to possess productive potency."

Institutionalists, argues Ranson, do not ascribe an autonomous productive potency to plant and equipment. They believe that productivity is instead a function of the growth of knowledge, its reflection in technology, and its application through institutions in the productive process. Institutionalists identify "capital" as "a community's technology and its technically serviceable institution." Incorporating the Veblenian dichotomy, Ranson cautions that "institutions that perform control functions that distribute status rather than produce income" do not have productive potency and are not then "capital." In sum, "by making the productivity of materials, skills, and equipment dependent on the level of technology and institutional efficiency, the institutionalist definition denies intrinsic productive potency to all three of the traditional factors, and makes the productive potency of all factors subject to human discretion."

The institutionalist theory of capital formation, as presented by Ranson, differs dramatically from the neoclassical formulation. Orthodox economists see capital accumulation occurring as a result of "altering the character of current production" by "decreasing the output of consumer goods (saving more) and increasing the amount of capital goods (investing more)." Institutionalist theory "holds that a community accumulates capital by altering the level and the character of its current production, increasing the community's mastery of technology and the efficiency of its technically serviceable institutions *without* saving, as traditionally defined."

In the remainder of the article, Ranson demonstrates, through a critique of an orthodox-oriented 1980 General Accounting Office publication that the institutionalist explanation of capital formation is more credible than that of orthodoxy. Given the dominance of the "savings theory of capital formation" in neoclassical theory the supplanting of such "savings" theory with the Keynesian-Institutionalist "debt creation theory of funding net investment" is one of the significant contributions of the Ranson paper.

Gregory Hayden, in his paper on the "Evolution of Time Constructs and Their Impact on Socioeconomic Planning," sets his topic for analysis as follows: "The primary focus of the institutionalist perspective is instrumentalist problem solving. Problems are delivered by the institutional process, and they are solved by altering the social structure.

To solve socioeconomic problems, planning is necessary. Important to planning is the question of *when* actions and events are to occur. To effect new social structures, actions and events must be properly sequenced. An analytical core of sequencing events is time analysis." Hayden is critical of the common view that holds that time is a flowing reality and is constantly passing. It shows up in neoclassicism, for example, in the mistaken contention that "education should be delivered to children on the basis of the outcome of a discounted time stream."

For Hayden, "time is not a natural phenomenon; rather it is a societal construct." In modern inquiry, "time does not flow, or go, or run from here to there in either a cyclical or linear pattern. It also does not bridge a spatial gap between points. . . . In traditional concepts motion and succession were thought to take place in time. Today motion defines time." "Time," he says, "is the duration of motion; it has no direction." He argues that "there is no future into which the world is destined to flow except in the sense of the 'after' that follows the 'before'." Old ideas of destiny and inevitability suffer in comparison. "The modern concept of time allows us to use clocks to regulate events rather than ourselves being regulated by the running clock of passing time. This expands the discretionary role and responsibility of modern planners."

Hayden explores emergent time constructs that are linear, cyclical or pendulous from a variety of cultures, East and West. Included especially is a critique of the neoclassical, Christian-Newtonian based view that time passes without qualitative changes but is to be used efficiently. This presumption is made operational "through the use of the geometric mean discounting formula." The paper concludes with a demonstration of the significance of the shift from "time discounting" to "timeliness" in a holistic frame of social inquiry. Incorporating systems analysis and diagraphic representations, he shows how critical is the astute ordering of "real time control systems." He explores the shift in inquiry from "event synchronization" to "social process sequencing."

William Melody's paper on "Information: An Emerging Dimension of Institutional Analysis," opens up an increasingly significant area of inquiry that heretofore has been left largely underdeveloped in economic scholarship. Yet "the functioning of society," he affirms, "depends upon information and its effective communication among society's members. Information, and the means for its communication, have a fundamental and pervasive influence upon all institutions." Institutional economists in particular, then, are in a most advantageous position to formulate and employ an "information" construct in economic inquiry.

In tracing the historic treatment of "information" by economists, he finds significant insights beginning with Adam Smith, and including Karl Marx and John Maynard Keynes. Little of note is contributed by neoclassicists with their unexamined assumption of "perfect knowledge." But in John R. Commons's concept of "transactions" and especially in the extensive contributions of Harold Innis, including his consideration of "time-biased" and "space-biased" communication and information systems, Melody finds precursors on whom to draw.

Melody examines in some depth the significance of information, both its generation and its control, in various market settings with particular attention to contemporary information markets themselves. Melody considers the impact of "advances in computer and telecommunication technologies" on the amounts and kinds of information made available. He explores as well the mushrooming expansion and increasing complexity of information in many forms; information becomes a commodity of exchange itself. Inevitably, normative assessments of content and public interest assessments of access become matters of public policy analysis. Institutionalists, through inquiry and their influence on policy, can "do more than just interpret the world. In the Commons tradition, they can participate in changing it."

Philip Klein, in his essay on "Power and Economic Performance: The Institutionalist View," says "we may define power according to the central problems considered in the most conventional view of economics—what to produce, how to produce, and for whom to produce. The greater one's ability to determine how any of these three questions, or their logical extensions, gets resolved, the greater is the individual in question possessed of what we call economic power." Power, then, is "one's ability to influence the way in which the economy operates to carry out the tasks assigned to it." The economy is a "system of power."

After an extensive canvass and assessment of various mainly mainstream orthodox and radical economic postures, Klein finds none that offer a credible and instructive analysis of economic power. The classicists, led currently by Milton Friedman, evade the issue by presuming a competitive-market, "democratic" allocation; power is not an object of inquiry except as government "intrusions" are treated as pathological concerns. In contemporary mainstream theorizing, the analytical contributions to understanding economic power are miniscule. Despite the "imperfect competition revolution" and an abandonment of laissez-faire notions, industrial organization analysis has not seriously addressed economic power as Klein defines it. Tests of performance remain conventional: "allocative efficiency" or "reasonable profits." The most recent apologia for private power is the "theory of contestable markets." Neoclassically based public choice theory applies orthodox microtheory to political processes; Klein argues that it would be more productive to apply political theory to the analysis of economic power. The neoclassical conclusion of public choice theory appears to be that "whatever the market failures," it is likely that "governmental activity will make it worse."

Klein then turns to a reconstruction of the institutionalist perception of economic power and its accountability. Recognition of the problem begins with Veblen's encompassing view. In Klein's words, "economic power emerges from comprehending the changing technology and deliberately manipulating the institutional response, often in the interest of a narrow group"—for Veblen, the "vested interests." Klein carries the institutional analysis forward by incorporating contributions of Commons, Ayres, Robert Brady, John Kenneth Galbraith, and Randall Bartlett. What emerges from this synthesis and from Klein's own contribution is a much more complete and instructive theoretical analysis to explain where economic power is held, how and through what institutions it is exercised, to what extent it can be held accountable, to what degree and in what form broad community objectives of resource allocation are accomplished, and how a normative assessment of the performance of centers of power can be made. This quest for what Klein calls "the higher efficiency"—a view of the public interest that incorporates instrumental valuing—does not generate final answers; the gain is a better managed economic process, more adequate levels of real income, more equitable income distribution, and greater democratic accountability. Klein concludes his essay by reminding us that, with the advent of multinational corporations that function as defacto private industrial governments, the universe of inquiry about economic power must now be global.

Rick Tilman closes this volume with his paper on "The Neoinstrumental Theory of Democracy." The democratic mode and ethic implicit in Klein's preceding analysis of economic power here become the explicit object of Tilman's essay. Democratic theory provides guidance for holding power accountable.

Tilman observes some theoretical (his word is "ideological") differences among institutionalists, in a larger context of general theoretical diversity, with regard to types of democratic theory. But the instrumentalist view of democracy, as reflected in Foster's writing, generates perhaps the most prevalent institutional referent. As Tilman expresses it, "Democracy is not a particular institution but a kind of process that

brings popular consent to fruition." Such popular determination of social policy permits choice *among* alternative ways of organizing the
economy and the policy. Its constants are procedural canons of intellectual freedom, open inquiry, access to information, and full delibera-
tion; it does not incorporate a recipe for an ismatic or utopian
economy.

With this instrumentalist identification of democratic processes in
mind, Tilman turns to Dewey and his followers to provide a fuller characterization of these processes. Some of the more significant insights
presented by Tilman are:

• Democracy "separates purposes from status conceived as hierarchy."

• Democracy accepts "the virtue of change in the interest of progress."

• In a democracy, "there are few, if any social structures that cannot
be abandoned or altered, for all social institutions are subject to the
collective will and to the test of usage."

• Instrumentalist democracy "is a naturalistic theory that employs
self-correction through judgment of consequences," and "the method
of self-correction searches for and adheres to public verification of its
processes and consequences."

• Democracy, in Dewey's words rests on "methods of consultation,
persuasion, negotiation, communication and co-operative intelligence."

Tilman continues his guided tour of instrumentalist democratic theory by exploring the normative dimensions as "proper human growth
and development," and by considering the "democracy-science analog"
in which experimental modes and self-corrective value judgments are
reflected in each. In consideration of the difficulties of getting democratic publics to organize and act, Tilman cites C. Wright Mills, to buttress insights of Dewey. He offers a brief critique of the neoclassically
rooted public choice theorists as "prescriptive elitists" who denigrate
the practice of democratic modes.

Tilman concludes his essay with a sobering yet hopeful assessment
of current threats to expanding the institutionalist mode and ethic of
democracy. Needed adjustments to bring democratic controls more
fully into realization will require fundamental changes in the present
dominion of corporate and political elites over economic institutions
and procedures.

Acknowledgments

The remaining task of acknowledgments in these introductory pages is indeed a pleasant one. Initial thanks go to the several dozen members of the Association for Institutional Thought and the Association for Evolutionary Economics who, early on, endorsed the idea of the project and suggested both topics and possible contributors. Thanks, in generous amounts, must go as well to those who graciously and enthusiastically accepted invitations and contributed papers to this collection, often when professional obligations elsewhere were already excessive.

Hearty thanks must go as well to those who served as "first readers" on the respective papers and offered constructive comments on early drafts. Wendell Gordon in particular read initial drafts of several essays. These individuals are identified in the author's own acknowledgments.

In addition, grateful appreciation is extended to members of the ad hoc Advisory Committee—Professors Bush, Hamilton, Hayden, Klein, Mayhew, Neale, and Trebing (introduced above)—who, in infrequent general meetings, and more often individually on the other end of the telephone, patiently offered counsel on matters of assignment, substance, and procedure in moving this project to its successful completion. Their supportive and encouraging suggestions were much appreciated, and in the main, were incorporated. Thanks go as well to Professors Robert Curry, John Henry, Philip Klein, Dale Bush, and Walter Neale for constructive comments on the Introduction.

Finally, a very special thanks must be extended from all individual contributors and myself to Anne Louise Jackson, production editor of the *Journal of Economic Issues,* for her dedicated and professional editing of the manuscripts for publication. Her workload was uncommonly heavy. We all gratefully acknowledge her most important contribution.

MARC R. TOOL, Editor
Journal of Economic Issues
Sacramento, California
May 30, 1987

References

Ayres, Clarence. 1944. *Theory of Economic Progress.* Chapel Hill: University of North Carolina Press.
Blaug, Mark. 1978. *Economic Theory in Retrospect.* 3d. edition. Cambridge: Cambridge University Press.

Part I

The Beginnings of Institutionalism

Anne Mayhew

The first institutionalists—Thorstein Veblen and John R. Commons —came to maturity in the decades following the Civil War, and both began to publish in the 1890s.[1] Veblen was born in Wisconsin in 1857 and Commons in Indiana in 1862. The Midwestern origins of both of these men have often been noted, as has Veblen's "frontier origin." It seems more important that they grew up in a rapidly changing— because rapidly industrializing—nation. The world they entered in maturity was not the world of their fathers; and this was markedly true of almost all Americans of the period, whether they lived in the Midwest or not.

Perhaps the most obvious manifestation and explanation of the changes was the decline in the relative importance of agriculture in American economy and society. In 1860 *and* in 1870, fifty-three percent of the labor force was engaged in agriculture. In 1880, the proportion was still 52 percent, but during the decade of the 1880s the percentage plunged to 43 percent and crept still further down in the 1890s.[2] During the 1880s the labor force increased by 34 percent, or by almost 6 million people, so that the increase in nonagricultural employment was dramatic indeed, as was the increase in nonagricultural output. Between 1839 and 1859, agriculture had contributed approximately 26 percent

The author would like to thank many for help, advice, and criticism, including Kathleen Brown, Emil Friberg, Jr., David Hamilton, Rick Tilman, and members of the Institutional Economics Workshop at the University of Tennessee. Special thanks are due Marc Tool for his thorough response to an earlier draft. As is always the case, Walter C. Neale served as critic and helper through all the drafts.

of national income, and manufacturing and mining 14 percent; but between 1880 and 1899, agriculture's share fell to 15 percent, while manufacturing and mining contributed 25 percent of a much larger national income.[3] Over the period 1870–1913, GNP grew at 4.3 percent and per capita GNP at 2.2 percent.[4] The growth in the labor force, the growth in output, and the relative decline in the contribution of agriculture were accompanied by substantial changes in the nature of both output and nonagricultural employment. The 1.6 percent annual increase in labor productivity between 1889 and 1919 is testament to improving technology and increased energy use. Table 1 shows another measure of the changing composition of the workforce. The increase in the relative number of engineers is but one example of many that could be given to illustrate the increasingly industrial nature of the U.S. economy.

Table 1. *A Measure of the Changing Composition of the Work Force.*

(1)	(2) Labor Force (1860 = 100)	(3) Engineers (1860 = 100)	(4) Column Three As Percent of Column Two
1880	157	245	156
1890	210	522	249
1900	262	803	306
1910	337	1,432	425

SOURCE: Stanley Lebergott, *The Americans: An Economic Record* (New York: W. W. Norton, 1984), Table 27.3 (p. 39). Column 4 computed.

The changes in social and economic organization were as dramatic as the changes in the amount and composition of output, and they were certainly more traumatic. In 1870 *and* in 1880, just over a quarter of the population lived in "urban places" and these had as few as 2500 people. By 1900, 40 percent of the population lived in such places, and by 1920 more than half the population was "urban" by this definition. In 1870, about half the "urban population" lived in cities of 50,000 or more: that is, only about one in thirteen Americans lived in a city with more than 50,000 people. By 1900, well over half the "urban" population, or more than one out of every five people, lived in places with populations over 50,000.

The end of the nineteenth century and the beginning of the twentieth was the period of the rise of "big business" and of the great "robber barons." It marked the end of the era when most manufacturing was carried out by single product, single plant firms that were owned and managed by the same individual or small group of individuals. The

corporate form of legal organization was adapted to the economic reality of the newly emerging multi-product, multi-plant, bureaucrat-
ically managed firm. The "robber barons" were the most visible feature,
but they were not the driving cause of the changes in business organization that included the growth of new forms of banking, the greater
importance of external finance for the firm, expanded markets, and new
forms of competition between firms with very substantial overhead
costs.[5]

The rise of big business was by no means cheered by most of those
who discussed it. The founders of institutionalism shared at least part
of the general concern. Both Commons and Veblen were, from their
early days, acutely aware of the economic changes and economic problems that were so much a part of the America in which they grew up.
In his autobiography, Commons observed, perhaps partly in bitter jest,
that his father's failure as a businessman could be given "a historical
justification. He could not fit himself to the Money and Credit economy."[6]

Commons and Veblen grew up in the midst of massive economic
change to a thoroughly commercialized "money and credit economy"
and their early interests reflect this. Commons came to his study of economics by way of a passion for the ideas of Henry George, an interest
in Richard Ely's "socialism," an active social conscience, and an interest in distribution.[7] He was, from the beginning, interested in organizing change through labor unions.[8] Veblen was less directly forthcoming
about his early interests in economics, but his first wife asserted that
their reading of Edward Bellamy's *Looking Backward* represented a
"turning point in their lives."[9] As much as Henry George's single tax
movement or Richard Ely's "socialism," Edward Bellamy's Utopian
scheme for a reordered world was a reaction to the traumatic changes
that accompanied the rapid and often disruptive economic growth after
the Civil War.

The New Ideas

In writing about the social and economic consequences of the industrialization of the United States, neither Veblen nor Commons relied
heavily upon earlier traditions of economic thought, nor upon earlier
justifications for economic reform. Instead, both relied upon the new
social science that was just emerging as they were attempting to understand the socioeconomic changes taking place in the world.

Four ideas have been critical to the development and separation of
institutionalist theory from neoclassical economic theory: evolution,
culture, cultural relativity, and instrumental valuing. All four were

thrown up from the ferment that created modern social science. In the years following the Civil War, virtually all American social thought was in one way or another affected by the ideas of Charles Darwin or Herbert Spencer, or at least by ideas attributed to them.[10] Ideas of natural selection and evolution found their way into households and university discussions of economic affairs as ways of explaining the experiences that came with the late nineteenth century. It is probably significant that William Graham Sumner, who found Spencer's ideas about the economic survival of the fittest attractive, was the son of an immigrant who had become unemployed as a result of the Industrial Revolution in Britain. It is probably also significant that Lester Frank Ward, who stressed man's ability to alter the course of evolution, was a poor boy who had acquired an education while working as a government clerk and attending night school.[11] Social Darwinism was a powerful justification for the rapid enrichment of some, as well as for the lack of security for many that was characteristic of the urbanizing, industrializing, market-dominated U.S. economy of the last decades of the nineteenth century.

The ideas of society and culture as evolving systems emerged from a combination of evolutionary thought and the greatly increasing knowledge of human variation over time and place that became available during the nineteenth century. In the United States, Lewis Henry Morgan had begun to record the evidence of social variation to be found among "living primitives." He not only recorded the kinship system of the Iroquois, he also classified and thereby "explained" it. He "divided all history into three main stages—Savagery, Barbarism, and Civilization—and correlated each with economic and intellectual achievements."[12] According to Robert H. Lowie,

> the idea of progressive development from savagery to civilization was much older than Darwin or even Lamarck. However, when evolution became not merely an approved biological principle but a magical catchword for the solution of all problems, it naturally assimilated the earlier speculations about cultural change as obviously congruous with its own philosophy. Similarly, the discoveries of prehistory neatly fitted into the evolutionary picture. Both biological theory and archaeological research powerfully stimulated the study of culture.[13]

Out of this study of culture came the ideas that served as the basis for anthropology.

Some parts of Morgan's scheme look strange and wrong to the modern reader. Any anthropologist can find serious fault with some of his propositions about kinship patterns and their correlation with other social patterns and with technology. What is important, however, is not how dated Morgan's ideas seem now, but how modern they seem when compared with what had gone before. Morgan grasped that the ways in which people saw, described, and related to their kin were both culturally specific and changed over time. He was not alone in beginning to understand culture in the modern anthropological sense. In 1871, Sir Edward Burnett Tylor defined culture as "that complex whole which includes knowledge, belief, art, morals, law, custom, and any other capabilities and habits acquired by man as a member of society."[14] The recognition that morals—as well as law, custom, and art—were learned as part of a particular culture was one of the set of ideas that became the core of modern anthropology, but its impact on other disciplines was also profound.

The new anthropological concept of culture had important and widespread effect because it carried the implication that the process of cultural evolution might not be over, that it might indeed be a process that never was over. Walter Goldschmidt's claim for anthropology does not seem exaggerated:

Anthropology has had a great impact on the moral philosophy of our time, an impact out of all proportion to the numerical and fiscal strength of the discipline. It has moved us away from biological thinking and toward an appreciation of the force of culture; it has made us aware of our own customs and beliefs as one of the many and apparently arbitrary modes of thought. In doing this it has promoted a cultural relativism, and this in turn has placed anthropology itself in the mainstream of an old scientific tradition. For as astronomy moved the earth away from the center of the universe and biology moved man out of his unique position in the living world, so, too, anthropology has removed Western man from the pinnacle and quintessence of human perfectibility and placed him with the Australian aborigine and the Hottentot as one of so many diverse cultural beings.[15]

The discovery of "cultures" necessarily entailed the discovery of our own culture, and that gave new perspective: once the ideas of culture and of evolution were accepted, the idea of cultural relativity followed.

Anthropology and sociology were disciplines defined by these ideas. Economics' longer heritage made acceptance of the new ideas difficult. As Veblen explained, economics was trapped in a tradition of natural law.[16] Neither the ideas of culture nor the ideas of cultural relativity could permeate a body of thought that was rooted in a hedonistic conception of human beings buffeted by natural laws that worked toward a predetermined social order. This impermeability was as characteristic of Marxist economics as of neoclassical economics, and it meant that economics continued to develop according to a different logic and quite apart from the other social sciences.

Veblen and the Idea of Culture

What made Veblen different—what made his economics unique and what leads Russett to call him "the complete Darwinian"—was that he was the first to approach the study of modern economics in the same anthropological spirit that Morgan pioneered in his investigations of the Iroquois.[17] Darwinism to Veblen meant more than a process of natural selection in which teeming masses of people were likened to teeming masses of other animals. It meant more than that one could divide mankind's past into stages, as the German historical economists had done. It meant that the culture of people living in Iowa in 1890 had evolved, and that, just as there was no natural way to count cousins or to trace descent, so there was no natural way to determine how the corn should be divided. Veblen was the first economic anthropologist, and what makes it so remarkable is that he did not study exotic peoples—it is always easier to see customs when they look foreign and therefore funny—but rather examined his own culture.[18]

Veblen understood that the variation in human society meant more than that societies change; he understood that human society was not tending to any end, spiritual or otherwise—that there simply was no end. The variations in human society that had become so apparent were the consequences of idle curiosity and "the adaptation of means to ends that cumulatively change as the process goes on."[19] Existing business organization, the robber barons, and the repeated economic crises were no more right, proper, or necessary than was the identification of some Iroquois as members of the hawk clan. If it was merely a "queer custom" that resulted in some Iroquois being brothers by virtue of being members of the hawk clan, and not brothers of others who were turtles, it was also a "queer custom" that allowed businessmen to claim a substantial share of the proceeds of a firm because they "owned" the firm. As Veblen saw it, all of these queer customs would change and, except for his brief activism during World War I and afterward, the challenge he accepted was to describe rather than to hasten or to direct the change.[20].

What Veblen did that has been of such enormous importance in the development of institutionalist theory was to take the notion of social Darwinism—of social evolution—and turn it into an unteleological, non-ethnocentric process of social change. Veblen observed that people were not only given to a wide variety of ideas and practices that could be explained only through the logic of the culture in which they existed; humans are also distinguished by skills in manipulating nature. Veblen saw the employment of these skills as a process that changed the ways people thought about the world in which they lived. He perceived that the "pragmatic" evaluation of truth, which Charles S. Peirce and William James described in philosophic terms, coexisted with inherited and unquestioned beliefs that were accepted only because they were part of the cultural heritage of the believers. He saw that this duality existed among the most sophisticated of scientists and the richest of robber barons as well as among primitive peoples. He thus added the idea of instrumental valuing to the ideas of culture, evolution, and cultural relativity and completed the quartet of essentially institutionalist ideas.

Veblen described the relationship between standards of scientific and philosophic inquiry and technology in this way:

> The changes in the cultural situation which seem to have had the most serious consequences for the methods and animus of scientific inquiry are those changes that took place in the field of industry.... The deity, from having been in medieval times primarily a suzerain concerned with the maintenance of his own prestige, becomes primarily a creator engaged in the workmanlike occupation of making things useful for man.... The "natural laws" which the scientists of that era make so much of are no longer decrees of a preternatural legislative authority, but rather details of the workshop specifications handed down by the master-craftsman for the guidance of handicraftsmen working out his designs.... The machine process has displaced the workman as the archetype in whose image causation is conceived by the scientific investigators. The dramatic interpretation of natural phenomena ... no longer constructs the life-history of a cause working to produce a given effect—after the manner of a skilled workman producing a piece of wrought goods—but it constructs the life-history of a process in which the distinction between cause and effect need scarcely be observed in an itemized and specific way, but in which the run of causation unfolds itself in an unbroken sequence of cumulative change.[21]

The machine process—the shift to industrial production and employment—altered the way people thought. This shift in thinking would then lead, Veblen thought, through the operation of idle curiosity, to further changes. Insofar as Veblen thought that progress had been made by mankind, it was progress through idle curiosity that was always guided and constrained by the standards of proof and truth of the day. But these standards of proof and truth were themselves changed by the changes in dealing with the "world-of-matter-of-fact." Thus Veblen's own evolutionary science was no more than the kind of thinking to be expected in a world of machines.

It should be emphasized that Veblen's view of the role that dealing with the world-of-matter-of-fact played in social evolution is not the same as Karl Marx's notion of historical materialism. Nor is Veblen suggesting simply that we humans tend to increase our capacity to produce goods faster than our antiquated institutions will allow us actually to produce. In Veblen's process, changes in dealing with nature lead not simply to economic conflict between classes, but to an entire alteration of the way in which we look at the world—to cultural change writ large. To put Veblen's view a bit flippantly: our opposable thumbs cause the world that we hold in our heads to be constantly altered.

Not only was Veblen almost unique among economists of his time in recognizing the importance of the notion of culture, he was also almost unique in attempting to account for social evolution as ongoing process. When Veblen contrasted "industrial employments" with "pecuniary employments," when he contrasted the "machine process" with "ceremonialism," and when he contrasted workmanship with "exploit" he was contrasting the two aspects of peoples' behavior that made social evolution a continuing process. The "cumulative change" of the evolutionary process was driven by pragmatic adaptation, while ceremonial refusal to engage in pragmatic evaluation slowed it down.

Commons and Evolving Institutions

Veblen was clearly a "social theorist of the first rank."[22] He combined the elements of the turn-of-the-century revolution in social thought in a way that makes his work of continuing importance. But he was not quite unique among economists in adopting and adapting the new ideas. John R. Commons, who took a different route and a different approach, arrived at some remarkably similar conclusions. Veblen was purely an academic even when he had no academic post. Commons was from the beginning an activist reformer. He, like Veblen, absorbed the debates and arguments of the new social sciences. Where Veblen gave importance to variations in customs and to showing his fellow man in the new anthropological light, Commons emphasized the possibility of changing things. Commons's theory followed his "participation in collective action." Neither his theory nor the way that he arrived at it paralleled Veblen's theory or approach. Veblen and Commons moved at angles to each other, but the paths of their thought intersected in a significant way, as Commons himself recognized.[23]

The genius of Commons lay in devising a theory about the ways in which people came into conflict, the ways in which those conflicts were settled, and the ways in which those settlements altered the social forms —the working rules—in which the subsequent cooperation and conflict of people would take place. As one might say today, Commons built a model of *process,* of repetitive conflict and conflict resolution, and made this the driving force of social evolution:

> my sources were my participation in collective action, in drafting bills, and my necessary study, during these participations, of the decisions of the Supreme Court. . . . I discovered that, of course, the decisions of these tribunals began with conflict of interests, then took into account the evident idea of dependence of conflicting interests on each other; then reached a decision. . . .
>
> Meanwhile I was trying to find what could be the unit of investigation which would include these three constituents of conflict, dependence, and order. After many years I worked out the conclusion that they were found combined together only in the formula of a transaction.[24]

Commons's long experience with legal processes of dispute resolution helped him to formulate a method to effect socioeconomic change in the United States. His wider acquaintance with the literature of the new social sciences allowed him to frame it in a way that, despite superficial appearances, is not culturally specific and can be easily adapted to describe processes of change elsewhere. Although Commons never wrote many words without returning to the specifics of Anglo-American legal processes, his discussions of social scientific and philosophical issues make it clear that he understood these processes in a broader perspective.[25]

The Legacy of Veblen and Commons

Both Veblen and Commons broke away more thoroughly than did others from traditional economic analysis. The period from the 1880s through the 1930s was a period when many economists were "unorthodox," either in advocacy of state involvement in economic affairs or in pursuit of new descriptions and descriptive techniques.[26] What Commons and Veblen passed on, however, was a more fundamental "unorthodoxy," one that is reflected in these passages from Wesley C. Mitchell's 1924 Presidential Address to the American Economic Association:

> it seems unlikely that the [new] quantitative workers will retain a keen interest in imaginary individuals coming to imaginary markets with ready-made scales of bid and offer prices. Their theories will probably be theories about the relationships among the variables that measure objective *processes.* . . . If our present beliefs are confirmed, that the human nature which men inherit remains substantially the same over millenniums, and that the *changes in human life are due mainly to the evolution of culture,* economists will concentrate their studies to an increasing degree

upon *economic institutions*—the aspect of culture which concerns them.
. . . The quantitative workers will have a special predilection for institutional problems, because institutions standardize behavior, and thereby
facilitate statistical procedure.

   With the growing prominence of institutional problems, the fundamental issue of welfare is inextricably involved. . . . The statistical worker is
in no better position than any other student to specify what mankind
should aim at; but in view of the multiplicity of our competing aims and
the limitations of our social resources his help in measuring objective
costs and objective results is indispensable to convert society's blind fum-
bling for happiness into an intelligent process of experimentation.[27]

I have not quoted at length because Mitchell's predictions about the
future of economics were accurate—sadly, they were not—but because
he summarized so well the radical departure from orthodoxy that Veblen and Commons passed on as their legacy.

Institutionalism and Other Radical Economic Thought

   An assertion that the institutionalist legacy deriving from Veblen and
Commons was drastically different from other economic thought, and
that both Veblen and Commons drew relatively little upon other traditions of economic thought is at odds with propositions easily found in
the literature. It is often asserted that American Institutionalism was
an offshoot of the German Historical School. It is also sometimes asserted that Veblen, and perhaps Commons, worked within the larger
tradition of which Marx was a major figure. Paul T. Homans was explicit: "The institutional movement in American economics is peculiarly a derivative from the work of Veblen. . . . Much of Veblen's
thought is compounded from the ideology of Marx and the historical
school."[28]

   It is easy to account for the belief that institutionalism and the German historical school are closely connected, but more difficult to justify
it. During the decades after the American Civil War a substantial number of those who later became leaders in academic social science went
to Germany for postgraduate study.[29] The ideas to which they were exposed there were and are important propositions in American institutionalism: "the historical approach was fundamental to the study of
political economy; economic activities constituted but one aspect of a
developing social organism and were intimately related to its religious,
political, and social activities."[30] Institutionalism shared with the German school a rejection of Ricardian economics and of the laissez-faire
policies that emerged from that economics.

It is not at all difficult to explain how these ideas and views could have developed among institionalists even in the absence of any exposure to the German tradition. However, ideas drawn directly from the German historical school were part of what the founders of institutionalism absorbed in the early stages of their intellectual careers. John Bates Clark, who taught Veblen when he was an undergraduate at Carleton, had studied in Germany just prior to going to that Minnesota academy and was, while at Carleton, still very much under the influence of the German tradition.[31] Richard T. Ely, who was one of the strongest proponents of the ideas of the German historical school, was on the faculty at Johns Hopkins when Veblen was a student there. Later Commons was a student under Ely at Johns Hopkins and continued his association with Ely for many years at Wisconsin.[32] There is thus a question about whether Veblen, Commons, and other institutionalists formulated issues and answers in ways that could only have been given by exposure to the ideas of the German historical school. There seems little reason to doubt Veblen's own word when he said that he was in substantial disagreement with the German historical economists. He knew the literature of the German Historical School well, as is evidenced by his reviews of works by Adolf Wagner, Gustav Schmoller, and Werner Sombart.[33] He also wrote critically of the school in "Why Is Economics Not an Evolutionary Science?" There he criticized the German school for its failure to develop a theory of process and so to become a modern science. Mitchell commented that

> Veblen's institutional approach has close relationships with that of the historical school; and yet the difference is of considerable importance. It arises primarily from the fact that Veblen has an analytic point of view of human nature which differed far more from the Benthamite tradition than did the view of human nature entertained by Schmoller; that is, the difference arises primarily from a different conception of human nature.[34]

Most of what is important and uniquely Veblenian is missing from the literature of the German historical school. While the German historical economists recognized the importance of economic change and the limited importance of Ricardian economics, they never developed a more general theory of the nature of that change. Veblen did. They were, even in their theoretical work, committed to developing a set of propositions that would guide and justify policies far more appropriate to Germany than to Britain, and they were far less committed to a general theory of economic process. This commitment is what Veblen noted in his essay entitled "Gustav Schmoller's Economics."[35] There he praised Schmoller for his efforts to develop a "post-Darwinian, causal theory of the origin and growth of species in institutions," but then criticized him because, instead of treating the likely consequences of the development of a large body of trained mechanics "in a scientific spirit, . . . he harks back again to the dreary homiletical waste of the traditional *Historismus.*" Veblen goes on to say, "It seems as if a topic which he deals with as an objective matter so long as it lies outside the sphere of every-day humanitarian and social solicitude, becomes a matter to be passed upon by conventional standards of taste, dignity, morality, and the like, so soon as it comes within the sweep of latter-day German sentiment."[36]

The relationship between the German historical school and the thought of John R. Commons was perhaps closer. Commons said that the "so-called Historical school . . . brought into the science the concepts of Custom, Property, and conflicts of interest. . . . The Historical School led to the Ethical and institutional schools. . . ."[37] However, the answer to the important question of whether or not Commons's work shows a marked influence from that school is not so clear. Commons remained associated with Ely for many years, and much of what he did and wrote was in the "Christian Socialist" spirit central to Ely's work.[38] The idea that the state (above all) and the church could provide solutions to economic problems was fundamental to the German political economists, and Ely brought that idea back to the United States as a proposition of fundamental importance. The first principle that Ely put in the prospectus for the proposed new American Economic Association in 1885 was this: "We regard the state as an agency whose positive assistance is one of the indispensable conditions of human progress."[39] A strong case can thus be made that Commons, with his continuing interest in reform and in the use of the state for that purpose, was furthering a transplanted version of the German historical school.

On the other hand, it is equally possible to ascribe his proclivities to his family. Both his parents had been keenly interested in politics; he already had the homegrown makings of a reformer before he became involved in Ely's Christian socialism. More importantly, it is clear that Commons, in his search for the processes through which reform might be achieved and in his efforts to teach people to use that process effectively, went far beyond the notion of the role of the state that Ely presented in the 1880s. His ideas of the collective will in action and of the transaction as the central unit of analysis are not inconsistent with the German tradition, but they do not derive from it.

Given the inadequacy of Ricardian economics to account for what was happening in either the United States or in Germany in the late nineteenth century, it is not surprising that groups of scholars in both countries pointed out its inadequacies. Nor is it particularly surprising that there were marked similarities in their analyses. Both were reactions to a period in which "the development of society and its order had become an immediate individual experience."[40] Homans was correct in seeing similarities between institutionalism, the German school, and Marxism because "The German historical school of necessity was deeply concerned with the changing structure of economic institutions and the progressive adaptation of life and thought to such change. Karl Marx's attention was centered upon the evolution of economic institutions in their relation to the distribution of power."[41] While a concern with changing institutions does mark an area of similarity between the German school, institutionalism, and some other schools of thought, Homans was not correct in thinking that this concern was an essential or identifying characteristic of institutionalism.

Institutionalism, Marx, and Socialism

If there has been a tendency by some to classify institutionalists as American members of the German historical school, others have wanted to see institutionalists, or at any rate those of the Veblenian tradition, as American Marxists or American socialists. The natural desire to find common ground among modern "heterodox economists" has reinforced the tendency to see Veblen in particular as a native-born radical whose thought was closely akin to that of Marx.[42] Veblen's scathing commentaries on businessmen and on American capitalism have led others who are not economists to see Veblen as closely akin to Marx.[43] Still others have wondered at the failure of an alliance to form between Veblen, his followers, and socialists.[44] All these arguments assume that Veblen's work was in the same radical tradition as Marx's. Veblen was a radical, but to equate him with others also classified as radical is entirely wrong. Furthermore, in thinking of Veblen as radical and akin to Marx, the much closer kinship between Veblen and Commons is minimized.

Although Veblen's radicalism, and particularly his view of the undesirable consequences of private property, make him seem an obvious ally of Marx, he rejected any possibility of such an alliance. He found Marx's thought rooted in the pre-Darwinian world of natural rights.[45] Marxism, Veblen said, was inconsistent with his own Darwinism. This inconsistency, he continued, arose from the contrast between the "unteleological Darwinian concept of natural selection" and the Marxian process of class struggle, which was "in fact a piece of Hedonism . . . related to Bentham rather than to Hegel."[46] Institutionalists do not ally themselves with Marxists because they view evolutionary social change as always ongoing and far more complex than is to be accounted for by any correction of distributional wrongs.[47]

Those who have identified themselves as institutionalists have often been keenly interested in reform. Many non-institutionalists and some who have regarded themselves as institutionalists have been inclined to see activism coupled with rejection of the *status quo* as the major trait of institutionalism. To the extent that "the desire to be of assistance in an intelligent scheme of social reform" has been seen as coupled with radicalism of analysis, it has appeared reasonable to expect an alliance, not only with Marx on the intellectual level, but with socialists on a political level.[48] What those who take this view miss is that the Benthamite origins of Marx's class struggle, the metaphysical notions of natural rights, and the labor theory of value blocked the absorption within the Marxist tradition of the notions of cultural relativity and cultural change that are so essential to modern social science and to institutionalism.

Institutionalism, Structuralism, and More Recent Theories of Development

Although it requires a substantial leap forward in time, it is worth noting that structuralism in Latin America, the work of Mahadev Govind Ranade in India, as well as the writing of the nineteenth-century Africans Africanus Horton and Edward Blyden, all are examples of theories of economic development and critiques of classical and neoclassical economics much like those of institutionalism.[49] Concern with changing economic institutions is undoubtedly the reason that ideas that seem closely related to American institutionalism have been spawned by the process of industrialization in other parts of the world. All have been reactions to changes associated with assimilation into the larger industrial world economy or to the rapid economic change that comes with industrialization.[50] Craufurd D. Goodwin suggests why the similarity between these bodies of thought and institutionalism is no accident, saying the work of Horton and Blyden

> may be claimed as an independent manifestation of the wide-spread questioning of economic science which began during the second half of the nineteenth century, identified with the historical school . . . and the institutionalists. . . . Attitudes common to the German, American, and West African thinkers included skepticism regarding current theory as a

universal guide to policy, belief in the relativity of most economic relationships to time and place, and an abiding interest in economic and social facts as an essential background to analysis. The West Africans' . . . intuition was of a very high order, and many of their policy conclusions are remarkably similar to those of present-day economists of developing countries.[51]

Both the processes of change and the difficulties of achieving the changes served to focus attention on institutions, their development over time, and their role in the process of economic growth. However, what makes institutionalism distinctive are the ways in which institutionalists have sought to explain change; it is the theory of change that combines Commons's notion of conflict resolution with Veblen's notions of idle curiosity and the instinct of workmanship, and both with instrumental valuing that sets institutionalism apart.

Institutionalism as an American Phenomenon

While the relationship of institutionalist thought to Marxism and to the German historical school has often been stressed, there has also been a not-entirely consistent stress upon the "Americanness" of institutionalism. There is, for example, a fairly common view that the conscious process through which the United States was created, the very low population/land ratio, and the social conditions associated with frontier life were what gave rise to the rather special intellectual tradition of which institutionalism is one part. It is not difficult to explain the appeal of this proposition because it is closely related to Ayresian institutionalist thought about the relationship of frontiers to institutional change and is very much part of a well-established American historiographic tradition. Clarence Ayres described frontiers as areas that were "free and easy," areas in which the constraints of "older mores and folkways" suffered "some reduction in importance."[52] He argued that Western Europe was "the frontier region of Mediterranean civilization" and that it was this frontier character that made the area the birthplace of the industrial economy. In the process he articulated a proposition that has had other applications, one of them being an explanation of the formation of institutionalism itself. J. Fagg Foster, for one, argued that institutionalist thought was essentially a twentieth-century phenomenon that grew out of a peculiarly American "common sense," differing from the habits of mind that allowed acceptance of "classical economics" in other parts of the world. In Foster's view it was the frontier, the self-sufficiency of the frontiersman, the "disinclination toward invidious distinctions" that the frontier caused, and the view of institutions as "created" that gave rise to this "common sense."[53] This view gains legitimacy from its similarity to the widely accepted proposition that there was something in the culture of the Midwest that produced so many of the major social thinkers of the United States in the late nineteenth- and early twentieth-centuries.[54]

Foster's argument is akin to the general Ayresian proposition about frontiers, but it is also very much part of the historiographic tradition that began with Frederick Jackson Turner's essay, "The Significance of the Frontier in American History."[55] Turner's was the classic statement of the proposition that free land altered both the individuals who settled on it and their society. When Foster suggested that there was an "American view" of the economy that rejected classical economic propositions and that this "American view" found later expression in institutionalism, he was espousing an essentially Turnerian view.

A difficulty with the Turner thesis as it has been used by Foster and others arises from the fact that the Turnerian view of conditions along the frontier owes more to American mythology than to accurate description. Despite the persistence of a very low population/land ratio, land was by no means so freely available after the Civil War, as is often assumed. The rhetoric associated with the passage of the Homestead Act has been persistent and powerful. However, by the time the Act was passed in 1862, land suitable for family farms was no longer easily and freely available.[56] Although the frontier was not declared closed by the Census Bureau until 1890, it had taken on a drastically different meaning for American farmers after the building of the railroads and after settlement reached the vicinity of the ninety-eighth meridian. Caught in an increasingly commercial agriculture, farmers had to buy land and other inputs, such as storage and transportation, for which they had to pay by selling their crops on what had become world markets.[57]

It was prior to the Civil War (and prior to the passage of the Homestead Act) that land was most freely available to settlers moving west. Whatever that movement did to the American character and to American thought, it did not result in an abandonment of the assumptions and concepts of British political economy. For most of the period when land was relatively free and when it was being settled rapidly, American intellectuals were remarkably conservative in their thought about the economy.[58] The low population/land ratio, the special problems faced by the new government in the years following the adoption of the Constitution in 1787, the rapid expansion of the population without the problems of urban misery obvious in England, all led to special American twists on the use of the classical British-derived economic theory—but American economic thought remained well within the boundaries of that thought until the 1880s. It is true that Alexander Hamilton and Friedrich List advocated a strong role for government and that Jacob Newton Cordozo, Alexander H. Everett, John Rae, and others dissented from the British emphasis on diminishing returns and the evils of unchecked population growth.[59] It is also true that Americans (both academic and otherwise) who wrote about economic matters in the period before the Civil War took positions on matters of public policy that were in some ways similar to those of twentieth-century institutionalists, but it is hard to find any methodological or philosophical similarities.

Rather than trying to explain institutionalism as a delayed, twentieth-century development of an especially American set of "common sense" economic ideas that prevailed in the nineteenth century, it seems better to see it as a product of the late nineteenth-century thought in the United States, while recognizing that earlier experience with creating a new nation and settling a largely empty land must have influenced the reaction to the growth of Darwinian and pragmatic thought in an increasingly industrial world. However, both pragmatism and the concern with social change were surely consequences of the growth of science and of the rapidity of socio-economic change that accompanied industrialization.

Populists or Muckrakers?

The last three decades of the nineteenth century in the United States were years in which problems associated with industrialization were phrased and understood as problems arising from the growth of big business, the price squeeze placed upon farmers, the turmoil associated with the rise of labor unions and their suppression, recurring financial crises, and the problems associated with immigration, urbanization, and corruption in government.[60]

Unfortunately, there has been a tendency to take the views of the founders of institutionalism to be essentially the same as those of the reformers of the period. Given Veblen's and Commons's strong criticisms of American capitalism, it is easy to think of them and their followers, and most importantly to think of their analyses, as part of this general American push for reform of a malfunctioning system. Commons was a reformer throughout his life, and it has been easy

enough to lump Veblen with the progressive critics of American society
of his time.[61] In the twentieth century, the followers of Veblen, Commons, and Wesley C. Mitchell were often keenly interested in reform.
Paul T. Homan, who was considered sufficiently authoritative on the
topic to have been chosen to write the 1931 *Encyclopaedia of the Social
Sciences* entry on "Institutional Economics," professed uncertainty
about any theoretical unanimity among institutionalists and fell back
upon reform as an essential sign that identified members of the school.
The "scent for problems" among institutionalists was "like that of bears
for honey," he said, and asserted that "the desire to be of assistance in
an intelligent scheme of social reform" was a major characteristic of
"the considerable proportion of the more capable younger economists"
who were associated with the school.[62] This close association between
a keenness for reform and institutionalism has made it even easier to
imagine that institutionalism somehow arose out of the same diagnosis
of the ills of the late nineteenth-century economy that gave rise to the
major reform movements of that period.

My proposition—a proposition that I set against the view that institutionalism was an offshoot of the reform movements of the late nineteenth and early twentieth centuries—is that the early institutionalists
did *not* share the general views about what had gone wrong with the
economic system of the gilded era. The farmers played the central role
in articulating the sources of trouble in the late nineteenth-century U.S.
economy. More than six out of every ten Americans still lived in "rural
territory" in 1890, and the political and general cultural clout of the
farmers was considerable.[63] As they became caught up in the changes
involved in the process of industrialization, they complained that they
were being squeezed between falling prices for their products and being
charged "too much" by increasingly monopolistic large firms. They
were particularly vociferous in their complaints against railroads and,
sometimes, against a monetary system dominated by "idle holders of
idle capital" who favored the gold standard.[64]

Although there were disagreements about the best ways to help the
farmers, there was wide agreement, among farmers and among those
who wrote or talked about them, that their problems stemmed from
the failure of agricultural prices to maintain a stable ratio to nonagricultural prices. Because this failure was attributed to the monopoly power
of the "robber barons" who controlled the railroads and the basic industries, the Sherman Act was seen as a major solution to the problems
of the farmers. Both William Letwin and Hans Thorelli, who have written most thoughtfully about the origins of the Sherman Antitrust Act,

repeat and espouse this view.[65] A related view that often creeps into the literature is that workers suffered a lowered standard of living. Actually, agricultural prices fell less rapidly than did non-agricultural prices and real wages rose, at least after 1880.[66]

Despite the rising real incomes of the bulk of the population, one of the lasting legacies of the period is the belief that the increased concentration of industry brought about some deterioration in the standard of living. This legacy has contributed to the fixation of standard economists upon the virtues of a nonexistent perfect competition. It has also been part of the continued populist and popular hostility to "big business."[67] Insofar as institutionalists are understood to be economists who are strong in their opposition to big business, they are understood to be economists who belong to this liberal left part of the political spectrum; they are understood to be "prairie populists."[68]

Neither of the founding fathers of institutionalism shared the populist and muckraking view of the turn-of-the-century economy. Writing in 1891, Veblen said

> Especially can it fairly be claimed that the result of the last few decades of our industrial development has been to increase greatly the creature comforts within the reach of the average human being. And, decidedly, the result has been an amelioration of the lot of the less favored in a relatively greater degree than that of those economically more fortunate. The claim that the system of competition has proved itself an engine for making the rich richer and the poor poorer has the fascination of epigram; but if its meaning is that the lot of the average, of the masses of humanity in civilised life, is worse today, as measured in the means of livelihood, than it was twenty, or fifty, or a hundred years ago, then it is farcical. The cause of discontent must be sought elsewhere than in any increased difficulty in obtaining the means of subsistence or of comfort.[69]

In an article published in 1892, Veblen observed that between 1872 and the early 1880s, wheat farming was "distinctly profitable." "How profitable," he continued, "is a question that does not admit of an intelligible answer, but there are indications that it was, perhaps, the most paying branch of American farming during a time when American farming paid unusually well."[70] Veblen also estimated that even after the price declines of the 1880s, wheat farming was still "mostly profitable," but his dating and even, in fact, the probably great accuracy of his estimates are of less importance here than is the fact that he did *not* share the view of farm distress that was so widespread.

In his discussion of the concept of reasonable value as determined by the courts, Commons made clear his view that the large corporations had not been "exploitative." Indeed, he found Veblen's views on the matter too critical of the performance of the large firms:

> Veblen was the first who builded upon the modern concept of intangible property, which he derived directly from the customs of business men who used the term. . . . He rested solely on the new concept of intangible property as the present value of the future bargaining power of capitalists.
>
> But he did not investigate the decisions of the Supreme Court. The Supreme Court of the United States, when cases arose, rested its decisions on this same new phenomenon of intangible property, not, however, on Veblen's exploitation, but on its own historic concept of reasonable value. In some cases this doctrine sustained the contentions of the capitalists, as in the United States Steel Dissolution Suit (1920). In other cases it greatly reduced the values contended for by the capitalists.[71]

Commons emphasized the extent to which corporations and the courts had been engaged in a process of establishing "reasonable value" in the face of the changing organization of production and the changing levels of output. In the passage above and elsewhere he argued that Veblen had erred in finding evidence for "exploitation."

Both Veblen and Commons did agree that "ownership" had taken on new meaning. In Commons's words, ownership meant the "power to restrict abundance."[72] In Veblen's words, "the proximate aim of the business man is to upset or block the industrial process at some one or more points."[73] But neither Veblen nor Commons attributed this power to "derange the industrial system" to a growth of big business that public policy could or should reverse. Veblen, in fact, saw virtues in the concentration of industry:

> So long as related industrial units are under different business managements, they are, by the nature of the case, at cross-purposes, and business consolidation remedies this untoward feature of the industrial system by eliminating the pecuniary element from the interstices of the system as far as may be. The interstitial adjustments of the industrial system at large are in this way withdrawn from the discretion of rival business men, and the work of pecuniary management previously involved is in large part dispensed with, with the result that there is a saving of work and an avoidance of that systematic mutual hindrance that characterizes the competitive management of industry. To the community at large the work of pecuniary management, it appears, is less serviceable the more there is of it. The heroic role of the captain of industry is that of a deliverer from an excess of business management. It is a casting out of business men by the chief of business men.[74]

Of course, Veblen did not like many of the actions of those who managed big business, and neither did Commons. But neither was anti-big business. They were simply not participating in the same realm of discourse that occupied populists and muckrakers. Veblen was concerned with the businessman's tendency to "derange the industrial system," to withhold abundance over the course of a business cycle that itself resulted from the pecuniary processes. His was not a concern with the alleged existence of an essentially one-time movement from a larger competitive to a smaller monopolistic level of output. The same can be said about Mitchell, about John Maurice Clark, and about Walton Hamilton. All recognized that, as Hamilton put it, the relevance of *laissez-faire* had passed and what was wanted was "an economics relevant to problems of control."[75] In recent decades Allan Gruchy has emphasized the proposition that the solution for the new economic order was *new* institutions of planning rather than a turning back to some hypothetical ideal of *laissez-faire*.[76]

Drawing a careful distinction between the early institutionalists and the populists and muckrakers is important because there is a tendency for institutionalists to be identified as economists who disapprove of existing institutions. Since most economists today know of Veblen only because of his reputation as social satirist and of Commons only because he was somehow associated with the labor movement, this tendency is reinforced. A clearer view of modern institutionalism emerges if it is understood that neither Commons, nor Veblen, nor Hamilton, nor their immediate followers shared the most vigorous and popular protest positions of their day.

Conclusion

The arguments presented in this essay may be briefly summarized. Institutional economic thought began in the United States in the last two decades of the nineteenth century when the early institutionalists drew upon that world of growing industrialization and rapid socioeconomic change for the substance of their analysis. Their methods and their perceptions of social processes—methods and perceptions that continue to give institutionalism its distinctive characteristics—reflected the wide acceptance of Darwinian thought and the new ideas in the social sciences that derived from and fitted with the new conditions. Ongoing change and human diversity and the related abandonment of natural laws governing human behavior and human society gave rise to the modern ideas of culture, cultural evolution, and cultural relativity. Institutional economics diverged from standard economics because it rested upon acceptance of these ideas. Institutional economics also diverged from other traditions in the social sciences because institutionalists placed great emphasis upon instrumental valuation as the driving force of cultural evolution.

Notes

1. I make no effort in this paper to provide a history of early institutionalist thought. Limitation of space has meant that I have focused primarily upon Thorstein Veblen and John R. Commons, and even there I have provided only a brief introduction to their work. For fuller accounts of the formation of institutionalist thought, I recommend Joseph Dorfman, *The Economic Mind in American Civilization*, Vols. 3 and 4 (New York: Augustus M. Kelley, 1969 [1934]); Wesley C. Mitchell, *Types of Economic Theory*, Vol. 2 (New York: Augustus M. Kelley, 1949), Chaps. 31–36 and 40–41; Wesley C. Mitchell, "Thorstein Veblen" and "Commons on Institutionalism," in *The Backward Art of Spending Money and Other Essays* (New York: Augustus M. Kelley, 1950); David Hamilton, *Newtonian Classicism and Darwinian Institutionalism* (Albuquerque, N.M.: The University of New Mexico Press, 1953); Allan G. Gruchy, *Modern Economic Thought: The American Contribution* (New York: Prentice-Hall, 1947), and *Contemporary Economic Thought: The Contribution of Neo-Institutional Economics* (Clifton, N.J.: Augustus M. Kelley, 1972).
2. Stanley Lebergott, *Manpower in Economic Growth* (New York: McGraw Hill, 1964), Table A-1, p. 510. These numbers and the ones in the sentences that follow are as reported by Lebergott for the labor force aged 10 and over.
3. Lance E. Davis *et al., American Economic Growth* (New York: Harper & Row, Publishers, 1972), Table 2.19, p. 55.
4. U.S. Bureau of the Census, *Historical Statistics of the United States, Colonial Times to 1970, Bicentennial Edition, Part 2* (Washington D.C., 1975) Series F 10–16.
5. For the importance of overhead costs and the professionalization and bureaucratization of management, see John Maurice Clark, *Studies in the Economics of Overhead Costs* (Chicago: University of Chicago Press, 1923); Alfred D. Chandler, J., *The Visible Hand* (Cambridge, Mass.: The Belknap Press, 1977); A. A. Berle, Jr. and G. C. Means, *The Modern Corporation and Private Property,* rev. ed. (New York: Harcourt Brace Jovanovich, 1968); Robert T. Averitt, *The Dual Economy* (New York: W. W. Norton & Co., 1968).
6. John R. Commons, *Myself* (New York: The Macmillan Company, 1934), p. 11.
7. Ibid., pp. 38–44.
8. See Commons, *Myself,* but also John R. Commons, *Institutional Economics* (New York: The Macmillan Company, 1934), Chap. 1, for Commons's account of his intellectual development.

9. Joseph Dorfman, *Thorstein Veblen and His America* (New York: The Viking Press, 1935) Chaps. 1–4 and p. 68 for comments about Bellamy. For further discussion of the relationship of Bellamy's work to Veblen's, see Rick Tilman, "The Utopian Vision of Edward Bellamy and Thorstein Veblen," *Journal of Economic Issues* 19 (December 1985): 879–98.

10. For accounts of the extent to which concern with Darwinism dominated social thought, see Richard Hofstadter, *Social Darwinism in American Thought* (Philadelphia: University of Pennsylvania Press, 1945) and Cynthia Eagle Russett, *Darwin in America: The Intellectual Response 1865–1912* (San Francisco: W. H. Freeman and Company, 1976).

11. Hofstadter, *Social Darwinism in American Thought*, Chap. 4.

12. Robert H. Lowie, *The History of Ethnological Theory* (New York: Holt, Rinehart and Winston, 1937), p. 56.

13. Ibid., p. 19.

14. Sir Edward Burnett Tylor, *Primitive Culture* (New York: Harper, 1958 [1871]), p. 1.

15. Walter Goldschmidt, *Comparative Functionalism: An Essay in Anthropological Theory* (Berkeley: University of California Press, 1966), p. ix.

16. In Thorstein Veblen, "Why Is Economics Not an Evolutionary Science?" pp. 56–61 in *The Place of Science in Modern Society* (New York: Russell & Russell, 1961), reprinted from *The Quarterly Journal of Economics* 12 (July 1898).

17. Russett, p. 148.

18. John P. Diggins, *The Bard of Savagery* (New York: The Seabury Press, 1978), p. ix.

19. Veblen, "Why Is Economics Not an Evolutionary Science?," p. 75.

20. Dorfman, *Thorstein Veblen and His America,* Chap. 19–22 discusses Veblen's brief and unsuccessful career as an activist. Those who emphasize Veblen's interest in fomenting revolutionary change usually cite this period and what he wrote during the years immediately afterward: for example, Rick Tilman, "Thorstein Veblen: Incrementalist and Utopian," *American Journal of Economics and Sociology* 32 (April 1973): 155–69.

21. Thorstein Veblen, "The Place of Science in Modern Civilisation," in *The Place of Science in Modern Civilisation,* pp. 1–31, reprinted from *The American Journal of Sociology* 11 (March 1906): 14–16.

22. Clarence E. Ayres, "Veblen's Theory of Instincts Reconsidered," in Douglas F. Dowd, ed., *Thorstein Veblen: A Critical Reappraisal* (Ithaca, N.Y.: Cornell University Press, 1958), p. 25.

23. In *Institutional Economics* Commons lays out his economic theory and, in the process, tells us a great deal about its sources and about how he perceived the relationship of his work to that of Veblen. Commons wrote that, to Veblen, "Darwinian evolution has no foreordained goal, but is a continuity of cause and effect without any trend, any final term, or consummation," which is true. Commons then goes on to say, "But Darwin had two kinds of 'selection' . . . : Natural Selection and Artificial Selection. Ours is a theory of artificial selection. Veblen's is natural selection." However, Commons said, "Veblen is compelled to introduce *purpose* into his instinct of workmanship and thereby to change from Darwin's 'natural' selection to Darwin's 'artificial' selection" (Commons, *Institutional Economics,* p.

657), which is not quite right. To Commons the distinction between artificial and natural selection is the presence or absence of "purpose," but
in Veblen's world of goal-less evolution, people's actions are certainly purposive. The important point here is that Commons was dealing in the same
ideas as was Veblen, although he saw those ideas from a different perspective. Commons divided contemporaneous social theorists into those who
accepted a Spencerian (and, in his view, Darwinian) interpretation of social
evolution as something that could not and should not be consciously altered and those who were for reform, those who favored "artificial selection." It is a tribute to Commons's commitment to reform that he could
not see that, to Veblen as social theorist, being for or against efforts to reform was beside the point. Yngve Ramstad, "Institutional Existentialism:
(Or More on Why John R. Commons Has So Few Followers)," *Journal of
Economic Issues* 21 (June 1987): 661-71, offers an interesting and convincing interpretation of Commons's view of directed social evolution, an interpretation that could be used to emphasize the congruity between
Veblen's and Commons's approaches (although Ramstad does emphasize
heavily the human direction of social change).

24. Commons, *Institutional Economics,* p. 4. For excellent explication of Commons's basic theory, see R. A. Gonce, "John R. Commons's Legal Economic Theory," *Journal of Economic Issues* 5 (September 1971): 80-95;
and R. A. Gonce, "The New Property Rights Approach and Commons's
Legal Foundations of Capitalism," *Journal of Economic Issues* 10 (December 1976): 765-97.

25. See, for example, his discussion of David Hume and C. S. Peirce in Commons, *Institutional Economics,* pp. 140-57.

26. See Dorfman, *The Economic Mind in American Civilization,* Vols. 3 and 4.

27. Wesley C. Mitchell, "Quantitative Analysis in Economic Theory," *The
American Economic Review* 15 (March 1925): 1-12, reprinted in *The Backward Art of Spending Money* (New York: Augustus M. Kelley, 1950), pp.
20-41. Italics added.

28. Paul T. Homan, "Economics, The Institutional School," *The Encyclopaedia of the Social Sciences* 5 (New York: Macmillan, 1931), p. 388.

29. For an interesting treatment see Jurgen Herbst, *The German Historical
School in American Scholarship* (Ithaca, N.Y.: Cornell University Press,
1965), particularly Chap. 6.

30. Ibid., p. 134.

31. Wesley C. Mitchell, *Types of Economic Theory,* Vol. 2 ed. Joseph Dorfman, (New York: Augustus M. Kelley, 1969), pp. 237-43; Paul T. Homan,
Contemporary Economic Thought (New York: Harper Bros., 1928), Chap.
1.

32. For the ongoing relationship between Commons and Ely after Commons
joined Ely at the University of Wisconsin in 1904, see Commons, *Myself;*
Richard T. Ely, *Ground Under Our Feet: An Autobiography* (New York:
The Macmillan Co., 1938); and Benjamin G. Rader, *The Academic Mind
and Reform* (Lexington: The University of Kentucky Press, 1966).

33. These and other reviews are reprinted in Joseph Dorfman, *Thorstein Veblen: Essays, Reviews, and Reports* (Clifton, N.J.: Augustus M. Kelley, 1973).
Veblen had read passages in the German encyclopedia from which Ely took
his lectures on the German historical school. He did not find Ely's lectures

superior to those passages and was, during his brief stay at Johns Hopkins, unimpressed with Ely (Dorfman, *Thorstein Veblen and His America*, p. 40).

34. Mitchell, *Types of Economic Theory*, p. 745. See also George H. Hildebrand, "Discussion of Joseph Dorfman, 'The Role of the German Historical School in American Economic Thought'," *American Economic Review, Papers and Proceedings* 45 (May 1955), p. 37.

35. Thorstein Veblen, "Gustav Schmoller's Economics," pp. 252–78 in *The Place of Science in Modern Society*, reprinted from *The Quarterly Journal of Economics* 16 (November 1901).

36. Ibid., pp. 274–75.

37. Commons, *Institutional Economics*, p. 115.

38. Dorfman, *The Economic Mind*, Vol. 3, p. 162, where he describes Ely as "fundamentally a Christian Socialist" and discusses the importance of this description.

39. The story of the founding of the American Economic Association, of its relationship to the German training of many of its founders, and of the subsequent debates about the principles for which it stood has been told in several places. See, for example, Dorfman, *The Economic Mind*, pp. 205–12.

40. Michael Hutter, "Early Contributions to Law and Economics: Adolph Wagner's *Grundlegung*," *Journal of Economic Issues* 16 (March 1982): 131–47, p. 131, uses the phrase to describe Germany.

41. Homans, "Economics, The Institutional School," p. 388.

42. Cf. E. K. Hunt, "The Importance of Thorstein Veblen for Contemporary Marxism," *Journal of Economic Issues* 13 (March 1979): 113–40. For a thorough survey of the literature comparing Marx and Veblen, see Forest G. Hill, "Veblen and Marx," in Dowd, *Thorstein Veblen: A Critical Reappraisal*, pp. 129–49.

43. Cf. John P. Diggins, *The Bard of Savagery*.

44. Donald R. Stabile, "Thorstein Veblen and His Socialist Contemporaries," *Journal of Economic Issues* 16 (March 1982): pp. 1–28.

45. E. K. Hunt tries, in "The Importance of Thorstein Veblen for Contemporary Marxism," to minimize the importance of Veblen's rejection of Marx as an intellectual ally. He argues that Veblen was wrong about the importance of the metaphysical Hegelian dialectic for Marx and that Veblen was not really a Darwinian (or was mistaken in being so). This does not deal with Veblen's view that Marx was fundamentally a Benthamite. Hunt also argues that Veblen was not truly "Darwinian" because Veblen's appreciation of cultural and aesthetic elements in evolution must mean that Veblen thought that values guided the evolutionary process. To take Veblen out of a non-teleological "Darwinian" camp and put him into the teleological Marxian camp Hunt must, however, ignore the mechanism of Veblen's evolutionary process.

46. Thorstein Veblen, "The Socialist Economics of Karl Marx and His Followers," pp. 409–30 in *The Place of Science in Modern Society*, reprinted from *The Quarterly Journal of Economics* 20 (August 1906). The quoted passages are from pp. 417–18.

47. Marc Tool, "Social Value Theory of Marxists: An Instrumentalist Review and Critique," *Journal of Economic Issues, Part One* 16 (December 1982):

1079–1107; *Part Two*, 17 (March 1983): 155–73.

48. The quoted phrase is from Homans, *Contemporary Economic Thought*, p. 415. I do not here address the relationships among political and intellectual positions. For a view that they are essentially the same, see Rick Tilman, "Social Value Theory, Corporate Power, and Political Elites," *Journal of Economic Issues* 17 (March 1983): 115–31, where he equates radical analysis with radical political position and thus converts "neoinstitutionalism" into a form of Marxism (p. 127).

49. John Adams, "The Institutional Economics of Mahadev Govind Ranade," *Journal of Economic Issues* 5 (June 1971): 80–92; James H. Street, "The Latin American 'Structuralists' and the Institutionalists: Convergence in Development Theory," *Journal of Economic Issues* 1 (June 1967): 44–62; James H. Street and Dilmus D. James, "Institutionalism, Structuralism, and Dependency in Latin America," *Journal of Economic Issues* 16 (September 1982): 673–89; and Craufurd D. Goodwin, "Economic Analysis and Development in British West Africa," *Economic Development and Cultural Change* 15 (July 1967): 438–51.

50. The British Historical School that struggled valiantly against the tide of British economic orthodoxy was part of the same process even though it emanated from the center of the established industrial world. For an account, see A. W. Coats, "The Historicist Reaction in English Political Economy, 1870–90," *Economica* 21 (May 1954): 143–53.

51. Goodwin, "Economic Analysis and Development" p. 451. See Phillip A. Klein, "An Institutionalist View of Development Economics," *Journal of Economic Issues* 11 (December 1977): 785–807, for a discussion of the similarities among institutionalist and development economists. Klein quotes R.A. Gordon's earlier observation that in development economics "Economics has truly 'gone institutional'."

52. Clarence E. Ayres, *The Theory of Economic Progress*, 2nd edition (New York: Schocken Books, 1962), p. 133.

53. Baldwin Ranson, ed., "The Papers of J. Fagg Foster," *Journal of Economic Issues* 15 (December 1981): 851–1052, and for this passage, pp. 863–65. See also Marcus R. Tool, "The Philosophy of Neoinstitutionalism: Veblen, Dewey, and Ayres," unpublished PhD. thesis, 1953, University of Colorado, for an extended discussion of the proposition that it was the special American character that gave rise to institutional thought.

54. See, for example, Hofstadter, *Social Darwinism in American Thought*, p. 53. I do not know if studies have been done to determine whether reformers came disproportionately from frontier environments, but it is part of unexamined American "common sense" that they did.

55. Frederick Jackson Turner, "The Significance of the Frontier in American History," in Turner, *The Frontier in American History* (New York: Henry Holt, 1920). The essay was originally delivered as a paper at a meeting of the American Historical Association in 1893.

56. For the classic article on this topic, see Paul Wallace Gates, "The Homestead Law in an Incongruous Land System," *The American Historical Review* 41 (1936): 652–81.

57. Anne Mayhew, "A Reappraisal of the Causes of Farm Protest in the United States, 1870–1900," *Journal of Economic History* 32 (June 1972): 464–75. The "frontiersmen" of the post-Civil War period bought and sold land just as they bought and sold their farm produce. One mythological aspect of

thought about the frontier almost surfaces in the Veblen family's history: Thorstein Veblen's father moved his family to a newly purchased farm of 290 acres in 1865, when Thorstein was eight. Dorfman says that "the land hunger of the rural Norwegian was finally appeased. Thomas Veblen had none of the acquisitiveness of the average American pioneer farmer who seized for its speculative value as much of the land as he could hold possession of and thereby made rural life dreary and isolated. While Thorstein Veblen was growing to maturity, his father was content to cultivate his 290 acres." Dorfman, *Thorstein Veblen and His America,* pp. 9–10. However, the average acreage per farm in Minnesota was 149 acres in 1860, 129 in 1870, and 145 in 1880—the average farm was half the size of the Veblen farm! In the literature about the American past, whether or not an author describes the purchase of a farm that contains 200 acres of "wild prairie land" as a speculative venture or as the heroic making of a farm often seems to depend upon whether the author approves or disapproves of the individuals who purchase (Dorfman, *The Economic Mind in American Civilization).*

58. Dorfman, *The Economic Mind in American Civilization,* Vols. 1 and 2 (New York: The Viking Press, 1946). See especially pp. 695–713 in Vol. 2 for Dorfman's summary of "the higher learning" in the years 1829–1861, the period when land was probably most freely available to the largest numbers. What he describes in those pages is allegiance to the ideas of the classical economists and extreme conservatives. Lest this be attributed solely to the dominance of Eastern schools with their religious ties, it should also be noted that Dorfman says, "If the West was a center of radicalism, it certainly did not show up in the writing of its economists in this period. They were, if anything, even more conservative in their underlying social philosophy than their eastern brethren" (Vol. 2, p. 934).

59. Dorfman, *The Economic Mind in American Civilization,* Vol. 2 and Henry William Spiegel, *The Growth of Economic Thought* (Durham, N.C.: Duke University Press, 1983), Chap. 27.

60. Samuel P. Hays, *The Response to Industrialism: 1885–1913* (Chicago: The University of Chicago Press, 1957) is a good, brief account of the interconnection of these and other issues. I am not going to try to relate the ideas of the founding fathers of institutionalism to "progressive thought." For one attempt to do so, see Rick Tilman, "Dewey's Liberalism vs. Veblen's Radicalism: A Reappraisal of the Unity of Progressive Social Thought," *Journal of Economic Issues* 18 (September 1984): 745–69.

61. See Rick Tilman, "Dewey's Liberalism vs. Veblen's Radicalism," *Journal of Economic Issues* 17 (September 1984): 745–69.

62. Paul T. Homan, *Contemporary Economic Thought* (New York: Harper Bros., 1928), pp. 414.

63. U.S. Bureau of the Census, *Historical Statistics of the United States, Colonial Times to 1970, Part I,* Series A 57–72, pp. 11–12. In this discussion I am drawing heavily on my article, "A Reappraisal of the Causes of Farm Protest in the United States, 1870–1900."

64. The phrase is from William Jennings Bryan's famous speech, "Cross of Gold," reproduced in William W. Letwin, ed., *A Documentary History of American Economic Policy Since 1789* (Garden City, New York: Doubleday & Co., 1961), pp. 248–56.

65. William Letwin, *Law and Economic Policy in America* (New York: Ran-

dom House, 1965); Hans Thorelli, *The Federal Antitrust Policy* (Stockholm: no publisher given, 1954).

66. See Douglass C. North, *Growth and Welfare in the American Past* (Englewood Cliffs, N.J.: Prentice-Hall, 1966), pp. 137–48 for the agricultural terms of trade and Stanley Lebergott, *Manpower in Economic Growth*, p. 163.

67. Glenn Porter, *The Rise of Big Business, 1860–1910* (Arlington Heights, Ill.: Harlan Davidson, 1973), pp. 1–26, is an excellent brief statement of the role that "big business" has played in American historiography and in American thought more generally.

68. John Adams, "Gailbraith on Economic Development," *Journal of Post Keynesian Economics* 7 (Fall 1984): 91–102, has an interesting discussion of how John Kenneth Galbraith (an institutionalist-as-liberal who is "for the people and against big business and foolish technocrats") fits this mold. Adams argues that institutionalists do not feel entirely comfortable with Galbraith because, even though he shares many of their views, he is primarily an "institutionalist-as-prairie-populist"—and that is *not* the essential characteristic of most institutionalists.

69. Thorstein Veblen, "Some Neglected Points in the Theory of Socialism," *The Place of Science in Modern Civilisation and Other Essays*, p. 391.

70. Thorstein Veblen, "The Price of Wheat Since 1867," *The Journal of Political Economy* (December 1892), reprinted in Joseph Dorfman, ed., *Essays, Reviews, and Reports*, pp. 347–48.

71. Commons, *Institutional Economics*, p. 651.

72. Ibid., p. 8.

73. Thorstein Veblen, *The Theory of Business Enterprise* (New York: Mentor Books, 1958, c1904), p. 21.

74. Veblen, *The Theory of Business Enterprise*, p. 29.

75. Walton H. Hamilton, "The Institutional Approach to Economic Theory," in *Industrial Policy and Institutionalism* (Clifton, N.J.: Augustus M. Kelley, 1974), p. 313. (No editor listed, but Hamilton's name in parentheses on the cover; Joseph Dorfman wrote the introduction.)

76. Allan Gruchy, "Government Intervention and the Social Control of Business: The Neoinstitutionalist Position," *Journal of Economic Issues* 8 (June 1974): 235–49.

Part II

The Philosophical Bases of Institutionalist Economics

Philip Mirowski

The precise nature of the relationship between the disciplines of economics and philosophy has yet to be explicated in detail. Certain family resemblances can be readily verified, and traced to a common lineage. Many of the precursors of Western economic theory, such as John Locke and Adam Smith, were self-identified moral philosophers; many other inhabitants of the pantheon of economic theory, such as Karl Marx and John Maynard Keynes, are recognized as having made substantial contributions to philosophy. Nevertheless, in the modern era, ontogeny does not recapitulate phylogeny; and the average economist in the late twentieth century would deny any necessary or close links between the two fields.

In economics, the facade of the repudiation of philosophical preconceptions is propped up by the widespread conviction that modern economics has successfully adopted the character and attributes of a *science*. This invocation of science is intended to settle all arguments once and for all and to expiate all sins. Of course, this has been a vain hope. Disputes over method, epistemology, and ontology have not been banished because an invocation of science merely impounds controversy under the rubric of "the philosophy of science," without really

The author would like to thank Anne Mayhew, Marc Tool, Ken Dennis, Bob Coats and especially Paul Dale Bush and Yngve Ramstad for their comments on an earlier draft. He wishes also to express his appreciation for permission to reprint parts of his book Against Mechanism *in this article.*

answering any of the hard questions. Once we can get beyond the lab coats and the particle accelerators and the rest of the clanking machinery, it is not at all clear that "science" is inextricably committed to any particular program or method or ontological construction. Indeed, once we get beyond the homiletic nostrums of Physics I, some exposure to the history of science demonstrates that there is no such thing as single "scientific method." Science may at various junctures be realist or it may be idealist; it may be rationalist or it may be empiricist; it may be monistic or it may be dualistic; it may be naturalist or operationalist or it may be instrumentalist; or, most bluntly, it may be true or it may be false. Nothing is substantially illuminated by the mere invocation of science by economists, although it has in the past proved useful in cowing certain critics.

A survey of the philosophical presuppositions of modern economics is made doubly difficult by the necessity of confronting the role of "science" in both revealing and obscuring the main points of contention. Thorstein Veblen, himself first trained as a philosopher, once began one of his articles with the deadpan sentence: "A discussion of the scientific point of view which avowedly proceeds from this point of view itself has necessarily the appearance of an argument in a circle; and such in great part is the character of what here follows" [Veblen 1969, p. 32]. Veblen's predicament is particularly poignant for the issues at hand because he was philosophically literate, he was the acknowledged progenitor of the institutionalist school of economics, and he chose to raise the issue of the philosophical preconceptions of the economics of his day by attacking its credentials as a science. Ever since that time, the institutionalist school has been distinguished from the general run of orthodoxy by a concern with the philosophical aspects of economic issues, especially in its role of a critic of neoclassical economics.

Nevertheless, things get stickier when one tries to briefly characterize the philosophical bases of institutionalist economics, either as it is presently practiced, or else as an ideal projection. (For some recent attempts, see Alan Dyer [1986]; Yngve Ramstad [1986]; and C. Wilbur and R. Harrison [1978].) In this article, the reader should be prepared for one very individual and idiosyncratic reading of the philosophical underpinnings of institutionalist theory: namely, that it has not yet found a way to break out of Veblen's ironic circle. The problem, as we shall argue in this chapter, is a failure of comprehension of the fact that institutionalist economics was the offspring of an entirely distinct philosophical tradition from that which gave rise to neoclassical economics. These two traditions have a profound conflict over their respective images of a "science," and therefore profoundly incompatible images of "economic man" and "rationality."

The Durkheim/Mauss/Douglas Thesis

The first urgent issue in the philosophy of economics is the question of the intelligibility of a separate discipline devoted exclusively to the explication of an abstract concept called "the economy," separate from other categories of social phenomena, and separate from the relationships we attribute to the physical or non-human world. These are the fundamental issues that any coherent discipline of economic theory must address: it must carve up reality, and have some claim to have carved artfully "at the joints"; it must have some resources to adjudicate boundary disputes with other disciplines, which requires a clear conception of its own theoretical object; it must nurture some epistemological conception of the economic actor and the economist and presumably reconcile them one with the other; and it must build bridges to the conceptions of power and efficacy within the context of the culture in which it is to subsist. Although it is not inevitable, in the past these requirements have been satisfied to a greater or lesser degree by positing a curious symmetry between the portrait of the economic scientist and the theoretical portrait of "rational economic man" in the particular school of economic thought. This symmetry exists on many levels, both formal and informal. It is the thesis of this chapter that once the pattern of this symmetry is understood, then the philosophical distinctions that divide and demarcate institutionalist economic theory from neoclassical economic theory become transparent; and further, one can go quite a distance in explaining the evolution of institutionalist thought in the twentieth century.

In order to organize the various themes in the philosophy of economics, and to explain our symmetry thesis, we shall have recourse to a very important generalization about human behavior that was generated not in economics, but in anthropology. In 1903, the anthropologists Emile Durkheim and Marcel Mauss proposed a hypothesis that has become one of the core tenets of research programs in the sociology of knowledge. They asserted that, in all primitive cultures, the classification of things reproduces the classifications of human beings [Durkheim and Mauss 1963]. Although the Durkheim/Mauss thesis was only intended to apply to primitive societies, and the original empirical ethnographic evidence they offered in its support was widely challenged and criticized, the thesis has been taken up and revised by the Edinburgh school of the sociology of science and applied to the history of *Western* science [Bloor 1982; Barnes and Shapin, 1979]. Recently the anthropologist Mary Douglas has further elaborated the hypothesis by asserting its antithesis: the social classification of human beings is often a mirror image of a culture's classifications of the natural world.

For purposes of brevity, we can summarize the complete Durkheim/ Mauss/Douglas (DMD) thesis in the format of the "vortex model of the sociology of science" [Mirowski, forthcoming]. Societies differ tremendously in the sources of inspiration and validation for their social and natural concepts, but they resemble one another quite dramatically in the way in which social and natural concepts are interlinked and in the manner in which belief in one set of concepts reinforces belief in the other. Theories of the physical world are shaped by the social relations within the culture that generates them, and these are used in turn to express in reified form the essence of that culture's ideal of order. This ideal of order consequently molds the expression of social concepts and classifications, eventually transforming the original notions of mastery and control in the social sphere. The circuit or vortex is completed by the persistent projection of anthropomorphic concepts onto "Nature," and the intended demonstration of the efficacy and legitimacy of structures in the social sphere through its purported success in the mastery of personified nature.

While this "vortex model" is a cornucopia of suggestions for the analysis of social life, for the history of science, and for various controversies in epistemology, it has its immediate effectiveness in helping to understand the preconceptions of institutional economics that concern us here. Divergent assumptions about the relationship of social concepts to natural concepts, and the relationship of the possibility of mastery and control to the reified concept of order are the fundamental distinguishing marks of institutional and neoclassical economic theory.

The discipline of economics in the Western world has always been caught in the thrall of the contemporaneous Western understanding of the physical world, particularly with respect to the concept of value.[1] It has been an even more recent phenomenon (say, since the early nineteenth century) that the idealized image of the method of natural science has played the predominant role in shaping the image of the economic actor in economic theory. However, at this juncture the cultural diversity of various Western societies has come into play: because there have been multiple variations on the theme of the correct scientific method, there have been equally numerous corresponding images of the "economy" and of the economic actor. Economic praxeology may recapitulate epistemology, but it can only do so within a specific cultural setting. Schools of economic thought may subsquently interpenetrate and cross-fertilize, but their initial integrity and specificity derives from their origins in a particular construct of our knowledge of the "external" world and hence of ourselves and other actors.

Rather than discuss the interplay suggested by the DMD thesis of the reigning scientific epistemology and the ontology of the economic actor at an extremely rarified level, it will be more efficient to demonstrate the thesis through the display of two relevant examples: that of Cartesian analytic philosophy and neoclassical economic theory; and the American variant of the Continental hermeneutic tradition in philosophy and institutional economics.

The Cartesian Tradition and Neoclassical Economic Theory

The Cartesian tradition in philosophy has made its appearance in the British and American contexts with the tendency toward "analytical philosophy," especially in the twentieth century. Although many of the modern tenets are not intended to be faithful representations of Descartes's original concerns, the "Cartesian tradition" does serve as a shorthand for a certain sequence of canonical texts and attitudes [Rorty, Schneewind and Skinner 1984]. We shall characterize this tradition by the following seven tenets [Cf. Tiles 1984; Bernstein 1983]: (a) Analytical Cartesian philosophy is not overly concerned with the thought processes of the individual scientist, nor indeed, of any group of scientists. Above all, it demands that science is mechanical and impersonal, and quarantines the context of discovery from the context of justification. (b) The process of inquiry is divided into "deduction" and "induction." Philosophy analyzes the former as a discrete set of logical statements, with concepts investigated only through their functions in isolated abstract statements. Philosophy is relatively helpless in analyzing induction because there is no guaranteed logic of induction. (c) "Logic" is interpreted to mean mathematical axiomatization. (d) There is an unbridgeable gulf between the philosophy of science and the history of science. The best one can do is to construct a *post hoc* "rational reconstruction" of what is, at best, a mess. Science perennially reconstitutes itself and therefore has no real need of history. (e) The role of philosophy is to prescribe and defend the right rules of scientific method. The *summum bonum* would be an automaton to which all disputes would be submitted and that would hence guarantee the validity of scientific work. (f) The separation of mind and body dictates that we know our own thought better than we can know the world. Hence all verification is the assuagement of personal doubt. This comes about by means of repeated personal contact with a stable external world, independent of any mediation by others as well as independent of the signs used to express such knowledge. (g) Knowledge, once attained, is passed along intact to other researchers. Knowledge is fully cumulative, the accretion of past individual researches [Cf. Tiles 1984; Bernstein 1983].

One important corollary of the DMD thesis is that the social theories that were prevalent in the culture dominated by the portrait of science made up of the seven points outlined above would project that image onto their understanding of their own social relations. If we cast our gaze upon the orthodox economics of Britain and America in the twentieth century, we indeed discover that the neoclassical portrait of the "rational economic man" conforms to the outline, very nearly point-by-point: (a) Neoclassical economics is not concerned with the actual thought processes of the individual economic actors. The actors are subject to an ideal of rationality that is mechanical and impersonal in the dual senses that constrained optimization imitates the "behavior" of the inert mechanical world in physical theory, and that interpersonal influences and processes of interpretation are ruled out by assumption [Mirowski 1984a; 1986a; forthcoming]. One must separate the context of socialization from the context of choice. (b) Rational choice is divided up into rational choice rules and independently given endowments. Neoclassical economics takes as its primary subject the logic of the former and is relatively silent about the latter because there is no logic of endowments that claims the allegiance of neoclassicals in general. (c) "Logic" is interpreted to mean mathematical axiomatization. (d) There is an unbridgeable gulf between neoclassical economics and the history of any particular economy. The market is always presumed efficient and therefore exhibits no hysteresis [Mirowski 1987b]. (e) Neoclassical economics prescribes and defends the right rules of market organization. The *summum bonum* is an automatic mechanism that coordinates the economy and guarantees its legitimacy. (f) The mind/body separation dictates that we know our own thought better than we know the world. Hence economic theory must be cast in the format of self-sufficient individual mental valuations brought in contact with a stable external world of commodities independent of any mediation or dependence upon signs. (g) Capital accumulation is treated as analogous to knowledge accumulation: an incremental aggregation of discrete units. Indeed, the former should be reduced to the latter in the guise of an inexplicable "technological change."

Our purpose here is not to put the DMD thesis through all its paces; nor is it our intention to discuss neoclassical theory in the detail warranted to seriously illustrate the above parallels.[2] All we wish to suggest for present purposes is that there exists a close correlation between the Cartesian epistemology and the structure of neoclassical economic theory: a familial resemblance that serves to fuse the natural world and the social world into a single coherent entity for the analytic Anglo-American mind. The social order of the economic world is reflected in the scientific order of the natural world; it hence comes as no surprise that Karl Popper has admitted that certain inspirations for his philosophy of science came from his particularly Western understanding of economics [Hands 1985].

If we accept this thesis as a provisional working hypothesis, the question of interest then becomes: how to account for the existence of heterodox schools of economic theory? Most germane to our present task, how can we understand the existence of the only school of economic thought indigenous to the United States, which is in many respects incommensurable with neoclassical economic theory—that is, institutionalist economics?

Pragmatism and Peirce

Prompted by the DMD thesis, our answer is to search for its philosophical foundations elsewhere than in the Cartesian analytic tradition. The origins of this phenomenon must be traced back a century to the situation extant in philosophy and science in the America of the Gilded Age. In the late nineteenth century United States, the predominant understanding of science was not that of the Cartesian tradition; indeed, as Bruce Kuklick put it, "In the late nineteenth century American philosophical circles there were more Hegelians of various sorts than you could shake a stick at" [Rorty, Schneewind and Skinner 1984, p. 132]. The main influences upon the idea of science in the Gilded Age came not from Britain or France, but rather from the Germany of the research universities. There the philosophy of science had not grown as separate and detached from social theory as it had elsewhere, and this was manifest in the three great movements in German philosophy: the dialectical idealism of Georg Friedrich Hegel, the historicist hermeneutics of Wilhem Dilthey, and a revival of neo-Kantianism. These traditions took root in the United States, and, by a very convoluted route, sprouted an indigenous school of philosophy in the United States called "Pragmatism." It is our thesis that this Pragmatic conception of

scientific endeavor and epistemology, which later induced a novel re-
interpretation of the economy and the economic actor, was consoli-
dated into an institutionalist school of economic theory in the first
three decades of the twentieth century.

Richard Bernstein has written, "It is still a popular myth, even
among philosophers, that positivism was a tough-minded variety of the
more tender-minded and fuzzy pragmatism" [Bernstein 1966, p. 168].
Judging by the *Dictionary of the History of Science,* the myth is still
popular, since that source defines "pragmatism" as "A variant of empiricism . . . foreshadowing both operationalism and the verifiability
principle of logical positivism." These impressions are unfortunate because they obscure the fact that it was the project of the pragmatists to
provide a systematic alternative to the Cartesian analytical tradition,
as well as to the naturalist doctrines characteristic of positivism. (We
shall see that this confusion has subsequently spilled over into economic controversies to the extent that, in some quarters, institutionalist economics is misperceived as a sort of naive empiricism.) The
situation is further muddied by the fact that the founder of pragmatism,
Charles Sanders Peirce, left no synoptic account of his philosophical
system. In this respect (as in some others as well: see H.S. Thayer [1981
p. 79]), he resembles that other towering figure of twentieth century philosophy, Ludwig Wittgenstein, in that he only bequeathed to us a disor-
ganized sheaf of disconnected, epigrammatic and oracular accounts of
his mature philosophy, which had to await publication until after his
death.

Reading Peirce is no fun; and therefore, most who have a passing
acquaintance with pragmatism base their knowledge on the more accessible but less reliable versions to be found in John Dewey or William
James, or worse, simply upon their own understandings of the collo-
quial connotations of "pragmatism." It is frankly impossible to do justice to Peirce's writings in the space allotted in this essay; there is no
reasonable substitute for reading his *Collected Papers* and the best of
the commentaries upon them such as that of Karl Apel [1981]. Both
because Peirce was the only pragmatist philosopher trained in mathematics and the physical sciences, and because it is our intention to
connect Peirce (through the DMD thesis) to the institutionalist conception of the economic actor, this discussion shall focus predominantly
on Peirce's philosophy of science.[3]

Because the Peircian corpus is so fragmented, it has been argued that
certain of his texts, especially those concerned with induction, might
be read as anticipatory of later neopositivist writings and of some as-

pects of Karl Popper [Rescher 1978, p. 52; Radnitzsky 1973, pp. xxv–xxvii]. Contrary to these suggestions, a survey of his entire work reveals that he was openly hostile to the Cartesian analytical tradition, and may be better understood as a sophisticated advocate of a hermeneutics of science and a semiotics of scientific practice. In highlighting Peirce's concern with the social aspects of science, we follow the lead of numerous modern commentators (John R. Commons, Alan Dyer, Apel, Bernstein, and R. Rorty) who have seen in Peirce a third alternative to the conventional rationalist/empiricist dichotomies [Commons 1934, p. 102; Dyer 1986; Apel 1981; Bernstein 1983; Rorty 1979].

The mainstream tradition of the philosophy of science in the twentieth century has found itself driven from pillar to post searching for the appropriate entity in which to ground the certainty of scientific knowledge. Early analytic philosophy began by touting the single linguistic term as the primary epistemic unit, but was fairly rapidly forced to retreat to the entire sentence or proposition as the lowest common denominator of scientific intelligibility. Complaints about the incoherence of an independent object language and the indeterminate consequences of scientific tests forced a further retreat to an entire conceptual scheme as the appropriate epistemological unit, but careful historical critiques, combined with skepticism about the notion of a self-contained theory, have prompted some philosophers to insist that only a research tradition in all its complex historical development can do justice to the various forms of knowledge claims of a working scientist. One amazing aspect of this progressive erosion of logical atomism in the philosophy of science is that Peirce essentially anticipated its form and consequences a century ago. His definition of "science" seems particularly relevant after the breakdown of logical atomism:

> What is Science? We cannot define the word with the precision and concision with which we define *Circle,* or *Equation,* any more than we can so define *Money, Government, Stone, Life.* The idea, like these, and more than some of them, is too vastly complex and diversified. It embodies the epitome of man's intellectual development . . . a particular branch of science, such as Physical Chemistry or Mediterranean Archeology, is no mere word, manufactured by the arbitrary definition of some academic pedant, but a real object, being the very concrete life of a social group constituted by real facts of inter-relation (Peirce 1958, pp. 37–39).

Peirce's insistence that "the very origin of the conception of reality shows that this conception essentially involves the notion of a *community"* could be read as being founded on the thesis that scientific research is irreducibly hermeneutic, and therefore recourse to an independent law-abiding world or to some innate preconception of truth is impotent to account for the *process* of scientific inquiry [Peirce 1934, p. 186]. Because the word "hermeneutics" is bandied about in a careless manner these days by literary critics, it might be prudent to provide a brief working definition for the present audience.

Hermeneutics is the theory of the process of interpretation, be it of a text, a doctrine, or a phenomenon, by a self-identified community of inquiry. Indeed, all coherent philosophies must possess some such theory of interpretation, be it explicit or implicit; however, this theory concentrates explicitly upon the role of shared tradition as the locus of continuity and quality control in the interpretative process; it therefore follows that the discipline of history is an indispensable accessory of hermeneutics.

Hermeneutics is a response to the gridlock of communication that often results when strongly disparate perspectives confront one another. The doctrine of hermeneutics arose from the experience of trying to "get into the other person's head," leading to a realization that comprehending an alien perspective often meant trying to grasp the whole of the other's experience. As Bernstein puts it, this "Hermeneutical circle" allows us to steer a course between objectivism and relativism [Bernstein 1983]. "Put negatively this principle means that there are no absolute starting points, no self-evident, self-contained certainties on which we can build, because we always find ourselves in the middle of complex situations which we try to disentangle by making, then revising, provisional assumptions. This circularity—or perhaps one might call it a spiral approximation towards greater accuracy and knowledge —pervades our whole intellectual life" [Rickman 1976, p. 11].

Hermeneutical philosophies freely admit that rival interpretative communities may harbor incommensurable readings of some text or phenomenon, but also recognize that there will be pressure to attempt comparisons as long as the communities are rivals, and that posterity may decide that traditions were eventually rendered commensurable. Hermeneutics reinstates the importance of diversity in the process of understanding to the extent of advocating the examination of alien or pariah traditions in the course of interpretation. Hermeneutics is also concerned with acknowledging the anthropomorphic element in human knowledge, viewing it as a fruitful and necessary aspect rather than an embarrassing and regrettable anachronism [Peirce 1934, p. 35n]. Finally, hermeneutics is generally hostile to the Cartesian tradition of analytic philosophy, especially the presumption of the mind/body dichotomy and the program of mechanical reduction [Peirce 1935, pp.

15–16]. Peirce was himself particularly scathing about the plausibility of the Cartesian program of radical self-doubt, which he termed a sham, merely formal, and incapable of altering any seriously held belief [Scheffler 1974, p. 20; Apel 1981, pp. 62–63].

It is important to understand that what one might call Peirce's brand of hermeneutics underwent revision and transformation over the course of his life, in part as a reaction to versions promulgated by William James and John Dewey. His disaffection with their readings and embellishments provoked him in 1905 to insist that he was not at all one of these "Pragmatists," but rather a "Pragmaticist," a label so contrivedly ugly that no one would be tempted to "kidnap" it [Apel 1981, p. 82]. Some of the fault for such a repudiation can be laid at Peirce's own door, if only because his early statements, and in particular his "pragmatic maxim," were phrased in such a way as to foster the impression of a transparent and banal common-sense philosophy of science. The pragmatic maxim of 1878 was stated as follows: "Consider what effects, that might conceivably have practical bearings, we conceive the object of our conception to have. Then, our conception of these effects is the whole of our conception of the object" [Peirce 1934, p. 1].

William James read the pragmatic maxim as equating those "practical implications" with the psychological responses of the user of the concept, and therefore misrepresented pragmatism as a species of individual psychological behavioralism, thus entirely neutralizing the hermeneutic aspects of the community of inquiry. John Dewey read the maxim as dictating that there was no such thing as a final end or goal of inquiry, a position that Peirce explicitly repudiated [Apel 1981, p. 88]. Others, less sophisticated, read the maxim as a celebration of a particularly American stereotype of a hard-nosed no-nonsense man of action, heedless of hesitation or tergiversation over fine points of reasoning. It must be admitted that some of Peirce's early writings seemed to encourage a crude know-nothingism: "pragmatism is generally practiced by successful men" or "Each of us is an insurance company" [Peirce 1934, pp. 21, 220]. However, in the face of attempts to portray pragmatism as a kind of crypto-capitalism in the sphere of science, Peirce went out of his way to insist that "the meaning of [pragmatism] does not lie in individual reactions at all."

Peirce divided the process of scientific inquiry into three categories: deduction, induction, and what he termed "abduction." He had very little of substance to say about deduction, although he did point out that no actual novelty, and therefore no progress, could be attained by deduction *mutatis mutandis* (Peirce 1958a, p. 47). Induction plays a much more substantial role in his system, and here Peirce brought his extensive experience as an experimentalist and his interest in probability theory into play in his discussions of empirical research. One important stabilizing influence on Peirce's community of inquiry was his postulate that *quantitative* induction was automatically self-correcting, albeit in the longest of long runs (Peirce 1935, p. 80; Rescher, 1978].[4] However, nothing in these writings gave any aid or comfort to naive empiricism. At one point he commented upon the limited role that experiment occupied in the rise of modern mechanics [Peirce 1935, p. 13]. He also observed that an hypothesis should not be abandoned immediately when contravened by empirical results, and that all good theories are always surrounded by a field of contradictory facts [Peirce 1958a, pp. 54, 60]. In these respects he appears to share contemporary concerns with the problem of the underdetermination of theory acceptance by the "facts," and with the Duhem/Quine thesis, which states that no hypothesis is definitively falsified because it can always be immunized to adverse tests by some adjustment in the ever-present auxiliary hypotheses that accompany it [Harding 1976]. Most significantly, Peirce stated that induction and deduction, either jointly or severally, could not account for the progress of scientific inquiry. That proficiency was reserved for the third mode, abduction.

"Abduction is the process of forming an explanatory hypothesis. It is the only logical operation which introduces any new idea; for induction does nothing but determine a value, and deduction merely evolves the necessary consequences of a pure hypothesis" [Peirce 1934, p. 106]. Of the three modalities of method, it is abduction that explicitly assumes a hermeneutic demeanor because it is the method responsible for creativity, interpretation, and innovation, which are historical processes made manifest in language and social behavior, subject to the self-discipline of a normative logic. This is why "the question of pragmatism . . . is nothing less than the question of the logic of abduction" [Peirce 1934, p. 121].

In order to discuss abduction, Peirce often employed the language of "instincts" or evolutionary talents, and these metaphors were often carried over into the works of Dewey, Veblen, and others influenced by pragmatism. Peirce's equation of abduction with instinct and meaning with habit probably strikes the modern reader as odd; but Peirce's unrelenting hostility to mechanical reductionism should signal that these passages are not to be read as anticipations of sociobiology [Apel 1981, p. 71]. Instead, they seem to posit the existence of a naive commonsense metaphysics that provided physics with its early fundamental hypotheses about natural law. Given Peirce's further thesis that natural laws themselves evolve, it follows that he would likewise expect the sources of inspiration for scientific hypotheses to evolve [Peirce 1935, p. 84]. Peirce expressly asserted that *physical* laws evolve over time because laws of homogeneity could only be discerned against the backdrop of stochastic phenomena, from which they would be emergent. One can only marvel at his prescience in this respect, since it was only well after his lines were written did physicists begin to plumb the significance of stochastic phenomena in quantum mechanics, cosmology, and elsewhere.[5]

No summary of Peirce's philosophy could be complete without some acknowledgement of his role as the founder of semiotics, the theory of the interpretations of signs and their interrelations. Peirce saw the sign relation as fundamentally triadic, as a relation between the denotation of a word, the designated object, and the interpreter. The importance of this triad for Peirce lay in his conviction that previous philosophers had attempted to understand language by concentrating attention on only one or two aspects in isolation, a practice he claimed served to quarantine the hermeneutic aspects of human inquiry. An important corollary of the triad was that it is impossible to discern the rules of sign-mediated behavior by simple external observation; in other words, there is no such thing as the passive observation of rule structures [Mirowski 1986a]. Not only did this anticipate the mature Ludwig Wittgenstein's critique of rules and language games, but it also has profound relevance for the positivist attempt to explain rule structures by mechanistic models.

Finally, in a philosopher so concerned with exploring the links between social processes and scientific inquiry, it should come as no surprise to discover that he also had a reasonable familiarity with the social theories of his day. It has not often been noted, however, that Peirce was hostile to orthodox economic doctrines, and downright livid when it came to hedonism and utilitarian doctrines [Peirce p. 43; pp. 59–60]. He wrote:

> [Jeremy] Bentham may be a shallow logician; but such truths as he saw, he saw most nobly. As for the vulgar utilitarian, his fault does not lie in pressing too much the question of what should be the good of this or that. On the contrary, his fault is that he never presses the question half far enough, or rather he never really raises the question at all. He simply rests in his present desires as if desire were beyond all dialectic [Peirce 1934, p. 98].

This single passage captures much of the gist of Dewey's subsequent and much more verbose and pedantic disquisition upon the role of values in the process of inquiry.

In a few essays, Peirce trained his sights on American political economy, accusing it of "an exaggeration of the beneficial effects of greed," and complaining of a tendency to want their "mammon flavored with a soupçon of god" [Peirce 1935, pp. 193, 194]. The presuppositions of utilitarianism offended his hermeneutic view of science in a number of ways: they denied the role of tradition in human understanding; they blithely ignored the incommensurability of valuations; they gave short shrift to the dependence of behavior on community interaction and semantic processes; they were incompatible with the idea of evolutionary change and with abduction; and they smacked of Cartesian mechanical reduction. Although Peirce was not concerned with sketching out an alternative political economy, in restrospect it would seem obvious that anyone deeply influenced by his thought would certainly be skeptical of the encroaching tradition of neoclassical economics.

The modernity of Peirce's package of concerns, or as he put it, his "architectonic," is striking. With some generosity of exegesis, one could credit him with the anticipation of the DMD thesis in certain respects because he saw that one of the most fruitful sources of abduction in science was the transfer of metaphor from one sphere of inquiry to another.[6] Nevertheless, Peirce was definitely out of synchronicity with the ragtime era of American culture. It is tragic that the theorist of the infinite community of science was himself expelled from that community in 1884, never to hold another academic position. He repaired to Milford, Pennsylvania in 1887, to reside in almost total isolation, scribbling away at manuscripts that remained unread and unpublished during his lifetime. In part because of this exile, it generally was either through William James or John Dewey that many learned about Pragmatism.

John Dewey

Dewey was the conduit through which many of the precepts of pragmatism migrated over to American social theory in the early twentieth century. From a certain point of view this was unfortunate because the quality of his thought was not often up to the standard of Peirce; nevertheless, he managed to achieve much greater influence and renown than Peirce. Peirce himself once rebuked Dewey for a lack of logical subtlety, despite the fact that Dewey (along with Veblen) was one of the few illustrious students during Peirce's stint at Johns Hopkins [Apel 1981, p.

5]. Even an enthusiastic supporter like Richard Bernstein was forced to admit: "imagination and insight must be explicated and modified in detailed analyses, and this is what Dewey failed to do for us. Insofar as philosophy requires the funding of fertile imagination with systematic elaboration, his philosophy fails" [Bernstein 1966, pp. 171–72].

Dewey insisted that, for philosophy, "the central problem is the relation that exists between the beliefs about the nature of things *due to natural science* to beliefs about values—using that word to designate whatever is taken to have rightful authority in the direction of conduct" [Thayer 1981, p. 166]. One can observe a familial resemblance to the concerns of Peirce here, but already, in contrast to Peirce's wide-ranging attempt to synthesize specific aspects of scientific practice with the social nature of inquiry, we discover exceptionally vague references to a monolithic "science" and a premature reduction of the social sphere to an ill-defined phenomenon of "values." For Dewey, as for Peirce, inquiry is pre-eminently a *process* whereby doubtful or unsettled situations become settled. Yet Dewey's definition of inquiry is surprisingly impersonal and very pedantic in the Germanic style: it is defined as "the controlled or directed transformation of an indeterminate situation into one that is so determinate in its constituent distinctions and relations as to convert the elements of the original situation into a unified whole" [Dewey 1938, pp. 104–5]. In this marriage of Hegel and Peirce, Thought comes perilously close to Thinking Itself, but is wrenched back from the Idealist precipice with the help of Peirce's pragmatic maxim of 1878. Dewey called this interpretation of reasoning "Instrumentalism," and defined it as follows:

> Instrumentalism is an attempt to constitute a precise logical theory of concepts, of judgements and inferences in their various forms, by considering primarily how thought functions in the experimental determinations of future consequences . . . it attempts to establish universally recognized distinctions and rules of logic by deriving them from the reconstructive or meditative function ascribed to reason [Thayer 1981, p. 169].

Unfortunately, Dewey spent much more time talking about this attempt to establish universally recognized et cetera, et cetera than actually suggesting a few concrete rules and exposing them to criticism. In effect, Dewey extended some of the hermeneutic themes found in Peirce to explicit application in social theory, especially generalizing the concept of habit into the broader concept of social custom. Many have observed that Dewey equated pragmatism with social psychology; and indeed, he seemed to approach philosophy as if it were a branch of a more encompassing instrumentalist social science [Apel 1981, p. 87; Thayer 1981, pp. 183–90]. Perhaps he felt that "valuations" were discrete empirical entities, the description of which could be left to the social scientist. He often wrote as if that were the case: "Valuations are empirically observable patterns of behavior and may be studied as such. The propositions that result are *about* valuations but are not themselves value-propositions in any sense marking them off from other matter-of-fact propositions" [Dewey 1939b, p. 51].

In retrospect, Dewey's numerous appeals to the scientific method appear awkward, strained, and pedantic. This reification of an abstract "Science" would have serious consequences for the later evolution of pragmatism. In place of actual training in any specific science or in the history of one of the sciences, Dewey's favored sources of inspiration were Hegel and Greek philosophy. The path of his intellectual evolution can be traced from the psychologistic idealism of his early career to a vague and politicized pragmatism towards the end of his life.

Dewey's crusade was to argue against the idea of truth as accuracy of representation, which took the form in his later life of an insistence that reality could not exist prior to and independent of the process of inquiry [Dewey 1939a, p. 308]. The idea of "warranted assertability" was as close as he ever got to Peirce's richer notion of the complex interaction of the interpretative community and the object of inquiry; in Dewey, this assumed the rather more prosaic cast of a comparison of scientific inquiry with a jury trial [Dewey 1939a, pp. 898–900]. Dewey followed Peirce in his skepticism concerning the Cartesian analytic tradition, but as was his inclination, he tended to reinterpret philosophical problems as amenable to translation into problems in psychology: "the older dualism of body and soul finds a distinct echo in the current dualism of stimulus and response" [Dewey, 1931, p. 233]. Dewey also imitated Peirce in viewing human inquiry as an evolutionary process, but diluted this legacy by transmuting the sweeping portrayal of the evolution of natural law itself into the diminished banality that "tool and material are adapted to each other in the process of reaching a valid conclusion" [Dewey, 1939a, p. 929].

Whatever one's opinion about Dewey's conception of science, it is demonstrably true that his work in social theory found a sympathetic audience in a United States that had previously associated evolutionary theory with either atheism or social Darwinism. Although it had remained a familiar idea in the Continental tradition of philosophy, it was a novelty to find an American arguing that, "History is the record of the development of freedom through the development of institutions. . . . Here we have instead an anticipatory criticism and challenge of the classical liberal notion of freedom, a deliberate, reflective and reactionary one. Freedom is a growth, an attainment, not an original possession, and it is attained by the idealization of institutions and law" [Dewey 1931, p. 285].

Dewey also maintained Peirce's hostility to utilitarianism, although his objections appeared to spring primarily from an aversion to the idea of given and immutable tastes:

> Not even the most devoted adherents of the notion that enjoyment and value are equivalent facts would venture to assent that because we once liked a thing we should go on liking it. . . . Desire and purpose, and hence action, are left without guidance, although the question of the regulation of their formation is the supreme problem of practical life. Values (to sum up) may be connected inherently with liking, and not yet with *every* liking but only with those that judgment has approved" [Dewey 1939a, p. 786].

As a champion of the importance of the process of change over static notions of optimality, Dewey became associated with groups opposed to economic laissez-faire notions; he was a vocal advocate of the position that classical liberalism had avoided all the hard questions of co-ordination and the definition of order by surreptitiously postulating that each citizen came naturally equipped with an innate complement of rights, desires, and powers that were sufficient to do the job (Dewey 1931, p. 281). It is relevant to later developments in economics that he saw this flawed predisposition as part and parcel of the larger Western predisposition to yearn for natural laws, which qualifies as a limited appreciation of the DMD thesis [Dewey 1939a, p. 745]. As he put it, "the existing limitations of 'social science' are due mainly to unreasoning devotion to the physical sciences as a model, and to a misconception of physical science at that" [Dewey 1939a, p. 949]. Unfortunately, here Dewey became tangled in his own dependence upon science, for not only was he incapable of describing the actual historical instances of practices within the physical sciences, but he was also bereft of any coherent description of the processes of promulgation of social order. This led him in later life to compound these weaknesses by proposing the *non sequitur* that the natural sciences would themselves provide the progressive ideals of social order [Dewey, 1939a, p. 791]. We might suggest that Dewey's appreciation of the DMD thesis must have been limited, because this latter prescription clashes with his earlier warnings about the "unreasoning devotion to the physical sciences as a model." Democracy was said to be a pronounced improvement over previous

modes of political organization because it deployed the same techniques as science to mediate freedom and authority [Dewey 1939a, pp.
358–60]. All social problems would be thus purportedly solved (or dis-
solved?) by the scientific method, because democracy was the analog
of the scientific method in the political arena. Dewey may simply have
meant that "democracy" was another name for the trial-and-error process that he thought characterized all inquiry, but, if so, it would portend a rather sloppy use of political terminology, and, moreover, it was
only an innocuous step to equate instrumentalism with social engineering.

The Pragmatic Tradition and Institutionalist Economic Theory

We now return to the DMD thesis in order to ask whether the alternative philosophical program of pragmatism did provide an alternative
template for rational economic man. In what follows, the essence of
Peirce will rather dominate the musk of Dewey, for reasons already
broached above: it is specifically philosophies of *science* that set the
tone for the ensuing portraits of man. As we did for the Cartesian tradition, we can generate a brief bill of particulars that characterize the
Pragmatic philosophy of science: (a) Science is primarily a process of
inquiry by a self-identified community, and not a mechanical legitimation procedure of some pre-existent goal or end-state. Science has con-
formed to no set of ahistorical decision rules, and for this reason history
and science are inseparable. Most of this would come under the rubric
of Dewey's "instrumentalism." (b) Possible methods of inquiry consist
of deduction, induction and abduction. No one method is self-sufficient
without the other two as complements. Abduction is the explicit source
of novelty, whereas induction and deduction provide the checks and
balances. (c) There is no single logic, but rather a logic of abduction, a
logic of deduction, and a logic of induction. (d) Because there are no
foolproof impersonal rules of scientific method, decisions concerning
the validity of scientific statements reside within the community of inquiry. The community of inquiry is the basic epistemological unit. (e)
Without a strict mind/body duality, science has an irreducible anthropomorphic character. This is not inherently a dangerous phenomenon.
Natural laws themselves evolve, as do the members of the community
of inquiry. Social and natural concepts interpenetrate; therefore hermeneutic techniques are a necessary component of scientific inquiry, on
the same epistemic level as mathematical techniques. (f) The study of
semiotics and the interrelation of signs constitutes an integral part of

the philosophy of science. (g) Because pragmatism must ultimately depend upon the community of inquiry, the Scylla and Charybdis between which it most frequently must negotiate are a defense of the status quo and an advocacy of a technocratic utopia.

Just as with our previous experience with the connection between the Cartesian tradition and neoclassical economic theory, here too the conception of the rational economic actor in institutionalist economics can be read off the pragmatic program. This reading is not nearly as easy as in the neoclassical case, however. This is because the neoclassicals have by and large practiced what they preached: their research praxis depends upon a close imitation of their colleagues, the natural scientists, many of whom hew to the Cartesian ideal as self-evident. The institutionalist school, on the other hand, has confronted the quandry that "pragmatism" has not generally been a popular epistemology among the physicists, and therefore they possess no obvious role models. In practice, the research praxis of institutional economics in the twentieth century displays little of the homogeneity and internal coherence across researchers of neoclassical economics, and therefore most of our characterization of institutionalism will be drawn from programmatic statements. In our drawing of parallels, we shall concentrate upon the first generation of institutionalist economists, roughly from Thorstein Veblen to John R. Commons. Proceeding point-by-point: (a) The economy is primarily a process of learning, negotiation, and coordination, and not a ratification of some pre-existent goals or end-state. Economic rationality is socially and culturally determined, and therefore history, anthropology, and economics are different perspectives upon the same inquiry. The economy itself may be conceptualized as the prosecution of inquiry by material means, with the community both constructing and discovering its values. (b) Economic actors are defined by their habits, customs, and "instincts," the physical or material relations that impinge upon them, and the expedients developed in order to adapt one to the other [Veblen 1934, p. 189]. This portrayal seeks to find a middle way between "nature" and "nurture." "'Instinct,' being not a neurological or physiological concept, is not statable in neurological or physiological terms. The instinct of workmanship, no more than any other instinctive proclivity, is an isolable, discrete neural function" [Veblen 1914, p. 28fn]. (c) There is no unique logic of choice. "Passion and enjoyment of goods passes insensibly and inevitably into appraisal. . . . Enjoyment ceases to be a datum and becomes a problem. As a problem, it implies intelligent inquiry into the conditions and consequences of the value-object; that is, criticism" [Dewey 1939a, pp. 260–61]. (d) Because there exist no innate rules of rational economic behavior, the only gauge of the validity of such behavior resides in the particular economic community. Laws are made by people, not nature. The appropriate epistemological unit is the institution. Institutions are transpersonal rules that endow individual economic actors with the ability to cope with interpretations of action and with change, or as Commons put it, "collective action controlling, liberating and expanding individual action" [Commons 1934, p. 70]. (e) Acceptance of the thesis that science embodies anthropomorphic concepts prompts the social theorist to incorporate hermeneutics or a sociology-of-knowledge approach when comparing certain incommensurable interpretations of the behavior of economic actors. Diversity of interpretations are as important for the viability of social structures as for simpler economic indices, such as profit or growth. (f) Because rule structures cannot be comprehended by external detached observation, economists must self-consciously engage in participant observation. Economics is based upon a theory of the semiotics of trade, production, and consumption, which serves to explain how actors interpret the significance of transactions. (Examples are Veblen's "conspicuous consumption" and Commons's typology of transactions.) (g) Institutional economics has displayed a periodic tergiversation between a defense of the status quo and an advocacy of a technocratic regime that reifies science as a unique principle of rationality.

These seven points do not capture the whole of institutionalist theory, but they do give some indication of the divergence of the conception of economic rationality from that characteristic of neoclassical theory. As previously noted, the first generation of institutionalists generally derived their pragmatism from James, Dewey and other sources more accessible than Peirce. This path of influence made a mark on their writings; among other more subtle effects, it induced an image of science that was excessively vague. This weakness, especially in Veblen and Ayres, resulted in a vulnerability to neoclassical complaints that their appeals to "science" were less legitimate than those of the neoclassicals, the difficulty being that both sides' conceptions of "science" were rarely made explicit. Somewhat later Commons made more explicit reference to Peirce's philosophy of science, and consequently built upon a more robust philosophical foundation. Nevertheless, Commons's book *Institutional Economics* signals the end of the first phase of the development of institutionalist economic theory. This watershed was not so much because of the merits or demerits of Commons's work as it was to the rapid decline of what remained of the pragmatist philosophy of science in the United States—it never really could have been described as enjoying a period of dominance—and its supercession by a Cartesian logical positivism.[7]

We now turn to summarize the interactions of pragmatism and the conceptions of science in the key institutionalist economists, Veblen and Commons.

Thorstein Veblen

It has been observed that Veblen owed a number of debts to the pragmatist tradition [Dyer 1986]. What has not been noticed is that Veblen's conception of science and economic rationality owes more to Dewey and James than to Peirce, and that many of his initial ideas grew out of a struggle with Kantian antinomies. In his famous essay "The Place of Science in Modern Civilization," Veblen wrote:

> Modern science is becoming substantially a theory of the process of cumulative change, which is taken as a sequence of cumulative change, realized to be self-continuing or self-propagating and to have no final term. . . . Modern science is ceasing to occupy itself with natural laws—the codified rules of the game of causation—and is concerning itself wholly with what has taken place and what is taking place. . . . A scientific point of view is a consensus of habits of thought current in the community [Veblen 1969, pp. 37–38].

The influence of Dewey and Darwin here is fairly self-evident, but the key to understanding Veblen's use of the term "natural law" derives from his first paper on Kant's *Critique of Judgement* [Veblen 1934, pp. 175–93]. Veblen was absorbed by Kant's problem of the conflict of freedom and determinism and thought he had struck upon a new solution to the problem, making use of the notions of "adaptation" and evolution. He wrote, "The principle of adaptation, in its logical use, is accordingly the principle of inductive reasoning." Peirce's "abduction" would have been the more appropriate term, curiously enough for a student of Peirce [Veblen 1934, p. 191].

As Veblen became acquainted with economic theory, it dawned on him that neoclassical theory was beset with the very same Kantian conundrum; namely, it purported to be a mechanistically deterministic theory predicated upon teleological principles. In his famous article on the "Limitations of Marginal Utility," he declared,

> [Neoclassical] theory is confined to the ground of sufficient reason instead of proceeding on the ground of efficient cause. The contrary is true of mod-

ern science, generally (except mathematics). . . . The two methods of inference—from sufficient reason and from efficient cause—are out of touch
with one another and there is no transition from one to the other. . . . The
relation of sufficient reason runs only from the (apprehended) future into
the present, and it is solely of an intellectual, subjective, personal, teleological character and force; while the relation of cause and effect runs only
in the contrary direction, and it is solely of an objective, impersonal, materialistic character and force. The modern scheme of knowledge, on the
whole, rests, for its definitive ground, on the relation of cause and effect;
the relation of sufficient reason being admitted only provisionally [Veblen
1969, pp. 237–38].

One might have expected a student of Peirce to see a third, transcendant, option: sufficient reason and efficient cause could have been
united by recourse to an evolutionary epistemology and ontology,
where both laws and our understanding of them jointly were altered by
the activity of inquiry. In the sphere of the economy, institutions, defined as habits of thought and action, could serve as the connecting link
between efficient cause and sufficient reason [McFarland 1986, p. 621].
Yet this was not the road taken by Veblen's subsequent intellectual career. Instead, he tended toward an increasingly pessimistic Manichaeism with sufficient reason as the darkness and efficient cause, now
conflated with Peirce's pragmatic maxim, as the light. Since there was
no necessary connection between the pragmatic maxim and "objective,
impersonal, materialistic" law, he was increasingly driven to a very idiosyncratic version of a theory of "instincts," especially "the instinct of
workmanship," a non-physiological entity whose "functional content
is servicability for the ends of life, whatever these ends may be" [Veblen
1914, p. 31]. The pragmatic maxim, which started out as a solution to
a difficult problem in metaphysics, ended up as a reified "instinctive"
entity.

Early in his career, Veblen's antinomies resonated with the pragmatist philosophy and produced some of his most profound work. For instance, *The Theory of the Leisure Class* may be read as a skillful
example of the pragmatic maxim, showing that the consequences of an
action are an important part of its interpretation, and wryly pointing
out that "serviceability" might actually be consistent with waste. "The
Economic Theory of Women's Dress" is a *tour de force* of Peircian semiotics. By *The Theory of Business Enterprise* another antimony was pos-
ited, pitting "the machine process" against pecuniary enterprise. This
antimony also resulted in fruitful economic theory, but the tendency
to conflate "science," efficient causal reasoning, and the working or engineering class made its first appearance [Mirowski 1985]. Progres-

sively, Veblen came to see the conflicts of science versus religion, efficiency versus waste, capitalist versus worker, and knowledge versus ignorance as all prototypes of one large dichotomy [Veblen 1914]. Everything seemed to conspire to drag down the march of scientific progress as Veblen got older, and this Manichaeism blunted his earlier sensitivity to the subtle interplay of science and culture —what we have dubbed Peircian hermeneutics—so that by the time he reached *Absentee Ownership,* he could write:

> The technology of physics and chemistry is not derived from established law and custom, and it goes on its way with as nearly a complete disregard of the spiritual truths of law and custom as the circumstances will permit. The reality with which technicians are occupied are of another order of actuality, lying altogether within the three dimensions of the material universe, and running altogether on the logic of material fact (Veblen 1923, p. 263).

Perhaps Veblen believed he could break out of the "logical circle" cited above by resorting to this lofty and other-worldly conception of science, and then using it to claim he himself was merely applying the "matter-of-fact" attitudes to the economic sphere. Instead of Peirce's community of inquirers, scientists became for Veblen almost automatons, closer to Dewey's Thought Thinking Itself. In a striking similarity to Marx, Veblen also wished to argue that there was a certain inevitability to the whole process: the matter-of-fact efficiency characteristic of the technician would necessarily clash with the anachronistic appeal to inefficiency propped up by the legitimation of natural law by the "Captains of Industry"; and Veblen intimated the technicians would defeat the business interests in the long haul [Layton 1962].

Although Veblen's writings are a fertile source of insights into economic theory, the Achilles heel of his later system was his naive conception of science and the exaulted place of the engineer. This epistemological weakness led to two further flaws: the first, that Veblen misunderstood that the neoclassical theory he so adamantly opposed had a more powerful claim to his brand of scientific legitimacy than he realized, because it later turned out that those self-same engineers would be attracted to the neoclassical brand of social physics; and second, that certain particular evolutionary or Peircian aspects of Veblen's thought stood in direct conflict with his later image of science.

The first flaw can go quite some distance in explaining the neglect of Veblen's profound critiques of neoclassical theory, particularly the theory of capital and the theory of production. Veblen clearly believed that natural law explanations were on the wane in physics, and that economics would eventually follow suit. Obviously, things haven't turned out as anticipated. Veblen's neglect of the hermeneutical aspects of science prevented him from understanding how deeply rooted natural law explanations are in the Western cultural matrix, and how significant they were in the nineteenth-century science he admired: in mechanics, in chemistry, and in energetics. In other words, Veblen had an inadequate comprehension of the DMD thesis.[8] Because of this, he could not comprehend the primal attraction of neoclassical theory, or the extent to which it was a model appropriated lock, stock, and barrel from nineteenth-century physics [Mirowski 1984a; forthcoming]. Veblen's assertions that he was a partisan of modern scientific methods appeared weak and unavailing compared to the shiny surfaces of neoclassical economic theory. The engineers, with whom Veblen was so enamoured, flooded into economics after his death and opted to work for the theoretical tradition that they recognized as closest to their previous training: that is, neoclassicism.

The second flaw in Veblen's epistemology was that he did not realize that some of the more intriguing aspects of his economic theory were in open conflict with his conception of science. In his early essay on Kant, he claimed that "the play of the faculties of the intellect is free, or but little hampered by the empirical elements in its knowledge," but did not maintain this insight on his later work using anthropological sources [Veblen 1934, p. 181]. He was also very scathing when it came to others' adherence to a naive sense-data empiricism, as in his critique of the German historical school, but oblivious to instances of it in some of his descriptions of science [Veblen 1969, p. 58]. In his profound series of essays on the preconceptions of economic science, he observed:

> Since a strict uniformity is nowhere to be observed in the phenomena with which the investigator is occupied, it has to be found by a laborious interpretation of the phenomena and a diligent abstraction and allowance for disturbing circumstances, whatever may be the meaning of a disturbing circumstance where causal continuity is denied. In this work of interpretation and expurgation the investigator proceeds on a conviction of the orderliness of natural sequence. . . . The endeavor to avoid all metaphysical premises fails here as elsewhere [Veblen 1969, p. 162].

This heightened awareness of the presumption of natural sequence was put to good use in Veblen's critique of the "obvious" neoclassical proposition that the value of outputs must necessarily be equal to the value of inputs, for example.

There are other Peircian themes in Veblen that languish in an under-developed state because of his epistemological position on science. His earliest work on the theory of the leisure class could be read as a prolegomenon a semiotics of economic transactions. The phenomenon of conspicuous consumption indicates that desires and wants cannot simply be read off of economic behavior (as has often been claimed under the rubric of "revealed preference"), but that the interpretative and intentional problems of the actors must also enter into the picture, undermining any unique reference for the concept of self-interest. In essays such as "The Economics of Women's Dress," he shows the hermeneutic practice of approaching familiar behavior as if we were producing an ethnographical report of the behavior of an alien tribe [Veblen 1934]. His conception of capital as an evolving linchpin of our economic system has interesting parallels with Peirce's idea that natural laws themselves evolve, and thus our interpretations are forced to evolve as well.

These possibilities did not receive the attention they may have deserved; instead, Veblen became associated in the public mind with the politics of the technocratic movement and a "soviet of engineers," as the extrapolation of his faith in a self-assured materialist science [Layton 1962].

John R. Commons

The Peircian legacy in the work of Commons was more self-conscious and more direct [Ramstad 1986]. In his magnum opus *Institutional Economics* he surveyed the philosophical traditions he saw as nurturing the primary schools of economic thought and argued it was time for recent advances in philosophy to prompt a new economic theory:

> In the stage of Pragmatism, a return is made to the world of uncertain change, without fore-ordination or metaphysics, whether benevolent or non-benevolent, where we ourselves and the world around us are continually in a changing conflict of interests. . . . Not till we reach John Dewey do we find Peirce expanded to ethics, and not until we reach institutionalist economics do we find it expanded to transactions, going concerns, and Reasonable Value [Commons 1934, pp. 107, 155].

Commons followed Peirce in many respects. He, too, was hostile to the Cartesian duality of mind and body and suspected that doctrine had served to obscure the problem of conflicts of interest in earlier economic thought [Commons 1934, pp. 16, 105]. For Commons, both truth and value were defined as the consensus of the relevant investigative community. Mind was not assumed to be a passive receptacle of sense impressions, contrary to neoclassical biases, but rather as an active inventor of meanings that displayed "an inseparable aspect of valuing, choosing and acting" [Commons 1934, p. 18]. Commons brought these philosophical convictions to bear in his economics, by isolating value as the central epistemological term in economics and by postulating that the definition of value is tentative and evolutionary, constructed by courts in the course of their adjudication of conflicts of interest.

Commons perceptively grasped the importance of the dichotomy between sufficient reason and efficient cause in Veblen's research program, and yet he rejected Veblen's reification of the dichotomy as an unbridgeable gap.

> Veblen's concept of a science was the traditional concept of the physical sciences which rejected all *purpose* in the investigation of the facts. The court's concept of a science was an institutional concept wherein the investigation must start with a public purpose as a primary principle of the science itself. Veblen's elimination of purpose from the scope of science was based on his interpretation of Pragmatism as set forth by James and Dewey. He does not seem to have known the Pragmatism of Peirce, which dealt only with the physical sciences, nor the Pragmatism of the courts, which more nearly followed Dewey [Commons 1934, p. 654].

This hermeneutical character of science is an important presupposition of Commons's economics. He insisted that "false analogies have arisen in the history of economic thought by transferring to economics the meanings derived from the physical sciences" [Commons 1934, p. 96]. If economists had not been so spellbound with the slavish imitation of the outward trappings of physics, they might have admitted that the structures and meanings they had constructed frequently conflicted with the interpretations of the actors so described, and that there had to be some rational means for reconciliation of such divergent constructions. All economic life is interpretative, and there is no more certain recourse than the interpretative practices of the community. This explains why Commons dubbed his theory "Institutional Economics": "we may define an institution as Collective Action in Control of Individual Action" [Commons 1934, p. 69].

Commons's theory of transactions follows directly from his embrace of what we have called Peircian hermeneutics, as it attempts to supply a theory of semiotics to explain the actors' interpretations of the meanings of legitimate transactions [Ramstad 1986, pp. 1083–86]. To portray a transaction as simple physical transport between two spheres of relative need assumes away all problems of rational cognition [Mirowski, forthcoming]. "It is significant that the formula of a transaction may be stated in terms of psychology. . . . All that is needed to shift it to institutional economics is to introduce rights of property; legal units of measurement; the creation, negotiability and release of debt; the enforcement of the two duties of delivery and payment by the collective action of the state" [Commons 1934, pp. 438–39]. In effect, Commons was invoking Peirce's dictum that every semiotic act must be analyzed according to the sign itself, the signifier, and the interpreter. In his taxonomy of transactions, the signifiers were the actual traders, the interpreters were to be the virtual buyers and sellers and the state apparatus, and the signs were to be the contracts, the debt instruments, and all the rest.

Once one sees the transaction for the complex social phenomena it is, it should become apparent that conflicts of interest and interpretation would be endemic. Hence, problems of coordination within a market system will be rife, and there will be an imperative for some notion of "Reasonable Value" to be negotiated. This concept of value can only be historical and contingent upon the evolution of the interpretative community.

Commons's legacy as an economist was consonant with his stated philosophical premises. As is well known, both he and his students were very active in legal and governmental circles, attempting to get courts and legislatures to recognize their role as experimenters as well as mediators. Commons openly advocated the gradual improvement of capitalism through governmental intervention. Many of the economic functions of the U.S. government that we take for granted today were the handiwork of Commons and his students in the first half of the twentieth century.

However, his greatest triumphs in the arena of practice were viewed in the next generation as liabilities in the arena of economic theory. His refrain that there were no "natural" grounds for economic institutions was read as implying that he left no systematic economic theory. The conjuncture of the decline of pragmatism in the United States in the 1930s and the rise of a particularly narrow form of positivism sealed the fate of the Commons wing of the pragmatist institutionalist program.

Post-1930s Institutionalism

The pragmatist view of science had fewer and fewer partisans in the United States from the 1920s to the 1960s. The causes of this decline are too complex to discuss here, but it is obvious that a Cartesian-style positivism rose to predominance and became the premier cultural image of natural knowledge.[9] The institutionalist school of economics found itself vulnerable in this harsh new climate. The rival tradition of neoclassical economics was patently more attuned to the trends in philosophy and science, and even went on the offensive, branding its rivals as "unscientific." In reaction to this threat, the "second generation" of institutionalists tended to distance themselves from their mixed heritage of Peircian pragmatism and Deweyan evolutionary social theory. Two prominent representatives of this reaction were Wesley Clair Mitchell and Clarence Ayres.

Mitchell was a student of Veblen, and received from him an extreme skepticism about the analytic claims of neoclassicism, a skepticism he maintained throughout his career. His early work on monetary history and business cycles were extrapolations of some major Veblenian themes, such as the divergence of financial from material expansion as a cause of macroeconomic instability. However, as Mitchell rose in professional standing, he became the advocate of a very unsophisticated notion of scientific endeavor, in the sense that Mitchell became an advocate of the economic scientist as a neutral and impartial gatherer of facts. One of his crowning achievements was becoming the prime mover behind the founding of the National Bureau of Economic Research, an organization originally dedicated to the nonpartisan support of the collection and analysis of quantitative economic data, such as the fledgling national income accounts.[10]

From some of his comments such as those in *The Backward Art of Spending Money,* it seems he thought that statistical analyses were somehow separate from and immune to the mechanical analogies imported by neoclassical theory [Mitchell 1937, p. 35]. Nonetheless, it is also clear that his formidable success in capturing funding and support for his bureau hinged crucially upon his willingness to make use of the appearance of scientific rigor. Largely because of Mitchell, by mid-century the institutionalist school was perceived as promoting a species of naive empiricism without any theory. Protests to the contrary were met with the challenge: where is your scientific theory?—which really meant, why are you not using the conventional techniques of physics (such as constrained maximization) as we do? Mitchell and his school, for the most part, had no coherent response, since he had already acquiesced to so much of the positivist program. (See, however, Rutledge Vining [1949] and Morris Copeland [1951]).

Clarence Ayres was another well-known institutionalist who stressed the later, more Manichean side of Veblen's legacy. Ayres explicitly traced his influence from Dewey: "It was from John Dewey that I first learned what that way of knowing is. It is what Dewey called the 'instrumental' process. This, as Dewey realized, is identical with what Veblen was calling the 'technological' process" [Ayres 1961, p. 29]. (See also McFarland [1986], p. 622). The reification of technology as the sole category of legitimate knowledge, begun by Veblen, was carried to its extreme conclusions by Ayres. In the process, the Peircian pragmatic maxim was stripped of everything but a crude instrumentalism that sought "to identify the intellectual procedures of science with the use of instruments and at the same time to identify the instruments of scientists with the tools which are still in wider use by artisans and craftsmen" (Ayres 1961, p. 277). While Dewey could hardly be accused of possessing an architectonic, this was certainly a misrepresentation of his position [Rutherford 1981]. Where Dewey wanted to portray scientific inquiry as a continuous questioning procedure, Ayres tried to portray it as the accumulation of certain and final knowledge by means of the accumulation of tools and artifacts. While this position had little to do with pragmatism, it did resonate with certain doctrines in the philosophy of science in the 1930s through the 1960s, such as Percy Bridgeman's "operationalism" and various attempts to define a neutral object language, and, therefore, it did attract adherents.

The central theme in Ayres's work is the tension and dichotomy between "ceremonial" and "technological" or "instrumental" processes [Waller 1982; Bush, 1983]. The distinction seems to reduce to an exhaustive partition of all social life into nonscientific and scientific endeavor, for Ayres insists that, "tribal beliefs, and the institutional and ceremonial practices in which they are objectified, are simulcra of scientific knowledge and technical skills" [Ayres 1961, p. 30–31]. Technology is by far the larger category, since it is defined, "in the broadest possible sense to refer to that whole aspect of human experience and activity which some logicians call operational, and the entire complement of artifacts with which mankind operates. So defined, technology includes mathematical journals and symphonic scores" [Ayres 1961, p. 278]. This work was more reminiscent of Auguste Comte's division of all human knowledge into three stages—the Theological or fictitious, the Metaphysical or abstract, and the Scientific or positive—than it was of any of the writings of Peirce or Dewey. Somewhat incongruously for an institutionalist, "ceremonial" practices and habits are equated with institutions, which are then invidiously contrasted with science. Religion, myth, folkways, and the status quo are at various times tarred with the brush of "ceremonial" status; but the most concise definition of the concept is provided by Anne Mayhew: "Ceremonialism is a failure to evaluate by testing consequences" [Mayhew 1981, pp. 515–16]. At the end of this road, the pale shadow of pragmatism has become— irony of ironies—a Popperian version of science.

Hence the subtle hermeneutics of Peirce, by way of Dewey, was reduced in Ayres's hands and those of his followers to a very prosaic materialism. "The 'we' who know are not the entire community, or even a majority of all the people . . . such knowledge exists, is a community possession, so to speak accessible to anyone who seeks access to it" [Ayres 1961, p. 34]. Knowledge was effectively a stock, and the role of community was diminished to the vanishing point. Science was treated as if it were the embodiment of a single method true for all time, although he was negligent when it came to describing precisely what the method consisted of [Ayres 1961, p. 51]. Ayres was prone to such *obiter dicta* as "nothing but science is true or meaningful," or "Any proposition which is incapable of statement in scientific terms, any phenomenon which is incapable of investigation by scientific methods, is meaningless and worthless as meaning and value are conceived in that universe of discourse" [Lepley 1949, p. 59]. Ayres did temper the harshness of this pronouncement by his reference to the relevant universe of discourse, but he had obviously come a long distance from Peirce's hermeneutics. This increasing stridency in the evocation of science became painfully incongruous to a positivist audience, and pushed institutional economics further and further out on a limb: how could they praise scientific discourse as the only relevant truth criteria and simultaneously eschew scientific practice as it was understood in the mid-twentieth century United States? Where was the mathematical formalism and axiomatization, the systematic hypothesis testing according to the canons of classical statistical inference, the mathematical models, and the style of studied anonymity of the physics report?

Revolutions in Science and Philosophy

A funny thing happened on the way to the Temple of Science. Just as neoclassicism and institutionalism were vying to be the sole legitimate claimant of the mantle of science, science itself changed dramatically. First in the theory of relativity, and then more dramatically in quantum mechanics and cosmology, physics was severely warping the complacent vision of natural law. The particularly Laplacean notion of rigid determinism came unstuck, and the prosaic conception of precepts or sense-data got lost in a whole sequence of counter-intuitive and perverse accounts of space, time, discontinuity, and the interaction of the observer with the natural phenomenon. Eternal verities, such as the conservation of energy and the supra-historical character of physical law were progressively undermined [Mirowski, forthcoming]. Things got so bad that physicists started going around telling people that there could be such a thing as a free lunch.[11] The amazing thing is that much of this drift had been anticipated by Peirce as part of his hypothesis that natural law was itself the product of an evolutionary process.

Philosophers of science felt the tremors under their feet in the 1960s. Analytical philosophy of science had not only been subject to devastating internal criticism, but historians of science such as Thomas Kuhn, Paul Forman, Richard Westfall and others were demonstrating that respected scientists of the past did not conform to the strict positivist code of correct scientific behavior. Perhaps because they were historians, they grew more curious about the hermeneutic aspects of scientific behavior. As Thomas Kuhn, wrote about scientists: "When reading the works of an important thinker, look first for the apparent absurdities in the text and ask yourself how a sensible person could have written them. When you find an answer, I continue, when those passages make sense, then you may find that more central passages, ones you previously thought you understood, have changed their meaning"· [Kuhn 1977, p. xii]. Now, if we have difficulties in understanding the paradigm scientists sanctioned by our culture, it is but a short step to assert that the contemporaries of pivotal scientists also had problems of interpretation and understanding their peers. Explicit rules of deduction and induction could not be expected to resolve this problem in all situations, and as a result the entire Cartesian portrayal of science came unravelled for philosophers [Suppe 1977; Laudan 1984; Rorty 1979, 1986].

By the 1980s, it was common to find historians, philosophers, and sociologists of science employing hermeneutic techniques [Latour and Woolgar 1979; Knorr-Cetina and Mulkay 1983; Radnitzky 1973; Ackerman 1985]. This development in turn encouraged philosophers to rediscover Peirce and to resuscitate the pragmatist tradition in the United States. Writers such as Richard Rorty, Richard Bernstein and Karl Apel have put pragmatism back on the philosophical map, proposing to reunite a theory of language and social interaction with a theory of scientific inquiry. As Rorty has written of the new pragmatism:

> [It] is the same as the method of utopian politics or revolutionary science (as opposed to parliamentary politics or normal science). The method is to redescribe lots and lots of things in new ways, until you have created a pattern of linguistic behavior which will tempt the rising generation to adopt it, thereby causing them to look for appropriate new forms of non-linguistic behavior—e.g., the adoption of new scientific equipment or new social institutions. Philosophy, on this model, does not work piece by piece, analyzing concept after concept, or testing thesis after thesis. Rather, it works holistically and pragmatically. . . . It does not pretend to have a better candidate for doing the same old things which we did when we spoke the old way. Rather, it suggests that we might want to stop doing those things and do something else [Rorty 1986, p. 4].

The irony of this revival was that the legitimate heirs of the tradition of Peirce in economics were basically unaware of it, remaining wedded in many instances to the Cartesian conception of science, which bartered away their legitimacy to neoclassical economics. Although many institutionalist economists maintained a lively interest in philosophical issues, they tended to get sidetracked into such controversies as the meaning of Milton Friedman's essay on the "methodology of positive economics" (an article so incoherent that it could support any reading), or else into behavioralism of a mechanistic cast, which neutralized all hermeneutic problems of interpretation.

Worst of all, the lavish praise of science that had been a hallmark of institutionalism from the 1930s to the 1960s grew more and more an embarrassment, both because of the overt scientism of neoclassical theory, and because of the increasing skepticism about the competence and benevolence of the technocrat in a society where the very institution of science seemed an instrument of subjugation and a juggernaut careening out of control. The tragedy was that institutionalism had lost sight of its bearings, making the mistake of pretending to be a better candidate for doing the same old things that were done when speaking the same old language. In consequence, the research agenda had been set by the neoclassical economists. It was a no-win situation.

The Modern Revival of a
Pragmatist Institutionalist Economics

There is one more nod to be made in the direction of the DMD thesis, and that is to discuss certain nascent hopeful trends in institutional economics. As the vortex model suggests, one might expect that profound transmutations of our "natural" concepts would be felt (perhaps with a lag) in the construction of social theory. I would like to argue that this is indeed the case in some recent institutionalist economic research, and that one might extrapolate from present trends to anticipate a full-scale repudiation of Cartesian philosophy of science and an increased reliance on hermeneutic conceptions of the economic actor as well as the role of the economic researcher.

Twentieth-century innovations in physical science have come quite a distance in denying a mechanically determinate world, reinterpreting our ideas of limitation and scarcity, and filling us with disquiet at the boundlessness of chance, chaos, and emergent novelty. Science is making us rudely aware of our role in constructing the world, or as Rorty puts it, "making truth." If the DMD thesis is any guide, then we should expect that this progressive awakening should eventually show up in economics. Because neoclassical economics is irreparably committed to the imitation of nineteenth-century physics, the DMD thesis predicts that it will find itself progressively isolated from cultural conceptions, defending an increasingly reactionary conception of Natural Order as mechanically deterministic and static. Institutional economics, on the other hand, with its Peircian pedigree, should be well-positioned to participate in the reconstruction of economic theory from a hermeneutic perspective. This reconstruction is not merely wishful thinking; there are signs that it is already well under way.

Notes

1. Evidence for this assertion is presented in detail in [Mirowski, forthcoming, chaps. 4–6].
2. See, however, Mirowski [1987a; 1988] and Piero Mini [1974].
3. I must stress that what follows is specifically my own reading of Peirce, although it shares many points with Karl Apel [1981]. We shall ignore in this essay questions of the wellsprings of Peirce's influences, or the tangled question of his metaphysics. We should caution, however, that some authors in the institutionalist literature, such as H. Liebhafsky, have tried to absolve Peirce of any Hegelian or Continental influence, a thesis I obviously find unpersuasive [Liebhafsky 1986, p. 13]. On this issue, see C.S. Peirce 1958b, p. 283; H.S. Thayer [1981] and Apel [1981, p. 201fn].
4. This assertion of the self-correcting nature of specifically quantitative induction is perhaps one of the weakest parts of the Peircian corpus, because it provides no cogent reason for the privileged character of quantitative evidence. On this issue, see Thomas Kuhn [1977]. Further, it is easy to

devise numerous situations where repeated measurement does not con-
verge upon any particular value. This would be true especially of non-
ergodic situations, such as those envisioned in Peirce's own "evolutionary"
laws.

5. Peirce made a number of observations on the role of conservation principles in the construction of the static mechanical world picture [Peirce 1935,
pp. 15, 20, 100]. It is interesting to compare these statements with the definition given below of an institution as a socially constructed invariant. See
also Mirowski [1984b]. The role of stochastic phenomena is discussed in
my unpublished manuscript, "Uncertain Wavering," discussion paper,
Tufts University.

6. Said Peirce:

> But the higher places in science in the coming years are for those who
> succeed in adapting the methods of one science to the investigation
> of another. That is where the greatest progress of the passing genera-
> tion has consisted in. Darwin adapted biology to the methods of Mal-
> thus and the economists. [James] Maxwell adapted to the theory of
> gasses the methods of the doctrine of chances, and to electricity the
> methods   of   thermodynamics. . . . [Antoine-Augustin]   Cournot
> adapted to policital economy the calculus of variations [Peirce 1958a,
> p. 46].

On this issue, see also Mirowski [1986b].

7. The reasons for the decline of pragmatism in the 1940s is beyond our mandate in this article, but see Thayer's *Meaning and Action,* where it is suggested that pragmatism's alliance with liberal social engineering, its
misconstrual of the pragmatic maxim as a methodological semantic principle, and Dewey's alliance with the logical positivists, particularly in his
Theory of Valuation, all served to cripple the program [Thayer 1981, pp. 560–
63; Dewey 1939b].

8. "Addiction to magical superstition or religious conceptions will necessarily
have its effect on the conceptions and logic employed in technological theory and practice, and will impair its efficiency by that much" [Veblen 1914,
p. 41]. Here Veblen clearly understands that science may be influenced by
culture as well as vice versa, but notice the derogatory language in reference
to non-science, as well as the unfounded assertion that cultural or teleological influences impair the efficiency of scientific logic. Where the DMD thesis posits a vortex, Veblen has two poles of a dichotomy, where one can
only pollute the other.

9. See footnote 7 above.

10. Conventional histories of economic thought have not given sufficient attention to the importance of the institutionalist school for the rise of
twentieth-century macroeconomics. Here, see Mirowski [1985]. The position of the National Bureau of Economic Research as a non-partisan pur-
veyor of data and research ended in the 1970s when Martin Feldstein was
installed as director and institutionalist themes disappeared from its
agenda.

11. "I have heard it said that there is no such thing as a free lunch. It now
appears possible that the universe is a free lunch." [Guth 1983, p. 215].

References

Ackermann, Robert. 1985 *Data, Instruments and Theory.* Princeton: Princeton University Press.

Apel, Karl. 1981. *Charles S. Peirce: From Pragmatism to Pragmaticism.* Amherst: University of Massachusetts Press.

Ayres, Clarence. 1961. *Towards a Reasonable Society.* Austin: University of Texas.

_____. 1962. *The Theory of Economic Progress.* 2d ed. New York: Schocken.

_____. 1963. "The Legacy of Thorstein Veblen." In *Institutional Economics.* Berkeley: University of California Press.

Barnes, B., and S. Shapin, eds. 1979. *Natural Order.* Beverly Hills: Sage.

Bernstein, Richard. 1966. *John Dewey.* New York: Washington Square.

_____. 1983. *Beyond Objectivism and Relativism.* Philadelphia: University of Pennsylvania Press.

Bloor, David. 1976. *Knowledge and Social Imagery.* London: Routledge & Kegan Paul.

_____. 1982. "Durkheim and Mauss Revisited." *Studies in the History and Philosophy of Science* 13 (Winter): 267–97.

Boland, Lawrence. 1982. *The Foundations of Economic Method.* Winchester: Allen & Unwin.

Brown, S. ed. 1979. *Philosophical Disputes in the Social Sciences.* Atlantic Highlands: Humanities.

Bush, Paul Dale. 1983. "An Exploration of the Structural Characteristics of a Veblen-Ayres-Foster Defined Institutional Domain." *Journal of Economic Issues* 17 (March): 35–66.

Cahn, S. ed. 1977. *New Studies on the Philosophy of John Dewey.* Hanover: University Press of New England.

Commons, John. 1934. *Institutional Economics.* New York: Macmillan.

Copeland, Morris. 1951. "Institutional Economics and Model Analysis." *American Economic Review* 41 (May): 54–66.

Dennis, Ken. 1982. "Economic Theory and the Problem of Translation." *Journal of Economic Issues* 16 (September): 691–712.

Dewey, John. 1931. *Philosophy and Civilization.* New York: Minton Balch.

_____. 1938. *Logic: The Theory of Inquiry.* New York: Holt.

_____. 1939a. *John Dewey's Philosophy.* New York: Modern Library.

_____. 1939b. *Theory of Valuation. Vol. 2 of International Encyclopaedia of Unified Science, no. 4.* Chicago: University of Chicago Press.

Douglas, Mary. 1970. *Natural Symbols.* London: Barrie & Jenkins.

_____. 1975. *Implicit Meanings.* London: Routledge Kegan & Paul.

_____. 1986. *How Institutions Think.* Syracuse: Syracuse University Press.

Durkheim, E., and M. Mauss. 1963. *Primitive Classification.* London: Cohen & West.

Dyer, Alan. 1986. "Veblen on Scientific Creativity." *Journal of Economic Issues* 20 (March): 21–41.

Eisele, Carolyn. 1957. "The Peirce-Newcomb Correspondence." *Proceedings of the American Philosophical Society.* 101: 409–25.

Field, Alex. 1979. "On the Explanation of Rules Using Rational Choice Models." *Journal of Economic Issues* 13 (March): 49–72.

_____. 1984. "Microeconomics, Norms and Rationality." *Economic Development and Cultural Change* 32 (July): 683–711.

Guth, Alan. 1983. "Speculations on the Origin of the Matter, Energy, and Entropy of The Universe," in *Asymptotic Realms of Physics*, ed. Alan Guth, et al. Cambridge: MIT Press.

Hands, D. 1985. "Karl Popper and Economic Method." *Economics and Philosophy* 1 (April): 83–99.

Harding, Sandra ed. 1976. *Can Theories Be Refuted?* Boston: Reidel.

Hollis, M., and E. Nell. 1975. *Rational Economic Man.* Cambridge: Cambridge University Press.

Knorr-Cetina, Karin, and Michael Mulkay. 1983. *Science Observed.* London: Sage.

Kuhn, Thomas. 1977. *The Essential Tension.* Chicago: University of Chicago Press.

Latour, Bruno. 1987. *Science in Action.* Cambridge: Harvard University Press.

Latour, Bruno, and Steven Woolgar. 1979. *Natural Order.* Beverly Hills: Sage.

Laudan, Larry. 1984. *Science and Values.* Berkeley: University of California Press.

Layton, Edwin. 1962. "Veblen and the Engineers." *American Quarterly* 14 (Spring): 64–72.

Lepley, Ray ed. 1949. *Value: A Cooperative Inquiry.* New York: Columbia University Press.

Levi, Albert. 1974. *Philosophy as Social Expression.* Chicago: University of Chicago Press.

Liebhafsky, H. 1986. "Peirce on the Summum Bonum and the Unlimited Community." *Journal of Economic Issues* 20 (March): 5–20.

Mayhew, Anne. 1981. "Ayresian Technology, Technological Reasoning, and Doomsday." *Journal of Economic Issues* 15 (June): 513–20.

McFarland, Floyd. 1986. "Clarence Ayres and his Gospel of Technology." *History of Political Economy* 18 (Winter): 617–37.

Meyerson, Emile. 1962. *Identity and Reality.* New York: Dover.

Mini, Piero. 1974. *Economics and Philosophy.* Gainesville: University of Florida Press.

Mirowski, Philip. 1981. "Is There a Mathematical Neoinstitutional Economics?" *Journal of Economic Issues* 15 (September): 593–613.

_____. 1984a. "Physics and the Marginalist Revolution." *Cambridge Journal of Economics* 8 (December): 361–79.

_____. 1984b. "The Role of Conservation Principles in 20th Century Economic Theory." *Philosophy of the Social Sciences* 14 (December): 461–73.

_____. 1985. *The Birth of the Business Cycle,* New York: Garland.

_____. 1986a. "Institutions as Solution Concepts in a Game Theory Context." In *Microeconomic Theory,* edited by Larry Samuelson. Hingham, Mass.: Kluwer-Nijhoff.

_____. 1986b. "Mathematical Formalism and Economic Explanation." In *The Reconstruction of Economic Theory,* edited by Philip Mirowski. Hingham, Mass.: Kluwer-Nijhoff.

_____. 1987a. "Shall I Compare Thee to a Minkowski-Ricardo-Leontief Matrix of the Hicks-Mosak Type?", *Economics and Philosophy* 3 (April): forthcoming.

_____. 1987b. "What Do Markets Do?" *Explorations in Economic History*
_____. 1988. *Against Mechanism*. Totawa, N.J.: Rowman & Littlefield.
_____. forthcoming. *More Heat Than Light: Economics as Social Physics*. New York: Cambridge University Press.
Mitchell, Wesley. 1937. *The Backward Art of Spending Money*. New York: McGraw Hill.
Morgenbesser, S. ed. 1977. *Dewey and His Critics*. New York: Journal of Philosophy.
Peirce, Charles S. 1934. *Collected Papers*, Vol. 5. Cambridge: Harvard University Press.
_____. 1935. *Collected Papers*, Vol. 6. Cambridge: Harvard University Press.
_____. 1958a. *Collected Papers*, Vol. 7. Cambridge: Harvard University Press.
_____. 1958b. *Collected Papers*, Vol. 8. Cambridge: Harvard University Press.
Polanyi, Karl. 1968. *The Great Transformation*. Boston: Beacon.
Putnam, Hilary. 1983. *Realism and Reason*. New York: Cambridge University Press.
Radnitzsky, G. 1973. *Contemporary Schools of Metascience*. Chicago: Regnery.
Ramstad, Yngve. 1986. "A Pragmatist's Quest for Holistic Knowledge." *Journal of Economic Issues* 20 (December): 1067–1106.
Rescher, Nicholas. 1978. *Peirce's Philosophy of Science*. Notre Dame: University of Notre Dame.
Rickman, H. P. 1976. "Introduction." In *W. Dilthey, Selected Writings*. New York: Cambridge University Press.
Rorty, Richard. 1979. *Philosophy and the Mirror of Nature*. Princeton: Princeton University Press.
_____. 1986. "The Contingency of Language." *London Review of Books* 3 (April): 3–7.
Rorty, R., J. Schneewind and Q. Skinner, eds. 1984. *Philosophy in History*. Cambridge: Cambridge University Press.
Rutherford, Malcolm. 1981. "Clarence Ayres and the Instrumentalist Theory of Value." *Journal of Economic Issues* 15 (September): 657–74.
Samuels, Warren. 1978. "Information Systems, Preferences and the Economy in the JEI." *Journal of Economic Issues* 12 (March): 23–42.
Scheffler, Israel. 1974. *Four Pragmatists*. New York: Humanities.
Suppe, Frederick. 1977. *Structure of Scientific Theories*. Urbana: University of Illinois Press.
Taylor, Charles. 1985. *Human Agency and Language*. Cambridge: Cambridge University Press.
Thayer, H. S. 1981. *Meaning and Action*. Indianapolis: Hackett.
Tiles, Mary. 1984. *Bachelard: Science and Objectivity*. Cambridge: Cambridge University Press.
Veblen, Thorstein. 1914. *The Instinct of Workmanship*. New York: Macmillan.
_____. 1923. *Absentee Ownership*. New York: Heubsch.
_____. 1933. *The Vested Interests and the Common Man*. New York: Viking.
_____. 1934. *Essays in Our Changing Order*. New York: Viking.
_____. 1969. *The Place of Science in Modern Civilization*. New York: Capricorn.
Vining, Rutledge. 1949. "Koopmans on the Choice of Variables." *Review of Economics and Statistics* 31 (May): 77–86.

Waller, William. 1982. "The Evolution of the Veblenian Dichotomy." *Journal of Economic Issues* 16 (September): 757–71.
White, Morton. 1949. *Social Thought in America.* New York: Viking.
Wilbur, C. and R. Harrison. 1978. "The Methodological Basis of Institutional Economics." *Journal of Economic Issues* 12 (March): 61–90.

The Theory of Human Nature

Hans E. Jensen

This article is based on three simple *postulata:* (1) all socioeconomic theories contain, explicitly or implicitly, a theory of human nature; (2) institutionalism is a socioeconomic theory; (3) institutionalism must, therefore, include a theory of human nature.

Given the third *postulatum,* one may pose the following question: what are the characteristics and essence of the institutionalist theory of human nature, and what role does such a theory play in institutionalist thought as a whole? I shall attempt to answer this question on the following pages. In so doing, I shall begin with a discussion of the concepts and theories of human nature that were formulated by Thorstein B. Veblen and John Dewey. The rationale for this particular commencement is that Veblen and Dewey exerted a strong influence on two prominent institutionalists when these two scholars formulated their concepts of human nature. I am referring to Clarence E. Ayres and John R. Commons. Ayres, for example, was greatly influenced by both Dewey and Veblen when he crafted his theory of human nature [Ayres 1961, pp. 28–30]. And Commons, who did not owe any intellectual capital to Veblen, cast his theory of human nature in a Deweyian mold [Commons 1959, pp. 150–51].

Ayres and Commons, in turn, had impact on the thinking of succeeding generations of those students of society who admitted, and admit, to being institutionalists. Consequently, the orgins of the modern insti-

The author wishes to thank Wendell Gordon and the Editor of this journal for valuable comments on an earlier draft of this article.

tutionalist theory of human nature must be sought in the works of Veblen and Dewey.

The Beginning of an Institutionalist Theory of Human Nature

According to Veblen, "instincts . . . are the prime movers in human behaviour." These "native proclivities alone make anything worth while, and out of their working emerge not only the purpose and efficiency of life, but its substantial pleasures and pains as well" [Veblen 1964, p. 1]. Veblen was well aware, however, that the concept of instincts had suffered a "disintegration" in the biological sciences, and that it was "of too unprecise a character to serve the needs of an exhaustive psychological analysis" [Veblen 1964, p. 2]. But Veblen did not propose to undertake biological investigations or to engage in exhaustive psychological analysis. His chosen task was that of inquiring "into the nature and causes of the growth of institutions." Such an inquiry, he argued, "will address itself to the growth of habit and conventions, as conditioned by the material environment and by the innate and persistent propensities of human nature" [Veblen 1964, p. 2]. And for "these propensities, as they take effect in the give and take of cultural growth," Veblen could find "no better designation than the time-worn 'instinct'" [Veblen 1964, pp. 2, 3].

How did Veblen conceive of instincts, and how did he categorize these human attributes? In formalizing his notion of instincts, he was influenced by the evolutionary biology associated with the name of Charles Darwin and by the works of the physiologist Jacques Loeb, the social psychologist William McDougall, and the philosopher-psychologist William James [Veblen 1908, pp. 36–36; 1964, pp. 3n, 4n, 12n]. Thus Veblen distinguished, on the one hand, between "'tropismatic'" impulses, which Loeb had defined as "blind instincts," and, on the other hand, "instinctive proclivities," which McDougall had identified as "certain innate specific tendencies of the mind . . . that have been slowly evolved in the process of adaption of species to their environment" [Veblen 1964, pp. 1, 5; Loeb 1912, p. 28; McDougall 1923, pp. 23–24]. And arguing à la James, who maintained that an instinctive "impulse . . . [is] acted out . . . for *the sake* of its results," Veblen averred that the "distinctive feature by the mark of which any given instinct is identified is to be found in the particular character of the purpose to which it drives." That is, "instinctive action is teleological," according to Veblen [James 1950, p. 390; Veblen 1964, pp. 4, 3]. Thus "Veblen moulded his own notions of human nature on Darwin, William James," Loeb and McDougall; notions that he found to be illustrated and confirmed by available "anthropological records" [Mitchell 1936, p. xxvi].

Given this parentage of his ideas concerning human nature, it was logical for Veblen to argue that instincts are "teleological categories" and that every instinct, "as contra-distinguished from tropismatic action" . . . "involves consciousness" and intelligence. [Veblen 1964, pp. 3, 4]. Thus whereas "tropismatic reaction" is a "simple reflex action," and hence without intelligent guidance, it is "a distinctive mark of mankind that the working-out of the instinctive proclivities of the race is guided by intelligence to a degree not approached by the other animals" [Veblen 1964, pp. 10, 5, 6]. And, speaking in a McDougallesque vein, Veblen observed that although "instincts are hereditary traits," they are not immutable because "the instinctive ends of life are worked out under any given cultural situation." In other words, instincts are conditioned by "the experience of past generations" [Veblen 1964, pp. 13, 7]. As Ayres put it: "Clearly when he spoke of instincts," Veblen had in mind "culturally significant patterns of behavior" that differ "very substantially" from those of all "other creature[s]" [Ayres 1958, pp. 28, 25].

To Veblen, therefore, the "complement of instinctive dispositions . . . makes up . . . 'human nature'," sometimes spoken of as the " 'spiritual nature' of man." Although this complement "fluctuates from one individual to another," in particular among "the civilised peoples" of the West, "there runs" through these latter populations a "generically human type of spiritual endowment, prevalent as a general average of human nature." In Veblen's view, this average human nature is dominated by six major "instinctive proclivities" [Veblen 1964, pp. 14, 15, 19]. These are: an " 'instinct of workmanship' "; an "instinctively . . . actuated . . . idle curiosity"; an "instinctive disposition" labeled "the parental bent"; a "proclivity to . . . acquisition"; a set of "self-regarding proclivities"; and "an habitual bent" that makes instinctive "habituation" possible on the part of human beings [Veblen 1957, p. 4; 1964, pp. 11, 25, 26, 27, 182, 204, 285].

Veblen pointed out that these "instincts are not to be conceived as severally discrete and elementary proclivities." On the contrary, instinctive dispositions of an individual "incontinently touch, blend, overlap and interfere" with each other. Moreover, in such a process of interaction, the various instincts are "subject to development and hence to modification by habit" [Veblen 1964, pp. 11, 38]. It was because of this modifying influence of habit that Veblen assigned an importance to the habitual bent that is matched only by that which he attached to the instinct of workmanship and the parental bent. These three proclivities are unique among all the relevant instincts in that each is "an auxiliary to all the other instincts, rather than an independent force," as Wesley C. Mitchell pointed out with special reference to the instinct of workmanship [Mitchell 1914, p. 24].

The "innate predispositions [of] the parental bent," the idle curiosity, and the instinct of workmanship become "instincts of serviceability" when they are powerful enough to elicit the cooperation of the habitual bent. In such a situation, the knowledge and information unearthed by idle curiosity "come to serve the ends of workmanship" and parental bent [Veblen 1964, pp. 48, 49, 88]. The result is a habitual "pursuit of efficiency in the ways and means of life" that leads to "increasing technological mastery" [Veblen 1964, pp. 48, 58] and hence to evermore "material welfare" for the community [Veblen 1944, p. 79]. The "control exercised over custom and usage by . . . [the] instincts of serviceability" may sometimes be "neither too close nor too insistent," however. That is to say, the habitual bent, and with it workmanship and allied instincts, may be overpowered by, and put into the service of, the "self-seeking" and acquisitive instincts [Veblen 1964, pp. 49, 45]. When that happens, the only "worthy employments are those which may be classed as exploit; unworthy are those necessary everyday employments into which no appreciable element of exploits enter" [Veblen 1924, p. 8]. In other words, "imbecile usages and principles of conduct" become encrusted in "disserviceable institutions" that "continue to hold their place in spite of the disapproval of native common sense" [Veblen 1964, p. 49].

Veblen concluded, therefore, that the major instincts work in such a fashion that they produce a "two-cleft systematisation of knowledge," namely "speculative" and "institutional" knowledge [Veblen 1942, pp. 45–46, 47], on the one hand, and "matter-of-fact," or "technological," knowledge, on the other [Veblen 1964, pp. 40, 41]. Over the ages, these two kinds of knowledge have given rise to, and perpetuated, two distinct and contrary types of behavior, namely "pecuniary and industrial" behavior, respectively [Veblen 1904, p. 315].

Dewey's Contribution to an Institutionalist Theory of Human Nature

Like Veblen's, Dewey's thinking was initially stimulated by German philosophers. But whereas Veblen received his early inspiration from the works of Immanual Kant, Dewey took his from ideas that originated with Georg W.F. Hegel [Tool 1953, Chap. 2, pp. 42–43]. Thus in an autobiographical sketch written in 1930, Dewey acknowledged that he experienced "at least a temporary conversion . . . to 'Hegelianism'" when he was a graduate student at Johns Hopkins University in the

1880s. And although he "drifted away from Hegelianism in the next fifteen years . . . [the] acquaintance with Hegel . . . left a permanent deposit in . . . his thinking" [Dewey 1930a, pp. 6, 8]. Like Veblen again, Dewey acquired a familiarity with the ideas of Darwin that left an even larger, permanent deposit in his mind. The "'Origin of Species'," said Dewey, "introduced a mode of thinking that in the end was bound to transform the logic of knowledge, and hence the treatment of morals, politics, and religion" [Dewey 1951, p. 2]. Especially, Darwinism pointed to the necessity of "explor[ing] specific values and the specific conditions that generate them" [Dewey 1951, p. 13]. That is to say, Darwinian biology "paved the way for a new psychology." It was for this reason that it was the "biological strand in William James's *Principles of Psychology* that influenced Dewey more than James's pragmatic writing" [Bernstein 1960, p. xxii].

Hence, when Dewey formulated his theory of human nature, he started from the proposition that human beings are biological organisms. It means that "there are always intrinsic forces of common human nature at work." But, he hastened to add, "culture" exercises a "pervasive and powerful influence . . . in shaping the concrete manifestations of every human nature subject to its influence." Dewey was convinced, therefore, that human nature can be understood "only as a system of beliefs, desires and purposes which are formed in the interaction of biological aptitudes with a social environment" [Dewey 1930b, pp. viii, viii, xi]. Consequently, human "behavior" can only be described as one "in which organism and environment act together, or *inter*-act" [Dewey 1938, p. 33]. This being the case, Dewey concluded that a correct theory of human nature must be one that "persists in securing and maintaining an equilibrium with reference to intrinsic human nature on one side and social customs and institutions on the other" [Dewey 1930b, p. viii].

By intrinsic human nature, Dewey meant certain "tendencies [that are] so integral a part of human nature that the latter would not be human nature if they changed. These tendencies used to be called instincts" [Dewey 1946, p. 187]. Dewey preferred to use the label "impulses," however, for those "instinctive activities" that constitute the "primitive, natural and inevitable" in human nature [Dewey 1930b, pp. 90, 89]. Thus in Dewey's theory, impulse replaced instinct, and he gave the following reasons for the substitution.

The use of the words instinct and impulse as practical equivalents is intentional, even though it may grieve critical readers. The word instinct taken alone is still too laden with the older notion that an instinct is always definitely organized and adapted—which for the most part is just what it is not in human beings. The word impulse suggests something primitive, yet loose, undirected, initial. Man can progress . . . precisely because he has so many "instincts" that they cut across one another, so that most service-able actions must be *learned* [Dewey 1930b, p. 105n].

What is it that is learned? "Habits," said Dewey, which he character-ized as "organized activities [that] are secondary and acquired, not native and original" like impulses. Habits are, however, "outgrowths of [the latter] unlearned activities which are part of man's endowment at birth." And, according to Dewey, in "learning habits it is possible for man to learn the habit of learning" [Dewey 1930b, pp. 89, 105n]. In this fact is rooted what Dewey called the "changeability of human nature" [Dewey 1946, p. 192].

Thus according to Dewey, human nature has two major, interacting elements: impulses and habits. Before I enter into an exposition of his explanation of how these two "pegs" shape human attitudes, ideas and behavior through their interaction, it is necessary to take a closer look at Dewey's concept of habits [Levitt 1971, p. 139].

As he put it himself, Dewey used the term in a sense that is "twisted somewhat from its customary use." In particular, he asserted that "rep-etition is in no sense the essence of habit" [Dewey 1930b, pp. 40, 42]. Rather, said he,

The essence of habit is an acquired predisposition to *ways* or modes of response, not to particular acts except as, under special conditions, these express a way of behaving. Habit means special sensitiveness or acces-sibility to certain classes of stimuli, standing predilections and aversions, rather than bare recurrence of specific acts. It means *will* [Dewey 1930b, p. 42, emphasis added].

Habit, therefore, "is an ability, an art" said Dewey; and he added significantly that it is one that has been "formed through past experi-ence" [Dewey 1930b, p. 66]. What is experience? First and foremost, experience "is the result, the sign, and the reward of that interaction of organism and environment which, when it is carried to the full, is a transformation of interaction into participation and communication" [Dewey 1934, p. 22]. Although it is undeniable that people interact with the physical environment, to "a very large extent the ways in which human beings respond even to physical conditions are influenced by their cultural environment" [Dewey 1938, p. 42]. In other words, it is in the "social environment" that human beings gain that experience that Dewey associated with participation and communication. Conse-quently, habits and "personal traits are functions of social situations" with the result that all of the "actions of an individual bear the stamp of his community as assuredly as does the language he speaks." That is to say, our "conduct is socially conditioned whether we perceive the fact or not" [Dewey 1930b, pp. 318, 20, 317, 316]. "Man, as Aristotle remarked, is a *social* animal" [Dewey 1938, p. 43].

And according to Dewey, habit is characterized by "stability." That is so, said he, because those "widespread uniformities of habit," which he called "customs," tend to "persist" because of the fact that "individuals form their personal habits under conditions set by prior customs." Consequently, the "nature of habit is to be assertive, insistent, self-perpetuating." Inasmuch as he conceived of "institutions as embodied habits," Dewey concluded that the strong "force" of "permanence and inertia that . . . belong[s] to acquired customs" has resulted in a situation in which the "force of lag in human life is enormous" [Dewey 1930b, pp. 108, 58, 108, 109, 108].

It is in their interaction with these "encrusted habits" that instinctive human impulses contribute to the formation of human behavior. These native impulses are "highly flexible" and plastic, however. Thus "although first in time," impulses "are never primary in fact; they are secondary and dependent." On the other hand, when it comes to "*conduct,* the acquired [element of habits] is the primitive" and, as indicated above, inflexible component of human nature. Dewey explained this "seeming paradox" in the following manner [Dewey 1930b, pp. 105, 95, 89; emphasis added].

> In the life of the individual, instinctive activity comes first. But an individual begins life as a baby, and babies are dependent beings. Their activities could continue at most for only a few hours were it not for the presence and aid of adults with their formed habits. And babies owe to adults more than procreation, more than the continued food and protection which preserve life. They owe to adults the opportunity to express their native activities in ways which have meaning. Even if by some miracle original activity could continue without assistance from the organized skill and art of adults, it would not amount to anything. It would be mere sound and fury [Dewey 1930b, pp. 89–90].

"In short," said Dewey, "the *meaning* of native activities is not native; it is acquired. It depends upon interaction with a matured social medium," namely, "habits" [Dewey 1930b, p. 90]. "War," for example, "does not exist because man has combative instincts, but because social conditions and forces have led, almost forced, these 'instincts' into this channel" [Dewey 1946, pp. 186–87].

What about economic behavior? According to Dewey, the "current economic psychology has . . . tremendously oversimplified the situation" by recognizing "but one type of motive, that which concerns personal gain." By the same token, in "economic theory," labor means "something painful, something so onerously disagreeable or 'costly' that every individual avoids it if he can, and engages in it only because of the promise of an overbalancing gain" [Dewey 1930b, pp. 122, 123].

Dewey did admit that there "is doubtless some sense in saying that every conscious act has an incentive or motive." He hastened to add, however, that "this sense is as truistic as that of the not dissimilar saying that every event has a cause. Neither statement throws any light on any particular occurrence." At most, it is "a maxim which advises us to search for some other fact with which the one in question may be correlated" [Dewey 1930b, p. 118]. And that other fact is that a human being "is an active being." Thus, although it is "absurd to ask what induces a man to activity generally speaking," when "we want to direct his activity . . . in a specified channel, then the question of motive is pertinent." In this context a "motive is then that element in the total complex of a man's activity which, if he can be sufficiently stimulated, will result in an act having specified consequences" [Dewey 1930b, pp. 119, 120].

Consequently, said Dewey, a "motive does not exist prior to an act and produce it. It is an act *plus* a judgment upon some element of it, the judgment being made in the light of the consequences of the act" [Dewey 1930b, p. 120]. How is the individual able to judge such consequences? He or she does so habitually. That is to say, other people react to an individual's act "in order to encourage him in future acts of the same sort, or in order to dissuade him—in short to build or destroy a habit." Consequently, Dewey maintained that a motive "is simply an impulse viewed as a constituent in a habit, a factor in a disposition." It was in this circumstance that Dewey found the source of the "unnatural emphasis on the prospect of reward" in the modern economic society [Dewey 1930b, pp. 121, 122]. This emphasis, said he, exemplifies "our leading proposition that social customs are not direct and necessary consequences of specific impulses, but that social institutions and expectations shape and crystallize impulses into dominant habits." A "real and important fact is thus contained in current economic psychology, but it is a fact about existing industrial conditions and not a fact about native, original activity" [Dewey 1930b, pp. 122, 123].

These conditions, then, are part of the whole institutional system that embodies customs and habits. And, as already mentioned, Dewey was convinced that custom is characterized by "inertia" and hence not very "susceptible to alteration" [Dewey 1930b, p. 107]. Hence he emphasized again and again that the "resistance to change comes from acquired habits" and not "from original human nature" [Dewey 1946, p. 190]. Despite this "fixity of human nature," there have been changes in human nature over time. "Civilization itself is the product of altered human nature" [Dewey 1946, p. 190]. But, cautioned Dewey, actual "social change is never so great as is apparent change. Ways of belief, of expectation, of judgment and attendant emotional dispositions of like and dislike, are not easily modified after they have once taken shape" [Dewey 1930b, p. 108].

In order to get his point across, Dewey contrasted the positions of the "conservative" and the "short-cut revolutionist" [Dewey 1930b, pp. 106, 107]. The former finds "in the [traditional] doctrine of native instincts a scientific support for asserting the practical unalterability of human nature." The latter, on the other hand, believes that it is possible to have "rapid and sweeping social change" through an alteration of habits by means of "education" [Dewey 1930b, pp. 106, 108, 106]. Both parties "rest their case," however, upon "just the factor which . . . weakens their respective conclusions." That is to say, "it is precisely custom," which the revolutionist assumes to be flexible, that "has greatest inertia, which is least susceptible to alteration; while instincts," which the conservative views as fixed, are "most readily modifiable through use, most subject to educative direction" [Dewey 1930b, p. 107].

How is such a direction to be brought about given the "stability and force of habit" [Dewey 1930b, p. 108]? This problem was particularly manifest in the realm of economic institutions. Thus Dewey was convinced that there was a need and "necessity of change in economic institutions" but that by definition, these institutions "offer serious obstacles to the change" [Dewey 1930b, p. 126]. Hence he was forced to ask himself: "Is there any way out of this vicious circle?" One way out might be the one that was followed in the past: to let the economic problems fester long enough so that "upheaval . . . [will] dislocate customs so as to release impulses to serve as points of departure for new habits" [Dewey 1930b, pp. 127, 126].

Needless to say, this solution was rejected by Dewey. Instead, he hoped that a "future new society of changed purposes and desires may be created by a deliberate human treatment of the impulses of youth." This, he said, "is the meaning of education" [Dewey 1930b, p. 96]. Unfortunately, "for the most part, adults have given training," that is, provided "certain skills," rather "than education" [Dewey 1930b, p. 96; 1946, p. 190; 1930b, p. 96].

It was partly for this reason that Dewey developed a life-long interest in education and schooling, subjects on which he wrote extensively (see

Dewey [1916; Axtelle and Burnett 1970]). As he put it himself, when developed, the "sciences of human nature and human relations" will have as their chief concern the "problem of how human nature is most effectively modified. . . . This problem is ultimately that of education in its widest sense" [Dewey 1946, p. 192].

Commons's Pragmatic Theory of Human Nature with a Negotiational Twist

Commons's economics has been described in several ways (see Gruchy [1947, pp. 152–54; Parsons 1986, esp. pp. 283–90; Rutherford 1983, pp. 721–22]). For the present purpose, however, the following *precis* by Richard A. Gonce is highly suggestive as an entree to a discussion of Commons's concept of human nature: "A certain interpretation of evolutionism, pragmatism, and an endeavor to embed economics within a theory of Anglo-American social organization are the hallmarks of Commons's economic thought" [Gonce 1971, p. 91]. In the context of this article, the key word is "pragmatism." The reasons are as follows.

First of all, Commons viewed himself as "a 'pragmatic' theorist—a theorist who places experience foremost in the *theories* of political economy" [Commons 1964, p. 175, emphasis added]. He used the term experience in three meanings, or contexts, however. First, in the sense used by the philosphical pragmatists, namely that experience influences human behavior. Second, and related thereto, in the sense that the (assumed) experiences gained by the actors in the economic drama must be incorporated as an explanatory variable in economic theory. It was for this reason that Commons argued that his "institutional economics is behavioristic" [Commons 1931, p. 654]. Third, in the sense that Commons's own thinking was greatly influenced by his varied experience as an observer, investigator, and shaper of labor-management relations, as a consultant to public officials and agencies at all three levels of government, as an author of social legislation, as an historian of the labor movement, as a legal historian, and as a doctrine-historian [see Commons 1964; Harter 1962, esp. pp. 9–24, 89–204; Mitchell 1935, esp. pp. 313–18]. Commons provided the following hint concerning at least one source of his thirst for experience in the actual economy.

> I had read Veblen's brilliant criticisms, beginning in 1895, on the theories of the classical, socialistic, and psychological economists, and his suggestion that an evolutionary theory of value must be constructed out of the habits and customs of social life. But he had not studied the decisions of

the courts which are based on these customs, and I went to work with my students digging directly out of the court decisions stretching over several hundred years the behavioristic theory of value on which they were working [Commons 1957, p. vii].

When he formulated his particular type of economics, Commons integrated the three types of experience so that they constitute a continuum, as it were, that runs through the entire corpus of his mature work. And it was in this process of integration that he was especially influenced by the pragmatists, particularly by Charles S. Peirce and Dewey. When, for example, he selected his empirical data, Commons viewed them as the result of human "action in all the economic transactions of bargaining, managing and rationing" [Commons 1931, p. 654], acts in which individuals engage in consequence of their socially conditioned experiential judgments. This notion that human beings act as they do because they possess "their own [culturally determined] 'conceptual schemes'" [Commons 1959, p. 98], Commons obtained from Dewey who, alone among all the Western philosophers since the days of John Locke, formulated a "social psychology of custom [that] may become negotiational" [Commons 1931, p. 655; 1959, p. 91]. When, however, he formulated his "own [conceptual scheme] by which he construct[ed] his science" for the purpose of gaining "scientific understanding of [the] negotiational psychology" of those engaged in transactions, Commons was influenced by "Peirce's Pragmatism [which] is none other than the scientific method of investigation" [Commons 1959, pp. 98, 91, 156]. Thus we "are compelled," said Commons, "to distinguish and use two meanings of pragmatism: Peirce's meaning of purely a method of scientific investigation" and Dewey's "meaning of the various social-philosophies assumed [and held] by the parties ... who participate in ... [economic] transactions" [Commons 1959, p. 150]. Thus when Commons undertook his Peirceesque investigations, he gained experience in the light of which he extended Dewey's theory and concept of human nature. This extension furnished Commons with a deeper understanding of those human behavior patterns that are experientially conditioned, an understanding that in turn influenced his research activities and added new dimensions to his interpretations. These intellectual developments on the part of Commons enhanced his personal experience, which enabled him to extend Dewey's theory still further, and so on. As Commons put it himself: "Not until we reach John Dewey do we find Peirce expanded to ethics, and not until we reach institutional economics do we find it expanded to transactions, going concerns, and Reasonable Value" [Commons 1959, p. 155].

Commons effected this latter expansion when he viewed the ideas of David Hume and Thomas Robert Malthus, especially those of the latter, in the light of Dewey's social psychology. With Malthus, whom Commons considered to be the "first scientific evolutionist, indeed the first scientific economist," began the "Age of Stupidity" that followed upon the "Age of Reason [that] ended in the French Revolution" [Commons 1959, pp. 246, 244]. Concretely, what Malthus did, according to Commons, was to convert Adam "Smith's divine abundance for the purpose of human happiness into divine scarcity for the purpose of evolving the human mind and moral character out of the 'clay of the earth'" [Commons 1959, pp. 245–46]. The "wage system" and "vice, misery, poverty, and war" were consequences of, or "accidental to," the "divine principle that population should increase faster than the means of subsistence." This is the Malthusian principle of population "which," said Commons, "is none other than the biological foundation of the principle of Scarcity" [Commons 1959, p. 246].

As far as Commons was concerned, however, the truly remarkable aspect of Malthus's thinking was that he did not conceive of humans as primarily rational beings, as did the mainstream classical and later neoclassical economists. Rather, according to Commons, Malthus argued that "the mass of mankind are rather stupid; that they are swayed by passions quite as much as by calculation," as Mitchell put it in one of his interpretations of Commons's institutionalism [Mitchell 1969, p. 725]. In Commons's own words, Malthus "introduced scarcity, passion, stupidity, misery, as fundamentals in economic science" [Commons 1959, p. 112]. In a setting of scarcity, human passion and stupidity produce conflicts. Malthus, therefore, "began the disillusionment of an Age of business cycles, overproduction, underproduction, unemployment" and political and "economic struggles of landlords, peasants, farmers, capitalists, and laborers" [Commons 1959, p. 250].

Once he read Malthus's works through lenses tinted by Dewey's theory of "Custom," Commons was in possession of those principal ingredients that he needed in order to construct a theory of human nature that would make it possible for him to change the "foundations of economics from abundance, sin, and holding for self, to scarcity, collective action, and withholding from others" [Commons 1959, p. 41; 1964, p. 60]. In this task of constructing a concept of human nature, Commons made a distinction between habit and custom. "Habit is individual repetition. Custom is a kind of social compulsion imposed on individuals by the collective opinion of those who feel and act alike" [Commons

1959, p. 153]. Commons expanded on these notions in the following manner.

[Thus] if we distinguish custom from habit, then custom is none other than education, for it is the repeated impressions of fellow beings from childhood, which impose conformity of habitual assumptions upon individuals. . . . Habit is indeed an individualistic term in that it is limited to experience, feelings and expectations of an individual; but custom is that portion of experience, feelings, and expectations derived from other persons who are collectively alike, which is education in the broadest meaning. Habit is repetition by one person. Custom is repetition by the continuing group of changing persons. It has a coercive effect on individuals, and . . . it accounts for practically all of . . . "those opinions that prevail upon mankind" [Commons 1959, p. 155].

Thus by virtue of being "born into this process of collective action," human beings "become individualized by the rules of collective action" [Commons 1970, p. 21]. Institutions are the locus of such actions and rules. Hence Commons defined an "institution as collective action in control, liberation and expansion of individual action" [Commons 1931, p. 649]. Each individual is therefore a thoroughly "Institutionalized Mind"; that is to say, he/she is conditioned to behave in accordance with those "Working Rules" that embody the "universal principles of cause, effect, or purpose, common to all collective action" [Commons 1959, pp. 73, 71]. In other words, institutionalized customs, and the rules associated therewith, are the forces that either bend and mold individual habits so that they conform to the rules of collective action or punish those individuals who do not mend their habits in accordance with these rules. In Commons's view, the processes involved are as follows:

Stated in language of the operation of working rules on individual action they are expressed by the auxiliary verbs of what the individual can, cannot, must, must not, may, or may not *do.* He "can" or "cannot," because collective action will or will not come to his aid. He "must" or "must not," because collective action will compel him. He "may," because collective action will permit him and protect him. He "may not," because collective action will prevent him [Commons 1959, p. 71].

According to Commons, collective action "ranges all the way from unorganized custom to . . . organized going concerns," or, in Gonce's terminology, from "[u]norganized institutions" to "organized institutions" [Commons 1931, p. 649; Gonce 1971, p. 84]. The former consist of individual "persuasions, coercions" and philosophically and ethically based individual "commands" that constitute "inducements" to individual action [Commons 1959, p. 700]. The organized institutions are the "Going Concerns, such as the family, the corporation, the holding company, the trade association, the trade union, the Federal Reserve System, [and] . . . the State" [Commons 1959, p. 70].

It is the organized institutions that are the really powerful conditioners of individual behavior because they alone can impose "Sanctions," which are those *"collective* inducements that require individuals to conform their behavior to that of others." This is the real "meaning of an Institution," said Commons, because an organized "institution is collective action inducing individual action" [Commons 1959, pp. 700–701, emphasis added].

Institutions and customs, and thereby human behavior, have been "continually changing in the history of civilization," however [Commons 1959, p. 701]. What has brought about such a change? Commons listed only one cause: "Customs have merely changed with changes in economic conditions" that followed in the wake of improvements in "technological efficiency" [Commons 1931, p. 651; 1970, p. 230]. Economic change and development result in new social groups and classes, new conflicts, institutional realignments, and changes in the mix of customs [Commons 1959, pp. 292–93]. As pointed out by Gruchy, this does not necessarily mean Commons argued that human beings are passively permitting their individual habits to be remolded mechanically by the unfolding power of economically induced change in customs [Gruchy 1947, p. 164].

The extent to which one absolves Commons from being an economic determinist in his explanation of human nature and behavior depends, however, on one's interpretation of the meaning of his concepts of "Willingness" and "Will" [Commons 1959, pp. 738, 648]. Sometimes Commons used these terms synonymously, as he did when he observed that "the human will, *or* willingness, was not recognized by the courts as existing in . . . statute law" [Commons 1970, p. 37, emphasis added]. In other, and more frequent, contexts, he used the term willingness to mean "the complex attributes of human beings" that enable individuals to exercise their will, an exercise that results in "Will-in-Action." In this setting, "the will . . . [is] the whole activity of human beings in their actions and transactions." The question is then to what extent the "will is free" [Commons 1959, pp. 738, 305, 739].

Commons admitted that in the case of individuals, the will is "subjective" and sometimes "capricious" and hence may "differ" from person to person. Economic life is characterized by "uniformity," however. But this uniformity is uniformity "of action . . . [in] transactions" and not uniformity of "emotions" [Commons 1959, p. 739]. And in carrying out transactions, which are in the domain of the "going concern," the "social force" of custom "compels individuals to conform" [Commons 1959, p. 638]. In other words, Commons concluded that custom "compels uniformity of action by all individuals within the jurisdiction" in question [Commons 1959, pp. 638, 740].

"But," said Commons in a significant statement, "no science requires absolute unformities in order to be a science." Hence he allowed for some "variabilities" in the behavior of individuals [Commons 1959, p. 741]. He hinted at the possibility that such differences might be because of different degrees of "insight" on the part of individuals. The reason he gave is that insight is "the emotional, volitional, valuing, intuitive, even instinctive, process" that, together with "habitual assumptions" and the "strictly intellectual process" of "rationalization," constitute what Commons called "Willingness" [Commons 1959, pp. 747, 748]. And, as already pointed out, he argued that willingness is the governor of will-in-action. He was certain, however, that differences in insight produce only "variable *degrees* of [that] conformity" of action that is imposed upon individuals by the institutional force of custom [Commons 1959, p. 740, emphasis added].

It may be concluded, therefore, that Commons was of the opinion that those aspects of human nature and behavior that are relevant from the point of view of the economist are determined largely by nurture rather than nature. Inasmuch as he explained that the former force emanates from customs embedded in institutions, it was logical and appropriate for Commons to label himself an institutionalist.

Ayres's Cultural Theory of Human Nature

Ayres belonged to a group of twentieth-century American heterodox economists who have been identified as "neo-institutionalists" by Marc R. Tool, Fritz Mann, and Gruchy [Tool, Chap. 7, p. 22; Mann 1960, p. 169; Gruchy 1969, p. 5]. According to Tool, the hallmark of neo-institutionalism is that key parts of Veblen's economics have been blended and fused with the "work of John Dewey and the philosophy of instrumentalism." And, said Tool, the "major . . . exponent of this integrated analysis of neo-institutionalism is Clarence E. Ayres" [Tool 1953, Chap. 1, pp. 3, 4]. Ayres was in a unique position to undertake such a task. He "grew up in the atmosphere of instrumentalism," a concept he associated with both Dewey's and Veblen's works [Ayres 1946, p. 189]. As Ayres put it, what "Dewey called the 'instrumental' process ... is identical with what Veblen was calling the 'technological' process" [Ayres 1961, p. 29].

Prominent among the elements integrated by Ayres are the Veblenian and Deweyian theories of human nature. He effected more than a fusion, however. He also extended the two pioneers' theories of behavior because neither, in Ayres's opinion, had provided a "clear and [fully] acceptable" behavioral proposition, "Dewey because of his preoccupation with Kant and the theory of knowledge, and Veblen because he allowed himself to be misled by McDougall and others, into explaining everything in terms of contrary instincts" [Ayres 1967, p. 4]. Thus taking off from Veblen and Dewey, and benefiting from the insights obtained by a host of other scholars since the days of the two pioneers, Ayres was confident that he was in a position to "offer a ... much simpler and more conclusive explanation" of human behavior *and* that he actually did provide such an explanation. Significantly, the core and centerpiece of this explanation consist of a concept of a behaviorally determined *and* behavior-conditioning "polarization of institutions and technology" [Ayres 1967, pp. 4–5].

Ayres started his inquiry into the essence and character of human nature by observing that the "science of economics must include the original nature of man among its major and constant occupations" because economics is "necessarily a description, an analysis, and even it may be a prediction of human behavior" [Ayres 1936, p. 224]. When Ayres used the term "the original nature of man" he was, like Veblen and Dewey before him, referring to the fact that man is "a biological species" that has "species endowment[s]" [Ayres 1952, p. 12; 1973, p. vi]. Among these is an "erect posture, in consequence of which the forepaws, with their uniquely rich enervation and finger flexibility," vest in humankind that capacity for "inveterate fingering and handling which is so characteristic of our species." Of even greater importance are the species endowments of "brain power," "memory power," and "propensity to use tools, and therefore to make things" [Ayres 1973, pp. vi, v–vi].

Ayres admitted that many other creatures "use various things in a tool-like manner." But no other animal retains and re-uses his 'tool'" like the human being does because the former's memory power is much less developed than is the latter's [Ayres 1973, p. vi]. Similar differences exist in the realm of habituation. "As a biological species, man has a capacity of forming habits" that may not be qualitatively different from that of some other creatures. In "degree, extent, and complexity," however, man's capacity for habituation is vastly greater than that of all "other animals" [Ayres 1952, p. 13].

It is this biological edge we have on other creatures—organically, perhaps, a very slight advantage—which just enables us to form language habits, and so cultural habits generally, and so to be social beings, living and acting in a manner that is progressively different from that of other creatures (and even our own past) as the body of *culture* of which *human nature* is a *function* grows in extent and refinement [Ayres 1952, p. 13, emphasis added].

Thus, whereas differences in biological endowments can explain why human beings are behaviorally different from all other species, such differences cannot explain why human beings may behave differently at the same place in different ages or at different places in the same age. "Men act as they do—they are what they are—because of the societies in which they live" [Ayres 1952, p. 13]. Their "activities themselves— as distinguished from the component physiological processes which they employ—are not transmitted in the genes, but are learned by each member of the species from the older members of the community into which he is born" [Ayres 1960, p. 60]. Hence according to Ayres, there are two routes for the transmission of human nature: the biological route and the socio-cultural route. The process in which the species endowments have been transmitted through the former channel has been such that no perceptible changes have occurred in these endowments at least since the beginning of Western "civilization . . . in the 'fertile crescent'" of the Middle East [Ayres 1952, p. 71]. On the other hand, during the same period, perceptible changes have been wrought to a large extent in man's "learned activities" in the course of their transmission through the socio-cultural channel [Ayres 1960, p. 59]. Consequently, as far as Ayres was concerned, the only aspect of human nature that is relevant for socioeconomic analysis is the historically evolved socio-cultural component. He emphasized this by stating again and again that *operationally* "human nature is a social or cultural phenomenon," and "not a biological one," because "man and society evolved together." It means, of course, that "men carry on their economic activities (of getting a living) as they do because they live in economies such as they do" [Ayres 1952, pp. 12, 11, 13].

When Ayres used the terms "social" and "cultural" as apparently synonymous, it was intentional. Thus, although he argued that there is a "bi-polarity that runs through all of . . . society and culture," he did not view society and culture as polar opposites [Ayres 1961, p. 77]. Defining the former "as an organized community" and the latter "as a body of activity patterns," he concluded that culture and society are "aspects of the same phenomenon. The creation of interpersonal relationships is a function of culture. All cultural action patterns define social relationships" [Ayres 1961, p. 76]. And using the word "culture" . . . "as we have learned [it] from the social anthropologists," Ayres put the same proposition in the following slightly different terms:

> Whereas the word "society" suggests a community of people and the structure of relationships by which they are bound together (and apart), the word "culture" has reference to the body of lore which pervades and sustains that system of relationships and which has been (in varying amounts) learned by all the members of the community. Language is such a body of lore and one which . . . illustrates [the fact that] culture exists independently of any particular human being [Ayres 1952, pp. 11, 12].

As intimated above, Ayres was of the opinion, however, that the "sum total of all that is learned—that is, the sum of all the activity patterns of the community," or the social behavior of its members, is dichotomized into "technological and ceremonial aspects" [Ayres 1960, p. 60; 1944, p. 100]. By "technology" he meant the "tool-using aspect of human behavior"; that is to say, "technology is first and foremost a type, or form, or aspect, of human behavior" [Ayres 1961, p. 77; 1952, p. 51]. "Thus," said Ayres, "'technology' must be understood to include all human activities involving the use of tools—all sorts of tools: the simplest striking stones of primeval man as well as the atom-splitting Bevatrons of present-day physicists; written language, books, and the symbols mathematicians manipulate, as well as marks in the sand, notches on a stick, or the fire built around the trunk of a tree to fell it" [Ayres 1962, p. xv].

Human tool-using skills, which are "tool-behavior," "are cultural" in that they are part of the "body of lore from which individual human beings learn whatever they learn" [Ayres 1952, p. 52; 1953, p. 282]. Tools are therefore extensions, as it were, of human behavior. In Ayres's words, "all technological behavior patterns are objectified in tools, instruments, formulas, and notations of many kinds; and that fact is very important, for it is the basis for economic development" [Ayres 1953, p. 282]. Why that is so, Ayres explained in the following manner.

> The technological process can be understood only by recognizing that human skills and the tools by which and on which they are exercised are

logically inseparable. Skills *always* employ tools, and tools are such *always* by virtue of being employed in acts of skill by human beings. Once the dual character of the technological process is understood, the explanation of its dynamism is obvious. Technology advances by virtue of inventions and discoveries being made—by men, of course. But all inventions and discoveries result from the combining of hitherto separate tools, instruments, materials, and the like. These are capable of combination by virtue of their physical existence [Ayres 1962, p. xv].

It means that technological behavior is a two-pronged behavior, so to speak. In the first place, tool-behavior—skills—is learned in the context of existing tools. Secondly, new skills—new types of technological behavior—are created in the processes of invention and discovery. For example, once separate chains, or lines, of inventions are juxtaposed at a certain point in time, a new combination is possible: "An automobile is a combination of a buggy with an internal combustion engine. The internal combustion engine itself is a combination of the steam engine with a gaseous fuel which is substituted for the steam and exploded by the further combination of the electric spark," and so on. And Ayres argued that "as regards the nature of process there is no difference between 'mechanical' invention and 'scientific' discovery. Scientific discoveries also result from the combination of previously existing devices and materials, laboratory instruments and techniques" [Ayres 1944, pp. 112, 113]. As far as the Ayresian concept of human nature and behavior is concerned, the important, and significant, point is that new types of transmittable technological behavior are created in the processes of invention and discovery. And because of their learnability and transmissibility, "knowledge and skills," that is, technological behavior patterns, "accumulate" [Ayres 1961, p. 112].

But, said Ayres, "what Veblen called ceremonialism" may "curb" inventions and thereby impede the growth and spread of technological behavior [Ayres 1962, p. xvi]. That is so because, whereas "efficiency" is the objective of technological behavior, "ceremonial adequacy" is, not surprisingly, the objective of "ceremonial activities" and behavior [Ayres 1961, p. 136]. Moreover, "and this is the most important consideration of all," said Ayres, "ceremonial organization is necessarily static. This means it stands in inevitable opposition to the dynamism of the technological process" [Ayres 1961, p. 137]. Thus Ayres agreed with Veblen that ceremonial behavior is "inherently past-binding" [Ayres 1963, p. 57]. That is so because it is based on legends and myths and beliefs of the past. Especially, said Ayres, the "concept of status . . . permeates the 'philosophies' which are indissociable from . . . all ceremonialism" [Ayres 1961, p. 135]. That human behavior in the twentieth century is still to a large extent ceremonial behavior, Ayres illustrated in the following manner.

Ceremonial adequacy requires that tradition shall always be honored regardless of consequences—that is, of mere technological consequences. The rule of seniority must be maintained regardless of the technical efficiency of the persons concerned, and no woman must ever be permitted to do "man's work" regardless of her apparent qualifications. In each case, however, all "right-minded" people "know" that the apparent advantages of following another course are illusory, and that in the end only the righteous prevail [Ayres 1961, p. 137].

Ayres insisted, however, that "the distinction of the technological and the ceremonial aspects of organized behavior is a dichotomy but not a dualism." That is to say, technological behavior and ceremonial behavior are "two aspects of what is . . . a single, continuous activity both aspects of which are present all the time" [Ayres 1944, p. 101]. But why? Late in his career, Ayres believed that he had found the beginning of an answer to the question of how "this extraordinary bifurcation of human mentality" had come about. He based his "conjectural explanation . . . on what has come to be known as the symbolic process" [Ayres 1961, p. 31].

By the symbolic process, Ayres understood the "response of an organism to a stimulus which is not the 'original' or 'natural' occasion of that response . . . but one which has come to be taken as representative—or symbolic—of it" [Ayres 1961, p. 89]. Once, for example, a "gesture, or mark has become associated in the experience of a group of people with some person, object or operation, its symbolic character is a fact that is independent of any member of the group." Thus a mark may "remain after all the human beings in whose experience it became a symbol have disappeared" [Ayres 1961, pp. 91, 92]. Being "counterparts of persons, objects, and operations," the numbers of symbols "increase in direct proportion to the spread of human operations, and by the same process" [Ayres 1961, p. 92]. One such process is that of invention in the realm of science and technology. As mentioned above, Ayres argued that inventions lead to new knowledge and new skills. Inventions also lead to an increase in the number of processes that become symbolized. Consequently, the advancement of science and technology has been closely associated with increases in the number of symbols and their uses. According to Ayres, the "emergence . . . of the science of chemistry from the mumbo-jumbo of alchemy" is illustrative of this phenomenon [Ayres 1961, p. 92].

Ayres was of the opinion, however, that the symbolic process was not confined to the realm of technological behavior. Thus he surmised that this process "is also the wellspring of all the phantasmagoria by which all human communities have been haunted since the beginning of time." That is, "myth-making, ritualism, and institutionalized conventions generally" may have their roots in a process that involved "the mysticizing of the symbolic process" with the result that "'ceremonial adequacy'" became an "imitation of technological adequacy." In other words, Ayres was leaning toward the idea that technological behavior and ceremonial behavior are of "joint origin, or common origin" [Ayres 1961, pp. 31, 95, 96–97].

Over the centuries, ceremonial "beliefs and practices have been embedded in the culture" through a process of institutionalization [Ayres 1961, p. 100]. Hence Ayres viewed an institution, "not as a structural category," but as an "aspect of social behavior" [Ayres 1952, p. 43]. The behavioral aspect of an institution stems from the fact that it is "a cluster of 'mores'" in the sense of "traditions which define right and proper behavior." The mores can serve this purpose because they are "accompanied by legends" that provide the rationale for the behavior sanctioned by the mores. It is, therefore, the "mores which sustain and implement all the distinctions of authority and status which it is the function of the typical institutions to establish." Hence institutions constitute a power system as exemplified by the "'typical' institutions" of the "family, the state, and the church" and the "corporation" [Ayres 1952, pp. 43, 44].

Inasmuch as all "the typical institutions derive from the legend-enshrouded past," present-day institutions "derive from pre-existing institutions and the immemorial past, of which they retain as much as circumstances permit" [Ayres 1951, p. 51; 1952, p. 44]. The fact that "present-day institutions are the 'residues' of ancient institutions" is indicated by the fact that "present-day society is divided into upper, middle, and lower strata" [Ayres 1951, p. 51]. In particular, said Ayres,

> In its distributive aspect, our economy is what it is because the institutional structure of Western society is what it is. Who gets what is wholly determined by that organizational structure. This is the universe of discourse to which terms such as wealth and investment are truly pertinent, and also such terms as dividends, interest, rent, salary, wages, parity payments, poor relief, and social security. All these terms designate the various groups and strata into which the community is divided by the prevailing institutional system [Ayres 1953, p. 283].

That which is distributed in accordance with the rules of the prevailing ceremonial behavior in contemporary society has been produced in consequence of those activities that are undertaken in consonance with the prevailing technological behavior in the same society. The latter type of behavior promotes change and the former resists change. "Thus what happens to society is determined jointly by the forward urging of its technology and the backward pressure of its ceremonial system" [Ayres 1962, p. xvii].

This is not the place to discuss Ayres's speculations about the future as a possible outcome of the ongoing struggle between ceremonial and technological behavior. It is the place to make the following three points, however. First, all of Ayres's analyses and discussions were based upon a concept of a dichotomous human nature that is split between the said two types of behavior. "The history of the human race," said he, "is that of a perpetual opposition of these forces, the dynamic force of technology continually making for change, and the static force of ceremony . . . opposing change" [Ayres 1944, p. 176]. Second, he argued that deceremonialization, deinstitutionalization, and "institutional decomposition" can occur only if there are advances in science and technology that are so rapid and pervasive that more and more people become increasingly occupied, in thinking and doing, in activities that are devoid of ceremonial and mythological contents [Ayres 1944, p. 193]. When that happens, technological behavior becomes more prevalent and more prominent relative to ceremonial behavior. And as far as Ayres was concerned this means that human beings will have "more knowledge—clearer and more certain knowledge—of what . . . existence means than any previous generation has had, and for obvious reasons" [Ayres 1961, p. 291]. Third, as pointed out by Paul D. Bush, human behavior is intimately connected with the valuations people make [Bush 1983, p. 36]. "What is at issue here," said Ayres, "are the basic 'value judgments' of our society and the institutions which embody them" [Ayres 1968, p. 342]. There is, therefore, only a short step from Ayres's theory of human nature to his theory of value. In Tool's words, Ayres "utilizes his analysis of the nature of human nature as an entree to a consideration of social value theory"; a theory that is discussed elsewhere in this symposium [Tool 1953, Chap. 4, p. 21].

Thus it may be concluded that Ayres acted in accordance with his own dictum that economics must include the nature of man as an endogenous variable, and as an independent variable at that [Ayres 1936, p. 224]. This maxim was accepted by those American neoinstitutionalists who took their clues from Ayres. In so doing, they added their own dimensions to Ayres's theory of human nature, however.

The Concept of Human Nature in Modern Neoinstitutionalism

The majority of those post-Ayres neoinstitutionalist writers who added to, or employed, the Ayresian theory of human nature may be divided into two broad groups: the "Texas School" and the "Colorado School" of neoinstitutionalists.

The Texas School

Ayres's theory of human nature constitutes the basis for those neoinstitutionalist works on human behavior that have been produced by some of his colleagues at The University of Texas at Austin and by a number of his former students elsewhere. Thus there is, at least in this sense, a "Texas School" of neoinstitutionalist economists. Echoing Ayres, Wendell Gordon observed, for instance, that the "starting point of economics is, or ought to be, an understanding of how people behave" [Ayres 1936, p. 224; Gordon 1980a, pp. 85–86]. Speaking in a similarly Ayresian vein, David Hamilton declared that all "human behavior is culturally conditioned behavior" and that it is dichotomized into "institutional behavior" and technological, or "tool behavior." Hence all "of human activity is a mixture of both institutional and technological behavior" [Hamilton 1962, pp. 50, 53, 57]. Hamilton also followed Ayres in maintaining that there is a continuous struggle between the technological and institutional aspects of human behavior: "By constantly facing us with new technology for which there is no ceremonial prerogative, the technological process erodes the institutionally structured behavior," but, on "the other hand, the institutional structure may be sufficiently rigid to prohibit just such a technological erosion" [Hamilton 1962, p. 60]. The "cultural processes of technology and institutions are [therefore] the forces through the interaction of which we achieve economic progress, the first being a dynamic cultural force and the other being a permissive force at best and, at worst, a retardant" [Hamilton 1986, p. 527]. And speaking at the midpoint of the decade of the 1980s, Hamilton confirmed his faith in the Ayresian approach: "At no time has an analysis centering on institutions and technology been more appropriate to understanding what is being experienced" [Hamilton 1986, p. 531].

Philip A. Klein, who has endeavored to extend the Ayresian theory into a "science of valuation," seems to agree with Hamilton that Ayres's theory of human nature is still an adequate and powerful explanatory device. Thus Klein observed that one of the objectives of a science of valuation is to establish "criteria for . . . allocative decisions." And he added that he was of the opinion "that Ayres's distinction between institutional and technological values was directed just at this point" [Klein 1974, pp. 802, 800]. In Klein's opinion, however, Ayres's theory of human nature can serve not only as a basis for a theory designed to explain how "accurately to translate dynamic choice into the total allocation of the economy," but due to its emphasis on the "relationship between technology and institutions," it is equally well suited as a foundation for development economics [Klein 1984, p. 544; 1977, p. 788].

James H. Street and Dilmus D. James endorsed Klein's proposition that Ayres's concept of a bifurcation of human behavior is a notion that throws light upon the economic processes and problems in underdeveloped countries. Thus they observed that the conception "of human behavior as characterized by habitual patterns resulting from cultural conditioning but capable of intelligent responses to changing realities . . . [is] distinctively incorporated" into their analysis of "developing economies" [Street and James 1982, pp. 673–75]. And, in a study of the Argentine economy, Street observed that Ayres "drew particular attention to the evaluative judgments that distinguish technological from institutional behavior," and that, when viewed from this point of view, it is clear that the Argentine economy "has been powerfully shaped by technological forces and institutional resistance" [Street 1974, p. 708].

As mentioned above, Gordon agreed with Ayres that an understanding of human behavior is the starting point for all economic reasoning. That is so, Gordon argued, because without such an understanding, a theory of value cannot be formulated; and without a theory of value, there can be no economics. As he put it: "It is important to note that we are talking about values." And inasmuch as he conceived of value as "a judgment made by an individual . . . regarding what is desirable or esteemed," Gordon posed the following question: "Who is this individual who makes judgments about values?" [Gordon 1980a, pp. 87, 37].

Gordon's answer to his own rhetorical question was that he had the individual economic actor in mind. It is this "individual who matters, at least if individuals are the actors and they think so." There is a further question, however, namely the question of "what makes the beast tick?" [Gordon 1980a, p. 38]. The following are those principal factors responsible for human behavior, according to Gordon. "The forces influencing the ever changing ideas about values [and hence the behavior] of individuals are here alleged to be (1) the individual's biological heredity, (2) the force of technology, (3) the inhibitions of institutional norms, and (4) the nature setting" (which involves resource availability) [Gordon 1980a, p. 38].

Gordon admitted that biological heredity "beyond doubt influences the individual's conception as to what is desirable or estimable" [Gordon 1980b, p. 35]. But, we *"are* our biological make up . . . because of a long drawn-out process of mutation and natural selection." And although a "few genetic accidents" may explain "some special differences" between individuals, most of human behavior is attributable to technological and institutional factors [Gordon 1980a, p. 38]. Hence Gordon quoted with approval Hamilton's observation that human attitudes and behavior, including conceptions of wants and their satisfaction, are "affected by both institutional (symbolic) and technological (tool using) considerations" [Gordon 1973, p. 267]. Moreover Gordon maintained, like Ayres, that technology, consisting as it does of "all tools and all mental skills," is an "evolutionary process with its own built-in dynamics" and that institutions are "static, . . . past-glorifying . . . creatures of habit" [Gordon 1980a, pp. 10, 11, 17].

Gordon added an important dimension to the neoinstitutionalist theory of institutional behavior, however. In so doing, he started from the Ayresian proposition that "an institution is a grouping of people with some common behavior patterns" and that "in this definition the emphasis is on the institutionalized *behavior* pattern" [Gordon 1980a, p. 16, emphasis added]. Gordon's main argument runs as follows.

An institution is, then, an agency endorsing a complex of standardized behavior norms (including the role of custodians of . . . technical knowledge) that continue to prevail until an outside power (technology or the pressure to modify exerted by other *institutions*) comes along to force their change [Gordon 1980a, pp. 16, 17, emphasis added]. . . . [As a result, institutional] resistances break down. . . . A period of institutional change is a crucial period when leadership can make much difference in influencing the direction of change. . . . The important problem is to develop judgment in deciding what to do in dealing with the new situation. What is the desirable direction, and what *policies* will lead in that direction? At times of institutional collapse *human will* can play an over-shadowing role in influencing the direction that the new pattern of *behavior* will take. In fact it is at such times that the individual will can exert a significant influence on the course of history [Gordon 1967, p. 63, emphasis added].

From the point of view of an Ayres-inspired theory of human nature, these are remarkable observations. When the said statements are viewed in the context of Gordon's conviction that society "has to have social and economic institutions" because behavior "has to be controlled and regulated," it is difficult not to reach two conclusions [Gordon 1980a, p. 21]. In the first place, the above-quoted Gordonian comments take on the hue of a more positive view of the institutionally determined aspects of human behavior than one finds in the works of Ayres. As Gordon has put it: "It is not useful categorically to stigmatize all institutions and their associate behavior norms as merely ceremonial, imbecile, useless, and bad, and to conclude that they should be abolished" [Gordon 1984, p. 370]. Secondly, and of greater importance from the point of view of the development of a general neoinstitutionalist theory of human nature, Gordon's special theory is one in which "technology and institutions play different but *not* precisely *contrasting* roles." Hence he was somewhat wary of the Veblen-Ayres concept of a dichotomy in human nature: "Dichotomizing does not satisfactorily get hold of how" technological behavior and institutional behavior interact, said Gordon, because "institutions, and the behavior norms they sanction at the moment, control the use . . . of evolving technical knowledge" [Gordon 1984, p. 370, emphasis added].

In other words, Gordon was moving away from a concept of sharply bifurcated human nature toward a concept of a unitary type of human nature. As a result, he argued that the institutional and technological aspects of human behavior blend in a manner that permits the former to be in closer rapport with technology as a tool-using process than was ever envisioned by Ayres. Gordon put it this way.

> Behavior is technological behavior, it is functional, if it contributes effectively to human welfare and progress as welfare and progress are conceived by the individual and/or by society. It is institutional if it is practiced because it is the tradition to do things in that manner. Institutionalized behavior is not necessarily undesirable, but it is "institutionalized behavior." And it is *not necessarily nontechnological* or nonfunctional *merely* because it is institutionalized [Gordon 1980a, p. 16, emphasis added].

In a response to the charge that "[i]nstitutionalists have been guilty . . . of neglecting biospheric constraints on the . . . state of human existence" [Spengler 1976, pp. 126–27], Anne Mayhew added a dimension to institutionalist thought that implies a modification of the Ayresian concept of human nature similar to that proposed by Gordon. The core of Mayhew's argument deserves to be quoted in full because of its (at least implied) consequences for a theory of human nature and behavior.

> Precisely because it is so confusing to say that "institutions inhibit progress" in the face of overwhelming evidence that on-going social arrangements are necessary, I use the phrase "ceremonial valuing" to de-

scribe the process that inhibits human progress, and because of the confusion that can arise from the use of the word *technology*, I use instead the phrase "instrumental valuing." . . . If the source of human progress resides in the *process* of instrumental valuing rather than in technological artifacts, then it is the *evaluation of the consequences* of any particular use of a tool that is progressive. Ceremonialism is a failure to evaluate by testing consequences [Mayhew 1981, pp. 515–16].

The positions of Gordon and Mayhew are remarkably similar to that taken by the advocates of what has been called the "'new' dichotomy." These proponents maintain that "tool application as human behavior can be evaluated for its instrumental *and* ceremonial aspects" [Waller 1982, p. 766]. The work that contains the new dichotomy grew out of that which has been hailed as J. Fagg Foster's contribution to "'the oral tradition in institutional economics'" [Tool 1986, p. 3]. I shall now, therefore, turn to a consideration of the relevant aspects of those contributions to a neoinstitutionalist theory of human nature that have been made by some of the members of what may be labeled the "Colorado School of Neoinstitutionalist Economics."

The Colorado School

What is sometimes referred to as the "Veblen-Dewey-Ayres-Foster tradition" of institutionalist economics, is here taken to mean that "reformulation" of "fundamental principles of economics on the Veblen-Dewey-Ayres base" that Foster undertook in the course of his professional life [Tool 1983, p. 156; 1977, p. 836]. The term "Fosterian tradition," on the other hand, is used to designate those contributions that have been made by some of Foster's students on the basis of his teaching. The appellation "Colorado School" is used as an umbrella term for both traditions.

Foster studied under Ayres at The University of Texas in the late 1930s and early 1940s when the latter was in the process of formulating and publishing his major contributions to institutionalism [Ranson 1981, pp. 854–55]. Foster was therefore present at the creation, as it were, and hence in a position to absorb and reflect on the results of Ayres's efforts to "identify the philosophical parameters of . . . Institutionalism" [Breit and Culbertson 1976, p. 7]. Being greatly in sympathy with, and impressed by, Ayres's ideas, Foster continued his reflections after he left Austin for Denver. Gradually, these reflections shaded into critical evaluations of Ayres's message with the result that Foster "substantially and substantively stretched the fabric of institutional thought in many areas," including that occupied by a theory of human nature [Tool 1982, p. 35].

Foster accepted the traditional institutionalist notion that each member of the human race is a "social creature." And that is so, he explained, because the "individual necessarily correlates his behavior with that of other persons" [Foster 1969, p. 859]. And he added:

> When patterns of correlated behavior become effectively operational, they are called institutions. In becoming operationally effective, patterns of correlated behavior (institutions) display a prescriptive effect. A particular prescription may be no more than a mild "ought to," and it may be a physically enforced "must." But in all cases, it is in some degree prescriptive. As institutions become firmly established, the component patterns of behavior become habitual—habits of thought and attitude and habits of action. That is to say, institutions are comprised essentially of mores and folkways [Foster 1969, p. 859].

As "prescribed patterns of human relations, patterns of correlated activities and attitudes," . . . "institutions are 'made up of' habitual actions and attitudes," said Foster. He insisted, however, that these patterns "are not *determined* by habit. Their determination is a matter of deliberate and guided action. The habituation follows; it does not precede" [Foster 1948, p. 933; 1949, p. 900]. Thus what Foster seemed to be saying is that sometime in the past institutions were set up as "arrangements", or, in the words of one of Foster's students, Marc R. Tool, as "structures" [Foster 1949, p. 900; Tool 1979, p. 74]. What is of relevance in the present context, however, is that, once in existence, institutions mold and determine individual behavior. Human nature in its behavioral aspects is controlled by institutionalized habits. And not all of these habits are ceremonial, according to Foster. He was able to take this position because he made a distinction between "technology" and "instrumental functions" [Foster 1969, p. 858; 1948, p. 932].

Foster used the term "technology" "to connote the not-man aspects of man's environment." Arguing *à la* Erich W. Zimmermann [Zimmermann 1951, p. 10], Foster identified these aspects as man-made resources and commodities: "man creates not only commodities but also natural resources." Both "are defined by human inventions and discovery" and hence the result of the application of "know-how to the economic process" [Foster 1969, p. 858]. In other words, technology is things. But "the technological aspects of human know-how" are in the realm of attitudes and prescribed patterns of behavior and therefore among the "fundamental determinants of . . . economic behavior" [Foster 1948, p. 932; 1969, p. 858]. This means, of course, that there are both "instrumental and . . . ceremonial functions of institutions" [Foster n.d. p. 908]. Hence, as rendered by another of his former students, the late Louis Junker, Foster's complete definition of an institution reads: an institution consists of "prescribed patterns of correlated human behavior with (a) instrumental aspects and (b) ceremonial aspects" [Waller 1982, p. 765].

Thus Foster came to a conclusion similar to that reached by Gordon and Mayhew: Human nature and behavior are shaped entirely by institutional factors because institutions are the locus of both ceremonial and instrumental behavior.

Some of Foster's former students have extended his theory of human nature still further. They are the ones who may be said to be working in a Fosterian tradition. Two of these, Junker and Paul D. Bush, developed independently and simultaneously such an extension, which both of them labeled "ceremonial encapsulation" [Bush 1983, p. 63n].

Briefly, their argument runs as follows: It is accepted that the human nature of individuals is determined by those institutions that prescribe the particular person's behavior. Institutions are the repositories of knowledge. Such knowledge may be used either ceremonially or instrumentally. Bush put it in this way:

> More precisely, knowledge is either "embodied" in instrumentally warranted patterns of behavior or "encapsulated" within ceremonially warranted patterns of behavior. Knowledge embodied in instrumental patterns of behavior is available to the community for use in problem-solving activities that sustain the life process of the community. Knowledge encapsulated within ceremonial patterns of behavior is either effectively withheld from the problem-solving processes, or, to the extent that it is permitted to be employed in the problem-solving processes, the legitimacy of its use is held to be the standard of "ceremonial adequacy" [Bush 1983, pp. 37–38].

Clearly, we have here a concept of an intra-institution dichotomy. Hence the term the "new dichotomy," which is claimed to be analytically superior to the old Veblen-Ayres dichotomy because it is cast as behavior, pure and simple [Waller 1982, pp. 766–69]. It therefore spells the end of those confusions alleged to be clinging to the old dichotomy, namely the confusion of institutional behavior with institutional structure and the confusion of technological behavior with tools and implements. As Mayhew put it, if "the source of human progress resides in the *process* of instrumental valuing rather than in technological artifacts, then it is the *evaluation of the consequences* of any particular use of a tool that is progressive" [Mayhew 1981, p. 515]. The inventors of the new dichotomy reach the same conclusion. "They say that any application of tools can [now] be evaluated; its adequacy for solving a problem can be adjudged from its consequences." In short, the new concept makes it possible for institutionalists to extricate themselves from a position in which they appear "to uncritically applaud any application of a tool or gadget as part of the technological process, irrespective of its impact on the life process" [Waller 1982, p. 766].

It may be concluded, therefore, that those modifications that have been made in the institutionalist concept of human nature by members of the Texas and Colorado Schools have been effected in response to an increasingly felt need for an enhancement of the power of the tools of their craft to deal with the problems of a changing world. As Mayhew put it: Ayres "did not address, and understandably so, the problems of the 1980s. This should not prevent an Ayresian institutionalist from doing so today" [Mayhew 1981, p. 519].

Conclusion

What conclusions does the above selective review of the contributions of the institutionalists and neoinstitutionalists entitle one to draw with regard to the present-day neoinstitutionalist concept of human nature? In the first place, it is fairly clear that today's theoretically oriented neoinstitutionalists do not speak with one voice. There are differences of opinion among them concerning the *extent* to which there is a dichotomy in the nature of the modern human being. Consequently, their views are differentiated with regard to the *extent* to which institutionalized behavior may produce *non*ceremonial results or consequences. These are differences of degree, however, rather than of substance. Hence that which separates neoinstitutionalists in their interpretation of human nature and behavior is slight in comparison with that which unites them.

The neoinstitutionalists are united in their criticism and rejection of the orthodox concept of human nature; a concept that is epitomized in the phrase "the economic man." This individual is presented in a widely used introductory text as a "fairly rational person" who seeks to achieve maximum satisfaction as an economic actor by playing two roles in the economic game. In the first place, the rational maximizer plays the part of a consumer whose "insatiable" wants are maximized "when she allocates her money income in such a way that the last dollar spent" on each of a variety of commodities will "yield equal amounts of additional, or marginal, utility"; a utility that the consumer measures "with units we shall call 'utils'." Secondly, the rational economic actor plays the part of a producer who strives to maximize her or his income through the sale of those productive services that are under her or his control. For example, the businessman is "motivated to seek [maximum] profits" [McConnell 1987, pp. 19, 73, 505, 508; emphasis deleted]. Similar ideas are presented in scholarly discourses at high levels of abstraction. Thus it is argued by the present-day practitioners of the highly mathematical "new classical economics" that human beings form "rational expectations" as a basis for their "maximizing behavior" [Klamer 1984, pp. 240, 241].

As intimated in the above discussion of the neoinstitutionalist, and institutionalist, concept of human nature, the architects of this concept have sought to replace the one-dimensional economic man with a multidimensional human being who, for want of a better term, may be labeled the "socio-cultural person." This individual is a complicated creature whose behavior and acts are determined largely by a socio-cultural environment that is evolving continuously under the impact of dynamic technological forces; forces that are the creations of those human beings who populate the society of which the individual is a member and an actively participating member at that. Because of the multidimensional character of the social psychology of the socio-cultural person, this individual pursues a multiplicity of goals and objectives. Hence the socio-cultural person is not, and cannot be, in single-minded pursuit of maximum satisfaction *à la* the economic man.

Moreover, by virtue of having formulated their concept of a multidimensional human nature, the neoinstitutionalists have willingly barred themselves from access to the apparatus by the use of which orthodox economists make predictions. As a result, the questions that are asked by neoinstitutionalist economists are radically different from those asked by orthodox economists. It follows, therefore, that the two schools employ equally dissimilar methods when they go about their business of seeking answers to their dissimilar questions. In other words, by formulating their particular concept of a multidimensional human nature, the neoinstitutionalists laid the foundation for, and constructed the core of, that which has become the principal contribution to an American body of heterodox economics.

References

Axtelle, George E. and Joe E. Burnett. 1970. "Dewey on Education and Schooling." In *Guide to the Works of John Dewey,* ed. Jo Ann Boydston, pp. 257–305. Carbondale and Edwardsville: Southern Illinois University Press.
Ayres, C.E. 1936. "Fifty Years' Development in Ideas of Human Nature and Motivation." *The American Economic Review: Papers and Proceedings* 26 (March): 224–36.

————. 1944. *The Theory of Economic Progress.* Chapel Hill: The University of North Carolina Press.

————. 1946. *The Divine Right of Capital.* Boston: Houghton Mifflin.

————. 1951. "The Co-Ordinates of Institutionalism." *The American Economic Review: Papers and Proceedings* 41 (May): 47–55.

————. 1952. *The Industrial Economy.* Boston: Houghton Mifflin.

————. 1953. "The Role of Technology in Economic Theory." *The American Economic Review: Papers and Proceedings* 43 (May): 279–87.

————. 1958. "Veblen's Theory of Instincts Reconsidered." In *Thorstein Veblen: A Critical Reappraisal,* ed. Douglas F. Dowd, pp. 25–37. Ithaca, N.Y.: Cornell University Press.

————. 1960. "Institutionalism and Economic Development." *The Southwestern Social Science Quarterly* 41 (June): 45–62.

————. 1961. *Toward a Reasonable Society.* Austin: The University of Texas Press.

————. 1962. "Foreword—1962." In *The Theory of Economic Progress,* by C.E. Ayres, pp. xiii–xxxiii. 3d ed. Kalamazoo: New Issues Press, Western Michigan University, 1978 [1944].

————. 1963. "The Legacy of Thorstein Veblen." In *Institutional Economics,* by Joseph Dorfman *et al.,* pp. 44–62. Berkeley and Los Angeles: University of California Press.

————. 1967. "The Theory of Institutional Adjustment." In *Institutional Adjustment,* ed. Carey C. Thompson, pp. 1–17. Austin: The University of Texas Press.

————. 1968. "The Price System and Public Policy." *Journal of Economic Issues* 2 (September): 342–44.

————. 1973. "Prolegomenon to Institutionalism." In *Science the False Messiah* and *Holier than Thou,* by C.E. Ayres, pp. iii–xii. Clifton, N.J.: Augustus M. Kelley [1927, 1929].

Bernstein, Richard J. 1960. "Introduction." In *On Experience, Nature, and Freedom. Representative Selections: John Dewey,* ed. Richard J. Bernstein, pp. ix–xlvii. Indianapolis and New York: The Bobbs-Merrill Co.

Breit, William and William Patton Culbertson, Jr. 1976. "Clarence Edwin Ayres: An Intellectual Portrait." In *Science and Ceremony:* The *Institutional Economics of C.E. Ayres,* ed. William Breit and William Patton Culbertson, Jr., pp. 3–22. Austin: The University of Texas Press.

Bush, Paul D. 1983. "An Exploration of the Structural Characteristics of a Veblen-Ayres-Foster Defined Institutional Domain." *Journal of Economic Issues* 17 (March): 35–66.

Commons, John R. 1931. "Institutional Economics." *The American Economic Review* 21 (December): 648–57.

————. 1957. *Legal Foundations of Capitalism.* Madison: The University of Wisconsin Press [1924].

————. 1959. *Institutional Economics.* 2 vols. Madison: The University of Wisconsin Press [1934].

————. 1964. *Myself.* Madison: The University of Wisconsin Press [1934].

————. 1970. *The Economics of Collective Action,* ed. Kenneth E. Parsons. Madison: The University of Wisconsin Press [1950].

Dewey, John. 1916. *Democracy and Education.* New York: Macmillan and Co.

————. 1930a. "From Absolutism to Experimentalism." In *The Structure of*

Experience, ed. John J. McDermott, pp. 2–13. Vol. 1 of *The Philosophy of John Dewey.* New York: G.P. Putnam's Sons, 1973.

————. 1930b. *Human Nature and Conduct: An Introduction to Social Psychology.* New York: The Modern Library of Random House [1922].

————. 1934. *Art as Experience.* New York: Minton, Balch and Co.

————. 1938. *Logic: The Theory of Inquiry.* New York: Holt, Rinehart and Winston.

————. 1946. *Problem of Men.* New York: Philosophical Library.

————. 1951. *The Influence of Darwin on Philosophy and Other Essays in Contemporary Thought.* New York: Peter Smith [1910].

Foster, J. Fagg. 1948. "Syllabus for Problems of Modern Society: The Theory of Institutional Adjustment." *Journal of Economic Issues* 15 (December 1981): 923–28.

————. 1949. "The Relation Between the Theory of Value and Economic Analysis." *Journal of Economic Issues* 15 (December 1981): 899–905.

————. 1969. "Economics." *Journal of Economic Issues* 15 (December 1981): 857–69.

————. n.d. "The Effect of Technology on Institutions." *Journal of Economic Issues* 15 (December 1981): 907–13.

Gonce, R.A. 1971. "John R. Commons's Legal Economic Theory." *Journal of Economic Issues* 5 (September): 80–95.

Gordon, Wendell. 1967. "Orthodox Economics and Institutionalized Behavior." In *Institutional Adjustment,* ed. Carey C. Thompson, pp. 41–67. Austin: The University of Texas Press.

————. 1973. "Institutionalized Consumption Patterns in Underdeveloped Countries." *Journal of Economic Issues* 7 (June): 267–87.

————. 1980a. *Institutional Economics: The Changing System.* Austin: The University of Texas Press.

————. 1980b. "Neoinstitutionalism and the Economics of Dissent." In *Institutional Economics: Essays in Honor of Allan G. Gruchy,* ed. John Adams, pp. 33–44. Boston: Martinus Nijhoff.

————. 1984. "The Role of Institutional Economics." *Journal of Economic Issues* 18 (June): 369–81.

Gruchy, Allan G. 1947. *Modern Economic Thought: The American Contribution.* New York: Prentice-Hall.

————. 1969. "Neoinstitutionalism and the Economics of Dissent." *Journal of Economic Issues* 3 (March): 3–17.

Hamilton, David. 1962. *The Consumer in Our Economy.* Boston: Houghton Mifflin.

————. 1986. "Technology and Institutions are Neither." *Journal of Economic Issues* 20 (June): 525–32.

Harter, Lafayette G., Jr. 1962. *John R. Commons: His Assault on Laissez-Faire.* Corvallis: Oregon State University Press.

James, William. 1950. *The Principles of Psychology.* Vol. 2. New York: Dover Publications [1890].

Klamer, Arjo. 1984. *Conversations with Economists.* Totowa, N.J.: Rowman and Allanheld.

Klein, Philip A. 1974. "Economics: Allocation or Valuation?" *Journal of Economic Issues* 7 (December): 785–811.

————. 1977. "An Institutionalist View of Development Economics." *Journal of Economic Issues* 11 (December): 785–807.

———. 1984. "Economic Policy and the Obligations of the Economist." *Journal of Economic Issues* 18 (June): 537–46.

Levitt, Morton. 1971. *Freud and Dewey on the Nature of Man.* Westport, Conn.: Westport Press [1960].

Loeb, Jacques. 1912. "The Mechanistic Conception of Life." In *The Mechanistic Conception of Life,* by Jacques Loeb, pp. 5–33. Chicago: The University of Chicago Press.

McConnell, Campbell R. 1987. *Economics: Principles, Problems, and Policies.* 10th ed. New York: McGraw-Hill [1960].

McDougall, William. 1923. *An Introduction to Social Psychology.* 16th ed. Boston: John W. Luce and Co. [1908].

Mann, Fritz Karl. 1960. "Institutionalism and American Economic Theory: A Case of Interpenetration." In *Readings in the History of Economic Thought,* ed. Ingrid H. Rima, pp. 164–75. New York: Holt, Rinehart and Winston, 1970.

Mayhew, Anne. 1981. "Ayresian Technology, Technological Reasoning, and Doomsday." *Journal of Economic Issues* 15 (June): 513–20.

Mitchell, Wesley C. 1914. "Human Behavior and Economics: A Survey of Recent Literature." *The Quarterly Journal of Economics* 29 (November): 1–47.

———. 1935. "Commons on Institutional Economics." In *The Backward Art of Spending Money and Other Essays,* by Wesley C. Mitchell, pp. 313–41. New York: Augustus M. Kelley, 1950 [1937].

———. 1936. "Thorstein Veblen." In *What Veblen Taught,* ed. Wesley C. Mitchell, pp. vii–xlix. New York: The Viking Press, 1947 [1936].

———. 1969. *Types of Economic Theory: From Mercantilism to Institutionalism.* Vol. 2, ed. Joseph Dorfman. New York: Augustus M. Kelley.

Parsons, Kenneth H. 1986. "The Relevance of the Ideas of John R. Commons for the Formulation of Agricultural Development Policies." *Journal of Economic Issues* 20 (June): 281–95.

Ranson, Baldwin. 1981. "John Fagg Foster." *Journal of Economic Issues* 15 (December): 853–56.

Rutherford, Malcolm. 1983. "J.R. Commons's Institutional Economics." *Journal of Economic Issues* 17 (September): 721–44.

Spengler, Joseph J. 1976. "Limits to Growth: Biospheric or Institutional?" In *Science and Ceremony: The Institutional Economics of C.E. Ayres,* ed. William Breit and William Patton Culbertson, Jr., pp. 115–33. Austin: The University of Texas Press.

Street, James H. 1974. "The Ayres-Kuznets Framework and Argentine Dependency." *Journal of Economic Issues* 8 (December): 707–28.

Street, James H., and Dilmus D. James. 1982. "Institutionalism, Structuralism, and Dependency in Latin America." *Journal of Economic Issues* 16 (September): 673–89.

Tool, Marcus Reed. 1953. "The Philosophy of Neo-Institutionalism: Veblen, Dewey, and Ayres." PhD. diss. Boulder: The University of Colorado.

———. 1977. "A Social Value Theory in Neoinstitutional Economics." *Journal of Economic Issues* 11 (December): 820–46.

———. 1979. *The Discretionary Economy: A Normative Theory of Political Economy.* Santa Monica, Calif.: Goodyear Publishing Co.

———. 1982. "J. Fagg Foster." *Journal of Economic Issues* 16 (June): 351–52.

_____. 1983. "Social Value Theory of Marxists: An Instrumental Review and Critique: Part Two." *Journal of Economic Issues* 17 (March): 155–73.

_____. 1986. "In Memoriam: John Fagg Foster 1907–1985." *Journal of Economic Issues* 20 (March): 1–3.

Veblen, Thorstein. 1904. *The Theory of Business Enterprise.* New York: Charles Scribner's Sons.

_____. 1908. "The Evolution of the Scientific Point of View." In *The Place of Science in Modern Civilisation and Other Essays,* by Thorstein Veblen, pp. 32–44. New York: The Viking Press, 1942 [1919].

_____. 1924. *The Theory of the Leisure Class.* New York: B.W. Huebsch [1899].

_____. 1942. *The Place of Science in Modern Civilisation and Other Essays.* New York: The Viking Press [1919].

_____. 1944. *The Engineer and the Price System.* New York: The Viking Press [1921].

_____. 1957. *The Higher Learning in America.* New York: Sagamore Press [1918].

_____. 1964. *The Instinct of Workmanship and the State of the Industrial Arts.* New York: W.W. Norton [1914].

Waller, William R., Jr. 1982. "The Evolution of the Veblenian Dichotomy: Veblen, Hamilton, Ayres, and Foster." *Journal of Economic Issues* 16 (September): 757–71.

Zimmermann, Erich W. 1951. *World Resources and Industries.* Rev. ed. New York: Harper and Brothers [1933].

The Theory of Institutional Change

Paul D. Bush

If institutional economics is truly an "evolutionary" economics, it is because it has the capacity to explain the phenomenon of institutional change and because it incorporates the principles of that explanation in both theoretical and applied inquiry. While it cannot be argued that all that has been labeled "institutional" economics in the past rests either explicitly or implicitly on a coherent theory of institutional change, contemporary institutionalists generally agree that such a theory is, and must be, the diagnostic characteristic of the institutionalist perspective.

The purpose of this article is to set forth a systematic statement of the institutionalist theory of institutional change. The theory presented is a synthetic statement of what the author understands to be (at its present state of development) the theory of institutional change that informs all analytically grounded contributions to the institutionalist literature. The classical foundations of the theory were laid by Thorstein B. Veblen, John R. Commons, John Dewey, and Clarence E. Ayres. Contemporary refinements of the theory are to be found in the works of J. Fagg Foster, William Dugger, David Hamilton, F. Gregory Hayden, Louis Junker, Philip Klein, Anne Mayhew, Walter C. Neale, Baldwin Ranson, Marc Tool, and others who have offered explicit dem-

The author wishes to thank William M. Dugger for his thoughtful comments on the initial design of this article, James A. Swaney for his careful review and critique of earlier works upon which this article draws heavily, and Marc R. Tool for his patience and encouragement in seeing this project through to the end. They are, of course, absolved of any blame for the deficiencies that careful readers will undoubtedly discover.

onstrations of the theory of institutional change in their theoretical and applied investigations. The theory, like the phenomenon it purports to explain, has undergone evolutionary change. As the intellectual pace in institutional economics has quickened in recent years, contributions to the theory of institutional change have likewise appeared at an increased rate. The following presentation attempts to capture not only those classical principles set forth by Veblen at the turn of the century, but also the most recent contributions that have extended the theory and pointed it in new directions.

The article is organized into six major sections. The first section presents a discussion of the institutional structure and the concept of "behavioral patterns." The second section is devoted to an explication of the "institutional" dichotomy, which is a fundamental tenet of most contemporary institutionalist analyses. The third section examines the concept of the "technological dynamic," which institutionalists believe identifies the basic evolutionary force in social change. The fourth section describes the manner in which "institutional space" is partitioned by the knowledge fund and the value structure of the institution. The fifth section develops the concept of "ceremonial encapsulation" and explains both "progressive" and "regressive" institutional change. The article concludes with some observations on the discretionary character of social evolution.

The Institutional Structure of Society

The theory of institutional change must begin with a theoretical formulation of the institutional structure. This section and the next are devoted to that formulation. The primary focus in both will be the significance of the value system of the society in determining the character of the institutional structure.

Definition of the Term "Institution"

"Society" may be thought of as a set of institutional systems. An "institutional system," in turn, may be thought of as a set of institutions. And an "institution" may be defined as *a set of socially prescribed patterns of correlated behavior*. In each of the above sentences, the term "set" refers to functionally interrelated elements.

Social Prescriptions

When employing this definition of an institution, institutionalists lay stress on the term "socially prescribed." While it is entirely possible for human behavior to exhibit random characteristics, institutionalists argue that all behavior within a community is ultimately subject to social prescriptions or proscriptions. This is especially true of all problem-solving (purposive) behavior. The community at large has a stake in the manner in which its tools and intelligence are brought to bear on its life processes. Those patterns of behavior perceived to be vital to the survival of the community are the most carefully prescribed and carry the heaviest sanctions.

It is a well-established point in the fields of sociology and child psychology that social conditioning begins prior to an infant's capacity to walk or talk.[1] Throughout one's life, the process of habit formation is the mechanism by which socially prescribed behavior is internalized. While some habits may be learned only through conscious effort, most habit formation is probably unconscious. Such unconscious habituation gives rise to the impression that certain patterns of behavior are "natural" and not amenable to discretionary change. The fruitless "nature" versus "nurture" debate is grounded in the misapprehension of unconscious habituation. Institutionalists hold the view that all socially relevant behavior is learned and is, for the most part, habitual.[2] While unconscious habituation may account for most observed behavior, particularly "traditional" behavior, this fact must not be allowed to obscure the discretionary nature of the social prescriptions that are thereby internalized. Socially prescribed behavior arises from social choices, and the critical history of any culture is the story of how these choices evolved in the life experience of the community. As will be argued at length below, institutional change is discretionary precisely because all social prescriptions are the outcomes of conscious choices made at some point in the life history of the culture.[3]

Behavioral Patterns

The term "patterns of correlated behavior" embodies two important concepts: (1) the notion that behavior within an institution is not random but purposeful and correlated; and (2) the notion that "values" function as the "correlators" of behavior within and among patterns of behavior. The term "behavioral pattern" (singular) may be thought of as two behaviors (or activities) correlated by a value. This conception of a "behavioral pattern" clearly indicates the social significance of "values." Values function as the standards of judgment by which behavior is correlated. Values not only correlate behavior within the behavioral pattern, they also correlate behavioral patterns with one another. The interconnection among behavioral patterns may be envisioned as the correlation of one behavior of one behavioral pattern by a given value with the behavior from another behavioral pattern. In essence, the interconnection among behavioral patterns is accomplished by a behavioral pattern.

In order to clarify these relationships, it may be helpful to symbolize a behavioral pattern as follows: $B^1 \; V^1 \; B^2$, where "B^1" is one behavior or activity, "B^2" is another behavior or activity, and "V^1" is the value that correlates B^1 with B^2. A second behavioral pattern might be identified as follows: $B^3 \; V^3 \; B^4$. The correlation of the first behavioral pattern with the second is accomplished through the use of an additional value, V^2, such that B^2 is correlated with B^3 through V^2, which produces a third behavioral pattern: $B^2 \; V^2 \; B^3$. Thus "behavioral patterns" (plural) are correlated by values, and the correlation of behavioral patterns entails a behavioral pattern. It is, then, the value system of the institution that provides the functional interrelationship of all patterns of behavior within the institution.[4] These comments on the nature of the correlation of behavior within and among behavioral patterns requires a further statement about the focus of the social prescriptions that give shape and form to the institutional structure. Clearly, what is prescribed are the values that will be employed as correlators of behavior. In other words, a given pair of behaviors or activities can be found in a number of different social contexts, but their relationship to one another will change depending on the value system under which they are correlated. This will be discussed at length below. Thus the diagnostic characteristic of an institution is the value structure that correlates the behavior within it. It follows from this that institutional change must entail a change in the value structure of the institution. This matter will also be explored at length later. But another concept fundamental to institutional analysis must be discussed first. It is the notion of the ceremonial-instrumental dichotomy.

The Ceremonial-Instrumental Dichotomy

Given the central importance of values to the structure of institutions, inquiry into the nature of institutions and the processes of institutional change is inherently normative. All inquiry involves interpretation, and interpretation requires judgment.[5] When the subject matter under investigation is the value system of society, interpretations and their attendant judgments must be made about the value system. The methodology of institutional economics faces this intellectual responsibility squarely by incorporating a philosophy of value that permits a straight-forward analysis of the value system. In contrast, all schools of mainstream economics attempt to evade this intellectual responsibility by purporting to adhere to the value-knowledge dualism in their methodologies. This positivist tenet is the foundation for claims of "objectivity" in mainstream economics. In the long history of the institutionalist critique of mainstream economics (from Veblen to Tool), this *wertfrei* methodology has been shown to be not only sterile, but counterproductive: normative considerations are not eschewed, they are merely suppressed, thereby obfuscating the true import of the inquiry; and the notion of "objectivity" is held hostage to the positivist dualism. As a consequence of these methodological strictures, mainstream economists have evaded the study of institutional structure (let alone institutional *change)* by relying on "methodological individualism."[6] The philosophical foundations of the institutionalist approach to the study of the value system of society is grounded in the classical works of Veblen and Dewey. Their works were synthesized and refined by Clarence E. Ayres. Ayres's student, J. Fagg Foster, and his student, Marc R. Tool, have brought "social value theory" to its present state of development. It is this particular line of institutionalist thought that informs the treatment of values in this essay.[7]

Ceremonial Values

The institutional structure of any society incorporates two systems of value: the ceremonial and the instrumental, each of which has its own logic and method of validation. While these two value systems are inherently incompatible, they are intertwined within the institutional structure through a complex set of relationships.

Ceremonial values correlate behavior within the institution by providing the standards of judgment for invidious distinctions, which prescribe status, differential privileges, and master-servant relationships, and warrant the exercise of power by one social class over another. The logic of the ceremonial value system, as Veblen put it, is one of "sufficient reason." Validation of ceremonial values is found in appeals to tradition and in the formulation of suitable myths (ideologies) that mystify the origin and legitimacy of their existence. Ceremonial values are by their very nature beyond inquiry in the sense that they may not be subjected to critical scrutiny. They may be rationalized through plausible argument, but they are never subjected to any sort of test of refutability. They are accepted on authority and regarded as absolute. Presumably, they emanate from human nature and, therefore, are not subject to human discretion. Patterns of behavior in which behaviors are correlated by ceremonial values are referred to here as "ceremonially warranted" patterns of behavior. The operative criterion by which such patterns of behavior are judged within the community is that of "ceremonial adequacy."

Instrumental Values

Instrumental values correlate behavior by providing the standards of judgment by which tools and skills are employed in the application of evidentially warranted knowledge to the problem-solving processes of the community. Using Veblen's language once again, the logic of the instrumental value system is that of "efficient cause." Instrumental values are validated in the continuity of the problem-solving processes. Patterns of behavior correlated by instrumental values are referred to as "instrumentally warranted" patterns of behavior. The criterion by which the community judges instrumentally warranted patterns of behavior is that of "instrumental efficiency."

Instrumental values are not, however, fixed or immutable. The problem-solving processes of the community, being dependent on the processes of inquiry and technological change, are inherently dynamic, requiring changes in habits of thought and behavior. As new patterns of behavior are required to accommodate the absorption and diffusion of new technology, instrumentally warranted patterns of behavior must change accordingly; and this requires changes in the instrumental values that correlate such behavior. H.H. Liebhafsky has referred to this capacity for change in the instrumental value system as "self-correcting value judgments."[8] A specific standard of judgment is warranted only as long as it provides for instrumental efficiency in maintaining the causal continuity of the problem-solving process. When such a standard loses its capacity to do so, it is replaced by a more appropriate standard. The process is "self-correcting" by virtue of the fact that the processes of inquiry upon which the problem-solving processes depend involve a conscious awareness of the method by which behavior is correlated. The causal continuity of the problem-solving process is, in principle, open to the surveillance of the community. When a sensed awareness of a disrapport between current instititional practices and instrumental efficiency arises within the community, the community has the capacity to opt for the discretionary change of those patterns of behavior that are no longer appropriate to the problem-solving processes.

The "Dialectical" Nature of Behavior

Whereas the value system of an institution is dichotomous, behavior is "dialectical" in the sense that Nicholas Georgescu-Roegen has used the term; that is to say, behavior may possess either ceremonial or instrumental characteristics, or possess *both* ceremonial and instrumental characteristics.[9] This fact adds considerable complexity to the forms that behavior patterns may take. As will be shown below, a ceremonially warranted pattern of behavior may incorporate instrumental behavior, and an instrumentally warranted pattern of behavior may incorporate behavior that has ceremonial characteristics.

A few examples may help to clarify the notion of the dialectical nature of behavior. Some examples of purely ceremonial behavior (B_c) would include: discrimination on the basis of race, color or creed; "wrapping oneself in the flag"; making a sacrificial offering; using deceit or coercion in manipulating the behavior of others; and kow-towing to those in authority. Some examples of purely instrumental behavior (B_i) would include: sawing a board; practicing the clarinet; painting a picture; dialing a telephone; programming a computer; using persuasion to obtain the cooperation of others; solving a mathematical problem; and taking medicine under a doctor's prescription. Three examples of behavior that possess both ceremonial and instrumental characteristics (B_{ci}) are: taking a bath; giving an order; and standing behind a lectern. Let us turn briefly to an explanation as to why each of the behaviors in this last set are dialectical.

The example of "taking a bath" is borrowed from Clarence Ayres's discussion of the "cult of the tub."[10] Noting Veblen's comments on the "ceremonial cleanliness" of the upper classes, Ayres discusses the ceremonial implications of the cult of the tub; but he also points out that whatever may be the ceremonial significance of cleanliness, regular bathing is instrumental to both personal and public hygiene. Similarly, the act of "giving an order" may at once announce one's status as well as perform the instrumental function of supervising the work of others. Most of us can tell the difference between the situation in which the boss issues orders just to remind everyone that he/she is in charge and the situation in which the boss issues orders that are instrumental to the supervision of an employee's work. Lastly, "standing behind a lectern" in a classroom clearly establishes the ceremonial status of the professor; but it is also an instrumentally efficient position from which to deliver a lecture.[11]

Whether a dialectical behavior will carry primarily ceremonial or instrumental significance in a given instance depends on the social context in which it occurs. Under the theory presented here, that social context is defined by the behavioral pattern in which the behavior is correlated with other behavior in the institutional arrangement. And that correlation is uniquely the function of the value that defines the behavioral pattern. If the value that correlates behavior is ceremonial, the dialectical behavior will take on ceremonial significance: thus, "taking a bath" performs the ceremonial function of displaying status; "giving an order" is intended to let everyone know who the boss is; and "standing behind a lectern" establishes the superior status of the professor over his/her students. If, on the other hand, the value is instrumental, the dialectical behavior takes on instrumental significance: bathing is understood to be necessary to maintenance of both personal and public health; orders are understood to be necessary to the instrumentally warranted process of supervision; and the physical location assumed by the professor is understood to be a function of his/her need to communicate effectively.

Types of Behavioral Patterns

The principle that the mode of valuation (that is, ceremonial or instrumental) will determine the ceremonial or instrumental significance of dialectical behavior is closely related to another important principle governing the formation of behavioral patterns in general. It was stated earlier that ceremonially warranted patterns of behavior can contain instrumental behavior and that instrumentally warranted patterns of behavior can contain behavior that has ceremonial characteristics. These possibilities emerge because there are a number of ways in which values and behaviors of a ceremonial or instrumental type can be combined. It has been demonstrated elsewhere that the number of possible combinations is finite.[12] Using the symbols introduced above, the possible types of behavioral patterns may be enumerated as follows:

Ceremonially Warranted Patterns	Instrumentally Warranted Patterns
(C-1) $B_c\ V_c\ B_c$	(I-1) $B_i\ V_i\ B_i$
(C-2) $B_c\ V_c\ B_i$	(I-2) $B_i\ V_i\ B_{ci}$
(C-3) $B_c\ V_c\ B_{ci}$	(I-3) $B_{ci}\ V_i\ B_{ci}$
(C-4) $B_{ci}\ V_c\ B_i$	
(C-5) $B_{ci}\ V_c\ B_{ci}$	

Several important observations may be made by reference to this tableau of behavioral patterns.

First, it should be noted that there are five possible types of ceremonially warranted behavioral patterns as compared with only three types of instrumentally warranted behavioral patterns. This reflects the fundamental differences in the two modes of valuation. The instrumental mode of valuing requires an open-ended process of inquiry capable of evaluating the consequences of the application of any particular standard of judgment in the correlation of behavior. The logic of instrumental valuation is, therefore, embedded in the causal continuity of the problem-solving process. This delimits the types of behavior to which instrumental values are relevant as correlators. The logic of instrumental valuation is relevant only to behavior that is somehow involved in the tool-skill nexus of the technological continuum. This is symbolized in the above tableau by the appearance of the *"i"* subscript in all behaviors shown in each of the three cases of instrumentally warranted behavioral patterns. Note the complete exclusion of any behavior exhibiting *only* a *"c"* subscript. In other words, instrumental valuation cannot rationalize purely ceremonial behavior. The values that correlate behavior in the pursuit of the arts and sciences cannot validly be made to justify such things as the imposition of invidious distinctions on the social structure of the community, the use of dishonesty and deceit in human affairs, or the denial of access to knowledge vital to the problem-solving processes of the community by vested interests.

In contrast, the ceremonial mode of valuation does not entail such limitations. As shown in the tableau, combinations of all three types of behavior can be correlated through ceremonial values. This is made possible by the very nature of the logic of ceremonial valuation. Resting as it does on the notion of "sufficient reason," the logic of ceremonial valuation may be used to rationalize any combination of behaviors. All that is required is a plausible argument to validate any particular correlation of behavior. The boundaries of the logic are as limitless as the human imagination. A particular pattern of behavior may be required "because the memory of man does not run to the contrary," or because "it is the will of God," or because "blacks are inherently inferior to whites," or because "it is consistent with the requirements of national security."

There should be no difficulty in seeing that purely ceremonial behaviors will be correlated by a ceremonial value. But what can be said about those patterns of behavior in which a ceremonial value correlates a ceremonial and an instrumental behavior? Such cases arise in C-2 and C-4 in the tableau. (Note that they do not arise in C-3 or C-5 where the ceremonial value gives ceremonial significance to the behaviors designated "B_{ci}.") In these instances, instrumental behavior is "encapsulated" within a ceremonially warranted behavioral pattern, thereby incorporating instrumental behavior in a ceremonially prescribed outcome.

Bronsilaw Malinowski provided a detailed description of such behavioral patterns in his account of the canoe-building practices of the Trobriand islanders.[13] According to Malinowski, two kinds of behavior are clearly involved in the canoe-building activities of the Trobrianders; one is ceremonial, the other instrumental. "The building of the sea-going canoe," he says, "is inextricably bound up with [the rituals of the Kula magic]. . . . the technicalities of construction are interrupted and punctuated by magical rites."[14] For example, before the tree from which the canoe will be carved can be felled, the magician must make an offering to the woodsprite that presumably inhabits the tree and utter an incantation designed to persuade the woodsprite to leave the tree. It is only after this ritual has been performed that the canoe builder can proceed to chop down the tree.

The Trobrianders are aware of the differences in the behavior of the magician and the craftsman. They apply instrumental criteria to the evaluation of the technical competence of the craftsman and the results of his efforts. It is clear that they understand that the rituals performed by the magician, however mystically potent they are presumed to be, "will not make up for bad workmanship." Nevertheless, the Trobrianders would never consider building a canoe except under the guidance of the Kula magic, for they believe that "a canoe built without magic would be unseaworthy."[15] It is the logic of magic and ritual, not the logic of the tool-skill nexus of canoe-building technology, that determines the correlation of the magician's behavior with that of the craftsman in the above example. In this instance, ceremonial considerations are dominant, and a ceremonially warranted standard of judgment correlates the behaviors of the magician and the craftsman. The instrumental behavior of the craftsman is "encapsulated" within a ceremonially warranted pattern of behavior. It should be obvious that there could be no instrumental warrant for this pattern of behavior because the technology of canoe-building is a causal continuum confined to the realm of evidentially demonstrable consequences within which the ritualistic behavior of the magician has no meaning.

The Concept of Ceremonial Dominance

The fact that an instrumental behavior can be encapsulated within a ceremonially warranted pattern of behavior leads to a broader set of considerations. In the case of the Trobrianders, Malinowski argues that magic is not merely an extraneous function "having nothing to do with the real work or its organisation." The presumed mystical powers of the magician give him the invidious status of a "natural leader whose command is obeyed, who can fix dates, apportion work, and keep the worker up to the mark."[16] In the language of present analysis, Malinowski is saying that the entire range of the division of labor in the canoe-building process is dominated by ceremonial considerations.[17] For the Trobrianders, the division of labor inherent in the technology of canoe-building is not a sufficient basis for the correlation of behavior. Something more is required to integrate the particular activities of canoe-building with other aspects of the culture; it is the function of magic to meet this requirement. Consequently, the instrumental warrant for the correlation of behavior inherent in the technology of canoe-building is dominated by a "higher order" of warrantability as the division of labor in this critical enterprise is required to meet the standard of "ceremonial adequacy."

This is the phenomenon of ceremonial dominance, and it is by no means confined to the Trobriand society. Institutional economists believe that it is a characteristic of all cultures. In modern, industrial societies, ceremonial dominance is rationalized not through magic but through ideologies. The magician's incantations are replaced by the harangues of the ideologue. Mystical potency is no longer perceived as the ability to drive out the demons of the lagoon; it is now perceived as the capacity to mobilize the *Herrenvolk,* or to awaken entrepreneurial spirit from its slumbers, or to inspire greater productive efforts by the new socialist man. All ideologies possess ritualistic language that serves to block inquiry and to mystify the warrant for socially prescribed patterns of behavior. Thus the *"untermensch"* may be sent to the gas chambers, "property rights" may be viewed as superior to "human rights," and "counterrevolutionaries" may be sent to the gulags.[18]

Clarence E. Ayres argued that ceremonially warranted patterns of behavior stifle progress precisely because they are "past-binding" and inhibit technological innovation.[19] He noted, however, that ceremonial practices are believed by members of the culture to be the source of instrumental efficiency; thus the Trobrianders believed that a canoe, no matter how well built, would not be sea-worthy unless the prescribed magic rituals were performed. This confusion abounds, Ayres said, because "'ceremonial adequacy' is an imitation of technological efficiency. The tribal medicine man purports to be altering the course of events in imitation of the tool activities by which technicians really do alter the course of events."[20] As indicated above, it is the encapsulation of instrumental behavior within a ceremonially warranted behavioral pattern that gives plausibility to this imitation of instrumental efficiency by ceremonial adequacy.

Ayres argued that the degree to which the ceremonial practices of the community inhibit technological innovation will vary from culture to culture and from one historical epoch to another. The fact that technological innovations appear to occur with greater frequency in one culture as compared to another is in part because of the relative degree of "permissiveness" in the ceremonial practices of the two cultures.[21] For example, the ceremonial practices of feudalism were less permissive of technological innovation than the ceremonial practices of the system of mercantile capitalism that emerged from the "cracks and crevices" of feudalism. The permissiveness of the ceremonial practices of a culture is a function of ceremonial dominance as defined above. In the analysis that follows, the phrase "index of ceremonial dominance" will be used to indicate the degree of permissiveness within the institutional structure. The two concepts are inversely related; thus a high index of ceremonial dominance would indicate that the institution has a very low degree of permissiveness with respect to technological innovation.[22]

The Dynamic Character of Technological Innovation

The foregoing analysis of ceremonial dominance required the premature introduction of the concept of technological innovation. Since this concept is fundamental to the institutionalist theory of institutional change, it requires careful consideration, and it is to that task the discussion now turns.

The Meaning of "Technology"

The term "technology" has been defined in various ways by institutionalists. While there is a continuity of meaning to the various definitions, the term continues to produce confusion and often heated dispute.[23] Part of the problem arises from the failure of institutionalists always to distinguish clearly technology as a process from the tools or machinery that embody technology. Sloppy conceptualization along these lines was encouraged by Veblen's (almost) invariant coupling of the words "machine" and "technology." Despite the fact that he habitually used the term "machine technology," it is clear that he never intended the term to be confined to "machines" as such. Accordingly, when speaking of the relationship of technological change to economic development, he says,

the changes that take place in the mechanical contrivances are an expression of changes in the human factor. Change in the material facts breed further change only through the human factor. It is in the human material that the continuity of development is to be looked for; and it is here, therefore, that the motor forces of the process of economic development must be studied if they are to be studied in action at all.[24]

Technology for Veblen was a process that arose out of the human proclivity for workmanship and the exercise of intellectual curiosity. It was embodied in the tool-skill nexus of problem-solving activities. The essence of technological change, therefore, was the change in "prevalent habits of thought" associated with a given state of the arts and sciences. Veblen saw technological change as a process of "cumulative causation." The problem-solving processes of the community generate innovations in the ways of "bringing material things to account," thereby changing the industrial environment in which the community works; and this changed environment produces further changes in prevalent habits of thought about how to conduct the community's affairs.

Clarence Ayres endeavored to explicate the broad implications of Veblen's notion of machine technology. Comparing Veblen's analysis with John Dewey's philosophy, Ayres argued that Veblen's conception of the technological process was the logical equivalent of Dewey's notion of "instrumentalism."[25] According to Ayres, Dewey faced the problem of formulating a concept that would "identify the intellectual procedures of science with the use of instruments and at the same time . . . identify the instruments of scientists with the tools which are in still wider use by artisans and craftsmen."[26] This is precisely what Veblen had accomplished in his overall treatment of the interplay of science and technology in his description of the manner in which the evolution of the scientific point of view had transformed society.[27] In Ayres's view, the confluence of the ideas of Veblen and Dewey require us to think of "technology" in the broadest possible terms. "So defined, technology includes mathematical journals and symphonic scores no less than skyscrapers and assembly lines, since all these are equally the product of human hands as well as human brains."[28]

This broadening of the conception of technology to incorporate the full sweep of the arts and sciences, does not render the notion vacuous; on the contrary, it enhances its theoretical precision. As Anne Mayhew has argued so convincingly, Ayres's integration of Veblen and Dewey brings us to the recognition that the essence of the technological process is "instrumental valuing."[29] The instrumental mode of valuation is the thread of continuity running through all of the arts and sciences which permits "the evaluation of the consequences of any particular use of a tool."[30] With reference to the foregoing discussion of the ceremonial mode of valuation, it is useful to note that Mayhew cites H.H. Liebhafsky's telling observation that ceremonialism inhibits progress precisely because it "inhibits ... the free inquiry necessary for instrumental valuing."[31]

Thus "technology" is broadly conceived in the institutionalist literature. This is consistent with the "holistic" nature of the institutionalist methodology, which facilitates an understanding of the workings of the economic system as a cultural process.[32] From this perspective, the fund of knowledge available to the community for problem-solving purposes is composed of the instrumentally warranted knowledge generated across the full range of the arts and sciences. "Technological innovation," therefore, can originate in any field of inquiry or creative endeavor. This broadened view of technology also encompasses the notion that the knowledge fund is expanded through the efforts of the entire community, not just some academic or scientific elite. The proclivities for workmanship and intellectual curiosity, the well-springs of the pursuit of instrumentally warranted knowledge, are the common heritage of all members of the community. Incremental contributions to the knowledge fund occur on a daily basis through the efforts of individuals found in all walks of life and at all levels of the socioeconomic structure of the community. This idea was captured brilliantly in a statement that Solomon Fabricant made before the Joint Economic Committee of the U.S. Congress in 1978.

In short, the high productivity of the American economy is the end result of a great many different activities involving decisions by millions of scientists, engineers, and technicians in laboratories and industry; educators in schools, universities, and training centers; managers and owners of production facilities; workers and their families and unions; and government officials. Increase of this country's output per hour over the long run is the result of the energy, ingenuity, and skill with which all of us, individually and as a Nation, manage our resources of production.[33]

The institutionalist view that "capital" can only be meaningfully identified as the "immaterial capital" of the knowledge and skills possessed by the community at large is founded on the kind of evidence to which Fabricant alludes in this statement.[34]

The Technological Dynamic

The technological process is inherently dynamic. Technological innovation creates new possibilities for inquiry and problem-solving. Whether it takes the form of ideas embodied in a new mathematical equation, a new physical implement, or a new technique for organizing problem-solving activity, technological innovation involves a change in behavior, and changes in behavior create new problems for the community in the correlation of behavior. This is the process that Veblen called "cumulative causation." He captures the essence of the process in the following passage:

> All economic change is a change in the economic community—a change in the community's methods of turning material things to account. The change is always in the last resort a change in habits of thought. This is true even of changes in the mechanical processes of industry. A given contrivance for affecting certain material ends becomes a circumstance which effects the further growth of habits of thought—habitual modes of procedure—and so becomes a point of departure for further development of the methods of compassing the ends sought and for further variation of ends that are sought to be compassed.[35]

The observation that the solution of one problem creates a whole host of new problems, trite though it may be, is nevertheless, pertinent. The expansion of the community's fund of knowledge is not only instrumental to the solution of problems, it is the means by which new problems are identified.

It would appear that anthropological research and studies of the history of technology support the proposition that technological innovation is developmental in the sense of being cumulative, combinatorial and accelerating in character. As a cumulative process, it exhibits a one-way time vector; the expansion of the knowledge fund through technological innovation is an irreversible process through time. This is true because the emergence of new technologies involves the combination of previously existing technologies. The time rate of technological innovation appears to approximate an exponential function, exhibiting a very flat curve through history until the last three centuries. William F. Ogburn, among others, attributed the exponential expansion of the community's knowledge fund to the cumulative nature of its growth. As Ogburn puts it: "The fact that material culture is accumulative, that is, new inventions are not lost but added to the existing stock, and the fact (if it be a fact) that the larger the stock the greater the number of new inventions, suggests at first glance the compound interest law."[36] Marc R. Tool uses a graphical presentation of this proposition in his book *The Discretionary Economy* to illustrate the "exponential growth in the knowledge of continuum."[37] These, then, are the major premises upon which the institutionalist hypothesis of the technological dynamic is based.

Clarence Ayres laid particular emphasis on the combinatorial aspect of technological innovation. The thrust of his argument is contained in the following passage:

> knowledge and skills accumulate. They do so . . . because knowledge and skills are objectified in tools and symbols. . . .
> The importance of such objectification of this whole aspect of culture is not merely that of accumulation. Rather accumulation is only the minor premise to innovation. The major premise is the combining of previously exisiting "culture traits" to form new ones.[38]

Ayres's emphasis on the idea that technological innovation is a combinatorial process bears a striking resemblance to Nicholas Georgescu-Roegen's conception of evolution as "the emergence of novelty by combination."[39] In both formulations, the evolutionary process is couched in terms of a "developmental continuity" that rises out of a combination of previously existing traits. Unlike the evolutionary processes of the biological and physical realms, the emergence of novelty by combination in human culture results from the choices made in the problem-solving processes. In other words, the rate and direction of social evolution is subject to the discretionary control of mankind. Using terminology established earlier in this discussion regarding patterns of behavior, technological innovation involves changes in instrumentally warranted patterns of behavior. Such changes are made possible by the mode of instrumental valuation, which permits changes in the standards of judgment by which behavior is correlated. J. Fagg Foster used the term "developmental continuity" to identify both the meaning of evolution and the method by which it was accomplished, that is, instrumental valuing.[40] Thus it can be seen that the institutionalist hypothesis regarding the technological dynamic is conceptually linked to the instrumental theory of value.

The Interface of the Knowledge Fund
and the Institutional Structure

At any given point in time, the institutional structure of society incorporates a given fund of knowledge that is distributed between ceremonial and instrumental patterns of behavior. Knowledge is either "encapsulated" within ceremonial patterns or "embodied" within instrumental patterns of behavior. This distinction in language is required to indicate that the index of ceremonial dominance determines the permissable use of existing knowledge in the community's problem-solving processes. The knowledge fund is translated into problem-solving activities through instrumentally warranted patterns of behavior. But because of the phenomenon of ceremonial dominance, only that part of the knowledge fund that can be reconciled with the existing value structure of the community would be sanctioned for problem-solving purposes. In other words, the instrumental behavior that is permitted within the community is required to meet the standard of ceremonial adequacy. Thus knowledge that cannot be reconciled with the need to justify existing patterns of status, power, and other forms of invidious distinctions would not be intentionally sanctioned.

While ceremonial dominance determines the ceremonial feasibility of the range of permissable behavior, it is the knowledge fund that determines the instrumental feasibility of problem-solving activities. When these two standards of feasibility are taken into account, the interface of the fund of knowledge with the institutional structure defines an "institutional space" that may be partitioned into four sectors delineating the ceremonial and instrumental feasibility of behavioral patterns.[41] These four sectors are presented schematically in Figure 1 and can be identified as follows:

Sector I.   In which the behavioral patterns are both ceremonially and instrumentally feasible.

Sector II.   In which behavioral patterns are instrumentally feasible but ceremonially nonfeasible.

Sector III. In which the behavioral patterns are ceremonially feasible but instrumentally nonfeasible.

Sector IV.   In which behavioral patterns are both ceremonially and instrumentally nonfeasible.

Each of these sectors will be discussed in turn.

Sector IV can be immediately disregarded since it is an empty set. Behavioral patter.   this sector, even if they could be imagined, are both ceremonially and instrumentally nonfeasible; they would not fall within either the myth structure or the technology of the community. Sector I, on the other hand, is that sector in which the actual institutional structure exists. The patterns of behavior in this sector are tech-

	INSTRUMENTALLY FEASIBLE	INSTRUMENTALLY NONFEASIBLE
CEREMONIALLY FEASIBLE	SECTOR I (Sector of Ceremonial Encapsulation)	SECTOR III (Sector of Lysenko Effects)
CEREMONIALLY NONFEASIBLE	SECTOR II (Sector of Lost Instrumental Efficiency)	SECTOR IV (Empty Set)

Figure 1. *The Partitioning of Institutional Space by the Interface of the Knowledge Fund and the Value Structure of the Institution.*

nologically feasible, and they meet the standard of ceremonial adequacy. Sector II defines, for a given state of the knowledge fund, the technological possibilities of the community that are denied to it by the existing level of ceremonial dominance. As will be shown below, it is into this sector that the community would move if "progressive" institutional changes reduced the degree of ceremonial dominance. Sector III may at first blush appear to be socially irrelevant, but as the subsequent discussion will show, it has always been a factor in human history, particularly in the history of the twentieth century. Sector III contains behavioral patterns that involve an extension of the myth structure that not even the ceremonial encapsulation of instrumental behavior can sustain without a loss of instrumental efficiency to the community at large. Such extensions of the myth structure will be referred to later as "Lysenko effects." It is into this sector that the community would move if "regressive" institutional change increased the degree of ceremonial dominance.

The Process of Institutional Change

This discussion has now reached the stage where the process of institutional change can be brought under direct inspection. Both the "regressive" and "progressive" forms of institutional change will be delineated. Fundamental to a discussion of either is the concept of "ceremonial encapsulation." In the case of "regressive" institutional change, a particular type of ceremonial encapsulation, the "Lysenko" type, will be shown to be the cause of what might be called the *absolute* "triumph of imbecile institutions over life and culture."[42]

Ceremonial Encapsulation

In the foregoing discussion of the technological dynamic, it was argued that the dynamic force for change in the institutional structure is the growth of the community's fund of knowledge. The phenomenon of ceremonial dominance, however, poses an obstacle to the absorption and diffusion of the new knowledge in the form of technological innovation. Consequently, a new discovery in the arts or sciences will be incorporated into behavioral patterns only to the extent that the community believes that the previously existing degree of ceremonial dominance can be maintained. Technological innovations will be permitted only if it is anticipated that they will not disrupt the existing value structure of the community. This will involve changes in behavioral patterns, but any increase of instrumentally warranted behavioral patterns will be offset by concomitant increases in ceremonially warranted patterns of behavior. The new ceremonially warranted patterns are required to "encapsulate" the increase in instrumentally warranted behavioral patterns. It is through this process that the community seeks to attain a *status quo ante* with respect to its value structure. Hence, ceremonial encapsulation, to the extent that it is successful, denies to the community those technological innovations that the existing knowledge fund is capable of generating, thereby depriving the community of higher levels of instrumental efficiency in the problem-solving processes.[43]

Two important qualifications must be introduced to the discussion at this point. First, it should be noted that the theoretical formulation of "ceremonial encapsulation" does not require the assumption that the community is omniscient in its effort to "encapsulate" new knowledge. There may be considerable slippage in the process, and technological innovations inconsistent with the existing value structure may indeed be adopted without a full comprehension of the consequences of doing so. To the extent that such innovations "slip through" the ceremonial net, so to speak, some amount of "progressive" institutional change (as defined below) will take place.[44] Second, it must be noted that both anthropological and contemporary studies indicate that all societies attempt to maximize the efficiency with which they employ their existing (ceremonially encapsulated) technology. Whatever the community's taboos may be that bound use of knowledge, the knowledge that is deemed ceremonially adequate is used to the fullest. If one must grow rice with little more than one's bare hands, it would be wise to study the rice-growing methods of the Vietnamese peasant. And if one must navigate among the South Pacific archipelagos in an outrigger canoe, it would be desirable to do so in one built by the Trobrianders. Veblen's "instinct of workmanship" appears to manifest itself even under the most trying ceremonial circumstances.

It is the attempt to preserve the existing value structure in the face of technological innovation that gives the ceremonial practices of the community what Ayres called their "past-binding" character.[45] This notion is similar to Ogburn's concept of "cultural lag," which he formulated to explain the lag in the correlation of adjustments between two interrelated aspects of culture.[46] The concept of ceremonial encapsulation offers a precise explanation of the cultural lag involved in the institutional response to technological innovation. It focuses on the fact that although "past-binding," the ceremonial practices of the community are "permissive" in the sense that some aspects of the expanding knowledge fund will be absorbed into the behavioral patterns of the community. As indicated above, this involves the effort to preserve the existing value structure. Thus it is the value structure that correlates behavior within the institution that "lags." Even though there is some technological innovation, as long as the value structure remains unchanged, it cannot be said that an "institutional change" has taken place. Under the logic set forth in the present analysis, an "institutional change" does not take place unless there is a change in the index of ceremonial dominance; which is to say, an institutional change occurs only when there is a change in the value structure of the institution.

There are three identifiable types of ceremonial encapsulation of the knowledge fund.[47] For purposes of identification, the three types of ceremonial encapsulation will be called: (1) the "past-binding" type, (2) the "future-binding" type, and (3) the "Lysenko" type.

The "past-binding" type. The first type of ceremonial encapsulation for which the term "cultural lag" is most appropriate involves the "past-binding" resistance of the traditions of the community to the absorption and diffusion of technological innovations. The community responds to unanticipated advances in the arts and sciences (either indigenous or borrowed from other cultures) by attempting to minimize the impact of the technological innovation on existing habits of thought and behavior. Since technological innovation requires changes in instrumentally warranted patterns of behavior, it carries with it a threat to the stability of the ceremonially warranted patterns of behavior that traditionally encapsulate the knowledge fund that is the common heritage of the community. In the face of this threat, conscious efforts are made to shore up the existing value structure by an elaboration of ceremonial practices designed to minimize the innovation's dislocation of the status quo. Veblen described this type of ceremonial encapsulation as follows: "The innovation finds its way into the system of use and wont at the cost of some derangement to the system, provokes new usages, conventions, beliefs, and principles of conduct, in part directed

advisedly to its utilisation or to the mitigation of its immediate consequences, or to the diversion of its usufruct to the benefit of given individuals or classes."[48] While this type of ceremonial encapsulation is
most easily identified in traditional, preindustrial cultures, which exhibit very slow time rates of technological diffusion, the cultural lags it
produces are also quite evident in modern society. For example, Ogburn argued that the historical delay in the development of workmen's
compensation laws, coming almost a century after the onset of the industrial revolution, constituted a major cultural lag.[49] But perhaps the
most widely recognized evidence of this type of ceremonial encapsulation in the standard economics literature is to be found in those studies
that report the frustration of the best-laid plans for economic development in less developed economies.

The "future-binding" type. The second type of ceremonial encapsulation involves the active development of technological innovations for
the purpose of strengthening and extending the control of vested interests over the life of the community. In this case, the introduction of
technological innovations into the life processes of the community is
carefully coordinated with the formulation of an appropriate mythology and related ceremonial practices that rationalize and enforce the
legitimacy of the control over the technology by the vested interests
that have captured it. The strategy is to promote, capture, and control
all those technological innovations that can reasonably be anticipated
to have a bearing on the ceremonially warranted exercise of power by
the vested interests over the life processes of the community. To the
extent that vested interests can maintain control over the process of
technological innovation, they effectively control the future of the community, hence the term "future-binding."

It is this second type of ceremonial encapsulation that has been the
main preoccupation of institutional economists from Veblen to the present. Veblen formulated the problem in terms of his distinction between "pecuniary" and "industrial" employments, in which the
ceremonially warranted pecuniary employments were dominant over
the instrumentally warranted industrial employments.[50]

Contemporary institutionalists have identified this type of ceremonial encapsulation in several recent works. F. Gregory Hayden has
offered extensive evidence of the capacity of giant enterprises in the
chemical, farm machinery, and agribusiness industries to encapsulate
science and technology for the purpose of increasing their own power
and profits at the expense of instrumental efficiency in maintaining a
healthy food chain, the conservation of viable agricultural acreage, and
the preservation of vital social and ecological systems.[51] The late Louis

J. Junker analyzed the ceremonial encapsulation of knowledge pertaining to diet and health by what he called the "American food power system." While many of the conclusions he drew in this study are highly controversial, he offered compelling evidence that those industries involved in the production, distribution, and sale of commodities and services relating to nutrition and health have the power to prevent the community from utilizing the complete fund of knowledge available for the proper maintenance of health and dietary practices. In the concluding paragraphs of his study, Junker summarizes the social significance of this "future-binding" type of ceremonial encapsulation as follows:

> As a general theoretical principle, the ceremonial-instrumental dichotomy posits the existence of a gap between the growing knowledge fund (and the value structure it entails) and the vested interests of the existing power system that governs and exploits its use. All the forces that encapsulate and control knowledge for the benefit of limited vested interests create master-servant relationships between themselves and the community at large, and this produces organized waste. Genuine knowledge sets the outer limits of human potential. But ceremonial forces encapsulate genuine knowledge, and thus the human potential, by confining the use of knowledge within the framework of the core values of the established power structure. This encapsulation reduces the community's flexibility and adaptivity to the potentialities of the new knowledge. In the case of the food power system, the encapsulation can lead quite literally to death.[52]

The Hayden and Junker studies, while focusing on specific industrial clusters, lay bare the underlying process of ceremonial encapsulation that is endemic to the economy as a whole. Other institutionalists have produced works that reveal the specific means by which the process contaminates the entire society.

William M. Dugger's study of "corporate hegemony" analyzes the social mechanisms by which this type of ceremonial encapsulation is transmitted throughout the community.[53] It is Dugger's contention that the corporation has become the dominant institution in American society and that this dominance is manifest in its hegemonic influence over all other institutions of the society. This hegemony is maintained, he says, "not through a conspiracy, but through four social mechanisms": subordination, contamination, emulation, and mystification. He identifies each as follows: "Subordination ties all institutions together so that noncorporate institutions are used as means to corporate ends. Contamination puts corporate role motives into noncorporate roles. Emulation allows corporate leaders to gain acceptance, even respect, in non-corporate leadership roles. And mystification covers the corporate hegemony with a protective (magic) cloak."[54] It is through these mechanisms, Dugger argues, that the corporate interests are able to control the availability and use of knowledge throughout the society. One of the most significant features of his analysis is his treatment of the ceremonial encapsulation of institutions of higher learning by corporate interests.[55] He shows how the university's instrumentally warranted social goals to pursue unfettered inquiry and to expand the intellectual horizons of its students have been subordinated to the ceremonially warranted corporate goals of industry-specific research and the vocationalization of the curriculum. Beginning with Veblen's *The Higher Learning in America,* institutionalists have stressed the critical importance of the educational system (most particularly, the system of higher education) to the development of society's capacity to adapt to growth in the knowledge fund.[56] Dugger's analysis reveals how this critical educational mission has been ceremonially encapsulated to the detriment of the community.

John Munkirs has also produced a powerful analysis of the American economy that comes to rest, in part, on his identification of the ceremonial encapsulation of technology by what he calls the system of centralized private sector planning (CPSP), which is dominated by giant financial and industrial corporations. One of his main contentions is that the reality of centralized private sector planning is only dimly perceived by policy makers and the public at large because their view of the real world is obscured by the mythical *Weltanshauung* of capitalist ideology. In the language of the present analysis, this ceremonially warranted perception of reality has impaired our society's capacity to develop instrumentally warranted social policies. Munkirs sums up the matter in the following passage:

> Unfortunately, in America, the real choices that our technological knowledge make possible (choices between different production and distribution systems, for example, centralized versus decentralized) have been circumscribed by, or encapsulated within, our capitalistic ideology and, in particular, by the values of self-interest, profit seeking, and laissez-faire. In brief, the particular type of centralized planning that exists in America today is due neither to technological determinism nor to conspiratorial machinations. Rather, CPSP is a direct result of combining the values of self-interest, profit seeking, and laissez-faire with certain technological possibilities.[57]

Munkirs's detailed analysis of the structure and functioning of the centralized private sector planning system provides dramatic evidence of the existence of "future-binding" ceremonial encapsulation throughout the entire economy of the United States.

While space does not permit an extended discussion of the subject, it must be noted that a driving force for "future-binding" ceremonial encapsulation in the twentieth century has been the military-industrial complexes of the nations of the world. Veblen set forth the first systematic analysis of the military-industrial complex in 1917. He demonstrated how the ceremonial preoccupation with nationalism, patriotism, and the pecuniary employments encapsulate technology and the industrial employments at the expense of life and culture.[58] Fortified by appropriately formulated myths (for instance, "the balance of powers," "mutually assured destruction," "strategic defense initiative"), the military-industrial complex has virtually unlimited capacity to produce, capture, and control modern technology. The degree of ceremonial dominance enjoyed by the military-industrial complex in the United States is indicated by the fact that most Americans take it for granted that not only national security but economic stability is dependent on a "strong national defense."

The "Lysenko" type. In the "past-binding" and "future-binding" types of ceremonial encapsulation, genuine knowledge is encapsulated by the ceremonial beliefs and practices of the community. In the "Lysenko" type of ceremonial encapsulation, on the other hand, the community attempts to achieve instrumentally nonfeasible outcomes through ceremonially warranted behavioral patterns. This is the extreme case of ceremonial practices imitating instrumental efficiency. Under the concept of institutional space set forth earlier, such an effort pushes the community into Sector III, which entails ceremonially feasible, but instrumentally nonfeasible patterns of behavior. Spurious "knowledge" is substituted for genuine knowledge, and ceremonially warranted patterns of behavior *displace* instrumentally warranted patterns of behavior in critical areas of the community's problem-solving processes.

This type of ceremonial encapsulation is called the "Lysenko" type, after Trofim D. Lysenko, whose name has become synonymous with the corruption and manipulation of science for ideological purposes. Lysenko was the Russian "agrobiologist" who argued that genetic change could be induced through the environmental conditioning of biological organisms. Although his theories were diametrically opposed to the evidentially warranted hypotheses developed over the previous century in the field of genetics, they were embraced by Stalin as the only biological theories consistent with Marxist-Stalinist ideology. Lysenko's theories became the official dogma in agronomy and the supporting biological sciences. The application of Lysenko's theories to the growing of field crops produced disastrous results; nevertheless, Lysenkoism dominated Soviet science for thirty years. But perhaps the most devastating effect Lysenkoism had on the reduction of instrumental efficiency in the Soviet Union was not its impact on the practice of agriculture, but its impact on the practice of science.[59]

History offers numerous examples of the "Lysenko" type of ceremonial encapsulation, but space limitations permit only a brief mention of two cases (one historical, and the other potential) that have emerged in the twentieth century. The most notorious historical case is, of course, the Nazi theory of Ayrian racial supremacy. The Nazis did not invent anti-Semitism and racism; these virulent forms of invidious discrimination were the cultural heritage of Europe. The Nazi innovation was to formulate a theory that would provide a cloak of "scientific" legitimacy for the racial laws adopted in the Third Reich. The new, spurious "science" displaced genuine science, thereby providing the intellectual foundation for the monstrous crimes against humanity that followed. Turning to the potential case, while it is perhaps not the same threat to civilization that the Nazi racial theories were, the so-called science of "creationism" is, nevertheless, a contemporary example of a "Lysenko" type of ceremonial encapsulation going somewhere to happen. Creationists, encouraged by the moral support of President Reagan, are engaged in a nationwide campaign to place "creationism on a par with classical evolution in public school instruction."[60] Aside from the damage this would cause to the teaching of science, one can only speculate on the broader social ramifications of a successful creationist campaign to substitute religious dogma for the processes of inquiry.

The Definition of Institutional Change

Institutional change takes the form of a change in the value structure of the institution. A change in the value structure may be measured theoretically by a change in the institution's index of ceremonial dominance. The index of ceremonial dominance reflects the dominance of ceremonially warranted values over instrumentally warranted values in the correlation of behavior in the behavioral patterns of the institution. An increase in the index of ceremonial dominance entails the displacement of instrumentally warranted values by ceremonially warranted values in the correlation of behavior. An increase in the index of ceremonial dominance signifies a "regressive" institutional change. A decrease in the index of ceremonial dominance entails the displacement of ceremonially warranted values by instrumentally warranted values in the correlation of behavior. A decrease in the index of ceremonial dominance signifies a "progressive" institutional change. As already indicated in the foregoing discussion of "past-binding" and "future-binding" ceremonial encapsulation, the index of ceremonial dominance may remain unchanged if ceremonially warranted patterns of behavior increase at a rate sufficient to encapsulate increases in instrumentally warranted patterns of behavior brought about by changes in the community's fund of knowledge. In such cases, there is no institutional change.

"Regressive" Institutional Change

The "Lysenko" type of ceremonial encapsulation (called a "Lysenko effect") generates "regressive" institutional change by causing the *displacement* of instrumentally warranted patterns of behavior by ceremonially warranted patterns of behavior, thereby raising the index of ceremonial dominance in the community. This is a quite different outcome from the institutional adjustments associated with either "past-binding" or "future-binding" ceremonial encapsulation. In those cases, the index of ceremonial dominance remains unchanged, and there is a *net increase* in the instrumental efficiency of the community, meager though it may be. In the case of a "Lysenko effect," there is a *net loss* of instrumental efficiency because there is no way to maintain legitimate scientific or technological practices in those parts of the community affected directly or indirectly by the intrusion of the spurious "science." The Russian agronomists and biologists who opposed Lysenkoism were expelled from the academies or worse. Agricultural practices were modified to meet the Lysenkoist criteria, and agricultural productivity declined. A similar fate befell the German scientists, intellectuals, and ordinary citizens who disputed Nazi dogma. Their options were: (1) remain on the faculties, join the party, and teach the despised doctrines; (2) speak out against these intellectual outrages and risk death or the concentration camps; or (3) emigrate. The loss of instrumental efficiency to the community was measured ultimately by the Holocaust and the death and destruction of World War II.

While one can be sanguine that "regressive" institutional changes are ultimately reversible, since the demonstrable adverse consequences of spurious "knowledge" cannot be long endured in the life processes of the community without a sensed awareness that something is amiss,

Veblen admonished us to remember that "history records more frequent and more spectacular instances of the triumph of imbecile institutions over life and culture than of peoples who have by force of instinctive insight saved themselves alive out of a desperately precarious institutional situation."[61] Lysenkoism lasted for thirty years in Russia; and while the Third Reich lasted for only twelve, the cost of reversing the "regressive" institutional changes it spawned were ultimately borne by the entire world.

Progressive Institutional Change

"Progressive" institutional change occurs when, *for a given fund of knowledge,* ceremonial patterns of behavior are displaced by instrumental patterns of behavior.[62] This entails an increased reliance on instrumental values in the correlation of behavior within the community, thereby lowering the index of ceremonial dominance. The displacement of ceremonial patterns by instrumental patterns of behavior moves the institution into Sector II, which was defined by the interface of the knowledge fund and the original index of ceremonial dominance. Sector II, it will be recalled, isolates that institutional space in which behavioral patterns are instrumentally feasible but ceremonially nonfeasible. In other words, this sector contains those behavioral patterns that the knowledge fund makes possible but which cannot be undertaken because of ceremonial restraints on behavior. "Progressive" institutional change involves technological innovations that break down those ceremonial barriers.

To reiterate, innovations in the arts and sciences bring about growth in the fund of knowledge, but the new knowledge is incorporated into the problem-solving processes only to the extent that it is possible for the community to maintain the previously existing level of ceremonial dominance. With the exception of the "Lysenko" type, the process of *ceremonial encapsulation* involves some technological innovation. This *is the first phase of institutional adjustment.* Even though the new instrumental patterns of behavior generated through the technological innovation are ceremonially encapsulated, they *are* integrated into the experience of the community. The new standards of instrumental valuing they bring to the problem-solving processes have demonstrable consequences that become known to the community. As the community becomes habituated to employing these new standards of judgment in the correlation of behavior, the learning process reveals new opportunities for their application elsewhere in the problem-solving processes. The diffusion of the new instrumental values throughout the community erodes the ideological foundations of those ceremonial practices that are dominant in the affected areas of activity. Eventually, instrumental standards of judgment displace ceremonial standards of judgment in the correlation of behavior in a range of problem-solving activities not contemplated in the original technological innovation. *"Progressive" institutional change is,* then *the second phase of the institutional adjustment* brought about by innovations in the arts and sciences.

Veblen's conception of "cumulative causation" explains the dynamics of the process that produces "progressive" institutional change. Technological innovation changes the objective circumstances of the community; the new set of circumstances alters habits of thought and behavior; these new habits of thought and behavior are projected into other areas of the community's experience, giving rise to further innovations in the arts and sciences, which, in turn, produce new technological innovations in the community's efforts "to turn material things to account."[63] Veblen believed that the change in the material circumstances of the culture brought about through the introduction of machine technology during the Industrial Revolution conditioned working people to think in terms of cause and effect. "The machine," he said, "throws out anthropomorphic habits of thought."[64] This affects not only the ability of working people to become consciously aware of the manner in which their behavior is correlated in the workplace, but also their ability to think in causal terms about broader social relationships that affect the life processes of the community. Machine technology creates the material circumstances that are inhospitable to those habits of thought that rationalize ceremonial patterns of behavior. "Its scheme of knowledge and of inference is based on the laws of material causation, not those of immemorial custom, authenticity, or authoritative enactment."[65] Thus the working people in an industrial society are less likely to submit to the kind of master-servant relationship that existed under feudalism. The industrial system gives rise to an "animus of insubordination" and the individual's status shifts from "subject" to "citizen."[66]

A critical factor in bringing about "progressive" institutional change is a sensed awareness within the community that there is a need to modify habitual patterns of thought and behavior in order to achieve a higher level of instrumental efficiency in the problem-solving processes. Veblen saw this sensed awareness arising out of the change in the material circumstances of the community brought about by the introduction of machine technology. Other factors affecting the material circumstances of the community can also bring about such a sensed awareness. Clarence Ayres stressed the importance of the "frontier experience" in breaking down the allegiance to traditional patterns of behavior.[67] Environmental catastrophes that disrupt the physical habitat of the community can also have a profound effect on the community's willingness to consider alternative patterns of behavior as a simple matter of survival. Finally, contact with other cultures through war or trade can induce a sensed awareness of new possibilities for social adaptation.[68]

One additional brief comment must be made on a subject that should be given detailed attention, and that is the dynamic interrelationship between "progressive" institutional change and growth in the knowledge fund. It is clear that there is a feed-back relationship between "progressive" institutional change and further growth in the knowledge fund. As the theory has been formulated so far, it is the change in the fund of knowledge, generated by the community-wide problem-solving processes (incorporating both formal and informal processes of inquiry), that provokes institutional adjustment. As the second phase of institutional adjustment ("progressive" institutional change) lowers the index of ceremonial dominance in the community, it becomes easier to absorb and diffuse technological innovations; *but it is also this process that accelerates the growth of knowledge.* As Milton Lower puts it, "knowledge increases in the degree that it is used."[69] The higher rates of technological innovation made possible by a lower index of ceremonial dominance provide the social environment conducive to the processes of inquiry throughout the culture. Thus, the growth of knowledge is both the cause and consequence of "progressive" institutional change. The dynamic relationship between the growth in knowledge and "progressive" institutional change is presented schematically in Figure 2.

The Limits to "Progressive" Institutional Change

There is, of course, nothing inevitable about "progressive" institutional change. Veblen expressed his generally pessimistic view about it when he warned of the "triumph of imbecile institutions over life and culture." The historical reality of "regressive" institutional change has already been acknowledged. Given the present state of the theory presented here and the level of empirical work associated with it, predictions regarding either the time rate or the direction of institutional

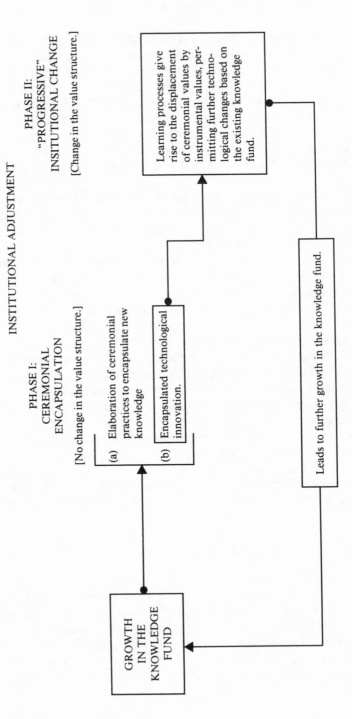

Figure 2. *The Dynamics of the Relationship between Growth in the Knowledge Fund and the "Progressive" Institutional Change.*

change on anything but the most narrowly defined range of cultural activity is probably impossible. Nevertheless, the theory does specify qualitative limitations on the generation and rate of institutional change. They are: (1) the availability of knowledge; (2) the capacity for understanding and adaptation; and (3) the principle of minimum dislocation.[70]

The availability of knowledge. The breadth and depth of the accumulated fund of knowledge available to the community clearly sets the limits to the feasibility of institutional change. The greater the fund of knowledge, the greater the potential for institutional change. Scientifically primitive societies do not exhibit rapid rates of "progressive" institutional change. The dynamics of technological innovation are at work in these communities as in any other, but the time rate of change is constrained by the paucity of the technological base from which the innovations must spring. "Cultural borrowing" can make a significant difference to the rate of change in any society since the transfer of technology from other cultures creates a quantum increase in the borrowing culture's knowledge fund.[71] The institutional consequences of this fact have been the focus of the institutionalist literature on economic development.[72] Development programs involving technological transfer from advanced to less-developed economies, in order to be successful, must anticipate the "progressive" institutional changes that will be required to accommodate the new technology; otherwise ceremonial encapsulation will significantly diminish the culture's ability to adopt and diffuse the technology.[73]

The capacity for understanding and adaptation. The ability of the members of the community to understand and adapt to the changes in habits of thought and behavior entailed by technological innovations affects the time rate of both the adoption and diffusion of the innovations. There must be some social mechanism to facilitate the changing of habits of thought if "progressive" institutional change is to occur. Veblen's analysis of the impact of the "discipline of the machine" on the institutional structure was premised on the fact that a broad cross-section of the population came into contact with machine technology on a daily basis. The workplace served as a "school of hard knocks" so to speak. Contemporary institutional economists lay greater stress on the educational system of the culture as the most important social mechanism performing this function. But, as the earlier discussion of Dugger's theory of corporate hegemony revealed, it is clear that the educational system can be so organized as to inhibit rather than enhance "progressive" institutional change. If it is organized along invidious lines that reflect the existing occupational structure, it will simply reinforce the status quo and contribute to increasingly sophisticated strategies for the ceremonial encapsulation of the knowledge fund. If it is to contribute to the community's capacity for understanding of and adaptation to advances in the knowledge fund, the educational system must be organized for that purpose. Baldwin Ranson states the matter plainly.

> Educational planners can promote economic progress by providing every-one with the skills necessary to master the best technology. That planning objective is not dictated by any occupational structure, but rather by the nature of technological progress: the more the community knows, the more it can learn. Transmitting the ability to adapt to evolving technologi-cal opportunities will maximize economic progress as well as educational excellence, not as measured by competitive superiority of one group over another, but by the growing potential for economic and social wellbeing of the entire community.[74]

In sum, the time rate of "progressive" institutional change is bounded by the community's capacity to learn the adaptive skills necessary to absorb technological innovation.

The principle of minimal dislocation. The principle of minimal dis-location is critical to an understanding of both the direction and rate of "progressive" institutional change.[75] The principle states that while technological change always involves dislocation in the institutional structure, the interdependence of the institutional structure is such that "progressive" institutional change is possible only if it involves a mini-mal dislocation of the behavioral patterns of the community. Techno-logical innovation in the context of "progressive" institutional change always involves the displacement of ceremonial patterns of behavior, and it may also involve the displacement of outmoded technology. Such dislocation of the institutional structure is inherent in the process. But those patterns of behavior that are displaced by the technological innovation are interlinked with other patterns of behavior (both cere-monial and instrumental) throughout the institutional structure of the society. As the earlier analysis of behavioral patterns indicated, the va-riety of forms that behavioral patterns can take introduce considerable complexity into the institutional structure. Ceremonially warranted patterns of behavior may contain instrumental behavior as well as cere-monial behavior.[76] Thus care must be taken not to displace ceremonial practices that encapsulate instrumental activities vital to the problem-solving processes of the community.

To illustrate the argument, recall the case of canoe-building in the

Trobriand culture. The division of labor within the culture as a whole that regulated not only the tasks of the craftsmen in building the canoe but also the correlation of canoe-building with other activities of the culture was ceremonially encapsulated by a system of magic and ritual. A "progressive" institutional change that would free the division of labor in canoe-building from magic and ritual, but would not somehow provide for the reintegration of canoe-building with other activities of the community still under the rule of magic and ritual, would entail a maximum dislocation of the institutional structure. The attempt to introduce an instrumentally warranted division of labor in one part of the culture would disrupt the instrumentally vital (but ceremonially encapsulated) division of labor on a culture-wide basis. It is highly unlikely that any community (scientifically primitive or advanced) would knowingly undertake institutional changes that entail a maximal dislocation of the institutional structure, but this does not preclude the possibility that errors in judgment or lack of knowledge could lead to maximal dislocation. Thus the principle of minimal dislocation provides insight into the problems that must be addressed in any form of social or economic planning.[77]

The Discretionary Character of Institutional Change

Marc Tool describes "progressive" institutional change as change that "provides for the continuity of human life and the noninvidious recreation of community through the instrumental use of knowledge."[78] This language is descriptively accurate of the process in which ceremonially warranted patterns of behavior are displaced by instrumentally warranted patterns of behavior under conditions of minimal dislocation. It is the institutionalist view that this is *in fact* what happens when the community alters its behavior to accommodate the use of existing knowledge. But it is also clear that Tool's language states a social value principle that is applicable to the formulation of social policy. It provides a criterion for selecting among alternative institutional arrangements when the purpose is to achieve genuine progress in the community's problem-solving processes. Thus the theory of institutional change presented here achieves a dual purpose: it provides an explanation of the process of institutional change while at the same time it reveals the social value criterion most appropriate to the planning of the process.

It would not be historically accurate to suggest that all institutional changes result from the conscious formulation of social policy, and it has not been the author's intention to make such an argument. What has been argued is that the evolution of a culture results from the choices made to adopt or not to adopt the technological innovations. The intentional choice to improve the instrumental efficiency of the community through the adoption of a technological innovation does not necessarily involve the intention to throw over some aspect of the ceremonial practices of the culture. The displacement of ceremonially warranted patterns of behavior by instrumentally warranted patterns of behavior is a consequence of the extension of instrumental valuing in the correlation of behavior. The "progressive" institutional changes that have brought modern cultures to their present stage of development may have appeared to have been quite unremarkable at the time of their occurrence. This is most likely to be true of the process of technological diffusion wherein the adaptation to new technology requires incremental adjustments in the habits of thought and behavior over a broad cross-section of the community. Nevertheless, no matter how subtle the process, it involves the making of choices, and these choices define the evolutionary continuum of the culture.

A conscious awareness of the nature of the choices made in the process of social evolution is a precondition to the planning of that process. By revealing the nature of these choices, the institutionalist theory of institutional change demonstrates that social evolution is subject to the discretionary control of mankind. It is this realization that informs the institutionalist approach to public policy formation. In the institutionalist view, social problems arise when the institutional structure is unable to accommodate the noninvidious application of instrumentally warranted knowledge to the support of the life processes of the community. The solutions to social problems take the form of "progressive" institutional changes that will alter those ceremonially warranted patterns of behavior that thwart the extension of instrumental valuing in the problem-solving processes.

Tool argues that the social value principle that emerges in this theory of institutional change has the greatest potential for successful application within a democracy polity.[79] Those habits of thought that make instrumental valuing possible are most likely to be nurtured in a system of democratic self-governance.[80] He cites three reasons for this affinity: (1) because democracy "encourages the development of distinctively human potentialities for creative and reflective use of the mind"; (2) because it "engenders an experimental approach to social change"; and (3) because "self-rule generates consequences that must be endured, a democratic public becomes increasingly self-conscious about the character of the value theory it employs."[81] As Ayres put it, "The essence of democracy is not the fact of majority rule, but rather the process by which majorities are formed."[82] For the institutionalist, the process by which majorities of a democracy are formed is identical with the process of inquiry upon which instrumental valuing depends. Thus, democracy is the political process most likely to nurture the conscious exercise of human discretion over the evolution of the society.

Notes

1. One of the earliest classics in the field is Charles H. Cooley's *Human Nature and the Social Order* (New York: Schocken Books, 1964 [1902]).
2. For an authoritative statement of the institutionalist position on the "nature versus nurture" debate, see William M. Dugger, "Sociobiology: A Critical Introduction to E. O. Wilson's Evolutionary Paradigm," *Social Science Quarterly* 62 (June 1981): 221–33.
3. This theme is developed most fully by Marc R. Tool in *The Discretionary Economy: A Normative Theory of Political Economy* (Santa Monica: Goodyear Publishing Co., 1979).
4. The notation used here for behavioral patterns was first developed by the author in "An Exploration of the Structural Characteristics of a Veblen-Ayres-Foster Defined Institutional Domain," *Journal of Economic Issues* 17 (March 1983): 35–66.
5. See John Dewey, *Reconstruction of Philosophy,* enlarged edition (Boston: Beacon Press, 1948 [1920]): and John Dewey, *Theory of Valuation* (Chicago: University of Chicago Press, 1939). See also, Jacob Bronowski, *Science and Human Values,* revised edition (New York: Harper & Row, 1965).
6. These matters have been discussed at greater length by the author in "The Normative Implications of Institutional Analysis," *Economic Forum* 12 (Winter, 1981–82): 9–29.
7. Space constraints do not permit a detailed review of this literature in this essay. For a systematic treatment of the institutionalist approach to value theory see Steven Hickerson's "Instrumental Valuation: The Normative Compass of Institutional Economics" in this volume.
8. H. H. Liebhafsky, *The Nature of Price Theory,* revised edition (Homewood: Dorsey Press, 1968), p. 523.
9. Nicholas Georgescu-Roegen, *The Entropy Law and the Economic Process* (Cambridge: Harvard University Press, 1971), p. 14.
10. Clarence E. Ayres, *Toward a Reasonable Society* (Austin: University of Texas Press, 1971), p. 241.
11. It is interesting to note that Veblen treated "conspicuous consumption" as dialectical behavior. Accordingly, he says, "an article may be useful and wasteful both, and its utility to the consumer may be made up of use and

waste in the most varying proportions. . . . It would be hazardous to assert that a useful purpose is ever absent from the utility of any article or of any service, however obviously its prime purpose and chief element is conspicuous waste." Thorstein Veblen, *The Theory of the Leisure Class* (New York: Augustus M. Kelley, 1975 [1899]), pp. 100–101.

12. See Bush, "An Exploration of the Structural Characteristics," pp. 39–42.
13. Bronislaw Malinowski, *Argonauts of the Western Pacific* (New York: E.P. Dutton, 1950 [1922]). See especially Chap. 5, "The Ceremonial Building of a Waga."
14. Ibid., p. 124.
15. Ibid., p. 115.
16. Ibid., p. 116.
17. This discussion of Malinowski's commentary should not be misinterpreted. It is not at all clear that Malinowski would have agreed with the treatment of his observations set forth here. See Clarence E. Ayres's remarks on Malinowski's analysis of the function of magic in the Trobriand culture in Ayres, *Toward a Reasonable Society*, p. 133.
18. Marc R. Tool provides an extensive analysis of the ceremonial functions of ideology in *The Discretionary Economy;* see especially: pp. 26–34, and pp. 275–78.
19. Clarence E. Ayres, *The Theory of Economic Progress* (Chapel Hill: University of North Carolina Press, 1944), pp. 177–202.
20. Ayres, *Toward a Reasonable Society*, p. 31.
21. Ayres, *The Theory of Economic Progress*, pp. 177–78.
22. A rigorous formulation of the index of ceremonial dominance appears in Bush, "An Exploration of the Structural Characteristics," pp. 48–51.
23. For example, see the exchange of notes between F. Gregory Hayden and Thomas R. DeGregori in the *Journal of Economic Issues* 14 (March 1980): 221–25. See also Warren Samuels, "Technology *vis-a-vis* Institutions in the *JEI:* A Suggested Interpretation," *Journal of Economic Issues* 11 (December 1977): 867–95; and David Hamilton, "Technology and Institutions are Neither," *Journal of Economic Issues* 20 (June 1986): 525–32.
24. Thorstein Veblen, "Why is Economics Not an Evolutionary Science," *The Place of Science in Modern Civilisation* (New York: The Viking Press, 1942 [1919]), p. 71–72.
25. Ayres, *Toward a Reasonable Society*, p. 277.
26. Ibid.
27. See Thorstein Veblen, "The Evolution of the Scientific Point of View," *The Place of Science in Modern Civilisation* (New York: Viking Press, 1942 [1919]), pp. 32–55.
28. Ayres, *Toward a Reasonable Society*, p. 278.
29. Anne Mayhew, "Ayresian Technology, Technological Reasoning, and Doomsday," *Journal of Economic Issues* 15 (June 1981), pp. 513–20.
30. Ibid.
31. Ibid., p. 514. The Liebhafsky observation was contained in a letter he had written to Warren Samuels and which Samuels quoted in his article, "Technology vis-a-vis Institutions." The Liebhafsky quotation appears on p. 887 of the Samuels article.
32. The term "holism" was first used in reference to institutional economics

by Allan G. Gruchy in *Modern Economic Thought: The American Contribution* (New York: Prentice-Hall, 1947). An excellent discussion of "holistic" methodology in institutional economics is to be found in Yngve Ramstad, "A Pragmatist's Quest for Holistic Knowledge: The Scientific Methodology of John R. Commons," *Journal of Economic Issues* 20 (December 1986): 1067–1105. In a passing remark, Ramstad indicates that the kind of approach the present author took in "An Exploration of the Structural Characteristics," (and, by extension, in this article) is incompatible with the "holistic" methodology. The author disagrees with Ramstad on this point, but this is not the place to argue the issue.

33. U.S. Congress, Joint Economic Committee, *Special Study on Economic Change*, Hearings, 95th Congress, 2d Session, June 8, 9, 13 and 14, 1978, (Washington: U.S. Government Printing Office), p. 517.

34. For some representative samples of the institutionalist view of the concept of capital, see: Thorstein Veblen, "On the Nature of Capital" in *The Place of Science in Modern Civilisation* (New York: Viking Press, 1942 [1919]), pp. 324–86; Louis J. Junker, "Capital Accumulation, Saving-Centered Theory, and Economic Development," *Journal of Economic Issues* 1 (June 1967): 25–43; Baldwin Ranson, "The Unrecognized Revolution in the Theory of Capital Formation," *Journal of Economic Issues* 17 (December 1983): 901–13; and William Dugger, "Capital Accumulation and Technological Progress," *Journal of Economic Issues* 18 (September 1984): 799–823.

35. Thorstein Veblen, "Why is Economics Not an Evolutionary Science?", in *The Place of Science in Modern Civilisation*, p. 75. See also W. F. Ogburn, *On Culture and Social Change* (Chicago: University of Chicago Press, 1964), p. 25; and Louis J. Junker, "Capital Accumulation, Savings-Centered Theory and Economic Development," p. 33. In footnote 33, on page 33, Junker provides a useful list of references on the notion of the exponential increase in the knowledge fund.

36. William F. Ogburn, *Social Change* (New York: The Viking Press, 1950 [1922]), pp. 103–42. See also, Thomas R. DeGregori, *A Theory of Technology* (Ames: The Iowa State University Press, 1985), p. 36.

37. Tool, *The Discretionary Economy*, p. 39. A smooth, continuous exponential function, such as that used in Tool's illustration, is an oversimplification, as he would readily admit. Most institutionalists would agree that in real time there can be discontinuities and "quantum leaps" in the rate of growth that require the qualification that the function is only a rough approximation of an exponential curve. This qualification does not, however, reach to the notion of "developmental continuity" discussed in the following paragraphs.

38. Ayres, *Toward a Reasonable Society*, pp. 112–13. Ogburn also stressed the combinatorial aspect of the growth of technology and cultural traits; see Ogburn, *On Cultural and Social Change*, pp. 25–26.

39. Nicholas Georgescu-Roegen, *The Entropy Law and the Economic Process* (Cambridge: Harvard University Press, 1971), p. 13.

40. This attribution of the use of the term "developmental continuity" to Foster is based on the author's recollection of Foster's lectures at the University of Denver. The recollection is corroborated by Baldwin Ranson's

reference to Foster's use of the term in his review of Marc Tool's *The Discretionary Economy,* which appeared in the *Journal of Economic Issues* 14 (September 1980), p. 764. Another student of Foster's, the late Louis J. Junker, commented extensively on the principle of continuity in his article entitled "Instrumentalism, the Principle of Continuity and the Life Process," *American Journal of Economics and Sociology* 40 (October 1981): 381–400.

41. This discussion of the partitioning of "institutional space" is based on a mathematical modelling of these relationships developed by the author in "A Veblen-Ayres Model of Institutional Change: A Provisional Formulation," a paper presented at the Annual Meetings of the Western Economic Association, Anaheim, California, 21 June 1977.

42. The language, "the triumph of imbecile institutions over life and culture" is, of course, Veblen's ringing phrase. See Thorstein Veblen, *The Instinct of Workmanship* (New York: Augustus M. Kelley, 1964 [1914]), p. 25.

43. The term "ceremonial encapsulation" has only recently been introduced into the institutionalist literature. The author and the late Louis J. Junker, unbeknown to one another, began using the term almost simultaneously in their teaching and writing. The author's first effort to define the term rigorously appeared in "A Veblen-Ayres Model of Institutional Change: A Provisional Formulation." The author presented an application of its use in "The Ceremonial Encapsulation of Capital Formulation in the American Economy," a paper presented to the Western Social Science Association, Lake Tahoe, Nevada, 27 April 1979, and extended the rigorous treatment of the concept in "An Exploration of the Structural Characteristics," pp. 35–66. For Louis J. Junker's theoretical formulation of the concept, see: "The Ceremonial-Instrumental Dichotomy in Institutional Analysis: The Nature, Scope, and Radical Implications of the Conflicting Systems," *American Journal of Economics and Sociology* 41 (April, 1982): 141–50; and "The Conflict Between the Scientific-Technological Process and Malignant Ceremonialism," *American Journal of Economics and Sociology* 42 (July, 1983): 341–52. The dates of these articles do not accurately reflect the time frame in which Junker began using the term since both were published several years after the papers on which they are based were presented to various professional societies. Junker's most detailed application of the concept of ceremonial encapsulation to a specific problem area is to be found in his "Nutrition and Economy: Some Observations on Diet and Disease in the American Food Power System," *Review of Institutional Thought* 2 (December 1982): 27–58. The author has commented on the origin of the concept and Louis Junker's pioneering application of it in an article entitled "On the Concept of Ceremonial Encapsulation," *Review of Institutional Thought* 3 (December 1986): forthcoming. Whether the term "ceremonial encapsulation" is merely a new way of referring to well-established concepts in the institutionalist literature or, for better or worse, an extension of institutionalist analysis into new intellectual territory is a matter that must yet be settled. For two important contributions to the deliberations on this point, see William T. Waller, Jr., "The Evolution of the Veblenian Dichotomy: Veblen, Hamilton, Ayres, and Foster," *Journal of Economic Issues* 16 (September 1982): 757–71; and Hans E. Jensen's article on the "Theory of Human Nature" in this volume, pp. 1039–73.

44. A special case of this kind of "slippage" is discussed as the "add on" process in Bush, "An Exploration of the Structural Characteristics," pp. 59–61.
45. Ayres, *Toward a Reasonable Society,* pp. 30, 137, and 233.
46. See Ogburn, *On Cultural and Social Change,* pp. 200–213. The similarities between the works of Veblen and Ogburn have been widely noted, and the notion of the cultural lag is often attributed to Veblen. He did not, of course, use the term. Ogburn denied that his formulation of the concept was influenced by Veblen. There are some fundamental differences between the Veblen-Ayres approach and Ogburn's. Whereas Veblen and Ayres postulate technological innovation as the dynamic factor generating the cultural changes to which there is a lagged cultural response, Ogburn argued that changes in those aspects of culture identified by Veblen and Ayres as "ceremonial" could be the dynamic cause of a lagged cultural response. Nevertheless, Ogburn's comments on this point do not appear to offer a serious challenge to the arguments made by Veblen and Ayres. Virtually all of Ogburn's own studies treat technology as the "independent variable"; and in those instances where he would appear to make ceremonial practices the independent variable, a case can be made that he failed to probe far enough along the chain of causal events to discover the technological innovation that produced the change in the ceremonial practices. As will be demonstrated in the following paragraphs, "regressive" institutional changes prompted by purely ceremonial considerations force the community into Sector III, and this results in a loss of instrumental efficiency. This line of analysis directly contradicts Ogburn's speculations. See William F. Ogburn, *On Culture and Social Change: Selected Papers,* ed. Otis D. Duncan (Chicago: The University of Chicago Press, 1964), p. 87.
47. This discussion of the three types of ceremonial encapsulation is based on the author's presidential address to the Association for Institutional Thought entitled "On the Concept of Ceremonial Encapsulation" (Albuquerque, New Mexico, 29 April 1983), a revised version of which appears in *The Review of Institutional Thought* 3 (December 1986): forthcoming.
48. Thorstein Veblen, *Imperial Germany and the Industrial Revolution* (New York: Augustus M. Kelley, 1964 [1915]), p. 25.
49. Ogburn, *Social Change,* pp. 213–36.
50. Veblen developed this theme originally in "Industrial and Pecuniary Employments," *Publications of the American Economic Association* 2 (1901): 190–235, reprinted in *The Place of Science in Modern Civilisation,* pp. 279–323; and expanded upon it later in *The Theory of Business Enterprise* (Clifton, N.J.: Augustus M. Kelley, 1975 [1904]).
51. F. Gregory Hayden, "A Geobased National Agricultural Policy for Rural Community Enhancement, Environmental Vitality, and Income Stabilization," *Journal of Economic Issues* 18 (March 1984): 181–221.
52. Junker, "Nutrition and Economy," p. 50.
53. It should be noted that while Dugger does not employ the term "ceremonial encapsulation" in his discussion of corporate hegemony, there can be no question that the term applies to his analysis. See William M. Dugger, *An Alternative to Economic Retrenchment,* (New York: Petrocelli Books, Inc., 1984). This point is clearly established by William T. Waller, Jr. in "Ceremonial Encapsulation and Corporate Cultural Hegemony," *Journal of Economic Issues* 21 (March 1987): 321–28.

54. Dugger, *An Alternative to Economic Retrenchment*, p. 57.
55. Ibid., pp. 135–42.
56. Thorstein Veblen, *The Higher Learning in America: A Memorandum on the Conduct of Universities by Business Men* (New York: Augustus M. Kelley, 1965 [1918]). This book is often dismissed by serious scholars and university administrators alike as Veblen's angry "letter to the editor" about those who made his life so miserable in academia. Yet the book is a systematic piece of institutional analysis and may be more relevant to institutions of higher learning today than when Veblen wrote it. For an excellent institutionalist commentary on the role of education in progressive institutional change, see Baldwin Ranson, "Planning Education for Economic Progress: Distinguishing Occupational Demand from Technological Possibilities," *Journal of Economic Issues* 20 (December 1986): 1053–65.
57. John R. Munkirs, *The Transformation of American Capitalism* (Armonk, N.Y.: M.E. Sharpe, 1985), p. 179.
58. Thorstein Veblen, *The Nature of the Peace and the Terms of Its Perpetuation* (New York: Augustus M. Kelley, 1964 [1917]).
59. For an authoritative account of Lysenkoism, see David Joravsky, *The Lysenko Affair* (Cambridge: Harvard University Press, 1970).
60. *Los Angeles Times*, 21 October 1980, Part I, p. 3.
61. Veblen, *The Instinct of Workmanship*, p. 25.
62. As Ayres put it: "the progressive advance of technology means a similarly cumulative diminution of the extent and importance in the affairs of the community of superstition and ceremonial investiture." *The Theory of Economic Progress*, p. 245; see also page 201 where he refers to the process as the "displacement of ceremonial by technological functions." Ayres did not specify the requirement of a given fund of knowledge. This is an analytical refinement that has been developed by the author. Putting the matter of "progressive" institutional change in the context of problem solving, Marc Tool states that "The resolution of a problem consists of the reduction or removal of ceremonial behavior and attitudes and the creation or extension of instrumental behavior and attitudes." See Tool, "A Social Value Theory in Neoinstitutional Economics," *Journal of Economic Issues* 11 (December 1977): 823–46 at p. 837; this essay is reprinted in Tool, *Essay in Social Value Theory: A Neoinstitutionalist Contribution* (Armonk, N.Y.: M.E. Sharpe, 1986), pp. 33–44; the quotation appears on page 47.
63. Veblen discusses the process of "cumulative causation" throughout his works, but perhaps the most pertinent of his remarks on the subject for present purposes is to be found in *The Place of Science in Modern Civilisation*, pages 74–75.
64. Veblen, *The Theory of Business Enterprise*, p. 310.
65. Ibid., p. 311.
66. Veblen, *Imperial Germany and the Industrial Revolution*, p. 100. The question as to whether Veblen, in giving this account of institutional change, failed to distinguish adequately between what has been called "functional" rationality and "substantial" rationality has been given careful consideration by Rick Tilman in his masterful study of C. Wright Mills. See Rick Tilman, *C. Wright Mills: A Native Radical and His American Intellectual Roots* (University Park: Pennsylvania State University Press, 1984), pp. 97–98.

67. Ayres, *The Theory of Economic Progress,* pp. 137 ff.
68. In one of his most remarkable essays, Veblen described in some detail the mental processes involved in achieving the "sensed awareness" discussed here. In "The Intellectual Pre-eminence of Jews in Modern Europe," Veblen argues that the cultural alienation of the European Jew gave rise to a "skeptical animus" among Jewish intellectuals that emancipated them from the ceremonial practices of both the Christian culture and their own traditional heritage. Being thus released from the "dead hand of conventional finality," they were free to explore truly innovative approaches in all of the arts and sciences. The intellectual transformation of the European Jew was, for Veblen, a metaphor for the emergence of the scientific habit of thought. See "The Intellectual Pre-eminence of Jews in Modern Europe," in *Essays in Our Changing Order,* ed. Leon Ardzrooni (New York: Augustus M. Kelley, 1964 [1934]), pp. 219–31. The essay originally appeared in *The Political Science Quarterly* 34 (March 1919): 33–42.
69. Milton D. Lower, "The Industrial Economy and International Price Shocks," *Journal of Economic Issues* 20 (June 1986): 297–312, at p. 311.
70. These three limiting conditions of "progressive" institutional change were discussed by Marc Tool in *The Discretionary Economy,* pp. 172–76. They were originally formulated by J. Fagg Foster and presented in his lectures at the University of Denver in the late 1940s and early 1950s. A severely truncated version of his treatment of them appears in Foster, "Syllabus for Problems of Modern Society: The Theory of Institutional Adjustment," *Journal of Economic Issues* 15 (December 1981): 929–35.
71. "Cultural borrowing" is the term Veblen used to identify this phenomenon in *Imperial Germany;* see especially pp. 19–43.
72. See, for example, Louis J. Junker, "Capital Accumulation, Savings-Centered Theory, and Economic Development," pp. 25–43; and Philip A. Klein, "An Institutionalist View of Development Economics," *Journal of Economic Issues* 11 (December 1977): 785–807.
73. While David Seckler may not regard himself as an institutionalist, he has provided solid evidence of the correctness of the institutional position on this point in his article entitled "Institutionalism and Agricultural Development in India," *Journal of Economic Issues* 20 (December 1986): 1011–1027.
74. Baldwin Ranson, "Planning Education for Economic Progress," p. 1063.
75. While there can be no question that J. Fagg Foster formulated this principle, it is clear that Clarence Ayres had an intuitive grasp of it, as indicated by the following statement: "It is also true that the sudden nullification of the ceremonial system of any community would produce a grievous state of disorganization." See Ayres, *Toward a Reasonable Society,* p. 138.
76. To reiterate the point by way of an additional example, it should be recalled that Veblen found a "non-invidious residue" even in the ceremonial labyrinth of organized religion. He commented favorably on the instrumentally warranted" sense of communion with the environment, or with the generic life process—as well as the impulse of charity or of sociability," which he found to be encapsulated in religious life. See Veblen, *The Theory of the Leisure Class,* p. 334.
77. A matter of some importance in any discussion of "minimal dislocation" is the environmental impact of the technological innovations contemplated in "progressive" institutional change. The principle of minimal dis-

location requires that any technology be compatible with the sustainability of the evolution of the ecosystem. This is a point that may not have been given sufficient attention by institutionalists in the past. Space limitations preclude any discussion of this vital issue. A most valuable discussion of this matter is to be found in James A. Swaney, "A Coevolutionary Model of Structural Change," *Journal of Economic Issues* 20 (June 1986): 393–400. The author's only quibble with this article has to do with Swaney's misapplication of the terms "ceremonial" and "instrumental" in his discussion of ecosystem feedbacks.

78. Tool, *The Discretionary Economy*, p. 293.
79. Tool, *The Discretionary Economy;* see, in particular, pp. 199–213, and pp. 315–36. See also his essay entitled "The Neoinstitutionalist Perspective in Political Economy," in Tool, *Essays in Social Value Theory*, pp. 3–30.
80. This theme runs throughout the institutionalist literature. It reflects the heavy influence of John Dewey's philosophy on American Institutionalism. Clarence Ayres viewed democracy as the system of governance most compatible with the emergence of the scientific point of view. See Ayres, *Toward a Reasonable Society*, pp. 281–94. The thesis was advanced most persuasively by the mathematician and philosopher Jacob Bronowski in his elegant little book *Science and Human Values*. While Bronowski was not an institutionalist, his philosophical writings have been most enthusiastically embraced by them.
81. Tool, *Essays in Social Value Theory*, pp. 25–26.
82. Ayres, *Toward a Reasonable Society*, p. 283.

Instrumental Valuation:
The Normative Compass of Institutional Economics

Steven R. Hickerson

Nobel laureate Gunnar Myrdal is, perhaps, the most widely known living economist who continues to make the case and the plea for the explicit articulation of value premises in the practice of social and economic science. "Valuations," he states, "are always with us. Disinterested research there has never been and can never be. . . . Our valuations determine our approach to a problem, the definition of concepts, the choice of models, the selection of observations and, . . . in fact, the whole pursuit of study from the begining to the end."[1]

Institutional economists accept this position and, generally, make every effort to respond to this plea. The value premises and the theory of value that institutionalists articulate and apply differs sharply, however, from the implicit premises of most other schools of economic thought. In keeping with the theme of this symposium, the primary purpose of this essay is to present the valuational foundations of institutional economics as clearly and cogently as possible. The objective is not to make invidious distinctions or comparisons with other premises or theories of value; nor is it to launch further institutionalist attacks on orthodox theory. Nonetheless, some comparison is necessary and conducive to the objectives at hand. Accordingly, this essay proceeds through discussion of the following three areas.

The author would like to thank Editor Marc Tool, Paul D. Bush, Andrew Larkin, and Nancy Fontana for helpful suggestions and comments in the preparation of this article. They are all absolved of responsibility for any remaining deficiencies.

First, the "value neutral" stance of orthodox economics is briefly examined. This standard of objectivity requires that the economist treat the object of inquiry as if it were so many molecules, atoms, or distant gaseous clouds of no "personal" interest to the investigator. Yet, following Werner Heisenberg, even the physicists now recognize that such scientific detachment is an impossibility. Here we will support the view that "value impregnation" is inevitable in economics.

Second, the institutionalist claim that an alternative path for economics is both possible and necessary is discussed. To the extent that economics, or any social knowledge for that matter, lays claim to purposefulness and policy relevance, valuative criteria and valuative discourse must coexist and interrelate with the theoretical and empirical facets of inquiry. Theory building and empiricism uninformed by explicitly articulated value premises are like loaded guns; we know they are very powerful but we know not where to aim them.

This question of aim leads to the third and most important area of consideration. The normative compass that guides institutionalists in their work is the instrumentalist theory of value that emerged through the works of philosophers William James, Charles Peirce and, most notably, John Dewey. It has received further extension, clarification, and application in the works of institutional economists from Thorstein Veblen and John R. Commons up to and including the present generation. Although some brief review of these latter contributions will be helpful, lengthy recapitulation is not the objective here. We seek, rather, to present an integrative contemporary formulation that ties together various dimensions of instrumental value theory. Accordingly, this portion of the essay addresses the following areas: (1) the cultural origins of value, (2) the instrumental value principle itself and its corollary rejection of the notion of a dichotomous relation between "the positive" and "the normative," and (3) the nature of the criteria and method of valuing that emerge from these principles, and that provide institutionalists their sense of purpose and direction. This discussion is highlighted through a brief comparison of the instrumentalist and the orthodox approaches to the problem of waste.

On the Standard of Objectivity in Economics

Our profession has inherited a deep-seated concern with attaining scientific stature and with maintaining the standard of scientific inquiry and objectivity. One needs only to consider the countless pages of print devoted to the discussion of economic methodology to appreciate the centrality of this preoccupation. But an inspection of the content of these pages reveals the contentious relationship between those who argue that economics is value neutral, at least in its theoretical guise, and those, such as Myrdal, who argue that value impregnation is an inevitability that must be squarely confronted in the work of the economist. A rehearsal of the argument in favor of the former position would be tedious and probably redundant to most readers. This is not our purpose.[2] We seek, rather, to support the view that value impregnation is, in fact, inevitable.

In defense of orthodox economists' claim to value neutrality, Professor Kurt Klappholz argues that, "Those who insist on inevitable 'value-impregnation' are often concerned to show the relevance of 'values' to economic research and policy discussion. This is true—indeed trivially true, since values are relevant to all human activities—but in no way affects the 'orthodox' claim of logical ethical neutrality."[3] He then proceeds to examine some of the arguments that have been made in favor of the value impregnation thesis, concluding that they can be "easily refuted." Since Klappholz's arguments are generally representative of the neoclassical position, I wish to provide here a critical examination of his supposed refutations. That is, to refute his "refutations."

Klappholz's first argument addresses Myrdal's well-known observation that the very formation of the questions to be asked about economic and social systems implies that the questioner is under the influence of some conception of *ought;* the questioner is influenced by values. Klappholz grants this, but argues that it does not affect the *logical* neutrality of economics. As he sees it, this may be true with respect to neutrality in some wider sense, such as that implied by statements like "economics is neutral as between ends"; but he also believes that "this sort of neutrality has nothing to do with logical neutrality."[4] His point is that if, as David Hume believed, a normative "ought" cannot be deduced from a descriptive "is"; and if, as most economists believe, theoretical economics consists wholly of descriptive statements, then economics is necessarily value free. The issue is whether or not the statements of economics, even in its positivistic and tautological theoretical guise, are genuinely descriptive, and if that means that they are therefore value neutral. Do the questions asked impregnate the *logic* of economic theory with implicit normative references?

The answer to this question is yes. When we ask such questions as "What conditions or practices facilitate efficiency or growth?" the obvious value referent is that these outcomes are "good," they are "desirable," they are an "ought." And, though we may or may not support these particular valuations, the fact remains that they are *normative* judgments. This implicit valuational legacy of orthodox economics rests on utilitarian foundations.[5]

But the implicit normative coloration does not stop there. It is deeply embedded in the *logic* of the inferences that follow. The emphasis on efficiency and the mode of its evaluation, for example, intrinsically values self-serving individualized choice while simultaneously devaluing collective choice and public goals.[6] The emphasis on efficiency permeates distribution theory as well. Orthodox economists conceive of this matter in terms of market measured productivity and compensatory factor pricing. The initial distribution of entitlements, power, and wealth is uncritically taken to be a reflection of past productivity. Yet, as Warren Samuels has demonstrated, this approach is replete with implicit antecedent valuations about the character of social order. In accepting market efficiency as the sole criterion in problem solving, orthodox economists implicitly preselect determinate solutions to the problems they chose to address. These "solutions" are founded, thus, in selective but implicit premises regarding whose interests count and whose do not.[7] Thus the whole train of logic beginning with the initial valuation of efficiency is value impregnated. Efficiency is defined with reference to the relation of input prices to output prices, while both these sets of prices are themselves reflections of the status quo distribution of entitlements and rights. Hence "economic solutions" are prechanneled by implicit antecedent value premises in favor of the status quo.[8]

Professor Klappholz's second argument is a presumed refutation of the hypothesis that, "Just as the selection of questions may be ideologically biased, so also . . . may be what we accept as a 'true' answer to these questions."[9] He concludes, however, that this is not a refutation of the orthodox position because, "the motives for accepting a statement as true or false can in no way affect its logical status (which depends on its having truth value, not on its being true)."[10]

This point turns on the meaning of the term "truth value," and that, presumably, turns on the potential for falsification. Thus statements with "truth value" might be of two types. Let us suppose that "type *A*" truth value statements take the form "if *P*, then *Q*," and that "type *B*" statements take the form "*P* is". Type *A* statements, then, are theoretical and deductive; type *B* statements are empirical. Both types of statements are potentially falsifiable, yet neither is as value neutral as Klappholz would have us believe.

Type *A* statements may become value impregnated in at least three ways.[11] First, they are founded in a particular vision of the economy and, thus, retain the ethics of that vision. It is a vision that treats the evermore efficient production of an everlarger output as the highest ideal. The objectivist truth criterion then withholds the blessing of scientific admissibility from all questions and methods not formulated in the service of this ideal. Secondly, the objectivity standard itself disguises the relationship between economic theory and the social consciousness that forms the values that are taken as givens. "[orthodox economics] was born as, and it remains an antistate polemic, an apologia for property as the bastion of liberty in the free market. Hence its preservation is linked to the preservation of the structure of property power. It is kept intact as an instrument for keeping intact vested interests and ongoing forms of social organization."[12] Finally, as economics has become increasingly technical (and, thus, as its standards of scientific admissibility have become correspondingly technocratic), it has become wedded to a view of reality that normatively endorses an evermore technocratic future.

Cartesian in its origins, orthodox economic thinking leans heavily on fictive mental constructs and a mechanistic *modus operandi* linking each fiction to the next. Inherent in this process has been a tendency for technique to perfect itself, often at the expense of content.[13] Orthodox economists, thus, have become the schizophrenic prisoners of their own conceptual apparatus. As citizens they espouse democratic self determination. Yet, as "scientists" they presume to exclude themselves from participating in the democratic dialogue concerning values and goals. Indeed, their very efforts to cast economic problems in purely technical terms fosters an environment in which values are seen as irrelevant. The result is decidedly undemocratic in its implicit prescription that authority be rendered unto technical specialists.[14]

Type *B* statements, empirical ones, appear to be even richer in "truth value" and objectivity, but they are no less value impregnated for it. Werner Heisenberg's well-known principle of indeterminacy indicates that observer and observed are not ontologically distinct. That is, the very act of observation of a phenomenon affects that which is observed. Modern physicists came to recognize that the human mind and the object of its study can no longer be regarded as ontologically separate the way Descartes would have wished it to be.[15] The principle holds with even greater force in economics where the phenomena studied are themselves the mere shadows of imagery and ideology projected by the mind's light.

One is told that all market relationships perpetually tend to a point of long run equilibrium; or that the rich have a higher propensity to save; or that

population increases as a function of higher-than-subsistence wages and
that man-hour productivity declines as a function of population increase;
or that history is the story of class struggle; or that power corrupts and
absolute power corrupts absolutely. In no instance is an experiment conceivable that would, through failure in the prediction of specific event or
any specific set of events, definitely refute such statements as these.[16]

Professor Klappholz concedes the problem of experiment construction stating that, "economists often attempt to test theories which, as
they stand, simply are not testable."[17] He goes on to state that this does
not necessarily mean they are tautological but, rather, that they are metaphysical, and that metaphysics is irrelevant to the logical fact-value
problem. To the institutionalist, however, this is a false distinction.
John Dewey's "naturalistic metaphysics" looks to the context in which
all human experiences (including valuation) are connected. An ontological separation of fact and value would suggest that experience, science, and knowledge are irrelevant to value.[18] This position is
untenable in that human action and experience are all part of a common matrix. They are, at once, both existential and valuational. Contrary to the notion that metaphysical preconceptions are irrelevant to
the fact-value question, they are both a fact in that they exist, and they
are also a source of motivation invoking the process of valuation.[19]

A third contention with which Klappholz takes issue is the claim that
economics is normative because it employs emotive language and persuasive definitions. As he puts it, "the notions of 'emotive language'
and 'persuasive definitions' may be relevant from the point of view of
psychology and sociology. . . . But it is clear that these notions, which
hinge on the motives for, and psychological effects of, using certain
words are utterly irrelevant to the logical status of different propositions."[20] To this, the institutionalist would counter that it is not just
the words, their use, and their definitions that are at issue, but the way
in which the entire linguistic structure of economic discourse encodes
certain messages. "As human experience finds its way into the vocabulary and structure of the language, the latter orients the vision, predis-
poses the user to certain attitudes and behavior."[21] Lexical and syntatic
structure can both influence, and are influenced by, the values and ideologies of a society. "The heart of language," as John Dewey put it, "is
not 'expression' of something antecedent, much less expression of antecedent thought. It is communication; the establishment of cooperation
in an activity in which there are partners, and in which the activity of
each is modified and regulated by the partnership."[22]

Finally, Klappholz goes on to discuss two additional sources of value
impregnation, and dismisses each as refutable. The fourth one, only

touched on here, involves Lord Robbins's denial of the possibility of interpersonal utility comparisons. Robbins's point, which leads ultimately to the orthodox economists' rejection of cardinal utility theory and its replacement with ordinal indifference curves and axiomatic theory, was that since interpersonal comparisons cannot be tested or validated they are normative and have no place in "pure science".[23] Klappholz himself points out that Robbins's argument confuses value judgments with untestable statements, but our criticism is more substantial. The very concept of utility is itself sterile and circular, offering no guidance in any referent external to itself for social policy. The various ordinal conceptions that subsequently came to replace utility fare no better. Whether it is cardinal "wants" or ordinal "preference" that are taken to be given, the result remains the same. "What is . . . is an existing pattern of wants and tastes. Since the purpose of an enterprise economy is to facilitate the satisfaction of wants, orthodoxy effectively recommends that 'what is' be used as a standard or criteria for judging 'what ought to be.' "[24] Thus, orthodoxy's "positive" perception of "is" becomes also its normative, and status-quo biased, prescription of ought.

In his fifth denial of value impregnation, Klappholz draws attention to the familiar argument that the "economist *qua* economist" cannot give imperative policy advice in view of the means/ends dichotomy. His position is that "if an economist were furnished with his 'client's' utility function, which, together with the possibility function provided by the economist, made it possible to derive the 'appropriate' policy, the resulting advice would be value free."[25] But consider the actual task of the economist in this more closely. In practice, the economist's advice will not be "If you do X then Y will occur," but rather, "If you do X then the probability that Y will occur is Z percent." The point here is that the economist must decide what is an acceptable margin of error. That decision must, and properly should, turn on a value judgment concerning the consequences of being wrong.[26]

The institutionalist position, then, is that all of these alleged refutations of the value impregnation thesis are untenable. The questions asked, the answers given, the linguistic structure of the logic, and even the choice made in accepting or rejecting particular hypotheses are all value directed. An alternative path seems both possible and necessary.

The Need For An Alternative Path

The question of value is really much larger and more significant than this difference of opinion over the value impregnation thesis suggests.

Joan Robinson seems to have appreciated this when she wrote "to eliminate value judgments from the subject-matter of social science is to
eliminate the subject itself."[27] She was, of course, correct in this observation and, unfortunately, this is precisely what economists have attempted to do, most particularly in the last two centuries. A brief
discussion of why this has been so will help clarify the need for an alternative path.

Economics was born of the intellectual spirit of seventeenth-century
Cartesianism, an epistemological outlook that made a sharp distinction
between reason and sense perceptions. Reason, in the form of mathematical and geometrical relationships, was taken to be a far more reliable source of knowledge and understanding than were sensory
observation and experimentation. In Descartes's world, constructs con-
trived within the mind were thought to be a more accurate representation of the world outside the mind than observation of and experience
with that outside world.

This Cartesian epistemology, with its dichotomization of reason and
experience, contributed heavily to the rise of the positive/normative
dichotomy. The very idea of such a split would have seemed strange
to Adam Smith, who was consistently hortatory in his work. But possibly by the time of David Ricardo, and certainly by the time of Nassau
Senior and John Stuart Mill, the vehicle of Cartesianism significantly
imposed the epistemological necessity of the positive/normative dichotomy on economic and social thought. Our immediate objective is
to: (1) draw the distinction between the Cartesian dichotomy on the
one hand and the positive/normative dichotomy on the other, and (2)
explain the relationship between the two and, in so doing, verify the
foregoing assertion that the former dichotomy imposed the epistemological necessity of the latter for orthodox economics.

René Descartes is widely recognized as having set out the epistemology of "correct" thinking in the modern world. Before Descartes's
observation was the main means of acquiring knowledge, appearance
and essence were presumed to be one and the same and, consequently,
experience and sensory perceptions were thought to be reliable guides
to "knowing." But events of the seventeenth century proved this to be
less than entirely correct. The travels of the great explorers proved the
world, which appeared to be flat, to be round; and Copernicus proved
that the earth revolved around the sun, though it appeared to be mo-
tionless. The Cartesian dichotomy grew from these revelations concerning the deceptiveness of appearance. It juxtaposed observation and
sensory experience of the world outside the mind, with thought, reason,

and deduction, the realm within the mind. Only the latter, thought Descartes, could be considered a reliable way of "knowing."[28]

The vehicle of this Cartesian way of knowing is logical deduction and mathematics. This method necessitates a rather high level of abstraction in the reduction of complexity to simplified *essences,* such as the reduction of the multiplicity of characteristics of all goods to the common denominator of utility, or the fictitious unity of capital so thoroughly expunged by the Cambridge Controversy. The point is that the Cartesian Method itself imposed the necessity of thinking according to such essences and that this, in turn, imposed the epistemological necessity of the positive/normative dichotomy. Let us first differentiate this dichotomy from the Cartesian, and then specify how the latter necessitated the introduction of the former.

The positive/normative dichotomy of orthodox economics posits a sharp chasm between the "scientific" analysis of that which "is" and "pontification" about that which "ought to be." This stands in contrast to the Cartesian dichotomy between reason and sensory perception. Where the former divorces "is" from "ought," the latter separates the empirical and the experiential from the realm of deduction and pure reason. In this latter realm resides the method of orthodox economics and here "[goals], values, [and] ends have no place ... because they have no meaning."[29] Normative issues were cast out of orthodox economics because "ought" is irrelevant to its method. On the one side of Cartesianism is the pure world of reason, the world of economic theory. On the other side is the world of matter and experience, observation and fact, the world of economic activities, institutions, and practice. The world of economic theory presents us with an array of optima, maxima, distributive justice, and consumer satisfaction, all of which undermine the râison d'etre of economics. If the world were in fact like the theory, there would be no need for economics, much less an avowedly normative economics. As Piero Mini puts it, "What *can* the economist suggest if the scientific branch of the discipline ... proves the inherent perfection of the economic order?"[30]

This situation was fraught with radical implications for, as Mini points out, under these circumstances, the only thing the economist could suggest is that the world be brought into line with the theory. Yet this would hardly do, for such a restructuring of the world would require far too activist a government for the laissez-faire minded economists. Thus, we would argue, the positive/normative dichotomy is little more than an expedient device necessitated by the Cartesian foundations of economics and designed to maintain its "intellectual equipoise."[31] This balance came at a very high price, however, as Mini discloses. For, in the process, economics had to give up its distinctive characteristics as the only social science founded on a view of man as a rational being. Both Lionel Robbins and Ludwig von Mises, for instance, in their eagerness to reassert the value-free nature of economic theory, were compelled to regard any goal as rational by definition: Robbins emphasizes that "economics is entirely neutral between ends. . . . Economics is not concerned with ends as such . . . the ends may be noble or they may be base." Von Mises is just as clear: "Modern economics makes no distinction among ends *because it considers them all equally legitimate.*"[32]

This is precisely where the institutionalist objection begins. Any ends; all of which are equally legitimate? Hardly! As this symposium on institutionalism makes clear, the human agent cannot be regarded as exogenous to the economic system, providing that system with "input" only in the form of "wants." Human beings, rather, are both products and producers of this larger system. Part of the distinctive mark that this system leaves on human beings is its valuations, for good or for ill. Valuations not only necessarily impregnate inquiry, they are also themselves a legitimate object of inquiry in that they are very much a part of the "output" of the system in question. That the cave dwellers of the South Pacific, the West German steelworkers, and Nebraska cattle ranchers have both differences and commonalities in their respective systems of value is not just a random fact, nor is it inconsequential. Both are cultural and systemic in origin and merit a central place in economic inquiry.

Furthermore, not all valuations are equally valid or legitimate. Values are the normative criteria by which "bettering" and "worsening" circumstances are differentiated; they define a public or social purpose. Yet some of the valuations imprinted upon thought by cultural and systemic phenomena are patently and demonstrably false and misleading in this regard. Institutional economists devote considerable attention to this topic and have now developed and elaborated the instrumentalist theory of social value. To this we now turn.

The Instrumentalist Theory of Value

A number of excellent historical accounts of the development of the instrumentalist theory of value are already available in the institutionalist literature.[33] This will allow us to be brief in the present sketch. Nonetheless, continuity requires that some background be provided here. We begin, then, with a brief recount of the contributions of Thorstein Veblen, John Dewey, Clarence Ayres, and Marc Tool.

It is a common observation that Veblen did not formulate an explicit theory of value and that, indeed, he often claimed detachment and disinterest in such. Whether such claims were intended to be taken seriously or, as seems more likely, were a part of Veblen's sardonic intellectual subterfuge remains an open question, but they are beside the point here. "In point of fact," as Marc Tool has stated, "much if not most of his [Veblen's] scholarly work was directed to a fundamental critique of prevailing social customs and business practices and the theory that gave each its credibility."[34] Obviously some principle of value was at work in his famous indictment of "imbecile institutions" as a threat to human progress, and this principle can be uncovered by examining two aspects of Veblen's work.

First, Veblen characterized several behavioral proclivities in his use and discussion of the term "instincts."[35] Among these proclivities are three—"workmanship," "the parental bent," and "idle curiosity," which he viewed as contributing to the progressive evolutionary development of human societies. These elements of our behavior add to the fullness of life and the continuity of culture and are, therefore, to be encouraged.[36] In clear contradistinction to these proclivities, however, are those that threaten to obstruct and perhaps even destroy that continuity. This is evident in the acquisitive and emulative practices of exploit, predatory warfare, and industrial sabotage. This juxtaposition of progressive and regressive traits suggests a principle with which to differentiate those practices and institutions that are meritorious from those that are not.

Secondly, and even more to the point, is what has come to be known as the Veblenian dichotomy. Veblen viewed the institutions making up the economy as roughly divisible into two groups, depending upon whether they served a genuinely productive purpose or merely an acquisitive one. "They are pecuniary or industrial institutions . . . serving either the invidious or the non-invidious economic interest."[37] Those institutions that serve the invidious interest reflect the predatory and acquisitive instincts and are, therefore, regressive. As a principle of business behavior this is, perhaps, best captured with the term "vendibility." The non-invidious interest, in contrast, is best captured with the term "serviceability." It is progressive and forward looking, with a technological dynamic that is disruptive of invidious institutions and their attendant myths and ceremonial behaviors. These dichotomous elements of social structure continuously contend for the support of the community in determining which will become or remain the dominant valuative criteria. Veblen's fundamental, if implicit, normative concern was to develop a way of differentiating those institutions and practices that are progressive and non-invidious, and that promote serviceability from those that are ceremonial and invidious and that promote *mere* vendibility.

Where Veblen may have been only suggestive regarding a principle of valuation, John Dewey was direct. Dewey recognized the purposeful and problem-directed nature of social inquiry and developed an instrumental logic to fit this task. Further, he fully and explicitly recognized the possibility of applying this same logic to the question of valuation.

In preparing the way for his statement of the instrumental logic of social inquiry, Dewey rejected two basic canons of positivistic thought. The first was the idea that matters of judgment or valuation are wholly personal and therefore unknowable and not amenable to the methods of science. He argued instead that valuations exist in fact and are empirically verifiable. The point, as Marc Tool has observed, is that, "since all social choices require the application of criteria, and since choices produce consequences, one may reflect upon the *character* of consequences emerging from the use of a criterion and thus the propriety of the criterion itself. Value judgments are brought within social inquiry."[38] Dewey also rejected the idea of a positive/normative dichotomy. This was grounded in the belief that: (1) to conceive of something as an "end" is to conceive simultaneously of the "means" of its achievement and, therefore, (2) it is wholly arbitrary to designate and isolate "means" from "ends" in the continuum of phenomena. Dewey also viewed both means and ends as arising from actual social experience. To posit a neat and inviolate divorce between worldly and experiential means on the one hand and some conception of ends that are the non-experiential stuff of tastes, utilities or other metaphysical ultimates on the other, runs counter to the continuity of experience as we actually find it.

For Dewey, then, what is required is an experimental value principle that is consistent with the view of social and economic phenomena as an evolutionary process. Valuative criteria arise from within the process itself; they are not externally imposed as some "self evident" metaphysical ultimate. The point is that value and valuing are regarded as observable phenomena carried on within the social process through the application of intelligence and action to problematic situations. They are not transcendant, isolated, or subjective. Emergent values, rather, are objectively tested to determine their success or failure in resolving problematic situations.

Clarence Ayres's central achievement in this area was his integration of Dewey's instrumentalism with Veblen's evolutionary theory of the economic process. Recognizing, as he surely did, that the purpose of Veblen's dichotomy was evaluation, Ayres's connection of this with Dewey's thought was both an extension and a modification. The result is an evidentially grounded principle of instrumental value. For Ayres, as for Dewey, means and ends form a continuum that arises from within the process of experience. There is, in this view, no dualistic separation between means conceived as experiential in origin and ends conceived in exclusively metaphysical terms. Thus Ayres made a clear distinction between genuine values, which are the technological stuff of experience, and ceremonial values, which are the product of cultural mores and institutionalized rank, status, and authority.

As Ayres states, "the values of each system have the character of the process in which they occur."[39] In the case of the experiential values, this character is that of *facts*. Bread, work, play, and love, for example, are all valued for precisely the same reason; experience demonstrates that each forms part of a continuous and mutually reinforcing system. Bread gives us the strength to work and play, but it takes work to create bread and play to relieve the tensions of work. Without the sustenance of bread, the discipline of work, and the relief of play we cannot develop the capacity for mature love. Yet, in the absence of love, bread, work, and play become hollow and meaningless. Each conditions and reinforces the other, while all are demonstrably and factually "good."

The ceremonial values, in contrast, are the result of the human capacity to create fictions and have, accordingly, that same character.[40] These derive from supernatural sources and serve to legitimize mystic rites in the observance of hierarchical status. Their "principal function is not that of getting things done, but rather that of preventing change."[41] Examples of this obstruction to change abound in the anthropological and historical record of other cultures. Ayres's point— and here it seems is where he connects Dewey's logic with the "referential content" of Veblen's dichotomy—is that such past-binding systems of valuation survive in modern industrial society.[42] To cite just one example, these false values often find expression today in the ingenious and obsessive efforts of corporate leaders, conservative politicians, and economists to preserve the popular illusion that competitively structured markets continue to operate quite effectively as a mechanism of social control, despite significant *factual* evidence to the contrary.[43]

The final segment of this brief history of institutional economists' contributions to the instrumental theory of value brings us more or less up to date. This, of course, is a reference to the work of Marc Tool.[44] Drawing not only from the aforementioned scholars but also from his teacher, J. Fagg Foster, Tool has formulated a comprehensive modern statement of this view.[45] In his well-received book, *The Discretionary Economy: A Normative Theory of Political Economy,* Tool suggests that following an instrumentalist theory of value, we should seek that which, "provides for *the continuity of human life and the noninvidious re-creation of community through the instrumental use of knowledge.*[46] Tool elaborates at some length on the meaning of this principle by breaking it down into both its explicit and implicit elements. In what follows we relate this principle to the areas specified earlier in this essay. These areas were, again, (1) the cultural origin of value, (2) the instrumental value principle itself, and (3) the nature of the criterion and method of valuing.

Cultural Origin

The expression that "values are cultural in origin" has a very specific and significant meaning to instrumentalists and it is important to distinguish this view from other interpretations. Communal human existence necessitates nontrivial choice and that choice, to the extent it is meaningful, must be grounded in criteria that are open to examination. Non-instrumentalists have pursued this examination of criteria mainly through one or the other of two modes, neither of which is credible or acceptable to instrumentalists.[47]

The first of these two modes is ethically absolutistic. Here the criteria of choice are taken to be congruent with a "natural order" that is an expression of divine design or an invariant materialist construct such as class or race. Those definitely are not what the instrumentalist has in mind, since they cannot be modified to accommodate changing cultural circumstance or new knowledge. Consequently, such criteria tend to be ceremonially past binding and discriminatory; they obstruct progressive cultural change.

The second approach is an ethically relativistic mode of which there are two variations. The first variation is of the individualistic variety. Orthodox economic theory represents this view in that it takes all acts to be rational and, therefore, an expression of some underlying criterion (such as utility maximization) that is deemed sufficient unto itself. Individual choices are not, in this view, to be tested against any larger body of knowledge or frame of reference. The second variation claims to be "cultural" in the sense that values are conceived as originating solely from the social practices of the specific group of people who happen to hold them. Neither of these variations are what instrumentalists have in mind. As Louis Junker states:

> In all the above cases we are faced with a necessary choice of either of two main courses. We are faced either with the acceptance of the assumption that the atomistic individual and his equally atomistic value expression are the first and last unit of calculation and the final reference point for evaluation of choices; or with the assumption that a culture's values are "true" because many people are committed to those values or to idea that the word "true" is itself irrelevant to the whole choosing process. Choices are just choices—period.[48]

But choices are not *just* choices as they are taken to be in either of these views. Values are cultural, but the cultural dimension of value and choice is more complex than the simple "social practices of those who happen to hold them" view. This latter view misconceives the very idea of culture.

Human beings are culture-building creatures. In this they are unique for creative capabilities and represent a step beyond the limitations of organic or biological adaptation to the stresses of the environment in the direction of intellectual adaptation. Intellect and the human capacity for speech, the creation of language, and the creation of tools have allowed for selective and purposeful adaptation. Thus, humans adapt according to their own ideas and conceptualizations. The result is ordered and purposeful conduct, exhibiting the formulation and application of theory, which is the distinguishing characteristic of human activities, as opposed to those of other biological organisms.

This kind of conduct arises when responses to problematic situations are measured and assessed in consideration of the future consequences of present action, rather than simply carried out impulsively or instinctually. The types of problematic situations in question here involve eking out sustenance, shelter, and security from an indifferent environment. This necessitates collective action in the development of a cooperative human way of living, and the collective regulation and coordination of individual behavior. The "individual," contrary to the atomistic view, is not antecedent to the group. Groups are not mere sums of individuals; rather, individuals are born to groups with an already existing pattern of response to these environmental exigencies.[49] Purposeful conduct, thus, is patterned and learned conduct addressed to situations presented by the complex of environmental stimuli. It is *evaluated* according to its anticipated consequences. Those actions that fail to produce the anticipated results are gradually discarded over time. Humans, in effect, build culture through a trial and error process of intellectual adaptation to their environment.

Culture, in this view, is a human creation, a human environment born of human recognition of the problems presented by the larger environment and of the intellectual adaptation that creates an orderly, secure, and meaningful way of life in the face of these problems. The continuity of this culture-building process and the consequential valuing central to that process is seen as the locus and source of value. The valuations emerging from this ongoing problem of adaptation are translated into social life through the various kinds of institutions that organize and regulate individual behavior. Over time, as we critically re-examine the structure and performance of institutions and the values supporting them, we come to realize that some of our traditional beliefs have not been "true," "genuine," or "instrumental" in the Veblen-Ayres-Dewey sense. Rather, they prove to have been false, that is, invidious or ceremonial. They have not permitted or contributed to the resolution of problems requiring intellectual adaptation. When and where the resistance of vested interests to proposed adjustments is not too great, such false values and the institutions erected upon them can be discarded and replaced by new ones more consistent with contemporary warranted knowledge. This is the essence of culture, cultural change, and the cultural origins of value. Values are cultural in origin, but they are not just the beliefs of people who happen to hold them. They are the outcome of intellectual adaptation to the continuing stream of problems presented by the environment.[50] This is also, I believe, a fair description of what Tool has in mind when he speaks of the "noninvidious re-creation of community." Such re-creation, however, is conditioned on the instrumental use of knowledge. We turn our attention now to the instrumental value principle itself.

The Instrumental Value Principle

In his reference to the idea that the re-creation of community is the result of the instrumental use of knowledge, Tool states, "The reference to 'instrumental use' of reliable knowledge . . . affirms the relevance of such knowledge in the identification and resolution of human problems . . . . [It] conditions and constrains the use of reliable knowledge to that which is pertinent and compatible with the remainder of the principle. . . . [It] embodies an insistence that economic and political problems be identified and approached as a matter of a difference between what our reliable knowledge indicates is possible and desirable and what current practice shows is going on instead."[51] The purpose of this segment of the essay is to extend this explanation somewhat.

To the instrumentalist, value is to be understood as continuous with the whole of experience. Value "is the consummatory phase of a situation which is initially problematic."[52] These situations arise when human activities are in some way disrupted by impediments or obstacles. We are continuously confronted with such frustrations, and our adaptation requires an analysis of the problem in the context of our general experience, and the formulation of aims that, it is hoped, will remove the obstacle and redesign the activity in a more instrumentally purposeful way. It is this interaction of human intellect with experiential problems that produces value judgments; that is, the selection of standards for the evaluation of circumstances. Problematic situations, in short, necessitate choice, and choice requires criteria. The method for selecting criteria depends upon intellect and cognitive perception of the whole system of relations among the elements of the situation and the possible outcomes of various different courses of action.

A plan of action based upon reflective inquiry and the formulation of a value judgment is devised according to means and ends.[53] It is important to note that these ends are not preconceived, *a priori*, or given in any way external to the inquiry process. They are, rather, products of the same intellectual process by which the means to their achievement are conceived. The so called fact/value dichotomy is perceived to be an indefensible obstacle, blurred as we recognize that the "scientific" and the "normative" aspects of inquiry form continuous and inseparable parts of a common process. John Dewey put it this way: "When physics, chemistry, biology, medicine, contribute to the detection of concrete human woes and to the development of plans for remedying them and relieving the human estate, they become moral; they become part of the apparatus of moral inquiry or science . . . At the same time that morals are made to focus in intelligence, things intellectual are moralized."[54]

The point is that there is a continuity of means and ends. We cannot envision an end independently of a simultaneous envisioning of the means to its achievement. This continuum and its emergent values are a cultural process, not some transcendental given. Value recognition results from the experiences of human beings in interacting with their environment and in trying to cope with the problems that arise in that interaction.

But, and this is the contribution of Veblen and Ayres, in that this continuum is very much a human process, there is always the possibility of errors of judgment. The distinction between ceremonial and technological values, echoed throughout all institutional economics, defines errors of judgment. Ceremonial values are past bound and invidious. Often they become camouflaged as transcendental ultimates that appear to legitimize invidious status hierarchies and exploitive relationships. However, since values are in fact experiential in origin, no error of judgment camouflaged as a transcendental truth "could in any way give priority of right or advantage to one person or group as opposed to others".[55]

"Value" is thus understood to be the criterion of an ongoing, cultural, trial and error process of "valuing." This is what is meant by the instrumentalist phrase "valuational process." The process involves inquiry and experience, leading to the formation of value judgments. These judgments involve the selection of standards or norms for the appraisal of circumstances. For institutionalists, this involves the application of the instrumental criterion to the choice of a course of action, which leads to consequences that constitute a new situation and a new beginning for the process.[56] Figure 1 illustrates this.

Figure 1. *The Valuational Process*

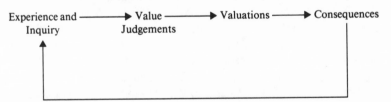

Source: Adapted from Paul D. Bush, "The Normative Implications of Institutional Analysis," *Economic Forum* 12 (Winter, 1981–82).

The ceremonial and instrumental modes of valuation can be contrasted as represented in Figure 1. Ceremonial values, again, are past bound and frequently camouflaged as transcendental ultimates. In contrast to the inquiry and experimentation that characterize the formulation of instrumental value judgments, the ceremonial values are ideologically based; they are prescribed by myth and ritual. Ceremonial values are, thus, habitual and conditioned by traditional practices; they reflect deferential concern with status, power, and custom. They come to be viewed as "natural" and are not, consequently, likely to be tested in the same crucible of experience as are instrumental value judgments. "Solutions," thus, are viewed solely as actions bringing institutional practices into conformance with ceremonial beliefs. From the instrumentalist perspective, in contrast, problems are resolved to the extent that invidiously and ceremonially warranted prescriptive (and proscriptive) facets of institutions are abandoned, and instrumentally warranted strucutral changes are introduced. This is "re-creation of community" in Tool's terminology, geared to the achievement of instrumentally warranted ends-in-view.

Ever since Veblen's spirited critique of price theory, orthodox economics has appeared to institutionalists to be little more than an exercise in the type of habitual conditioning that exhibits and sustains ceremonial values. A brief comparison of the respective approaches of the two schools to a real world issue should help bring this contention and the discussion in the foregoing paragraph into clearer relief. The issue to be considered here is the economic conception of externality and waste.[57]

From the neoclassical point of view, competitive market structures render the marginal benefits of an activity equal to its marginal costs. That constitutes an optimal outcome. Nothing (neither good nor service) that carries a positive price tag can, by virtue of the normative presumptions of this model, be classified as wasteful production. That is, anything someone is willing to pay for is definitionally "of value," simply by virtue of this willingness. Further consideration of the consequential merits or demerits of the good or activity are ruled out. Thus, there is no waste. The foregoing presumes, of course, the absence of "market imperfections" such as externalities, public goods, and nondiscriminating monopolies.[58] But the point is that the entire neoclassical argument centers on the preservation of a ceremonial valuation of the inviolate beneficiality of rational choice, individualistic consumption, and laissez-faire social policy.[59] Each of these underlying valuations are grounded, as Andrew Larkin has shown, in tautological and truncated reasoning. As a result:

In the neoclassical perspective, environmental problems are relegated to the category of externalities. . . . But the so-called externality is perceived as external only when one adopts the market-centered, voluntary exchange perspective. If the theory takes a more encompassing perspective, viewing markets as among the many imperfect institutional forms, what was formerly seen as an externality becomes another form of institutionalized behavior. Under this encompassing perspective, environmental problems become open to inquiry without the pre-selected market solution; a greater variety of options becomes available, thus enriching the problem-solving process. Indeed, reliance on the market often precludes solution of environmental problems because the market and its associated effects are among the causes of the problem.[60]

From an instrumentalist perspective, the problem of waste takes on a very different look. Again, instrumentalists regard the cultural process of intellectual adaptation to the problems presented by the environment as the point of origin for value analysis. This inquiry process provides the criteria with which institutions are judged. "We use instrumental criteria to judge the adequacy of institutions; we do not use institutions themselves as criteria. This is the mistake of the neoclassicist who uses the institution of the market as a criterion."[61]

The market itself is not a value; it is an institution, the performance of which is to be evaluated according to the criteria provided by the instrumental valuation process. But the market mentality of the neoclassical view enshrines this particular institution as a judgmental standard because it is the allegedly efficient vehicle for maximizing utility. Such "enshrining" is a mistake. While specific institutions may perform in service of instrumental values at a particular time and place, they tend to become counter-serviceable, ceremonial, or invidious as advancing social and technological complexities render them obsolete.[62] With regard to the example of waste, reliance upon the market mentality tells us an "optimal" solution will be forthcoming if only we "let the market work." Yet further inquiry into the operational implications of such a solution is precluded by the traditional limited scope and alleged value neutrality of orthodox economics. Externality and waste are all too often attributable to physical causes alone. This is the result of Western mentality and the logic of orthodox economics, both of which conceive of the problem as a by-product of the application of science and technology to material progress. This is unfortunate for it precludes analysis of social causes, most specifically the institutionalization of externality and waste *through the market,* the professed solution of the neoclassicals. When, as in the case of market capitalism, the economy becomes disembedded from social relationships, it becomes determinative of those relationships. A pecuniary logic comes to dominate the community such that, rather than serving as an instrument to social value, it becomes identified *as* social value.[63] James Swaney identifies the result.

> Externality is, then, symptomatic of erosion of instrumental functions of community by the market mentality and its application over time. Nuisance externalities result from lack of concern for immediate neighbors. Supply externalities are exacerbated by faith in market solutions (engendered by the market mentality) and lack concern for general others (in this case, future generations). Environmental externalities, particularly in the case of industrial pollution, result when strict adherence to the letter of the law or willful violations of the law serve as operational notions of fair play.[64]

Instrumentalists, then, would look to the *social* causes of externality and waste in their analysis of the problem, and to a values-directed redesign of institutions as the only meaningful sort of solution. At the very least, one suspects, this would entail a democratization of the twisted system that presently exists, wherein knowledge and information are controlled by vested interests and distorted by corporate media.[65] "The continuity of human life and the noninvidious re-creation of community" require nothing short of this. Ongoing value formation in accord with the best available knowledge leads quite logically to the exercise of human volition in the adaptation and change of institutions; not to a myopic and wrongheaded refusal to abandon the outmoded institutions of the past. It will be slim comfort to our children and grandchildren to know that we fouled the world they will inherit "optimally." And for this reason, we believe, the instrumentalist theory of value offers a more suitable path.

Conclusion

Our intent has been to present a reasonably cogent statement of the instrumentalist theory of value as the normative compass of institutional economics. In this we have proceeded in three stages. The first was a reconsideration of the standard of objectivity in economics. Numerous economists, most notably Myrdal in recent times, have argued that value impregnation is an inevitability in economics. The neoclassical response to this position has been less than enthusiastic, with the counterargument centering on four themes: (1) do the questions asked normatively impregnate the logic of economics? (2) are the answers given to these questions pre-selected through some antecedent and implicit normative preference? (3) does the language of economic discourse encode certain normative messages? and, (4) do economists unconsciously interject normative coloration into their policy advice? The orthodox position has always been that normativism does not slip through into any of these areas; economics is value free. Institutionalists have always taken issue with this claim, and this essay has continued in that tradition through an exposition of the flaws in the claims to ethical neutrality in each of the four areas mentioned.

The second area we addressed was the need in economics for an alternative path, a path that openly addresses the inescapability of value judgment and, indeed, the need for such judgments to be made and openly examined. Here the epistemological underpinnings of classical economics were shown to have ultimately given rise to the sharp positive/normative split of the neoclassical era. In the hands of such well-intentioned, but wrongheaded, economists as Robbins and von Mises this led to the belief that economists can only study means, not ends. The ends of utility maximization are beyond inquiry. Instrumentalists reject this idea on the grounds that values, or ends, are not just a reflection of individualistic desires and, therefore, an "input" into the economic system. Values, or ends, are an "output" of the larger cultural milieu and they are not all equally valid or legitimate. We do, because we must, choose *among* wants, desires, and preferences. Because values serve as criteria for defining "better" or "worse," logically they cannot all be valid.

Values, we argued, are not transcendental or natural. They originate, rather, in the cultural process of intellectual adaptation to problematic situations. The instrumental value principle, then, facilitates the process of valuing. It is a trial and error process through which inquiry and experience lead to the formation of value judgments and to courses of action (institutional adjustments) designed to correct problems that are subject to continuous assessment. This continuous testing and redesign of institutional structure through recourse to the instrumental value is the route to problem solving, not only of waste disposal problems but also problems of stability, equity, and the production and distribution of real income.

Notes

1. Gunnar Myrdal, "What is Political Economy," in *Value Judgment and Income Distribution,* ed. Robert A. Solo and Charles W. Anderson (New York: Praeger Publishers, 1981), pp. 41–53.
2. However, some of the most influential works to support this view include, in chronological order, John Stuart Mill, *Essays on Some Unsettled Questions of Political Economy* (1844), 3d ed. (London: Longmans Green and Co., 1877); John Neville Keynes, *The Scope and Method of Political Economy,* 4th ed. (London: Macmillan, 1917); Lionel Robbins, *An Essay on the Nature and Significance of Economic Science,* 2d ed. (London: Macmillan, 1935); Milton Friedman, "The Methodology of Positive Economics," in *Essays in Positive Economics* (Chicago: University of Chicago Press, 1953); and T.W. Hutchison, *'Positive' Economics and Policy Objectives,* (London: Macmillan, 1964).
3. Kurt Klappholz, "Value Judgments and Economics," *British Journal for the Philosophy of Science* 15 (1964): 97–114, as reprinted in *The Philosophy of Economics: An Anthology,* ed. Daniel M. Hausman (Cambridge: Cambridge University Press, 1984), pp. 276–92.
4. Ibid., p. 279.
5. In this regard see: James Bonar, *Philosophy and Political Economy in Some of Their Historical Relations,* 3d ed., (New York: Humanities Press, 1922 [1893]); Piero V. Mini, *Philosophy and Economics: The Origins of Economic Ideas* (Gainesville: University Presses of Florida, 1974); Joan Robinson, *Economic Philosophy,* (Chicago: Aldine Publishing Co., 1962); Thorstein Veblen, "The Limitations of Marginal Utility," *Journal of Political Economy* 17 (November 1909): 620–36; Clarence Ayres, *The Theory of Economic Progress* (Chapel Hill: University of North Carolina Press, 1944); Marc R. Tool, "The Social Value Theory of Orthodoxy: A Review and Critique," *Journal of Economic Issues* 14 (June 1980): 309–26. The list could go on.
6. Robert A. Solo, "Values and Judgments in the Discourse of the Social Sciences," in *Value Judgment and Income Distribution,* pp. 9–40.
7. Warren J. Samuels, "The Historical Treatment of the Problem of Value Judgments: An Interpretation," in *Value Judgment and Income Distribution,* pp. 57–69. Samuels has treated this issue at length in numerous writings. Among these are: "Ideology in Economics," in *Modern Economic Thought,* ed. Sidney Weintraub (Philadelphia: University of Pennsylvania Press, 1977), pp. 467–84; "The History of Economic Thought as Intellectual History," *History of Political Economy* 6 (Fall 1978): 305–23; "Normative Premises in Regulatory Theory," *Journal of Post Keynesian Economics* 1 (Fall 1978): 100–114; and "An Economics Perspective on the Compensation problem," *Wayne Law Review* 21 (November 1974): 113–34.
8. William M. Dugger, "Property Rights, Law, and John R. Commons," *Review of Social Economy* 38 (April 1980): 41–53.
9. Klappholz, "Value Judgments and Economics," p. 280.
10. Ibid.
11. These specific points are developed in John D. Wisman, "Toward a Hu-

manistic Reconstruction of Economic Science," *Journal of Economic Issues* 13 (March 1979): 19–48. Institutionalists have presented similar arguments for nearly a century, beginning, of course, with Veblen. A few other more recent works that make similar points include Larry Dwyer, "The Alleged Value Neutrality of Economics," *Journal of Economic Issues* 16 (March 1982): 75–106; R.L. Heilbroner, "Economics as a Value Free Science," *Social Research* 40 (Spring 1973): 129–43; and Philip A. Klein, "Economics: Allocation or Valuation?" *Journal of Economic Issues* 8 (December 1974): 785–811.

12. Solo, "Values and Judgments in the Discourse of the Social Sciences," p. 29. See also, George C. Lodge, *The New American Ideology* (New York: Alfred A. Knopf, 1976), *passim.*

13. Mini, *Philosophy and Economics, passim.*

14. Wisman, "Toward a Humanistic Reconstruction of Economic Science," pp. 33–35.

15. Walter A. Weisskopf, "The Method is the Ideology: From a Newtonian to a Heisenbergian Paradigm in Economics," *Journal of Economic Issues* 13 (December 1979): 869–84.

16. Solo, "Values and Judgments in the Discourse of the Social Sciences," pp. 19–20.

17. Klappholz, "Value Judgments and Economics," p. 280.

18. James Gouinlock, *John Dewey's Philosophy of Value* (New York: Humanities Press, 1972), p. 10.

19. Ibid., Chap. 1. Also see John Dewey, *The Quest for Certainty* (New York: G.P. Putnam's Sons, 1960); *Experience and Nature* (Chicago: The Open Court, 1925); and *Logic: The Theory of Inquiry* (New York: Holt, Rinehart and Winston, 1938). Additionally, see Albert Hofstader, "Concerning a Certain Deweyan Conception of Metaphysics," in *John Dewey: Philosopher of Science and Freedom,* ed. Sidney Hook (New York: Barnes and Noble, 1967), pp. 249–70.

20. Klappholz, "Value Judgments and Economics," p. 281.

21. Andre Rambouillet, *L'enseignement de la civilization francaise* (Paris: Hachette, 1973), p. 20. Cited in Richard G. Fritz and Judy M. Fritz, "Linguistic Structure and Economic Method," *Journal of Economic Issues* 16 (June 1982): 355–69.

22. Dewey, *Experience and Nature,* as cited in *Intelligence in the Modern World: John Dewey's Philosophy,* ed. Joseph Ratner (New York: The Modern Library, 1925), p. 810.

23. Klappholz, "Value Judgments and Economics," p. 282.

24. Tool, "Social Value Theory of Orthodoxy."

25. Klappholz, "Value Judgments and Economics," p. 284. In fairness to Klappholz, though, he does go on to say that the economist cannot reasonably expect to be furnished with a set of policy ends that would make such a deduction possible.

26. Dwyer, "The Alleged Value Neutrality of Economics."

27. Joan Robinson, *Freedom and Necessity* (New York: Vintage/Random House, 1971), p. 122.

28. Mini, *Philosophy and Economics,* p. 135.

29. Ibid.

30. Ibid., p. 129.

31. Ibid., p. 133.
32. Ibid., p. 134.
33. See, for example, Marc R. Tool, "A Social Value Theory in Neoinstitutional Economics," *Journal of Economic Issues* 11 (December 1977): 823–846, and F. Gregory Hayden, "Social Fabric Matrix: From Perspective to Analytical Tool," *Journal of Economic Issues* 16 (September 1982): 637–62.
34. Tool, "A Social Value Theory in Neoinstitutional Economics," p. 825.
35. It is important here that the reader understand that modern usage would preclude the application of the term "instinct" to the concept at hand because of its hereditary implications. Veblen inferred nothing hereditary, genetic, or "natural" in his use of the term. The reference, rather, is to the cultural conditioning and habitual modes of behavior that channel these proclivities into acceptable modes of expression.
36. Tool, "A Social Value Theory in Neoinstitutional Economics," p. 826.
37. Thorstein Veblen, *The Theory of the Leisure Class* (New York: Random House/Modern Library, 1934), p. 208.
38. Tool, "A Social Value Theory in Neoinstitutional Economics," p. 829.
39. C.E. Ayres, *Toward a Reasonable Society: The Values of Industrial Civilization* (Austin: The University of Texas Press, 1961), p. 103.
40. Ibid.
41. Ibid., p. 126.
42. Tool, "A Social Value Theory in Neoinstitutional Economics," p. 835.
43. Some of this contrary evidence can be found in the following works: Adolf Berle and Gardiner Means, *The Modern Corporation and Private Property* (New York: Macmillan, 1940); John M. Blair, *Economic Concentration* (New York: Harcourt, 1972); John M. Blair, *The Control of Oil* (New York: Pantheon, 1976); Edward S. Herman, *Corporate Control, Corporate Power* (Cambridge: Cambridge University Press, 1981); John R. Munkirs, *The Transformation of American Capitalism: From Competitive Market Structures to Centralized Private Sector Planning* (Armonk, N.Y./London: M.E. Sharpe, 1985); Charles R. Spruill, *Conglomerates and the Evolution of Capitalism* (Carbondale and Edwardsville: Southern Illinois University Press, 1982).
44. In addition to Tool, other very important contemporary instrumentalists include Paul D. Bush and Louis J. Junker. See, for example: Paul D. Bush, "The Normative Implications of Institutional Analysis," *Economic Forum* 12 (Winter 1981–82), pp. 9–29; Paul D. Bush, "An Exploration of the Structural Characteristics of a Veblen-Ayres-Foster Defined Institutional Domain," *Journal of Economic Issues* 17 (March 1983): 35–66; Louis J. Junker, "Instrumentalism, the Principle of Continuity and the Life Process," *American Journal of Economics and Sociology* 40 (October 1981): 381–400; and Louis J. Junker, "Nutrition and Economy: Some Observations on Diet and Disease in the American Food Power System," *Review of Institutional Thought* 2 (December 1982): 27–58.
45. See *Journal of Economic Issues* 15 (December 1981). This entire issue was devoted to the previously unpublished papers of J. Fagg Foster.
46. Marc R. Tool, *The Discretionary Economy: A Normative Theory of Political Economy* (Santa Monica: Goodyear Publishing Co., 1979), p. 293.
47. See Junker, "Instrumentalism," *passim.*

48. Ibid., p. 383.
49. John R. Commons, *Institutional Economics,* Vol. 1 (Madison: University of Wisconsin Press, 1961), pp. 73–74.
50. John Dewey, *Theory of Valuation,* (Chicago: University of Chicago Press, 1939), *passim.* See also Gouinlock, and Lawrence K. Frank, "Culture and Personality," in Sidney Hook, *John Dewey,* pp. 88–105.
51. Marc R. Tool, *Discretionary Economy* p. 296–97.
52. Gouinlock, *John Dewey's Philosophy of Value,* p. 125.
53. See Bush, "The Normative Implications of Institutional Analysis," p. 18.
54. John Dewey, *Reconstruction in Philosophy,* (Boston: Beacon Press, 1959), pp. 173–174.
55. Gouinlock, *John Dewey's Philosophy of Value,* p. 150.
56. Bush, "The Normative Implications of Institutional Analysis," p. 18.
57. See: Andrew Larkin, "Environmental Impact and Institutional Adjustment: Application of Foster's Principles to Solid Waste Disposal," *Journal of Economic Issues* 20 (March 1986): 43–61; Ken McCormick, "Towards a Definition of Waste in Economics: A Neoinstitutional Approach," *Review of Social Economy* 44 (April 1986): 80–92, at p. 81; James A. Swaney, "Externality and Community," *Journal of Economic Issues* 15 (September 1981): 615–27; and Larry D. Swanson, "Shifting the Burden of Environmental Protection," *Journal of Economic Issues* 18 (March 1984): 251–74.
58. McCormick, "Towards a Definition of Waste in Economics," p. 81.
59. Larkin, "Environmental Impact and Institutional Adjustment," *passim.*
60. Ibid., pp. 46–47.
61. Ibid., p. 49.
62. See: Steven R. Hickerson, "Complexity and the Meaning of Freedom: The Classical Liberal View," *American Journal of Economics and Sociology* 43 (January 1984): 91–101; Steven R. Hickerson, "Complexity and the Meaning of Freedom: The Instrumentalist View," *American Journal of Economics and Sociology* 43 (October 1984): 435–42; and Steven R. Hickerson, "Justice and the Social Economist: An Instrumentalist Interpretation," *International Journal of Social Economics* 12 (1985): 90–103.
63. Swaney, "Externality and Community."
64. Ibid.
65. Swanson, "Shifting the Burden of Environmental Protection."

References

Bush, Paul D. 1983. "An Exploration of the Structural Characteristics of a Veblen-Ayres-Foster Defined Institutional Domain." *Journal of Economic Issues* 17 (March): 35–66.
Dwyer, Larry. 1982. "The Alleged Value Neutrality of Economics." *Journal of Economic Issues* 16 (March): 75–106.
Foster, J. Fagg. 1981. "The Relation Between the Theory of Value and Economic Analysis." *Journal of Economic Issues* 15 (December): 899–905.
Fritz, Richard G. and Judy M. 1982. "Linguistic Structure and Economic Method." *Journal of Economic Issues* 16 (June): 355–69.

Hayden, F. Gregory. 1982. "Social Fabric Matrix: From Perspective to Analytical Tool." *Journal of Economic Issues* 16 (September): 637–62.
Heilbroner, Robert L. 1970. "On the Possibility of a Political Economics." *Journal of Economic Issues* 4 (December): 1–22.
_____. 1984. "Economics and Political Economy: Marx, Keynes, and Schumpeter." *Journal of Economic Issues* 18 (September): 681–96.
Klein, Philip A. 1974. "Economics: Allocation or Valuation?" *Journal of Economic Issues* 8 (December): 785–811.
Larkin, Andrew. 1986. "Environmental Impact and Institutional Adjustment: Application of Foster's Principles to Solid Waste Disposal." *Journal of Economic Issues* 20 (March): 43–61.
Myrdal, Gunnar. 1978. "Institutional Economics." *Journal of Economic Issues* 12 (December): 771–84.
Neale, Walter C. 1982. "Language and Economics." *Journal of Economic Issues* 16 (June): 355–70.
Petr, Jerry L. 1984. "Fundamentals of an Institutionalist Perspective." *Journal of Economic Issues* 18 (March): 1–18.
Rutherford, Malcolm. 1981. "Clarence Ayres and the Instrumental Theory of Value." *Journal of Economic Issues* 15 (September): 657–74.
Seligman, Ben B. 1971. "Philosophic Perspectives in Economic Thought." *Journal of Economic Issues* 5 (March): 1–24.
Stanfield, J.R. 1984. "Social Reform and Economic Policy." *Journal of Economic Issues* 18 (March): 19–44.
Swaney, James A. 1981. "Externality and Community." *Journal of Economic Issues* 15 (September): 615–27.
Swanson, Larry D. 1984. "Shifting the Burden of Environmental Protection." *Journal of Economic Issues* 18 (March): 251–74.
Tilman, Rick. 1974. "Value Theory, Planning and Reform: Ayres as Incrementalist and Utopian." *Journal of Economic Issues* 8 (December): 689–706.
_____. 1983. "Social Value Theory, Corporate Power, and Political Elites." *Journal of Economic Issues* 17 (March): 115–32.
Tool, Marc R. 1977. "A Social Value Theory in Neoinstitutional Economics." *Journal of Economic Issues* 11 (December): 823–46.
_____. 1980. "The Social Value Theory of Neoclassical Orthodoxy: A Review and Critique." *Journal of Economic Issues* 14 (June): 309–26.
_____. 1982. "Social Value Theory of Marxists: An Instrumentalist Review and Critique: Part I." *Journal of Economic Issues* 16 (December): 1079–1107.
_____. 1983a. "Social Value Theory of Marxists: An Instrumentalist Review and Critique: Part II." *Journal of Economic Issues* 17 (March): 155–73.
_____. 1983b. "Equational Justice and Social Value." *Journal of Economic Issues* 17 (June): 335–44.
Waller, William T., Jr. 1982. "The Evolution of the Veblenian Dichotomy." *Journal of Economic Issues* 16 (September): 757–71.
Weisskopf, Walter A. 1979. "The Method is the Ideology: From a Newtonian to a Heisenbergian Paradigm in Economics." *Journal of Economic Issues* 13 (December): 869–84.
Wisman, John D. 1979. "Toward a Humanistic Reconstruction of Economics." *Journal of Economic Issues* 13 (March): 19–48.

Part III

The Concept of Technology
Within the Institutionalist Perspective

Milton D. Lower

Institutionalism is an evolutionary science. The broadest theoretical aim of institutionalism—since Thorstein Veblen posed and answered the question "Why is Economics Not an Evolutionary Science?"—has been to repair this indicated defect in the process of socioeconomic inquiry. The concepts and methods of institutionalist inquiry have been developed since the late nineteenth century with conscious reference to paradigmatic changes in the life sciences precipitated by the Darwinian revolution.

Veblen, John R. Commons, and others who might be considered founders of the institutionalist approach, undertook to recast social inquiry—especially economics, which was most in need of such reconstruction—according to the new conception of "cumulative causation." The approach and the achievement of the post-Darwinian sciences consisted, according to Veblen: "on the one hand, in their refusal to go back of the colorless sequence of phenomena and seek higher ground for their ultimate syntheses, and, on the other hand, in their having shown how this colorless impersonal sequence of cause and effect can be made use of *for theory proper,* by virtue of its cumulative character" [Veblen 1919a, p. 62].

The most difficult task that confronts social scientists aspiring to "borrow" grand conceptions from the natural sciences, is the framing of concepts and methods genuinely appropriate to the different subject matter. This, in turn, is largely a question of framing key concepts at the appropriate *level of generalization,* or within the appropriate *universe of discourse,* for "doing" the science. The most serious errors arise when concepts are framed too *narrowly,* in two distinct senses. In one case, the resulting theory may be of insufficient generality and scope to embrace the substantive universe of social arrangements and changes therein. Secondly, and worse, theory may be framed too narrowly to comprehend the *behavior* to be accounted for—that is, purposive human behavior, ranging from the antecedent causes of human intent to the ongoing consequences of action. Traditional economics committed both errors, when it adopted Newtonian mechanics for its model, with the "economic man" as its unit of analysis.[1]

Obviously, this is not to say that every act of social inquiry must have generalizing aims even in an evolutionary framework. Nor is it to say that there cannot be a number of different social science disciplines delineated according to particular research interests. But there can be no evolutionary social science without a core concept of "what evolves," which also distinguishes the continuities in social life from other ranges of causal relations describing human life and behavior at the physical, biological, or psychological levels.

For such a core concept in evolutionary economics, the institutionalists borrowed an idea distilled by the anthropologists from a multitude of taxonomic human "laboratories" around the world: the *concept of culture.*[2] As Clarence Ayres would put it many years later:

> Culture, the organized corpus of behavior of which economic activity is but a part, is a phenomenon *sui generis.* It is not an epiphenomenon, a result of something else, explicable in other and non-cultural terms. It is the stuff of social behavior, the universe of discourse of the social sciences, the aspect which the data of observation assume at that level of generalization [Ayres 1944, p. 96].

The concept of *technology,* in all the uses for which institutionalists employ it, refers to an aspect of culture. In the final analysis, therefore, the institutionalist concept of technology cannot be fully grasped apart from the manner in which technology is conceived to articulate with the rest of cultural life—specifically with the "institutedness" of cultural behavior. Much of the volume in which this paper appears may fairly be said to be concerned with that question, and a full treatment of the concept of "institutions" by Walter C. Neale follows immediately. For the purposes of this article, these questions will be addressed as necessary in the discussions to follow of certain contextual meanings of the concept of technology.

Three broad contexts will be discussed to clarify the general concept. The first is "technology and cultural evolution," which introduces the institutionalist conception that technology is not only an aspect of culture, but the dynamic force in a process of cultural evolution that is continuous with biological evolution. The second context is that of "technological progress." This discussion explores in more detail the functional characteristics of the process of technological change that give it a cumulative, dynamic, and progressive character. The specific implications of technology for an evolutionary economics are also discussed in this context. Finally, the context of "technology and instrumental behavior" is analyzed, highlighting institutionalist conceptions of the theory of knowledge and of "instrumental valuation."

It should be clear from this statement of meanings yet to be explored that the word "technology" as commonly used does not begin to convey the content of this concept within institutionalist theory. Throughout the development of this evolutionary approach, leading contributors have grappled with the problem of how to convey the meaning more clearly, in face of the conventional wisdom of technology as "gadgetry" or as individual "creativity." While other groups of social scientists have independently developed or have adopted some of the contextual meanings, none has combined them coherently. Indeed, in this article, the distinctive contribution of institutionalism to social science is held to reside in its discovery of the *general* theoretical significance of technology as the foundation for a unified theory of cultural evolution, technological progress, and instrumental valuation.

This general framework of ideas, while it is a logic fully supported by observation, is never taken by institutionalists as a *substitute* for a genetic accounting of the cumulative causation at work in particular cultural circumstances. Hence, in the applications of institutionalist theory or in the uses of a central concept such as technology, the approach is quite different from that in sciences that, appropriately or inappropriately, employ mechanistic concepts and theories. Where such mechanistic concepts are applied inappropriately—without empirical referents, for example, as the concepts of supply and demand are applied in orthodox economics—events are explained by parable, based on reasoning merely "parallel to" the preconceived "general theory."

Nonetheless, empirical research problems may be suggested to those using this theoretical approach. To the extent these are recast to coincide with relatively stable regularities in the evolved institutional situation, accurate predictions of some events may be possible. Hence, there arises a spurious, but often credited, claim to predictability for the theory itself.

In the nature of the case, an evolutionary theory cannot be predictive of discrete "facts," since evolutionary events are non-repeatable. By the same token, however, an evolutionary approach yields the only valid means of discerning the *direction* of cultural events. Mechanistic models are constrained to assume, contrary to fact, that cultural events are infinitely repeatable, and even reversible, movements to and from stasis. This is an especially debilitating characteristic in circumstances of rapid or large-scale technological and institutional change.

In any case, it is the direction, and also the *pace,* of cultural change—but not the fact of it—that is legitimately at issue. All cultures display relative stability in some aspects of social life, and the same overall process of cumulative causation that explains technological revolutions explains the "institutedness" of social and economic arrangements. It should be noted that such institutionalization of cultural patterns constitutes an *alternative,* evolutionary explanation of any observed regularities in culture that are treated as "repeatable" events in mechanistic models of socioeconomic behavior.

The study of, and strategic intervention in, this process of cumulative causation defines the institutionalist research and policy agenda. Clearly, it is beyond the scope of this article to delve deeply into this growing body of evolutionary research or into the policy *issues* that largely define the work of evolutionary or institutional economists, including the work of this institutionalist. The reader is reminded that this article appears in the *Journal of Economic Issues,* sponsored for two decades by the Association for Evolutionary Economics. The concept of technology has been a central organizing concept for that entire literature and much more.

Technology and Cultural Evolution

The concept of technology within institutionalist theory derives prime theoretical significance from the dynamic role that technological change is conceived to play in cultural evolution. Perhaps needless to say, at this level of generalization, there are no functional distinctions to be made between "technology" and "science," or "tools" and "skills," or, for that matter, "means" and "ends." The conception is one of a cumulative "technological life process" and of evolving potential, not one of evolved "technologies." The latter bear a relation to the process of technological and cultural evolution that is approximately that of taxonomic species to biological evolution—extinct, specialized, or emergent. All are worthy of assiduous study with the general conception in mind.

Without pushing the analogy to biological evolution too far, it might be said that technology and technological "mutation" function somewhat as the "genetic material" of cultural evolution. Beyond mere analogy, it is widely recognized at the frontier between the biological sciences and the cultural sciences that cultural evolution is not only continuous with biological evolution in the human species, but for practical purposes has superseded it.

As Julian Huxley noted some years ago, a rare exception to the "unity" of the process of evolution occurred with "the emergence of mental capacities to the level where they begin to affect the future course of events." With this change, Huxley noted:

> Then there is the capacity for progress, in the sense of advance which permits further advance instead of leading eventually into blind alleys of specialization. Progress in this sense is unique, since only one progressive line has continued into the present epoch: the line leading to man. This line is also unique in that it has enabled life to transcend itself, by making possible a second mechanism for continuity and change, in addition to the genetic outfit. . . . This is man's method of utilizing cumulative experience, which gives him new powers of control over nature and new and more rapid methods of adjustment to changing circumstances [Huxley 1953, p. vii].

In this process, technological change is clearly the "cumulative experience" that has prevented human life from settling into "blind alleys of specialization." That this has involved a major shift in the nature of human methods of adjustment, as Huxley noted, is a point reinforced by Thomas R. DeGregori: "Evolution is sometimes thought of as the adaptation of the organism to the environment or changes in it. In a very real sense, technology involves the adaptation of the environment to the organism" [DeGregori 1985, p. 14].

It is clearly a "different sort of organism" that is so capacitated, and, in a logical sense, the point at which this shift in the character of human adaptation occurred also defines the point at which humans became "tool-using animals." Nonetheless, as the author just cited notes, while humans are considered to have been tool users for at least 2.5 million years, it may be preferable to consider "technology" as having arisen much later, when tool-using and tool-making became, in Walter Goldschmidt's phrase, "learned means" by which humans utilize the environment [DeGregori 1985, pp. 16–18].

Veblen imparted this concept of technology as *knowledge* to institutionalist thinking in all of his work. In "Why is Economics Not an Evolutionary Science?" Veblen emphasized the role of technological "habits of thought" as the basis for cumulative economic change, including changes in the "ends" for which economic activity is undertaken.

> All economic change is a change in the economic community—a change in the community's methods of turning material things to account. The change is always in the last resort a change in habits of thought.... A given contrivance for effecting certain material ends becomes a circumstance which affects the further growth of habits of thought ... and so becomes a point of departure for further development of the methods of compassing the ends sought and for the further variation of ends that are sought to be compassed [Veblen 1919a, p. 75].

Veblen's fullest development of this idea, which he recast as "immaterial equipment," came later, in two articles on "the nature of capital," to which it will be worth returning in a later context. However, a quotation from that source suggests two points of direct relevance here. First, the concept of technology as knowledge is a *comprehensive* but not an "idealistic" way of viewing the matter. Secondly, it is a thoroughly "cultural" concept. Veblen wrote:

> Wherever a human community is met with ... it is found in possession of something in the way of a body of technological knowledge,—knowledge serviceable and requisite to the quest of a livelihood,—comprising at least such elementary acquirements as language, the use of fire, of a cutting edge. ... This information and proficiency in the ways and means of life vests in the group at large; and apart from accretions borrowed from other groups, it is the product of the given group. ... It may be called the immaterial equipment ... of the community [Veblen 1919c, p. 325].

In the next section dealing with the concept of technology as "technological progress," further consideration will be given to the Veblenian concept of technological knowledge. In closing this discussion of technology and cultural evolution, however, a third point from the quotation above—which seems incidental in the context—must be noted. Toward the end of the passage, Veblen refers to accretions of knowledge "borrowed from other groups." This concept of the "cultural borrowing" of technology was hardly incidental to Veblen's contribution to the institutionalist concept of technology or to intellectual advancement in general. While Veblen himself "borrowed" the general idea of cultural borrowing from the anthropologists, his *Imperial Germany and the Industrial Revolution* remains the definitive theoretical account of the phenomenon in the culturally complex setting of modern economic development [Veblen 1915].

While Veblen recognized that all sorts of cultural elements can be and are borrowed, he found great significance in the fact that late nineteenth-century Germany—a backward economy, with a "modernizing" dynasty—was able to surpass Britain industrially by acquiring British technical knowledge, while not acquiring the obsolescent pecuniary institutions that had grown up around the technology. Though Veblen may have overgeneralized the case—in its applicability to other developing nations—the case was brilliantly made for Germany, and elsewhere, prospectively, for Japan [Veblen 1934].[3]

What the thesis of *Imperial Germany* relates to is a proposition central to the institutionalist conception of technology and cultural evolution: While technology is a phenomenon in and of culture, there is also a *trans-cultural* aspect to the technological process that is not evident in other cultural phenomena.

In whatever ways cultural groups adapt environments to life purposes, they necessarily employ working principles that are not themselves culture-bound, but that interrelate cultural activities with the "uniformities of nature" [Ayres 1961, pp. 92–93]. Such technologies thus become available to that culture, and, through cultural borrowing, to any other culture, as ways and means that can be adapted to a widening range of purposes through combination with other working principles.

Technological Progress

The degree of emphasis accorded to general concept formation or to descriptive and applied phases of scientific inquiry has varied greatly among institutionalists, as it does among practitioners of any science. Each phase is, of course, sterile without the other, especially in an evolutionary science. In this sense, it implies no invidious comparison to say that the most profound contributions to institutionalist *theory* to date have been those of Clarence E. Ayres, and that his principal contributions appear in *The Theory of Economic Progress* [Ayres 1944].

By the criteria of those who aspire to a "general equilibrium theory" of the economy, neither Ayres nor any of his institutionalist predecessors or followers has been engaged in "theory." Veblen was recognized by the economics profession in his day as a brilliant, but essentially misguided, critic of prevailing theory. In selective recognition of his alternative theoretical scheme, assorted "Veblen effects" have even been appended to the main mechanistic system [Lower 1980, pp. 82–83, 100].

No one could deny that John R. Commons had mastered "economic theory." But his efforts to transmute its static exchange concepts into processual ones—such as the social "transaction," the "going concern," and "collective action in control of individual action"—were in the end "unfathomable" to the economic theorists [Commons 1934, pp. 52–121; Ramstad 1986, p. 1067].[4]

To mention only one other example, while Wesley Mitchell's life work was to build, on Veblenian foundations, "a general *theory* of the money economy," he is honored by economists mainly for the (undeniably great) contributions he made to economic statistics as a means to this larger end-in-view [Schumpeter 1952, p. 330]. Thus, according to Milton Friedman, while the judgment that Mitchell was "primarily an empirical scientist rather than a theorist . . . is valid . . . , [in a sense] Wesley Mitchell's empirical work is itself a contribution to economic theory—and a contribution of the first magnitude" [Friedman 1952, p. 237].

Despite a century of such failed communication, institutionalists and evolutionary economists have proceeded with the difficult task of developing general theoretical concepts appropriate to the analysis of cumulative causation and consonant with the real world of change. Ayres was a major contributor to this line of development in general, but more directly than anyone since Veblen, to an alternative conception of the economy. *The Theory of Economic Progress* was a major contribution to the theory of cultural change, but it was also a call to substitute the "logic of technology" for the "logic of equilibrium" at the center of economic theory.

The contributions of Ayres to institutionalism and to the concept of technology are themselves an instance of the principle underlying his theory of progress—which he called the "tool-combination principle." They represent, in large measure, a combination of the intellectual tools of two predecessors—Veblen and John Dewey. These ways and means for understanding were in turn combined with the materials derived from a lifelong study of the history of science, technology, invention, and the arts.

On the frontispiece to *The Theory of Economic Progress,* Ayres chose to quote a brief passage from Veblen's previously cited article, "Why is Economics Not an Evolutionary Science?" The passage read: "There is the economic life process still in great measure awaiting theoretical formulation" [Ayres 1944, frontispiece; Veblen 1919a, p. 70]). Clearly, Ayres accepted Veblen's research program as his challenge and shared Veblen's turn-of-the-century assessment that the task remained to be done.

Veblen went on in this article to ask what had been accomplished to date by economists "in the way of inquiry into this economic life process." His answer was that:

> The ways and means of turning material objects and circumstances to account lie before the investigator at any given point of time in the form of mechanical contrivances and arrangements for compassing certain mechanical ends. It has therefore been easy to accept these ways and means as items of inert matter . . . serving the material ends of man. As such they have been scheduled and graded by the economists under the head of capital. . . . [Veblen 1919a, p. 71].

The critical implications of this with respect to the concept of capital will be noted here only in passing. However, this question is so central to evolutionary economics that a separate article by Baldwin Ranson, setting forth an institutionalist reconstruction of the theory of capital formation, is included in this volume. In the quotation from Veblen above, the particular contradiction pointed to is that between the orthodox concept of "capital" and Veblen's emphasis on technology as knowledge. However, this might appear as an opposition of "knowledge" to "tools," which would then suggest a line of questioning. If technology is knowledge, or "immaterial equipment," and not mechanical contrivances, is this equivalent to saying that technology is "skill," and not "tools"? And is technological progress, then, a matter of the progressive accumulation of skills? If so, how did Ayres derive from the work of Veblen a "tool-combination principle" that he explicitly referred to as a technological "law of progress"? [Ayres 1944, p. 119].

In the first place, Veblen cannot be charged with having bought the premise of this series of questions—namely, that knowledge, immaterial though it might be, is "skill" apart from "tools." Veblen's quarrel with the orthodox concept of capital runs very much deeper than the materiality or immateriality of technology *per se*. The gist of Veblen's discussion following the citation above is that the concept of capital—by which the orthodox economists "scheduled and graded" mechanical contrivances—contained no hint of a concept of cumulative technological development at all. "Capital" is essentially a category of distribution, not production or development—a particular institutional arrangement "to engross, or 'corner,' the usufruct of the commonplace knowledge of ways and means" [Veblen 1919c, p. 332].

As to the relation between technological knowledge and mechanical contrivances properly seen *as tools*, Veblen clearly believed there was a relationship of complete interdependence in the process of techno-

logical development. This was apparent in a passage quoted in the previous section of this article, where Veblen said that a given contrivance
for effecting certain ends "becomes a circumstance which affects the
further growth of habits of thought" [Veblen 1919a, p. 75]. The growth
of technological knowledge so induced pertains not only to the "means"
but to the "ends" for which economic activity is undertaken.

It was this *interdependence* between tools and knowledge upon which
Ayres built his theory of economic progress, incorporating the instrumentalist philosophy of Dewey. Dewey had shattered the traditional
notion of separate "realms" of knowledge and activity, demonstrating
the unity of practical and scientific knowledge as an interaction between
the knower and the known. His analysis of the method of the experiment established that genuine knowledge is produced by the use of
tools and instruments, and in no other way [Dewey 1929].

But if all knowledge is *produced* by the skilled use of tools, then—
among many other implications—it is merely foolish to ask if skills are
something apart from tools. As Ayres wrote in a paper for the American
Economic Association in 1953:

> All skills are cultural. They are part—and surely a not insignificant part—
> of the body of lore from which individual human beings learn whatever
> they learn. But it is true that all technological behavior patterns are ob-
> jectified in tools, instruments, formulas, and notations of many kinds; and
> that fact is very important, for it is the basis of technological development
> [Ayres 1953, p. 282].

Thus, contrary to much popular belief and much of the literature of
economics, it is not the heroic efforts or the genius of skilled individuals
—however essential (but also constant) these may be—that is the underlying basis of technological development. It is the sheer objective
existence and proliferation of tools. As Ayres went on to say in this
particularly clear statement:

> All culture derives from past experience. But because technology is objec-
> tified in physical tools and appartatus, it is always capable of progressive
> development. Every tool contains—within itself, so to speak—the pos-
> sibility of being applied in new situations, to different materials and in
> different ways from its historic use. This process is the universal pattern
> of invention and discovery. All new devices are combinations of old ones,
> and so are all the discoveries of the scientists and all the creations of the
> artists [Ayres 1953, p. 282].

With this tool-combination principle, Ayres added another dimension to the institutionalist concept of technology—as clearly as the air-

plane added a new dimension to the kite and the internal combustion engine. As noted earlier, Ayres referred to this principle as a "law of progress," which he explained to mean simply that, as in a mathematical progression, each member of the series is derived from the preceding member by the same operation [Ayres 1944, pp. 119–20].

A particulary good analogy would be the simple Fibonacci series: 1, 1, 2, 3, 5 . . . n, in which each member is the sum (combination) of the two preceding members. Although the operation that produces the series is additive, the series very soon converges on a geometric progression, suggesting the acceleration that has observably occurred in the tool-combination process.

Ayres was careful to point out that any mathematical analogy to the process of tool combination will be just that. The point is that, *like* the relationship between members of a progressive series, there is a *functional* relationship between new working principles and the previous working principles that they observably combine. That functionality is the continuum of technological and scientific knowledge, and it is a progressive development in the strictest sense.

The *condition* for this cumulative development is the physical existence of tools and instruments, which are "imprinted" with the working principles of their use. The term "imprinted" is used here in a very broad sense. However, Ayres elsewhere pointed to a literal extension of the idea in regard to the *increasing* objectification of tools: "Having found a primitive artifact, archaeologists can infer what it was used for. . . . But since the development of written language, and especially since the development of alphabetical printing . . . , everthing men do and think has become objectified" [Ayres 1961, p. 112].

The extraordinary detail on the history of invention and discovery with which Ayres supports the principle of tool combination in his numerous writings cannot be conveyed here. Nor is it possible to explore the many subleties and anomalies in the history of invention that are made intelligible by this principle—such as the role of chance, or "serendipity," simultaneous invention, the role of amateurs, cross-fertilization through culture contact, and so on [Ayres 1944, pp. 112–19].

Among the implications is what Ayres sometimes called the "contingent inevitability" of technological progress: "Granted that tools are always tools of men who have the capacity to use tools and therefore the capacity to use them together, combinations are bound to occur. Furthermore it follows that the more tools there are, the greater is the number of potential combinations" [Ayres 1944, p. 119].

That a *functional* continuum, a cumulative and accelerating process of tool-combination runs through *history,* is a startling idea. Functional, or "law," explanations and historical, or "genetic," explanations are commonly supposed to be mutually exclusive [Brown 1963, pp. 54–56]. Yet, in retrospect, there can be and is a "logic" to at least *a part of* what happened in history. Moreover, this *progress* is not only not "teleological"—involves no "intention in nature" such as earlier conceptions of progress—but is specifically found to be wholly independent of the intentions of "heroic" inventors.

Again, this is not to say that people—generally gifted people of great skill, as Ayres acknowledged—do not make the combinations that are made. The point is simply that such a statement, however interesting or significant for discourse on individual creativity, has no *standing* in the analysis of cultural phenomena, which precede and condition phenomena on the individual level. In short: "The whole analysis must proceed on the level of generalization of culture rather than of individuality in order for the principle of technological progress to be understood at all" [Ayres 1944, p. 112].

If the proliferation of tools suffices to explain much of what happened in history, and if there is a contingent inevitability to technological progress, does this mean that the tool-combination principle "predicts" the future? Certainly not. Nor has any such claim ever been made by Ayres or other institutionalists. Such claims would, indeed, be contrary to the cultural and evolutionary premises of institutionalist theory.

The "inevitability" of technological progress is one of *direction,* as determined by the logic of the process; and it is *uni*directional precisely because it also occurs in history—in the one-way process of cultural evolution. More particularly, in retrospect we know that it has been technological progress that has *imparted* direction to the evolution of culture.

Contingency stems from two sources, one of which might be said to precede the evolution of technology and culture, the other of which is wholly cultural. The first contingency is obvious: human life and then culture have always gone forward on the "premise" of human life itself. The security of life for *Homo sapiens* was enormously enlarged with the onset of culture, from whenever that might be dated; and the technological process has been the source of the progressive adaptability and hence security of human life in a converging world culture since that time [Ayres 1961, pp. 207–27].

This has been the overall direction of things for human life as a whole, even though what Veblen referred to as the "usufruct of the community's knowledge" for invidious purposes—by power-wielding priesthoods, classes, dynasties, corporations, or nations—has prompted the use of practically every instrument in the generic human tool kit for one or another crime against humanity. The enormity of the maladaptions that may be undertaken is, of course, commensurate with the technological potential for adaptation.

And now, of course, we have "the bomb," which poses in its extreme form contingency number one, and may indeed limit further progress of technological knowledge through the disappearance of human life. This "ultimate invidious usufruct of knowledge" would also have to be seen, however, as the extreme form of the *second* source of contingency. This is the continuous coexistence with technology, in all cultures, of a general mode of behavior that is inhibitive of technological change and adaptation.

This opposition—between technological behavior and what Veblen, and Ayres after him, conceived as "ceremonial behavior"—is central to the institutionalist approach and to any attempt to trace out empirical processes of "cumulative causation" in cultural change. Since these are concepts of two interactive "behavior functions," a fuller discussion of their universality and their interaction in all cultures will be postponed to the next section of the article, which is directly concerned with the concept of technology as "instrumental behavior." There the questions of valuation that arise from the concept of technological progress can be examined in their proper *behavioral* context.

For purposes of historical analysis, institutionalists have generally focused on the broad activity *complexes* to which these behavior functions give rise—technological progress and institutionalized resistance. These terms—or the shorthand and problematic terms "technology" and "institutions"—have been used, especially in the framework of evolutionary economics, since Veblen first formulated the distinction [Ayres 1944, pp. 178–88; Hamilton 1986, pp. 525–32]. This conflict between technological progress and institutionalized resistance to change, in the many economic contexts in which Veblen analyzed it, has long been known as the "Veblenian dichotomy" [Gruchy 1947, pp. 120–22].

We are now prepared to examine the implications of technological progress for evolutionary economics—and for what Ayres, addressing himself to the broader economics profession, called "the role of technology in economic theory" [Ayres 1953]. These implications, of course, pertain to the empirical economy, or to what Karl Polanyi called the "substantive" economy [Polanyi 1957]. Both Veblen and Ayres, and perhaps a majority of institutionalists, have been primarily concerned with the modern "industrial economy"—which is, of course, also characterized in Western countries by market institutions and, *in that aspect,* treated by standard economic theory as *the* economy [Ayres 1952].

A common ground of all of evolutionary economics is that market institutions do not constitute "the" economy. The book in which the above cited article by Polanyi appears—*Trade and Market in the Early Empires*—is a masterful demonstration of this point, based upon institutional analysis of a wide range of historical economies, by scholars with an orientation to economic anthropology. Evolutionary economics in the Veblen-Ayres tradition has established the same point by tracing the evolution of the *industrial* economy as a function of technological progress. These two lines of evolutionary economics converged in the active involvement of researchers in the economic development of less-developed countries.

In that part of his work that has received perhaps greatest recognition from non-institutionalist economists [Cf. Robinson 1964, pp. 112–16], Ayres applied the concept of the tool-combination principle to the institutional situation in medieval Europe to provide a full accounting of the "industrial evolution" of the modern economy [Ayres 1944, pp. 125–54]. Again, the empirical richness of the explanation cannot be conveyed, but the conclusion is easily stated.

Medieval Europe—rather than any other cultural area—was the setting of events culminating in the "industrial revolution" because this "frontier" was the legatee of the entire past development of technology in Mediterranean civilization, but not of its ceremonial complement. It was then "almost completely severed from the institutional power system of its parent. The result was unique" [Ayres 1944, p. 137].

This explanation of the origins of the industrial economy stands in direct contradiction to the whole range of theories that attribute the "rise of industrial capitalism" to one or another of the institutional underpinnings of market economy. As Ayres noted:

An understanding of technological process is sufficient to establish the reverse. It is already clear that technological innovation played the decisive part in establishing the institutions of capitalism. By making industry paramount in modern life, the industrial revolution has made the captains of industry powerful. Power is certainly important. The process of institutional adaptation to technological change is therefore tremendously important as well as subtle and complicated, and special attention must therefore be given to it [Ayres 1944, p. 154].

The different conception of the *origins* of industrial capitalism that proceeds from a proper understanding of the role of technology also has implications for the manner in which the industrial economy—not to mention economies without market institutions—should be analyzed at any point in time. The traditional market model is without a concept of technology, as Veblen was the first economist to emphasize. Even otherwise insightful contemporary mainstream economists, doing useful and relevant work, may resort to purely pedagogical constructs of "technological change" such as: "movement of the production-possibility frontier in the northeast direction" [Balassa 1961, p. 13].

Even as the industrial revolution was in full swing, Adam Smith—while attributing the improvement in "productive powers" and the wealth of the nation to the "division of labor"—finally had this quasi-technological factor depend more basically still on the commercial categories he called "extent of the market" and, most particularly, the "accumulation of stock" [Smith 1937, pp. 3–21]. Thus was set in motion a scheme of thought that struggles to this day, unsuccessfully, to "factor" technological progress without recognizing that it is a tool-combination process.

As Veblen was unremitting in pointing out, what has instead been "factored" is the pecuniary entitlements to the product of modern industry. This taxonomic scheme is then falsely extended to all economic activity. Hence: "a gang of Aleutian Islanders slushing about in the wrack and surf with rakes and magical incantations for the capture of shell-fish are held, in point of taxonomic reality, to be engaged on a feat of hedonistic equilibration in rent, wages, and interest. And that is all there is to it" [Veblen 1919d, p. 193].

The concept of technological progress has implications, then, at the most fundamental level of economic theorizing. The economy cannot be factored. Not only is this true with respect to "capital"—the pecuniary concept in orthodox theory that does duty for "technology"—but it is true for all the "factors of production."[5]

In Veblen's critique of the concept of capital, cited earlier, he noted that "material contrivances" should be taken to include not only capital goods, and the "land in use," but also "the useful minerals, plants, and animals." Continuing, he observed that: "To say that these minerals, plants, and animals are useful—in other words, that they are economic goods—means that they have been brought within the sweep of the community's knowledge of ways and means" [Veblen 1919c, p. 329].

"Natural" resources, then, are simply another aspect of technological knowledge—materials "imprinted" with working principles—and, as such, grist for the tool-combination process. Elsewhere in this volume,

Thomas DeGregori provides a full development of the institutionalist theory of resources, under the title: "Resources Are Not; They Become."

It is perhaps to the credit of the economic mainstream—rather than otherwise—that it has moved gradually to unify the factors of production, however unconvincingly, under the heading of "capital" [Neale 1984]. Capital has a certain institutional reality, at least, in a capitalist economy. While some have objected that the term "human capital" can properly be construed only as "slave," the concept is in fact an admission that the brute human capacity for work—the labor factor—is always "augmented" by technological knowledge.

The most promising development to date, however, was the 1960s discovery by economists in the field of growth accounting that the "residual"—read "consequences of technological progress and institutional resistance not encompassed by the presently conceived augmented factors"—is the "coefficient of our ignorance" [Balogh and Streeten 1966, p. 138]. However, for some twenty-five years now, the forward thrust of new techniques of measurement has contended with the vested interest that investigators have in the factors theory, with disappointing results for economic knowledge.

The literature attempting to explain declining "productivity" growth in the United States, for example, is a morass. Edward Denison, the dean of American growth accountants, found in these circumstances that the explanation of declining growth given by the "residual" is larger than the decline to be explained [Denison 1979, p. 3; Lower 1982, pp. 633–34].

The basic difficulty, again, is that the factors of production are in reality factors of distribution—hence market, and not industrial, categories [Veblen 1919d]. To resolve the incompatibility between theory and measurement in the evolving industrial situation, it must be recognized that:

> The self-regulating market is a mechanism that implements the existing technological and institutional situation, to some extent and in certain particular respects. It does not create that situation on either the technological or the institutional side, and the equilibrium it (sometimes) reaches only registers the relative stability of the prevailing situation [Ayres 1953, p. 284].

Of course, an evolutionary economics cannot be construed—any more than the concept of technological progress can be—as a "purely economic" matter. Especially with respect to the forward "policy" aspect of economic inquiry, the search for a unified conception of cultural knowledge and action must continue. With the logic of technology at the center of economic theory:

> The problem of general economic and social policy is that of making the most of our tools, of their potentialities as well as their present efficiency, by whatever institutional adjustments may prove necessary and possible. The complexity and difficulty of the task is axiomatic. That it is not impossible, our present level of achievement bears witness, notwithstanding all its manifold perplexities [Ayres 1953, p. 287].

Technology and Instrumental Behavior

The theory of knowledge, action, and valuation that informs institutionalist perspective in general, and the concept of technology in particular, is that which evolved in the United States in this century under the name of "pragmatism" and, at the hands of Dewey, "instrumentalism." Earlier in this volume, several authors addressed key aspects of the philosophical underpinnings of institutionalist thought; and leading contributors to institutionalism have been uncommonly explicit about the philosophy of science that underlies their work.

For the purpose at hand, it would be neither desirable nor feasible to recapitulate the philosophical grounds for the concept of technology as instrumental behavior. The focus must be limited to the evolved idea that all cultural behavior is of one of two types: "instrumental behavior" or "ceremonial behavior." One of these behavior functions— instrumental behavior— is "problem-solving" behavior. Invariably, if the problems and the solutions are real, it is therefore tool-using, knowledge-producing behavior. Such behavior is, by virtue of the use of tools and the production of knowledge, a social process; and its processual significance derives not from particular problems solved but from the cultural means-ends *continuum* in which those problems are solved. It is the behavior function that gives rise to technological progress and cultural evolution.

From the distinction between two modes of knowing and doing there is further implication: One of these modes of doing—the technological or instrumental behavior function—exhibits, "matter-of-factly" as Veblen would say, a universalistic method of *valuation* applicable to all human doing. This non-culturally relative process of "instrumental valuation" embodies the full significance of the concept earlier set forth in evolutionary terms, that technology is *trans-cultural.*

While the grounds of the pragmatic or instrumental theory of knowledge cannot be explored in any detail, mention must at least be made of the revolution it wrought in traditional conceptions of theory and practice, knowledge and action. These traditional conceptions—including much in the prevailing worldview of science—treated knowledge and action as pertaining to separate realms of "mind" and "body," of the "ideal" and the "material." The theory of knowledge this perpetuated was what Dewey called the "spectator theory of knowledge," and it was this that was overthrown by his analysis of the instrumental method of knowing actually employed in experimental science [Dewey 1929, p. 23].[6]

Knowledge is not, then, acquired by peering into an ordained "Nature"—whether physical, biological, or social. As in the practical activities by which people have purposefully employed tools since the dawn of culture, the "known" in the most secure theoretical sciences is a *consequence* of human intent and action. "If we see that knowing is not the act of an outside spectator," Dewey wrote, "but of a participator inside the natural and social scene, then the true object of knowledge resides in the consequences of directed action" [Dewey 1929, p. 196].

The instrumental behavior function, which was earlier described as an evolutionary life process and a tool-combination process, thus turns out to be continuous with—and indistinguishable in any but the invidious senses of "mind" and "body," or "theory" and "practice"—from the process of inquiry in the scientific laboratory. Technology and science are one.

But there is another mode of cultural behavior, and it has equally been present in the organized activities of man since, in Huxley's phrase, "the emergence of mental capacities to the level where they begin to affect the future course of events" [Huxley 1953, p. vii]. This behavior function is what we have been calling "ceremonial behavior." While Veblen must be credited with the discovery of ceremonialism as a universal behavior function in conflict with technological behavior, this "Veblenian dichotomy" should perhaps also be regarded as a matter that was ripe for "simultaneous invention," a phenomenon that is itself explained by the principle of tool combination.

In any case, whether by borrowing or by simultaneous invention, this idea lay also at the heart of Dewey's thesis in *The Quest for Certainty* [Cf. Ayres 1944, p. 99]. The opening words of this work, which went on to revolutionize the theory of knowledge, were:

Man who lives in a world of hazards is compelled to seek for security. He has sought to attain it in two ways. One of them began with an attempt to propitiate the powers which environ him and determine his destiny. It expressed itself in supplication, sacrifice, ceremonial rite and magical cult. ... The other course is to invent arts and by their means turn the powers of nature to account; man constructs a fortress out of the very conditions and forces which threaten him. He builds shelters, weaves garments, makes flame his friend instead of his enemy, and grows into the complicated arts of associated living. It is a commentary on the slight control man has obtained over himself by means of control over nature, that the method of action has been felt to manifest dangerous pride, even defiance of the powers which be [Dewey 1929, p. 3].

There is of course a difference between the main uses of this dichotomy by Veblen and by Dewey. Dewey's scientific purpose was to show that the ceremonial way of seeking security from hazards—the quest for certainty—still distorted the modern understanding of the fundamental nature of knowledge, and also of valuation. The instrumental theory of knowledge and valuation was itself an instrument to supplant this futile and destructive quest [Dewey 1929, pp. 254–86; Dewey 1939].

Veblen's evolutionary economics employed the dichotomy—presented largely in the form of "industrial" *versus* "pecuniary" and "honorific" aspects of behavior; or "workmanship" *versus* "leisure" in the special sense of abstention from useful work—for analysis of economic culture. Further usages included "serviceability" as opposed to "disserviceability"; "industry" *versus* "exploit" or "predation"; instrumental consumption *versus* "conspicuous" leisure, consumption, and waste; and many more paired meanings.

The conceptual purpose of the dichotomy in Veblen's work as a whole must be seen as a means to distinguish the "technological life process" as a universal mode of behavior from the ceremonial "usufruct" of technology—which was, like Dewey's "quest for certainty," often destructive of life and culture. In this sense, as will be made explicit later, it is difficult to see how it can be denied that Veblen also had an operational concept of instrumental valuation.

As should be clear from the above, Veblen's conception of ceremonial behavior was at bottom one of "invidiousness" in a sense that is easily broadened—and was broadened by him—to the employment of the material means of life for any merely relative advantage. However, his first and most famous book, *The Theory of the Leisure Class,* highlighted the more direct forms of invidious distinction—in symbols of prowess, dress, consumption, leisure, tastes, and the like [Veblen 1899].

Dewey, like Veblen, clearly had an encompassing concept of ceremonial behavior; but his immediate focus was on the residue of ceremonialism in modern philosophy and science, which was a residue precisely of the "consumptive" or "leisure class" form of invidiousness. With respect to the spectator theory of knowledge, Dewey noted:

> The whole scheme hangs together with the traditional depreciation of practical activity on the part of the intellectual class. In reality, it also condemns intelligence to a position of impotency. Its exercise is an enjoyable use of leisure. The doctrine of its supreme value is largely a compensation for the impotency that attached to it in contrast with the force of executive acts [Dewey 1929, p. 214].

With Ayres, all of the earlier meanings of the dichotomy were unified. At the same time, Ayres provides a clearer understanding of the relationship *between* the instrumental and the ceremonial behavior functions. With respect to certain widespread confusions on this point, Ayres wrote:

> This difficulty could be resolved if it could be clearly understood that the distinction of the technological and the ceremonial aspects of organized behavior is a dichotomy but not a dualism. That is, it undertakes to distinguish two aspects of what is still a single, continuous activity both aspects of which are present at all times. Indeed, they bound and define each other as do the obverse and reverse of a coin [Ayres 1944, p. 101].

This is an absolutely crucial distinction in the *behavioral* context of the concept of technology. It was precisely the metaphysical *dualism* of traditional philosophy that Dewey had set as the "problem" for his inquiry on scientific knowledge. This problem was resolved by the demonstration that knowing is doing. The proper distinction is between this knowing and doing process—the continuum of technological and scientific inquiry—and the quest for certainty. This is not a dualism because both are behavior going on within culture. Moreover, they typically go on within the *same* behavioral complexes, as when Veblen's "gang of Aleutian Islanders" are found "slushing about in the wrack and surf," wielding *both* rakes *and* magical incantations for the purpose of capturing shell-fish.

Nonetheless, the behaviors are clearly distinguishable as to antecedents, as to the framing of purpose and means, and most importantly, as to consequences. This is what is meant by saying they are two behavior *functions.* Instrumental behavior, as should be clear from what has been said, derives from previous knowing and doing. It frames purpose in regard to an objective "lack" or " problem" in the situation, employs tools and instruments as means, and has as its consequence both the resolution of particular problems and the production of further knowledge. The "ends" become "means" in further knowing and doing—hence Dewey's "means-ends continuum."

Ceremonial behavior is re-enactment, and its purposes as well as its antecedents are given by what has gone before. "Ceremony," in the ordinary sense of the term, is only one aspect, and one greatly attenuated by centuries of advancement in technological knowledge. However, the behavioral mode is described by Ayres as fully manifested in several other ways familiar to any social scientist.

It is manifested in social stratification and in all hierarchical organization. Within stratified systems, status or rank, as well as the proper behavior pertaining thereto, are prescribed by the "mores." Social stratification and the mores are, in turn, sustained by an ideology, or "system of tribal beliefs, which purport to explain the magic potency which distinguishes people of higher ranks and the awful consequences which are believed to follow infractions of the mores" [Ayres, 1962, p. xvi]. Systems of indoctrination that begin in infancy emotionally condition members of every community to accept the beliefs, mores, and systems of rank. Even where awe-inspiring mystic rites and rituals have become attenuated, ceremonies as such still solemnly confer what Veblen called "ceremonial adequacy" on the various ranks at rites of passage and on religious and other occasions.

The continuity in ceremonial behavior is a static continuity, inherently resistant to change. Ceremonial purpose is not framed as "ends-in-view" in a continuum of means-ends activity, but as the re-enactment of cherished "values." Such purpose does not stand in any direct—much less directed—relationship to the uniformities of nature or to ongoing change.

Ceremonial purpose and conduct relate to the imagined world of unchanging verities described in the system of tribal beliefs. This requires nothing less, according to Veblen, than that "life is conceived as a scheme of conformity to a purpose outside and beyond the process of living" [Veblen 1919e, p. 108]. Apart from the simple ceremonies that employ fetishes (or pseudo-tools) to propitiate invisible forces, ceremonial behavior is "without visible means" to its "transcendent" ends.

Ceremonial behavior and thought thus *dualize* the knowing and doing process in what Dewey called a "quest for certainty" [Ayres 1944, pp. 224ff]. The "ends" of activity in a dualized conception necessarily belong to the "higher" realm of mind, while the "means" belong to the inferior realm of activity—in modern versions, "mere" technology. Social inquiry still suffers from the conception—the prevailing one not that long ago—that its task is the discovery in Nature of the proper "ends" of human conduct: for example, consumption is the "end" of all economic activity. In such a dualized scheme of thought, technology easily appears as an exogenous "disturbance" of equilibrium—but equally as a "means" to given "ends."

Ceremonial behavior, therefore, is not without consequences. It includes, but is more than, passive "archaism." The behavior function that re-enacts and "re-enforces" the mores, beliefs, and systems of rank, also reinforces and extends a system of *social power*. The maintenance or expansion of such a system, to the differential advantage of those ceremonially adequate to run it, depends economically and in other ways on gaining the "usufruct" of some part of the community's knowledge.

The uses of technological knowledge occur under cultural conditions in which the purposes of activity are in part instrumental, or problem-solving, and partly ceremonial. Hence, directly, or at some remove from the immediate activity, there are two different perspectives, also at "cross-purposes," regarding the technical "means" at hand. They are means to matter-of-fact "ends-in-view" and to "ends" in the ceremonial sense.

In varying degree, in every culture, the *adaptive power* of the technology—its working principles in relation to the uniformities of nature—is brought under control for ceremonial and invidious "ends." The main thrust of Veblen's analysis of the modern capitalist economy was that the pecuniary aims of business—including the prevailing system of social stratification and economic rewards—were at odds with the technological proficiency of industry. The pecuniary purpose required limits on the evolving technological potential for mass production and consumption of genuinely useful output. The options included direct curtailment of production, or "waste" on a scale sufficient to dispose of output through conspicuous consumption or war [Veblen 1904]. It is hardly clear that these dilemmas have yet been resolved.

It is noteworthy, however, that in the same penetrating analysis that yielded these insights, Veblen developed the concept of "the cultural incidence of the machine process" [Veblen 1904, pp. 302–73]. This tendency to matter-of-fact behavior and habits of thought, in the population actually touched by the evolving technological system, was derived from "reading the machines," in a time when the underlying population barely read the printed word. It is anything but clear that this process has ended.

These are the two behavior functions. If we set aside what we know of the technological life process and its direction, then the usufruct of the squaw's knowledge of ways and means, for the manly pursuits of war and pecuniary advantage, may appear as the whole of history. If this *had* been all that happened in history, then Dewey (and Veblen) would still be right that the quest for certainty is a futile quest. It would still be true that the transcendent "ends" or "collective representations" of particular cultures and cultural groupings misrepresent what *did* happen and offer no guide to what *ought* to happen.

This is the level of understanding reached by "cultural relativism": human life is quaint—if sometimes ugly—and questions of value can be settled only by the bashing of heads. However, we cannot set aside what we know of trans-cultural evolution or technological progress. Nor is it true that we know nothing about the universal mode of instrumental valuation.

But what, precisely, does the knowing and doing process tell us about the "values" we ought to hold? The answer to this question is: nothing. But the defect is in the question. We should no more expect a behavioral process to yield specific "values" in the static and finished sense of that term, than we should expect the theory of technological progress to predict the next machine, or the theory of biological evolution to "name" the next animal.

The question *ought* to be: What does the knowing and doing process tell us about the *process of valuation* that accompanies and completes it? And what does the entire instrumental behavior function tell us about the way the human race has in fact achieved whatever it has achieved? What does the technological life process tell us about the method and the criterion by which genuine valuation—as opposed to the fabrication of transcendentals—has always gone on in human culture?

The institutionalist answers to these questions have themselves "evolved" in the clearest intellectual sense of the term. For Veblen, the idea of instrumental valuation was implicit in his concept of "the economic life process," but was seldom made explicit. To the extent he tried to formulate it under the heading of the "instinct of workmanship," he ran afoul of the general scientific currents then disposing of the notion of instinct—even though he was at pains to explain he did not mean it that way [Ayres 1963, pp. 56–57].

Nonetheless, Veblen knew the meaning of "waste," in consumption and also in production. In his first book, he set forth an inchoate criterion of instrumental valuation in defining what was *not* waste in consumption, and this suffused all of his later work: "The test to which all expenditure must be brought in an attempt to decide that point is the question whether it serves directly to enhance human life on the whole —whether it furthers the life process taken impersonally. For this is the basis of award of the instinct of workmanship" [Veblen 1899, p. 99].

In Dewey, it is difficult to say where the theory of knowledge leaves off and the theory of valuation begins, which is *processually as it should be.* Just before closing the key chapter on "The Supremacy of Method" and beginning the next on "The Construction of Good," Dewey wrote that:

> The final import of the conclusions as to knowledge resides in the changed idea it enforces as to action. The distinction once made between theory and practice has meaning as a distinction between two kinds of action: blind and intelligent. Intelligence is a quality of some acts, those which are directed; and directed action is an achievement, not an original endowment. The history of human progress is the story of the transformation of acts which, like the interactions of inanimate things, take place unknowingly to actions qualified by understanding of what they are about; from actions controlled by external conditions to actions having guidance through their intent:—their insight into their own consequences [Dewey 1929, p. 245].

Just here the method of instrumental valuation has been defined. It is the *same* as the method of scientific knowing. Knowing is a purposive act; and we *know* through insight into the consequences of this action, whether in the laboratory or in "practical" problem-solving. This is the method of intelligence. But this is also the method of instrumental valuation, as is implicit in Dewey's words. Later he wrote, explicitly: "Valuations exist in fact and are capable of empirical observation, so that propositions about them can be verified" [Dewey 1939, p. 58]. Since valuations are themselves consequential, they are subject to the same investigatory process as facts, and testable by future experience.

Ayres was given to posing this linkage of "fact" and "value judgment" in somewhat jarring terms, in order to make the unfamiliar point: "By intent every judgment is a determination of fact. Every decision intends to take account of facts, and every choice has as its prototype the mechanic's choice of the right tool" [Ayres 1944, p. 219]. That choice is never the "final judgment." Nor is the right tool always available. Sometimes this "lack" is apparent—for example, while using a pipe wrench ōn a bolt or nut, for want of a crescent wrench. The more significant case is the problem for which there is no known solution. Inquiry on the consequences of proposed solutions must precede the value judgment, or if one is tentatively made, it must be tested. The relevant complex of tools and knowledge must be brought to bear. By virtue of the tools and knowledge employed, the process of instrumental valuation is also a cultural process—even for the lone mechanic. The character of this ongoing process of valuation makes it, like genuine knowing, a "self-correcting" process [Gordon 1980, pp. 43ff.].

The instrumental theory of valuation, like the concept of technological behavior generally, is a conception of a *process* that goes on in all of human culture. It is not a theory of the elusive *quality* of "value," such as has occupied the mainstream of economic thought [Liebhafsky 1986, p. 16]. Still less is it a theory of the "values" that ought to be held, on any *authority* whatsoever [Ayres 1961, 119–21].

Indeed, there is no ground for treating the problem of values *in relation to* authority at all. While value is inherently a relational concept, this misconstrues what it always and everywhere relates *to*. As Ayres wrote in *Toward A Reasonable Society:* "Moral significance arises only *within* the *system* of human activities. Given our existence as a species, and given the system of activities by which we live and to which we are irrevocably committed, the problem of values is that of the relation of any given activity or interest to that system" [Ayres 1961, p. 117].

This brings us to the crucial question [Ayres 1961, p. 119; Liebhafsky 1986, p. 18]. As Ayres wrote: "What is at issue here is the *criterion of value"* [Ayres 1961, p. 119, italics added]. Just as the criterion of scientific *truth* is a process—

the process of inquiry in which mankind has been continuously and cumulatively engaged throughout the ages. . . . : When we seek to determine whether anything is good or bad, or whether any act is right or wrong, we are seeking clear and certain knowledge of its *causal bearing on the life process of mankind.* The criterion of value, like the meaning of causality and the criterion of clarity and certainty, derives from the process itself [Ayres 1961, pp. 120, 122, italics added].

Conclusion

The theory of instrumental valuation completes the concept of technology within the institutionalist perspective. The "technological life process" thus becomes a concept with clear and consistent meaning in the processes of cultural evolution, of progressive development in history, of the criteria of truth and value in human behavior. All of these meanings are derived from the observable characteristics of the process itself.

As was noted in the introduction, this concept provides the foundation for a general or unified theory of cultural process. However, technology is not the only concept in the institutionalist tool kit and does not alone constitute a theory of cumulative causation in culture. As the discussion of instrumental and ceremonial behavior makes clear, the concept of technology has *explanatory* and *policy* value in concrete cultural circumstances only as a dichotomous aspect of culture. This is so despite the fact that over sufficiently long periods, technological progress is the salient aspect of what happened in history.

In short, the *problems* for inquiry under the general theory arise in ongoing cultural circumstances, in the interaction between technological and ceremonial behavior. This pertains not only to policy *issues,* but to every "problem of inquiry" regarding what is *so,* has been so, or is likely to be so in evolving socioeconomic systems.

For such evolutionary inquiry, there is no substitute for an empirical analysis of the situation at hand, which takes account of the achieved technological potential and the full range of culturally relative behavior and interests at play. In this institutional analysis of substantive societies and economies—or of fields of operations therein—the prevailing "usufruct" of technological knowledge is itself seen to be instituted in the scheme of cultural life.

The problem of directing cultural change, perhaps especially in traditional societies, is the difffiult one of inducing new combinations on the existing base of evolved technologies, or of introducing new technological knowledge from outside the system. Alternatively, in conditions of rapid technological change, as in most advanced economies, it is the equally difficult problem of "institutional adjustment" [Thompson 1967; Foster 1981a; Foster 1981b].

The applications that institutionalists have made of the concept of technology—within this broad scheme of evolutionary social science—have ranged widely. Depending upon the problems set for inquiry, more or less emphasis has been placed upon specifically technological or specifically institutional aspects of the cultural situation; and conceptions of institutions, as well as the concept of technology, have evolved in this process of inquiry.

But from the earliest contributions of Veblen and Commons, through hundreds of relevant and useful studies of every conceivable problem of the industrial and industrializing economies, and finally in a burgeoning literature in the *Journal of Economic Issues* during the past two decades, these have been the coordinates of an emerging general theory that now clearly defines the institutionalist perspective.

Since Ayres published his mature statement of the instrumental theory of valuation in 1961, it can no more be said that: "There is the economic life process still in great measure awaiting theoretical formulation" [Veblen 1919a, p. 70]. The never-ending task that has remained is the furtherance of that process—of the problem-solving potential it has always embodied—in a world still deeply mired in the conflict and misery of a false quest for certainty.

Notes

1. Traditional economists assumed a very particular institutional framework as "given and immutable," which, as Veblen said, "limits their inquiry in a particular and decisive way. It shuts off the inquiry at the point where the modern scientific interest sets in" [Veblen 1919b, pp. 239–40]. But the narrowly drawn "hedonistic conception of man," while essential to "mechanize" human response in the model, was absolutely fatal to scientific inquiry, cutting it off at the point where psychological intent was (presumably) formed—with no means of testing such propositions. This had the further effect of leaving human action and its consequences entirely out of account. As Commons noted, such "ideal types" as the economic man are in fact pedagogical, not scientific concepts. They convey a certain understanding or "fellow-feeling" with respect to some aspect of shared experience (for those who share it), but cannot substitute for scientific hypothesis formation and testing in an ongoing situation [Commons 1934, pp. 724 ff. Lower, 1980, pp. 89-90.]

2. The characterization of "culture" as a "core concept" of institutionalism is taken from the December 1986, presidential address of Anne Mayhew to the Association for Evolutionary Economics, entitled "Culture: Core Concept Under Attack." The address was published in the June 1987, issue of the *Journal of Economic Issues*. Mayhew provides further discussion of the cultural and conceptual background of institutionalist thought in this volume.

3. Veblen seems to have found the evidence compelling that one nation borrowing cultural elements from another will selectively borrow technological knowledge. As he noted: "The borrowing community or cultural group is already furnished with its own system of conceits and observances—in magic, religion, propriety, and any other line of conventional necessity" [Veblen 1915, p. 37]. However, this writer found that, in Chile's modern industrialization effort, the selectivity has run almost entirely in the opposite direction, through a process of "dysfunctional institutional adaption" [Lower 1970, especially pp. 159–70].

4. Yngve Ramstad notes that Commons's development of concepts has been regarded as "confused" by orthodox critics and "convoluted" and difficult even by sympathetic institutionalists (including Ramstad). This difficulty is held, with substantial merit, to stem from the fact that "Commons appears to be the prototypical holist" [Ramstad 1986, p. 1069]. That institutionalism in general is "holistic" in the rather broad sense that Allan Gruchy gave to the term in his *Modern Economic Thought* seems beyond dispute [Gruchy 1947, especially pp. 26, 56, 550–65]. But Commons seems

to carry what Ramstad aptly calls his "multi-level, part-whole mode of explanation" to extremes that are not essential to the holistic concept and method. As the thrust of this article indicates, this institutionalist believes that one can tarry a while on any particular level and that institutionalists who have done so at the general level have contributed much to conceptual clarity—especially with respect to the concept of technology.

5. Significantly, the same conclusion follows from any analysis of the economy according to cumulative causation. Thus, Karl Polanyi's brilliant work, *The Great Transformation* [Polanyi 1944], which was published the same year as *The Theory of Economic Progress,* examined the "rise and fall of market economy" according to the "commodity fictions." These were the fictions—effectively *enacted into law* and actively enforced under "laissez-faire"—that land, labor, and money are commodities, that is, that they are produced for sale. Without these fictions, the market cannot function on the "resource market" side as in the orthodox "factor theory." These fictions were so destructive of man, habitat, and enterprise that social movements protective of each cumulatively transformed market economies into mixed economies.

6. It is important to note that Dewey's theory of knowledge is in effect experimentally verified. It is supported by the same evidence in quantum mechanics that supports "Heisenberg's principle of indeterminacy." Heisenberg demonstrated that position and velocity cannot both be known, since neither can be known without measurement by the investigator, which alters either position or velocity. This is not a matter to be overcome by better methods of measurement. We know by doing, and uncertainty is a uniformity of nature [Dewey 1929, pp. 201ff].

References

Ayres, C.E. 1944. *The Theory of Economic Progress,* 3d edition. Kalamazoo, Michigan: New Issues Press, 1978.

————. 1952. *The Industrial Economy: Its Technological Basis and Institutional Destiny.* Cambridge, Mass.: The Riverside Press.

————. 1953. "The Role of Technology in Economic Theory." *American Economic Review* 43 (May): 279–87.

————. 1961. *Toward a Reasonable Society: The Values of Industrial Civilization.* Austin: University of Texas Press.

————. 1962. "Forward—1962." In *The Theory of Economic Progress,* 3d edition, pp. xiii–xxxiii. Kalamazoo, Michigan: New Issues Press.

————. 1963. "The Legacy of Thorstein Veblen." In *Institutional Economics: Veblen, Commons, and Mitchell Reconsidered,* pp. 45–62. Berkeley: University of California Press.

Balassa, Bela. 1961. *The Theory of Economic Integration.* Homewood, Ill.: Richard D. Irwin.

Balogh, Thomas, and P.P. Streeten. 1966. "The Coefficient of Ignorance." Reprinted in *Education and the Development of Nations,* ed. John W. Hanson and Cole S. Brembeck, pp. 137–48. New York: Holt, Rinehart and Winston.

Brown, Robert. 1963. *Explanation in Social Science.* Chicago: Aldine Publishing Co.

Commons, John R. 1934. *Institutional Economics,* Reprint edition. Madison: University of Wisconsin Press [1961].

DeGregori, Thomas R. 1985. *A Theory of Technology: Continuity and Change in Human Development.* Ames, Iowa: The Iowa State University Press.

Denison, Edward G. 1979. "Explanations of Declining Productivity Growth." *Survey of Current Business,* part 2, 59 (October): 1–24.

Dewey, John. 1929. *The Quest for Certainty: A Study of the Relation of Knowledge and Action.* New York: Minton, Balch and Company.

———. 1939. *Theory of Valuation.* In the *International Encyclopedia of Unified Science,* Vol. 2, No. 4. Chicago: University of Chicago Press.

Foster, J. Fagg. 1981a. "The Theory of Institutional Adjustment." *Journal of Economic Issues* 15 (December): 923–28.

———. 1981b. "The Fundamental Principles of Economics." *Journal of Economic Issues* 15 (December): 937–42.

Friedman, Milton. 1952. "The Economic Theorist." In *Wesley Clair Mitchell: The Economic Scientist,* ed. Arthur F. Burns, pp. 237–82. New York: National Bureau of Economic Research.

Gordon, Wendell. 1980. *Institutional Economics: The Changing System.* Austin: University of Texas Press.

Gruchy, Allan G. 1947. *Modern Economic Thought.* New York: Prentice-Hall.

Hamilton, David. 1986. "Technology and Institutions are Neither." *Journal of Economic Issues* 20 (June): 525–32.

Huxley, Julian. 1953. *Evolution in Action.* New York: Mentor Books.

Liebhafsky, H.H. 1986. "Peirce on the *Summum Bonum* and the Unlimited Community; Ayres on 'The Criterion of Value'." *Journal of Economic Issues* 20 (March): 5–20.

Lower, Milton D. 1970. *Institutional Bases of Economic Stagnation in Chile.* PhD. diss., The University of Texas at Austin.

———. 1980. "The Evolution of the Institutionalist Theory of Consumption." In *Institutional Economics: Essays in Honor of Allan G. Gruchy,* ed. John Adams, pp. 82–104. Boston/The Hague/London: Martinus Nijhoff Publishing.

———. 1982. "The Reindustrialization of America." *Journal of Economic Issues* 16 (June): 629–36.

Neale, Walter C. 1984. "Technology as Social Process: A Commentary on Knowledge and Human Capital." *Journal of Economic Issues* 18 (June): 573–80.

Polanyi, Karl. 1944. *The Great Transformation.* Reprint. Boston: Beacon Press [1957].

———. 1957. "The Economy as Instituted Process." In *Trade and Market in the Early Empires,* ed. Karl Polanyi, Conrad M. Arensberg, and Harry W. Pearson, pp. 243–70. Glencoe, Illinois: The Free Press.

Ramstad, Yngve. 1986. "A Pragmatist's Quest for Holistic Knowledge: The Scientific Methodology of John R. Commons." *Journal of Economic Issues* 20 (December): 1067–1105.

Robinson, Joan. 1964. *Economic Philosophy.* Garden City, New York: Doubleday Anchor Books.

226 Milton D. Lower

Schumpeter, Joseph A. 1952. "The General Economist." In *Wesley Clair Mitchell: The Economic Scientist,* ed. Arthur F. Burns, pp. 321–40. New York: National Bureau of Economic Research.
Smith, Adam. 1937. *The Wealth of Nations.* New York: The Modern Library.
Thompson, Carey C., ed. 1967. *Institutional Adjustment: A Challenge to a Changing Economy.* Austin: University of Texas Press.
Veblen, Thorstein. 1899. *The Theory of the Leisure Class.* New York: Modern Library [1934].
_____. 1904. *The Theory of Business Enterprise.* 2d ed. New York: Charles Scribner's Sons [1936].
_____. 1915. *Imperial Germany and the Industrial Revolution.* New York: The Viking Press [1954].
_____. 1919a. "Why is Economics Not an Evolutionary Science?" In *The Place of Science in Modern Civilization and Other Essays,* pp. 56–81. Reprint edition. New York: Russell and Russell [1961].
_____. 1919b. "The Limitations of Marginal Utility." In *The Place of Science in Modern Civilization and Other Essays,* pp. 231–51. Reprint edition. New York: Russell and Russell [1961].
_____. 1919c. "On the Nature of Capital." In *The Place of Science in Modern Civilization and Other Essays,* pp. 324–86. Reprint edition. New York: Russell and Russell [1961].
_____. 1919d. "Professor Clark's Economics." In *The Place of Science in Modern Civilization and Other Essays,* pp. 180–230. Reprint edition. New York: Russell and Russell [1961].
_____. 1919e. "The Preconceptions of Economic Science: I." In *The Place of Science in Modern Civilization and Other Essays,* pp. 82–113. Reprint edition. New York: Russell and Russell [1961].
_____. 1934. "The Opportunity of Japan." In *Essays in Our Changing Order,* ed. Leon Ardzrooni, pp. 248–66. New York: The Viking Press [1954].

Institutions

Walter C. Neale

The words *institution* and *institutional* are central to institutionalist theory. Not only does the root word give us our name, but also and importantly it and its cognates run through our writings. We have a term that we find important, but it lacks clear meaning. Our founding fathers did not use the words regularly or in well-defined ways.[1] One may enjoy Thorstein Veblen's attitude when he remarked, "An institution is of the nature of a usage which has become axiomatic and indispensable by habituation and general acceptance. Its physiological counterpart would presumably be any one of those habitual addictions that are now attracting the attention of the experts in sobriety," but one

Never before has the author's beatriceandsidney debt to Anne Mayhew been as great, and I owe particular thanks for frequent and careful readings and criticism to Baldwin Ranson and Marc Tool, and to Kathleen Brown (graduate student in History, University of North Carolina-Chapel Hill) and Emil Friberg (graduate student in Economics, also at the University of North Carolina.) The issues discussed in this essay have long concerned me, and the list of my debts of gratitude to others is lengthy. Some are cited in the footnotes herein, but I should mention especially John Adams, the members of the Conference on Problems of Economic Change (1966–1970), Wendell Gordon, Gregory Hayden, Don Kanel, Milton Lower, John Munkirs, Harry Pearson, Baldwin Ranson, William Schaniel, and Marc Tool among economists; Richard N. Adams and Walter Goldschmidt in anthropology; and Barbara S. Neale and Edgard Polome among linguists. Among scholars no longer living, other than the founding fathers of institutionalism and their immediate successors cited herein, I should declare special debts to Karl Polanyi, my mentor in these matters, and to Bronislaw Malinowski and A.R. Radcliffe-Brown, whose contributions on these issues are perhaps insufficiently appreciated today. And there have been generations of graduate students whose responses have been a great help.

227

is hardly sure of the limits of the concept and even less sure of the mechanisms by which institutions work or of their consequences.[2] John R. Commons says

> we may define an institution as Collective Action in Control of Individual Action.
> Collective action ranges all the way from unorganized Custom to the many organized Going Concerns, such as the family, the corporation, . . . the trade union, the Federal Reserve System, . . . the state. . . .
> Collective action is even more universal in the unorganized form of Custom than it is in the organized form of Concerns. Yet even a going concern is also a custom.[3]

Wesley C. Mitchell remarks, "'Institutions' is merely a convenient term for the more important among the widely prevalent, highly standardized social habits."[4] Quite consistent with these characterizations, and explicitly closer to the argument in this essay, is Walton Hamilton's classic statement that an institution "connotes a way of thought or action of some prevalence or permanence, which is embedded in the habits of a group or the customs of a people. . . . Institutions fix the confines of and impose form upon the activities of human beings. The world of use and wont, to which we imperfectly accommodate our lives, is a tangled and *unbroken web of institutions.'*[5] The terms, it is clear, have been used somewhat differently, but not inconsistently, by different institutionalists. In addition, *institution* is widely used in all the social sciences, but again without a well-defined meaning, whether across the social sciences or within any one of them.

This vagueness often makes no difference. We use many words with broad and often not even consistent referents—our languages are living perceptions, not logical constructs. But when a root word appears central to a theory it is worth struggling to give it as clear a meaning as we can. The purposes of this essay, then, are to present a view of the idea of *institutions* that will encompass the ways in which the term has been used, while giving it greater clarity and some operational precision, and to discuss some of the issues that arise in the use of the term.

The Core Idea

"*Most* of what people do is *governed* by the *institutions* of their society" is a proposition to which institutionalists subscribe. Because no institutionalist has ever polled his colleagues on the subject, one cannot say how much *most* is, but it certainly lies between 85 and 99 percent (at least 95 percent is this author's guess). Thus when we say that "most of what people do is governed by the institutions of their society," we are using the term in a much broader sense that those who say that "the institutions of a society modify behavior." The institutionalist proposition is very much what social scientists mean when they speak of culture (and learning the rules that govern is what they mean by enculturation). What institutionalists have been emphasizing is that culture governs all—not in the sense that bees' instincts are supposed to govern precisely their every action, but in the sense that a culture defines the permissible and the forbidden, defines right and wrong, the admirable and its opposite, gives content to these definitions with rules for behavior, and so provides opportunities as well as limits. A culture is collective action, a collective legacy of patterns of action, just like a language, which allows freedom of thought but not of grammatical expression (and which is also collective action with a history).

Thus *govern* does not mean "as the springs of a pinball machine govern the movement of the ball." People do consciously manipulate the rules and values of their institutions in their efforts to achieve their ends. The institutions constitute the arenas in which people try to accomplish their aims. Institutions imply "you may" as well as "thou shalt not," thus creating as well as limiting choices. When Martin Bronfenbrenner, citing Commons's phrase "collective action in control of individual action," says that Commons "leaves in limbo such 'individualist institutions' as free markets and property rights," he misses the point because he assumes a contrast or inconsistency between *controlled* (as in *governed*) and liberty or with opportunity.[6] But as Commons frequently said, a liberty for one person is an exposure for another. A private property right implies a duty incumbent upon all others. Thus "free markets" are *not* ignored in his analysis; rather, they are among the institutions controlling or governing people's access to goods and services. My property in my house controls everyone else's access to shelter in my living room, and it burdens me with obligations to keep my dog away from the meter reader, to pay taxes, to keep the steps in repair for the postman, and so on. These opportunities and restraints, sometimes limiting and sometimes enlarging the range of permissible activities, are all rules controlling or governing what people do.

One may speak of individualism or individual motives, but it is within the constraints and meanings given by institutions that the individual feels and responds and plans. And this is equally true whether the individual is selfish, loving, patriotic, or the reverse; and whether the individual is functioning within the family, as part of a business firm, or as a member of Congress.

Institutions are the "habits of use and wont" (the phrase is Veblen's) that allow people to act with a high degree of confidence in their expectations of how other people will respond to their actions, and that allow other people to interpret actions and to respond intelligently. Institutions give meaning and continuity to actions and assure that each action fits with some of the actions of other people to maintain ongoing processes. It is for these reasons that J. Fagg Foster characterized institutions as "prescribed patterns of correlated behavior."[7]

Confusion about the roles of institutions in economies arises because there are in fact two different root meanings to the terms *economic* and *economics*.[8] On one side there is the meaning of *economizing,* meaning least effort, least cost, most output. It is from this root that standard theories of the firm, of factor markets, and of consumer choice derive. Economics becomes the study of the logic of economizing, and thus of maximizing. This is the root meaning to which Karl Polanyi attached the rubric "formal," as in "logical." On the other side there is the meaning of what people do to provide themselves with the material means of achieving their ends. This is the root meaning to which Polanyi attached the rubric "substantive." A substantive economics—institutional economics—becomes the study of econom*ies,* of how people go about provisioning themselves, whether as individuals or as members of groups with common purposes. No universal aim, no universal method or logic is assumed. Rather, what people want to achieve and how they go about it—the institutions that govern provisioning—become the subjects of study.

The view that the proper study of economists is the study of substantive economies is basic to institutionalism. "For the purpose of economic science," Veblen argued, "the process of cumulative change that is to be accounted for is the sequence of change in the methods of doing things—the methods of dealing with the *material means* of life" (italics added).[9] Commons put emphasis upon family and state, as well as upon firms and unions, upon the resolution of conflicts by institutions, and upon management and rationing as "social relations of superior and inferior."[10] Wesley Mitchell asserted that "orthodox economic theory . . . is not so much an account of how men do behave as an account of how they *would behave* if they followed out in practice the logic of the money economy."[11]

These propositions express a fundamental contrast between institutionalism and standard economic thought. Standard economists regard economic behavior as universal over time and place. Institutional economists regard it as specific to time and place. The standard economist holds that economic behavior is maximizing (and *vice-versa).* The institutional economist thinks of the economy as the ways in which a society provisions itself. The standard economist derives his explanations in large part from the assumed motive of all individuals: to wit, maximizing something good, like profit or satisfaction. The institutionalist focuses upon the rules and opportunities for action and the limits to action, simply assuming that each individual is always moved by one or another purpose. The contrast is important: motives are, of course, the reasons why an individual acts in any particular case, but the person's specific aims or passions do not determine specific acts. What specific acts are chosen depends upon the institutional context: the particular "rules of the game" in the particular system that each individual tries to manipulate to realize his goals.

Upon this much (and perhaps much more) institutionalists would agree. But "this much" still leaves questions open: about the identification of institutions and the relationships of institutions to ideas; about the origins of institutions; about the role of motives in the analysis; about the functional relationships among institutions; about how the different uses of the terms are related; and about how institutions change.

The Identification of Institutions

Many problems in interpreting the terms arise because an institution is not "something out there," like a cow or a Buddhist temple. Rather, it is a way of subdividing the social and cultural organization of a society into components meaningful to the participants in that society, and hence to observers and to analysts of the society. In a broad way *institution* implies an observable arrangement of people's affairs that contrasts with characterizations of people's activities deriving from assumptions, intuitions, or introspection. The term also implies specificities of time and place and contrasts with universals (or general characterizations). This means that the American middle-class family is an institution, but love or reproduction are not. An institutionalist would certainly call an accounting firm such as Price Waterhouse an institution and might call modern accounting an institution, but not "economic" profit or Ricardian rent. It is when one moves beyond the broad contrasts that the lack of clarity emerges. Is *marriage* an institution? If it is, can *American middle-class families* also be an institution? Is *banking* an institution? And the *American banking system* as well? And the *Federal Reserve System?* The *Board of Governors* of the Fed? Or *Citibank?* Is *double entry bookkeeping* an institution?

Such questions arise because it is impossible to define a reality. Only concepts such as "an equilateral triangle" can be defined. A cow or cows, a family or families, cannot be defined. They can be characterized, so that one can recognize cows and families, but one cannot define either—except operationally: that is, as directions for *identifying* a cow or a family.

The elements of an institutional analysis of social and economic organization and of changes therein are specific concepts of an *institution* and the *rules* and *folkviews* that identify an institution. I shall attempt to define both the concepts and their constituent sub-concepts operationally, in order to make possible general cross-cultural or intertemporal comparisons and to help to isolate the particular activities and ideas in which change is likely to occur.

An *institution* is identified by three characteristics. First, there are a number of *people doing*. Second, there are *rules* giving the activities repetition, stability, predictable order. Third, there are *folkviews*—most certainly what Walton Hamilton meant by a "bundle of intellectual usages"—explaining or justifying the activities and the rules.[12]

The *people doing* can be seen doing and are thus identified.

The *rules* are identified by ordering the doings into repetitive event sequences. The analyst observes and records what happens and can, after a number of observations, state that in such-and-such a kind of situation this person will do thus-and-such and another will do thus-and-so, with some variation in the detail and style with which it is done.

This is more obvious in cases of anthropologists observing the more exotic societies, but it is also how good social scientists study their own societies. A great danger when studying our own society is that we will take "short-cuts" and use "known-to-all" patterns rather than consciously try to observe the doings in order to sort out the rules the way we would in studying another society. There is the same danger when organizing our own society's folkviews (see immediately below).

From the observation of activities and the construction of testable rules of regularity one does not understand the institutional organization being observed. Coming to a factory, manipulating machines, leaving, doing the same five days in a row but then skipping two can be described without understanding the meaning of the activities (and of course the factory can be described without using the term or knowing what a "factory" is). One can also learn about the remarks made at different times during the day under different conditions and report a regular pattern. It should be recognized that speech itself is as much an observable activity as bodily movement and manipulation of objects.

Knowing the rules is, however, insufficient for understanding (knowing when to participate and being able to explain why one is participating), and even insufficient for identifying an institution—consider how easy it would be to confuse dancing for fun at a party, dancing for rain in a religious ceremony, and dancing for money, on the evidence of the dancing alone.

The *folkviews* provide the further element needed for identification, and they give us the information we would need to participate intelligently in the activities of the society. The folkviews *justify* the activities or *explain* why they are going on, how they are related, what is thought important and what unimportant in the patterns of regularity. Folkviews, like rules, can be discovered by observation, but here the eye is a minor instrument and the ear a major one. The analyst asks questions and listens to the answers.

What is wanted is not the truth, in the sense that the folkviews reported reflect the reality of the society, although that would be nice to have. What one wants to know is how the ideas of a culture interpret events and explain the world around them.[13] When people lie, they lie within the context of the ideas of their culture. If respondents were to lie about their own beliefs, the replies are as "objectively" misleading as any misinformation, however acquired—but the lies themselves would be significant indicators of values in the folkview system. The answers reflect the beliefs of the participants about how and why the activities are carried on *or* beliefs about what justifies or ought to justify the activities. Suppose, for instance, that some people, perhaps including the investigator, doubt that many in a culture go to church because it is "the Christian thing to do." Would it then not be the folkview? On the contrary, it would still be the folkview—at a minimum the standard to which these people feel it appropriate to appeal for explanation and justification. Hypocrisy may not even be implied, but rather inferred by the doubting reader, whose own folkviews of what it means to be a Christian may color the doubter's interpretation.

Nor should one object because one can question the meaning of statements, or because one must ask and listen in the particular language of those who believe in the folkviews, with all this implies about the investigator "understanding" the language or about the peculiarities of viewpoint implicit in any particular language. The language—the ways and times and places and situations in which the components of a language are used—is itself an integral part of the folkviews, and folkviews are as translatable (or untranslatable) as any language.

In operational procedure the answers elicited by the question

"Why?" are folkviews. Answers to the questions "How?" or "What?" are the rules. In the terminology of linguistics the identification of rules and folkviews by interview would be the identification of "lexical clusters." "God's will," "to stay healthy," "because that's the way the world is" are all lexical clusters that are here termed folkviews. But if one were to ask a professor "What do you do in class when the bell rings?" and the usual reply were "I dismiss the class and go to my office," one would have identified a lexical cluster indicating a rule—a what, not a why. When one finds a common pattern of reply to how or what and to why questions—"we go to church on Sunday morning" and "because that is the Christian thing to do"—one can state that the people in this culture regard church and Christianity as part of the same institutional structure and the investigator is on warning that other replies involving church, Christianity, and Sunday are likely to reflect the same complex of inter-related activities and folkviews. (To call this a "religious" institution or subsystem is a matter of convenience—we have not established an activity religious of itself, nor have we found a "religious function"—but we follow conventional terminology in such cases.)

An institution is a mental construct. Unlike the elements in such mental constructs as "normal profit," the components of an institution may be observed, but an institution itself cannot be observed as a whole. Rather, what one can observe are the activities of people in *situations*. A situation is the total relevant context in which a participant in a society finds himself at any moment. It includes the social rules and the cultural folkviews as well as the physical or natural environment and it is "structured" by the prior acts (verbal as well as physical) of the participants and others. The relevant context is this whole environment as perceived by the participants. Thus in inviting people to dinner I do not perceive as relevant the fact that one guest's father died a decade ago, but in offering "one for the road" I do recognize as relevant the fact that my guest will have to drive his babysitter home. The *perception* of the total context is defined by the folkview of relevancy—ideas of cause and effect and of decency and morality.

An institution may thus be regarded as a grouping of situations in accordance with the "organizing ideas" of the folkview, and it is probably the case that participants usually think of themselves (although they would not express it just this way) as actors in situations—"I'm in a class," not "I am participating in an institution." We can therefore say that classroom situations plus department meeting situations plus faculty-student meetings group together to make the university "an educational institution." Although the regular patterns of activity in the three kinds of situation differ, people, in explaining all three situations, refer to the folkview of what a university is and what it is supposed to accomplish. By contrast, we learn that a church discussion group situation is not part of a university institution (or we decide to regard it as part of a different institution) because, although the observed doings of the participants seem similar to those observed in classroom situations, the participants nevertheless use a different folkview in explaining what they are doing.

It is thus possible to proceed with an institutional analysis in two ways: one that breaks down the total social structure into components that we call institutions; and another that builds up larger components (again, the institutions) from smaller components (situations). The fact that people do differentiate situations into such groupings—and it is basic to an institutional analysis that in fact they do so—means that one can analyze (predict) actions, or the limits of actions, only by understanding how the people in a culture organize and differentiate their institutions, or (the same thing) how they allot situations to different institutions.

Summary Statement

Each constituent of an institution can be observed, or can be stated as testable predictions of event sequence: (1) people doing; (2) the rules, including the situations in which they are followed; and (3) the folkviews explaining the rules. The folkviews indicate which activities belong within which institutions and substantiate or correct first approximations made on the basis of similarity of patterned actions. The folkviews may overtly or consciously delimit the groups of situations or activities that call forth and constitute the institution, or they may only identify the institutional range by implication: that is, when respondents refer to the same set of folkviews (justifications, explanations) in response to questions about a range of situations and actions, the similarity of the answers is evidence that the activities are linked in what we call an institution.

It may be worth emphasizing here that it makes no difference to this point whether the rule is technological and cross-culturally understandable (oiling a machine), or social or ceremonial and culturally specific (shaking hands or genuflecting). All have regularity, a stable pattern. Similarly, the explanation may be plausible or even utterly convincing by the investigator's standards, or it may be wildly improbable if not downright impossible by these standards—again, it makes no difference, for the folkview still identifies the sets of activities understood by the participants as somehow "the same" or linked.

We then operationally identify an institution by the common rules governing sets of activities (activities in "like" situations) and by the explanations given for the rules, and make explicit what is implicit in Walton Hamilton's characterization of institutions cited in the introductory part of this essay.

Some Benefits of This Approach

The method of identifying suggested here is consistent with the definitions and characterizations that institutionalists have suggested or used. It should not be regarded as an alternative, but rather as a fuller formulation, an articulation of what has been implicit in the work of institutionalists all along. Thus J. Fagg Foster's "prescribed patterns of correlated behavior" characterizes the rules and points to their function in integrating activities within an institution. And, so long as one is familiar with the rules and with the associated folkviews, Foster's characterization will serve.

The fuller, operational method has several virtues when one cannot assume familiarity with the system:

(1) An institution is identified (or a specific institution defined) only for the particular culture under examination.

(2) The procedure does not depend upon the folkview of the investigator (although, of course, the folkview will strongly influence the investigator's choice of topics to investigate).

(3) We do not need to introduce generalized social functions or to assume logical requirements for the survival of a social structure such as the ones developed by Talcott Parsons.[14] Neither do we need to accept Bronislaw Malinowski's seven-fold basic "needs," varying from the necessary correlation of metabolism through food to the secondary "commissariat" social function to the more doubtful correlation of the need for physical activity with games.[15] *However,* neither do we foreclose the possibility of using such ideas if they seem appropriate.

Actually, Foster's "continuing factors" appear to be very much the sort of thing Malinowski had in mind when he used the term "needs." In his introduction to Foster's "John Dewey and Economic Value," Baldwin Ranson explains Foster's emphasis on what Foster called *continuing factors:* "theory must distinguish continuing factors from those that are situational and temporary . . . wants and institutions are always situationally determined and thus are not genuine continuing factors. He [Foster] identifies as continuing factors the functions that must be carried out in order for the life process to continue. For example, providing nourishment to the body is the function that eating food must carry out, while the particular materials identified as food by any culture are situationally determined and may change as dietary knowledge advances."[16] This seems to be exactly what Malinowski meant by the "commissariat function" (except that, whatever determines the diet, the evidence is strong that the "determining situation" cannot be the biospherical environment except as an outer limit on possible foodstuffs).[17]

(4) We do not need to identify or to assume classes of generalized types of activity such as economic, religious, or political. These are in fact classifications deriving from our own folkviews, which have, of course, been influential in structuring our institutions of markets, churches, and governments. Certainly human survival requires provisioning, but, as Veblen said, "There is no neatly isolable range of cultural phenomena that can be rigorously set apart under the head of economic institutions, although a category of 'economic institutions' may be of service as a convenient caption, comprising those institutions in which the economic interest most immediately and consistently finds expression, and which most immediately and with the least limitation are of an economic bearing."[18]

(5) As a corollary of the point immediately above, this approach avoids, in the comparative studies of economic and social systems— whether over time or as among places—the problems of prejudging which institutions are to be compared or whether certain institutions are comparable. Which institutions are to be compared will follow from the investigator's formulation of the issues and from the facts of how the societies compared organize their activities. The investigator thus asks questions about the organization of agriculture, the distribution of goods, the organization of people's efforts (work included), the support of children, rules and folkviews governing relations with the mystical and divine, and so on. One does not ask about the economy but about making and distributing and using things, on some occasions generally and on others specifically in regard to farming or to industrial organization or to control of people and nature. One does not ask about "economic institutions" but about the economic *aspects* of institutions. When one asks, for instance, about farming in ancient Mesopotamia, it turns out that the key institution is the temple.[19] The focus of interest is on an economic aspect of the temple (as it would be if one asked about the building of temples). Doubtless the Mesopotamians thought

of their temples as what we would call religious, but the question of whether temples were religious institutions simply does not arise—they were an ancient Mesopotamian institution with what we call economic and religious (and other) aspects.

(6) We do not need to build analyses upon the motives of the actors. We do not even need to consider their motives (although we are not barred from doing so). We might, indeed, simply use two "all-purpose proxies" for any and all motives—(a) the desire to continue to participate in an institutional arrangement, and (b) the desire to use the institution to achieve one's personal aims, whatever they may be.

Activities are governed by rules, not motives. Motives lead people to engage in particular activities, but what they do and how they do it depend upon the structure of institutions. If people do not follow the rules, they get "the chop," so they must follow the rules in order to stay in the system. When people want to achieve personal aims—to become richer or more powerful, to be cheered by crowds, to be loved by their parents and children—they decide how best to act within the rules so that they achieve their aims. "The presence of this or that motive," says J. R. Stanfield, "is not the important factor in institutional analysis. Rather, it is the institutional structure within which motives operate" that is important.[20] (I also discuss motives below—see pp. 1192-94.)

(7) The suggested method of identifying institutions also allows us to answer the questions raised earlier about whether one could call both American banking and the Board of Governors of the Federal Reserve System institutions. Using this method of identification, it becomes quite sensible to treat the American banking system, the Federal Reserve System, its Board of Governors, or Citibank as an institution, or some or all as institutions, depending upon one's focus of interest. The logical postulate is that institutions are not necessarily exclusive of each other, although many institutions in fact will be. Thus a large grouping such as the American banking system can be treated as an institution if the investigator is dealing with the whole system; and, equally or simultaneously, components such as the Board of Governors or Citibank can be treated as institutions if the investigator is focusing on these components. We may enjoy this freedom or flexibility because the identification of any one of these groupings or components as an institution is separate from the identification of any other. When discussing the relationships of one institution to another—and institutions are always related to one another in a society—one can simply point out that there is a relationship of hierarchy and scope among these institutions:

no confusions need arise. Similarly, there need be no confusion between the identification of the American family and the American
middle-class family; and when one is considering the relationships of
either to the American banking system (or to Citibank), the relationships will not be ones of hierarchy or scope (I leave it to scholars dealing
with families and banks to sort out what the relationships are).

There are dangers in using this freedom or flexibility. One should be
wary indeed of treating general classifications such as *marriage* (as opposed, say, to the American family) or *banking* (as opposed, say, to the
American banking system) as institutions. Such general classifications
derive from views about inherent functions or nature, not from observations of people acting. *Marriage* or *banking* as general classifications
are conclusions from comparisons of specific institutions—as when we
might (wrongly) decide that the association among sexual relationships is
so closely correlated across cultures that we would like to use a general
term for this fact.

Marriage can serve to point to the dangers of starting by assuming a
general institution (which is itself apt to derive in significant part from
specific views of function, as it does in this case). While the correlation
to which I referred at the end of the last paragraph is high, it is not
perfect. Walter Goldschmidt, drawing on Kathleen Gough, points out
that among the Nayar sub-castes of the Kerala coast of India the "husband" is defined by the *tali* rite, the wife enjoys a number of simultaneous sexual partners, a child is legitimized when one of these sexual
partners pays a fee to the midwife, and all the while, as the Nayar say,
"No Nayar knows his father." The children are raised by the matrilin-
eage.[21]

This certainly does not mean that we cannot have an institutional
analysis of sexual relations and child-rearing among the Nayar. In fact,
as Goldschmidt argues, there are very close relationships among the
systems of sexual access, of child-rearing, of inheritance, of caste, of
military service, and of farming. The lesson that I derive from Goldschmidt's analysis is that we can compare *like* activities among
cultures—sexual access, child-rearing, money creation, plowing, disposing of the harvest—but should let the information about each society determine how we express the institutional composition of each
society.

We call the American family an institution because the doings and
the rules and the folkviews so define it for Americans (although today
one should certainly avoid including two parents in an operational

identification). What we are saying is that we have identified an institution that the natives (Americans) denominate *family,* not that we have found a case of the universal institution *family* in America.

The Benefits Illustrated

John R. Munkirs, in his *The Transformation of American Capitalism,* illustrates how using institutions as the unit of analysis makes a difference.[22] It also illustrates the sort of quantitative analysis that Mitchell favored; and it illustrates how institutionalist analysis is often done with little use of the terminology associated with institutionalism.

Munkirs finds that a new economic institution has emerged in the United States, an institution that he calls centralized private planning. He makes this discovery by a quantitative analysis of the frequency and circumstances of the contacts, both direct and indirect, among officers of major corporations and by an analysis of the ways in which formal and informal planning instruments (stocks, debts, directorships, trusteeships, and transfers and registrars) can be used to coordinate the actions of different companies. The institution he describes is an inevitable consequence of the flows of information that the contacts create, in contrast to models of interlocking boards of directors and to models of "finance capitalism."

Centralized private planning works through a centralized private planning core consisting of seven banks, four insurance companies, and one diversified financial corporation. Associated with these twelve financial institutions are *at least* 126 non-core corporations ("at least" because some industries were omitted because Munkirs lacked the time and money to do the research; because the presentation of the data became unwieldy; and because wholly owned subsidiaries are not listed). These associations are based on direct and indirect interlocks among the corporations defined far more broadly than has been done in studies of interlocking boards of directors. Thus membership in the same family constitutes an interlock, as does membership on the board of another company by a senior officer who is not on his own company's board, and membership on a third company's board by officers from two other companies. The basic criterion of linkage between and among companies is that there exist relationships that make it impossible not to believe that information flows from one to another among the whole 138 companies. The proposition supporting the view that there is cooperation among these companies is that one cannot believe that all these contacts and all this information is not put to use by the companies and that the flow of information would not be allowed if the companies were not cooperating. (Munkirs's additional evidence of cooperation strongly supports the proposition that the companies cooperate—plan a large number of mutually satisfying arrangements—but not that they have any national plan.)

How is his analysis a study of institutions? And what difference does it make? First, it identifies *people doing* as they participate in the management of corporations and in the deliberations of boards of directors. Secondly, right along with the identification of the people, there is a sorting out of the rules or regularities for inter-corporate meetings and exchange of information and views. All this is done without reference to the motives of the participants (although one is free to guess at their motives), and it portrays how the system must lead to cooperation whatever the particular intentions of any participant. Perhaps more important, the system could not be derived from the motives of the actors.

What is lacking is a presentation of the folkview of the corporate officers. This is hardly surprising, for several reasons: Munkirs conducted research on the basis of publicly available documents only, and the folkviews are so likely to imply violation of our anti-trust laws—and even our publicly held beliefs about businessmen—that one would hardly expect accurate public statements of the officers' views about what they were actually doing.

The quantitative establishment of an institution or of institutions of centralized private sector planning and a planning core hardly exhausts Munkirs's analysis of these institutions. (The descriptions of how stocks, boards of directors, debts, trusteeships, and transfers and registrars structure the situation and function to ensure cooperation remind one of lessons in how to play bridge—which may explain why the largest number of adoptions of Munkirs's book as a text have been by MBA programs). One knows how the 138 corporate institutions have created a private planning institution. And here again Munkirs calls upon no motives and no conspiracies to explain the origin of the institution. Rather, his account is of how the institution evolved from the use of and the opportunities provided by the previously existing institutions of ownership and finance. There are other rather striking aspects of his analysis: the private planning institution is not a variant upon classic propositions about interlocking boards of directors but is a system of information flows; and the twelve institutions of the central planning core do not dominate the other 126 corporations—rather, the 126 dominate the core, which acts as their agent. It was only by trying to sort out the ways in which (the rules that governed how) the system worked that Munkirs discovered this new institution.

Other Issues and Corollaries

Motives

It is common to try to explain activities by reference to the motives of the actors. One might ask, "Why not put a knowledge of motives to use in analyses?" The answer is multifold. Motives may vary much from person to person. We do not know enough—certainly those of us untrained in psychology or psychiatry do not know enough—to make accurate judgments.[23] In many cases we do not know the motives. The Hebrews made their reasons for leaving Egypt quite clear, but neither they, the pharaohs, nor the priests of ancient Egypt have told us how the Egyptian peasants felt. Emphasis upon motive can lead to silly analyses (as when Henry VIII's marital history is attributed to sex mania instead of the rules of dynastic politics—despite the fact that he had his native-born queens in bed before he had them on the throne). Knowing the motive cannot tell us what action to expect if we do not know the rules governing the consequences of action.

If motives cannot be used to predict actions without knowledge of the rules, they certainly cannot be used to explain the structure of institutions in a society. The following sections on "The Origins of Institutions" and "Institutional Change" outline some institutionalist thinking on the structure of institutions, but here I discuss the relationship of rules to motives and action.

Analogies with games might be appropriate. The rules of bridge prescribe what the players must do (lay down the hand if dummy) and what they must not do (fail to follow suit if they can). The rules also prescribe the consequences of actions, but they allow a latitude of permissible actions from among which players may choose. Good players use a knowledge of the rules, of probabilities of the distribution of cards, of opponents, and a capacity for concentrated memory to win. These are the players who are good at using the "institution" of bridge, whatever their motives, and may be among those exemplifying the desire to use the "institution" to achieve personal ends.

Lesser players make more mistakes. Failing to get trumps out is not against the rules, but a pair that fails to do so loses far more often than it wins. Such a pair is not prohibited from playing any more, but if they always make so many errors that they spoil the games, they are apt to be quietly ignored when games are organized. They will certainly be barred from games if they do not follow suit or if they communicate with partners outside of the rules for bidding or for recriminating after the hand is played. But so long as they do not violate these rules (the implicit rules of reasonable competence and attention to the play of the game and the explicit rules of bridge), they may continue to play. Some players may wish to achieve great things, the motives of others are sufficiently described as a desire to continue to participate.

It is to the point here that questions about the play of a game are questions about rules, conventions, and performance, not about motives. The proper and meaningful response to "Why did you lead the six of clubs?" is not "Because I wanted to maximize my income." Rather, a proper answer is of the order, "Because you led a high club." That response is the appropriate one whether the personal motives are greed, desire for prestige, love of the game, an urge to compete, or a desire to get along with friends who like to play bridge. Actually the onlooker who knows the personal motives of each player but not the rules will make very poor guesses about what will be led, while the onlooker who knows bridge and has not a clue about the personalities of the players will predict "the six of clubs" correctly much of the time.

Note also that similarities in devices and forms do not allow us to use our knowledge of one game to understand another game. Bridge is played with the same fifty-two cards as is poker. In both games it is often useful to the players to know about the psyches of the other players. But the rules of bridge and the rules of poker are quite different. A poker player picks up a hand with four fives and a glow suffuses his innards. A bridge player picking up a hand with three sets of four of a kind and no face cards feels no glow.

As we have good and middling and passionate and merely contented players in games, so we have fine mothers, brilliant statesmen, great runners, and rich robber barons participating in institutions. And we also have parents who are content to get along with their children and keep them out of jail, politicians who are content to be cooperative backbenchers in parliaments, people who are content to jog, and people who are content to drive a bulldozer or manage a hamburger stand. Why or how well a person performs a role is a matter of character, psychology, and competence or style—so that precisely what people do varies, but always within the limits set by the rules of institutions.

The identification of an institution and the knowledge we so gain about how it works allows us to avoid or evade the problems raised by the use of motives to explain. If someday we can use motives more effectively in analyses of society, fine, and let us at that future date use motives; but meanwhile we can do much without trying to integrate them into an analysis.

Origins of Institutions

We may set at rest immediately some issues about origins. First, one simply cannot account for the origins of institutions in general or of many specific institutions. Amongst the Hebrews we find institutions of a pastoral society already established when the Biblical accounts begin. As Sir Henry Maine pointed out more than a century ago, there were operating institutions when our earliest knowledge of western Indo-European society commenced with the Homeric epics.[24] Eighty years after Maine wrote *Ancient Law*, Bronislaw Malinowski was pointing out that there was no way we could know the historical origins of non-literate societies:

> the persistent search for "origins" and "historic causes," in the nebulous realms of undocumented, unrecorded historic past or evolutionary beginnings of a people who neither have a history nor have left any traces of their previous evolution. . . . history explains nothing unless it can be shown that an historical happening has had full scientific determination and that we can demonstrate this determination on the basis of well-documented data. In ethnology or history, only too often, the hunt for the "true cause" lies in completely non-determined, because non-charted, realms of hypothesis, where speculation can roam freely, unhampered by fact.[25]

It would not be foolish to assume that there were institutions with a long history when our ancestors showed up in Olduvai Gorge. Arguments from rationality, and certainly from our ideas of what might be reasonably rational, are pointless—they derive from modern ideas combined with historical ignorance and are no more than prejudice garbed as thought. It is for this reason, among others but especially for this reason, that institutionalists totally reject the arguments of the "new institutionalists," which are but neo-classical efficiency arguments set in an historical void.[26]

Second, the origins of many institutions can be traced historically where we have the records—for the history of American capitalism, for instance, or for the history of modern banking institutions—but even in such cases one is necessarily entering the study *in medias res*.[27] It was for this reason that Walton Hamilton commented that "an institution has no origin apart from its development."[28] In short, all reconstructions of origins must be founded upon the historical record, not upon assumptions.

Third, we may be able to account historically for changes in many institutions where we cannot account for the origins. This will be the case, for instance, in the histories of the institutions of private property or family in many societies, where we can know much about how these institutions have changed but always find that Foster's "prescribed patterns of correlated behavior" already existed when the historical records began.

Functional Relationships Among Institutions

An institution does not stand alone. It fits into the system of institutions, so that changing the rules of one institution means that the rules of other institutions must adapt and so change. This is implied by the point made earlier, that one can treat institutions in a general way (the American banking system), or in a highly specific way (the Board of Governors of the Federal Reserve System), but the nature of functional relationships bear spelling out.

The argument here is not that there are discrete, specific, and universal functions that institutions in any society must fulfill, a view often taken in sociology and sometimes in anthropology.[29] There can, of course, be no denying that every society must provide for the maintenance of its members, for teaching its offspring to speak, and so on. What is not so much denied as ignored, avoided, or evaded is the proposition that we can (even should?) list and account for these necessary functions. Rather, an institutional analysis concentrates upon explaining how the institutions within each specific society are related to each other. The relationships among institutions are *functional* in that each takes over where "the writ of rules" of another "ceases to run"— the functions of any one institution are to provide the rules and folkviews governing activities that are not governed by the rules and folkviews of another institution. This also means that changes in the rules governing one set of institutional situations are likely to lead to changes in the rules governing other kinds of situations, and that the changes in one set of rules will certainly affect actions under other sets of institutional rules.

Consider some examples. In the United States a change in the rules of the school system—say, a requirement that children start attending school at age five, or lengthening the school day—will mean that the rules of family life will have to change to correspond with the new circumstances created by the change in school rules. There may also be changes in the functions performed by the two sets of institutions. For instance, teaching children to tie their shoes could become a duty of teachers instead of parents, or this teaching could now be shared indifferently between teachers and parents. The change in the age at which children start school or in the length of the school day could be consequences of changes in the rules governing the employment of women. However, a longer school day would probably not *force* changes upon the rules of family life so much as allow (and tempt) more women to become "working wives." And then, more working wives would probably hasten the emerging changes in the rules governing how credit institutions evaluated applications from women. And so on.

Take another kind of case. The National Labor Relations Act not only created a new institution, the National Labor Relations Board; it also set in train necessary adjustments in the way that judicial institutions responded to cases involving unions and labor relations. There were also changes in the folkviews to which unions, managements, and courts appealed to explain or justify their actions. Whether these changes in folkviews were a consequence of the changes in rules or whether emerging changes in folkviews led to changes in the rules can be debated, as can answers to questions about what anterior causes changed the rules or folkviews.

In these cases a large element of self-conscious intent is certainly implied. However, conscious awareness of the functions of an institution is not necessary, and in fact will often be absent. For instance, I think most people would reply "schools" if asked, "What institution has the function of educating children?" Yet the two most important things that we teach children are to use their limbs and hands and to speak their mother tongue, and both are taught by families. If asked, "What institutions settle disputes in the United States?" the likely reply would be "the courts." Yet legislatures, in setting the rules, play a major role in deciding who will benefit and who will bear a burden. And then, market institutions now settle disputes over sharing society's material product that officers of guilds or the course of peasant rebellions settled in the middle ages. More recently, legislatures in the western countries have altered the shares in society's material product by legislatively "adjudicating" the levels of social security taxes and benefits.[30]

The points here are that each institution is related to others, that each governs activities not governed by other institutions, and that a society's entire set of institutions are functionally related to provide rules and folkviews for all the activities in which members of the society engage.

Institutions and Ceremony Versus Technology and Instrumentalism

Institutionalists, especially those in the Veblenian tradition, have often contrasted the terms *instrumental* and *technological* with *institutional* and *ceremonial,* and have emphasized the "past-binding" nature of institutions.[31] Clarence Ayres contrasted *technological* with *institutional.* Veblen attached the qualifier *imbecile* to the term *institutions.* Both equated *institutional* with *ceremonial.* Among institutionalists who trace their intellectual descent from Veblen through Ayres, these contrasts have been called the *dichotomy,* probably far more frequently in an oral tradition than in the literature. One consequence has been that institutionalists have occasionally treated such general disparagements of many institutions or many aspects of institutions as if ceremonial imbecility were the defining or essential trait of all institutions. This in turn leads to a tendency to say, "If a social arrangement is imbecile, then it must be an institution." Actually, the arrangement is very probably an institution, *but not* because it is imbecile. Rather, all institutional arrangements have ceremonial and probably most have imbecile aspects, but most, if not all, probably have technological aspects. For instance, there are aspects of the nuclear power industry that strike many of us as imbecile, and the computation of probabilities of fires and meltdowns now look almost purely ceremonial (and perhaps imbecile if not meretricious), but the nuclear industry nevertheless manipulates nature to produce electricity.

It would almost certainly be better if, from the beginning, the term most often used had been *instrumental* instead of technological, but Veblen wrote rather early to have chosen instrumental (and it probably was not such a fun word for him to use). Similarly, the use of *ceremonial* from the start, instead of institutional, to express the noninstrumental aspects of activities, would have been a happier choice. It might indeed be happier if, in future, institutionalists used instrumental and ceremonial; but, in understanding the arguments as they have developed from the past, we do have to deal with the vocabulary with which the past has endowed institutionalism.

The essential point is that institutionalists subscribe to the instrumental theory of valuing: that is, to the proposition that valuing emerges in the processes of trying to solve problems, in contrast to such other putative sources as intuition (conscience?), revelation, or unanalyzable tastes. Whether the problem is how to cut meat, how to protect one's group from raiding enemy groups, or how to regulate the flow of automobile traffic, people try out tools and systems and adopt solutions that seem to be improvements upon the existing state of affairs. *Instrumental* and *technological* refer to these problem-solving processes. In the Veblenian tradition, *ceremonial* (and institutional, and sometimes ritual) refer to beliefs and practices that derive from the past and are accepted rather than tested as solutions to problems.

This then—the contrast between the currently problem-solving instrumental and the backward-looking ceremonial—has become *the dichotomy.* Among those in the Veblenian-Ayresian tradition the use of the word *dichotomy* has certainly served to emphasize the contrast. It has, however, in combination with the use of institutional instead of ceremonial, sometimes led to statements that sound as if the speaker or writer thought that institutional and technological were incompatible, almost *things* rather than contrasting *aspects* of all institutions. Another, associated problem has been an easy slippage from the view that people originally arrive at values by the instrumental processes of testing, to the view that many values held by institutionalists are instrumentally tested. This slippage occurs when we fail to recognize that institutionalists inherit ceremonial values just as everyone else does.[32]

One must always remember that problems arise within contexts of ongoing systems, are solved in such contexts, and the solutions become parts of ongoing systems. There are always ceremonial aspects to any ongoing system and its institutions. This means that the problems, their solutions, and the ongoing systems must all inevitably contain ceremonial or ritual elements. Thus, in the simplest of cases, people learn to use knives to cut meat (instrumental technology), but Americans hold the knife in the right hand, the English in the left hand (ceremonial—it makes no difference to the meat or the mouth which hand is used). The analysis is a bit more complicated when considering the rules governing traffic. Most of the world drives on the right hand side of the road, but the English and a few others drive on the left. All law abiding drivers stop for the red lights that are often above, sometimes to the side, but never below the green lights. Both systems work to reduce collisions, and are thus instrumental. But left or right seem to work equally well; and a Martian might ask, "Why not put the red light beneath the other lights, where it would be closer to the driver?" Since these rules appear to be neither intuitive nor revealed, they must be something else. Postulating that there has been an association with ideas inherited from the past (untested ceremonial elements), while awfully vague, does seem more meaningful than postulating tastes. It also fits Walton Hamilton's statement that people "see with their ideas as well as with their eyes. . . . [and] meet events with a wisdom they already possess, and that wisdom belongs to the past and is a product of a by-gone experience."[33]

In the Ayresian tradition institutions are always past-binding. "There is no such thing," wrote Ayres, "as an institution (or a set of institutions) that is 'appropriate' to a given technology in any but a negative sense."[34] An institutional structure can only be "permissive, not dynamic."[35] For instance, "inheritance remains as a feature of the modern institutional structure . . . performing no useful (industrial) function whatever and 'better adapted' to the present technological scene than chivalry only in the sense that . . . it has not yet fallen so directly afoul of industrial technology as to have become intolerable."[36] That institutions are past-binding seems not only certain and important but also necessarily true. Any institution or set of institutions emerged as an instrumental solution (the instrumentalism modified, of course, by the then existing institutions) to problems that have already been solved and thus necessarily reflects the past rather than the present or the future. The similarity of Ayres's style to the irony that marked Veblen's writings is clear, but the clarity of irony can blind a reader to the wider context. Between the two passages just quoted, Ayres has a lengthy discussion of institutions. At one point he remarks that "institutions such as the family must be understood to contain tool-activities as well as ceremonial usages."[37] At another point, discussing whether science is an institution, Ayres says, "Scientists as members of a profession have become institutionalized. . . . but surely science as a mode of behavior is qualitatively different from respectable family life."[38] Ayres's point, I take it, is that the National Science Foundation has both instrumental and ceremonial aspects. Perhaps funding research is instrumental, but elements in the peer review process are ceremonial. Nonetheless there are institutionalists who think (myself among them) that the existence of the NSF and its procedures do encourage advances in technology, and only in probably too narrow a sense can one say that the NSF as an institution—meaning in its ceremonial aspects—is at best permissive.

There may appear to be a conflict between this Ayresian view and the way Commons emphasized volition and the will-in-action. It is possible to read Commons as holding that institutions are suited to the present and future. His assertion that Veblen left no room for purpose (volition) in social processes can be taken to lend support to this interpretation (an assertion that is not correct in respect of Veblen but revealing of the importance that Commons attached to volition or the will-in-action as a prime mover in social relations).[39] In addition, Commons's description or model of how rules are changed by decisions of an authority can be read to imply that the institutions that provide the authority and its power to change the rules are forward-looking. However, what Commons argued was that people have objectives and self-consciously seek to achieve them, both as individuals and as members of groups. Neither Veblen nor Ayres nor, I think, any other institutionalist has ever argued that people do not have purposes in using institutions or that the instrumental valuing that changes institutions is purposeless.[40] (What Veblen and Ayres held—the view permeates their work—was that there is no discernible, given purpose in the history of the universe or the history of our species and that intent did not determine consequence.)[41] Commons's model of *how* changes are made is in no way inconsistent with a view that existing institutions are never so well adapted to the present and the future as they could be. In fact, it can be argued that the conflicts that cause the authority to change the rules are themselves evidence that the existing rules are inappropriate (if not actually "intolerable").

Institutional Change

First, institutions change in response to new technologies. Patterns of courtship changed with the introduction of the automobile. The criteria of sexual morality changed with the advent of effective contraception. The nature of the corporation changed with the advent of the railway. Prior to the middle decades of the nineteenth century, the corporation was typically a body with public responsibilities: the New England township would be a prime example. More rarely, a group with primarily economic aims would be incorporated: the East India Company and the turnpike companies would be prime examples, but even in such cases responsibilities for governance or other duties were attached to the corporations. The enormous size and therefore costs of the railways led to the development of the market for private bonds and to the spread of the corporation as an economic agent whose liability for debt was limited.

Institutions change within the context of existing rules and folkviews, adapting some rules and folkviews and creating some new ones. Thus the need to finance railways led to new ways to start corporations, to adaptations of the older system of joint stock ownership, to easier systems for acquiring and disposing of shares, and frequently to the absence of a public duty as a major requirement for incorporation. But these new ways developed from existing corporate forms, and thus "free incorporation" of economic agents was both a consciously introduced institutional change and an institutional change whose particular form and content derived in large part from existing institutions.

A major case of institutional change is the emergence of the self-regulating market system during the latter part of the eighteenth century and the first half of the nineteenth century. In *The Great Transformation* Polanyi argued that the inclusion of markets for land (nature), labor (people), and capital (money, which gives power to organize and control) was an adaptation by a commercial society of the expensive new machines using great amounts of inanimate energy. The costs of these machines meant that the owners had to be able to get the inputs they needed when they needed them—that is, to be able to buy, rent, or hire them at any time—and to cut costs quickly when the inputs were not needed (that is, to fire labor). Polanyi concentrates upon the creation of a labor market, the market for land having already been largely created by the enclosures of the 1790s, and upon the establishment of the gold standard as a "self-regulating" financial system.[42]

It is possible to spell out or extend the underlying argument, in a way that Polanyi did not do explicitly, in order to show how existing institutions change. Much of the new system was given shape by existing institutions. Two closely related sets of institutions limited and directed the changes. First, the existing system of land holding and enclosures determined that nature would be privately owned. Second, the system of commercial markets and the institutions of private property determined that the machine technology would be fitted into a system of markets. Third, the evolving system of liberal government determined that the role of government should be severely restricted. Fourth, the institutions of private property determined that the costs that could be quickly cut when inputs were not needed would be the cost of labor. The rules and folkviews of private property required that rents and interest be paid to owners even if the resources or capital were not being used. Workers, however, did not have similar institutionalized property rights. Outdoor relief under the Elizabethan Poor Laws could have been changed into a property right to a job, but workers lacked the political power to endow themselves with an inalienable right to be employed. Thus do generations of budding economists learn that fuel, power, raw materials, and labor are naturally variable costs, while site and capital equipment—meaning *rent,* amortization, *interest, and insurance*—are of course fixed costs.

In addition to the events and circumstances generated within a culture, it should by now be apparent that contacts between different cultures may be a source of institutional change. This proposition derives support from the history of Europe's colonies over the past two centuries and more, as well as from the economic histories of Germany and Japan, who borrowed technologies from other cultures.[43] While the cases of Germany and Japan illustrate the effects of technological change, the founding, growth, and democratic organization of the Indian National Congress do not appear to owe any direct debt to technology. Rather, they seem to have emerged from contacts with British political institutions and the folkviews of British government. The history of modern India seems to present a case where institutions themselves induce change; but still a case where the change is in response to new experiences, as well as a case where the institutional substance of Indian democracy did not evolve in the same way or into the same forms as did the institutional substance of British democracy.[44]

Conclusion

While institutionalists have used *institution* to convey the idea that people's actions are shaped by and reflect culturally inherited but evolving social rules or relationships, the word has never enjoyed a precise meaning. This essay has proposed what, I hope, is a significant step toward providing a clearer meaning for the term. I have stressed the need for an operational definition because an operational definition helps analysts to escape their own cultural preconceptions and to avoid troublesome questions about generalized social functions and motives. It also allows a clear explanation of how institutions are identified. Furthermore, such a definition is entirely consistent with the different, but not inconsistent, ways in which contributors to the institutionalist tradition have used the term.

Notes

1. I have found William T. Waller, Jr., "The Evolution of the Veblenian Dichotomy," *Journal of Economic Issues* 16 (September 1982): 757–72, a helpful, clear, and concise account of the origins and changes in the use of *institution* among institutionalists. For citations of many uses of the terms in this journal, see Warren J. Samuels, "Technology Vis-A-Vis Institutions in the JEI: A Suggested Interpretation," *Journal of Economic Issues* 11 (De-

cember 1977): 867–95. It should, however, be noted that, while the words run through our writings, many publications of many institutionalists do not use the words. Thus the frequent use of the words is strong *prima facie* evidence that the author is an institutionalist, but their absence is not evidence that the author is not an institutionalist.

2. Thorstein Veblen, *Absentee Ownership and Business Enterprise in Recent Times: The Case of America* (London: George Allen & Unwin, 1924, [c1923]), p. 101.

3. John R. Commons, *Institutional Economics* (New York: Macmillan, 1934), pp. 69–70, 72.

4. Wesley C. Mitchell, "The Prospects of Economics," in *The Backward Art of Spending Money and Other Essays,* chap. 16, pp. 342–85 (New York: Augustus M. Kelley, Inc., 1950), p. 373; reprinted from *The Trend of Economics,* ed. R. G. Tugwell, pp. 3–34 (New York: F. S. Crofts & Co., 1924).

5. Walton Hamilton, "Institutions," in *Encyclopaedia of the Social Sciences,* ed. Edwin R. A. Seligman and Alvin Johnson, vol. 8, pp. 84–89 (New York: Macmillan, 1932), italics added. Among the earlier institutionalists the word *habit* was clearly used with a different range of meanings than we are apt to attach to it today.

6. Martin Bronfenbrenner, "Early American Leaders—Institutional and Critical Traditions," *American Economic Review* 75 (December 1985): 13–27, p. 19. Bronfenbrenner follows Commons, as I did early in this essay, in capitalizing the initial letter of each noun; here, and in the subsequent quotations from Commons, I have decapitalized in the interests of clarity.

7. For his use of the phrase, see J. Fagg Foster, "The Effect of Technology on Institutions," *Journal of Economic Issues* 15 (December 1981): 907–13, pp. 907–8.

8. For a fuller treatment of the two root meanings of "economic" and the consequences for the study of economics, see Karl Polanyi, "The Economy as Instituted Process," in *Trade and Market in the Early Empires,* ed. Karl Polanyi, Conrad M. Arensberg, and Harry W. Pearson, chap. 13, pp. 243–70 (Glencoe, Ill.: The Free Press, 1957).

9. Thorstein Veblen, "Why Is Economics not an Evolutionary Science?" in *The Place of Science in Modern Civilization and Other Essays,* pp. 56–81 (New York: Russell & Russell, 1961); reprinted from *The Quarterly Journal of Economics* 12 (July 1898): 70–71.

10. Commons, *Institutional Economics,* p. 679, for the phrase. For the general characterizations, Commons's writings, *passim.* Although Anne Mayhew (see her essay in this volume) casts doubt upon the importance of the German Historical School in the development of American institutionalist thought, Commons surely did get the idea from somewhere that one should madly capitalize initial letters of lots of nouns.

11. Mitchell, "The Prospects of Economics," p. 371. Italics added, to emphasize that Mitchell did not believe that people did behave in this way.

12. Hamilton, "Institutions," pp. 88–89.

13. Paul Bohannan, *Social Anthropology* (New York: Holt, Rinehart & Winston, 1963), pp. 11–14, discusses what he calls there "key terms" (and has called "organizing ideas" in conversations). Pages 25–31 are also highly relevant to this discussion. The anthropologist F. G. Bailey made the same point when he said (in comments at a Conference on South Asia at the

University of Illinois, 1970) that "anthropology is about 'wording' the world." Both were talking about core concepts in what are here called folkviews—how a people see the world in which they live, and how they see the institutions that organize their activities.

14. Talcott Parsons and Neil J. Smelser, *Economy and Society: a Study in the Integration of Economic and Social Theory* (Glencoe, Ill.: The Free Press, 1956), pp. 16–19. See also Talcott Parsons, *The System of Modern Societies* (Englewood Cliffs, N.J.: Prentice-Hall, 1971), pp. 4–26, and specifically pp. 4–8. The arguments are more clearly stated in Guy Rocher, *Talcott Parsons and American Sociology* (New York: Barnes and Noble, 1975), pp. 40–51.

15. Bronislaw Malinowski, *A Scientific Theory of Culture and Other Essays* (New York: Oxford University Press, 1960, [c1944]), section 10 of the title essay.

16. Baldwin Ranson, introduction to J. Fagg Foster, "John Dewey and Economic Value," *Journal of Economic Issues* 15 (December 1981): 871–97, p. 871.

17. See C. Daryll Forde, *Habitat, Economy and Society* (New York: E. P. Dutton & Co., [c1934]), chap. 22 and pp. 463–66.

18. Thorstein Veblen, "Why Is Economics Not an Evolutionary Science?" pp. 56–81 in his *The Place of Science in Modern Civilization and Other Essays* (New York: Russell & Russell, 1961); originally published in *The Quarterly Journal of Economics* 12 (July 1898): 77.

19. For the case I have in mind, see Henri Frankfort, *The Birth of Civilization in the Near East* (Garden City, N.Y.: Doubleday Anchor Books, 1956, [c1951], chap. 3.

20. J.R. Stanfield, *The Economic Thought of Karl Polanyi: Lives and Livelihood* (New York: St. Martin's Press, 1986), p. 60. On the role and relevance of motives, one should read Stanfield's discussions, pp. 59–61 and 82–83.

21. Walter Goldschmidt, *Comparative Functionalism* (Berkeley: University of California Press, 1966), pp. 15–26, 92–201. The quoted phrase is on p. 98. The book is the best analysis I have read on the topic of its title.

22. John R. Munkirs, *The Transformation of American Capitalism: From Competitive Market Structures to Centralized Private Sector Planning* (Armonk, N.Y.: M.E. Sharpe, 1985).

23. A psychologist (Gustav Triandis, University of Illinois-Urbana) once replied to my question, "What is a motive?" with the statement, "A motive is that black box that makes different people respond differently to the same stimulus"—hardly encouraging for those who wish to give motives a primary place in social analyses.

24. Henry Sumner Maine, *Ancient Law* (Gloucester, Mass.: Peter Smith, 1970, [c1861]), p. 2.

25. Bronislaw Malinowski, *A Scientific Theory of Culture*, pp. 117–18. See also pp. 19–20.

26. Anne Mayhew, "The First Economic Revolution as Fiction," *Economic History Review*, 2d series, 35 (November 1982): 568–71.

27. John R. Commons, *Legal Foundations of Capitalism* (Madison: University of Wisconsin Press, 1968 [c1924]), chaps. 6–8, where he traces the history of Anglo-American market and property institutions from 1066 in successive chapters on "The Rent Bargain," "The Price Bargain," and "The Wage Bargain," are perhaps the prime examples of this kind of recon-

struction of the origins of specific institutions. For a recent, small example of the same kind of effort in this journal, see Walter C. Neale, "The Evolution of Colonial Institutions: An Argument Illustrated from the Economic History of British Central Africa," *Journal of Economic Issues* 18 (December 1984): 1177–87. Abbot Payson Usher, "The Origins of Banking: The Primitive Bank of Deposit, 1200–1600," *Economic History Review* 4 (1934): 399–428, and Rondo Cameron, ed., *Banking in the Early Stages of Industrialization* (New York: Oxford University Press, 1967), would be good examples of the latter.

28. Hamilton, "Institutions," p. 84.
29. See footnotes 14 and 15.
30. These points are made by Commons, *Legal Foundations of Capitalism.* It was Harry Pearson (oral communication, many years ago) who started me reading Commons by pointing out that Commons treated all organizations, *including markets,* as means of settling disputes. The argument has recently been made in conveniently short space with succinct clarity by David W. Bromley in "Resources and Economic Development: An Institutionalist Perspective," *Journal of Economic Issues* 19 (September 1985): 779–96, and Don Kanel in "Institutional Economics: Perspectives on Economy and Society," *Journal of Economic Issues* 19 (September 1985): 815–28.
31. For more extended discussions of the issues raised here see David Hamilton, "Technology and Institutions Are Neither," *Journal of Economic Issues* 20 (June 1986): 525–32; Anne Mayhew, "Ayresian Technology, Technological Reasoning, and Doomsday," *Journal of Economic Issues* 15 (June 1981): 513–20; and Baldwin Ranson, "The Place of Institutions in Institutional Analysis" (paper presented to the joint annual meeting of the Western Social Science Association and the Association for Institutional Thought, Albuquerque, New Mexico, 1983).
32. See Wendell Gordon's presidential address to the Association for Evolutionary Economics, "The Role of Institutional Economics," *Journal of Economic Issues* 18 (June 1984): 369–81, and especially pp. 378–80 for a warning on this score.
33. Hamilton, "Institutions," p. 88.
34. C. E. Ayres, *The Theory of Economic Progress* (New York: Schocken Books, 1962 [c1944]) p. 187.
35. Ibid., p. 177.
36. Ibid., p. 188.
37. Ibid., p. 182.
38. Ibid., pp. 183–84.
39. Commons, *Institutional Economics,* p. 651. Also, p. 655, "Ours is a theory of artificial selection. Veblen's is natural selection."
40. On these matters see Wesley C. Mitchell, "Commons on Institutional Economics," in *The Backward Art of Spending Money,* footnote 4, p. 333.
41. And see Gordon, "The Role of Institutional Economics," note 32.
42. Karl Polanyi, *The Great Transformation* (Boston: Beacon Press, 1957, [c1944]).
43. The literature on colonial history is replete with examples of "the western impact." For an example in the institutionalist tradition, see Walter C. Neale, "The Evolution of Colonial Institutions," note 26. Thorstein Veb-

len's accounts of the cases of Germany and Japan—in his *Imperial Germany and the Industrial Revolution* (Ann Arbor: University of Michigan Press, 1966, [c1915]) and "The Opportunity of Japan," *The Journal of Race Development* 6 (July 1915), reprinted in *Essays in Our Changing Order,* ed. Leon Ardzrooni, pp. 248–66 (New York: Augustus M. Kelley, 1964, [c1934]—are seminal, but almost any economic history of these two countries over the last 120 years will provide persuasive evidence.

44. For a more detailed discussion of these issues the reader is invited to consult the essay in this volume by Paul Dale Bush, pp. 1075–1116.

Human Resource Development and the Formulation of National Economic Policy

Vernon M. Briggs, Jr.

One of the more insightful explanations for economic progress in industrialized nations during the last half of the twentieth century has been the recognition of "human resources as the wealth of nations."[1] The notion has long enjoyed a rhetorical appeal by politicians in democratic societies. But awareness that the principle has enormous economic implications for national and international well-being has essentially been a post-World War II phenomena. Increasingly, policymakers in industrialized nations have realized that the human resource development of their labor forces is the key to efforts to address such difficult issues as efficiency, equity, stablilization, and growth. Nations with limited physical resources, such as Japan and Germany, have sustained superior economic performances in this new era largely because they have been forced to develop their human resources. All industrial democracies have come to appreciate the wisdom of Ray Marshall's observation that "developed, educated, motivated people are an unlimited resource . . . [while] undeveloped, uneducated, unmotivated people are a monumental drag on an economy in the internationalized information era" of contemporary times.[2]

For most of its history, the field of economics has paid little attention to the contribution of human resources to the production process. Workers were assigned an essentially passive role. It was simply assumed that, since the demand for labor is a derivative of the demand

257

for goods and services, the workers could adjust somehow to the technologically imposed requirements of the job. The labor supply was viewed as having a weak influence on job design. During periods in which societies were primarily agriculturally based (as they were during the era of the classical writers from Adam Smith to Karl Marx), the assumption that the labor supply was essentially homogeneous was generally acceptable. Most jobs required little in the way of skill or knowledge and most workers possessed little of either. The same can be said for the job creation process associated with the mechanization of industry during the century following the Industrial Revolution (including the period when classical economics gave way either to Marxist or neoclassical economics depending upon one's politics). The substitution of machinery for the historic dependence by pre-industrial societies on animal and human muscle power resulted in the creation of millions of jobs that required very little in the way of skill or education from the work force. Karl Marx, and later Thorstein Veblen, bemoaned the resulting alienation of workers as the "instinct for workmanship" was gradually factored-out of their working lives. Both described what was essentially the urbanization and proletarianization of the work force because of the onset of the industrialization process.

In the early twentieth century, the addition of continuous process production techniques associated with the advent of the assembly line only exacerbated the dimensions of the prevailing employment patterns. It did not alter them. The economy of the United States was still in its adolescence. Mass production provided a means of producing consumer goods and of offering them at low cost to a consuming public that at the time possessed very few material goods. Except during the years of direct United States involvement in World War I, there was essentially no military budget to consume valuable economic resources. Millions of unskilled blue-collar jobs were created largely in manufacturing, mining and construction. Most required little in the way of human capital endowments. Furthermore, most of the new manufacturing and construction jobs were centralized in the urban centers of the Northeast.

The ensuing labor reform movements of the early twentieth century focused primarily on efforts to remove the sharp edges of the industrialization process. There was no perceived need to develop the human resource potential of the labor force. To the degree that the United States had any human resource policy at the time, it was essentially the open-door immigration policy (until 1924) that admitted millions of unskilled and poorly educated workers to staff the factories, mines, and construction sites, as well as to work in agriculture. The emergence of institutional economic thought in the United States during this period (with the exception of Veblen who, like Marx, saw the proletarianization process as inevitably giving way to a new socialist society) was primarily concerned with reforming the existing society. But these reforms—as typified by the humane contributions made by John R. Commons and his fellow members of "the Wisconsin School"—were designed to achieve a "reasonable" and harmonious society.[3] Commons did not believe in centralized planning. He and his followers thought that evolving institutional arrangements such as trade unionism (with its emphasis on achieving a collective bargaining contract), protective labor legislation, court decisions, industrial commissions with arbitration powers, personnel departments, and shop councils at work sites would provide *ad hoc* planning mechanisms. These efforts, they believed, would suffice to provide pragmatic ways to address the inevitable human adjustment problems associated with the advances of industrialization. There is mention only by implication by Commons and his associates of any need to focus upon the development of the employment potential of the nation's labor force. Commons's lasting contribution was his advocacy of a real-world problem solving approach as the justification for the study of labor economics. He did not, however, change the view of orthodox economics—that workers were a quantitative necessity but a qualitatively passive agent to the production process.

Likewise, the coming of the "new economics" of John M. Keynes in 1936 did nothing to alter the prevailing perspective.[4] As revolutionary as were the assumptions and policy prescriptions of Keynes, his analysis had nothing to say about the qualitative nature of the supply of labor. The macroeconomic theory that has subsequently evolved from Keynes's conceptualization was premised upon the singular importance of labor demand. The "employment policy" of Keynes and his followers has meant that the application of fiscal policy measures alone could sufficiently manipulate the aggregate purchasing power of society to stabilize the economy. But in the 1930s, with its mass unemployment and price deflation, there was no real need to worry about human resource development. The primary human resource concern was the under-utilization of the abundant supply of qualified labor that was already available.

The Recognition of the Importance of Human Resources

Three separate developments have occurred during the post-World War II era that have contributed to the recognition that human resource development may be the key to economic progress in the emerging era of computerization and automatic control. These have been the introduction of the concept of human capital to the study of the labor allocation and income determination process; the linkage of human resource development to economic growth; and the recognition of the growing significance of structural change in the labor market as a specific economic policy issue. Institutional economists have been very wary and openly critical of the human capital approach; they have accepted the findings pertaining to human resource development and economic growth; and they have been instrumental in their advocacy of the need to recognize the importance of human resource development as the key response to structural change of the economy. Each approach warrants brief mention.

The Human Capital of Individuals

Except for purely classical ideologues, most economists who have studied the labor market of the United States have been dissatisfied with the simplicity of orthodox economics. As the popular saying goes, "when Adam Smith's 'invisible hand' is applied to the labor market, it becomes all thumbs." The labor market is composed of widely differing types of labor demand for various kinds of workers and of a labor supply that consists of individuals with widely differing aspirations, talents, skills, locational preferences, and educational experiences. If classical theory postulates that the labor force is homogeneous, then there is very little for conventional demand and supply analysis to explain. But if both differentiated labor demand and labor supply exist, the explanation of how labor is allocated and rewarded becomes far more complex.

In an effort to salvage a market-oriented analysis, contemporary advocates of neoclassical economics concluded that only slight modifications were necessary in the orthodox perspective.[5] Their revised view essentially argues that the principle characteristics that differentiate the experiences of members of the labor force are skill and education. Differential economic returns to workers can be explained by the differences in their respective productivities. As there are costs incurred in the process of acquiring marketable skills and knowledge, the attainment of these attributes by an individual can be viewed as an investment in human capital. Proponents of this approach regard it as a positive theory of the labor market that explains how things are—not the way things should be. With this slight adjustment, the advocates feel content with the revised neoclassical analysis of how the forces of demand and supply operate in the labor market. Human capital proponents do not believe that human beings should be considered commodities. Nonetheless, they hold that employers actually do view workers as commodities whose labor services are purchased on the basis of their respective human capital endowments. Human capital theory seeks to bridge the gap between income determination and income distribution by asserting that variations in the human capital investments of individuals explain variations in individual income. The policy conclusion is that general expenditures on education and training can enhance the opportunities for higher incomes for labor force participants.

Institutionally-oriented writers have been openly critical of the human capital approach from its onset. Michael Piore, for instance, has claimed that human capital and the study of labor economics are fundamentally distinct. He has said that labor economics "is an applied field concerned with the solution of particular problems" while human capital theory "is applied theory concerned with the application of certain principles."[6] Uniformly, institutionalists, have felt that it is patently naive to believe that the human capital approach is a positive theory that is any more free of normative judgments than any other theoretical approach.[7] But more substantively, critics have attacked the simplicity of the human capital approach—like its broader neoclassical paradigm—for its avoidance of any recognition of the significance of complex institutional practices and historical factors that influence labor market operations.[8] There is no allowance made for the ways that societal institutions (for example, schools, businesses, unions, government, or the military) can limit through their customs, practices, and policies the efforts of individuals to maximize opportunities to improve themselves. Nor is there any recognition of the historical barriers that have been placed in the paths of subgroups of the labor force to attain levels of human capital or to apply equally those human capital attributes that they do possess. Studies, for example, have found that many such workers often already have human capital endowments that exceed the limited range of jobs that are generally available to them.[9]

Lester Thurow, who once was an avid advocate of the human capital approach, has subsequently become one of its sharpest critics.[10] Thurow notes that the labor input to the production process is so "peculiar" in its characteristics that it simply cannot be analyzed according to the same criteria applicable to physical factors of production. Human beings have preferences that are formed in a social environment. These preferences foster likes and dislikes that are often interdependent.

Thus, when human beings are involved, their behavior cannot be fully judged by simply using income as a measure of economic performance or behavior or as an indicator of satisfaction. In addition, the productivity of human beings often depends on personal motivation and effort. It is not technologically determined. Likewise, human capital cannot be separated from its owner (for instance, to earn a football player's wage, you must be able to excel in playing football). Further, whereas physical capital can only produce goods and services, human beings both produce and consume human capital (for example, significant consumption expenditures are made for improving health, acquiring education, or searching for a better job). Thurow also notes that many important decisions concerning human capital acquisition by individuals are made by other people (that is, parents and society) and, because human beings are mortal, the age and physical condition of an investor in human capital has much to say about the possibility of acquiring and using particular skills and education. There is a high premium placed on making many human capital decisions early in one's life, whereas such considerations are unimportant for investors in physical capital. Human capital, it turns out, often represents a collection of assets rather than a single asset. Moreover, not every investor in human capital has the same set of production techniques (some individuals have natural talents while others cannot acquire the same abilities no matter how hard they try or how much they spend). Thus, Thurow concludes "a human capital model of investments can be constructed but when it is completed it will have little relation to the model used for physical investments."[11]

Consequently, institutionalists have seriously questioned the appropriateness of the human capital approach with its feedback to traditional neoclassical analysis.[12] The issue involves much more than theoretical carping. Although human capital theory seems logical in its surface reasoning, it is flawed in its diagnosis of labor market outcomes and deficient in its application to the experiences of major subgroups of the labor force. With respect to diagnosis, it places full responsibility for differential market outcomes on individuals for their assumed differential investments in their human capital. It postulates, for example, that the poverty, underemployment, and unemployment of low-income minority workers is their fault (that is, they underinvested) when, in fact, the opportunities for self-improvement may have been inadequate or unavailable. By also attempting to link the education and training of individuals to income rather than to productivity, it is impossible to determine if higher earnings are the result of actual human capital endowments or of the mere possession of certain job credentials. In other instances, persons who already possess adequate skills and educations are denied equal opportunities to apply these abilities. The theory cannot explain why a subgroup such as Hispanics has a considerably higher income than do blacks even though blacks have significantly higher educational attainment levels than do Hispanics. The same can generally be said for the earnings experiences of many women relative to many men. Critics of the human capital approach assert that the explanations are more likely to be found in institutional practices and historical influences in the labor market that cause, rather than merely reflect, the differential experiences of certain individuals and of major groups within the labor force.

Human Resources and Aggregate Economic Growth

Most economists with differing intellectual orientations agree with the conclusions from studies relating human resource development with aggregate productivity increases and economic growth. Relying upon the seminal work done by Edward Denison, it is now clear that the growth of the U.S. economy stems largely from the contributions of the nation's human resources.[13] Of the six groups of sources that he identifies as making positive contributions to U.S. economic growth from 1929 to 1982, the labor inputs account for nearly half—47 percent—of the growth rate (34 percent came from an increase in the amount of work done because of the numbers, working hours, and characteristics of the workers, while an additional 13 percent is attributed to the increase in the level of education). If advances in knowledge (which added 26 percent to the growth of the economy) are included among the human resource contributions, the total human resource contribution increases to 73 percent. A similar study by Anthony Carnavale in 1983 found that 75 percent of the improvement in productivity in the United States since 1929 can be attributed to human resource development activities such as on-the-job training, education, formal training and health.[14] Thus, while economists in general and public policymakers in particular have focused upon physical capital as the explanation for long-term economic growth, it has actually been human resource development that has been the major contributor. Denison, for instance, found that increases in physical capital added only 17 percent and land improvements added zero to long-term economic growth.

Thus, the idea that human resources are a nation's most important asset is no mere political cliché. It is a fact of economic life that deserves prominence in policy formulation. As will be discussed subsequently, recognition of the necessity to focus economic policy upon human resource development is a relatively recent concept as has been the process of forging the institutional practices and organizations required to foster this relationship.

A Response to Structural Change

A major contribution that institutional economists have made to directing public attention and policy toward the necessity to adopt a human resource strategy has come from the contention that the employment structure of the U.S. economy since the end of World War II is being radically transformed. The causes are diverse but, in the main, they stem from rapid changes in technology; the fact that science itself has become a major source of innovation; enhanced foreign competition; substantial increases in the size of the labor force; dramatic changes in the gender and racial composition of the labor force; major shifts in consumer tastes away from goods toward services as revealed by their emerging expenditure patterns; the revival of mass immigration; and the accelerated growth in governmental expenditures on national defense.[15] The resulting influences have caused major industrial shifts of employment patterns from goods production to the provision of services; of occupational patterns from blue collar to white collar employment; and geographic shifts from rural to urban areas, as well as from the historic employment concentrations in the urban Northeast to new concentrations in the urban Southeast and urban Southwest.

Many observers believe that these shifts in employment patterns are responsible for the pronounced secular rise in the "prosperity unemployment rates" that the nation has sustained since the end of World War II (that is, every period of prosperity—with the sole exception of the years during the height of the Vietnam War in the late 1960s—for the past forty years has been accompanied by a higher level of aggregate unemployment than the previous period). Moreover, the unemployment experiences of subgroups of the labor force have not been evenly distributed. Youths and minorities, have, for example, sustained significantly higher unemployment rates than have been revealed by the rising aggregate unemployment measure. The same can be said of many workers in selected inner-cities and rural areas. Those workers with low levels of education and training, inadequate work experience, and those from groups that have endured past experiences with discrimination have had the greatest difficulty finding adequate employment and comparable income opportunities.

Recognizing the emergence of a secular increase in unemployment, however, has been easier than securing agreement among economists about what is causing the phenomenon or what to do about it.[16] Since the 1930s, Keynesian macroeconomics has sought to lay claim to the resolution of problems of economic stabilization. Thus, macroeconomists asserted in the 1960s that the problem was inadequate demand that required a fiscal policy solution (that is, reliance on a massive tax cut).[17] Likewise, during this same period the monetarists, led by Milton Friedman, boasted that they had the proper policy panacea.[18] These two policy approaches vied for support from mainstream economists.[19] But when substantial rates of inflation and unemployment occurred simultaneously in the 1970s, both schools of thought were intellectually stymied and forced to revert to baroque refinements of theoretical principles rather than to confront directly the economic problems of the times. Nevertheless, the teaching of economics in the United States has been based upon the contention that fiscal and/or monetary solutions are the proper responses to changing economic conditions in the labor market.

In contrast, a number of labor economists contended throughout this era that it was the changing structural conditions in the labor market that were the explanation for the deterioration of employment conditions. These structural factors meant that the supply of labor could not adjust automatically to the changing character of labor demand. Hence, they contended that these structural conditions had to be squarely addressed.[20] They prescribed interventionist human resource policies that were directly focused on facilitating the labor adjustment process. Advocates of human resource development have not attacked the need to adopt parallel policies designed to stimulate the demand for labor. But they have claimed that exclusive reliance upon such measures is likely to be insufficient to provide full employment for an economy in the midst of structural transformation.[21]

Ironically, Keynes was fully aware of the limitations of his proposals. He stressed the fact that his analysis was essentially a short-run diagnosis. It was based on the assumption that the size of the labor force, the capital stock (both human and physical), the state of technology, the degree of competition, and the tastes for consumption of goods and services are all assumed to be constant.[22] In the short run, such assumptions may be acceptable, but over the long run they obviously are not. Keynes clearly recognized this limitation. He labeled these parameters as composing the "social structure" that "determines the distribution of national income."[23] In other words, he recognized that changes in these structural conditions require policy responses other than fiscal policy. But the modern-day disciples of Keynes have overlooked his expressed warnings and have sought to convert his analysis into a long-run prescription for achieving stabilization.[24] They have acknowledged the existence of structural problems but they have contended that there is always some element of structural problems in any dynamic economy. They deny that these conditions have worsened in the contemporary era. Much the same can be said for the monetarism of Milton Friedman. It too is a single remedy approach. It simply assumes (or asserts) that a competitive domestic economic system with flexible international exchange rates must only adhere to a steady growth in the nation's money supply to achieve non-inflationary full employment. Labor force adjustment is assumed to be automatic. Thus, little mention is made by either macroeconomists or monetarists of the supply of labor and how it might adjust to widespread and sustained structural changes.

Despite the confidence—or arrogance—of both macro and monetarist economists that demand policies alone can guide the economy, labor economists of an institutional bent have not been convinced. They have argued that the structural changes in the economy require specific labor market responses. It is argued that in the emerging economic environment, the types of jobs that are most rapidly increasing in number are those that place a premium on skill and education; those that are disappearing are the ones that require little in the way of human capital endowments. Moreover, the geographical distribution of the growth of jobs has been uneven. Thus, it is to be expected in such dynamic circumstances that unemployed people and vacant jobs can coexist on both a short- and long-term basis.[25] Thus, there has been support for a policy approach that focuses on labor market policies—such as occupational training, re-training, up-grading, work experience, education (at all levels), improved labor market information systems, and voluntary labor relocation programs. There has also been growing recognition of the employment significance of such other critical areas of public concern as health, welfare, housing, speech therapy, counseling, social rehabilitation, child care, legal services, and transportation. The package of reforms also has included measures to assure equal employment opportunity practices. Thus, the overall objective has been to develop public policies that are intended to enhance the employment potential of labor force participants. As opposed to the general approach of fiscal and monetary policy, the human resource approach seeks specific remedies for specific individual circumstances. Different groups in the labor force have different needs. Hence, a menu of policy options needs to be offered. By introducing the concept of "employability" into the labor policy lexicon, it has also been implicitly recognized that no longer are such issues as unemployment, underemployment, and poverty to be considered the sole province of economists. Other disciplines and professions also have key roles to play in the policy formulation and application processes.

Throughout the 1960s and 1970s, the growth of human resource policy was strongly supported by governmental action despite the reticence of many mainstream economists about the need for a human resource strategy. Congress and a series of administrations (Kennedy through Carter) were openly supportive of providing programmatic substance to these ideas. In addition, the U.S. Department of Labor during this era undertook a massive research agenda to spawn policy-oriented programs, to sponsor demonstration projects, and to create an evaluation system to assess the effectiveness of the results.[26] It was a period of social experimentation that, as one might expect, included both successes and failures.[27]

In the early 1970s, still another tact was added to the human resource program endeavors. It was the revival of direct job creation. At first the support was based on the fact that job creation could be used as a countercyclical employment device just as it had been during the New Deal era of the 1930s. But by the mid-1970s, such programmatic actions were also viewed as having a counterstructural potential. Namely, there are certain subgroups of the labor force that have difficulty finding jobs even during periods of general economic prosperity. Providing jobs in the public sector could serve as a means of on-the-job training for persons who lacked both skills and work experience. The jobs that were provided could also be designed to provide needed public services that were generally underfunded (in urban areas) or unavailable (in rural areas). Moreover, during the period when the nation was confronted with both inflation and unemployment, job creation programs could be targeted precisely to those groups and regions that had higher-than-average unemployment rates so as to provide needed jobs while not contributing to inflationary labor market pressures. Despite political criticism of some of the administrative aspects of these efforts, the research studies of the economic effectiveness of these job creation programs were uniformly favorable.[28]

With the election of the Reagan Administration, however, this era of public support for interventionist human resource strategies essentially came to an end—or at least a pause. The Reagan Administration has sought to reduce domestic social expenditures in order to enhance the nation's defense posture. All public sector job creation programs were terminated and expenditures on publicly supported training programs were sharply reduced. Education programs, especially those designed for low-income students, were curtailed. For awhile, there were even attempts to abolish the Department of Education from the federal bureaucracy. As for economic policy, the administration fell back upon conventional macroeconomics as embodied by a series of massive tax cuts plus pursuit of a more competitive domestic environment (as manifested by efforts to de-regulate the economy and to pursue a free-trade international policy) to resolve employment problems.[29] In the wake of these endeavors, unemployment soared in 1981 and 1982 to the highest levels experienced since the 1930s (almost 11 percent). Even when a "recovery" did begin in 1983, the aggregate unemployment rate remained in excess of 7 percent throughout the mid-1980s. Unemployment rates for minorities and youths soared to astronomically high rates throughout this period.

It is likely that the nation is going to pay a high price for the interregnum in public support for human resource development. Unlike fiscal policy actions and money supply manipulations that can be altered in relatively short order, human resource policies and programs require long-range planning and continuity in financial commitments. Training and educational institutions involve the need for facilities, materials, equipment, staff, and administrators. But the most difficult problem to overcome is the fact that it takes highly trained people to train and to educate the untrained and the uneducated. Erratic support for human development programs can only make more difficult the task of attracting and retaining qualified trainers and educators. The same can be said for the parallel need to develop qualified program administrators and to attract a cadre of academic scholars to the field to generate problem-solving ideas and to assess programmatic effectiveness.

If the structuralists are correct in their assessment, it is likely that public support for this approach will again revive in the near future. To paraphrase Winston Churchill, it is hoped that the Reagan Administration's disinterest in human resource development is not the beginning of the end but, rather, merely the end of the beginning of efforts to adopt an active human resource policy at the national level. The remainder of this essay is devoted to outlining the course that a renewed human resource approach could assume.

Dimensions of Human Resource Development

There are three separate policy approaches to the study of human resource economics. One pertains to the quantitative dimensions, which are concerned with the aggregate amount of human resources that are actually available and utilized to produce the nation's goods and services. The second is the qualitative dimension, which is concerned with the opportunities for development of the latent employment potential of the individual, as well as the collective employment capabilities of society's available human resources. The third is the necessity to assure there are no artificial barriers imposed on the labor market that prevent equal opportunity both to access to the societal institutions responsible for human resource development and to employment in the jobs that allow persons to apply their acquired abilities.

The Quantitative Dimension

The quantitative dimension of a nation's human resources are transmitted to the economy through its population by means of participation in the labor force. The population is composed of those people who are born within the country plus the net difference between those who immigrate minus those who emigrate. In the United States, immigration has, since the mid-1960s, again emerged as a significant contributor to the nation's population growth. As the demographer Leon Bouvier has recently observed "immigration now appears to be almost as important as fertility insofar as U.S. population growth is concerned."[30] Thus, in the United States (but unlike most other industrial nations), immigration is of major contemporary consequence.[31] Although there is emigration from the United States, no such data has been collected since 1958. There is no question, however, that immigration exceeds emigration by several multiples, so that net immigration is known to be positive even though it cannot be specifically measured.

The Population-Labor Force Issue. The conversion of some portion of the population into an available labor force is measured by statistical definitions that measure availability and not well-being.[32] This means that there is a minimum age set for a person to be counted in the labor force. There are also standards that are set to determine those persons of labor force age who are not confined in institutions, and who are able, available, and actively seeking employment. Those who find work for a defined minimum number of hours are counted as being employed; those who meet all other standards for job search but who do not meet the minimum hour requirement are unemployed.

Thus, at any given time, there is some reserve portion of the population of labor force age who constitute potential human resource contributors to production of output for the economy but who are not being utilized. Most serious of these are those persons who are officially classified as being unemployed. The inability of an economy to provide employment for available workers represents the epitome of human resource inefficiency. Thus, one key aspect of national human resource policy must be to press for policy measures that are designed to obtain full employment. Consequently, as indicated earlier, fiscal and monetary policies that are specifically designed to maintain a high level of labor demand do have a quantitative human resource dimension: namely, the utilization of all available human resources already qualified to fill any jobs that are created as a direct consequence of these policies under changing economic circumstances.

The issue of the underutilization of human resources also has efficiency overtones. Of most concern are the problems of "discouraged workers" (that is, persons who give up active job search but who want to work if they thought they could find employment) and involuntary part-time employment (that is, persons who work part-time but who want to work full time). The former are not counted as being employed or unemployed, while the latter are counted as being fully employed. There is also the issue of underemployment—the situation wherein workers are employed in jobs that require skills and education below those that the workers already possess. Presently there is no measure of this underemployment because the concept is not easily quantifiable. The difficulty of measurement does not mean that the problem is unimportant. In fact, there are significant signs that underemployment is widespread in rural areas and in many inner cities.[33] A comprehensive human resource strategy must include efforts to reduce all of these categories of underutilization and underemployment.

Although quantitative measures of human resources focus on availability, full employment and full utilization of available human resources may still be insufficient goals. Available measures of human resource utilization do not relate income and earnings to employment. Consequently, it is possible for the spouse of the highly-paid president of General Motors to be unemployed (and, thus, be a subject of quantitative concern because an available human resource is not being employed), while a fully employed family head may be unable to earn a salary sufficient to pull his or her family above a poverty level (but not be a subject of specific quantitative concern because the resource is counted as being employed). Hence, a complete human resource strategy should look beyond mere utilization measures to examine the economic welfare of the employed human resources as well. Proposals to link employment and earnings in order to acquire a measure of actual economic "hardship" have been made but, to date, they have not been accepted as an official policy concern.[34]

The Immigration Issue. In those few countries of the world—of which the United States is one—that continue to accept significant numbers of new immigrants each year, immigration constitutes an important aspect of human resource policy. With the exception of Israel, which uses immigration policy as a means of national security and for religious acommodation purposes, most of the remaining nations use immigration to meet specific labor market needs (for instance, to meet skill shortages or to settle unpopulated areas where worker shortages exist). In these cases, there is also a tendency (as in Canada) to annually adjust the number of immigrants to be admitted on the basis of aggregate labor market conditions (when unemployment is low or declining, immigration levels are allowed to increase; when unemployment is high or rising, immigration levels reduced). In the case of the United States, however, immigration policy—for a number of unique institutional reasons—has been allowed to function independently of its economic consequences.[35] It has been allowed to become a purely political policy. Not only is mass abuse of the admission system tolerated by illegal immigration, but the legal system is predicated largely on the basis of family reunification rather than on demonstrated labor market needs. Moreover, legal admission levels are fixed so that there is no effort made to relate the number of immigrants admitted each year to prevailing economic conditions. If annual immigration flows were of minor importance, there would be little reason for concern. But as immigration accounts for at least one-third of the annual growth of the U.S. labor force in the 1980s, immigration is not a subject of minor human resource consequence. Comprehensive reform of the entire immigration policy of the United States is a contemporary imperative.

The Qualitative Dimension

In a period of economic transformation, democratic nations like Germany, France, Sweden, and Japan have recognized the need for an "active" human resource policy to complement efforts to achieve full employment of all available human resources.[36] Experience has demonstrated to the governments of these nations that labor market adjustment to rapidly changing industrial, occupational, and geographic employment patterns cannot be assumed. The United States has taken tentative steps in this direction, but, as will be discussed below, has tended to focus its efforts on passive policies designed to help those "left behind" by economic change. Helping the economically disadvantaged is a noble and a necessary aspect of a human resources development strategy, but it is an incomplete approach if similar undertakings are not available to all income stratums of the labor force who need assistance.

The overarching difference between the state of human resource development policy in the United States and that of other major industrial democracies is philosophical. In these other nations, the underpinning of their human resource endeavors is the belief that all accidental victims of social and economic change or of cyclical fluctuations in the economy are a societal responsibility. It is society's obligation to train (or retrain), to educate (or reeducate), to relocate, or to compensate those workers who find themselves unemployed or underemployed through no fault of their own. In most instances, these nations have adopted some form of national economic planning or industrial policy that includes necessary labor market adjustment policies as key elements. But, in the United States, the tendency is to place the responsibility on individuals and local communities to respond to these changing economic conditions on their own. There is little or no economic planning (except in the special areas of national defense and national highway construction). There is an aversion to economic planning in general and to human resource planning in particular. Reliance upon individual and community adjustment to the conditions of the marketplace remains the policy norm—especially in the 1980s. There is periodic political talk during election years about the need to re-order national "priorities" (which is precisely the language embodiment of the planning ideal) but there have been no steps at the national level to formalize the procedures necessary to establish and to achieve any set of national priorities. The political power (or lack of it) of vested interest groups to exert lobbying strength to achieve *ad hoc* objectives remains the *modus operandi* in the United States for setting and pursuing most non-defense related economic objectives.

The exception to this generalization about interventionist human resource policy has been the limited and piecemeal programs enacted between 1961 and 1981. During this period, the federal government initiated a variety of endeavors to directly assist in labor force adjustment. In response to a campaign pledge made by President John F. Kennedy, legislation was passed in 1961 designed to assist distressed geographic areas (that is, areas with above average unemployment rates). Included in the assistance package were federal funds to provide occupational training to citizens who might be hired by private sector enterprises that agreed to locate in these designated areas. This legislation was the "nose under the tent." It opened the door for a virtual plethora of human resource development legislation. These initiatives included overhauling existing vocational education and vocational rehabilitation programs, expanding and opening up apprenticeship training to minorities and women, providing federal funds to aid elementary, secondary, and higher education, creating health care programs, establishing nutrition and food stamp programs, providing preschool education to children of low-income families, as well as remedial adult education programs, and initiating economic development assistance to regions, communities, and neighborhoods.

In the training field, one of the most ambitious undertakings was the adoption of the Manpower Development and Training Act (MDTA) of 1962 and its subsequent liberalizing amendments. This legislation is of special interest because it was originally enacted in direct response to fears that rapid technological change (caused largely by automation) was a major explanation for structural changes in employment patterns.[37] This pioneering legislation was primarily designed to provide occupational retraining at the public expense for displaced workers to find private sector employment. In a way, it was intended to be a new form of social insurance for semi-skilled persons with prior work experience. With the coming of the Vietnam War, however, the employment patterns that had caused this concern were at least temporarily reversed. Both manufacturing sector jobs and blue collar occupations that had been declining for over a decade, were revived because of the sharp increase in defense and defense-related spending. The original clientele for MDTA, therefore, appeared to have vanished.

In the meantime, however, the civil rights movement had come into full blossom with the passage of the historic Civil Rights Act of 1964. After the initial euphoria had passed and the political and social barriers to black participation in American society had dissipated, the monumental challenges to the achievement of economic equality became starkly vivid. The concept of equal employment opportunity embodied in the Act assumed that minorities were *already* qualified for available jobs. Some were. But too often, the legacy of past denial of opportunities to acquire sufficient human resource preparation had left many from these groups unqualified, uninformed, unaspiring and disproportionately concentrated in declining industries and occupations. In the wake of the obvious need to address the massive human resource development deficiencies that had been forced upon the black population by past *de jure* and *de facto* discrimination, the Johnson Administration shifted the focus of MDTA in 1967 to serve the employment needs of the "economically disadvantaged." This was an historic turning point. Rather than returning to serve the broader needs of the labor force when the Vietnam War was over and the structural changes in the economy once more revealed themselves, these publicly supported training programs continued to focus on the employment needs of the "economically disadvantaged." Ostensibly, the training programs were for adults and youths from low-income families without regard to race. But as minorities in general and blacks in particular were disproportionately concentrated in the low-income population, they dominated the clientele.

In the process of concentrating on the employment needs of the "economically disadvantaged," however, these remedial programs acquired a stigmatizing image that implied that human resource programs were only for those people unable to help themselves. As a consequence, when the Reagan Administration came to power in 1981 with a determination to reduce federal spending on social programs, these programs did not have a politically powerful enough constituency to withstand the assault. The programs were drastically reduced in both their substance and in their level of financial support. Had the full potential of a national human resource development policy been in place to assist *all* income groups in need, it is unlikely that this dismantling process could have been accomplished.

Assuming that the federal government may someday renew the process of actively supporting human resource development, the qualitative dimensions of a human resource strategy should embrace three concepts: salvage; a preventive maintenance; and long-run educational development.

The Salvage Function. Despite the aforementioned efforts to reduce their numbers, there remain a number of individuals and subgroups of the population that are unprepared to find employment on a regular and self-supporting basis. In many instances, it is necessary for a civilized and generally prosperous society to financially support these persons—usually, however, at only marginally sufficient levels. Without targeted programs to develop their human resource abilities, these people are essentially doomed to play out their lives in poverty. There are also other persons who lack sufficient skills and education (because opportunities to acquire them were unavailable or inadequate, or because of a personal failure to take advantage of opportunities that did exist), which means that they are often forced to survive in the sizeable "irregular economy" of narcotics dealing, prostitution, gambling, and theft. Not all poor people or all "street hustlers" are amenable to a rescue attempt by human resources programs. But as long as there are sufficient numbers, a salvage strategy to provide a life-line of opportunity to prepare for legitimate employment is in order. For not only is it a socially worthy undertaking to reduce human suffering but, as indicated earlier, there is also the pragmatic economic reality that uneducated and poorly skilled workers can become "a monumental drag" to a post-industrial society.

Although a number of labor force issues could be cited where a salvage response seems warranted, three illustrative problems stand out in the mid-1980s: the declining black male labor force participation rate, the growth in the number of female-headed households and the feminization of poverty, and the mounting level of adult illiteracy. The corrective factors associated with each of these concerns are unlikely to be resolved by reliance on standard fiscal and monetary solutions. Each of these deserves a brief elaboration.

Historically, the labor force participation rate of black males exceeded that of white males for every age cohort. Beginning in the 1950s and since then, the reverse trend has developed. Consequently by 1985, the overall black male labor force participation rate was 70.8 percent while the comparable rate for white males was 77.0 percent. All things being equal, there is no reason why white males should now have higher participation rates for every age cohort than do black males or why white males should have a considerably higher overall rate. But, of course, all things have not been equal. Black workers are clustered disproportionately in declining industries in the inner cities of about twelve major urban areas, in addition to being scattered throughout much of the rural South. Jobs in general are scarce in these areas. But jobs are especially hard to find if one has few skills and a poor education and if there are limited opportunities to acquire or to develop latent abilities. Too often, this has been the case for black males. The process of finding a job that can provide adequate income is made more difficult if there are lingering practices and practitioners of racial discrimination. Under these conditions, an inordinate number of black males apparently have despaired from seeking work in the regular economy. There is, of course, an ominous societal implication to the secular decline in their participation rates. If adult black males are not at work, or in school, or in the military, what are they doing to survive?

The second group of special concern is female heads of households—especially those with families below the poverty level. In 1985, 10 million families were headed by females (because of divorce, separation, widowhood, or having children born out of wedlock). Of these, 6 million had children under the age of eighteen living with them. One of every three families headed by a woman was living in poverty (compared to one of thirteen for all families). In the labor market, the female single parent is often plagued by educational deficiencies, high unemployment, and low earnings. It is unlikely that many of these female family heads would be able to improve their employment and income opportunities without specific programmatic assistance.

Overlapping the issues of the nonparticipation of black adult males and the employment difficulties confronting female single parents is a third salvage problem: adult illiteracy. Although the 1980 Census—relying primarily upon written responses to a written questionnaire—concluded that the nation is almost 100 percent literate, these findings have been seriously questioned. Indeed, based upon studies that have focused squarely upon the issue of literacy, the U.S. Department of Education reported in 1983 that 23 million adults are totally or functionally illiterate and that another 23 million adults are only marginally literate at best.[38] Other studies released in the early 1980s have placed these numbers even higher.[39] The situation is believed to be so severe that the National Commission on Excellence in Education, appointed by President Ronald Reagan, concluded its 1983 comprehensive report by saying that the future welfare of the nation is "in peril" and chose to title its report, *Nation at Risk*.[40]

The economic consequences of mounting levels of adult illiteracy among the labor force are much more severe in the emerging service-oriented society than was the case when the goods-producing sector dominated the employment generation process. The bulk of employment opportunities provided by the goods-producing industries in the first half of the twentieth century did not require much in the way of educational and verbal skills from its jobs seekers. But the service economy is based much more upon verbal than manual skills. Thus, the literacy gap has emerged at a time when changes in the labor market are placing a premium on communication skills. Service industries and technologically-oriented businesses require workers to handle comprehensive tasks that are often based more on reading, writing, and listening than on manipulative skills. Thus, there is an inherent threat to the evolving viability of the economy because of widespread adult illiteracy. It entails more than a loss in potential worker productivity because of the limited availability of employment opportunities for such people. Adult illiteracy also contributes to the incidence of workplace accidents, the provision of poor quality products and services to customers, and the loss of management and supervisory time. Even the U.S. Department of Defense has been forced to spend "thousands of dollars to convert weapon manuals into easy-to-read comic books for military recruits who are expected to handle complicated equipment."[41] Hence, even the nation's ability to adequately defend itself may be at stake.

As if the number of functionally illiterate adults were not bad enough, it is estimated that their ranks are actually swelling by about 2.3 million persons a year.[42] Growing adult illiteracy has been attributed to the declining standards of the nation's educational institutions from elementary through college levels. Another cause has been the epidemic of teenage pregnancies over the past decade, which contributes to the school "drop-out" problem. Whatever the reasons, it is estimated that about one million teenagers leave schools each year without sufficient literacy skills. But the largest source of growth in the ranks of the functionally illiterate is immigrants who cannot speak English and who, in many cases, are illiterate in their own native language. This is especially the case with would-be workers who enter the nation illegally from Mexico and the Caribbean Basin. It also applies to many of the recent refugees admitted from Southeast Asia and from many of the post-1980 asylees and asylee-applicants from Cuba, Haiti, El Salvador, and Guatemala.[43]

Thus, there is an urgent need to undertake a national program geared to the attainment of educational competency. It was estimated that in 1985 about 75 percent of the unemployed persons in the United States have inadequate reading and writing skills.[44] Until these basic deficiencies are addressed, it is very difficult—if not imposssible—to provide the related skill acquisition needs of this significant segment of the adult population. It is also doubtful that any reasonable application of traditional monetary or fiscal policy could alone create sufficient employment opportunities to employ so many illiterate persons.

The Preventive Maintenance Function. In a period of labor market transformation, there is an acceleration in the process by which traditional industries and occupations decline and new ones rise to take their place. As discussed earlier, there are multiple new forces affecting employment patterns in the United States. The service sector of the economy has soared from accounting for 31 percent of the employed labor force in 1900 to 69 percent of employed labor force in 1984. The Bureau of Labor Statistics estimates that 90 percent of the growth in employment between 1985 and 1995 will be in the service sector.[45] But there is a pervasive myth that must be debunked: it is that service sector jobs are dead-end and low paying. Some are, of course, but so are some in the goods-producing sector (for example, in agriculture and textile manufacturing). The reality is that 80 percent of the professional and managerial jobs in the entire economy are to be found in the service sector. While it is true that there are growing service employment opportunities in such low-paying industries as fast-foods and nursing home care, there are also substantial employment increases being realized in high-paying jobs in computer services, legal services, and advertising, as well as average-paying jobs in insurance, wholesale trade, and auto repairing.[46] In general, the shift to a service-based economy will lead to an upgrading of the skill and educational requirements of the labor force from what hitherto existed.

The rapid shift to a service economy also has implications for the location of jobs. Goods-producing industries tend to cluster in specific geographic areas. But the key characteristic of services is that they must be produced locally. Thus, the shift from goods to services has contributed to the de-centralization of employment away from its historic concentration in the urban Northeast to other regions. Shifting national defense expenditures have also affected the geography of jobs. Historically, through the Korean Conflict of the 1950s, major non-personnel defense expenditures were made on steel and wheeled vehicles. Since the 1960s, however, the bulk of non-personnel expenditures has shifted towards missiles, rockets, and aircraft. These weapons often require that some phase of their construction be accomplished out-of-doors and that they be tested either over water or in remote areas with low populations. The result has been a shift in employment opportunities to the Southeast and Southwest.

In an environment of rapid shifts in employment patterns, it is necessary to recognize that both job and occupational changes will occur frequently over one's working life. Indeed, a typical worker entering the labor force in the mid-1980s can be expected to change jobs six or seven times and to change occupations three times over his or her working life. In this context of flux, there is a need to have in place a human resource system that can provide job retraining, up-to-date labor market information, ample opportunities for educational upgrading, and relocation assistance to promote the readjustment process for those who cannot easily, if at all, make these transitions. The system should not just help the working poor. It should also be designed to assist all income groups who become vulnerable to unemployment.

Traditionally, decisions pertaining to selecting careers, receiving training, securing education, and locating jobs have been left to individuals. But in a climate of rapid changes in employment patterns, there is a need for a preventive maintenance system of human resource programs to mitigate fear, hardship, and inefficiencies. Included in this public system would be programs to gather and disseminate up-to-date job information, as well as to provide job counseling. The federal government can also analyze and forecast labor demand patterns, as well as publicize the associated job requirements. It can also assist the adjustment process by actually financing occupational retraining and educational upgrading opportunities for adults. There are major institutional barriers that confront individuals who must re-adjust to changing employment conditions on their own. First, the personal financial cost of acquiring new training and additional education can be substantial. Secondly, there is often a lack of appropriate adult training and educational facilities in local areas that are in tune with national labor market needs. And thirdly, there is a lack of assurance that, if an individual has to make an unassisted new career decision, and undertakes a lengthy retraining process, new opportunities will actually be available.

An ideal preventive maintenance system would also include a comprehensive program to facilitate labor mobility from areas of worker surplus to areas of labor scarcity. Voluntary relocation programs are part of human resource initiatives in Western Europe, but they have not passed the pilot experimental stage in the United States. The resistance to such efforts is political, not economic. Because of the "one-man, one vote" principle that allocates political power, politicians are loathe to support programs to move their constituents to other political jurisdictions no matter how serious their employment needs. In contrast, politicians are willing to support almost any endeavor to attract industry to their jurisdictions (for instance, "enterprise zones," tax abatements, the issuance of industrial bonds, and the creation of industrial parks) but will oppose most efforts to move workers out. Often the efforts to attract new industries are unsuccessful, or insufficient, or the new industries bring their workers with them and only "cream" the local labor supply for new hires. The needy workers of the local area, therefore, are often left with the prospect of seeking some form of income maintenance or of relocating elsewhere on their own. When workers who are not in the higher occupational echelons relocate on their own initiative, the decisions are frequently made on the basis of kinship ties rather than as a response to demonstrated labor shortages. A guided relocation program would involve the use of trained experts to screen and to refer for voluntary interstate transfer those workers who can fill job vacancies in localities where jobs actually exist. Such a process can eliminate much of the waste, hardship, and disorderly search for new jobs that confront some workers who have been dislocated from their former employment.

In each of the above instances, the justification for public interventions is based on the belief that they can enhance the actual workings of the labor market. The process does not counter revealed market conditions but, rather, serves to facilitate the efficiency of the adjustment process by addressing the institutional obstacles.

Long-Run Educational Development. Ultimately, the foundation of a human resource strategy for a rapidly changing economy must be built on the quality of the nation's overall education system. As one study of the economic implications of the computer age concluded in 1983, "a highly literate work force, not necessarily college-trained, is precisely what is needed for worker flexibility and adaptability in the post-industrial society, with its ever more rapidly changing circumstances."[47] The study noted that what is often overlooked in discussions of Japan's emphasis on education is that their primary and secondary education system is not intended to create an educational elite but, rather, to generate a high *average* level of capability *throughout* their society.

It is not necessary at this juncture to detail the litany of indictments contained in the studies that have catalogued the serious failures of the contemporary U.S. educational system.[48] Blame for the past is less important than responsibility for the future. The extensive institutional reforms that are needed, however, involve far more than the public expenditure of increasing sums. They entail major educational changes in teacher preparation, compensation, and certification; in administrative practices and the distribution of decision-making power; in curriculum development; in disciplinary practices; and in academic standards for assessing student performance and promotion. They also involve the need for greater emphasis on "drop-out" prevention, as well as the need to provide lifetime educational opportunities that are accessible for more adults. And, they include the necessity to make access to education at all levels contingent on the ability to learn and not on the ability to pay. In other words, extensive institutional changes are essential if education is to contribute to the answer and not worsen the problem of contemporary labor force adjustment.

Any serious effort to reform the nation's education system so that it can become congruent with meeting long-term economic needs must ultimately be linked to some degree of national economic planning. To this end, there is an implicit need for the adoption of an overall industrial policy for the nation of which education and training policies would be a vital component.[49] Although the topic is controversial, there can be little purposeful long-term educational preparation of the labor force for employment if there is little direction provided as to where the economy is thought to be going.

Equal Employment Opportunity

The discussion of human resource development up to this point has been predicated on the assumption that qualified workers will have equal access to job openings. Experience, however, has demonstrated that it cannot be realistically assumed that labor markets function solely on the basis of merit and productivity. It has also been revealed that the roots of discrimination run deep into the institutional practices that prepare workers to compete in the labor market. Hence, mechanisms to monitor employment practices and patterns and to redress wrongful actions must be a fundamental component of any serious human resource development strategy. Without these assurances, there is little logic in public efforts to develop the human resource potential of significant segments of the labor force.

Although there is no dispute among economists over the principle that workers should be employed on the basis of their productive capabilities and not their personal characteristics, there has been extensive disagreement over what constitutes discrimination and how extensive an issue it is. The perception of the nature of the issue, as well as the assessment of its magnitude, are important because they define the nature of the appropriate remedies and determine the degree of importance to be assigned to the problem.

Until the late 1950s, neoclassical economics essentially ignored the issue of employment discrimination in the labor market. In a competitive environment, employment discrimination is an irrational act and the theory assumes rational behavior. But during these same years, as the conditions were occurring that would spawn the civil rights movement, Gary Becker introduced a refinement of neoclassical theory.[50] He conceded that some employers may have "a taste for discrimination" that may be reflected in their employment decisions. This "taste," however, is seen to be an entirely exogenous factor that is beyond the purview of economic analysis. There is no indication as to what creates it or what forces perpetrate it. Becker's analysis was welcomed by neoclassical theorists because it implied that, if discrimination is eradicated, labor markets will function in their assumedly competitive manner. Becker, however, defined discrimination in a very limited way: it existed only in those circumstances where two workers of a different race (or any other arbitrary distinction) who both have equal productivities are paid differently. If productivities differ, then there is no discrimination, since rewards are merely reflecting differential human capital endowments. Becker's analysis, therefore, was more a theory of wages than a theory of discrimination.

Numerous major refinements were soon offered by other neoclassical economists.[51] These refinements, however, revealed considerable disagreements. As Ray Marshall has noted "they [that is, neoclassicalists] agree only on the form of the theory, not on the details or even the major conclusions."[52]

By far, the most complete statement of the revised neoclassical theory was offered by Kenneth Arrow.[53] Essentially, Arrow rejected the idea of "tastes for discrimination" and instead introduced the notion of "statistical discrimination" as the explanation for continuing racial and gender differences in the labor market. That is to say, employers use group characteristics as a proxy for individual characteristics. Initial differences in productivities could be taken as a given and reinforced over time to become a "perception of reality." But what is the basis of these "beliefs"? Arrow suggested cognitive dissonance. But as Marshall notes, it is difficult to see how beliefs in a supposedly rational paradigm could persist if they were merely perceptions of reality that experience demonstrated to be erroneous. Likewise, the revised theory does not give any indication about what gives discriminators the power to discriminate in a competitive market system. Presumably there must be in a competitive system at least one employer who would act rationally and not practice discrimination. If so, such an employer would drive all firms who practice discrimination out of business. For these and other reasons, there are really no useful anti-discrimination policies that flow from the revised neoclassical model. Accordingly, the neoclassical model has rendered no contribution to real-world efforts to address one of the major labor market issues of this generation.

Neoclassical theory makes no distinction between overt and covert discrimination. It ignores completely the consequences of discrimination that occur when institutional practices deny equal access to jobs, training, and information to certain subgroups of the labor force. As a consequence, those groups that are discriminated against may not have the opportunity or may not aspire to seek the necessary skill and educational requisites. It was these practices that the National Advisory Commission on Civil Disorders unanimously found in 1968 to be the principle barrier confronting the integregation of blacks into the economic mainstream.[54] Similar claims have been made about the obstacles that confront other racial minorities in particular and women in general. By failing to stress the difference between overt discrimination and institutional discrimination, it is possible that discriminators can practice covert discrimination while claiming to be objective in their employment decisions.

When the Civil Rights Act of 1964 was passed, it, too, incorporated a perception that the problem of discrimination was manifested only through overt actions. Discrimination was viewed as being unambiguous. Hence, when passed, the Act was written in language that simultaneously sought to outlaw discriminatory actions while trying to protect the rights of employers to choose the most qualified labor force available, as well as to protect the job security rights of present employees. The gross inadequacies of this perception of both the problem and the scope of the appropriate remedies were soon revealed by the outbreak of civil disorders in urban centers across the nation in the mid-1960s. They occurred at a time when aggregate unemployment was considerably lower (in the mid-3 percent range) than it has been ever since. The message was clear: equal employment opportunity meant more than simply full employment—the *sine qua non* of neoclassical, Keynesian, and monetarist paradigms. It meant that there had to be changes in the racial and gender composition of employment patterns, as opposed to an exclusive policy focus merely on the level of employment. As a black leader once expressed it: "after all, we had full employment back on the plantations."

The finding of the Commission on Civil Disorders was that "white racism" as manifested by institutional discrimination was the chief barrier to the attainment of equal employment opportunity. This conclusion opened an entirely new policy era with respect to the issue of employment discrimination. The findings were not original, as other scholars (especially in sociology and psychology) had earlier made the same point. But the fact that a national commission composed entirely of political moderates could so boldly and clearly make the charge gave credence to the proposition.[55] It meant that a declaration of words to prohibit labor market discrimination would not suffice to provide equal employment opportunity. Labor market interventions would be required.

Although the Commission spoke only of the predicament of blacks, the message to varying degrees applied to other groups that had also sustained discrimination. The heritage of past denial of opportunities raises difficult questions such as stifled occupational aspirations, the effects of unequal educational quality, the absence of labor market information channels, the lack of opportunity to acquire skills in the newer and more technologically-oriented industries and the expanding managerial and professional occupations, and the paucity of formal job credentials. As for the actual implementation of equal employment opportunity at the work site, institutional discrimination raised difficult questions concerning recruitment, screening, and training practices of employers. Many of these practices were viewed by employers as legitimate methods to attract, cull, and prepare a qualified labor force. Thus, as Peter B. Doeringer and Michael Piore have warned, "the inherent equity of an attack upon racial discrimination is not always as clear to those within the market as it is to outsiders, and efforts to eliminate racial discrimination are often viewed by the employers and employees as an assault upon the instruments which effect labor market adjustment and preserve job security."[56] The process of actually securing changes in employment practices, therefore, has proven to be both difficult and slow.

Without diverting into a lengthy discussion of how equal employment opportunity policy has evolved, it suffices to say that by the mid-1980s it has reached a crossroads. Equal employment opportunity policy, as manifested by the development of affirmative action programs, has always been premised on the assumption that qualified workers from previously excluded groups do exist. Public policy can only ask that job credentials be job-related and that employment practices be fair. For many women and for some minorities this is all that has been necessary to open up employment opportunities where they previously did not exist. It is essential that these efforts continue, as it is unlikely that the principles of equal employment opportunity have yet been fully institutionalized to the degree that they can be taken for granted. On the other hand, until the lingering human resource development issues addressed elsewhere in this essay are fully supported and funded, it is unlikely that significant changes in racial employment patterns are going to occur. In fact, there is ample reason to fear that they are going to deteriorate.

The Final Dimension

The aforementioned themes have sought to highlight the critical role that human resources assume in the development of industrial societies in general and in the United States in particular. They have also focused upon programmatic efforts to assure that the latent abilities of the work force are given the opportunity to be developed and to be impartially employed. But the accomplishment of these tasks will be of little consequence if there is not parallel concern for the type of world in which these endeavors are an evolving part.

The goal of human resource development should be to provide opportunities for individuals to become better informed—in the sense both of one's personal ability to be prepared for employment and one's broader awareness of the quality of the society of which he or she is a part. The nation is entering a period of economic revolution in the means and methods of production. The answers to the problems of the past appear to have little relevancy to those of the present. The same can be said for the relevancy of past academic paradigms depicting the operation of the economy. The pressure to use science as a form of innovation and to encourage the technological application of the ensuing outcomes is not coming from the competitive sectors of the economy. Instead, the generative forces stem primarily from the oligopolistic private sector, the public sector at the federal level (especially as manifested by its expenditures on advanced forms of defense weaponry) and, the quasi-public support given by the federal government to private profit and non-profit enterprises for scientific research and development. As Robert Heilbroner has noted, the spectacular growth since World War II in scientific discovery and technological application "is no longer a spontaneous product of market forces."[57] Perceptively, he warns that "the idea that technology is benign in its social impact may be the most tragic of all contemporary faiths."[58] Technology and science have become commanding realities that are reshaping the relationship of human beings to their natural environment. Educational institutions, in addition to their vocational mission, must inspire labor force participants to pursue life-long self-education, as well as to transmit the obligation to their leaders to require that the forces of science and technology be used for tolerant, compassionate, and peaceful purposes. It is imperative that the uses of these forces be the result of decisions made by an informed citizenry and not by an opinionated or indifferent society. Otherwise, the progression of industrialization could lead to calamitous human consequences. As Carlo Cipolla has warned, "the mass schools of the industrial world tend to teach techniques that leave the spirit barren."[59] He adds that "there is nothing more dangerous than technical knowledge when unaccompanied by respect for human life and human values."[60] As one witnesses the advent of genetic engineering, robotics, nuclear power, genetic screening, artificial intelligence, laser-based weaponry, and space stations (to recite only a few science-based technologies) into societies that are still dominated by intolerance and aggressiveness, there is justifiable reason for alarm.

If human resources are truly "the wealth of nations," their development carries with it the parallel responsibility to recognize that their contribution to the economy must enhance the quality of life on this planet and not lead to its enslavement, impoverishment, or extinction.

Notes

1. Frederick H. Harbison, *Human Resources as the Wealth of Nations* (New York: Oxford University Press, 1973).
2. Ray Marshall, "The Role of Appprenticeship in an Internationalized Information World." Paper presented at the Conference on *Learning By Doing* sponsored by The International Union of Operating Engineers, the U.S. Department of Labor, and Cornell University. Albany, New York, 6 April 1986, p. 1.
3. John R. Commons, *Institutional Economics: Its Place in Political Economy*, Vol. 2 (Madison: University of Wisconsin Press, 1961), Chap. 10.
4. John M. Keynes, *The General Theory of Employment, Interest and Money* (New York: Harcourt Brace and Company, 1958).
5. See, Theodore W. Schultz, "Investment in Human Capital," *American Economic Review* 51 (March, 1961): 1–17; Theodore W. Schultz, *Investing in People: The Economics of Population Quality.* (Berkeley: University of California Press, 1981); and Gary Becker, *Human Capital* (New York: National Bureau of Economic Research, 1964).
6. Michael J. Piore, "The Importance of Human Capital Theory to Labor Economics—A Dissenting View." *Proceedings* of the 26th Annual Winter Meetings (Madison: Industrial Relations Research Association, 1973), p. 253.
7. See, for example, Eli Ginzberg, "Expanding the Knowledge Base for Informed Public Policy" in *Employment and Training R&D*, ed. R. Thayne Robson, (Kalamazoo, Michigan: The Upjohn Institute for Employment Research, 1984), p. 3; See also Gunnar Myrdal, *Objectivity in Social Research* (New York: Pantheon Books, 1969).
8. David M. Gordon, *Theories of Poverty and Underemployment* (Lexington: D.C. Heath and Company, 1972) Chap. 3 and Peter B. Doeringer and Michael Piore, *Internal Labor Markets and Manpower Analysis* (Lexington: D.C. Heath and Company, 1971), Chap. 2.
9. For example, see Bennett Harrison, *Education and Training in the Urban Ghetto* (Baltimore: The Johns Hopkins University Press, 1972), Chap. 1; Ivar Berg, *Education and Jobs: The Great Training Robbery* (Boston: Beacon Press, 1971) Chapters 2,3 and 9; Gordon, *Theories of Poverty and Un-*

deremployment, Chap. 4; and Doeringer and Piore, *Internal Labor Markets,* Chap. 2.
10. Compare Lester C. Thurow, *Investment in Human Capital* (Belmont, Calif.: Wadsworth Publishing Co., 1970) with Lester C. Thurow, *Dangerous Currents: The State of Economics* (New York: Random House, 1983), Chap. 7.
11. Thurow, *Dangerous Currents,* p. 180.
12. For example, see Ray Marshall, Vernon M. Briggs, Jr., and Alan King, *Labor Economics: Wages, Employment, Trade Unionism, and Public Policy* (Homewood, Ill.: Richard D. Irwin, 1984), 5th ed., Chap. 12.
13. Edward F. Denison, *Trends in American Economic Growth, 1929–1982* (Washington, D.C.: The Brookings Institution, 1985).
14. Anthony Carnevale, *Human Capital: A High Yield Corporate Asset* (Washington: American Society for Training Directors, 1983).
15. Eli Ginzberg, "The Mechanization of Work," *Scientific American* 247 (September 1982): 66–75; Howard Fullerton and John Tshetter, "The 1995 Labor Force: BLS's Latest Projections," *Monthly Labor Review* 108 (November 1985): 17–25; Ray Marshall, "Labor Market Implications of Internationalization," in *The Internationalization of the U.S. Economy: Its Labor Market Policy Implications,* ed. Vernon M. Briggs, Jr., (Salt Lake City: Olympus Publishing Company, 1986) pp. 1–27; Joyanna Moy, "Recent Trends in Unemployment and the Labor Force, 10 Countries," *Monthly Labor Review* 108 (August 1985): 13–14; Philip Rones, "An Analysis of Regional Employment Growth 1973–1985," *Monthly Labor Review* 109 (July 1986): 3–14; Carol Leon, "Occupational Winners and Losers: Who Were They During 1972–80," *Monthly Labor Review* 105 (June 1982): 18–28; G. T. Silvestri and J. M. Lukasiewicz, "Occupational Employment Projections: The 1984–95 Outlook," *Monthly Labor Review* 108 (November 1985): 42–59; Vernon M. Briggs, Jr., "Employment Trends and Contemporary Immigration Policy," in *Clamor at the Gates,* ed. Nathan Glazer (San Francisco: Institute for Contemporary Studies, 1985), pp. 135–60; Robert W. DeGrasse, *Military Expansion and Economic Decline,* (Armonk, N.Y.: M.E. Sharpe, Inc. 1983).
16. Clair Brown, "Unemployment Theory and Practice: 1946–1980," *Industrial Relations* 22 (Spring 1983); 164–85.
17. See Walter Heller, "The Administration's Fiscal Policy," and Otto Eckstein, "Aggregate Demand and the Current Unemployment," in *Unemployment and the American Economy,* ed. Arthur M. Ross, (New York: John Wiley & Son Inc. 1964), pp. 93–115, and 116–34, respectively.
18. See Milton Friedman, "The Role of Monetary Policy," *American Economic Review* 58 (March 1968): 1–17 and Milton Friedman, *Capitalism and Freedom* (Chicago: The University of Chicago Press, 1962), pp. 53–55.
19. See Milton Friedman and Walter Heller, *Monetary vs Fiscal Policy* (New York: W. W. Norton & Co., 1969).
20. Charles C. Killingsworth, "The Fall and Rise of the Idea of Structural Unemployment," *Proceedings* of the 31st Winter Meetings of the Industrial Relations Research Association (Presidential Address) (Madison, Wisconsin: Industrial Relations Research Association, 1979), pp. 1–13; and Ginzberg, "The Mechanization of Work," pp. 66–75.

288   Vernon M. Briggs, Jr.

21. Charles C. Killingsworth, "Full Employment and the New Economics," *Scottish Journal of Political Economy* (February 1969): 1–27.
22. Keynes, *The General Theory of Employment, Interest and Money*, Chap. 18.
23. *Ibid.*, p. 245.
24. For example, see Walter Heller, *New Dimensions of Political Economy* (New York: W. W. Norton & Company, 1967) and Arthur M. Okun, *The Political Economy of Prosperity* (New York: W. W. Norton and Company, 1970), Chap. 2.
25. Charles Holt, *The Unemployment-Inflation Dilemma: A Manpower Solution* (Washington: The Urban Institute, 1971), Chaps. 5 and 6.
26. Howard Rosen, "An Administrator's Reflections," in *Employment and Training R & D*, pp. 73–104.
27. For a review of these efforts, see Eli Ginzberg, ed., *Employing the Unemployed* (New York: Basic Books, 1980); see also John E. Schwartz, *America's Hidden Success: A Reassessment of Twenty Years of Public Policy*, (New York: W. W. Norton & Company, 1983), pp. 44–58; and Robert Taggart, *A Fisherman's Guide: An Assessment of Training and Remediation Strategies* (Kalamazoo: The Upjohn Institute, 1981).
28. Vernon M. Briggs, Jr., "The Revival of Public Service Employment in the 1970s: Lessons for the 1980s." *Proceedings* of the 34th Winter Meetings of the Industrial Relations Research Association (Madison, Wisc.: Industrial Relations Research Association, 1982), pp. 258–65.
29. John L. Palmer and Isabel V. Sawhill, eds., *The Reagan Record* (Cambridge, Mass.: Ballinger Publishing Company, 1984).
30. Leon F. Bouvier, *The Impact of Immigration on the Size of the U.S. Population* (Washington, D.C.: Population Reference Bureau, 1981), p. 1.
31. Vernon M. Briggs, Jr., *Immigration Policy and the American Labor Force* (Baltimore: The Johns Hopkins University Press, 1984).
32. For definitional details and a review of the major policy issues surrounding these definitions, see National Commission on Employment and Unemployment, *Counting the Labor Force* (Washington: U.S. Government Printing Office), 1979.
33. For example, see Harrison, *Educational and Training in the Urban Ghetto;* and Vernon M. Briggs, Jr. "The Rural Labor Force, Unemployment and Underemployment Issues" in *The Economic Evolution of Rural America*, both published in *Hearings* before the Subcommittee on Agriculture and Transportation of the Joint Economic Committee of the U.S. Congress (Washington, D.C.: U.S. Government Printing Office, 1985), pp. 226–27.
34. Sar A. Levitan and Robert Taggart, *Employment and Earnings Inadequacy* (Baltimore: The Johns Hopkins University Press, 1974) and Robert Taggart, *Hardship: The Welfare Consequences of Labor Market Problems* (Kalamazoo, Mich.: The Upjohn Institute for Employment Research, 1982).
35. Briggs, *Immigration Policy*, Chap. 8.
36. See, Robert Haveman and Daniel Saks, "Transatlantic Lessons for Employment and Training Policy," *Industrial Relations* 24 (Winter 1985): 20–36; Bernard Casey and Gert Bruche, "Active Labor Market Policy: An International Overview," *Industrial Relations* 24 (Winter 1985): 37–61;

and National Council on Employment Policy, *Comparative Labor Market Policies of Japan, West Germany, United Kingdom, France and Australia,* ed. Howard Rosen (Salt Lake City: Olympus Press, 1985).
37. See Charles C. Killingsworth, "Automation, Jobs, and Manpower: The Case for Structural Unemployment," in *The Manpower Revolution,* ed. Garth L. Mangum (Garden City, N.Y.: Doubleday & Company, 1966), pp. 97–116. See also, Garth L. Mangum, *The Emergence of Manpower Policy,* (New York: Holt, Rinehart and Winston, 1969).
38. The studies are cited in Jonathan Kozol, *Illiterate America,* (Garden City, N.Y.: Anchor Press/Doubleday, 1985), pp. 7–12.
39. Ibid. (see citations in the "Notes" section on p. 227).
40. National Commission on Excellence in Education, *Nation at Risk: The Imperative for Educational Reform,* A Report to the U.S. Department of Education (Washington, D.C.: U.S. Government Printing Office, 1983).
41. "Hearings Accents Problem of Work Force Illiteracy," *Daily Labor Reporter,* No. 149 (2 August 1985), p. A-10.
42. Ibid.
43. Briggs, *Immigration Policy,* p. 159–66 and 220–22; and Ellen Sehgal, "Foreign-Born Workers in the U.S. Labor Market: A Special Survey," *Monthly Labor Review* 108 (July 1985): 18–24.
44. "Hearings Accents Problem of Work Force Illiteracy."
45. "Service Sector is Diverse, BLS Chief Says," *Daily Labor Reporter,* No. 75 (18 April 1986), p. A-6.
46. Ibid.; see also Leon, "Occupational Winners and Losers."
47. Edward A. Feigenbaum and Pamela McCorduck, *The Fifth Generation: Artificial Intelligence and Japan's Computer Challenge to the World,* (Reading, Mass.: Addison-Wesley Publishing Company, 1983), p. 147.
48. National Commission on Excellence in Education, *Nation at Risk;* see also Thomas Sizer *Horace's Compromise: The Dilemma of American High Schools* (Boston: Houghton Mifflin Co., 1984); National Board of Inquiry, *Barriers to Excellence: Our Own Children at Risk* (Boston: National Coalition of Advocates, 1985); Association of America Colleges, *Integrity of the College Curriculum* (Washington, D.C.: Association of American Colleges, 1985); Ernest L. Boyer, *High School: A Report on Secondary Education in America* (New York: Harper & Row, 1983); National Institute of Education, *Excellence in American Higher Education* (Washington, D.C.: National Institute of Education, 1984); National Science Board, Commission on Precollege Education in Mathematics, Science and Technology, *Educating Americans for the 21st Century,* (Washington, D.C.: National Science Board, 1983); National Commission on Student Financial Assistance, *Signs of Trouble and Erosion: A Report on Graduate Education in America* (Washington, D.C.: National Commission on Student Financial Assistance, 1983).
49. R. D. Norton, "Industrial Policy and American Renewal," *Journal of Economic Literature* 24 (March 1986): 1–40. See also Robert R. Reich, *The Next American Frontier* (New York: The New York Times Book Co., 1983).
50. Gary S. Becker, *The Economics of Discrimination* (Chicago: University of Chicago Press, 1957 [1971]).

51. For the most comprehensive review of this literature, see Ray Marshall, "The Economics of Racial Discrimination: A Survey," *The Journal of Economic Literature* 12 (September 1974): 849–71. See also Ronald L. Oaxaca, "Theory and Measurements in the Economics of Discrimination," in *Equal Rights and Industrial Relations,* ed. Leonard J. Hausman, *et al* (Madison, Wisc.: Industrial Relations Research Association, 1977) pp. 1–30.

52. Marshall, "The Economics of Racial Discrimination," p. 849.

53. Kenneth J. Arrow, "Models of Job Discrimination" and "Some Models of Race in the Labor Market," Chaps. 2 and 6, in *Racial Discrimination in Economic Life,* ed. A. H. Pascal, (Lexington, Mass: D.C. Heath, 1972).

54. National Commission on Civil Disorders, *Report of the National Advisory Commission on Civil Disorders,* (New York: Bantam Books, 1968).

55. Vernon M. Briggs, Jr. "The Report of the Commission on Civil Disorders: A Review Article," *Journal of Economic Issues* 2 (June 1968): 200–210.

56. Doeringer and Piore, *Internal Labor Markets and Manpower Analysis,* p. 136.

57. Robert L. Heilbroner, "The Impact of Technology: The Historic Debate," in *Automation and Technological Change,* ed. John T. Dunlop (Englewood Cliffs, N.J.: Prentice Hall, 1962), p. 22.

58. Ibid., p. 25.

59. Carlo Cippola, *The Economic History of World Populations* (Baltimore: Penguin Publications, 1962), p. 109.

60. Ibid., p. 117.

Resources Are Not; They Become:
An Institutional Theory

Thomas R. De Gregori

In common usage, as well as in traditional mainstream economics, material inputs for production have been thought of as physical resources. Classical economists defined the factors of production in material terms. Land was the "original and indestructible powers of the soil." Resources were "natural" and given. If land and mineral resources are material, then at least in a global sense they are fixed and finite. From an institutionalist perspective, however, following in the tradition of Clarence Ayres and Erich Zimmermann, "resources are not; they become." In the process of becoming, then, they are neither fixed nor finite, and, as we shall demonstrate, the process of becoming is one that is as much ideational as it is material.[1]

The material or physical aspect of resources exists before they become resources. Arguing from "the principle of indestructibility of matter," a view that would have to be modified in light of current physics, Ayres argues that "there is no such thing as a 'new material'." There are, however, new resources. "The history of every material is the same. It is one of novel combinations of existing devices and materials in such a fashion as to constitute a new device or a new material or both."[2] This creative process of fashioning the material and non-material stuff of our environment in a form usable and serviceable to human beings is determined by science and technology. It is the sum total of human

291

knowledge and capability that is the prime resource and the one that defines all others.

Technology and Resource Creation: The Concept

To say that the term "resources" essentially has no meaning apart from a relationship to human beings does *not* mean that all things have a right to exist only to the extent that they serve human beings. We can speak about the living resources of planet Earth. We can argue that we *ought* to preserve and protect them. Calling them resources and saying that we should act in certain ways, then, means that there can be an operational meaning to the effect that it is in our best interest to preserve as large a genetic heritage as possible. This is an intelligent, sensible argument that many conservationists and environmentalists put forward. We can also argue that other living things have *rights* apart from their service to us.[3] For the sake of consistency in the use of language, we should not use the term "resources" when we are making specific reference to the rights of other creatures.

It is ironic that most mainstream economists have taken a position on resources that is not too different from that of the institutionalists. This was noted by Ayres four decades ago and resulted in some "confusion" for a discipline in which scarcity is the cornerstone.[4] Economists generally maintain that the issue of finite resources is not an interesting question. Reference is made to price changes, substitution, greater efficiency, and discovery. Occasionally, even science and technology are mentioned. Yet, without technology, one cannot indefinitely substitute one resource for another. Substitution alone merely delays reaching finite limits.

Mineral resources is not the only area in which the institutionalist perspective has become orthodoxy. The ideas of science-based agriculture, or of certain technologies as "land augmenting" or that investment creates arable land, make sense in a functional theory of resources, but not in one that assumes land as "natural" or as the non-human, non-manmade factor of production.[5] Direct investment creates arable land in many ways: by increasing crop intensities (more than one crop per season) through irrigation, or by developing crops with shorter growing seasons, or by creating higher yields in a particular crop because of improved seed. The basis for these resource-creating investments is the ongoing research in agriculture, which most agricultural economists find to be an investment that has paid extraordinary returns in recent years.

The focus on scientific research as a means of resource creation goes to the very heart of institutional economics. Wesley C. Mitchell stated precisely what should be a fundamental principle of all economics. "Incomparably greatest among human resources is knowledge. It is greatest because it is the mother of other resources."[6] Mitchell's claim is true both as a historical proposition and as an operating principle for policy.

Resources are not things or stuff or materials; they are a set of capabilities. These capabilities use the stuff of the material and nonmaterial universe in a life-sustaining manner. These capabilities define a functional relationship that we call resources. This relationship is what Zimmermann referred to as the "fundamental concept of resources."[7] The relationship implies the prior physical existence of both humans and the material (or non-material) substance. Absent from the relationship, the term "resources" is meaningless. Humans are the active agent, having ideas that they use to transform the environment for human purposes. Resource, then, is a property of things—a property that is a result of human capability.

Logically, one resource—food—had to pre-exist the others. Before hominids, there were proto-hominids, and obviously their survival presumes the use of food resources. Beyond this very basic precondition, ideas precede, not only all other resources (including all other food resources), but also the emergence of homo sapiens. Proto-hominids had ideas and began to use certain objects in their environment, such as stones. This idea and subsequent action established the functional relationship that allows us to call the stones resources. Others saw possibilities of fashioning these stones so that they were more usable. The greater the usability, the greater the resource character of the stones. Tools are, then, used to create still newer and better ones, thus continuing the process of resource enhancement. The stones had not changed, but ideas, skills, and behavior had, and these literally created the resource.

These new tools allowed for more effective exploitation of the environment. New edible materials became accessible, for example, tubers in rock-hard earth or large animals, and for humans these became food resources. The ability to harvest more food from an area increased the resource character of that land. This process continued through the domestication of plants and animals and on up to the present. It was agriculture that created arable land and not the reverse.

This simple illustration shows the dynamic interactions and reinforcing feedback mechanisms involved in the human generation of ideas and their embodiment in the process of technology and in the creation of resources. Other animals use tools, but both the tools and the resources they create are functionally limited. Humans engage in a dynamic open-ended process called technology. In a recent book of mine, I make an analogy to signals and language. Other animals have closed systems of communication using signs or signals; only humans have the dynamic, open-ended process of language.[8]

Tool-using created resources. It also created homo sapiens; for the use of tools favored certain members of the proto-hominids who had large areas of the brain controlling the hand that made the tools. This gave a direction to evolutionary processes and established another dynamic feedback relationship because with improved hands and brains one can make better tools.[9]

Tools may have been instrumental in our emergence as homo sapiens; they also made further evolutionary change unnecessary. Until the emergence of technology, living creatures exploited a limited number of resources in an environment. Environmental change wiped out resources and those life forms that could not evolve and adapt. Evolution is the means of adapting to change, and it is the means that allows movement from one environment to another. A sucessful species is one with the capability of exploiting its environment for continued survival. A failed species may be nothing more than a victim of an environmental change that was too rapid or dramatic to allow for evolutionary change.

With ideas and with the technology in which those ideas are embodied, resource creation can be continuous, and adaptation does not depend upon chance biological change. From a rather limited range of habitat, humans have spread around the globe, inhabiting every conceivable climate and environment. Unique among mammals, we have done this without speciation. The ways in which we use a technology to make an area habitable for humans, to make clothing, shelter, food, and materials, can only be described as resource creation. The very concept of habitability for an area that was previously uninhabited can only have meaning through resource creation.

Historic Concerns about Resources

Concern for the availability of resources is as old as the human endeavor itself. In the quote cited above about knowledge being the mother of other resources, Mitchell adds: "The bulk of man's resources are the result of human ingenuity aided by slowly, patiently, and painfully acquired knowledge and experience."[10] Various stones and pebbles became resources when humans learned to use them to make tools. These same materials ceased to be resources when humans acquired new skills in taking previously worthless earths and smelting them into metals. The new tools allowed humans to exploit more fully their environment and thereby to create still more resources. And so it has been ever since—humans create resources and use them to create still other resources. For all human beings are (virtually by definition) tool users. The very use of tools presupposes both resources to make them and resources to be exploited by them. The use of tools is central to the process of maintaining and sustaining human life. Peoples and cultures achieve levels of population density and styles of life based upon their use of tools, technology, and resources. Rarely, if ever, can a people abandon a technology and its resources and return to an older pattern without loss of life (that is, a lowered population density) and living standard. The ongoing concern for a secure supply of resources is vital to the very life and lifeways of a people. "All forms of life other than human beings deal only with renewable resources," and only humans have found a way to use so-called non-renewable resources.[11] Contrary to the doomsday critics, this is a strength and not a weakness of the human endeavor.

For a significant period in United States history, lack of access to resources was not a primary concern. An abundant natural endowment (as defined by the existing technology) and a seemingly endless frontier contributed to this attitude. By the beginning of the present century, this perspective began to change with the putative closing of the frontier in 1890. In the late 1920s, fear was expressed in official circles that we might be exhausting domestic sources of critical resources.

After World War II, domestic resource exhaustion was not the only resource concern of the United States. Continued uninterrupted access to foreign sources no longer seemed certain. A series of official commissions and studies testifies to the intensity of these resource concerns. The most famous and important of these studies is the Paley Commission Report (officially entitled *Resources for Freedom*), a comprehensive five-volume report issued in 1952.[12]

The Paley Commission began with the question, "Has the United States of America the material means to sustain its civilization?"[13] It found that:

> In area after area the same pattern seems discernible: soaring demands, shrinking resources, the consequent pressure toward rising real costs, the

risk of wartime shortages, the ultimate threat of an arrest or decline in the standard of living we cherish and hope to help others to attain. If such a threat is to be averted, it will not be by inaction. After successive years of thinking about unemployment, reemployment, full employment, about factory production, inflation and deflation, and hundreds of other matters in the structure of economic life, the United States must now give new and deep considerations to the fundamental upon which all employment, all daily activity, eventually rests: the contents of the earth and its physical environment.[14]

The issues of resource dependency gained a far wider constituency in the 1970s, reaching far beyond official circles. Phraseology featuring the "limits to growth" or an "era of limits" were in popular currency, as sophisticated computer models cranked out conclusions arguing that world-wide resource exhaustion was but decades away. The petroleum crisis also brought to the United States public a vivid sample of the meaning of resource dependency. In the 1960s, there also emerged doomsday and catastrophist theories, which I have attacked in other articles for the failure (fortunately) of their dire prophecies.

By the early 1980s, despite the utter failure of the doomsday prophesies, the proponents of alternate technology came up with newer, presumably more profound, reasons to be opposed to modern technology. Jeremy Rifkin, in his book, *Entropy,* boldly proclaimed "a new world view" in his subtitle.[15] The inexorable law of entropy in thermodynamics requires that matter and energy flow from high to low, from structure to randomness and from heterogeneity to homogeneity. Thus we move from order and complexity to chaos. Since this is a law of the cosmos and of the planet, it is not exactly clear in Rifkin how we could have achieved our current state of complexity and organization from which descent is inevitable. Similarly, Kirkpatrick Sale argued in *Human Scale* that smallness is an inherent biological virtue.[16] Unfortunately for Sale, he has no solid biological evidence to offer for his thesis. One source that he uses, J. B. S. Haldane's "On Being the Right Size," does speak of the advantages of smallness, but then turns to the advantages of bigness. Evidently, the author of this large book on smallness did not finish the Haldane essay before quoting it.[17]

Someone once joked that Karl Marx had carried classical economics to its logical absurdity. Much the same can be said of Sale and Rifkin. For the very logical structures that they conjured gave rise to implications the exact opposite of what they advocated. If resources are fixed and finite, then entropy does condemn us to inevitable and ineluctable decline. There is one thing that entropy and scientific and technological inquiry teach us; namely that no process such as recycling or conservation can be one hundred percent effective. Renewability is, at best, only partially successful. At each turn of the cycle, some bit of order becomes disorder, soil is lost, or a resource is dissipated. Thus, not only are we faced with decline, but also, in the case of Rifkin, we are at a loss to explain how we ever achieved an elevated status from which decline is possible. This decline occurs with constant population; any population growth accelerates the process. Negative population growth delays, but does not prevent, decline.

There is a more respectable and persuasive argument for renewability. In these, the constraints are relaxed, and we have a slightly open system for natural processes to create resources, but at a slow pace. Aquifers are recharged by rain; running water provides sources of energy; soil is created; and new species evolve to replace those that die out. Thus, it is not fixed limits but carrying capacity of a constrained, but open, system that determines sustainability. If we view carrying capacity as purely a "natural" process, then unfortunately, humans transcended these limits at least 10,000 years ago with the development of agriculture. We do not merely harvest the environment, we transform it. In so doing, we have altered the carrying capacity of the environment.

Viewed in these terms, carrying capacity refers not to the environment as it is, but to the environment as it can be. The issue, then, is what technologies are best able to transform the environment for human purposes on a sustainable basis.

This brings us back to the argument of fixed, finite resources. A technology predicated upon fixed, finite resources is one that dooms us to decline. It does this to the extent that it fulfills the assumptions of many of the theorists who advocate it and to the extent that it supplants the technologies that have been deemed to be bad. (This generalization does not apply to the technologies created by the many dedicated workers who are not operating out of cosmic concerns of grandiose philosophical theories but merely trying to solve practical problems.) However, just as the concept of carrying capacity has a technological component, so does that of resources. Resources are not fixed and finite because they are not natural. They are a product of human ingenuity resulting from the creation of technology and science.

Obviously, at any given time, with a given technology, there is a sense in which resources are fixed and finite. Given these parameters, we can say that some countries are better endowed with resources, be they mineral, soil, or energy, than others. We said "in a sense," for even under the constraint of a given technology, changes in prices can dramatically alter resource availability. In defining the resource endowment of a country, furthermore, it is difficult to distinguish between the rich resources, such as ore deposits, that may even have been found by expatriates, and the arable land resources that were created by investments in applied technology.

The idea of "carrying capacity" has in usage a relatively precise meaning. In a given ecosystem, up to a set number of animals can be pastured or so much water can be drawn from an aquifer with the "natural" regenerative forces allowing for sustainable use. Beyond these limits, an inevitable accelerating decline begins. As such, the concept is useful, cautionary, and scientific. Unfortunately, the term has acquired a more common parlance. We, meaning earth's human inhabitants, must live within our energy budget or within the carrying capacity of the planet. Simply stated, we must live within limits. If these statements are to be accepted as anything other than truisms, then there is the unstated assumption that the resource boundaries established by various policy advocates are fixed by nature. Like other statements of fixed, finite resources, it denies the possibility for technological innovations that alter the boundary conditions.

Technology and Resource Creation:
Some Empirical Evidence in Minerals and Food Supply

By the mid-1970s, a series of studies and events appeared to lend scientific support and empirical evidence to the view that resources were being exhausted and that population was outrunning both food supply and resources. Studies such as the Club of Rome-sponsored *The Limits to Growth* used systems analysis and computer models to demonstrate that the mineral resources upon which civilization is based were being rapidly depleted and that some would be exhausted in a matter of decades unless corrective actions were taken.[18] The rapid rise in food prices in the early 1970s, accompanied by decreasing carryover food stocks and then followed by the oil embargoes and rapid escalation in price, all seemed to confirm the most dire forecasts.

In 1974 and 1975, there was a world conference on population and another on food production. Their conclusions were consistent with the temper of the times. World population had reached 4 billion with ever-increasing numbers being added, so that the dire prophecies of Malthus may have been delayed, but seemed now to be a reality. Famines, as severe as the one that struck the Sahel in Africa, would become frequent and involve more people until it became a permanent global condition. Added to all of this was a rising chorus of concerns about various forms of environmental contamination and destruction. Many argued that the enterprise of being human was about to enter resource bankruptcy unless it was saved by conversion to small-is-beautiful new age ideologies and pursuits. The most frequently cited villain was technology.

The irony of these dire forecasts of resource exhaustion was that they came at the end of a period in which the known reserves of most minerals had increased substantially. It is true that population growth rates were increasing during this period. But it was also true that birth rates were falling at record rates of decline and that the cause of global population increase was a dramatic and unprecedented decline in death rates. Despite record rates of population growth, food supply was growing even more rapidly, thereby raising world per capita food consumption. Per capita income was also growing throughout the globe. *The Limits to Growth* study was based on 1970 data and presumably should have reflected the sizeable increases in known mineral reserves that had accompanied the rapid increase in world industrialization and resource use. From the late 1940s to the late 1960s, reserves of iron ore increased 122.1 percent, manganese 27 percent, chromite 675 percent, copper 179 percent, and lead 115 percent.[19]

In the 1960s and 1970s, it was consistently found that the real price of most minerals had been falling throughout this century when measured in either the price of labor or in percent of total labor and total capital involved in extractive industries.[20] In 1986, the cost of all metal raw material for all uses came to $80 per person.[21] Similarly, the long-term trends of real food costs and food as a proportion of individual budgets showed a sustained downward movement, even despite the short-term upward movement of the early 1970s. In short, by all measures of scarcity, traditional or non-traditional, virtually all items in the class of economic inputs called land and natural resources were becoming less scarce and not more scarce, as had been predicted by the classical economists and echoed by contemporary catastrophists.

Not all of those who were forecasting a "new era of limits" were blind to the data. It was recognized that technology had rather consistently found new resources as we were seemingly running out of old ones. It was also recognized by some that food production had been growing faster than population and that generally standards of living had been increasing. But as the refrain went, we were living off capital and not income, since we were rapidly drawing down precious stocks of resources that had been slowly accumulated by natural processes. The very accelerated growth in well-being that was conceded was an acceleration in resource depletion that would bring us to limits within which we must learn to live. If such limits are exceeded, an inevitable decline of civilization will follow.

Others argued that growth since World War II was historically atypical (which it certainly was insofar as rapidity of change) and that this growth was the result of a fortuitous confluence of favorable events. In agriculture and food supply, for example, there were the "green revolutions" in wheat and rice, there was a run of favorable weather, the price of petroleum for fertilizer and energy was cheap and often falling, and there were still virgin fertile lands to bring under cultivation. These were all one-time conditions, the benefits of which were now realized and were unlikely to be replicated. Similiar fortuitous one-time only events were postulated to explain our overall economic fortune. Petroleum had provided an era of cheap energy that explained so much of our well-being, and its presumed imminent depletion presaged the closing of an era. The party, we were told, was over. Thus, while some used bad news to forecast economic catastrophe, others used good news to portend the same outcome. In the literature of the mid-1970s, however doomsday was forecast; there was an immediacy and an overwhelming sense of urgency for virtually instantaneous change in mental outlook, patterns of behavior, and economic policy.

The question remains whether or not we did make a historic transition in the 1970s because these one-time fortuitous circumstances were exhausted. As the accompanying table shows, from 1975 to 1985, most known mineral reserves increased, some rather substantially. Even for some that have experienced sizeable decline, the explanatory reasons are definitely not resource exhaustion. Tin, which shows the largest decline, has just experienced a virtual collapse of its market. Mines are being closed in Malaysia and Thailand, and Bolivia may exit the market entirely because capacity and production far exceed demand. Given that Brazil is emerging rapidly as a major, if not dominant, producer, it is not at all clear whether the data reflect the full extent of Brazil's known resources.

After World War II, many were fearful of exhausting high grade iron ore deposits. Since iron is the fourth largest constituent in the earth's crust or 5 percent of the crust by weight, there was never fear of exhausting it, only that lower grade ores would make the price prohibitive. Because of pelletization and other technological changes and the finding of new reserves, iron ore reserves substantially increased between World War II and the early 1970s. The apparent decline in re-

Table 1.

Mineral Name	RESERVES			(%△ based on year 1975)
	1975	1976	1985	
Bauxite	17 B/T	24 B/T	23.2 B/T	+ 36%
Chromium	1.9 B/T	2.9 B/T	7.5 B/T	+294%
Cobalt	2.7 M/T	2.9 M/T	9.2 M/T	+240%
Columbium	22 M/P	22 B/P	9.1 B/P	−58%
Copper	450 M/T	506 M/T	525 M/T	+17%
Ilemenite	580 M/T	771 M/T	734 M/T	+26%
Iron Core	259 B/T	255 B/T	206 B/T	−20%
Lead	160 M/T	160 M/T	143 M/T	−10%
Manganese	6 B/T	6 B/T	12 B/T	+100%
Molybdenum	13 B/P	19.1 B/P	25.9 B/P	+99%
Nickel	60 M/T	61 M/T	111 M/T	+85%
Phosphate Rock	18 B/T	20 B/T	34 B/T	+88%
Platinum-Group Metals	561 M/O	560 M/O	1.2 B/O	+114%
Rare-Earth Metals	7.7 M/T	7.7 M/T	48 M/T	+523%
Rutile	13.7 M/T	37 M/T	133.4 M/T	+881%
Tantalum	110 M/P	130 M/P	76 M/P	−30%
Tin	10.2 M/T	10.2 M/T	3 M/T	−70%
Tungsten	3.9 B/P	4 B/P	3.5 M/T	−10%
Vanadium	21.4 B/P	21.4 B/P	36.5 B/P	+70%
Zinc	150 M/T	175 M/T	300 M/T	+100%

SOURCES: For 1975 and 1976— *Commodity Data Summaries,* Bureau of Mines, United States Department of the Interior, 1976 & 1977; for 1986—*Mineral Commodity Summaries,* Bureau of Mines, United States Department of the Interior.

B/T = Billions of Tons   M/T = Millions of Tons
B/P = Billions of Pounds   M/P = Millions of Pounds
B/O = Billions of Ounces   M/O = Millions of Ounces

serves comes at a time when, at every stage of the process, from ore production to iron and steel, there is considerable excess capacity. More significantly, the relative importance of iron and steel is decreasing with the emergence of ceramics, composites, other metals, and a variety of specialty materials.

Using price as a measure of scarcity, we find that all categories of commodities, minerals, and various types of agricultural outputs have experienced, with few exceptions, decade-by-decade declines in real prices, so that the mid-1980s real prices for all categories are lower than they were in 1950.[22] The last decade fluctuations were such that the 1984 index of commodity prices in U.S. dollars was lower than in any year since 1976. In real terms, the measured decline was even greater, even allowing for the strong dollar as a measuring stick.[23] From 1980 to 1985, prices of metals decreased 30 percent, while the overall index of commodities fell 24 percent. "Moreover, real commodity prices so far in the 1980s have averaged about 16 percent below the average for the 1970s and in 1985 were about 20 percent below the average for 1960–1980."[24] Even if we question the faith that some mainstream economists have in price as the sole and absolute measure of scarcity, it is difficult to imagine the mechanism that would allow for these declines in prices in the world of increasing scarcity described by the limits-to-growth theorists. After all, an element of their prophecies that should not be forgotten is the higher real price we would have to pay for everything.

If there is one characteristic that tends to define the world's commodity markets, it is overcapacity and oversupply. World food production in 1985 set a new record, as it has for approximately thirty of the past thirty-five years. The record was both for total and for per capita production. Production in 1986 may be off somewhat, but still the problem in most parts of the world (except for Africa) is low prices and huge, unsold and presumably unsaleable mounds of surpluses of foodstuffs. Even in Africa, some countries such as Zimbabwe are accumulating surpluses of hard-to-sell, coarse grains. Asia, a region we have traditionally identified with poverty, hunger, and famine, is becoming a surplus food producer, even allowing for rising levels of domestic consumption because of rapidly rising incomes.[25] Asia is also the region we generally consider to be at the limits of environmental carrying capacity. Asia, more than almost any other area in the third world, has "created land" by increasing yields in existing areas far more that it has created land by bringing new lands under cultivation. If there is hunger in the world—and so there is, in abundance, even in wealthy countries—it is because of maldistribution of food, not insufficient global production. Hunger has always been with us, but today it is more rare, even though it receives much well-deserved media coverage. Hunger continues to exist today, not for the reasons predicted a decade ago—namely, that we were on an unsustainable consumption binge—but because we have not yet found a way to provide to everyone the capacity to earn sufficient income to obtain what is generally available.[26]

The metals markets are still suffering from overcapacity, even though there have been systematic closings of mines and production facilities in many metals. As this is being written, the real price index for metals (in a basket of currencies) is less than 80 percent of what it was in 1980.[27] Losses for some traders on the London Metal Exchange have been heavy. "Copper consumption seems set to decline by 2 percent during this year, while mine production is rising."[28] Ironically, the main hope from the perspective of the producers is that the low prices, having led to reduced exploration, will in time give rise to shortages.[29] Cobalt, which had risen to $50 per pound on the spot market in 1978 (because of political disruptions in Zaire), had fallen to $3.70 in August 1986 before rebounding to $6 per pound with some help from an attempt at cartelization by Zaire and Zambia.[30] Even the $6 price may be difficult to sustain because world production capacity is about 50 percent greater than demand.

It is close to a decade and a half since *The Limits to Growth* was published and well over two decades since catastrophic predictions of reaching limits became popular beliefs, yet no empirical evidence has yet emerged to support the thesis. In fact, the preponderance of evidence is pointing in the other direction. Since the surface area of the globe and the concentration of minerals in its crust are fixed (except for possible minuscule geological changes), the primary explanation for the increase in resources and output is technology. Studies such as *The Limits to Growth* were sufficiently specific in their forecasts that the data already available falsify a significant portion of them. Nobody could have accepted any portion of the doomsday literature of the 1960s and 1970s and believed that in the mid-1980s the world would be in surplus in most commodity production. Yet, though less shrill in tone, the belief in declining resource availability and in the limits to the earth's carrying capacity still predominate in the media. No matter how overwhelmingly the march of time emphatically refutes doomsday forecasts, there remains that lingering belief that good fortune has allowed us to delay the seemingly inevitable. But our luck will not last forever, and the inevitable will inevitably arrive.

A concept of fixed, finite resources provides the mindset that allows people to refuse to accept evidence of decreasing resource scarcity. The institutional theory of resource creation provides the necessary framework for correctly understanding the evidence. It is the only theoretical perspective that allowed us to forecast the trends of the post-World War II period. If some mainstream economists in recent years have joined the bandwagon, so much the better. However, it should be clear that, though mainstream economics can explain short-term trends by techniques such as substitution and increasing efficiency, their basic theory of finite resources does not allow for indefinite resource expansion. If some economists are now using the term "resource creation," then we should cheer and remind them of its origin. Similarly, the concept of "land augmentation" is another way of speaking of science and technology creating resources. Touting the institutionalist origins of such significant concepts is not for some purpose of creating intellectual property rights. Its purpose is to show the strength and power of a body of ideas. For whether or not humans have the food and other raw materials to continue the process of civilization is no small matter. The world has experienced a global revolution in food production, population growth, death rate decline, life expectancy increase, and per capita income increases of unprecedented proportions—all of which was understandable and predicted in institutional theory. If unmet need exists despite overproduction and overcapacity, then the problem is one of creating purchasing power, as institutionalists have long argued.[31] A body of theory with this strength should reasonably be called upon to formulate the policies that will allow the continuation of resource creation and civilizational advance.

Technology and Resource Creation: Arable Land and Mineral Resource Creation

Land as a human resource is created by technology (and science) in the same manner as minerals become resources. The first tools that allowed people to hunt and to harvest the land more intensely increased the resource character of that land. Stone tools that permitted early man to dig out roots from the rock-hard savanna soils made those roots into a human resource, and, with the domestication of plants, some of the wet, insect-invested river bottoms acquired the potential to be agricultural land. Agriculture created arable land.

The history of human migration and settlement is a history of people creating arable land by devising new means and new technologies to produce food. Theodore Schultz has long argued that some of the world's best agricultural land once had poor soil. "The original soils of western Europe, except for the Po Valley and some parts of England and France, were in general very poor in quality. As farmland, these soils are now highly productive." To Schultz, the inherent qualities of soils do not explain why agriculture is outstanding in some parts of the world and poor in others. He maintains that "a substantial part of the productivity of farmland is man-made by investments in land improvements."[32] N.W. Pirie voices essentially the same idea, that "good farmland is usually created by skilled farming."[33]

There are many ways of creating new land. Bringing uncultivated land into production is only one. Irrigation can not only bring cultivation to arid lands, it can also frequently add a second or third crop season to the agriculture of a region. Breeding crops with shorter growing seasons, allowing for an extra crop, is yet another way. Research has been, and continues to be, carried out to find or breed crops that are more tolerant of salt or can withstand the stress of acidity from aluminum-toxic soils. Biotechnology and other new breeding techniques give promise that not only will current trends be sustained, but that in the future they may even accelerate.[34]

A hundred-year decline in the real price of food is likely to continue. Clifford Lewis notes that "despite the weakness of data about global food trends, it is clear that global food production has grown at a generally increasing rate since the early decades of the 19th century and has consistently outstripped increases in global population." Lewis's data shows that the real price of wheat (in 1967 dollars) fell from $3.09 in 1890 to $2.10 in 1960 to $1.10 in 1982. There have been "temporary disruptions" in this downward trend, but they have been "when peace has not prevailed."[35]

The frontiers of technological research are as promising for the creation of new material resources as they are for the creation of land. Materials science is emerging as a prime area of research, as new technologies in every area of endeavor have performance demands that require material with specific qualities. Minerals previously little used are becoming vital to technological processes. Our ability to process these minerals is advancing as rapidly as the new materials that we are creating. Silicon chips, fiber optics, and ceramics have turned raw materials long in vast abundance into major resources. One of the problems with the metals market is in fact that these new "resources" are substituting for traditional ones, such as copper, decreasing the demand for them. In the case of fiber optics, the new material performs its task better, more efficiently, more reliably, and at a far lower material resource cost.

Even without new and improved technologies for resource utilization, there are additions to resource reserves because of new finds. The process of resource discovery is also subject to scientific and technological advances. Advances in geology, such as plate tectonics, and in geography give us new understanding of how various ores are formed, sorted, and where they are likely to be found. Remote sensing from satellites has added new dimensions to mapping and discovering minerals, though at times it is easier to be more enthusiastic about the potentials of remote sensing than is yet warranted by the data. Airborne and ground surveys, using a variety of technologies, aid in the search for new material sources.

Contrary to the pessimists, not only is technological change continuing, but the rate of change itself is accelerating.[36] Unchanging technology is resource-using. Changing technology is resource-creating. The history of technology and human societies today testify to these basic conditions. Thus, the growth in resources and the decline in their real price are not fortuitous, or accidental, or temporary, or paradoxical, but fundamental to the process of technological change. Because it is fundamental, it is reasonable to believe that the continued advances in science and technology, which everyone expects to occur, will create the resources necessary to sustain it. Furthermore, if the process is not entirely automatic, we can use our intelligence to structure the process so that we realize the full resource-creating potential of technological change.

The Life Process and the Conditions of Life

In the discourse on institutional economics, particularly in the writings of Veblen and Ayres, reference was made to the life process. Institutional economics was evolutionary economics drawing inspiration from the late nineteenth century post-Darwin period, rather than from the static conceptions of the eighteenth century. It is interesting that many of the current theories on life's origins make these references more appropriate than could be realized at the time. The first life forms "fed" on already existing organic matter, using it in chemical fermentation for life-sustaining energy. Clearly, there was a limited resource, as life was "consuming" organic matter faster than it was being created. Later, procaryotes would evolve photosynthesis, a new energy source that overcame the original resource constraint. Similar to human problem-solving endeavors, the solving of one problem creates new ones. The oxygen that was earlier being given off was creating an ozone layer that was shielding out the ultraviolet light that was creating organic food. To anaerobic procaryotes, moreover, oxygen was a deadly pollutant. Fortunately for us, eucaryotes evolved that were more efficient in energy use and were aerobic.[37]

To the extent that this scenario is correct, then the conditions (that is, the resources) for life as we know it did not exist; they were created by the evolution of life itself. The solution of some problems created others, but still we can understand problem-solving in an expanded energy-opportunity context. At any one point, "resources" are fixed and finite, and life seems doomed either to exhaust resources or to succumb to its own waste. The process that we are describing is one of emergent evolution. Had there been some kind of intelligence operating in or observing the early procaryotes, it would have proclaimed the limits to growth and the end of life. All logic and reasoning lead to one inevitable conclusion—death. Absolutely nothing in the situation could yield to any inquiry the hope for continuity. It is only after the transformation has occurred that one can begin to understand the process.

The same can be said for hunting and gathering humans. A widely respected thesis is that hunters and gatherers had reached the limits of their potential, creating a food crisis.[38] Where a growing population of hunters and gatherers are pushing the limits of the environment, there is again nothing that an intelligent observer could find in the situation that offered any escape from self-destruction. It is only in retrospect that we can understand the resource creating power of technology.

Having observed these and other processes, we can derive a theory of technological change and of the types of resource creation and other forms of novelty that emerge. This is, of course, part of what evolutionary economics is all about. It is a theory that, at least in outline form, helps us to understand the process and therefore to have an understanding of emerging possibilities. It clearly should make us aware that resources are not fixed and finite, and they definitely are not natural. As long as we do not run out of ideas, then we are not likely to run out of resources.

The assumption of fixed, finite resources has caused many to make catastrophic predictions of resource exhaustion. Fortunately, where these prophesies have been sufficently specific to be testable, the passage of time and events has falsified them. It has been my argument in several papers that the technologies the prophets offered as resource-conserving in fact would create the problem they claimed to be solving. Living within limits is inherently self-defeating, as the above illustrations demonstrate. Another principle, entropy, has been offered into the argument and guarantees decline.

The life process and the technological process form an enclave of negative entropy. Energy is taken from a source (that is, the sun) that would be experiencing increasing entropy in any case, and is used to build order and complexity (negative entropy). It is interesting that among the earliest recorded and recovered legends is that of ancient Sumerians and Babylonians about the separation of land from water, order from chaos. This legend celebrates the human achievement of negative entropy and the creation of arable land resources. Throughout the ancient Middle East and on into Greek and Roman culture was the basic proposition that was later expressed as *nihil ex nihilo*—out of nothing comes nothing. Creation out of nothing was impossible. Our idea of resource creation is consistent with that usage. Creation of resources is the creation of order out of chaos, the imposition of our ideas and will upon pre-existing substances.

The dynamic resource-creating power of technology has been central to evolutionary economic thought. It is ironic that mainstream economics has borrowed some modest semblence of this theory, or at least its conclusion, to counter the limits on growth theorists or the catastrophists. We might be wise to follow Ayres's lead and use this opening to raise more fundamental questions. If resources are not fixed but created, then the nature of the scarcity problem changes dramatically. For the technological means involved in the use of resources determines their creation and therefore the extent of their scarcity. The nature of the scarcity is not outside the process (that is, natural), but a condition of it.

Understanding the creative powers of technologies can be infectious to other areas of economic thought. Of the many definitions of capital, technology has to be a key component if we are to comprehend the dynamics of economic change. The other factor, labor, is increasingly addressed, not as a raw unit of measure of other things, but as human capital. Knowledge and skills, the very essence of technology and resource creation, are receiving attention for their critical role in the development process. Even entrepreneurship is about someone allegedly having a better idea.

Technology and Resource Creation: A Liberating Idea

Technology as ideas and as the creator of resources is not only correct, it is also liberating. It provides a conceptual basis for understanding the fact that the resource base of civilization has expanded, not contracted, with use. It gives us the kind of operational understanding necessary to frame the policies to sustain this resource-creating process. It provides a reasonable basis for optimism that the human endeavor can continue and can expand. It is, finally, the key component of a structure that challenges traditional ways of thought about the economy and opens new possibilities for creative inquiry and dialogue.

A little over two centuries ago, Adam Smith had a series of liberating ideas. The very title of his magnum opus, *An Inquiry into the Nature of Causes of the Wealth of Nations,* argues for the liberating idea that all nations can prosper and that nations need not impoverish their neighbor in order to succeed. He defined wealth as the annual produce of a nation, not merely of its sovereign. And he defined a relationship through markets by which those who participated in economic activity were supposed to be beneficiaries of it. Smith was inquiring into the causes of wealth in his economy, yet in reality he was in the first ferment of an industrial transformation that was to give concrete meaning to his liberal idea.

The idea of scarcity, which some conceive to be the fundamental organizing principal of economics, is a static concept and is counter to the liberating potential of Smith's ideas. To the extent that some see scarcity as based upon the principles of nature, then we are back to the concept of fixed, finite resources. The theory of technology as resource creating is dynamic. It removes scarcity as an organizing principle of economic inquiry. While it may be true that we do not have infinite resources from which to choose and to allocate, neither are we dealing with fixed resources. They are finite but unbounded. The very economic/technological processes that use "scarce" resources are also creating them; as we have argued, this historic process of allocating, and using, has created far more than it has used. If we define efficiency according to scarcity then we are dealing with a closed system. If we define efficiency according to the technology of resource creation, then we are describing and creating the conditions for an open-ended process.

The resource-creating power of technology is a never-ending problem solving process. It is a process by which people make choices and have even greater opportunities to make choices. By implication, the idea that problem solving continues indefinitely means that there will always be problems around to be solved. The critics of modern technology have confused using resources with using them up and see the existence of resource problems as an argument against modern technology. The simple fact is that without technology, there are no resources and therefore no resource problems. But the resource problems of human existence will only be terminated with the ending of the human endeavor itself. So-called alternate technologies that are resource conserving but not resource creating engender more problems than they solve.[39]

The biggest resource problems that technology creates are the hypothetical ones. The empirical argument that begins "if present trends continue" can inevitably demonstrate a future crisis if technology is held constant.[40] To counter that technology has historically made resources more available does not necessarily address the specifics of future resource needs and opportunities. Very simply, we can learn much from the historic process of technology that allows us to predict many aspects of the future course of events, as well as to plan and take action to make those events more favorable to the human enterprise.

Since we have described the process as one of emergent evolution, then, there are emergent possibilities that we cannot predict. Further, if the thesis is held true that we create the conditions of our existence, it is equally true that we can destroy the conditions of our existence. This has always been the case; it is only in modern times that it has been dramatically obvious. Of course we can do it in many ways. The one most frequently noted is to destroy ourselves with nuclear weapons. Out of fear of the unknown future, we can also do it by failing to carry forward resource-creating technology that is the basis for the sustainability of human civilization. It is our destiny to choose our future; not to choose is itself a choice as the existentialists have told us. What Albert Camus said about the individual is true for humankind: the most important choice we face is whether or not to commit suicide. Camus meant this as an affirmation, "as a lucid invitation to live and to create, in the very midst of the desert."[41] Similarly, we can understand technology transfer and economic development as a collective affirmation of the worth of life and the life process.

Technology, resource creation and emergent evolution engender not a world of unknown future but of emerging possibilities. Our destiny is not in being but in becoming. We as humans have turned adversaries into allies. What greater threat was there to primate life and habitat than fire? Yet fire was controlled and turned into a tool for converting ores into metals (that is, making clay into pottery and other dirts into ores) and for making the cold climates fit for human life. Ergot, a plant disease that threatens human life, is now used as a cure for migraines. Poisons from plants have been turned into life-saving or supporting drugs. The list is endless, and so is the future potential of humankind. Those who would turn us aside out of some fictitious fear of resource exhaustion would protect us from the dangers of the unknown but would also deny us its possibilities. The liberating idea of technology and resource creation is the human potential that is there, if we are aware of it and if we frame our policies accordingly. We will exhaust resources if we exhaust creative imagination. Technology as ideas and resource creation means that Descartes was more correct than he could possibly imagine when he said *cogito ergo sum,* that is, I think therefore I am. We think therefore we are and, more importantly, can be.

Notes

1. Quote from Erich Zimmermann, *World Resources and Industries* (New York: Harper & Bros., 1951), p. 15.
2. C. E. Ayres, *The Theory of Economic Progress* (Chapel Hill, N.C.: The University of North Carolina Press, 1943), p. 113.
3. One can find instances throughout human history of conservation and the protection of other species. Far more prevalent has been the wanton destruction of the environment and other life forms. As I argue in my book, *A Theory of Technology,* modern science and technology have created the understanding and conditions that have fostered the current wildlife and conservationist movements. Thomas R. De Gregori, *A Theory of Technology: Continuity and Change in Human Development* (Ames, Iowa: Iowa State University Press, 1985).
4. Ayres, *The Theory of Economic Progress,* p. 113.
5. Theodore Schultz, *Transforming Traditional Agriculture* (New Haven, Conn.: Yale University Press, 1964), is seen by many as the seminal work on science-based agriculture that generated a vast amount of empirical, theoretical, and applied work in world agriculture.
6. Wesley C. Mitchell, "Conservation, Liberty, and Economics," in *The Foundations of Conservation Education* (New York: National Wildlife Federation, 1941), p. 1.
7. Zimmermann, *World Resources and Industries,* p. 129.
8. De Gregori, *A Theory of Technology,* pp. 9–13.
9. Ibid., p. 12. The thesis used here is derived primarily from the work of Sherwood Washburn.
10. Mitchell, "Conservation, Liberty, and Economics," quoted in p. 1, Zimmermann, *World Resources and Industries,* p. 9. See also Robert C. Cowen, "Minerals: Breaking the Import Habit, Part 2: Knowledge, the Essential Raw Material," in *The Christian Science Monitor,* 12 January 1982, pp. 12–13.
11. Isaac Asimov, *A Choice of Catastrophes: The Disasters that Threaten Our World* (New York: Simon and Schuster, 1979), p. 291. Asimov notes that the word *metal* comes from the Greek, "to reach for," (p. 294), which is what humans do with metals and other resources; they reach for a better way of life.
12. *Resources for Freedom,* Communication from the President of the United States, Transmitting the Report of the President's Materials Policy Commission, June 1952, Washington D.C.: U.S. Government Printing Office, 1952. Five volumes, Doc. 527, 82nd Congress, 2nd Session.
13. Ibid., Vol. 1, *Foundations for Growth and Security,* p. 1.
14. Ibid. As in Dickens's *A Tale of Two Cities,* "It was the best of times, it was the worst of times . . . in short, the period was so far like the present period."
15. Jeremy Rifkin, *Entropy: A New World View* (New York: Viking, 1980).
16. Kirkpatrick Sale, *Human Scale* (New York: Coward, McCann and Geoghigan), 1980.
17. J. B. S. Haldane, "On Being the Right Size," in J. B. S. Haldane, *Possible Worlds* (New York: Harper & Row), 1928.

312   Thomas R. De Gregori

18. Donella H. Meadows et al., *The Limits to Growth: A Report for the Club of Rome's Project on the Predicament of Mankind* (New York: Universe Books), 1974.
19. DeGregori, *A Theory of Technology*, p. 61. Data are derived from J.S. Carman, *Obstacles to Mineral Development* (New York: Pergamon Press), 1979. Detailed data on population growth and food supply can be found in DeGregori, *A Theory of Technology*, Chap. 9, pp. 114–22 and p. 49.
20. H.J. Barnett and C. Morse, *Scarcity and Growth: The Economics of Natural Resource Availability* (Baltimore: Johns Hopkins University Press for Resources for the Future, 1963), and William Nordhaus, "Resources as a Constraint on Growth," *American Economic Review* 64 (May 1974): 22–26.
21. Max Singer, "How Dependent is the U.S. on Strategic Minerals?" *The Wall Street Journal*, 14 August 1986.
22. *World Development Report 1986* (New York: Oxford University Press for the World Bank, 1986), p. 7.
23. *World Economic Outlook*, April 1986, Washington, D.C.: International Monetary Fund 1986, pp. 139–45.
24. Ibid., pp. 139 and 141.
25. Leonard A. Pauleno, *Food in the Third World: Past Trends and Projections to 2000* (Washington, D.C.: International Food Policy Research Institute), Research Report 52, June 1986, pp. 41–42. Late projections for some food crops, such as wheat, hold the possibility that 1985/1986 may also set new records. Andrew Gowers, "World Harvest Record Forecast," Financial Times (London), 10 December 1986. And *World Agricultural Supply and Demand Estimates*, (WASDE-200), United States Department of Agriculture, Economic Research Service, Foreign Agricultural Service, 10 December 1986.
26. See Nicholas Eberstadt and Clifford M. Lewis, "How Many Are Hungry?", *The Atlantic*, May 1986, pp. 34–38, for an analysis of current greater food availability. See also Irma Adelman, "A Poverty-Focused Approach to Development," in *Development Strategies Reconsidered*, ed. John P. Lewis and Valeriana Kallab (New Brunswick, N.J.: Transaction Books, 1986), pp. 52–53, for data showing that the proportion of the world's population living below the poverty level fell from 39.8 percent to 22.4 percent between 1950 and 1980, even though inequality was increasing.
27. *Financial Times (London)*, 4 November 1986.
28. *The Economist (London)*, 4 October 1986, p. 75.
29. Ibid.
30. *Financial Times (London)*, 20 November 1986.
31. See for example Louis Uchitelle, "A Worldwide Glut Crisis," *The New York Times*, 17 December 1986.
32. Theodore W. Schultz, Lectures in Agricultural Economics, Washington, D.C.: Economic Services Bicentennial Lecture Series Committee, 1977, pp. 16, 17.
33. N.W. Pirie, "The World Food Supply: Physical Limitations," in *Readings From Futures: A Collection of Articles From the Journal Futures*, ed. R. Jones (Guilford Surrey, England: Westbury House, 1981), p. 305.
34. DeGregori, *A Theory of Technology*, Chap. 10.
35. C. Lewis, "Global Food Security: A Manageable Problem," *Development*

Digest, 21 (July 1983): 106–121, at pp. 106, 107. See also Per Pinstrup-Andersen and Peter B.R. Hazell, "The Impact of the Green Revolution and Prospects for the Future," *Food Reviews International* 1 (1985): 1–25, and Frederick H. Buttel, Martin Kenney and Jack Klopperburg, Jr., "From Green Revolution to Biorevolution: Some Observations in the Third World," *Economic Development and Cultural Change* 34 (October 1985): 31–55.

36. John H. Lienhard, "Some Ideas About Growth and Quality in Technology," *Technological Forecasting and Social Change* 27 (1985): 265–81.

37. DeGregori, *A Theory of Technology,* pp. 3–9. These conclusions are drawn from many authors and reflect no individual inquiry by me.

38. Mark Nathan Cohen, *The Food Crisis in Prehistory: Overpopulation and the Origins of Agriculture,* New Haven, Conn.: Yale University Press, 1977.

39. On the rather limited gains from "appropriate" technologies, see R.S. Eckaus, "Appropriate Technology: The Movement Has Only a Few Clothes On," *Issues in Science and Technology* 3 (Winter 1987): 62–71.

40. In fact, it can be argued using data from work such as that of Lienhard, that historically, trends are more sustainable than the particular technologies driving them. For example, for any major endeavor today, such as computation or information transfer, it is clear that the trends over the last forty years were absurd or scientifically impossible and not sustainable under the known technologies of the time. That today we have such capabilities, or even greater capabilities, is the result of emergent possibilities of new technologies. Just since the completion of this article, developments in superconductivity have occurred that promise to greatly increase the resource character of barium, yttrium, and possibly lanthanum. Most of the material composites having superconductivity are ceramics, which are relatively cheap. Increasing efficiency in the transmission and use of electricity will also increase the resource character of the "stuffs" used to create electricity. All these factors will contribute to a continuing expansion in resources and a downward movement in real prices—and as problems of application are overcome, we will find new uses and unexpected possibilities for development.

41. Albert Camus, *The Myth of Sisyphus and Other Essays* (New York: Vintage Books), 1953, p. v.

The Institutionalist Theory of Capital Formation.

Baldwin Ranson

There is probably no term in economics which has given rise to so much controversy as capital.

——Palgrave's *Dictionary of Political Economy.*

Controversy over the term "capital"—both among orthodox economists and between orthodox and heterodox economists—has not abated since it was remarked in Palgrave's dictionary nearly a century ago. But the intervening years have provided accumulating evidence of what the controversial issues are and the grounds on which the major contending interpretations rest. This article will propose a definition of capital and a theory of capital formation found persuasive by a number of institutional economists, explain the grounds on which the theory rests, and distinguish it from the orthodox definition and theory.

The term "capital" came into the business vocabulary of Europeans in the Middle Ages. It then referred to the principal of a money loan, an interest-bearing sum of money. The loan was an asset yielding income to the lender. But recognition that money is barren led to doubts by social analysts that loans could or should yield income. In order to legitimize such "capital," the business term was extended by economists to objects considered genuinely productive, from which barren money might derive income-yielding ability.

In the mid-1700s, the Physiocrats applied the term capital to stocks

The author was greatly assisted in formulating this article by constructive criticism of Walter Neale, Christopher Niggle, and Marc Tool.

315

of unconsumed assets. They also called those stocks accumulated values or advances, by which they meant essentially what we today call discretionary income. Although they held land alone to be genuinely productive, they recognized that land would yield more output when worked by well-equipped, than by ill-equipped, farmers. Consequently, Physiocrats considered accumulated stocks of unconsumed assets as potentially productive of further income when advanced to support agriculture.

British economists identified as capital a somewhat narrower stock of unconsumed assets than the Physiocrats' discretionary income. They explicitly treated capital as one of three factors of production, as the stock of things employers provided workers to carry on production—materials, tools, and the wage fund accumulated for employee consumption. German and Austrian economists emphasized a still narrower stock of assets: instrumental capital used in roundabout production processes, from which they excluded the "consumer goods" included by British usage.

Karl Marx denied that stocks of assets produce income, although he admitted that well-equipped workers produce more output in a given time. He held labor alone to be productive, while capital simply gave its owners the right to extract unpaid labor power from workers. The income-generating power of money and real capitals, their self-expanding exchange value, he found to be evidence of exploitation rather than of productive potency.

In the twentieth century, John Maynard Keynes treated as capital all goods on hand, but primarily concerned himself with the inventories entrepreneurs accumulated in search of financial gain. In contrast, some American economists broadened the term to cover all sources of income streams—including organizations, human skills, and even technology itself. Such non-material income sources are often called human capital.

Despite this diversity of referents for the term "capital," all display common traits, showing that economists have intended the word to refer to objects fulfilling a single economic function—an intention foreign to evolving business usage of the same term. Each referent has been a human-created object thought indispensable (in combination with other factors *not* created by humans) to the continuity of production: a factor within human discretion that must be maintained if output is to remain constant, that must be expanded if growth is to occur, and that must be improved if development is to occur (the expansion or improvement being called capital formation, capital accumulation, or investment). This historical usage suggests that, for economists, the function of the term has been to identify man-made agents thought to possess productive potency. Accepting this historical intention, institutional economists derive their definition of capital from their theory of production.

Institutionalist Definition

At the core of the institutionalist theory of production is technology. Technology is the total stock of human know-how applicable to physical facts. It is operational scientific knowledge, the body of techniques capable of producing real income. It has grown cumulatively throughout history, and is clearly a continuing factor in human experience, although each community employs only a small fraction of the total stock. The fraction or level of technology employed by a community specifies a complex of materials, skills, and equipment (traditionally identified as land, labor, and capital) available for production. Thus technology serves the function of capital.

Economists do not explain the physical-engineering substance of technology. Instead they seek to explain the patterns of correlated behavior (institutions) through which it is disseminated, applied, and improved. Technology is disseminated and improved largely through educational and research institutions, while it is applied through economic institutions.

To the extent that they correlate behavior to productive ends, institutions have productive potency and serve the function of capital. But institutions also perform control functions that distribute status rather than produce income. Because institutions display this dual nature, careful analysis is required to determine which behavior patterns are productive and which are not.

Observing that production occurs when a knowledge stock is applied through correlated behaviors, institutionalists arrive at their definition of capital. The man-made agents possessing productive potency are a community's technology and its technically serviceable institutions.

Thorstein Veblen initiated this institutionalist pattern of thought when he challenged the convention of imputing to capital goods (meaning the massive plant and equipment so awe-inspiring to contemporaries of the industrial revolution) an autonomous productive potency [Veblen 1961, pp. 324–51]. He argued that the productivity of capital goods (the "material equipment" of industry) depended on the level of technology (the "immaterial equipment" of industry, especially as embodied in skilled workers). But few economists have made use of Veblen's insight, perhaps in part because of the awkwardness of calling technology or the workers who have mastered it "immaterial equipment."

Orthodox economists have also come to recognize the productive potency of technology, but they do not mean by it what Veblen did. Theodore Schultz proposes including technology along with every other source of income to individuals as capital [Schultz 1971, Chap. 2]. He does not consider technology to be a state of the industrial arts that makes a whole complex of materials, skills, and equipment useful; rather, he uses the word to refer to any unit of knowledge or skill that can command a price. This position is diametrically opposed to (and intended to counteract) the view that the productive efficiency of materials, skills, and equipment is a function of the level of technology. By fragmenting technology into its individual embodiments, and imputing productive potency to each fragment, Schultz loses sight of the technological continuum, and insists on a microeconomic foundation for theories of production and capital formation. By calling technology and technically serviceable institutions capital, institutionalists insist on a macroeconomic foundation for the theory of production and capital formation—a unified theory of the productivity of land-labor-capital, which Schultz rightly recognizes as rendering irrelevant the core of accepted economic theory.

Traditionally, capital is considered a human-created factor of production that is combined with factors beyond human discretion (land and labor). This tradition permits economists to ignore the fact that the productivity of land and labor is also a human creation, thereby denying the necessity of theories of land formation and of labor formation as parts of a comprehensive theory of production. It also permits them to engage in marginal productivity analysis, which assumes that output results from combining the potencies intrinsic to each independently productive factor.

The institutionalist definition permits neither of these practices. By making the productivity of materials, skills, and equipment dependent on the level of technology and institutional efficiency, the institutionalist definition denies intrinsic productive potency to all three of the traditional factors, and makes the productive potency of all factors subject to human discretion. The prevailing level of technology specifies which objects will be productive; materials, skills, or equipment embodying a level of technology above that mastered by a community are unusable, while those embodying a lower level are obsolete. Accumulating stocks of objects beyond what is useful for near-term output is unlikely to raise a community's productive potential, because any technically competent community can, in the absence of social obstructions, provide itself with whatever materials, skills, and equipment are known to exist. Thus, institutionalists call technology and productive institutions capital, but not their embodiments used in production or control.

As happens frequently in economics, the institutionalists are trying to present a new theory with a term used in old theories and in daily business practice—which is why controversy over the term capital is inescapable. To communicate the new theory requires insistence on the error of traditional production theory in locating human discretion in but one of the factors of production, and calling that factor capital; and it requires demonstrating that the productive potency traditionally assigned to capital in fact inheres in technology and institutions.

Institutionalist Theory

A theory of capital formation must explain how a community can accumulate capital, meaning man-made agents possessing productive potency. Institutionalists accept this function for capital formation theory, but do not accept the orthodox explanation of how or why these indispensable agents are formed.

The orthodox theory holds that a community accumulates capital by altering the character of its current production, decreasing the output of consumer goods (saving more) and increasing the output of capital goods (investing more). Saving and investing occur when individuals come to value future income more than present income, and when business enterprise gives effect to this choice. This theory is criticized below. The institutional theory holds that a community accumulates capital by altering the level and the character of its current production, increasing the community's mastery of technology and the efficiency of its technically serviceable institutions *without* saving, as traditionally defined. Such investment occurs when a community creates more productive institutions.

A community invests or "accumulates" capital in the form of technology when more of its population masters the prevailing level of technology, or when a significant fraction of its population masters higher levels of technology. The first possibility has been unimportant historically but is increasingly important today. In traditional societies, only small leisure classes have been exempt from mastering and apply-

ing the prevailing technology. The masses acquired the skills necessary
to design, produce, operate, and maintain the materials and equipment
used in production. But in modern societies the most advanced technology has become the possession of highly trained engineers (usually
employees of corporations or governments). Large groups of people are
deprived of adequate technological competence, while small groups of
experts design increasingly complex equipment that requires little skill
and fewer workers to operate. Policies reversing this trend toward increasingly narrow expertise by making widely available a modern technological education would accumulate capital in every community.

Accumulating higher levels of technology occurs largely through
what Clarence Ayres called the "principle of combination," which explains the inherently developmental character of technology: the more
a community knows (and the more people in a community who know),
the more likely new combinations will arise that will extend knowledge
[Ayres 1978, pp. 111-15]. Throughout human history, technological
progress has resulted from accidental combinations, such as melting
copper and tin together to produce bronze. Occasionally advances in
knowledge have resulted from purposive trial-and-error combinations.
But in the last several centuries, the process of discovery has become
more subject to discretion through correlating scientific inquiry with
technological inquiry. Scientific inquiry is the search for general principles in special-case observations, while technological inquiry is the
search for special-case applications of scientific principles. Creating
new institutions in which a growing proportion of the population learns
to engage in both forms of inquiry would promote capital accumulation
and should be called investment.

A community "accumulates" capital in the form of institutions when
it learns how to correlate behavior more efficiently. More efficient economic institutions permit increasing the rate of output with the prevailing technology (a primary aim of operations research, for example),
while more efficient educational institutions raise production possibilities by diffusing skills necessary to apply, borrow, or improve
technology (the aim of land-grant colleges a century ago and of research
universities today). Given the current understanding of technological
inquiry, a community can design educational institutions expressly to
raise its level of technology, and it can design economic institutions
that will employ the rising production possibilities. The resulting full
employment of the highest technical competence will produce any desired output with the minimum labor time, thus freeing the maximum
possible human time for inquiries that may contribute to further technological progress and institutional adjustment.

Institutionalists recognize that applying modern technology requires large quantities of material equipment, and they recognize that acquiring such equipment requires large quantities of money. But they do not follow orthodox economists in considering these phenomena to constitute the theory of capital formation. The possibility of both producing and using material equipment is contingent on the community's technological mastery, not on any potency inherent in the equipment. Decisions to produce more of current kinds of equipment are evidence that the productive potential of the prevailing technology has not been fully exploited, making such decisions relevant more to a theory of unemployment than to a theory of capital formation. Decisions to spend money for net investment signify that new debt must be created, making such decisions relevant more to a theory of banking than to a theory of saving.

In short, the institutionalist theory of capital formation asserts that a community accumulates the agents possessing productive potency by all activities that raise its level of technology and its effectiveness in coordinating behaviors that apply technology. The theory locates creative potency not in business accumulations of past outputs or of money, but in workmanlike operation of industrial and educational institutions.

Clarification by Contrast

Since this statement of the institutionalist theory of capital formation employs definitions and patterns of thought that are not widely familiar, its meaning may be clarified by presenting one particular statement of the orthodox analysis (the central pattern of which is described in Ranson [1983]) and contrasting major points of the two theories.

In 1980, the General Accounting Office published a report to the Congress of the United States: *An Analytical Framework for Federal Policies and Programs Influencing Capital Formation in the United States.* The report was intended to show policymakers how the federal government could promote more rapid capital formation. It presents the orthodox theory with a clarity and brevity that permit easy identification of the points disputed by institutional economists.

The GAO report defines capital as produced goods used in further production, which sounds like the business-oriented definition often used by classical and Keynesian economists: physical assets through the use of which a profit is sought [U.S. General Accounting Office 1980]. But the definition intended is broader: capital is subdivided into business, consumer, public, and human components, and later money is casually included [U.S. General Accounting Office 1980, p. 37]. Consequently the definition embraces material goods, intangible assets (including money), and acquired talents and skills—all of which can be accumulated by individuals driven by the profit motive. Institutional economists find this definition both too broad—including intangible assets that are barren—and too narrow—excluding the community's level of technology as well as its technically serviceable institutions, which are man-made agents of production that cannot be accumulated by individuals.

The report's "capital" is formed by the activity of net investment, meaning producing goods faster than they are replaced. Net investment is considered important because the stock of produced goods so accumulated, along with technical progress, is assumed to be the primary source of increased productive capacity: "In the modern economy, technical progress and capital formation are the two main ways in which productive capacity grows. Moreover, capital formation facilitiates technological progress by embodying technical advances in new capital goods" [U.S. General Accounting Office 1980, p. 9].

The institutionalist theory agrees that technical progress is an agent of economic growth, and therefore labels that achievement capital formation. But it denies that accumulating stocks of goods facilitates technological progress. All applications of technology require embodying it in materials, humans, equipment, and consumer goods, but embodiment is not a source of technical progress. Accumulating stocks that embody the current technology is not the way to learn more.

The GAO report sees net investment as the result of a demand for new "capital" and a supply of "resources"—apparently meaning the traditional three factors of production. These two forces represent both the profit motives of individuals and society's desire for and ability to produce a stock of goods; they are coordinated in a market for loanable funds. The report explains the formation of business "capital" in some detail, stating that all the other types are subject to the same determinants.

Demand is the specification of the maximum prices potential buyers are ready, willing, and able to pay at various rates of purchase. Decisions to order capital goods are based on calculations of the costs and benefits individuals expect at each rate. As long as the expected yield of owning or leasing capital goods exceeds their costs, it pays to invest.

Businesses, of course, make such calculations, but institutionalists deny that they reveal a community's desire for new plants and equipment, to say nothing of its desire for higher levels of technology. Instead, they reveal the grounds on which businesses choose to keep the community's technology partially unemployed. Since only a fraction of the community's population has discretion to order the large-scale equipment often required in the application of technology, and since that fraction can often gain by keeping such goods scarce or unemployed, its judgments reveal neither what the community desires nor what is desirable for the community.

The latter question is the one institutionalists address first when trying to decide what resources to devote to new plants and equipment, or more importantly, to better technology and institutions. What is desirable are those forms and quantities of equipment that permit effective application for human betterment of the current best technology. For example, providing abundant electricity to all human groups is desirable at present, because participation in modern productive activities is impossible without it. Thus building a world-around integrated electric generating system would make a great contribution to world productive capacity and human developmental continuity. It would be desirable even if producing and operating the most efficient equipment—perhaps wind turbines or solar collectors—would not be profitable to electric companies. Recognizing that whatever is technically feasible is financially possible, institutionalists are unconcerned with business judgments that such a system would or would not pay [Foster 1981, p. 966–67]. They are concerned with helping communities understand what is desirable so that the highest level technology will be applied in directions that contribute to community well-being, regardless of market demand.

Supply generally means that specification of the minimum prices individual sellers are ready, willing, and able to take at various rates of sale. But in the orthodox theory of net investment, what is supplied is not "capital" goods but "resources" that have been saved and are available for investment. Thus, the GAO supply curve specifies the minimum interest rates potential savers are ready, willing, and able to accept in exchange for not consuming various fractions of their real or money incomes. The decision to save is based on calculations businesses and households make of the costs and benefits expected at each possible rate of saving. When the expected yield of saving exceeds the benefit of current consumption, it pays not to consume.

Institutionalists flatly deny that saving—refraining from consuming all of current income—makes available either real or money resources for subsequent net investment, although it appears to do so for individuals. Saving does accumulate "individual liquidity stocks" of goods or money, but does not raise the "collective security stock" relevant to a community's productive potency [Heinsohn and Steiger 1984, p. 53; Junker 1967]. The error arises from ignoring the bilateral nature of aggregate-level transactions when identifying referents for saving.

In real terms, part of current income typically enters a community's inventory of goods produced-and-not-consumed. Such a difference between the rates at which income is produced and consumed is traditionally defined as saving. But the rate of inventory growth is defined as investment. Using these definitions, the rate of real saving is simultaneous with and equal to the rate of net investment (an identity on which Keynes insisted but which is usually ignored). (Compare Foster [1981, pp. 950–52] and Parguez [1984, p. 85]). Real saving does not precede and make possible real investment; rather it is another name for a single bilateral transaction. The buyers of the new inventory may be called investors, while those from whom the inventory is bought may be called savers, since their money income was generated by nonconsumption transactions. But it is incorrect to think that there are savers who do something before and apart from investors.

The activity of real saving (which is simultaneously investment) makes some sense in a primitive agricultural community, where output is in a form that could be either eaten or saved for future use. Each grain of one season's crop not consumed becomes available (if safely stored) for planting next season. But in a modern community, the size of next season's crop is not dependent on the frugality with which this season's crop is eaten, and investment does not mean storing seed. Instead, output depends on the technical efficiency of a vast complex of economic activities—most of which are far removed from, and all of which are independent of, the farmer's seed stock.

The orthodox theory also treats saving in money terms, as the GAO supply curve readily shows, which makes no sense in either a primitive or a modern community. When an individual reduces his rate of spending of money income, in an effort to accumulate funds with which to finance investment, the instantaneous effect of the reduced rate of spending is an equally reduced rate of receiving somewhere in the economy. Saving money accumulates liquidity for the individual, but lowers community income without raising liquidity for the community. It does not create unobligated funds that are then available to finance investment. A community's ability to purchase any form of output depends on the size of its money stock, but never on some fraction of its funds that were received but not spent.

Nor does failure to spend all of one's money income free real "resources" that are then available to produce plant and equipment. Instead, it chokes the channels of trade, leaving entrepreneurs with disappointed expectations that often force them to reduce production. In short, all of the activities traditionally called saving discourage production without in any way facilitating or making possible capital formation.

In truth, the only aggregate activity in a modern economy to which the supposed effect of saving can apply is the spending of newly created funds on goods produced but not consumed. Funds to finance net investment are made available by new debt, not by failures to spend. The money value of new investment must always equal the rate of spending of new debt—which is the meaning of savings Keynes intended when he argued that saving is equal to investment. But the rates of thus saving and investing are determined by the willingness of the banking system and the government to create new debt, not by the willingness of "savers" to refrain from consuming. As with "capital," so with "saving": orthodox economists are led into error by careless semantics and an erroneous theory of production.

Having denied that the constructs of demand and supply reveal a community's desire for or ability to produce more plant and equipment or better technology or better institutions, there is no need to consider the GAO report's analysis of equilibrium between market forces in a market for loanable funds. The money market appears as a minor institution for distributing funds created elsewhere in monetary economies. But it might be useful to present the institutionalist response to the report's proposals for government spending and taxing policies.

The report grants that it is impossible to predict precisely the effect of government expenditures on private capital formation, but it lists four channels of possible influence. First, the government itself invests when it spends on roads, dams, parks, and the like. Institutionalists agree completely.

Second, through transfer payments to low-income people, the government may reduce the community's propensity to save and its actual rate of saving, thereby reducing the community's ability to invest. Institutionalists disagree completely. What is called a community's propensity to save is a misleading label for the fraction of a given income not consumed. It has nothing to do with the ability to finance or to produce more output. Transfer payments to low-income people will raise the community's propensity to consume and encourage business to spend more, which will raise investment and consumption activities, as well as the consequences of those activities—saving and income. On the other hand, were the government to try to raise the propensity to save, efforts to spend less would lower both aggregate income and actual saving and investment—the gap between what is produced and what is consumed.

Third, government purchases a different mix of goods and services than would private buyers, which might encourage or discourage the production of particular capital goods. Institutionalists agree, and would argue that government is more likely than are private buyers to spend on education, research, and institutional adjustments that improve technology and the serviceability of institutions.

Fourth, assuming the natural rate of unemployment hypothesis is correct, government spending will often push the economy beyond its normal capacity to produce, putting pressure on real interest rates and crowding out private investment spending. Institutionalists entirely disagree. This argument presumes that market economies tend to operate at a technologically determined full capacity rate. That presumption is false. Decisionmakers in market economies notoriously operate below capacity because their personal gain is not maximized by full use or advancement of the technological capacity of the community. The argument further presumes that the real interest rate measures both the availability of resources for producing future income and the social valuation of future income. Earlier paragraphs have shown why institutionalists find this presumption to be false.

Conclusion

Economists borrowed the term "capital" from business usage in the Middle Ages. Since then they have tried to give it precise technical meaning as the name of all man-made agents thought to possess productive potency. As their theories of production have evolved, different economists have assigned different referents to the term, and consequently have produced conflicting theories of capital formation to explain the maintenance, growth, and development of human-created objects thought indispensable to the continuity of production.

Although numerous economists have recognized major shortcomings in the orthodox theories of production and of capital formation [cf. Harcourt 1972; Nelson 1981] none but institutionalists have rejected the very foundations of those theories—the market forces of supply and demand thought to reflect the facts of scarcity and given wants—and developed alternative foundations for more accurate theories—explaining the role of technology and of institutions in the production process. Because individual self-interest is not competent to coordinate behavior so that a prevailing technology will be fully employed or efficiently advanced, institutionalists argue that public decisionmaking bodies must take responsibility for identifying what is technically feasible and for adjusting institutions so that the best technology will be applied to producing the most desirable level and character of income. The institutionalist theory of capital formation is necessary for efficient operation of the discretionary economy.

References

Ayres, Clarence. 1978. *The Theory of Economic Progress.* Kalamazoo, Mich.: New Issues Press, Chap. 3.
Chase, Stuart, 1938. *The Tyranny of Words.* New York: Harcourt, Brace & World, Chaps. 14, 15.
Commons, John R., 1961. *Institutional Economics.* Madison: University of Wisconsin Press, Chaps. 8, 9.
Dewey, John, 1962. *Individualism Old and New.* New York: Capricorn Books, Chap. 6.
Foster, Gladys Parker, 1986. "The Endogeneity of Money and Keynes's *General Theory.*" Ph.D. diss., University of Colorado.
Foster, John Fagg, 1981. "The Papers of J. Fagg Foster." *Journal of Economic Issues* 15 (December): 857–1042.
Fuller, R., Buckminster, 1969. *Utopia or Oblivion.* New York: Bantam Books, Chap. 8.
———, 1981. *Critical Path.* New York: St. Martin's Press, Chaps. 3, 6.
Gordon, Wendell, 1984. "The Implementation of Economic Development." *Journal of Economic Issues* 18 (March): 295–314.
U.S. General Accounting Office, 1980. *An Analytical Framework for Federal Policies and Programs Influencing Capital Formation in the United States.* Washington, D.C.: Superintendent of Documents, 23 September.
Hamilton, Walton, 1930. "Accumulation." In *Encyclopedia of the Social Sciences,* Vol. 1. New York: Macmillan.
Harcourt, G.C., 1972. *Some Cambridge Controversies in the Theory of Capital.* Cambridge: Cambridge at the University Press.
Heinsohn, Gunnar, and Otto Steiger, 1984. "Marx and Keynes—Private Property and Money." *Economies et societies* (18 April): 37–72, serie *Monnaie et Production,* pp. 37–72.
Junker, Louis, 1967. "Capital Accumulation, Saving-Centered Theory, and Economic Development." *Journal of Economic Issues* 1 (June): 25–43.
Keynes, John Maynard, 1936. *The General Theory of Employment, Interest, and Money.* New York: Harcourt, Brace & World, Chaps. 12, 16.
Moulton, Harold G., 1935. *The Formation of Capital.* Washington, D.C.: Brookings Institution.
Nelson, Richard, 1981. "Research on Productivity Growth and Productivity

Differences: Dead Ends and New Departures." *Journal of Economic Literature* 19 (September): 1029–64.

Parguez, Alain, 1984. "La dynamique de la monnaie," *Economies et societies,* serie *Monnaie et production* (18 April): 83–118.

Pearson, Harry W., 1957. "The Economy Has No Surplus: Critique of a Theory of Development." In *Trade and Market in the Early Empires,* ed. Karl Polanyi, New York: Free Press.

Ranson, Baldwin, 1983. "The Unrecognized Revolution in the Theory of Capital Formation." *Journal of Economic Issues* 17 (December): 901–13.

Schultz, Theodore, 1971. *Investment in Human Capital.* Glencoe: The Free Press.

Veblen, Thorstein, 1961. "Industrial and Pecuniary Employments," and "On the Nature of Capital." In *The Place of Science in Modern Civilization.* New York: Russell and Russell.

_____, 1973. *The Theory of Business Enterprise.* Clifton, N.J.: Augustus Kelley, Chap. 6.

Evolution of Time Constructs
and Their Impact on Socioeconomic Planning

F. Gregory Hayden

The primary focus of the institutionalist perspective is instrumentalist problem solving. Problems are delivered by the institutional process and solved by altering the social structure. To solve socioeconomic problems, planning is necessary. Important to any planning is the question of *when* actions and events are to occur. To effect new social structures, actions and events must be properly sequenced. An analytical core of sequencing events is time analysis. John R. Commons stated that, in addition to knowing what to do, the economist who has the power and responsibility for planning "must know *what, when, how much* and *how far* to do it at a particular time and place in the flow of events. This we designate the principle of timeliness."[1] This is not consistent with the common approach to time analysis. The more common approach leaves us at the mercy of passing time.

An experiment worth performing is to ask a group of university sophomores to take out a piece of paper and write a brief answer to the following question: What is time? In the years I have performed this experiment, only once has a student referred to what had been learned in a physics course. Again and again the students express the common bias of Western feelings regarding time. "Time is eternally passing." "Time is flowing past almost unnoticed." As one sophomore so vividly

The author wishes to express his appreciation to the Social Science Journal and to the Journal of Economic Issues for permission to reprint parts of past articles in this article.

explained, "the second that is here now will soon be going over the mountains and travel on to California." Most of us are not so graphic in our explanation about passing time but most of us believe the common misconception that time is a flowing reality that is constantly passing. The common view is wrong. We have not seen time flowing by, no one has measured it flowing by, heard it, or even recorded any telltale signs of its passing, yet the Western mind continues to hold to the common view. The flowing stream of time is so vividly believed that people seriously consider that the loss of aircraft over the Bermuda Triangle could be because of warps in the time stream, and neoclassical economists seriously recommend that education should be delivered to children on the basis of the outcome of a discounted time stream.

Time is not a natural phenomenon; rather it is a societal construct. What exists in society are duration clocks and coordination clocks selected by society, and the sequencing of events as scheduled by societal patterns.

In modern paradigms, time does not flow, or go, or run from here to there in either a cyclical or linear pattern. It also does not bridge a spatial gap between points. Time is a relative concept that relates one motion to the duration of another motion—a clock. In traditional concepts, motion and succession were thought to take place in time. Today motion defines time. The duration between successive events is measured by still another motion, such as atomic vibrations or hour clocks or color changes. The successive events are not connected by any rope of time or temporal plane. With so many items in motion, the universe is full of clock candidates. Since these items are moving in a multitude of directions, we might want to say that time is multidirectional. But that would be inaccurate. Time is the duration of motion. It has no direction.

There is no future into which the world is destined to flow except in the sense of the "after" that follows the "before." This certainly removes a good bit of the glow of destiny, inevitability, and evolutionary progress contained in the old concepts of time and future. Or, stated differently, the modern concept of time allows us to use clocks to regulate events rather than ourselves being regulated by the running clock of passing time. This expands the discretionary role and responsibility of modern planners.

Social-Cultural Time Constructs

To find social time it is necessary to observe the cultural symbols and institutions through which human experience is construed. Our own Indo-European language imposes the concept of time on us at a very early age, so it is difficult to identify with the concept of timelessness. Societies do exist without a consciousness of time, but most societies possess some concept of time. Conceptualizations of time are as varied as the cultures, but most can be categorized by one of three images. Time in the broad sense is viewed as a line (linear), a wheel (cyclical), or as a pendulum (alternating phenomenon). But within these central images, numerous other distinctions are made. One is tense. Is there a past or present or future, or all three? If more than one, to which is the society orientated and in what way? Another is continuity. Is time continuous or discontinuous? Does the continuity or hiatus have regularity? Another is progressiveness. Is evolutionary transformation expected with the passage of time? Still another is use. Is time used for measuring duration or for punctuality? In addition, the metaphysical distinctions are numerous. Is there a mode for measuring time? Is it reversible or irreversible? Subjective or objective, or both? Unidirectional? Rectilinear?

Various Cultural Times

These distinctions come into focus when one studies various cultures. The Pawnee Indians, for example, have no past in a temporal sense; they instead have a timeless storehouse of tradition, not a historical record. To them, life has a rhythm but not a progression.[2] To the Hopi, time is a dynamic process without past, present, or future. Instead, time is divided vertically between subjective and objective time. Although Indo-European languages are laden with tensed verbs and temporal adjectives indicating past, present, and future, the Hopi have no such verbs, adjectives, or any other similar linguistic device.[3] The Trobriander is forever in the present.[4] For the Trobriander and the Tiv, time is not continuous throughout the day. Advanced methods of calculating sun positions exist for morning and evening, but time does not exist for the remainder of the day.[5] For the Balinese, time is conceived in a punctual, rather than a durational, sense. The Balinese calendar is marked off, not by even duration intervals, but rather by self-sufficient periods that indicate coincidence with a period of life. Their descriptive calendar indicates the *kind* of time, rather than what time it is.[6] The Maya had one of the most complicated systems of time yet discovered. Their time divisions were regarded as burdens carried by relays of divine carriers—some benevolent, some malevolent. They would succeed each other, and it was very important to determine who was currently carrying in order to know whether it was a good time or a bad time.[7] (Was this an early explanation of business cycles?) The most common explanations of time among human societies, however, are the cyclical ones.

Cyclical Time

Two examples of cyclical time are those of the ancient Greek and Indian. Socrates believed his teaching was not new—he had repeated it in cycle after cycle for many lives. Aristotle denied the logical possibility of movement in a straight line to infinity and believed that the only everlasting continuous motion is circular motion. An example of cyclical time still in existence is found in India.

As in most Indian thought, spirituality plays a major role. For the Western mind to absorb the meaning of Indian time requires more than the average mental and emotional stability in order to survive. To begin with, one is dealing with more than one cycle, with more than one God, with numerous qualities and quantities of time, and with astronomical figures. For example, one day and one night for Brahma, in which a universe arrives and is destroyed, is equal to 4,320,000,000 human years, and this pattern will exist for 100 years of Brahma. But this is only the beginning; there are time cycles within the great cycle, with the *Mahayuga* consisting of four ages, each of which is longer than our historical records. One thousand *Mahaygas* make up a *Kalpa* and fourteen *Kalpas* make up a *Manvantra,* and on and on and on.[8] For the present purpose it is enough to note that man and history become quite insignificant in comparison to time. This has a tremendous impact on social and economic life. At birth, each person receives a *dhrama*—a moral code and duty appropriate to a given status and pattern of life.

> The joint belief in station and association obligation *(dharma)* and in the related cycle of existence *(karma)* serves as cement in uniting the caste system, and *jajmani* economic system, and all superior/inferior relations. . . .
> The idea of *karma* is additionally associated with a cyclical view of human and natural history. Annual crop and seasonal changes are circularly recurrent. . . . A man's life also is a cycle, and *karma* emphasizes the rhythm of life and death and rebirth. Because the world is viewed in terms of recurring cycles, the notion that a society might advance systematically in any way (i.e., the concept of "progress") does not naturally present itself.[9]

Clearly time concepts in India affect the economy there as do the time concepts in any society.

Western Time: Traditional

As stated above, Western temporal constructs are consistent with the idea of the linear flowing stream. "But in the broad sweep of human existence, that way of constructing the dimension of time is relatively rare."[10] The traditional Western linear time-stream came into being with Christianity; however, seeds of it had been alive for some time. For example, in the third century B.C., Strato said, "day and night, a month and a year are not time or parts of time, but they are light and darkness and the revolution of the moon and sun. Time, however, is a quality in which all these are contained."[11] This quote illustrates the appearance of flowing time to explain succession. Through the experience of succession, the appearance of time as a separate eternal entity suggests itself. The reality exists only in the appearance.

What was left of cyclical time among the Romans died with Christ. Christ was not a mythical entity. He was on earth and a part of history. Since he died as a man and for all, he could not die again as in cyclical time. Time must be linear. His death "was a unique event. It had happened, once, here on earth, in a certain place at a certain time, and any suggestion that it could happen again was a whisper from the devil."[12]

Augustine rejected Aristotle's connection of time and motion, and avoided any confusion of temporal with spatial concepts. He argued that time was found in the soul and in the mind. Christ died for our sins and man now moved forward into a sacred prophecy-fulfilling future.[13] History would flow from one prophesied interval to the next until the final judgment. Christianity became an onward religion. "The time series is linear . . . in the sense that it had a definite beginning at the creation of the world; it will have a definite end when Christ returns at the Last Day; and between these two limits it manifests, at least in a general way, the working out of a consistent Divine Plan. . . . The movement towards its fulfillment does give a direction and purpose to the time series."[14] Time gave Christians opportunity. "The certitude that time is useful and opportune clearly belongs to the conscious tradition of Christians; for them time is not an inert thing nor is its course a simple chronological unfolding without aim."[15]

The place of the individual Christian was, first, to order his whole life down to the last detail with a view of growing in the love of God, and second, he must ever be alert to accept God's grace.[16] Thus the idea of the atomistic individual concerned with growth and progress along the inevitable stream of time becomes apparent. In order to build God's community for His glorification on earth and the saving of souls, a positive work ethic was necessary. One was to be judged not only for good works but for good work as well. A Benedictine monastery's appreciation of labor is revealing: "Labor was to be man's greatest joy and the instrument of his union with God. Industry was the key to the upbuilding of the new world that Benedict created. . . . Everything was seen as an aspect of work."[17]

Since so much building, caring, and praying needed to be done, with no idea how much time was left, time became precious to the medieval mind. Both the individual and the Kingdom could be called before all the preparation was completed. "Thus, early Christian ideology also created a fertile ground for technological innovation and its employment for earthly improvements."[18] The more that could be done with passing time, the better. Since individual and community were committed to sacred and earthly accomplishments, accountability and measurement became important. The Christian Middle Ages achieved "an ordered society, sustained by a common and not ignoble belief, in which the individual was not lost but discovered himself, not suppressing but releasing joyous energies, reaching to the sky in the shape of cathedral towers, for the glory of God."[19]

Although the object of the glory has changed considerably, Christian time remains. It is a passing time without qualitative changes, to be used efficiently. At one time the object of the efficiency may be commercial interests, at another technology, at another Mammon, but the concept of time has not much changed.

The enlightment really did not alter traditional time concepts. Newton's time was Christian time, and despite Leibniz's argument that time is relative and that instants apart from things are nothing, the traditional concept of time was predominant in the scientific community until much later. Not until Einstein dealt with time on micro and macro levels did the scientific community change. However, the traditional view remains predominant today as the "common sense" view of time, and as the neoclassical view. Neoclassical assumptions regarding time are a continuation of its religious predecessor.

In neoclassical thought, individual consumption replaces religious glorification; thus the present becomes more important and pressure exists for individuals to get their fill before their time runs out. This is part of the transition from "biblical time" to "merchant time."

Neoclassical Time-Stream Discounting

Neoclassical thought puts its temporal construct into operation through the use of the geometric mean discounting formula. Consistent with its tradition, neoclassicalism borrowed the discounting tool from the world of capitalist finance. It was appropriate for the financier's portfolio analysis, but it is not appropriate as an evaluative tool for social policy. A review of the basic premises and assumptions involved in using the discounting technique makes it clear that they are not consistent with modern science. They are:

Isolation. Time analysis should be built around an isolated extrapolation or projection of segregated benefit and cost flows as opposed to an analysis of process integration. This stems from the analysis being atomistic and isomorphic, instead of holistic.

Importance. Time discounting should occupy a position of major importance in social evaluation. If resources constrain an analysis, then the research and organization of data for discounting should be the last to be eliminated. Thus, enormous research effort has gone into determining the correct discount rate for water projects, with very little research focusing on matters such as the effect of water projects on the quality of community life.

Measurability. What is important is measurable. Matters that are represented by numbers are the most important.

Consumer Desire. Evaluation of merits and flaws, benefits and costs, should be consistent with a philosophy that promotes consumer desire, even in those cases where there is no vehicle for registering such consumer desire.

Valuing Benefits and Costs. Both benefits and costs can be valued by the same common denominator. Pecuniary prices can serve as this common denominator, which takes account of relative scarcities and surpluses.

Closed Future. The future is closed, which assumes that there is a future out there, instead of assuming that there are numerous potential futures.

Big is Beautiful. More is better than less. The passage of time requires progress. The greater the present worth, the more superior a project is judged to be. The present worth is increased by increasing net benefits.

Existence of Time Preference. Neoclassicalists assume, tautologically, that since interest rates accompany saving and consumption by individuals, it follows that individuals have independent time preferences.

Time-Preference Judgment. Individuals have an inherent, intuitive, internal ability to judge time, both durational and continuous. Individuals have independent time preferences and can make judgments regarding them.

The Present is Most Important. The present gets top priority. Even though the additional hospital beds, for example, will not be needed for five years, they should be discounted *through* time and assigned a value for the present period when they are not needed.

Linear Proportionality. In addition, the correct fit for the time preference function is the linear proportionality of the geometric mean formula. Thus, time-stream discounting also assumes that social time preferences are expressed best through percentage rates.

The Commonality of Clocktime. The same time-measurement scale (clock) has the same meaning in different systems and across different institutions or can be used as a common denominator of different systems. This assumption means it is not necessary to develop a clock consistent with the system.

A Common Discount Rate. The same discount rate is correct for costs as well as benefits, and is correct for all kinds of costs and benefits.

The Existence of Time. Time exists as part of the physical world. Therefore, discounting can take place *over* time and *through* time, and events can take place *in* time. Humans, as well, are *in* time.

Commodity Value. Because time exists, it can be scarce. Because it is scarce, it can and should be valued as a commodity.

Rectilinearity and Forward Flowing. Time in neoclassical theory is what usually is identified as the Christian or Indo-European conceptualization of time. It is one-directional, moving into the future in a linear fashion. Time was switched on in the beginning and is still running.

Unidimensional and Absolute Character. Time is one-dimensional in its nature, texture, rate, structure, setting, and the like. These characteristics remain absolute in the neoclassical analysis.

Flowing Stream. Time is a flowing stream; thus the nomenclature "time stream analysis." Like so much of the rest of neoclassical theory, time, as a stream, comes from Newton. In the beginning of the *Principia* he said, "Absolute, true and mathematical time, of itself, and from its own nature, flows equally without relation to anything external." Although this statement is consistent with traditional Christian thought starting at least as early as Augustine, once Newton articulated it, i reified time and ascribed to it the function of flowing. Although from the beginning this reification was challenged and denied by others of equal fame such as Leibniz, Kant, Einstein, and Planck, they never were able to remove it from the public mind because of the general cultural and religious reinforcement. Later generations of physicists, astronomers, and philosophers were able to erase traces of Newtonian time from their models, but it is still basic to neoclassical time analysis.

Continuously Passing Time. Not only is it a stream, but the stream is continuously passing—running on and on and on. Flowing. Flowing. As the moralist cautions, "Make the most of time. Use it before it goes."

Infinite. Time is an infinite open set. The stream without definable banks is also without final destination.

Time Hypostatization. Many of the above assumptions are a result of what logicians refer to as time hypostatization. To hypostatize time is reification along with the creation of qualities and attributes. The neoclassicalist reification of time is a confusion between time and the experience of succession or sequence.

Time Spatialization. In conjunction with hypostatization, it is also necessary to practice time spatialization in order to see the neoclassical time-streams flowing ever outward. To spatialize time is to attribute spatial qualities to time or to confuse the spatial relations among things with the temporal relations among events.

Integrated Definitions. As in Christian time, duration, continuity, and sequence are integrated into one common definition. Time, usually designated by T, is an endless rectilinear stream made up of moments. An event takes place in a moment in T and a sequence of events is spread over the stream of moments. The interval between moments is duration, usually designated by t, thereby defining t as a piece of T. In this definition, reversibility and irreversibility are ignored.

Space-time Continuum. Separation of time and space. Although all sciences—from physics to anthropology—recognize the impossibility of separating time and space, the neoclassical discounting formula does not provide for a means to integrate the spatial aspects of the space-time continuum.

Western Time: Modern

To understand the modern concept of time, let us begin by conducting an imaginary experiment. Let us for a moment imagine that our sensing faculties are suspended in a universe of nothingness. Now look out into the empty space. There is no time. Now suspend one stationary item in the nothingness. There is still no temporal dimension. "If we try to imagine ourselves in a world without sound or movement, with nothing stirring, without even our breathing or heart-beats, we must agree that we cannot have Time there. Time may not be merely something happening, but unless something is happening, there cannot be

Time."[20] Now let us allow our suspended item to make one move and stop. What was the length of the move? We can see the length of the distance, but there is no measure for the temporal duration because there is no other motion to use as a time clock. If a second item is added to this universe, its rate of movement can be used as a measure of the duration of the first item's movement. We now have a relative time clock. We see that time is relative and duration is relative to another motion. Now let us fill the universe with items moving in a multitude of directions, in a multitude of spatial patterns, and at a multitude of rates. Now the universe is full of potential clocks and full of time dimensions. Since these items are moving in a multitude of directions, we might want to say time is multidirectional. However, as stated in the introduction, that would be incorrect. Time is the duration of the motion. It has no direction. The multitude of moving items is not flowing into the future. The earth is rotating around the sun, the bus is traveling about the city, and the barking dog is running about the yard. With this in mind, philosophers sometimes refer to reality as an infinity of layers of now. But to this author the words "infinity," "layers," and "now" suggest the old ideology. Reality cannot be broken into layers. Layers implies up and down, thus implying direction to time, and we are right back into the original problem of hypostatization and spatialization. In truth, the earth, the dog, and the sun are processing in the here and now. They are not flowing anywhere and neither is time.

Time becomes the duration between the "after" that follows the "before." For example, one of the dog's feet hits the earth after the other, or one tool development follows the other, and these durations can be measured with some other motion. This certainly takes some of the glamour out of the old concept of future, but more importantly, it also removes the idea of the inevitability of the future and removes some of the urgency of constantly being concerned that our lives are coming to a close. The old concept informs us that time is passing, and if we do not hurry, time will be wasted and the future will pass us. As stated above, the modern concept of time allows us to use clocks to regulate events rather than ourselves being regulated by the running clock of passing time. Humans can slow growth without feeling guilty of cheating posterity. This places men and women squarely in the decision-making roles of deciding when events should take place. In the old view of time, the relation of "earlier than" and "later than" was absolute and permanent because if an event is ever earlier than another event by a definable interval, it is always earlier, and by that interval. Yet we know that the sequence of events can be changed, reversed, slowed, accelerated, or destroyed. Modern time concepts do not provide for inevitable patterns.

One of E.F. Schumacher's shortcomings, this author believes, was his failure to identify the importance of the temporal construct held in the consciousness of the people he was asking to alter their commitment to growth. Because he did not identify the main determinate of the constant push for activity and accomplishment, he could not recommend a viable solution or policy. He could not tell us why we felt compelled to do what we were doing.

Time Analysis Should be Consistent With Holistic System

In modern thought, time is no longer an exogeneous concept but rather another element in the sociotechnical system. When we are planning for a complex sociotechnical system that is constantly evolving, we should not seek a single mechanistic synthesizer of temporal concerns.

Different Clocks for Different Institutional Processes

In order for a social plan to sequence and coordinate social delivery successfully with concomitant "linking-points," planners should be aware that different temporal conditions occur for different kinds of institutional experience. There can be a difference in temporal rhythm and temporal clock from institution to institution. Not only does time change from society to society, it changes among institutions, especially in a complex society. *"Time scales* may differ greatly over the hierarchical levels of a large system."[21] One time and one clock do not exist across institutions as is assumed in neoclassical thought. One institution may require an even temporal rhythm in the movement of resources, people, and goods. Another may require a relentless pace. Still another may go in impatient jerks, alternating between tremendous bursts of intense activity and long durations of plodding activities.

A simple example of different clocks in our society is the example of baseball and the effect of baseball games on transportation delivery systems. Baseball pays no heed to the hour clock, or to Einstein's atomic vibrations for that matter. Baseball has its own special time. It depends on outs, not minutes. Six outs to an inning, rather than sixty minutes to the hour. The duration of a game is determined by the correct number of innings, which may be two to five hours in non-baseball time. This difference in clocks complicates the delivery of transportation and police for taking the fans home while meeting the needs of those on alternative clocks. If the existence of alternative clocks and time are ignored, as in neoclassical analysis, problems are created.

Temporal variation in Brazil is related by Manfred Max-Neef. For example, he explained the frustration he had experienced in a Brazilian town. He was the only person in town who regularly lived by the dictates of a watch while the time of others was regulated by events. "In the short term, by daily events: things are done before or after mass, before or after school classes, after the Town Hall meeting, and so on. The long term is planned and regulated in tune with the religious and patriotic feasts of which there are, of course, a lot. A person's involvement with the preparation of a feast is a duty that takes precedence over any other type of commitment."[22] Max-Neef has found that the lack of concern for different temporal constructs in Third World countries can lead to a serious "human state of temporal asynchrony. These asynchronies produce varying degrees of anguish and anxiety, according to the importance given by the person concerned to the bonds of frustrated communication."[23]

However, Max-Neef pointed out that different times need not lead to frustration. To avoid the frustration, it is necessary to be sensitive to, and to integrate the different space-time dimensions in the social system. Social time integration is emphasized in the final section of this article. However, for now let us review the integration of alternative space-time that Max-Neef found in the town of Tiradentes, Brazil. He said:

> Time was there, of course, and so was space; but there was something different as well. I had the strong sensation that I was living a "contemporaneousness of the not-contemporary." The mules and the cars, the Chafariz and the television, the sun-dial and my Casio lithium watch. All widely diverging eras co-existing in the midst of a space of incredibly generous perspective. I remembered having been in many old cities before, and my sensation was almost always "time asynchronic": i.e. modern life going on at its usual rapid pace in museum-like surroundings. Here it was different. Times seemed to be synchronized because of the basically tranquil pace and style of the people's forms of human interaction. People were not *in* a space; they integrated *into* their space. They defined their own space and made up their own time, thus generating a splendid space-time coherence. It suddenly occurred to me that it was probably very difficult to develop gastric ulcers in a place of this kind. Sometime later I was to discover several forms of space-time disruption, yet this initial impression remained the overriding one for as long as I lived in Tiradentes.[24]

Individual Subjective Time Is Not Acceptable

For economic and social decisionmaking, one of the most dangerous analytical techniques available in dealing with time is the old philosophical technique of turning to individual intuition. "[Henri-Louis] Bergson, an original and bold if rather reckless philosopher, based a whole philosophy on the idea that outer or chronological time is unreal and that reality can be found only in our inner sense of . . . psychological time, the unceasing and creative flow of which we have an immediate apprehension."[25] Nicholas Georgescu-Roegen made this same basic mistake. He said, "there is no other basis for Time than 'the primitive stream of consciousness'."[26] The problem with this approach is that the analyst is right back where he started; for intuition is only the well filled with our sociocultural groundwater. As Einstein and Infel said,

> The method of reasoning dictated by intuition was wrong and led to false ideas of motion which were held for centuries. Aristotle's great authority throughout Europe was perhaps the chief reason for the long belief in this intuitive idea. . . .
> The discovery and use of scientific reasoning by Galileo was one of the most important achievements in the history of human thought. . . . This discovery taught us that intuitive conclusions based on immediate observation are not always to be trusted.[27]

The first ability one must acquire is to look outward—not intuitively— for the human being has no internal time or internal time clock. Time clocks are social and time concepts are cultural.

Robert E. Ornstein pointed out how early psychologists made the mistake of looking inward for a biological clock (similar to William Stanley Jevons's search for an internal utility calculator). He stated:

> Many psychologists, ignoring that ordinary temporal experience is personally and relativistically constructed, have searched for an internal organ of duration rooted in one biological process or another. This postulated "organ" has been termed a biological clock. Again, this search follows from the "sensory-process" paradigm of how we experience time, used primarily by those who would try to determine the "accuracy" of our time experience in relation to the ordinary clock. Such thinking confuses, once again, a convenient construction with reality.[28]

Social psychologists find that each year people in the United States have a poorer perception of the rate at which events are happening.

That is, they underestimate by a greater amount each year the interval of calendar time between when they expect events to happen and when they actually happen. This psychological phenomenon was an integral part of Toffler's book, *Future Shock,* in which he explained that futures are coming at us too rapidly for people to prepare for them psychologically. But for the present purpose, this phenomenon certainly should make suspect any attempt to base social planning in a technological society on a personal conception of time or time preferences.

French speleologist Michel Siffre found that after staying in a subterranean cave, which was dark and far out of sight and sound of his fellow humans, without any means of recognizing succession or discovering how clock time was passing, the length of the underground stay was completely misjudged. In Siffre's case, "He found to his astonishment that he had been far longer in his cave than he had imagined. We must note first that no intuitive sense of time had worked for him; that little watchman from the unconscious had gone off duty. . . . Then, his psychological time had lost touch with clock and calendar time."[29]

The reach for psychological time tends to sidetrack any real attempt to solve the problem of social time. First, social life cannot be coordinated with psychological time. The railroad uses clock time for its train schedules—not psychological time. Second, as Priestly pointed out, psychological time crams into one category too many quite different sorts of experiences.[30]

An additional problem with attempting to develop a succession concept that depends on individual time is that individual time changes with the individual's basal brainwave rate. "All that we experience as external reality is apparently nothing more than patterns of neuronal energy firing off inside our head."[31] Time, therefore, is not even a constant—even given a constant social situation—within an individual brain. In "ordinary" waking moments the brainwave rhythm, beta, is firing at approximately twenty-four frames per second (to use a movie projector concept). However, if slowed to a firing rate of ten waves per second, or alpha rate, the second hand on the clock appears to have slowed to approximately half its former speed. If the blasts are slowed to theta, or five blasts per second, time seems to stand still. "When brainwaves are still, time stands still, and when time stands still the illusion of motion becomes impossible . . . to the individual."[32] Time and motion correspond to the individual's current brainwave rhythm. In various states of consciousness, time and motion may be slowed, increased, intermitted, or run backward. By reducing the rate of spheroid blasts, as in meditation, one can fall through the gaps between the firings, and, to use current jargon, become "spaced out." Thus, if we are to follow Georgescu-Roegen's suggestion to use stream-of-consciousness, we will first have to know whether it is at the alpha, beta, theta, or delta rate.

Psychological predilections for time preference can be allowed to run free and wild, and even lead and lag, but if social clocks are not coordinated by an objective social time outside and above the individual psyche, then a slight miscalculation of timing, for example, can place one jumbo jet in the path of another. Individual preference, basal rate, or intuition about time or the speed of the plane are not important. To deliver air transportation safely, pilots and controllers must be coordinated on a common system.

Timeliness Requires Planning Decisions Be Above
the Atomistic Level at the Holistic Level

In determining the most timely delivery of social programs, it is necessary to take a holistic and organic view of institutions. Depending on individual perceptions, attitudes, and preferences with regard to time and time allocation is very misleading. Individual survey results have no correlation with what institutions actually require. F. Stuart Chapin, Jr., discussing Stuart Cullen's work on this issue, has said, "since much of the average weekday is tied up in routines over which people have little day-to-day control, the sequence of a day's activities in the life of an individual is 'pegged' around key structuring episodes. . . . Stuart Cullen sees both practicalities and conceptual problems standing in the way of applying utility-maximizing concepts or in explaining behavior in terms of preference analysis."[33] Chapin expanded on this issue saying, "rarely do preference studies present choice alternatives in the framework of constraints under which choices must be made. In study after study where preferences are followed up in an investigation of actual behavior, the correspondence between behavior has been of relatively low order."[34] This result would not surprise holistic social scientists. For that reason Chapin recommends the holistic approach for sequencing urban public programs. He said, "the view taken here runs counter to the reductionism bias in much of present-day scientific inquiry. But this view is not so much in reaction to these biases as it is a bias in the opposite direction, a strong belief in the necessity of a combinatorial emphasis of 'whole cloth' view which defines the contingencies of human activity in terms policy makers can recognize, evaluate, and project."[35]

In addition, the individual varies according to numerous matters such as race, class, recent employment, income, past achievements, and all those matters that color attitudes, estimates, and preferences. However, regardless of class, race, or employment record, the trains have to run on schedule.

From Time Discounting to Timeliness In a Holistic Frame

For society to function, it must be an integrated process—integrated into an organized effort by social forces. Before a construct can be designed to assist in temporal evaluation and decisionmaking, it must be understood, as Karl Polanyi emphasized, that society is an integrated system. Planning is the process of instituting new projects into the integrated system so that the right amount of social goods and services are delivered at the right point in the social system. This calls for Polanyi's concept of sufficiency: earmarking a sufficient amount to fill the needs of the system.

Time, if it is to be integrated usefully into social planning, should be what usually is connoted by the word "timely." Timeliness requires that we ask the question: Which projects will deliver the right amount of social goods and services at the right point in the social process to allow for the integration, maintenance, and improvement of the social fabric? It is not a matter of the neoclassical "firstest-with-the-mostest" criterion, but rather planning for the coincidence or congruence of the delivery system with need. For example, let us assume that we are able to discern that social forces are such that the future includes a great increase in lung disease in ten years. Timeliness requires that our plan provide for the delivery of the needed care in ten years. That care is not of value today when it is not needed. When planning is done on a substantive basis, rather than a pecuniary one, it becomes apparent that a pneumonectomy cannot be provided today and reinvested for a greater output of pneumonectomies later when needed. The sociotechnical system itself must define the temporal entities such as time clocks and temporal sequencing of events. How much, when, and how fast are questions that should be answered by system needs instead of a maximization principle. Therefore, "timeliness" best connotes the temporal concept that should guide project evaluation. If railyards or school buildings are needed at one point in the system evolution, that is when they should be delivered, not at an earlier point in order to increase the dividend found by a geometric mean discounting technique.

Project Evaluation for System Integration

For planning purposes, evaluation should assist in making decisions about the coordination of collective social motions and activities, and about the sequencing of events. When the social sequencing approach is emphasized, time is no longer thought of in relation to continuity, but rather in relation to duration between sequential events. A time clock is not measuring a continuous stream of moments, but rather is a motion that has been chosen as the instrument for measuring the duration of other motions, or duration between events.

To accomplish such temporal evaluation, three concerns must be implemented into the evaluation. First, Walter C. Neale's definition of the function of an institution becomes very important to integrated systems planning.[36] For Neale, the function of an institution concerns the interaction of one institution with another, and the mutual reinforcement of the institutions. Thus the function of alternative policies and programs must be judged to be in accordance with the needs of other system components. The new process should be structured to fit in another process, both along and across sequences. How much is needed depends on what is to be provided to other institutions. More is not always better.

Second, and closely related, is the knowledge acquired from anthropology regarding flow levels. "The flows of goods, services, information, and people through the network both structure and maintain . . . community relationships."[37] Formal models emphasize rates, but institutionalist ones emphasize the integration of levels.[38] For example, the flow of real outputs will exist only if there is an adequate flow of productive inputs, and the output will be sold if there is an adequate flow of buying power. "Only the values of levels are needed to describe fully the condition of the systems," because societies organize around levels.[39] "Rates do not control other rates without an intervening level; no rate variable depends directly on any other rate variable. A rate equation is a pure algebraic expression."[40]

Third, consistent with and necessary for integrated systems and temporal fit, is the structuring of a system without surpluses.[41] An excess either of food or pollution is wasteful. Waste is misallocated surplus that does not fit the system; pollution ceases if the system is structured properly. For example, urban sludge can be turned into a valuable resource if the system is redesigned to recycle it back into agriculture in a timely manner. If a system is structured properly, surpluses do not exist.

Real Time Control Systems

Temporal evaluation that judges whether a project correctly sequences the delivery of impacts with system needs is consistent with
the basic concepts of computer science real time. Real time systems
relate to the sequential events in a system, rather than to clock time.[42]
The system itself defines when events should happen. Real time systems have been used mainly to monitor and control systems by mini-
mizing response time to system deviations. For example, if the
monitoring device in a multi-color sheet-fed press (which uses advanced real time systems) detects a color deviation from the established standard, the control system brings the color back to .
conformance. Or, as another example, the chemical effusion that pre-
pares plants for winter dormancy and enables them to germinate when
the last frost has passed is a real time system. A failure of this real time
system would cause a plant's extinction. Plants have of necessity
evolved appropriate timing mechanisms to insure their survival. As the
length of the day changes, leaves take account of it through the blue
pigment phytochrome. Through the interaction of phytochrome and
the internal daily rhythms of the plant, there is a change in the production of the inhibitory growth chemical abscisic acid, which plays an
important role in the regulatory physiology of the plant. The plant
would be in trouble if it attempted to maximize the net present value
of abscisic acid instead of coordinating and controlling in a real time
sense with ecological needs. As Harold Sackman has stated, "control is
the process of assuring the conformity of plans and events. Real time
control requires that the response of each element of the control system
is such that the combined effect of all elements produces results that
are sufficiently expeditious to preclude failure of the system."[43] Sackman emphasized that real time control is structured around events in
an operating system, and does not try to force events to fit into tempo-
rally invariant molds.[44] The continual monitoring of real time control
systems "reaches its epitome with computer-based systems, where the
computer can act as a built-in laboratory to collect information automatically on how well the system is performing, whether it is achieving
its goals or not. But this has to start originally with a plan."[45]

Sackman saw real time as a step toward fulfilling John Dewey's philosophy. He said, "the twentieth century is witnessing the development
of a new and practical attitude toward time, an attitude of designing
and constructing the fixture through planning and control. Dewey
sensed the demise of spectator attitudes toward time and anticipated
the trend toward working control."[46]

Sackman also predicted that a concern for real time control would guide the evolution of other real time developments.[47] That is the purpose in this section: to develop real time evaluations that must precede project selection and real time control. Of course, real time control will still be necessary after system implementation.

Real Time Evaluation

In order to synthesize the concerns of Polanyi and Sackman into a real time evaluation, let us begin by looking at a simplified Matrix and Environmental Residuals for Energy Systems (MERES) flow chart (represented in Figure 1) of corn cob gasification and electric generation, and use it as an illustrative vehicle.[48] Figure 1 depicts the extraction of corn ears and the processing of electricity from the cob. The sequence of activities is identified across the top of the figure and a trajectory of processes to accomplish these activities is identified by the horizontal lines. Depending on the circumstances, different processes may be required to accomplish the same activities. For example, different methods may be used in the same plan to store the cobs.

The system is maintained by a sufficient flow through a production process, not by the flow of a time stream. The flow in the process changes with the production mode. Unlike the assumption about the one-dimensional undifferentiated time stream, the material flow through the instituted processes is differentiated and quite defined. The flow does not, as Newton said about time, flow from its own nature. Neither does it, to call on Newton again, flow "without relation to anything external." It flows according to the instituted process sequence of the activities across the top of Figure 1. The sequence is not designed around a linear time path. Some of these processes, such as gasification and generation, take place continuously throughout the Gregorian calendar. Sequences are designed by investigators; corn cob gasification is designed around a sequence of activities that change the form of energy from stored photosynthesized energy to electrical energy.

Real time evaluation requires system compatibility. Assume, for illustration, that it is decided that alternatives X, Y, and Z are to be evaluated to improve the cob gasification system. To accomplish such an evaluation, Figure 1 can be converted to a diagraph such as Figure 2, and collapsed onto a sequential axis as in Figure 3. The sequence of Figure 3 becomes the system clock. The system sequence acquires system meaning when we know about the flow levels at different points in the sequence. How many trucks need to arrive at the field and when, for example, depends on the yield of the corn and the technology of the

348

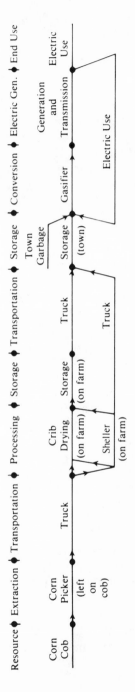

Figure 1. *Corn Cob Retrieval and Gasification Energy System*

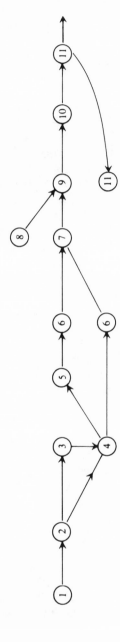

Figure 2. *Diagraph of Cob Retrieval and Gasification*

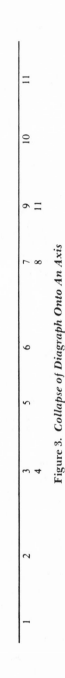

Figure 3. *Collapse of Diagraph Onto An Axis*

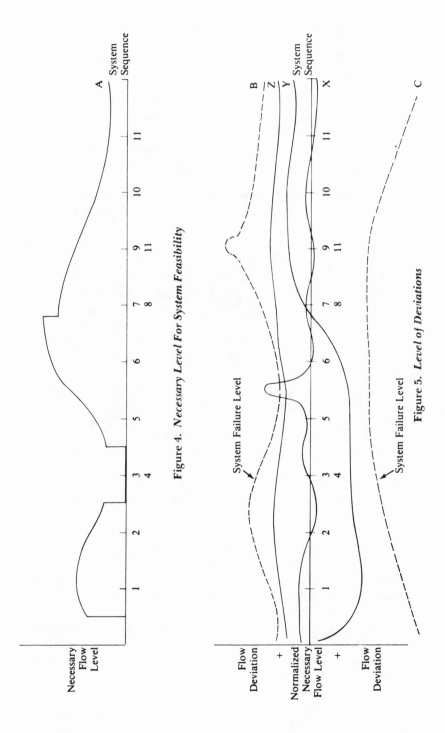

Figure 4. *Necessary Level For System Feasibility*

Figure 5. *Level of Deviations*

corn picker. Once the requisite, sufficient, or allowable levels are determined, evaluation can begin. There can be, for example, requisite levels of income and allowable levels of pollution. A composite of all three levels is designated as the necessary level in Figures 4 and 5.

As indicated in Figure 4, the necessary level may vary over the system sequence. Since it indicates the level needed to make the system feasible, it can be collapsed and normalized along the system sequence axis depicted in Figure 3. The flow at node 6 in Figure 5 would be at a much greater level than at node 2, but both are equal from the view of system requirements; therefore they both fall on the horizontal axis in Figure 5.

The axes both above and below the feasibility level are positive in order to determine how much a scenario trajectory deviates from the feasibility level. Zero points in numbering are, of course, arbitrary and it is equally arbitrary to assume that deviations are positive in one direction and negative in the other. Deviations from a norm can be damaging to a system irrespective of their direction. In all social systems of prescribed behavior, there is a spectrum of permissible deviation from the norm. Two important deviations to consider in evaluating alternatives are critical level and delivery specificity. The critical level is the extreme extent of deviation allowable. For example, if more garbage and cobs are delivered than can be gasified, then health and rodent problems develop. If, on the other hand, too little is delivered, the system must shut down and electrical generation is no longer feasible. Delivery specificity designates how specifically delivery must fit the recipient node. The more finely tuned the technological system and the level of mechanization, the less tolerance for variance. Lines B and C in Figure 5 represent a composite of both critical tolerance and delivery specificity.

To evaluate alternatives X, Y and Z represented in Figure 5, we want to select the one with the least deviation from the norm. This can be determined by the sum of the differences between the trajectory and the system sequence axis, except in those cases where the trajectory penetrates the critical level represented by B and C. This would eliminate alternative X, even though it would have the lowest sum of differences. Obviously alternative Y would be selected. The idea is to fit a selected norm represented by the horizontal axis rather than maximize a function from an axis.

Alternative Y was selected on the basis of a real time trajectory of one impact. Any real world problem, in contrast, would have multidimensional impacts for each alternative. The character of the problem will define the kind of indicator used to measure social impacts. With a real time approach to temporal evaluation, social indicators, instead of pecuniary prices, can be used as the measurement unit to compare alternative programs.

The real time concept applied to project evaluation is a step forward in time analysis. However, additional steps are needed to reach the level of social planning and system coordination necessary in the modern technological society.

From Event Synchronization to Social Process Sequencing

With the aid of the general summary contained in Figure 6, we can discuss the evolution of our time concepts, both in terms of the past and in terms of a needed future. *It can be summarized as an evolution from event synchronization to social process sequencing.* The evolution of technology is indicated across the top of Figure 6, the instruments or measures of time are along the left side, and the temporal concepts are arrayed outward from the intersection of the two axes. Figure 6 serves as a general summary of the relationship between technological

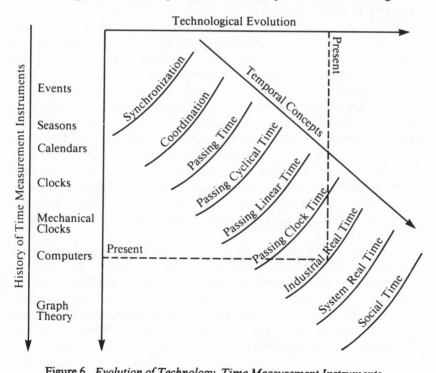

Figure 6. *Evolution of Technology, Time Measurement Instruments, and Temporal Concepts*

evolution and temporal constructs; as technology changes, both the instruments for measuring time and temporal concepts change. The ordering of time concepts in Figure 6 does not mean to imply all the earlier concepts fade away upon the adoption of the more recent.

As stated above, in the simplest technological societies, only a few events had to be synchronized in order to facilitate social life. Time existed only when those events had to be synchronized or when historical occurrences had to be recorded. It did not exist the remainder of the day, week, or year. There were no clocks or a sense of time sequencing. Neither was time divided into units such as weeks or hours. There was no need for such measurements. Sandor Szalai points out that even today "in quite a number of poor African and Asian countries the overwhelming majority of the rural population has no access whatsoever to clocks, public or private, and cannot read time."[49] According to Max-Neef, the same is true in Latin America. He states, "the bond of the peasant with time is different, and has different meanings and consequences, from that of the urban individual, especially one who lives in a metropolitan business industrial environment. There is no doubt that the famous (and very destructive) slogan 'time is money' has no meaning whatsoever for a peasant."[50]

With the evolution of nomadic and agricultural societies, sociotechnical processes became more complex, thus more synchronization and coordination were needed. Planting, harvesting, and warfare require more refined coordination. In addition, because the seasons became more important to when and where the tribe moved or when crops were planted, the seasons replaced events as the main time instrument. This added a natural rhythm and a sense of passing to time as seasons changed with some regularity. The regularity was noted and divided in smaller units. Seasons were turned into calendars and hour dials were developed as the various heights of the sun were recorded. Even at this, time was not a continuum. According to Szalai "Nobody ever cared in Athens or Rome to divide the *night* into hours. What for? With the exception of a few guardsmen and revellers, the use of time stopped when darkness set in."[51]

The regular rhythm of an organized society gave the sense of events passing along a time continuum. However the rate of technological change was so slow that life seemed to be repeating itself from year to year and from generation to generation. Therefore, the time construct was thought to be circular. As new technological combinations began to appear more rapidly, it became obvious that society was changing. Therefore, the time continuum ceased to be circular and began to move forward, finally becoming linear. The linear continuum became evenly divided into hours and minutes of uniform passing time. "The need for taking account of minutes, not to speak of seconds, arose only when people had already got accustomed to living 'by the clock' and to adapt their daily life, even 'minute' details of it, to the tick-tock of this mechanical device."[52] With the triumph of linear time,

> present time was "compressed" until it was merely a point sliding continuously along the line which runs from past to future. . . . Present time became fleeting, irreversible and elusive. Man for the first time discovered that time, whose passing he had noted only in relation to events, did not cease even in the absence of events. As a result, an effort had to be made to save time, to use it rationally and to fill it with actions useful for man. The bells from the belfry, ringing out at regular intervals, were a constant reminder of the brevity of life, and a call to great actions which could give time a positive content.[53]

In the industrial era the clock is not just a measure or symbol of passing time. In the minds of that era it *is* passing time, both operationally and as conscious proof of the passing of time. The clock's 24-hour-per-day, 60-minutes-per-hour and 60-seconds-per-minute has given the impression of an evenly divided flowing time to those living in an industrial society. Clock time, in conjunction with industrial society, has "established a clock work of its own that imposes its beat even more powerfully on everyday activities than the natural rhythm of the alternating nights and days and of the changing seasons had imposed itself on life in traditional agricultural civilization."[54] The commitment to and dependence upon the clock by industrial society should not be a surprise because the clock is a machine itself and, according to Clarence Ayres, "the clock has been called the master pattern of all subsequent expedients in the field of power driven machinery."[55]

Technological advancement allowed for the development of science as well as industry. Since science was emphasizing the relativity of time, the scientific findings were inconsistent with the belief in absolute clock time. We might believe these findings would have made people more conscious of taking control of their own temporal arrangements. However, that has not been the case. "Social life in the industrially developed parts of the world, and especially in modern industrial surroundings, shows an ever-growing dependence on the clock and an ever-growing independence of the calendar."[56]

Although social life continues with clock time, industrial processes are now being changed to real time. This has come about because of the continued expansion of science and technology. It is the result of the integration of holistic science, instrumentalist philosophy, computer science, and computerized industrial production processes. "Contemporary science was criticized as being narrowly compartmentalized around Aristotelian subdivisions of subject matter. The case was developed for science oriented around real-world events and concerned with the regulation and control of events in real time."[57] As stated earlier, the system determines the measurement instrument. It is not dependent upon the clock of passing time. Real time is defined in a system context that takes account of the appearance, duration, passage, and succession of events as they are interrelated within a system. Real time concerns temporary and situationally contingent events amenable to regulation and control. In addition "it results in an extension of human mastery over such events."[58] As real time is extended in industrial and computerized systems, its concept will begin to affect more and more spheres of social and personal life. As the author recommended above, the next step should be to extend the use of real time for project evaluation. With the spread of real time, the computer will replace the clock.

Technological evolution, along with holistic science, will continue to change temporal constructs and extend real time in use and in concept. The extension will be used for socio-technical-environmental space-time planning and coordination. "Relative space is inseparably fused to relative time, the two forming what is called the spare-time manifold, or simply *process.*'[59] More and more, it is understood that local, regional, national, and supranational processes must be coordinated and controlled if humans are to solve problems. This will lead to system real time and beyond that to social time, where the events are not just sequenced by the system but the socio-technical-environmental system is determined by the conscious temporal concept of timeliness through discretionary social institutions.

The Lapps are currently suffering an income loss because of radiation contamination of their reindeer grazing area by the Chernobyl nuclear plant incident in Russia. The Mexicans have been suffering a loss of water because of the United States Colorado River dam system, which loses more water through evaporation than it preserves. These are supranational events that could have been foreseen and avoided with the application of scientific inquiry and the development of institutions such as international inspections of nuclear plants and water projects. The inquiry necessary for completing such scenarios was not completed because of the pell-mell rush for development and growth to fulfill the incessant command of passing time. That can change. Time can be tamed, inquiry enhanced, and institutions created. Human mastery over events can be and will be expanded, given the requirements of recent technology.

Space, time, location, and movement cannot be separated. Therefore, these concepts cannot be separated in our planning. "Without movement, whether tangible or intangible, there are no spatial relations, the main object of study in much of geography. Mere co-existence in space without any effect of one body or process on another is like time without change, or rather like change not producing other changes. . . . Space (and time) seem to be discovered by movement, especially by *locomotion.*"[60]

When we are talking about events and movement with regard to time and space we are, as the institutionalists have emphasized, talking about holistic processes. When it is understood that social processes are policy-based, then it is understood that process planning is necessary. For example there is a multinational interest, confirmed by treaties and other agreements, in the ducks, geese, and cranes that travel the flyways and staging areas of the United States. Yet the staging areas—wetlands, potholes, rivers, marshes—are constantly being destroyed, thereby leading to high rates of death and disease among the birds. If we want the birds, then their migration patterns must be coordinated with the environment and with human activity patterns. Events such as drawing irrigation water from the river, providing an adequate water flow in the riparian wetlands, and the arrival of the birds must be sequenced in time, space, and location, or the birds will not survive.

The kind of planning necessary for our interdependent technological system requires a different level than the simple one that just tried to fill the passing time of the clock with production events. We must now adjust and coordinate our beliefs, environment, technology, and so forth. It seems this is a step beyond real time where the system is used as the clock. This could be called social time where the system itself is structured.

Traditional time concepts and clocks are not sufficient for the space-time coordination that will take place in the future. "It is not unreasonable to argue that the very fact that we conceptualize human activity as forming a stream flowing through time (and space) suggests that a classification into activity types, sets or modules is either not possible or that it produces a severe and unacceptable abstraction of reality."[61] In order to successfully plan, coordinate, and monitor we must change the mode of conceptual notion and abstraction. The "clocks" of the future are more likely to be akin to computerized matrices, graphs, and diagrams. The basic reason graph theory is suggested as the likely format of our time instrument is that graph theory does not conceptualize society as flowing along in a stream, and it treats events as discernable entities. In addition, graph theory

> is a general modeling system for relations. . . . The use of the graph underlying a situation enables us to strip off *initially* unessential details. Even when some information is lost in looking only at the graph, this method of modeling may bring new insights by directing one's attention to the structural aspects of the relations being studied. Where theory exists about the nature of structural relations a graph or diagraph theoretic approach provides a means for testing theory. Where no theory exists or in the more likely situation of ill-defined theories in the social sciences, graphs and diagrams may generate well-defined schemes. Sometimes it is useful to concentrate on part only of the relation being studied; instead of the whole graph, one looks at a *sub-graph* formed by deleting some vertices and/or edges from the original.[62]

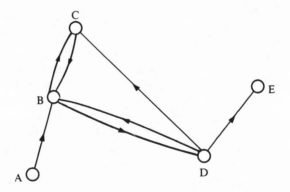

Figure 7. *Sample Diagraph*

A diagraph like Figure 7 can be used to represent the sequence of relations and the direction of deliveries among the components of the social system. Such articulation can be used to plan communication networks, or transportation systems, or pollution controls, or whatever needs to be coordinated in a timely manner.

The author has provided articles elsewhere on the use of matrices and diagraph theory for expressing institutional theory, defining socio-economic processes, and conducting geobased planning in conjunction with remote sensing and computer mapping.[63] The social fabric diagraph is consistent with activity sequencing called for by social time. Activity sequence

> puts social events into a system which is ideally timed by the succession of events relevant to that system, that is by *social time*. In other words, reference to universal or clock time becomes secondary to the internalized timing which is defined by the nature of activity sequence structure. We have yet to develop a timing system which is internalized to the relationship between events in a socially relevant cycle. Clock time still dominates.[64]

Sequence methodologies will help us determine and sequence the elements in our institutional structure and process. As W.E. Moore explained:

> Much of social behavior depends for its orderly qualities on common definitions, assumptions, and actions with regard to the location of events in time. Certain activities, for example, require simultaneous actions by a number of persons, or at least their presence at a particular time. . . . Thus one element of temporal ordering is *synchronization*. Other activities require that actions follow one another in a prescribed order; thus *sequence* is a part of temporal order . . . frequency of events during a period of time is critical; thus *rate* is also one of the ways that time impinges on social behavior. For all of these elements of social coordination the term *timing* is useful . . . timing is an intrinsic quality of personal and collective behavior. If activities have no temporal order, they have no order at all.[65]

To order our social systems, we must leave behind passing time, and ultimately move beyond real time to social time. In this way we can achieve the planning necessary for a supranational technological society.

Notes

1. John R. Commons, *Legal Foundations of Capitalism,* Madison: University of Wisconsin Press, 1968 [1923]), p. 379.
2. Thomas J. Cottle and Stephen L. Kleinberg, *The Present of Things Future:*

Explorations of Time in Human Experience (New York: The Free Press, 1974), p. 166.

3. Richard M. Gale, "Human Time," in *The Philosophy of Time*, ed. Richard M. Gale (Garden City, N.Y.: Anchor Books, 1967), p. 30.

4. Cottle and Kleinberg, *The Present of Things Future*, p. 166.

5. Ibid., p. 167.

6. Ibid., p. 168.

7. J.B. Priestly, *Man and Time* (Garden City, N.Y.: Doubleday & Company, 1963), p. 160.

8. Ibid., p. 172.

9. John Adams and Uwe J. Woltemade, "Village Economy in Traditional India: A Simplified Model," *Human Change* 39 (Spring 1970): 49–56.

10. Cottle and Kleinberg, *The Present of Things Future*, p. 162.

11. Priestly, *Man and Time*, p. 152.

12. Ibid., p. 158.

13. Ibid.

14. J.L. Russell, "Time in Christian Thought," in *The Voices of Time*, ed. J.T. Fraser (London: Allen Lane, The Penguin Press, 1968), p. 66.

15. Germano Pattaro, "The Christian Conception of Time," in *Cultures and Time* (Paris: The UNESCO Press, 1976), p. 189.

16. Russell, "Time in Christian Thought," p. 66.

17. Geddes MacGregor, *The Hemlock and the Cross: Humanism, Socrates, and Christ* (Philadelphia: J. B. Lippincott, 1963), p. 91.

18. George C. Lodge, *The New American Ideology* (New York: Alfred A. Knopf, 1976), p. 58.

19. Priestly, *Man and Time*, p. 166.

20. Ibid., p. 64.

21. Kenyon B. DeGreene,*Sociotechnical Systems: Factors in Analysis, Design, and Management* (Englewood Cliffs, N.J.: Prentice-Hall, 1973), p. 207.

22. Manfred A. Max-Neef, *From the Outside Looking in: Experiences in 'Barefoot Economics'* (Uppsala: Dag Hammarskjold Foundation, 1982), p. 150.

23. Ibid., p. 140.

24. Ibid., p. 150.

25. Priestly, *Man and Time*, p. 69.

26. Nicholas Georgescu-Roegen, *Analytical Economics: Issues and Problems* (Cambridge: Harvard University Press, 1966), p. 69.

27. Albert Einstein and Leopold Infeld, *The Evolution of Physics*, (Forge Village, Mass.: Simon & Schuster, 1938), p. 6.

28. Robert E. Ornstein, *The Psychology of Consciousness* (New York: Harcourt Brace Jovanovich, 1977), p. 105.

29. Priestly, *Man and Time*, p. 67.

30. Ibid., p. 69.

31. Keith Floyd, "Of Time and the Mind," *Fields*, 10 (Winter 1973–74): 47–57.

32. Ibid., p. 50.

33. F. Stuart Chapin, Jr., *Human Activity Patterns in the City: Things People Do in Times and Space* (London: John Wiley & Sons, 1974), p. 9.

34. Ibid., p. 10.

35. Ibid.

36. See Walter C. Neale's article, "Institutions," elsewhere in this volume.

37. F. Gregory Hayden with Larry D. Swanson, "Planning through the Socialization of Property Rights: The Community Reinvestment Act," *Journal of Economic Issues* 14 (June 1980): 351–69, at p. 354.
38. Howard H. Pattee, "The Role of Instabilities in the Evolution of Control Hierarchies," *Power and Control,* ed. Tom Burns and Walter Buckley (Beverly Hills: Sage Publications, 1976), p. 172.
39. DeGreene, *Sociotechnical Systems,* p. 61.
40. Ibid.
41. Harry W. Pearson did not define an excess of unwanted entities as surpluses; however the concept of surplus used here is intended to be consistent with his concept of relative surplus. See Harry W. Pearson, "The Economy Has No Surplus: Critique of a Theory of Development" in *Trade and Markets in Early Empires,* ed. Karl Polanyi, et al., (Glencoe: The Free Press, 1957), pp. 320–341.
42. *Real time* is something of a misnomer; a term more descriptive of the concept is *system time.*
43. Edward A. Nelson, "A Working Definition of Real-Time Control," P-3089 (Santa Monica: The Rand Corporation, 1965), p. 18.
44. Harold Sackman, *Computers, System Science and Evolving Society: The Challenge of Man-Machine Digital Systems* (New York: John Wiley & Sons, 1967) pp. 223–35.
45. Harold Sackman, "Futurists on the Future," *Los Angeles Business & Economics* 6 (Summer 1981): 21–36.
46. Sackman, *Computers, System Science and Evolving Society,* p. 42.
47. Ibid., p. 43.
48. Matrix of Environmental Residuals for Energy Systems is explained in: Council on Environmental Quality, *MERES and the Evaluation of Energy Alternatives,* publication 041–011–0026–2 (Washington, D.C.: U.S. Government Printing Office, 1975).
49. Sandor Szali, "Time and Environment: The Human Use of Time," *The New Hungarian Quarterly* 19 (Summer 1978): 138–39.
50. Max-Neef, *From the Outside Looking in,* p. 139.
51. Szali, "Time and Environment," p. 134.
52. Ibid.
53. A.J. Gurevich, "Time as A Problem of Cultural History," *Cultures and Time* (Paris: UNESCO, 1976), p. 242.
54. Szali, "Time and Environment," p. 135.
55. Clarence E. Ayres, *The Theory of Economic Progress,* (New York: Schocken Books, 1962 [1944]), p. 144.
56. Szali "Time and Environment," p. 133.
57. Sackman, "Futurist on the Future," p. 250.
58. Ibid.
59. J.M. Blaunt, "Space and Process," *Professional Geography* 13 (1961): 1–7, quoted in Edward L. Ullman, "Space and/or Time Opportunities for Substitution and Prediction," *Transactions Institute of British Geographers,* New Series 4 (1979): 121–37.
60. Ullman, "Space and/or Time Opportunities for Substitution and Prediction," p. 127.
61. Don Parkes and W.D. Wallis, "Graph Theory and the Study of Activity

Structure," in *Human Activity and Time Geography,* ed. Tommy Carlestein, Don Harkes, and Nigel Thrift (New York: John Wiley & Sons, 1980), p. 78.

62. Ibid., p. 81.

63. F. Gregory Hayden, "Social Fabric Matrix: From Perspective to Analytical Tool," *Journal of Economic Issues* 16 (September 1982): 637–62; F. Gregory Hayden, "Organizing Policy Research Through the Social Fabric Matrix: A Boolean Digraph Approach," *Journal of Economic Issues* 16 (December 1982): 1013–26; and F. Gregory Hayden, "Integration of Social Indicators Into Holistic Geobased Models," *Journal of Economic Issues* 17 (June 1983): 325–34.

64. Parkes and Wallis, "Graph Theory and the Study of Activity Structure," p. 77.

65. Ibid., p. 76.

Information: An Emerging Dimension of Institutional Analysis

William H. Melody

The functioning of society depends upon information and its effective communication among society's members. Information, and the means for its communication, have a fundamental and pervasive influence upon all institutions. The economic characteristics of information and communication systems affect the nature of the information that is generated and the conditions under which it is used and interpreted.

In the broadest sense, the social, cultural, political and economic institutions in any society are defined according to the characteristics of the shared information within those institutions. In the narrower economic sense, perhaps the most important resource determining the economic efficiency of any economy, industry, production process, or household is information and its effective communication. The characteristics of information define the state of knowledge that underlies all social and economic processes. They provide the foundation upon which explanations of social reality are structured.

Information is as central to the study of the functioning of economic systems as is air to the study of the functioning of the human body. Yet throughout the history of economic thought, information has received relatively little direct attention. Like air, information generally is assumed to be absolutely essential, but nevertheless pervasive, costless, and seldom worthy of special attention. If, in some circumstances, information is artificially restricted, economists of all stripes generally conclude that this is undesirable. It is assumed, sometimes naively, that

361

expanded information cannot help but improve the efficiency of any economic system.

In neoclassical theory, the fundamental assumption of "perfect information" or "perfect knowledge" typically is noted so that the analysis can proceed quickly to the important economic issues.[1] Institutional economists do not assume away the information issues, and on occasion draw attention to information deficiencies as part of explanations of economic problems. But even they only rarely have looked more deeply into the significance of information structures in society for the evolution of economic and social institutions. It is apparent that the structure of economic and political institutions in society creates serious information problems. Yet very little is known about the relations between information structures and other institutional characteristics, or how changing information structures affect the rise and fall of particular institutions.

It is indeed ironic that a profession that devotes itself to the pursuit of knowledge about the economic system has paid so little attention to the significance of information as a crucial factor affecting the performance and direction of change within the system. This article examines the concept of information within the context of the institutionalists' perspective. It illustrates the role that information has played in the work of selected leading institutionalists and argues that greater attention to the role of information offers promising possibilities for enriching the study of economic institutions. It also examines how new information and communication technologies are being applied in a manner that is likely to fundamentally alter the existing structure of economic institutions and to stimulate the development of a wide variety of "information markets" in a new rapidly growing sector of the economy.

In the economics literature the terms "information" and "knowledge" tend to be used interchangeably. To many people the term "knowledge" implies the notion of truth, or at least a higher level of intelligence or expertise. Such usage is not intended here. The terms will be treated essentially as synonyms meaning "to be aware," that is, to be informed. "Knowledge" sometimes denotes an aggregation of a range of different types of information, as in "the stock of knowledge," thus permitting information to be examined as having both a stock and a flow dimension. Communication adds an important spatial dimension to information and often introduces fundamental changes in the structure of information flows and the quality of the information communicated.

Information and Institutions

An institution, as succinctly described by Walton Hamilton "connotes a way of thought or action of some prevalence and permanence, which is embedded in the habits of a group or the custom of a people" [Hamilton 1968, p. 84]. Its dynamic character is vividly captured by Wesley Mitchell: "as ways of working shift, they will engender new habits of thinking, which will crystallize into new institutions, which will form the cultural setting for further cumulative changes in ways of working, world without end" [Mitchell 1936, p. 310].

Institutions reflect the patterns of interaction between and among individuals, acting within or between groups, or through formal organizations. Patterns of interaction may be determined by custom, law, organizational role or some other guideline for behavior. It is the patterns of interaction that maintain an institution, and changes in patterns of interaction bring about changes in institutions. The essence of this interaction is the communication of information.

Both the definition and structure of all institutions are significantly influenced by the state of information. Institutions are created from the development of a desire to share information, thereby cultivating patterns of interaction, that is, communication or information exchange. Institutions become structured in particular ways to achieve desired internal and external information flows. The institutional structure changes when, for whatever reason, the information flows change. Institutions die when the incentive or the ability to maintain the information flows and communication links ceases. Institutions can be described according to their informational characteristics, and one way to study institutional change would be to focus directly upon an institution's changing information structure.

Equally significant for economic analysis is the fact that institutions also generate information for the external environment that is employed by other institutions and individuals for decision making. For any particular institutional structure in society, there will be an associated information structure that will influence how that society functions. Some institutional structures will provide conditions and incentives conducive to the creation and diffusion of more information than others. The structure and quality of information is likely to change as a result of changes in institutional structure. If institutional change is desired, it may be necessary to change the information structure as a prerequisite to, or as an essential aspect of effective institutional change.

The importance of information flows and communication patterns to the establishment and maintenance of particular institutions has been well understood by policy makers since earliest times. Trade routes and communication links were deliberately designed to maintain centres of power and to overcome international comparative disadvantages. Britain still benefits substantially from its historically established communication links with its former colonies, long after the empire's formal demise. Universal telephone service was adopted as a policy objective in the Communications Act of 1934 to encourage economic and social interaction within the United States and to promote nationhood. The mandate of the Canadian Broadcasting Corporation includes a requirement to promote national unity. The European Economic Community is attempting to foster a new European identity by promoting increased communication and information exchange (including trade) among its member countries, in an attempt to ward off growing economic and cultural penetration of Europe, primarily by the United States. Those factors that influence information and communication structures are central to the study of all institutions, and sometimes are controlling with respect to economic institutions.

The Dimensions of Information

For purposes of economic analysis, information can be viewed from a number of different perspectives. One is as an overall enviromental condition, that is, the general descriptive information that provides the institutional background for economic decisions, such as news about political and social developments, the state of war and peace in the world, the crime rate, general employment levels in the economy, *et cetera*. Although such information is not tied directly to most individual decisions on economic matters, this background information provides assurance that the general institutional environment is reasonably stable. It provides the confidence for individuals to go ahead with decisions that will be made using other more direct and detailed information, and narrower and more precise decision criteria that are applicable only in a reasonably stable institutional environment.

The total body of this type of information provides a certain protection that minimizes the risk of short-term disaster. It is essentially a public good. It represents the broad information structures upon which the economy builds. It is a type of information "commons." The size and structure of the information commons may vary substantially among societies and among groups and sectors within societies. In developed countries, the information commons tends to be much more extensive than in developing countries. The characteristics of the information commons, including the type and structure of the information generated, and the terms and conditions for access to it are matters of fundamental importance to the study of institutional change. A change in the size and structure of the information commons may be an essential component of plans designed to promote desired changes in the institutional structure of society.

Many decisions require only instrumental, ephemeral information of no lasting decisional significance—for example, the price of strawberries in the local market today. Although any particular piece or bit of such information is relevant and applicable only to a single, specific short-run decision, it may be necessary to establish a communication system by which such information can be supplied on a continuing basis, as through stock quotation or press wire services, television and radio stations, the telephone network. The structure of the communication system established, in turn will cultivate particular patterns of interaction—that is, institutionalized behavior. In this instance the structure of the communication system established for supplying the information may influence the essential character of the institutional interactions more than the information itself.

Some information is of more lasting value and is stored in the memories of people, in books, on film, on computer tapes and in other ways. From a societal standpoint the accumulation of information represents the total stock of knowledge. It is increased as a result of improvements in science and technology, developments in the arts and letters, an improved understanding of the workings of society, and in other ways. From this perspective, technology can be represented as a particular application of stored information in the total stock of knowledge. New technical artifacts simply represent the physical embodiment of a particular set of information drawn from the state of knowledge. Considerable research is directed toward creating new information that will add to society's stock of knowledge. The accumulation of science and technological information in particular is seen as a stepping-stone to the accumulation of capital and economic growth. Most education and training involves an attempt to diffuse portions of the existing stock of knowledge throughout society.

The most significant application of the concept of information is with respect to the long-run accumulation and diffusion of knowledge in society. Its direct connection to the economic problem of the long-run accumulation of capital is through the concept of technology. If capital accumulation is stimulated by the application of new technologies, then the accumulation of information is at the heart of the capital accumulation process. In like manner, information is directly connected to the economic concern for the long-run diffusion of wealth and income. The diffusion of knowledge through education and training is not just a type of analysis where the information diffusion happens to run parallel to the diffusion of wealth. The diffusion of knowledge is an essential component of the process of diffusing wealth and promoting economic development.

It is of course necessary to note that not all information contributes to the stock of knowledge. But neither does all investment contribute to the stock of capital. There are crucial structural and qualitative aspects of both concepts that require careful consideration.

The concept of information also provides a common ground for relating economic issues to the social, political, and cultural aspects of institutions. Information is often a component of social, political, and cultural analysis, and where it is not, a manageable extension of the analysis often can capture it. The major difficulty that has persisted has been in linking up economic concepts with those of the other social sciences. The concept of information not only can enrich more narrowly based economic analysis, but also can provide a link to the other social sciences.

Information in the Evolution Of Economic Thinking

It is not possible to provide here a comprehensive review of the treatment of "information" in the history of economic thought. However an overview of selected landmark and illustrative applications will provide an appropriate historical context for addressing current issues.

Adam Smith, Karl Marx, and the classical school of economists were primarily concerned about the long-run accumulation of capital in a dynamic economic system and its implications for society. Although the concept of information was seldom used as a focal point for their analyses, the implications of information and communication systems upon economic institutions and economic growth were recognized frequently. In his classic explanation of how the division of labor is limited by the extent of the market, Smith noted the influence of the communication system as a crucial factor in determining the extent of the market, and thereby the division of labor: "As by means of water-carriage a more extensive market is opened to every sort of industry than water-land carriage alone can afford it, so it is upon the sea coast, and along the banks of navigable rivers, that industry of every kind naturally begins to subdivide and improve itself."[2]

In Smith's analysis of economic development he recognized that the diffusion of knowledge through the learning process was the corner-stone of development. The development of particular skills was essential to the division of labor. This information process would stimulate an increase in the productive powers of labor and the accumulation of capital.

Marx made frequent reference to the role of communication systems in the evolution of capitalism. In *Grundrisse,* he stated:

> the more production comes to rest on exchange value, hence on exchange, the more important do the physical conditions of exchange—the means of communication and transport—become for the costs of circulation. Capital by its nature drives beyond every spatial barrier. Thus the creation of the physical condition of exchange—of the means of communication and transport—the annihilation of space by time—becomes an extraordinary necessity for it.[3]

Marx frequently drew attention to the fact that improvements in the means of communication facilitate competition among workers in different localities and turn local competition into national. He argued that the opportunities created by the development of transport and communication facilities tended to drive capitalism in the direction of ever more remote markets until a world market is reached. He even foreshadowed the development of markets in information itself:

> Institutions emerge whereby each individual can acquire information about the activity of all others and attempt to adjust his own accordingly, e.g., lists of current prices, rates of exchange, interconnections between those active in commerce through the mails, telegraphs, etc. (the means of communication of course grow at the same time). This means that, although the total supply and demand are independent of the actions of each individual, everyone attempts to inform himself about them, and this knowledge then reacts back in practice on the total supply and demand.[4]

In contrast, the neoclassical school, in attempting to tighten up its analytical apparatus, established the assumption of "perfect information" or "perfect knowledge" in neoclassical theory, thereby restricting their frame of reference to static analysis, freezing technological options and the state of knowledge. The fundamental dynamic issues of the long-term accumulation of capital and economic growth over time, and under conditions of changing information, technology, and institutions were simply excluded from consideration.

It should be noted that there have been attempts to break out of the straitjacket of neoclassical theory by relaxing its most suffocating assumption of perfect information, while still retaining its basic analytical structure. For example, there has been a recognition that neoclassical theory depends crucially on the characteristics of the structure of property rights that have been assumed [Demsetz 1967]. Efficient markets must be supported by an efficient system of property rights. Unfortunately the usual solution is to assume a perfect market in tradeable property rights. In addition, Kenneth Arrow, Kenneth Boulding, Friedrich von Hayek, Fritz Machlup, Jacob Marschak, George Shackle, Herbert Simon, Jack Hirshleifer, Donald Lamberton and others have exposed further weaknesses and limitations of neoclassical theory arising from its assumption of perfect information. These critiques, coming primarily from neoclassical economists, have painted neoclassical theory further and further into the corner as a unique theory, so abstracted from reality as to be of little, if any relevance.[5] Nevertheless, the neoclassical school continues to perform more and more elegant intellectual pirouettes in its attempts at theoretical restoration of the perfect information assumption.

Institutional economists and most Keynesians have carried on in the tradition of Smith, Marx and the classical economists. They too examine the long-term development of the economy within analytical frameworks where issues of information and communication in the economy are recognized as significant aspects of the institutional structure. Imperfect information forms an integral part of Keynesian analysis. For example, Keynes's explanation of wage rigidity rested primarily on the fact that labor would rely on information of wage-rate experience (that is, historical information) in negotiations for future wage-rates, not on perfect information about future labor markets. Keynesian analysis often considers the deficient, real world information that decision makers actually rely on as an important factor in the analysis. Similarly, business cycle theorists from all schools of economic thought have recognized the crucial influence of lagged information on current decisions as a determinant of the course of economic development.

In addressing the long-term dynamics of capitalism, Joseph Schumpeter focused upon the "creative destruction" of technological change as a primary force bringing about change in economic, social, and political institutions. He spawned a growing field of research directed to explaining innovation and diffusion processes in the evolution of the economy, in which the diffusion of information plays a significant role, for example, through patents. This has led to the study of science and technology policies that might promote the accumulation of new knowledge that will stimulate the invention and innovation of new technologies.[6] Although this line of research is not often associated with institutional economics, it is operating within the same theoretical framework.

For the most part, institutional economists have tended to treat information and communication in much the same manner as the classical economists and the Keynesians. Where and when it has been revealed as a significant factor in the analysis it has been recognized and incorporated. Veblen, for example, emphasized that consumer preferences were learned and conditioned by the information environment, and that the conditions of supply were primarily determined by the institutional implications of technical change. He rejected the fundamental assumptions in neoclassical theory with respect to information as applied to both demand and supply in establishing his overall analytical framework for institutional economic analysis. Within this general overall analytical framework, the accumulated and shared information within the institutional structure of society becomes a major determinant of the conditions of demand and supply.

John R. Commons extended the analysis to encompass institutional reform through government regulation, that is, "collective action in restraint, liberation, and expansion of individual action'' [Commons 1934, p. 73]. But effective regulation requires information with respect to the potential implications of various reform possibilities and standards of regulation. Although Commons was directly involved in the design of many social reforms, and painstakingly gathered substantial empirical information as a basis for those reforms, he did not really focus directly upon the state of information as a key factor in his institutional analysis. Nevertheless, it must be observed that many of the social reforms arising from Commons's research had the effect of expanding the information available to less powerful groups in society, thereby improving their negotiating power.

For most of the current generation of institutionalists, the structure of information in society is not a major issue directing their research, although information deficiencies do arise reasonably frequently as part of explanations for inequalities in society. For a few, information has become more central. For example, Philip A. Klein has concluded that concentrated corporate wealth and power corrupts the flow of information to the general public. This prevents the real "emergent values" of the majority from arising and a "higher efficiency" level in the economy from being achieved. Klein's institutional reform centers on the information structure in society so that the nation's decision making is more informed and more sensitive to the real values of the majority of consumers [Klein 1985].[7]

Harold A. Innis

Harold A. Innis was one of the few economists to attempt a full integration of evolutionary economics and information and communication into a social science based institutional analysis.[8] His early work in the 1920s on the economic history of Canada showed how the westward expansion of Canada was influenced by an extension of the transport and communication system to meet political and economic objectives [Innis 1923]. His next work showed how the economic development of Canada was influenced by the demand for furs in Europe, Canada's unique geographical characteristics, and the drive of technology to exploit the fur resource [Innis 1956].

He then turned to the implications of the development of mechanized communication, beginning with printing, publishing, and mass communication via radio. He showed how the enormous expansion of a commercially based printing press, and an emphasis on freedom of the press, had tended to support institutional changes such as the growth of monopolies, the entrenchment of biased viewpoints and the extension of compulsory education. He argued that these developments tended to intensify nationalism, constrain freedom of speech, and resist the power of thought. The press and radio broadcasts to the world, he argued, do not address the individual or facilitate dialogue.

Finally Innis broadened his scope of inquiry to a study of the history of communication in the development of civilizations. He focused particularly on the role communication systems have played in extending the power of "empires." He argued that in any society the media of communication greatly influences the forms of social organization and thereby the patterns of individual association. New competing communication media alter the forms of social organization, create new patterns of association, develop new forms of knowledge, and often shift the centers of power.

In his books *Empire and Communications* and *The Bias of Communication* Innis observed that any medium of communication is "biased" in its tendency to permit control over extended periods of time or over extended geographical space [Innis 1964; 1972]. He argued that communication and information systems used in ancient civilizations such as parchment, clay, and stone were durable and difficult to transport. These characteristics are conducive to control over time, but not over space. These systems are time-biased. Paper is light, less durable, and easily transportable with reasonable speed. It is spatially biased; it permitted administration over great distances, and therefore, the geographical extension of empires.

In cultural terms, time-biased media are associated with traditional societies that emphasize custom, continuity, community, the historical, the sacred, and the moral. They are characterized by stable, hierarchical social orders that tend to stifle individualism as a dynamic for change, but permit individualism in the rich expressiveness of language and the range of human emotion. Time-biased communication systems are found in societies with rich oral traditions or with sophisticated writing technologies where access is limited to a privileged few.

Space-biased communication and information systems, for example, the modern media of print, telephone, radio and television, have an orientation toward the present and the future, the expansion of empires, an increase in political authority, the creation of secular institutions and the growth of science and technical knowledge. They are characterized by the establishment of systems of information exchange and mass communication that are extremely efficient, but which cannot convey the richness, diversity, and elasticity of the oral tradition.

Innis concluded that the particular technology of communication and information systems, depending upon their bias, tended to confer monopolies of authority and knowledge either on religion, through sacred order and moral law, or on the state, through the technical order and civil law. An overemphasis, or monopoly of either time- or space-biased modes of communication was the principle dynamic of the rise and fall of empires. Such a bias toward either time or space produced instability in society. A stable society was possible only with the development of mechanisms that preserved a balance between the time and space orientations.

Innis was unique among his contemporaries in recognizing the high degree of interdependence between economic institutions and communication and information systems. He noted that communication patterns and information flows are central to economic development. He argued that communication technologies are the building blocks for most other technologies in the economic system. At the same time he recognized that economic incentives and market forces have powerful influences on communication patterns and information flows, which cannot be ignored in any realistic analysis of communication and economic development [Melody, Salter and Heyer 1981, Chap. 1].

In recent years there have been only a few economists working directly at the intersection of economics and communication and information institutions. Leaders among these include Herbert I. Schiller and Dallas W. Smythe. Schiller has documented many of the evolutionary changes in social institutions that are beginning to unfold as the new information and communication technologies are introduced and has examined the relations between changing information and communication institutions and economic and political developments [Schiller 1981]. Smythe, a pioneer in the exploration of the economics of communication, has drawn particular attention to the role of the mass media in creating and conditioning consumer preferences and in molding public opinion and has examined its significance for economic theory of all kinds.[9] Smythe also has examined the implications of U.S. domination of the information and communication environment in Canada for Canadian economic dependency, Canadian collective consciousness, and the development of economic policy that contains desired "cultural screens" [Smythe 1981].

Information and Markets

The concept of information in institutional analysis is not discrete, standing alone or alongside the economic concepts. Rather it is an integral part of most economic concepts used by institutionalists. Information is an important dimension of other concepts, including such key concepts as "technology," "consumer preference," and, as has been shown above, the fundamental concept of "institution." Economists ignore the information dimension of these concepts at their peril, as it may be crucial for the effective application of the more familiar economic concepts.

This can be illustrated by reference to one of the most important concepts in economic analysis, that is, the "market." Throughout history, the notion of the market has preoccupied economists. Different schools of economic thought conceive of market relations differently, but a concern for the nature of market relations and their implications always has rested at the very heart of economics.

The general definition of a market is the provision of exchange opportunities between buyers and sellers. Without exchanges, or transactions, there is no market. The rate of exchange is the market price, which is determined by the conditions of supply and demand. Certain aspects of the market can be examined as an abstract exercise in logic by assuming that the only matter of significance is a single exchange price at a moment in time, and then varying the number of buyers and sellers—and quantities supplied and demanded—under conditions where each has perfect information and is maximizing short-run profit. This grossly oversimplified analysis, typical of neoclassical theory, tells us something about the nature of market exchanges, but it also leaves out alot. It focuses on a few surface characteristics of markets and a method of calculation, ignoring the institutional foundation of the market and many important structural aspects of markets, all of which are essential to preparing the ground for the ultimate market exchanges.

An exchange can only take place if there is a commodity, or service, to be traded. Trade requires ownership, that is, enforceable property rights in the commodity being traded. The specific characteristics of property rights in tradeable commodities have varied significantly over the last several centuries and do so today among different countries, and even among localities within countries. The notion of property rights, as C.B. MacPherson has demonstrated, embodies a large collection of specific rights that define the terms and conditions for the use and exchange for property [MacPherson 1978]. It is a dynamic concept subject to ongoing change, as current debates in many countries relating to changes in patent and copyright laws demonstrate. The vast majority of goods and services that are exchanged do not carry with them total freedom for the owner of the property to do with it whatever he or she pleases. Zoning regulations, product safety standards, and cultural norms illustrate some of the constraints on the terms and conditions of trade.

This is an area where the work of Commons is so instructive. Examining more deeply the concept of the market exchange, Commons enriched it by treating it as a social relation rather than a statistical artifact. He defined the social relation as a "transaction," rather than a simple exchange, thereby capturing a sense of the real world participants in the exchange as something more than abstract entities. The participants were "going concerns," engaged in the exchange of ownership rights in accordance with a set of "working rules." The working rules specified a system of rights and obligations for citizens in their transactions with others. Much of Commons's research was directed to gathering detailed information about the nature and determinants of "transactions." Then economic problems could be addressed by taking legal or other steps to change the underlying structure of rights and obligations embodied in working rules and ownership. Commons was working at the institutional foundation of markets rather than focusing on surface manifestations.

Commons's analysis may have been enriched if he had paid more attention to the information dimension of his concepts, because differences in the informational aspect of the neoclassical concept of "exchange" and Commons's concept of "transaction" are significant. The information associated with a market "exchange" in neoclassical theory is essentially limited to price information. That is the key, if not the only factor governing the exchange. The market "transaction" involves much more information that is not readily available, and therefore not recognized by the concept of exchange. Although Ayres is certainly right in criticizing the "obsession of our science with price theory," one of the difficulties of digging deeper into the institutional foundations of economic concepts is that the information aspects tend to become more significant, but also often more difficult to assess [Ayres 1944].

The historic debate in economics between the relative merits of the market versus central planning as the best mechanism for allocating resources most efficiently in society hinges upon the role attributed to information and communication. Hayek's seminal 1945 article, "The Use of Knowledge in Society," cogently presented the case for the superiority of the market. He stated:

> The various ways in which the knowledge on which people base their plans is communicated to them is the crucial problem for any theory explaining the economic process. And the problem of what is the best way of utilizing knowledge initially dispersed among all the people is at least one of the main problems of economic policy—or of designing an efficient economic system. [Hayek 1945, p. 520].[10]

The system that is most efficient, argued Hayek, depends "mainly on the question under which of them we can expect that fuller use will be made of the existing knowledge" [Hayek 1945, p. 521]. The knowledge that is needed is the overwhelmingly massive amount of detailed unorganized information with respect to the particular circumstances of individual buyers and sellers. Such information cannot hope to be captured in time, if at all, to facilitate coordinated central planning. The beauty of the price system is that it is a mechanism for capturing and communicating all this detailed unorganized information that reflects the myriad of individual buyer and seller, day-to-day decisions under continuously changing circumstances.

Economists cannot disregard the "unavoidable imperfection of man's knowledge and the consequent need for a process by which knowledge is constantly communicated and acquired" [Hayek 1945, p. 530]. Argued Hayek, "To assume all the knowledge to be given to a single mind in the same manner in which we assume it to be given to us as the explaining economists is to assume the problem away and to disregard everything that is important and significant in the real world" [Hayek 1945, p. 530].

Most neoclassical economists marvelled at the triumph of the market, but rejected Hayek's advice. Having accepted the fact of real world information deficiencies to shoot down the central planning option as horribly imperfect, most neoclassical economists have fled from the challenge of examining information deficiencies in real world market systems, preferring to maintain the idealistic perfect information assumption. This of course begs the real issue that Hayek raised. To the best of my knowledge, there has been no serious testing of Hayek's information hypothesis, either by neoclassical or institutional economists, although the work of Machlup can be seen as offering potentially relevant insights on this issue [Machlup 1980–1984].

Hayek assumed perfect knowledge on the part of individual buyers and sellers with respect to their own individual alternatives, preferences, circumstances, and ability to maximize their own best interests. He relaxed the perfect knowledge assumption only with respect to the knowledge that individual buyers and sellers would have about the behavior of all other buyers and sellers or about the complex set of market interrelations in the economy. But he also assumed that individual supply and demand would be unaffected by developments about which the individual sellers and buyers had no information. Thus, he assumed that individual demand was independently determined, and not influenced by the demand of others or any other external events.

The problem Hayek addressed then was how to use this known "perfect information" that individuals had about their own circumstances most efficiently to allocate resources in the economy. But the advantage Hayek claims for the market only applies to a condition of perfectly competitive markets. When markets are imperfect, individuals do not have sufficient information to know what will best serve their own interests. Boulding makes the point well.

It is one thing to look at a price tag and to know that any amount can be bought or sold at this price. It is quite another thing to discover a demand function, which is a set of *possible* prices and *possible* quantities, only one of which is given in present experience. Thus making what seems like a simple extension of the model from perfect markets to imperfect markets actually involves us in an information problem of first magnitude. We move from a situation where the information required for the making of a rational decision is a simple number such as a price, given by simple observation, to a situation where the information required is a set of functional relationships which are *not* given by simple observation, because what needs to be known is not what *is* but what *might be*. Of course, what needs to be known for a rational decision is always what "might be." In the case of perfect competition, however, the happy situation prevails that what might be can be deduced immediately from what is at the moment. In the case of imperfect competition this is not so. In one case we are driving a straight road and can easily project our present direction for miles ahead; in the second case we are driving a twisting mountain track where we cannot see more than a few feet round the bend, and where the position of the moment tells us very little about where we might be next week. [Boulding 1960, underscoring in the original].

Moreover, even if the prices in imperfect markets did capture the perfect knowledge by individual buyers and sellers with respect to their individual circumstances, those market prices would not bring about an efficient allocation of resources. Under monopoly conditions, for example, this information would simply result in a monopoly price. In imperfect markets, a requirement for an optimal allocation of resources would be that prices not be set on the basis of this limited set of perfect knowledge by individual buyers and sellers.

In addition, Hayek's assumption about independent atomistic decision making based on individual preferences made in a vacuum, and uninfluenced by other individuals, institutions, and developments in the economy, is necessary to keep his market alternative from being defeated by the same information complexity problem that he attributes to central planning. In addition, Hayek does not address the issue of coordinating non-price information, a common function for social institutions; nor does he entertain the possibility that in some circumstances collective decisions may yield better results for all individuals than the sum of individual decisions. Moreover, since information does not conform to the classical properties of privately supplied commodities, it is likely to be underproduced relative to what would obtain if it were a perfect private good [Arrow 1962; Samuelson 1954]. Further, many types of information take on the characteristics of public goods.

Hayek clearly has not demonstrated the superiority of the market as the most efficient system for allocating resources. He has drawn attention to one aspect of the problem that has highlighted an advantage of coordination of certain types of information through market prices. But his real contribution has been to focus debate in this long-standing economic controversy upon the role and characteristics of information in the institutional structure, a crucial aspect of the issue that far too often is neglected. It is disappointing that the debate on this important information issue has not been sharpened significantly since Hayek's article. An efficient allocation of resources in society will require an institutional structure that contains elements of both planning and markets. It is important that the structure be designed to reflect the comparative advantage of each in the areas to which they are applied. On the basis of the present state of knowledge, economists can offer precious few guidelines on this fundamental policy issue.

More recently, O. E. Williamson has used an updated version of the Hayek analysis to argue the opposite case. He has introduced the concept of "transaction costs" to neoclassical theory in recognition of the fact that in imperfect markets involving complex technologies, the costs of negotiation may become significant. Although Williamson claims that his concept of transaction costs is drawn from Commons, and that his analysis represents the "new institutional economics," the concept does nothing more than recognize that market transactions are not free (a traditional assumption of neoclassical theory). Institutional issues are not even addressed.

According to Williamson, transaction costs are driven up by bounded rationality, opportunism and asset specificity, that is, inadequate information, a failure of communication, and a high degree of uncertainty. Because market transactions are too complex and costly it is more efficient to integrate vertically and horizontally, thereby avoiding the market and the necessity for settling on a price. By avoiding the market, large conglomerate corporations will be in a better position to plan and to supply their products more efficiently. Apparently large-scale planning is now superior to the market in coordinating economic activity. Williamson does not attempt any empirical tests of his theory; nor does he discuss the relative merits of public versus private planning. His case rests upon assumptions about the information and communication characteristics of the market transaction in a technologically advanced economy. The information and communication aspects of this issue definitely need attention from institutional economists.

Some Characteristics of Information
in the Information Economy

Some authors believe that society is moving beyond industrial capitalism to an information-based economy.[11] In fact, detailed investigation certainly would show that societies have always been information-based. The oral traditions of the most primitive tribes were rich in information. The changes of recent years have been primarily in the market characteristics of information. First, the technology of generating, processing, and transmitting information at drastically reduced unit costs has provided quantum leaps in the capacity to supply information. Second, in the real economic markets—if not the economic theories—it has been discovered that many kinds of information heretofore not provided through formal market systems, have high exchange market values. It is now profitable to search for many new kinds of information that, in times past, were not sought because it was not profitable. Information that previously was outside the market and not included as economic activity has now been drawn into the market.[12]

The rapid rise of information markets is made possible by the interaction of advances in computer and telecommunication technologies. Advances in the computer industry have pushed back the intensive limit of the market by reducing the costs of generating more and more kinds of data. Advances in telecommunication have pushed back the extensive geographical limit to encompass global markets. However, it is important to distinguish the economic implications of the new technology facility systems that provide the infrastructure within which information is generated and processed, and over which it travels, and the information services themselves—the content that is provided over the facility systems.

In the narrow economic sense, the facility systems of computers, satellites, fibre-optic cables, terminals, and so forth, are no different, as a production process, than any other production or manufacturing process. What renders the facility systems important is that the information services must be provided over them. Therefore, the efficiency of the facility system is a significant factor influencing the efficiency of the information services provided over them. A nation with an efficient facility system may have major advantages in the competition for global information markets that will cut across most information services.

Information as an Economic Resource

The stock of knowledge in society, the skills and education of the populace, the detailed factual information relating to such things as science and technology, the working of production processes, the interrelationships among the different sectors of the economy, represent a primary resource. The value of this stock of knowledge to society depends upon how pervasively it is spread throughout that society and upon the institutions for maintaining, replenishing and expanding the stock of knowledge, that is, its educational and training system and research generating new knowledge. Economic benefits come in the form of improved decision making throughout the economy.

Once information has been generated, the cost of replicating it is very much lower than the cost of generating it in the initial instance. The consumption of information by one user does not destroy it, as occurs with almost all other resources and products. The information remains to be consumed by others, the only additional costs being those associated with bringing the same information and additional consumers of it together under conditions where it can be consumed, that is, learned. And once a given level of penetration is reached, a multiplier effect comes into play with many types of information, as the information is spread throughout society outside the formal processes of learning and training. Hence, although the costs of adding to the stock of knowledge may be very great, there are generally very significant economies in diffusing that information throughout society, and to other societies, if the incentive exists to do so. The implications of this economic characteristic of relatively low-cost replication of information can be extremely beneficial under some circumstances, such as the spreading of knowledge, but it creates special problems and difficulties under other circumstances.

Much of the information that has become important as a resource input to industrial and commercial production processes is specialized information sought to provide "inside" knowledge of the behavior of purchasers of a firm's products, suppliers of a firm's other resources, competitors, government regulators, and the like. In essence, in imperfect economic markets, this inside information for private consumption strengthens the negotiation and marketing position of the organizations that have access to it. Such information may or may not be costly to obtain, but its economic value clearly lies in its scarcity—in the monopoly of information. Once such information becomes generally known to all interested parties, its economic value dissipates drastically.

Specialized information services for the private consumption of a restricted clientele are springing up daily. They range from special research studies of the details of international markets for a group of transnational corporations to confidential assessments of the negotiating strength of a specific customer, competitor, labor union, or government regulatory agency for a specific negotiation. Because of the low cost of replication of such information—usually the cost of using the nearest copying machine—and the relative ease of information theft, which does not require the physical removal of the information, the value of such information can be extremely tenuous without extreme security. The same economies of information replication that can facilitate the spreading of knowledge throughout society can lead to the rapid destruction of the economic value of many kinds of specialized knowledge.

Information as Final Consumer Product

The characteristics of information as a final consumer product vary depending upon what kind of information is desired, by what users and for what purposes. Perhaps the greatest potential expansion of the information market now underway is for specialized data that can: (1) facilitate decision making, for example, shopping selections; (2) permit greater efficiency in the performance of certain activities, for example, banking; and (3) provide new forms of entertainment, for example, video games. The combination of specialized data banks, computer programs and advanced telecommunication systems make possible individual access through the market to specialized information for private consumption. The economic incentive for the act of promotion and expansion of such systems is very great, given the drastically reduced unit costs of adding subscribers to systems already established.

The new technologies also make possible the creation of specialized data banks of detailed personal information about individuals for selected users like credit bureaus or government agencies. In many instances, the market value of this information is greater if access to the information is restricted. This has raised concern that the new market conditions for information make it both profitable and efficient for invasions of personal privacy.

Many governments already have taken steps to attempt to restrain the march of information markets into the details of people's personal lives and to regulate the conditions of access to certain kinds of data banks, such as, credit, medical, and tax files. The pursuit, sale and use of information in accordance with the incentives of the marketplace apparently is not going to be unrestricted. In the Commons tradition, a change in the working rules of social interaction will modify the institutional nature of these transactions.

The mass entertainment market, most pervasively illustrated by television, takes on somewhat different characteristics. The economies of information replication are very substantial. The costs of copying program information already created is nominal, and the cost of serving larger audiences rather than smaller ones is minimal. With satellites, the additional cost of transmission to more locations is reduced to the cost of the receiving terminals. With the new telecommunication technology, the economies of replicating existing information have become enormous. In addition, the market value of mass entertainment information is not based on restricting access to this information, but in promoting it. Those restrictions that do exist from time to time are tools to maximize profit through discriminatory pricing, rather than attempts to restrict the scope of the market.

News, as a particular form of public or mass information, has very similar economic characteristics to mass entertainment. The major differences are the time sensitivity of the economic value of most news and the fact that most news is sold as an intermediate product by news agencies to distributors such as newspapers and television stations. Finally, we should recognize those unique information markets where purchasers pay to have selective information sent to influence third parties, that is, advertising. This, of course, introduces a special problem of the quality of the information because frequently the market incentive is to supply misleading information.

Some Implications for Industrial Structure
and Market Development

Information markets can be classified into two general categories: (a) those in which maximum market value is achieved by the maximum dispersion of the information; and (b) those in which maximum market value is achieved by restricting information to specialized users who value its scarcity and seek a monopoly of specific information. The former is represented primarily by information provided to the public for mass consumption and is best illustrated by entertainment television; the latter is represented by the generation of specialized information that provides a valuable knowledge differential relative to adversarial interests, and is illustrated by confidential assessments of the strengths and weaknesses of negotiating adversaries.

The maximum dispersion category is characterized by extremely low costs of information replication. With increasing costs for generating original information and reduced costs of replicating it from previous already low levels, the economic incentives to expand the market for existing information to a global basis are increased. In application, this means, for example, that the economic incentive to dump old U.S. television programs in greater quantities and in more countries is increased. The differential cost to other countries of choosing to produce original material at home instead of purchasing U.S. network reruns, is increasing significantly.

The second category, markets based on creating a monopoly of certain information, is less influenced by the low costs of information replication, although buyers with similar interests may economize by sharing in certain information purchases. Rather, information generation becomes a focal point for competing interests attempting to obtain a competitive advantage. As such, it imposes a cost on all competitive and adversarial interests if they hope to maintain their relative positions in the market. An opportunity is provided to buy an information advantage. A barrier to entry is created for those who cannot afford to compete at the information game. Since most major market transactions in international commerce ultimately boil down to bilateral monopoly, or oligopoly negotiations, the new information possibilities have the potential for significantly affecting the results of such negotiations. Transaction costs of the Williamson variety may simply be a manifestation of the tendency of oligopoly markets to create artificial barriers to entry that appear in the form of increased transaction costs.

The production characteristics of relatively high costs of establishing most data services and relatively low costs of extending the market for services already created provide a powerful force toward centralization of control and monopoly. Thus, competitive forces in many information markets are likely to be rather weak. This, in turn, can be expected to raise important issues of government policy with respect to information monopolies.

As a commodity, information can be extremely tenuous. The quality of information may vary substantially. And quality control may be impossible. It is certainly impossible to know in advance whether information you are receiving is truthful and accurate. If you knew, you would not be buying the information. And for many types of information, it will be impossible to assess the quality of it even after the fact. The risks of carelessly assembled, false, misleading and biased information are increased because of the inherent characterisitics of information as a marketable commodity.

The extension of the market to encompass information as a commodity also opens a market in its shadow for misinformation. The more valuable formal information becomes to decision-makers, the more devastating misinformation can be. If demands for positive information to enhance a firm or government agency's relative position can be met through the market, then the same objective could be achieved by purchasing misinformation and having it sent directly to an adversary.

Public Policy Issues

The successful development of information markets for the benefit of all sectors of society will require major adaptations by both private and public institutions. If markets in tradeable information are going to work efficiently and equitably, they must be developed upon a foundation of public information that provides the education and training necessary for citizens to function effectively as workers, managers, consumers and responsible citizens. Determining the appropriate adaptations, both by the public and the private sectors, to the new information and communication environment is a crucial task to which institutional analysis can contribute significantly.

Many individuals and organizations can benefit substantially from the rapid expansion of the information and communication sector, but at least some are likely to be disadvantaged, in both relative and absolute terms, especially if traditional public and social services are displaced, downgraded or made more expensive. To illustrate, a considerable portion of the information now accessible through public libraries is subject to commoditization and sale in private markets, where it would be accessible only through telecommunication-based information services. In recent years, many libraries have expanded access to a variety of bibliographic databases. But they have cut back their physical holdings of government reports and statistics, general research reports and studies, periodicals, and even books. This has facilitated research projects with the funding support to pay for computer searches and acquisition of the desired material. But most academic researchers, students, and the lay public can rarely afford to use computer searches, and are increasingly frustrated by the more limited access to hardcopy resources.

The telephone system is being upgraded to the technical standards of an integrated services digital network (ISDN) that is more efficient for the plethora of new information services required by sophisticated high volume users. But it may be significantly more expensive for small volume users and users with only local telephone service requirements. This could make it more difficult to extend basic telephone service coverage to a larger proportion of the population [Melody 1986].

The characteristics of information markets create special problems associated with the technological transfer of computer and telecommunication technologies to developing countries. The market incentives are to sell new technology facility systems in developing countries to establish the infrastructure for both the domestic and international communication of information services. Given the established base of information in the technologically advanced countries, and their lead in establishing new information services, the information flows are predictable. Final consumer information, such as television programs (often accompanied by advertising), is likely to dominate the flow from developed to developing countries. Specialized information markets that create value as a result of the monopoly of information is likely to generate a dominant flow of information about developing countries to developed countries and transnational corporations. Indeed these trends have already been documented.[13] These conditions in the information market will facilitate the penetration of developing country markets for the full range of economic goods and services by those organizations that have access to the specialized information. Of course, it may place developing country firms and agencies at an increased competitive disadvantage in their own countries because of an information deficiency about conditions there.

A major challenge for public policy will be to find methods to ensure that developments in the information and communication sector do not exacerbate class divisions in society and that its benefits are spread across all classes. This will require new conceptions and operational definitions of the "public interest" and of public services, new interpretations of the requirements of social policy, and the design of new institutional structures for its effective implementation.

Conclusion

The concept of information has been central both to economic problems and to economic theory of all kinds. In most circumstances, information issues have not been formally recognized because they are embedded as an integral part of more familiar economic concepts. But, as has been demonstrated above, the solution to many classic economic debates rests on the analysis, or assumptions, with respect to the information aspects of the problem.

The rapid improvements in information and communication technologies that are now being implemented throughout the world portend fundamental changes in society's economic, political, social, and cultural institutions. The growing importance of mechanized information and communication, and of the global markets that they permit, will force economists of all schools of thought to examine more carefully the information dimensions of their theories.

For institutional economists, conditions could not be better. Dynamic institutional change is forcing the concerns of public policy to pay more attention to those issues that institutionalists study. In the evolving institutional structure of society, opportunities are appearing for institutionalists to develop their research so as to inform public policy decisions. Now they have an opportunity to do more than just interpret the world. In the Commons tradition, they can participate in changing it!

Notes

1. George J. Stigler has observed:

> One should hardly have to tell academicians that information is a valuable resource: knowledge *is* power. And yet it occupies a slum dwelling in the town of economics. Mostly it is ignored: the best technology is assumed to be known; the relationship of commodities to consumer preferences is a datum. And one of the information producing industries, advertising, is treated with a hostility that economists normally reserve for tariffs or monopolists [Stigler 1968, p. 171].

2. Smith [1977], quoted in G. J. Stigler, *Selections from The Wealth of Nations* (New York: Appleton-Century-Crofts, 1959), p. 15.
3. Marx [1977], quoted in Yves de la Haye, *Marx and Engels on the Means of Communication.* (New York: International General, 1979), p. 125.
4. Ibid., pp. 102–3.
5. See Lamberton [1984]; also Lamberton [1971].
6. See Nelson and Winter [1982] and Freeman [1982].
7. See also Gruchy [1986, at pp. 813 and following].
8. See Melody, Salter, and Heyer [1981].
9. Dallas W. Smythe, "Communications: Blind Spot of Economics," in Melody, Salter, and Heyer [1981].
10. See also Arrow [1974].
11. See for example: Bell [1973] and Porat [1978].
12. See Melody [1985].
13. See for example: Pipe [1979a] and Pipe [1979b].

References

Arrow, K.J. 1962. "Economic Welfare and the Allocation of Resources for Invention." In *National Bureau of Economic Research: the Rate and Direction of Inventive Activity: Economic and Social Factors,* pp. 609–25. Princeton University Press.

———. 1974. "Limited Knowledge and Economic Analysis," *American Economic Review* 64 (March): 1–10.

Ayres, C.E. 1944. *The Theory of Economic Progress: A Study of the Fundamentals of Economic Development and Cultural Change.* Michigan: New Issues Press, Western Michigan University.

Bell, Daniel. 1973. *The Coming of Post-Industrial Society: A Venture in Social Forecasting.* New York: Basic Books.

Boulding, K. E. 1960. "The Present Position of the Theory of the Firm." In *Linear Programming and the Theory of the Firm.* Ed. K. E. Boulding and W.A. Spivey, pp. 1–17. New York: Macmillan.

———. 1966. "The Economics of Knowledge and the Knowledge of Economics," *American Economic Review* 56 (May): 1–13.

Commons, John R. 1934. *Institutional Economics: Its Place in Political Economy.* Madison: University of Wisconsin Press.

Demsetz, H. 1967. "Toward a Theory of Property Rights," *American Economic Review* 57 (May): 347–59.

Dorfman, J. 1934. *Thorstein Veblen and His America.* New York: Viking.

Freeman, C., ed. 1982. *The Economics of Industrial Innovation.* London: Frances Pinter.

Gruchy, Allan G. "The Cremona Foundation and the St. Mary's College Conference on Institutional Economics." *Journal of Economic Issues* 20 (September 1986): 805–23.

Hamilton, Walton H. 1968. "Institution." In *International Encyclopedia of Social Sciences,* Vol. 3. New York: MacMillan.

Hayek, F.A. von. 1945. "The Use of Knowledge in Society," *American Economic Review* 35 (September): 519–30.

Innis, Harold A. 1923. *A History of the Canadian Pacific Railway.* Toronto: Toronto University Press.

———. 1956. *The Fur Trade in Canada.* Toronto: University of Toronto Press [1930].

———. 1964. *The Bias of Communication.* Toronto: University of Toronto Press [1952].

———. 1972. *Empire and Communications.* Revised by Mary Q. Innis. Toronto: University of Toronto Press [1950].

———. 1973. "The Work of Thorstein Veblen." In *Essays in Canadian Economic History.* Ed. Mary Q. Innis, pp. 17–26. Toronto: University of Toronto Press [1929].

Jussawalla, M. and Lamberton, D.M., eds. 1982. *Communication Economics and Development.* New York: Pergamon Press.

Klein, P.A. 1985. "A Reappraisal of Institutionalism—its Critics and Adherents." Statement presented to the Conference on Institutional Economics, June.

Koopmans, T. C. 1957. *Three Essays on the State of Economic Science.* New York: McGraw-Hill.

Lamberton, Donald M. 1984. "The Emergence of Information Economics." In *Communication and Information Economics*. Ed. Meheroo Jussawalla and Helen Ebenfield, pp. 7–22. New York: North Holland.

———, ed. 1971. *Economics of Information and Knowledge*. Middlesex: Penguin.

Machlup, F. 1980–1984. *Knowledge: Its Creation, Distribution, and Economic Significance*. Princeton, N.J.: Princeton University Press.

Macpherson, C.B., ed. 1978. *Property: Mainstream and Critical Positions*. Toronto: University of Toronto Press.

Marx, Karl. 1977. *Grundrisse: Foundations of the Critique of Political Economy*. London: Penguin Books [1939–1941].

Melody, William H. 1985. "The Information Society: Implications for Economic Institutions and Market Theory." *Journal of Economic Issues* 19 (June): 523–39.

Melody, William H., L. Salter, and P. Heyer. 1981. *Culture, Communication, and Dependency: The Tradition of H.A. Innis*. Norwood, N.J.: Ablex.

———. 1986. "Telecommunication: Policy Directions for the Technology and Information Services." *Oxford Surveys in Information Technology*, Vol. 3,

Middleton, K., and M. Jussawalla. 1981. *Economics of Communication: An Annotated Bibliography with Abstracts*. New York: Pergamon Press.

Mitchell, Wesley C. 1964. *What Veblen Taught: Selected Writings of Thorstein Veblen*. New York: Sentry Press Reprints of Economics Classics [1936].

Nelson, R.R. and, S. Winter. 1982. *An Evolutionary Theory of Economic Change*. Cambridge, Mass: MIT Press.

Newman, Geoffrey. 1976. "An Institutional Perspective on Information." *International Social Science Journal* 28: 466–92.

Pipe, G. Russell. 1979a. "National Policies, International Debates." *Journal of Communication* 29 (Summer): 114–23.

———. 1979b. "Transnational Information Flows." *Intermedia* 7.

Porat, M.U. 1971. *The Information Economy*. Washington: Office of Telecommunications, U.S. Department of Commerce.

———. 1978. "Global Implications of Information Society." *Journal of Communication* 28 (Winter): 70–80.

Samuelson, P.A. 1954. "The Pure Theory of Public Expenditure." *Review of Economics and Statistics* 36 (November): 387–89.

Schiller, Herbert I. 1981. *Who Knows: Information in the Age of the Fortune 500*. Norwood, N. J.: Ablex, 1981.

Schumpeter, Joseph A. 1954. *A History of Economic Analysis*. Ed. Elizabeth Boody Schumpeter. New York: Oxford University Press.

Smith, Adam. 1977. *An Inquiry into the Nature and Causes of the Wealth of Nations*. 5th ed. New York: Modern Library.

Smythe, Dallas W. 1981. *Dependency Road: Communications, Capitalism, Consciousness and Canada*. Norwood, N.J.: Ablex.

Stigler, George J. 1968. *The Organization of Industry*. Homewood, Ill.: Irwin.

Veblen, T. 1919. "The Place of Science in Modern Civilization." In *The Place of Science in Modern Civilization*. New York: Viking.

Power and Economic Performance:
The Institutionalist View

Philip A. Klein

Economists rarely define economic power with precision. In general
we may take it that economic power refers to the ability to influence
decisionmaking. To possess economic power is to be able to exercise
significant control over the decisionmaking process. Economists generally agree, for example, that the Sherman Act was designed to do
something about "too much" power to set market prices. The public,
to take another example, generally regards Dwight Eisenhower's celebrated farewell address warning of the dangers inherent in the "military
industrial complex" as referring to a threat to the viability of the system
emanating from constellations of power. There are other examples. It
is fair to say, however, that with few exceptions, power is not a central
concern of mainstream economists today.

Microeconomics texts continue to present a picture of how the market system operates that makes relatively few references to market failures. Referring to them as "market imperfections" manages to remove
a good deal of the sting that might adhere to the charge that concentrations of economic power make allocation, as in fact it occurs in our
economy, quite different from the competitive ideal. (Indeed, if one factors in modern technology, the competitive ideal may no longer be an
ideal.)

---

*The author wishes to thank William M. Dugger, Jerry L. Petr, and Marc R. Tool for
their helpful comments on an earlier draft.*

389

In both macroeconomics and microeconomics, questions are raised about what the economy could achieve technologically, about what we collectively wish our economy to do, about the relation of these two, and about how to judge economic performance. Questions about the extent to which, either by means of prices in the market or by any other allocation mechanisms, we are in fact managing to get from our economy what we would like to get from it, are not easily posed, let alone answered. Instead of attempting to factor in the role that economic power plays in total resource allocation, mainstream economics often moves in precisely the opposite direction—searching for ways to blur more and more the line between what we have and what we want from our economy.[1]

This article will argue that power is a major factor today affecting the way our economy confronts its tasks. Furthermore, the view taken toward power and its impact on the economy can be directly related to the central thrust of modern institutional economics, in contrast to classical economics, current mainstream economics, and radical economics.

What do economists mean by power? Conventional mainstream economics begins with a competitive model in which the deployment of power is presumed to be precisely what has been institutionally sanctioned. Note that it is not equal, nor has equality in the distribution of power ever been part of the competitive model. Competitive producers are initially presumed to have equal power in the sense that they are all of the same size, have the same degree of control over resources, and are equal in their ability to offer products in the market. But the consumers in this model are certainly not equal. When "demand," as opposed to "desire," is expressed by "one dollar, one vote," surely then the more dollars one controls the more "power" one has.

This simple consideration of even conventional competitive theory suggests, of course, the essence of economic power—the ability to influence allocation. We may define power, therefore, according to the central problems considered in the most conventional view of economics—what to produce, how to produce, and for whom to produce. The greater one's ability to determine how any of these three questions, or their logical extensions, get resolved, the greater is the individual in question possessed of what we call economic power. Concentration of power is, therefore, partly a mathematical matter. If there are N persons in an economy, any departure from $1/N$, say, in answering basic economic questions represents some concentration in economic power. We shall see that economic power has ramifications far beyond this arithmetic beginning.

Power must be distinguished from authority. Power is technological and authority is institutional. One economist distinguished these terms this way: "Power means the ability to decide, to influence, to control . . . . *Authority* resides in those who have the weight of law, custom, and of society's deepest values vested in them."[2] When a judge says, "By the power vested in me by the state of *Z*, I pronounce you husband and wife," he really means the authority. The power to say "I pronounce you husband and wife" is possessed by virtually everyone, but it lacks significance until it is institutionally sanctioned by the granting of the authority to make this pronouncement legally (culturally) meaningful. We shall see that a major difficulty in economic analysis is to confront realistically the extent to which power is exercised—perhaps tacitly or covertly—in the absence of the authority to use it. The illegal exercise of power is a major factor in any analysis of how the economy operates and is an addition to the consideration of how the legal impact of power on economic activity affects total allocation.

Some Definitions

Some time ago I defined economic power simply as "disproportionate control over the decision-making process."[3] We here use "disproportionate" merely to denote the deployment of power according to criteria that may not have any explicit societal confirmation. In the polity, "one man, one vote" is explicit, and approved, but can be wholly or partly overwhelmed by influence that is concentrated and that, therefore, can control votes. In the economy, "one dollar, one vote" is affected by the distribution of income, which is determined by myriad forces, only some of which are explicitly societally sanctioned. Constellations of power acquired deliberately by large units in pursuit of their own goals, can be "disproportionate" in this sense, even though the "appropriate distribution of power," in the sense of being socially sanctioned, may itself be complex and is certainly far from "equal." By power, we mean essentially, then, one's ability to influence the way the economy operates to carry out the tasks assigned to it. For this reason, Warren Samuels has called the economy a "system of power," arguing that the power system can be defined according to resource allocation, income distribution, and the determination of basic economic results, such as the level of income, output, employment, or prices. In all of these, the question of "whose interests count" is what we refer to when we speak of economic power.[4] A part of economic power, therefore, in modern mixed economies surely involves affecting the role of the government in making the basic economic decisions alluded to above. This is what Randall Bartlett has termed "influence." He has written, "The production of influence . . . involves attempts by agents to increase their real incomes by altering relevant decisions made in the public sphere."[5] The assumption that what is at issue is acquiring more of the real income may unduly limit the notion of influence. Keeping competitors out, influencing the "wants" of consumers, affecting the outcomes of elections so as to maintain certain views in the elected officials, or preventing the election of officials with other views—all these and the myriad other ways in which power or influence is exerted may be related to real income and its distribution only in the very long run, if at all.

It is clear, therefore, that mainstream economic theory rarely, if ever, confronts the full panoply of factors that affect the power structure of an economy. Even when competitive assumptions are dropped, the presumed behavior of economic agents seldom encompasses anything like the complete catalogue of factors affecting resource allocation in the modern economy.

For example, in modern times it is by no means unusual for a prospective president, vice president, or cabinet officer to choose or to be required to put personal family holdings in large corporations into "blind trusts." Having done so, do these individuals make decisions affecting resource allocation in the same way they might have made them had they not had the experience of owning significant shares in certain corporations? The answer is by no means clear. The economic impact might be different had they not had these connections or had they instead been forced to divest themselves of shares in a trade union or a consumer cooperative. We suggest only that this state of affairs has profound implications for the way economic power is in fact deployed in the economy and how, therefore, it affects resource allocation.

In a sense, the institutionalist's concern with power and its implications for the economy is an extension of the more general unwillingness among institutionalists to follow orthodox economists in their *ceteris paribus* assumptions. A critical basic distinction between evolutionary and orthodox economists revolves not on any difference of opinion concerning the necessity to simplify and generalize in developing theory, but over assessing the simplifications and the generalizations utilized against the reality to which the theory must be applied. If the critical imperfections that require better public policy are consistently subject to excessive oversimplification in the pursuit of spuriously precise or general theory, the procedure becomes self-defeating. From the earliest fixation on perfect competition to the newest developments in rational expectations theory, mainstream economics has too often taken this path, with the result that public policy lags drastically and major economic problems go largely unattended. The implications for economic performance lurking in the existence of our current power structure are most conspicuously included in this charge. All this suggests that a good institutional analysis of the role of economic power in the operation of the economy could fill a major void in current economic analysis.

Power and Policy: The Locus of Power

We shall see that mainstream economics, therefore, despite some exceptions, has consistently taken the power system as it in fact emerges from the economy as appropriate or as institutionally sanctioned, and therefore not requiring debate. In mainstream theory, the actual locus of power is coterminous with where it is assumed to be. Things are what they seem. The convenience of this perspective is undeniable. The appropriateness depends largely on whether one follows mainstream economics in regarding the economy as largely an allocating mechanism, allocation being narrowly defined, or if one follows institutionalists in regarding the economy as a valuational mechanism concerned as well with analyzing the path followed by an economy through time.[6]

The point is that the power system in the U.S. economy, to stay close to home, is regarded by the mainstream in a way that is analogous to the way physicists regard the law of gravity. How prices are set, how resources are allocated, in short, how societal inputs become societal outputs—all this is surely affected by the actual power structure we have. "Radical economists" can be distinguished perhaps because they take a particular (and disapproving) attitude toward the power structure. It does not follow that the "positive economics" that mainstream economists revere can appropriately begin by taking an approving attitude. The extant power structure could be regarded dispassionately, but it is not. This confusion produces much of the further confusion between normative and positive, and surely obfuscates the path of analytical progress in considering where the participants in the economy might collectively wish to see it head.

Political scientists can presumably with profit and candor consider the road to a better functioning and more democratic polity; psychologists can scarcely consider what it means to be "well-adjusted" without considering the nature of the society to which the individual must adjust. Economists alone, among social scientists, begin by assuming that "what is," is a value-free base from which to analyze (in our case economic) performance.

Approaches to Power

If one begins, as we have, by thinking of economic power according to the degree to which one can affect the basic allocational function assigned to the economy, it is possible to draw certain useful parallels with political science. The polity is devoted to basic decision making, in this case, in the area of governance. We have defined economic power, similarly, to refer to the degree to which individuals or individual units affect the decision making process. "Powerful" individuals in the executive branch, for example, are "close to the President." Charles E. Lindblom and Robert A. Dahl, who have done work together and separately, are typical of this perspective in political science.[7]

Dahl, for example, has suggested that "a key characteristic of a democracy is the continuing responsiveness of the government to the preferences of its citizens, considered as political equals."[8] From this basis one can define political power as the disproportionate responsiveness of the government to a unit holding power. One specifically compares the powerful unit to other units to measure the degree of power inequality in the political units. There is simply no comparable parallel in economics (either normative or positive), because there is no unambiguous notion of what being considered "economic equals" would mean. Holding an accumulation of dollars, that is, votes (wealth), brings with it disproportionate influence on government, in the sense that holding one million dollars may connote much more (or less) influence than would be suggested mathematically by the holding of one thousand dollars. The power of, say, General Motors, is not encompassed by equating it to several million consumers with dollar holdings equal to the dollar holdings of GM. In a well-known study, C. E. Lindblom comments on the interrelations between economic and political power. He notes that conflict between business and electoral controls is partially obscured because they are not really independent, but coordinated. The polity accommodates the business interests so that electoral activity and business-interest group activity merge.

> One of the conventional insensitivities of contemporary social science is revealed in scholarly works on interest groups ... many such works treat all interest groups as though on the same plane, and in particular they treat labor, business, and farm groups as though operating at some parity with each other. ... No other group of citizens can compare with

businessmen, even roughly, in the polyarchal process. . . . The ease with which executives can bring corporate assets to the support of . . . activities is a remarkable feature of politics in market-oriented polyarchies. It has no rationale in democratic theory.[9]

Lindblom goes on to suggest that business people succeed in remarkable degree in persuading citizens that they want what business people want. Institutionalists have long made a similar point. John Kenneth Galbraith, for example, noted that "production creates the wants it seeks to satisfy." He called it the "dependence effect." Subsequently, he developed the notion of the "technostructure," which, as a matter of policy, excludes from decision making the corporate owners, creditors, workers (usually unions), consumers, and the government.[10]

Our concern with all this should be clear. In assessing the performance of the polity, political scientists must inelucatably confront these matters. In the process, a reasonably clear notion of what power means and how pervasive power affects the most fundamental operation of the system must be contemplated. Finally, while we shall note some concern with certain aspects of power (particularly in applied fields of mainstream economics) there is nowhere any real concern with or analysis of the implications of power on the fundamental operation of the economic system. Instead, the actual deployment of power is part of the status quo and is fundamentally accepted and incorporated into the base from which economic analysis is undertaken and on which it is ultimately evaluated.[11]

Classical Economics

In this critical sense, the vaunted *wert frei* neo-classical positive economics Lord Robbins did so much to popularize is by no means without its own normative baggage.[12] We surely need not pause long to consider the approach to power of classical and neo-classical economics. Even mainstream economists who may understand little of what early American institutionalism meant know principally that they disapproved of conventional price theory and its assumptions. In a new assessment of Thorstein Veblen, John Commons, and Wesley Clair Mitchell, Martin Bronfenbrenner recently commented, "when we try to define institutionalism pragmatically as whatever these three leaders hold in common, we are reduced to little beyond dissatisfaction with the standard or mainstream economics of their orthodox contemporaries."[13]

But Bronfenbrenner tries to move beyond this and produces a listing of early institutionalist objections to conventional economic theory. The first objection is that standard economics is "basically an apologia for the status quo and for the vested interests."[14]

While the institutionalist's objections to price theory are well known, the point we have been at pains to establish—that classical "positive economics" took a profoundly normative attitude toward the *prevailing* economic power system—was not appreciated, although Gunner Myrdal, among others, has made it.[15] It is still not appreciated. Milton Friedman has written more than perhaps any other modern economist on the positive nature of the neo-classical system as it pertains to current mainstream economics. Like a political scientist who assumed that because we call our system a democracy it has insignificant departures from the implications of "one man, one vote," Friedman assumes that the basic deployment of power in the economy is consonant with the allocational implications of one man, one vote, translated into economic terms. As we have seen, this may begin with "one dollar, one vote"—but even this understates the role of economic power.

Friedman's position is well known and needs little attention here. In *Capitalism and Freedom,* for example, he noted,

> The characteristic feature of action through political channels is that it tends to require or enforce substantial conformity. The great advantage of the market, on the other hand is that it permits wide diversity. It is, in political terms, a system of proportional representation. Each man can vote, as it were, for the color of tie he wants and get it; he does not have to see what color the majority wants and then, if he is in the minority, submit.[16]

This succinctly summarizes the essence of the assumed democratic allocation of conventional economic theory. It represents the valuation implication of competitive price theory, (the invisible hand, et cetera). It presents a world in which Pareto optimality is an acceptable welfare standard, and in which concern with the impact of economic power, our main concern here, is nowhere to be seen. It is, finally, the world in which positive economics can be viewed as totally *wert frei*, a perspective we have already considered.

It may, of course, be argued that Friedman was more concerned with current mainstream economics than with the neo-classical or classical economics we have been considering. In this connection, we may note that if economic power cannot be conveniently ignored in connection with earlier economic thought, it surely cannot be ignored in connection with an analysis of current economic activity. It is to this we now turn.

Current Mainstream Economics

It can be argued that today there is no economy left in the industrialized world in which a significant part of total resource allocation has not been removed from the market and placed in the public sector. There is no economy in which the public sector does not provide for national defense—the area about which no one from left to right would argue that "the market" should provide. But there are other areas for the public sector in every economy as well—some role for "welfare," however defined, some regulatory functions, et cetera.

If one focuses on current mainstream microeconomic theory, one can certainly buttress the old notions that (1) the mainstream continues to dwell excessively on the competitive model (which abstracts from concern with economic power), and that (2) institutionalists (among others) are still concerned with power. The inadequacies of conventional price theory continue to be what they have always been and we shall not retrace this familiar ground here.[17] Instead we shall consider several areas of current concern in mainstream economics in an effort to see whether present concern with concentrated economic power can be viewed there as more realistic.

Industrial Organization

The field of industrial organization has been traditionally the area where efforts to develop public policy have caused mainstream economists to drop the traditional assumptions of micro-theory with their reassuring laissez-faire implications for public policy. Traditional concern focused on how to achieve the results promised by theory but threatened as soon as economies of scale were recognized as making efficiency in competitive markets unlikely in much of the manufacturing sector of a modern economy.

The aftermath of the "imperfect competition revolution" in theory led to concern with what sort of public policy to develop for imperfectly competitive markets.[18] That the theory on which such policy need be based was never as satisfactory as competitive theory, has made the policy debates in industrial organization that much more difficult.

We neither can nor need to review the policy deliberations in industrial organization in detail here to make the major point required: in this field, concern with the kind of economic power we are discussing has never been very prominent; there have always been ways to approach the problem that enabled economists to reach soothing conclusions; the efforts to confront economic power that have been developed

frontally there are, in most ways, weaker now than they were a generation ago. These points can be substantiated relatively succinctly.

Traditional industrial organization approached the task of developing public policy proposals during the years following World War II.
Developed by E. S. Mason, and adumbrated by Joe S. Bain, F. M.
Scherer, and others, it related market structure and conduct to economic performance. The dimensions of each of these basic categories
was spelled out in some detail, but ultimately the test of acceptability
revolved around performance—allocational efficiency, profit rates,
rates of progress, and so forth.[19] Here the ways to dispel concern with
what concentrated businesses were doing to the presumed allocational
splendors emanating from the way in which our economy in fact operated have become myriad. J. M. Clark made a significant start many
years ago by transmogrifying the "perfect competition" that it was clear
we did not have (despite the attention given to it in price theory
classes), into "workable competition."[20] This is a much more slippery
concept in which public policy could be viewed benignly if the market
results led to a system that could be regarded as "reasonably or work-
ably competitive"—for example, profits were not too high, rates of progressiveness were reasonably high, and cost reductions appeared to be
mostly passed on to consumers. The degree to which significant departures from textbook competitiveness escaped serious concern and in
which lax policy was considered successful was probably rather high.

There were voices in the industrial organization field who echoed the
concerns of institutionalists. Corwin Edwards, for example, was much
concerned with what he called "excessive power," and at one point advocated a public policy alternative that would have been a major departure from the selective use of the antitrust laws that characterized much
of the policy proposals emanating from industrial organization specialists. He suggested that we "establish a rebuttable presumption against
bigness in excess of some relatively high level of size. Assuming that
bigness is typically dangerous and therefore objectionable, such a policy would tolerate the large enterprise only where bigness could be
shown to be necessary to the public interest.[21]

This approach, like the approach advocated much earlier by Henry
Simon (either establish industries that are atomistically competitive or
nationalize them), would have changed radically the industrial and economic landscape of the American economy, particularly the manufacturing sector, so as to leave it virtually unrecognizable. It would have
required large enterprises to justify their size or face dissolution. The
broad unworkability of such an approach emerges from the dominant

role of large enterprises in determining channels of influence, manipulating all other participants in the economic process and so forth. It would fly in the face of the fundamental institutional verities of the U.S. economy, which we referred to earlier, which mainstream economics consistently subsumes in "positive economics" despite its large normative implications, about which political scientists occasionally write, and about which institutionalists have consistently been concerned.

More recently, E. S. Herman has updated the work of A. A. Berle and Gardiner Means and reached the same sort of disquieting conclusions reached by Corwin D. Edwards. Corporate power has been maintained and even enhanced, with serious implications for the impact corporations have on the welfare impact of total allocation.[22]

The field of industrial organization has now moved beyond the structure-conduct-performance paradigm, but not to the kind of concern Edwards epitomized. William J. Baumol, John C. Panzar, and Robert D. Willig have, for example, developed the notion of "contestable markets." This notion begins with the earlier assumptions concerning the ability of extant firms to prevent new firms from entering the market. "Perfectly contestable markets" are markets that are "accessible to potential entrants," and such entrants can actually enter and serve customers with costs and prices like those of existing firms. "The power of potential competition to extend the beneficent sway of the invisible-hand is the central theme of our book."[23]

It is clear that, however useful within a relatively narrow range this formulation may be, it is singularly lacking in the sweep or clarity of the Edwards perspective. It fails to address the larger power question of concern to us here. It can serve as a justification for wide departures from the kind of competitive theory in which the invisible hand could legitimately be regarded as safeguarding the public interest within a system peopled by self-interested units. Baumol, et al. argue:

> Perhaps the most noteworthy implication of contestability theory is that a wide difference in appearance between a particular market and the form of perfect competition need not deprive the invisible hand of its power to protect the public interest. With the abandonment of the unrealistic standard of perfect competition as the model of market behavior, many old rules of thumb which have served as guides for antitrust agencies must be permitted to fall by the wayside. Whatever the appearances . . . we can no longer accept as *per se* indicators of poor market performance evidence such as concentration, price discrimination, conglomerate mergers, nor vertical or horizontal integration. . . . In contestable markets all of the ostensibly questionable phenomena that have been listed *can* be desirable

and should, indeed, be presumed so, with the burden shifted to those who
in any particular case maintain the contrary.[24]

This view is virtually opposite from Edwards's "rebuttable presumption" and, not surprisingly, the authors concluded that "contestability
analysis leans on those who advocate extension of the domain of
laissez-faire.'[25] It does not lean, however, in the direction of institutionalist concerns with the implications of pervasive power concentration
over how the system operates globally and over how responsive it is to
the collective will of all its participants.

So viewed, contestability is another approach, comparable in its impact on public thinking to workable competition. The latter is a view
incorporating the notion that products compete (as steel versus alumi-
num) so that market concentration measurements are misleading. Indeed John Kenneth Galbraith's early concept of countervailing power,
developed in his book *The Affluent Society,* is yet another such approach, and there are others. All these have the effect of eliminating the
fears departures from competition in industry historically have raised,
and that have made so complex the efforts to reconcile the automaticity
of the welfare implications of pure competition with the actualities of
markets in the real world. Institutionalists have never been sanguine
about these efforts in micro-theory. There is little to justify greater optimism about the parallel efforts in the applied field of industrial organization.[26]

Finally, we may note that from time to time voices in industrial
organization raise concerns that institutionalists can recognize and
easily relate to.

> Corporations do not simply pursue their own self-interest within the ex-
> isting institutional framework. They also pursue their self-interest in *at-*
> *tempting to determine the nature of that institutional framework.* . . . it can
> be argued that corporate gains are more than just disproportionally *active.*
> They also seem to be disproportionally *rewarded.* When they lean their
> great weight on the government's dinner table, it typically tilts in their
> direction.[27]

Also typical is the ultimate conclusion reached. Having raised the
question of what economic power, its concentration, and its deployment, do to the essential functioning of the system, the issue is all too
frequently simply dropped. Subsequent evaluation of the performance
of the economy reverts to traditional notions such as misallocation
leading to "deadweight loss," the virtues (or vices) relative to various
efforts at regulation, and so forth. While these can and are judged var-

iously, the critical question of how power might affect the basic operation of the system, and of its ultimate impact on what I have elsewhere called the "higher efficiency" of the system (to which we shall return in a subsequent section) is simply finessed.[28]

In a similar vein, a recent study of the costs of monopoly power concluded "the costs of monopoly power, calculated on an individual firm basis, are on average large. . . . A large part of this problem lies not in the height of monopoly prices and profits *per se*, but in the resources wasted in their creation and protection."[29]

The authors go on to note that one line of reasoning against attempting to change this situation is that these efforts stimulate large "defensive expenditures" on the part of the affected businesses. They conclude by noting that this question is difficult to answer, but that the costs of and benefits of alternative antimonopoly policies must be pursued. However, such pursuit is not, as we have noted, a major effort in the modern field of industrial organization. Either the question is defined away in some manner, as in the notion of contestable markets, or it is simply not addressed. In this respect industrial organization is an appropriate reflection of the mainstream micro-theory from which it stems (even if, as we have noted, some concerns having an institutionalist slant are from time to time voiced by a few industrial organization specialists).[30]

Public Choice Theory

In the past thirty years there have been a number of efforts in mainstream economics to apply economic reasoning to the allocation that occurs in the public sector. Because they all are concerned with allocation under conditions where traditional competitive conditions do not pertain and where the decisions are not necessarily made in markets, we must consider briefly the implications of such an approach—broadly construed—for the treatment of economic power.

In a sense, public choice theory is an outgrowth of public finance, the applied field within mainstream economics that explicitly considers how market-oriented economies (most particularly, our own) allocate in the public sector. It is fair to say that public finance customarily accepts the mainstream distinction between the normative and the positive, recognizes that economics views equity largely in distributional terms, and finds Pareto optimality surpassingly useful.[31] As such, it is not unfair to say that concern in public finance with the implications of the basic power system for the effectiveness with which the system serves all its participants is not highly developed.

Public choice theory, therefore, may be viewed still as a part of public finance. It is concerned with how governmental decisions affecting resource allocation are made. There is now a journal, *Public Choice*, which tells us that the field is concerned with "the intersection between economics and political science. It started when economists and political scientists became interested in the application of essentially economic methods to problems normally dealt with by political scientists. It has retained strong traces of economic methodology, but new and fruitful techniques have been developed that are not recognizable by economists."[32]

A leading early figure in the effort to apply economic methods to political decisionmaking was Anthony Downs (who now is on the Board of Editors of *Public Choice*). One can, of course, debate the usefulness of applying neo-classical economic methods to political decisionmaking. Some years ago I observed, "Anthony Downs may have shown what economic logic can do for political science; the potential in the reverse direction may well be greater."[33]

Other major figures in the development of public choice theory have been James M. Buchanan and Gordon Tullock, who have in general viewed governmental intervention as producing inefficient results—often, they argue, as inefficient or more inefficient than the "market failures" that stimulated the initial intervention. Anthony Downs, on the other hand, has argued that voter ignorance can produce too little rather than too much intervention, a position not far from Galbraith's.[34]

In general, public choice theory has been developed in an attempt to establish the position that whatever the market failures, or presumed failures that appear to justify governmental intervention, it is always possible that governmental activity will make a bad situation worse.[35]

While, in general, public choice theory regards itself as contributing to positive rather than normative analysis, it almost invariably concludes that the useful role of government is limited and is thus usually apt to prefer *laissez-faire* to interventionist economic policy. Thus, it is essentially normative.

A recent effort within public choice theory to analyze the behavior of those with some degree of economic power is termed "rent-seeking." Developed by Tullock, Richard Posner and Anne O. Krueger among others, rent-seeking suggests that much inefficiency is introduced into a modern economy by the competitive efforts of monopolists.[36] Welfare economics in mainstream economics regards rents as payments to resource owners in excess of opportunity costs. Welfare losses are analyzed as the confiscation of part of the consumer's surplus. Modern rent-seeking theory concentrates on the fact that the effort to acquire rents leads to distributional fights that do not add anything to the welfare of the consumers in the economy. Efforts to acquire these rents can take all sorts of forms—such as bribery, fraud, or coercion. "Rent-seeking involves social waste . . . rent seeking, as such, is totally without allocational value."[37]

In general, it seems fair to say that while these efforts deal with developments that have occurred in applied mainstream economics because of perceived failures in the market, most have rationalized very limited intervention, if that. Moreover, as an area where institutionalist concern with the impact of concerted economic power on the functioning of the economy would likely surface, we may say that this concern of institutionalists is rarely expressed and consistently either ignored or downplayed.

Radical Economics

The radical economists (Marxists, neo-Marxists, et cetera) take the same perspective as institutionalists on the significance of economic power in the manner in which the economy fulfills its role in society. A major point we shall attempt to substantiate here is that the distinction between institutionalist and radical economists is not so much in the difference in perspective from which they examine the role of power in economic activity as in the conclusions they draw from that examination. (One well-known American radical economist, Howard Sherman, would perhaps disagree with this distinction. He classifies social scientists as "conventional," as dogmatic Marxists, and as "non-dogmatic Marxists." In his view, conventional social scientists encompass both conservatives and liberals, (and presumably include institutionalists, although he does not use the term). One presumes, too, that he includes all non-Marxists who accept too much of the status quo to justify distinguishing among them. The second group is what he calls "dogmatic Marxists," and these are too inflexibly in the original Marxist mold to be credible. The third group, in which he places himself is the "non-dogmatic Marxists," whose critiques of capitalism are "humanist.")[38]

Traditional Marxist thought is founded in class-bound units—the capitalists, who had power, the laboring class, which was powerless. Economic activity revolved around little else than the tensions built up by the development of power. "The capitalist mode of production and accumulation, and therefore capitalist private propery, have for their fundamental condition the annihilation of self-earned private property; in other words, the expropriation of the labourer."[39]

Paul M. Sweezy, one of the best known of American post-World War II radical economists, has similarly viewed "capitalist class interests" as deriving from ownership of the essential property, and has moreover regarded the state as co-opted to protect these interests. "The state in capitalist society has always been . . . the grantor of capitalist property relations. In this capacity it is unmistakably the instrument of capitalist rule."[40]

"Capitalist class rule," of course, refers to the economic power that emanates from ownership of wealth, and suggests it is a pervasive conditioner of economic performance.

If class warfare was the heart of the Marxist analysis of economic operation, power was, therefore, the coin of the realm that conditioned the outcome of the struggle. The notion of exploitation is basic to Marxist analysis and what it measures primarily is the degree of economic power obtained by some participants in the economic process at the expense of others. Exploitation is precisely what those with a great deal of power could do and, therefore did do, to those who had little or no economic power.

On reflection, it is apparent that the essential dynamic in Marxist analysis has always been in the origination of profit in surplus value—value produced by labor but never given to labor. Marxist analysis of capitalist operation necessarily revolves around competition to acquire this surplus value. All this ultimately reflects the power emanating from differential relations among the means of production. The distribution of power conditions and determines the ultimate development of capitalism.[41] One need not impute evil intentions to the capitalists. They act as they do because of their relationship to the means of production (as do the workers). Change is not possible without altering the relationship of participants to the means of production. Exploitation consists, it follows, in Marxist terms, of wresting the surplus value away from the workers.[42] This represents the ultimate deployment of power.

Placing power (derived from ownership of productive means) in the pivotal analytical role in economics characterizes radical economics still. Thus, for example, a self-proclaimed recent analysis of the U.S. economy suggests that its basic characteristics are not necessarily the inevitable concomitants of an advanced industrial system. "The villain is not the existing state of technology and productive capacity, but the power relations in society which dictate . . . the ends of productive effort, the uses to which technology is to be put, and the very criteria by which some technologies are methodically developed and others are left dormant."[43]

Similarly, Douglas F. Dowd follows in the radical tradition by regarding power as one's ability to control the decisionmaking mechanisms. For, Dowd power, therefore, derives from ownership of the means of production, and its influence and impact is pervasive throughout the system.[44] Far from regarding the institutional milieu as the value-free neutral setting typical for mainstream economists, radicals like Dowd regard the setting as permeated with the values emanating from the way power is deployed in the system. Radicals, in effect, do not regard the system we have as "positive," with proposals for change constituting "normative" views of that system. That institutionalists share some of this perspective should be clear.

But institutionalists do not share it all. Radicals have quite specific ideas usually about the changes to be wrought in the system to bring it into line with the radical vision of the ideal society. In this, perhaps, they are merely following in the original Marxist tradition, in which the classless society was scarcely a positive (as opposed to a normative) vision of the future. Radicals have a reasonably clear view of what their ideal future society would look like.

In this, Dowd is perhaps typical. He refers to the "layers of oppression, injustice, violence, material and spiritual deprivation, and repression" in this country and comments, "Now the United States can be compared to an onion, whose layers when peeled away finally reveal little worth preserving."[45] He urges the development of an American revolutionary socialist movement. He recognizes that in the United States there is not now a "revolutionary movement [that is] . . . a socialist movement with the strength to cause and carry through a revolution." The strategy he proposes is not necessarily undemocratic—he urges "an analysis . . . that convinces the largest percentage of the population of the need for socialism." All of this would reassure a "social reconstruction of revolutionary proportions." Can this be carried out through resort to the ballot box? Does it require force and violence? Would it ultimately be imposed on the present "owners of the means of production"?[46] It is not entirely clear in the Dowd formulation.

Similarly, Samuel Bowles, David Gordon and Thomas Weisskopf, three radicals who analyzed U.S. economic activity in a rather widely discussed book, begin with a model of a business-dominated source of economic power employed by other radicals, and offer a rather detailed normative prescription for the society they propose. That society incorporates what they call an "economic bill of rights" (the right to economic security and equity, to a democratic workplace, to shape our economic futures, to a better way of life) and conclude:

> Our Economic Bill of Rights cannot be separated from the analysis of which it rests. We have argued that symptoms of economic decline in the United States reflect a real structural crisis—a crisis resulting from the erosion of the postwar corporate system and its relation of domination. Some kind of restructuring is necessary . . . (trickle-down economics represents) corporate efforts to restore their power. . . . a detailed democrative alternative . . . (is presented).[47]

The strategy for change they propose involves "popular mobilization around a democratic alternative." As the next section will be at pains to suggest, it is in both the degree of rejection of present society, and in the strategy for change that radical economists would appear to be most easily differentiated from institutionalists.

Institutional Economics

If one regards American institutionalism as having been established by Thorstein Veblen, John R. Commons, and Wesley Clair Mitchell—the usual view—it is clear, particularly in the work of Veblen, that the impact of economic power on the system has always been a basic tenet of institutionalist thought, conditioning the entire manner in which economic activity unfolds. The role of power is as fundamental as it is with radical economists, but it is different. Institutionalism has always stressed the impact of a dynamic technology and the institutional response. Economic power emerges from comprehending the changing technology and deliberately manipulating the institutional response, often in the interest of a narrow group. Veblen called such groups "the vested interests."

Power and the Value Premises of
Institutional Economics

Surely one of Veblen's major contributions to how we view the modern economy was his emphasis on the commanding and pervasive role played by what he called the "vested interests." For Veblen, power was derived from owning wealth.

> The population . . . falls into two main classes: Those who own wealth invested in large holdings and who thereby control the conditions of life for

the rest; and those who do not own wealth in sufficiently large holdings, and whose conditions of life are thereby controlled by these others. It is a division, not between those who have something and those who have nothing—as many socialists would be inclined to describe it—but between those who own wealth enough to make it count, and those who do not.[48]

Veblen employed an anthropological perspective in assessing the process of economic performance—the impact of power on the myriad aspects of that performance—its technological development, its willingness to utilize modern technology, its changing value, its attitudes toward production and consumption, its view of "wants," its distinction between luxuries and necessities, its notions of welfare and acceptable, as well as optimal, economic performance—all this was dynamic and interrelated. The basic factor is that it was critically affected by economic power, its deployment, and its changing nature. Compare this approach, for example, to the mainstream approach, which subsumes what it wishes to say about power in the deviation of price from marginal cost.

John R. Commons, though he differed in many respects from Veblen, had a similar notion about the pervasive consequences of economic power. It is often forgotten that one of Commons's earliest books was concerned with how to make the political apparatus of the country more responsive to social betterment in the face of the obstacles in the form of economic power.[49] Contrasting the contradictory forces exhalting "an ideal of human brotherhood and equality" on the one hand, with "an industrial condition fast solidifying class distinctions," on the other hand, Commons concluded, "The conviction is growing that in some way the government, as city, state, or nation, is to be an important place in solving these contradictions."[50]

As his views developed, Commons called the U.S. system "banker capitalism," and commented, "It is an economic government of bankers more powerful than the political government."[51] Obviously it was not all bankers or only bankers, but the banker-supported corporate structure to which he was referring. This system formed the foundation for the possession and use of economic power.[52]

This approach to economic analysis has, to begin with, profound consequences for the traditional mainstream distinction between normative and positive economics referred to earlier. To assume that an acceptance without comment, even for purposes of study, of "what is" constitutes the adoption of a non-normative approach is clearly inadequate, even though this is precisely what traditional mainstream economists have always done. To begin economic analysis by making no comment whatsoever about "what is" *is* to take a position. Hence the traditional approach, which sweeps under the *ceteris paribus* rug community taste, community incomes, the distribution of wealth, and so forth, and its decision to analyze welfare questions within the confines of Pareto optimality is not value free. It is not neutral or "positive." It in fact assumes away the area where public policies may well be most effective, where welfare standards are least clearly understood or formulated, and where much of the essential allocation of any industrial economy in fact occurs.

This is part of the heritage that economics carries from its long effort to emulate the physical sciences. It may well be that one can take a "value-free position" toward, say, the law of gravity. Acceptance of this premise explains why objects fall, why objects float in space, why the tides work as they do. The fact of or the existence of gravity can thus be viewed "positively" in a way that superficially, at least, makes much more sense than does the viewing positively of income and wealth distributions, the ownership of resources, or the distribution of decision making power in modern industrialized market economies. In economics, to make no comment at all on the world as it is is *not* to be positive rather than normative. Silence (or silent acquiescence) is a highly normative position to take.[53]

In short, it is the way the power system operates in the modern economy that underscores the futility of assuming that silent acquiescence in the status quo constitutes a valid "positive" basis for economic analysis. It turns out to be profoundly normative.

On the other hand, the institutionalist insistence on recognition of this aspect does not make institutionalist analysis coterminous with radical analysis. Radical economists have a clear objective that they do not hesitate to label normatively as "good." For Marx, it was "the classless society." Institutionalists in the Ayresian tradition, which is to say institutionalists influenced (as most have been) by the perspective of John Dewey, have no "ends in view," but view economic activity processually. As we will seek to develop here, the institutionalist view not only eschews teleology, but is often cast as judging economic performance over time, in light primarily of the changing views of its participants, assuming that the participants have accurate information and are free to develop and express their views in ways that are economically meaningful, and in ways that can be regarded as consonant with a democratic decisionmaking system.[54]

Power and the Past

We have seen that, for institutionalists, the existing power system is a fundamental and explicit conditioner of how that system will perform. If institutionalists have viewed economies in processual terms, stressing the impact a changing technology has on the prevailing institutional structures, power is a major ingredient through which this interactive process emerges. It is at bottom the technological process that alters the production possibilities and that conditions how, in western industrialized economies, the corporate system develops. This is an essential inheritance from Veblen: the machine process conditions both the industrial and the corporate system. In one sense, surely, the possibilities opened up by technological developments enable those who gain power from this process to create the divergences between the industrial process and the pecuniary process that figure so prominently in Veblenian analysis. It is the impact of technological change on the operation of the means of production that enables their owners to acquire the power that subsequently conditions the operation of the entire system. We have seen that this view of the role of economic power was a hallmark of the perspective of the founders of institutionalism. It is a preeminent reason why from the start they regarded the perspective of mainstream economics as inadequate.

This orientation was no less critical in the next generation of institutionalists. Ayres commented:

> The power-system and its legendary background, the system and theory of capitalism, is not the author of the industrial technology by which the modern community gets its living and on which it therefore completely depends. It is the residue of our ceremonial past, and as such it is an impediment to economic progress as ceremonial properties have always been. . . . it . . . define(s) the problem of value and welfare which industrial society has now to face.[55]

The power system, in sum, depends on the technological process for its possibilities, but embodies the institutional adjustment to those changes. Modern corporations are not imaginable in the absence of large-scale industrial units. Ultimately, the power system has its greatest impact on wealth and property relations. In this way, it defines or structures always the emerging value problem society confronts.

So put, the role of power concentrations is preeminent, and places the value problem 180 degrees from the orthodox approach to value that places the power system within the *ceteris paribus* constraints and embraces Pareto optimality. So viewed, can the world of orthodox theory truly be regarded as a contribution to positive analysis?

A contemporary of Ayres who saw the role of economic power in similar fashion was Robert A. Brady. A heterodox economist clearly in the Veblenian rather than the Marxist tradition, he regarded business as "a system of power." Indeed, it was the preeminent determinant of the power system that in turn conditioned the operation of the economy and the society within which it was found. The flavor of Brady's perspective is perhaps conveyed by the following passage:

> Free in large part of direct investor control, managements . . . may be able greatly to rationalize productive operations . . . management now largely swings free from all direct controls other than those which may be imposed upon it by governmental authority; this fact will and apparently does mean that the executive and managerial end will be handled by paid functionaries, the better to allow the leading figures within the ranks to focus the massed power of their pendulous corporations upon larger issues of policy. Business leadership not only acquires political interests, but it turns to the political arena already backed by enormous, fully mobilized, and easily focused power.[56]

Ayres and Brady were, of course, not the only members of their generation of institutionalists to be concerned about economic power and its impact on the system. Indeed, the chief legacy of Veblen to institutionalism was his concern about the impact of concentrated power on how the system operated, most particularly in causing a deviation of industrial (technological) and pecuniary values and goals. This divergence has been fundamental in coloring the approach, the assumptions, and the overall perspective taken by institutionalists. This concern is often highlighted today by the impact power has on the ways government affects the private economy, and by the analytical perspective taken by institutionalists toward this relationship.

Power and the Government

From our examination of the past, it is clear that institutionalists have traditionally been concerned about the relationship between economic power and the state. Throughout the work of institutionalists there is a consistent, if progressively complex, recognition that concentration of economic power in the private sector requires a governmental sector that can somehow marshall and reflect the collective wishes of the participants as they would be expressed in the absence of concentrated economic power. This is clearly a complex and ongoing task.

As long ago as 1896 Commons was concerned that "government, to be an agent for social reform," requires the "confidence of the people," and this can be obtained only if government is "representative in character."[57] By 1972 the thinking of institutionalists concerning the relationship of power and the state had progressed to:

> when we make power and therewith politics a part of our system, we no longer can escape or disguise the contradictory character of the modern state. The state is the prime object of economic power. It is captured. Yet on all matters I have mentioned—the restrictions on excessive resource use, organization to offset inadequate resource use, controls, action to correct systematic inequality, protection of the environment, protection of the consumer—remedial action lies with the state.[58]

It is clear that the contemporary debate about the appropriate role for the government revolves largely around the way the debaters see the private sector operating, and this in turn is determined more or less directly by how they see private power in action. Milton Friedman, for example, makes it clear that in general he really does believe the market reflects "voluntary exchange." He grants the possibility that there are "technical monopolies"—public utility type units in which competition and efficiency cannot coexist. Even here he argues that as between government regulation and monopoly, "private monopoly may be the least of the evils."[59]

Friedman simply has no place for the kind of governmental intrusions that Galbraith, to take an opposite viewpoint, enumerates. Friedman recommends that the government get out of many areas it now regulates, a position that has found increasing favor in many quarters in recent years, as the "deregulation movement" has gained strength. In the final analysis, where Galbraith fears the deployment of private power and calls for government to provide protection from it, Friedman argues that the major threat to free institutions may well lie in "the economic powers already concentrated in Washington."[60] Clearly, what Friedman must be arguing is that the call by Commons in 1896 to make government responsive to the people has failed, and that the government, far from being responsive, is the chief threat. Although many mainstream economists would not follow Friedman this far, it is clear that a major difference between institutional and mainstream economists concerns the possibilities for reducing the inefficiencies as well as the perceived inequities in the operation of the system by using public power to offset or counter private power. That there can be inefficiencies at any level of activity, private or public, ought to go without saying; that the inefficiencies are necessarily endemic in public activity and cannot be reduced is a position taken only by convinced mainstream economists. That private power can constitute a sufficient threat to the efficiency of the system to justify efforts to develop public policy to cope with it is an enduring theme among convinced institutionalists. We should note that the argument here concerns efficiencies. Inequities engendered in large part by private power concentrations are also of concern to institutionalists. Mainstream economists either ignore or downplay these concerns, and, in the extreme, argue that the market defines equity better than any other agency. While in recent years we have heard talk about "a social safety net," it has not been defined clearly or consistently in mainstream quarters.

The Institutionalist Focus

Institutionalism, we have seen, has consistently been concerned about the impact of economic power, and has consistently recognized that the basic operation of an industrial economy cannot be realistically —let alone adequately—comprehended unless explicit attention is directed to the ways power impinges on economic performance.[61] Economic power, we noted earlier, led mainstream economists by the 1930s to develop theories of imperfect competition.[62] These markets were imperfect, after all, largely because of the existence of more power on the part of participants than could be consonant with the conditions postulated in the theory of competition. But oligopoly theory as it developed has always been the self-acknowledged least satisfactory part of conventional micro-theory. In recent years the earlier theories of oligopoly have given way to new efforts influenced by game theory.[63] Models of conjectural interdependence and bargaining have proliferated.[64] The outcomes of these models may be either an equilibrium or non-equilibrium condition, and the results may be regarded as stable or unstable. But they are rarely related to the broader questions that have consistently concerned institutionalists—how well is the economy serving its participants, insofar as the standards the participants would set for themselves in ideal circumstances (full information, et cetera). Because of the imperfections in the system, these standards are applied only imprecisely. In all this, judging economic performance for institutionalists is not unlike appraising the functioning of the polity for political scientists applying "ideal democratic theory."

Power results from factors like modern technology that cut with a two-edged sword, both making possible kinds and quantities of production unthinkable in earlier times, and creating all sorts of possibilities for thwarting or altering the overall responsiveness of the system to the collective wishes of its subjects, as well as the overall ways the economy performs in carrying out allocation. Because the emergent economy subsumes all sorts of consequences from the way concentrated power affects it, to regard the economy "which is" as positive is, we have stressed, to take a profoundly normative view. We have examined this at some length. On the other hand, to take an *explicit* or static view of what the "economy should be" is to be unduly restrictive in judging economic performance. Institutionalists have consistently been processual—the economy, like Dewey's means-end continuum, is always in process of *becoming.* Unlike radical economists, as we have seen, there is no ideal timeless state to which institutionalists can refer as an appropriate "end." (As radicals place "the classless society.") The bedrock perspective of institutionalist analysis is recognition of the ceaseless change in both technology and institutional response to that change. In consequence, there are no "ideal" institutions to which we move. The family, the law, government—all are constantly changing in greater or lesser degree.

In consequence, what institutionalists stress is the direction of change, (movement along a technologically conditioned continuum) and the forces shaping and conditioning this movement. The "ideals" toward which the system moves are themselves dynamic. Equity, for example, is a major characteristic by which to judge economic performance. Concentrated power has as a preeminent consequence the likely result of either retarding movement toward greater equity, or of creating movement toward greater inequities. But this does not mean that there is a static "state of equity" toward which societies move. We do not always at all times wish the same "equity," but over time economies move toward greater equity, under ideal circumstances—it being understood thereby that equity is itself a dynamic standard.

The polity might elect officials to public office who will perform well or poorly by a given standard. The test of democracy is how responsive to the wishes of the participants is the decision making system at any given time. Similarly, economists ask how well does the system present the alternatives, inform the participants, et cetera. Unlike radicals, institutionalists as institutionalists do not have static absolutist standards to insert in judging performance. They must judge in light of their best assessment of technological possibilities, of the collective wishes of the participants, and their assessment of the extent to which the wishes of the participants are based on full information and energized by candidates desirous of serving the interest of their constituents as they understand them at any given time. Even at this level of generality there are problems. How does the ideal political system operate in making decisions too complicated for the average participants to absorb the requisite information? The difficulties here explain why public referenda on all issues do not necessarily represent the ideal decision making mechanism for the ideal democratic state. Defining what participants *would* wish if they have such information is, at best, partly a subjective process, but it is nonetheless important.[65]

The Impact of Power on Allocation as a Politico-Economic Process

So viewed, it is clear that the realities of economic power in the modern world of necessity make the operation of total resource allocation a politico-economic process.

In this connection I once commented:

> The economy itself and the choices it offers its participants are both affected by power concentrations. Moreover, the total choosing system is partly economic (dollar votes) and partly political (ballot box votes), and *both* operate differently than they would were power and wealth not concentrated. It is as inappropriate to focus on "free markets," as though markets really were free (making a few ancillary comments about "imperfections"), as it would be to focus on free elections, making a few ancillary comments about imperfections in the democratic process.[66]

An essential task for the economist is to cut through the ways economic power distorts the allocative process from what it would be otherwise. This presupposes that analytic devices exist for ascertaining what allocative patterns might look like were the participants in economic activity fully informed, allowed—indeed encouraged—to be socially sensitive and aware of alternatives and possibilities. This system would not produce any static "ideal allocation," but it would *move* in consonance with technological change toward *better* and more democratic allocative results. This means that in judging the allocative performance of the economy and how it confronts concentrated economic power, we suggest that the perspective taken is part of the common institutionalist perspective—namely, economies are processual, with no "final ends," and hence no final allocative states that can be regarded as ideal. Institutionalists consider the total allocation process in general, and the impact on it of economic power in particular, as a reflection of emergent values. Here institutionalists do have some precedents. Anthony Downs made something of a breakthrough in suggesting some years ago that the methodology and perspective of economics could fruitfully be applied to government decisionmaking in the public sector. The thrust of much of what we have been saying here is that the approach of political science, insofar as it considers the political process as it actually operates and assesses its performance in light of where we would like the political process in a democratic system ideally to take us, could with profit be applied to the tasks of political economy as well.[67]

The kind of political science approach being contemplated here is epitomized by the work of Randall Bartlett, who raises clearly the economic challenge of making an imperfect democratic system work better: "The implicit assumption of a fixed and independent political structure underlying economic analysis is invalid and unsubstantiated. The distributions of political power and the distributions of wealth are inexorably intertwined, even in a democratically organized state based upon a free market system."[68]

While this may suggest that any politico-economic system in the real world will undoubtedly fall considerably short of the ideal of democratic and free market theory in its pure form, it need not be interpreted to mean that progress toward that ideal cannot be made. Reaching that ideal will require explicit recognition of the thwarting and warping of the objectives of idealized systems caused by the power concentrations that mainstream economics continues implicitly to favor. This occurs when real world activities are blunted through such devices as the assumption of Pareto optimality. In this respect (and perhaps *only* in this respect) the implication of much of current political science—that the system we have falls considerably short of the ideal system—represents a healthy step in the direction of more fruitful analysis.[69] This is clearly parallel to what the institutionalist assessment of economic power attempts to do.

Economists have paid remarkably little attention to allocation in the public sector except as a solution, however unsatisfactory, to "market failures." For this reason the recent backlash has promoted "privatization" as a solution to "government failures." Institutionalists need begin with no preconceptions that "ideal allocation" must be left to either the private or the public sector.

Decisionmaking will, of necessity, be divided between the private and the public sectors. There is no presumption that allocation in either sector is superior *per se* to that in the other, nor that it is preferable. Allocation should be left to whichever sector can carry it through with the greatest likelihood of its being accomplished according to the freely expressed wishes of all the participants. In this view, institutionalists are unlike both radical and mainstream economists. In common with the former, however, they recognize that the realities of economic power and its deployment in the modern world require that unfettered private allocation mechanisms be both regulated and controlled in certain areas and supplanted by public allocation in others.

Economic Power in a Global Setting

If the dynamic of technological change has produced one cliché for our time, it is surely that the world is getting steadily smaller. It is impossible any more even for mainstream economists to assume with comfort that we live in "a closed economy." Surely institutionalists have made a major contribution to the literature addressing the implications of spreading economic power beyond national borders for the operation of the major domestic economies in the western world. We have earlier referred to Eisenhower's celebrated farewell address on the dangers lurking in the "military industrial complex." Seymour Melman, in a long series of books, has analyzed the impact that maintaining a more or less constant state of military readiness has had on the U.S. economy—on its failures, successes, and on the directions it has taken. He argues forcefully that the foreign policy of the United States, as well as other economies organized in roughly the same manner, has been seriously distorted by the global requirements of militarism, closely tailored to the internal motivations of large corporate powers in the United States.[70]

The other thread to the story of the international ramifications of concentrated power, of course, has been the spread of multinational corporate activities. Indeed, a major implication of multinational corporate growth is that not only is economic power enhanced thereby, but the corporations involved manage to escape effective control by any national government. The result has been the creation of a new supra-national power structure that has significant implications for the themes developed here. Many of the questions raised about the impact of concentrated economic power on what we call "the higher efficiency" (see below) are exacerbated by the internationalization of economic power and influence. One of the most persuasive students of these problems has commented: "The internationalization of the activities of the largest corporations has enhanced their power. . . . The domestic size of large firms tends to be exaggerated insofar as their markets and facilities are located abroad, but the multinational dispersion of international corporations increases their mobility and freedom from effective government control."[71]

There can be no doubt that technological progress has, among other things, made the institutional response of multinational corporations into a major new threat to the possibility of harnessing the fruits of technological development for the enhancement of what we identify below as "the higher efficiency."

Conclusions: Power and the Higher Efficiency

Institutionalists have a more complex standard by which to judge economic performance than the narrow allocative efficiency of mainstream economists. Recognizing that wants are not "given," but emerge in the process of the dynamic interaction that characterizes activity in a modern industrial economy, and recognizing that the values that emerge in this interactive process are part and parcel of the emergent value structure of the larger society, institutionalists must confront this value system.

Previously I have suggested that any economy ineluctably has some standards of equity, some standards of freedom, a notion of security, and a standard of humaneness (or compassion).[72] While any economy reflects current standards with respect to all of these, these are not static standards; they are in a constant process of change. A task of the public sector is to do what the private sector obviously cannot do—to assess and reassess the degree to which the private sector is performing in a way that is consistent with current standards in each of these dimensions. This social monitoring is a major activity within the public sector.

It is at once apparent that constellations of power in the private sector can severely distort the total allocational thrust of the economy. The degree to which the economy tolerates thwarting of any of its current standards of performance is what determines in part the degree to which public sector activity is urged. This is an application of the basic institutionalist view of technological change and institutional adjustment. *Both* are in constant change. President Reagan discovered early in his administration that his plans to alter social security coverage ran afoul of the then-existing standard of compassion or humaneness being applied in our economy. "Minimal welfare standards," like other dimensions of economic performance, are in constant flux, but in this case had advanced beyond what the Reagan plan envisaged, and the latter was hence judged to be unacceptable.

Institutionalists need not argue that standards for judgment must be perfect. It is sufficient that they are in the process of becoming better or more sensitively attuned to the changing performance of the economy as it actually operates. We have argued that economic power is deployed in ways that alter total allocation. This might enhance some aspects of performance while thwarting others, perhaps causing it to diverge even further from the current standards than would otherwise be the case.

The unavoidable task of economists is to monitor this performance in light of these standards. It is crucial to realize that failure to comment on the standards or on changes in them (the conventional "positive" approach of mainstream economists) is a profoundly normative stance. If technology produces the ferment that leads to change, it also produces the opportunities for constellations of power to alter total allocation and so to more successfully thwart the emerging objectives of the system.

At bottom, an economy is always and at all times *a system in process of becoming.* Failure to realize this, and failure to realize the critical role of economic power in affecting the pace and timing of the system's fundamental dynamics is regarded as a pitfall in conventional approaches that institutionalists try to avoid.

For institutionalists, this is less than ideal, as indeed it is for other economists or social scientists generally surveying human progress. If there are no static ideals or "goods," there are myriad ideals in the form of "less bads." Ongoing technology defines the path. We may thus say with certainty, for example, that with current resources and technology, infant mortality could be lower, pollution could be reduced, conservation could be advanced, longevity could be increased (death rates in various directions could be reduced), illiteracy could be reduced, education could be improved, slums reduced, poverty reduced, housing improved, social services improved, and so on. If the private sector exhibits failures of will, or other failure, the quintessential role of the polity can be to see that sufficient economic power is implanted in the public sector to achieve more of these objectives. In a sense we are engaged presently in a public debate about whether such power *ought* to be located in the public sector or reattached firmly and exclusively in the private sector, where the allocational results may well be unpredictable and will, in any case, not be subject to any economy-wide valuational review. In any case, all of the improvements enumerated above are technologically possible. That improvement in one area might reduce the rate of progress in another is entirely possible. They all reflect aspects of economic performance, and so judging all of these is part of *economic* analysis. They cannot be left in the sterile confines of *ceteris paribus*. They are all aspects of "the life process." Affirming the life process is quintessentially Veblenian, and epitomizes the value stance of institutionalism. Conventional economics seems emaciated by comparison—with its finessed value questions, its assumption of a given income and wealth distribution, of given consumer taste, and other critical factors, its assumption that consumers are sovereign, and that firms that strive only to satisfy expressed demands. If institutionalists cannot define "the ideal" in static or level terms, the *direction* of progress is clear. That power constellations are deployed in the modern world so as to make human potential and human achievement diverge significantly can and has been shown quite clearly. The *rate* at which the gap ought to be closed, assuming we agree it should be closed at all, is the fundamental choice that economies, as choosing mechanisms, must make. Assessing the answer as it emerges from the dynamic interactive process we call the economy is no easy measurement problem. It is the supreme challenge to modern economics. Where and how it is being best answered is a question we must leave to each reader.

Notes

1. This is surely the role currently being played by rational expectations exponents and the new classical economists. It is not clear that microeconomics has ever gotten beyond the blurring of this critical distinction, which explains why mainstream economists devote so much time to positive economics—"what is," and so little to normative economics—"what ought to be."
2. Douglas F. Dowd,*The Twisted Dream* (Cambridge, Mass.: Winthrop Publishers, 1974), p. 58.
3. P. A. Klein, "Confronting Power in Economics: A Pragmatic Evaluation," *Journal of Economic Issues* 14 (December 1980):871–96, at p. 873. William M. Dugger has suggested that "power shall refer to the ability to tell other people what to do with some degree of certainty that they will do it." W. M. Dugger, "Power: An Institutional Framework of Analysis," *Journal of Economic Issues* 14 (December 1980): 897–907, at p. 897.
4. Warren Samuels, *The Economy as a System of Power,* Vol. I, *Corporate Systems,* (New Brunswick: Transaction Books, 1979), p. iii.
5. Randall Bartlett, *Economic Foundations of Political Power* (New York: The Free Press, 1973), p. 144.
6. That the economy is a valuational, rather than a narrowly allocational instrumentality, is a bedrock assumption in institutional thought. Compare

for example, P. A. Klein, "Economics: Allocation or Valuation," *Journal of Economic Issues* 8 (December 1974): 785–811.

7. Compare, for example, Robert A. Dahl, *A Preface to Democratic Theory* (Chicago: University Chicago Press), 1956; Robert A. Dahl and Charles E. Lindblom, *Politics, Economics, and Welfare* (New York: Harper, 1953); Charles E. Lindblom, *Politics and Markets* (New York: Basic Books, 1977); Robert A. Dahl, *Polyarchy* (New Haven: Yale University Press, 1971.)

8. Dahl, *Polyarchy,* p. 1.

9. Lindblom, *Politics and Markets,* p. 194.

10. J. K. Galbraith refers to "the dependence effect" in *The Affluent Society* (Boston: Houghton Mifflin, 1958), p. 153. The more general exclusion of other groups from the decisions of the technostructure is developed in J. K. Galbraith, *Economics and The Public Purpose* (Boston: Houghton Mifflin, 1973), p. 93.

11. Some of these ideas are developed more fully in Klein, "Confronting Power in Economics: A Pragmatic Evaluation."

12. Lionel Robbins, *The Nature and Significance of Economic Science* (London: Macmillan, 1946).

13. Martin Bronfenbrenner, "Early American Leaders—Institutional and Critical Traditions," *American Economic Review* 75 (December 1985): 13–27, at p. 19.

14. Ibid., p. 19.

15. Gunnar Myrdal, *Against the Stream* (New York: Pantheon Books, 1973).

16. Milton Friedman, *Capitalism and Freedom* (Chicago: University of Chicago Press, 1962), p. 15. Quoted in an interesting article, Zahid Shariff, "Reflections on Taxpayers' Revolt," *Administration and Society* (November 1982): 299–300.

17. We may note that a recent and typical book, William Sher and Rudy Pinola, *Microeconomic Theory: A Synthesis of Classical Theory and the Modern Approach* (New York: Elsevier North Holland, 1981) manages to discuss at length what constitutes good theory (logical, deductive), repeating all the conventional assumptions (profit maximization, perfect knowledge, homogeneity, et cetera)—including a careful distinction of perfect and imperfect competition—without ever discussing economic power, its possible concentration, or how it might complicate the operation of a real economy in the modern industrialized world. This approach is by no means distinctive; if it were it would be inappropriately mentioned here. It is appropriate precisely because it is typical.

18. Joan Robinson, *The Economics of Imperfect Competition* (New York: Macmillan, 1933) and E. Chamberlin, *The Theory of Monopolistic Competition* (Cambridge, Mass.: Harvard University Press, 1933) are the classic works in this area.

19. Compare Edward Mason, "Price and Production Policies of Large-Scale Enterprise," *American Economic Review,* Supplement., (March 1939): 61–74; Joe Bain, *Industrial Organization* (New York: Wiley and Sons, 1959); F. M. Scherer, *Industrial Market Structure and Economic Performance* (Chicago: Rand McNally, 1970 [1980]). For a useful review of this work see Douglas F. Greer, *Industrial Organization and Public Policy* (New York: Macmillan, 1980), Chap. 1.

20. The term, "workable competition" was introduced by J. M. Clark, "Toward a Concept of Workable Competition," *American Economic Review* 30 (June 1940): 241–56.
21. Corwin D. Edwards, *Maintaining Competition, Requisites of a Government Policy* (New York: McGraw-Hill, 1949), p. 131.
22. E. S. Herman, *Corporate Control, Corporate Power* (Cambridge: Cambridge University Press, 1981).
23. William J. Baumol, John C. Panzar, and Robert D. Willig, *Contestable Markets and the Theory of Industry Structure* (New York: Harcourt Brace Jovanovich, 1982), p. 13.
24. Ibid., p. 477.
25. Ibid., p. 476.
26. A prime apologia for the corporation was produced recently by Neil Jacoby, who studied the modern corporation, listed and then dismissed virtually every possible threat posed by the corporation to modern society that has been raised by institutionalists (though he does not include them by name), radicals, and liberals. Jacoby concludes, "For many centuries, the corporate form has been used to organize man's economic drives as well as to satisfy his psychic and social needs. We have every reason to believe that the corporation will survive and flourish as a social institution long into the future." Neil H. Jacoby, *Corporate Power and Social Responsibility* (New York: Macmillan, 1973), p. 270.
27. Douglas F. Greer, *Industrial Organization and Public Policy,* (New York: Macmillan, 1980), pp. 434, 441. Italics in original.
28. At one point Greer estimates that the misallocation of resources resulting from market power might reduce consumer surplus in the amount of 7–10 percent of GNP. The loss is the result of excess profits, excess wages and salaries, inefficiency, and misallocation (Greer, *Industrial Organization and Public Policy,* pp. 480–81). While 7–10 percent of GNP might be regarded as significant on its own terms, if coupled with the ability of powerful units to affect the institutional framework, the damage to the overall performance of the economy—from the vantage point of concerns of institutionalists—would appear to be considerably larger and more disturbing.
29. Keith Cowling and Dennis C. Mueller, "The Social Costs of Monopoly Power," *The Economic Journal* 88 (December 1978): 727–48, at p. 744.
30. A typical industrial organization conclusion might be the following, based on a study of the relationship between concentration and profitability: "It is not clear that U.S. antitrust policy restricts concentration very much. However, if it does, it is more likely to reduce efficiency, raise prices and reduce owner wealth." Sam Peltzman, "The Gains and Losses from Industrial Concentration," *Journal of Law and Economics* 20 (October 1977): 229–63.

   Institutionalists (along with *some* industrial organization adherents, as our analysis of views might suggest), are not likely to find this conclusion one that disposes of the matter, particularly the notion that reducing owner wealth is *per se* an indictment of potential public policy.
31. Richard and Peggy Musgrave, in one of the more thoughtful public finance texts of recent years, note that "Economists, over the last fifty years, have

increasingly held that a theory of just or equitable distribution is not within the purview of economics but should be left to philosophers, poets, and politicians." The Musgrave's general attitude is that this is impractical. "Economists who are concerned with public policy can hardly detach their thinking from equity issues." They tend to concentrate their concern with equity on distributional issues, however, rather than on the more basic allocational questions that would concern institutionalists. While their view is nonetheless one of the broader public finance views, the questions we have been wrestling with here—namely, how to make the system perform in a fashion more consonant with the emergent values of the community— appear to go beyond their concern. See Richard and Peggy Musgrave, *Public Finance in Theory and Practice,* 3d. ed. (New York: McGraw-Hill, 1980), pp. 89, 91.

32. *Public Choice* (Dordrecht, The Netherlands: Martinus Nijhoff), inside back cover of every issue.
33. P. A. Klein, "Confronting Power in Economics," *Journal of Economic Issues* 14 (December 1980): 871–96, at p. 891.
34. A useful summary of this controversy on the appropriate amount of government intervention is to be found in Edgar K. Browning and Jacquelene M. Browning, *Public Finance and the Price System,* 2d. ed. (New York: Macmillan, 1983). Compare especially Chap. 3, "Public Choice." Compare also J. Buchanan and R. D. Tollison, *Theory of Public Choice* (Ann Arbor: University of Michigan Press, 1972), and Anthony Downs, *An Economic Theory of Democracy* (New York: Harper and Row), 1957.
35. Compare, for example, Browning and Browning, *Public Finance and the Price System,* p. 84.
36. The early work includes Anne O. Krueger, "The Political Economy of the Rent-Seeking Society," *American Economic Review* 64 (June 1974): 291–303; Gordon Tullock, "The Welfare Costs of Tariffs, Monopolies, and Theft," *Western Economic Journal* 5 (June 1967): 224–32; Richard A. Posner, "The Social Costs of Monopoly and Regulation," *Journal of Political Economy* 83 (August 1975): 807–27.
37. James Buchanan, "Reform in the Rent-Seeking Society," in *Toward a Theory of the Rent-Seeking Society,* ed. James M. Buchanan, Robert D. Tollison, and Gordon Tullock (College Station: Texas A&M University Press, 1980), p. 359.
38. Howard Sherman, in his book *Radical Political Economy,* nowhere refers to institutionalism or institutionalists, except for a brief reference to Veblen. He does refer to Galbraith at one point as a "liberal." It is clear that Sherman disagrees with the Galbraithian conclusions. He believes that Galbraith is too optimistic concerning the possibility that the evils of the modern corporation can be reduced through "internal change." Sherman himself appears to favor "patient, non-violent, socialist education." It is not clear how this might differ from "patient, non-violent institutionalist education." See Howard Sherman, *Radical Political Economy* (New York: Basic Books, 1972), pp. 104–5; 198.
39. Karl Marx, *Capital* (New York: The Modern Library, 1906) p. 848.
40. Paul M. Sweezy, *The Theory of Capitalist Development* (New York: Oxford University Press, 1942), p. 349.

41. For a recent restatement of the Marxist economic analysis of capitalism, see Jacques Gouverneur, *Contemporary Capitalism and Marxist Economics,* (Totowa, N.J.: Barnes and Noble, 1983), for example, Chap. 1.
42. A mathematical Marxist analysis of capitalist operation is provided in John E. Roemer, *Analytical Foundations of Marxist Economic Theory* (Cambridge: Cambridge University Press, 1981). See especially Chap. 2.
43. Richard C. Edwards, Michael Reich, and Thomas Weisskopf, eds., *The Capitalist System* (Englewood Cliffs, N.J.: Prentice-Hall, 1972), p. 3.
44. Historically for Dowd this means that "The American businessman was able both to create and to control the political and social ('normative') sources of power, i.e., the system of government, the political system, and religious and educational institutions all accepted the directions and values established by business." Douglas F. Dowd, *The Twisted Dream* (Cambridge, Mass.: Winthrop Publishers, 1974), p. 248, footnote 7.
45. Douglas F. Dowd, *The Twisted Dream,* p. 301.
46. Ibid., p. 298.
47. Samuel Bowles, David M. Gordon, and Thomas Weisskopf, *Beyond the Wasteland* (Garden City, N.Y.: Anchor Press/Doubleday, 1983), p. 380.
48. Thorstein Veblen, *The Vested Interests and the Common Man* (New York: Heubsch, 1920), pp. 160–61. Quoted in Allan G. Gruchy, *Modern Economic Thought* (New York: Prentice Hall, 1947), p. 97.
49. His solution was what he called "proportional representation," designed among other things to cope with "a political philosophy teaching the infallibility of the majority." If his faith in proportional representation would not garner much support today, it is nonetheless noteworthy that he was worrying before the turn of the century about the interface between economic progress and how the political system confronted the distribution of the fruits of that progress—a traditional concern of institutionalists, as well as many of today's less traditional political scientists. See John R. Commons, *Proportional Representation,* (New York: Thomas Y. Crowell, 1986 [1907]). Reprint edition (New York: Augustus M. Kelley, 1967), p. 227.
50. Ibid.
51. John R. Commons, *Institutional Economics* (Madison: The University of Wisconsin Press, 1959), p. 895.
52. Allan G. Gruchy has commented, "Commons orients his system around the concept of economic power, because he finds that property in the twentieth century has come to mean 'economic power' rather than 'economic utility.'" Gruchy, *Modern Economic Thought,* p. 219.
53. There have been surveys, for example, that have found that large numbers of college students assume that they and their classmates will cheat on exams. That they do not comment on this in determining their own actions is scarcely to suggest that they are not taking a value position.
54. Judging what is democratic in a system in which dollar votes are unequally distributed, in which there are no normative implications surrounding equality of wealth or income, and in which ascertaining what the participants would prefer if well informed and *actually* "free to choose," rather than free only in the myopic perspective of Friedman, is perhaps the most complex challenge facing the modern economy.

55. Clarence E. Ayres, *The Theory of Economic Progress* (Chapel Hill: The University of North Carolina Press, 1944), p. 202.
56. Robert A. Brady, *Business as a System of Power* (New York: Columbia University Press, 1943), pp. 310–11. It is interesting to note that the book is dedicated to Mitchell, "Who, without knowing it, . . . had . . . much to do with (its) writing."
57. Commons, *Institutional Economics,* p. 233.
58. John Kenneth Galbraith, "Presidential Address to the American Economics Association," *American Economic Review* 63 (March 1973): 1–11, p. 10.
59. Friedman, *Capitalism and Freedom,* p. 28.
60. Ibid., p. 202.
61. Many of the ideas in this section were developed in an earlier article, cited above, Klein, "Confronting Power in Economics: A Pragmatic Evaluation." In the connection cited we may note that a recent volume of work by institutionalists on the impact of power on economic performance is entitled *The Economy as a System of Power,* ed. Warren Samuels (New Brunswick, N.J.: Transaction Books, 1979).
62. We referred to this earlier. See footnote 18.
63. Following the publication of J. von Neumann and O. Morgenstern's *Theory of Games and Economic Behavior* (Princeton, N.J.: Princeton University Press, 1944), game theory as an approach to oligopoly markets was developed in works such as R. Dorfman, P. Samuelson, and R. Solow, *Linear Programming and Economic Analysis* (New York: McGraw-Hill 1958); and W. Baumol, *Economic Theory and Operations Analysis,* 4th ed. (Englewood Cliffs, N.J.: Prentice Hall, 1977).
64. "Public choice" adherents have given attention to bargaining models as well as others; see for example, James M. Buchanan and Gordon Tullock, *The Calculus of Consent* (Ann Arbor: The University of Michigan Press, 1962), Chap. 8.
65. If radicals profess to know that the ideal society is one that is classless, or one in which distribution follows the dictum of from each according to ability and to each according to need (presuming that ability and need are both definable), institutionalists have no such absolute and static standards. It is true that Galbraith on occasion seems to be suggesting that he (Galbraith) is singularly blessed in escaping "the conventional wisdom." In general institutionalists judge the system according to *movement* toward the perceived objectives of the participants. Whether such movement is as fast as individual institutionalists might wish, or in accord with their individual judgments is problematical. The ultimate conclusion is that one must hope that in the long run such a process is in accord with the judgment of the participants as a whole, and that this collective judgment moves rapidly in directions consonant with the value system that developing technology presents.
66. Klein, "Confronting Power in Economics; A Pragmatic Evaluation," p. 890.
67. See Anthony Downs, *An Economic Theory of Democracy* (New York: Harper and Row, 1957). I developed this view at some length in "Confronting Power in Economics."
68. Randall Bartlett, *Economic Foundations of Political Power* (New York: The Free Press, 1973), p. 198.

69. We have earlier here suggested that this effort was one objective of J. K. Galbraith's "Presidential Address to the American Economic Association."
70. See for example, Seymour Melman, *The Permanent War Economy* (New York: Simon and Schuster, 1974).
71. E. S. Herman, *Corporate Control, Corporate Power* (Cambridge: Cambridge University Press, 1981).
72. P. A. Klein, "Institutionalist Reflections on the Role of the Public Sector," *Journal of Economic Issues* 18 (March 1984); 45–68.

The Neoinstrumental
Theory of Democracy

Rick Tilman

The development of democratic theory and practice in the English-speaking world has been a long and arduous process, as old as the British Constitution itself; but at present there is no definitive theory of democracy in the western world, only theories of democracy.[1] However, since it is the neoinstitutional perspective on democracy that will be explored here, it is important to recognize that institutionalists have never been united on the meaning of their own doctrinal tradition or of its relationship to democratic theory and practice. In fact, since Walton Hamilton coined the term "institutionalism" in 1916, at least two ideological tendencies have been present in the movement. Evolutionary economics contains liberals on the one hand, such as John Commons, Clarence Ayres, Wesley C. Mitchell, and Hamilton himself, and, on the other hand, radicals like Thorstein Veblen and J. K. Galbraith in his neosocialist period. This is not to suggest that institutionalism has been polarized into two camps; it is to state, however, that ideologically and programmatically Commons and Veblen, for example, had widely divergent views. It is largely the need for institutionalists to present a united front against political conservatives and neoclassical economists that prevents them from adequately recognizing their own diversity and squarely facing its political and ideological implications.

The author wishes to thank Paul Goldstene, Michael Clarke, Baldwin Ranson, Vernon Mattson, Laurence A. Tool, and Marc R. Tool for helpful comments on an earlier draft.

The bifurcation in institutionalist thought between reform capitalism and socialism has direct relevance for understanding the evolving neoinstitutionalist theory of democracy. From the radical wing of the movement comes the question as to whether or not a genuine democracy is possible within a system wedded to capitalist property relations. From the liberal wing comes an articulation of the means-ends dilemma, which is essentially the question of political and economic feasibility.[2]

It would be too simplistic, however, to maintain that contemporary neoinstitutionalists can be divided into two explicitly ideological groupings, the one prescribing reform capitalism, the other democratic socialism.[3] Instead, it appears that the majority of evolutionary economists are neither reformists nor advocates of economic collectivism. Indeed, most probably belong to a large intermediate grouping that cannot accurately be labeled either liberal reformist or socialist. This grouping is skeptical about ideological labels, critical of past failures of welfare and regulatory state collectivism, but is, as yet, unconvinced of the feasibility of large-scale transformations of corporate property and power. Although committed to neoinstitutionalist doctrine, it wishes to keep its political and policy options open, particularly during a period like the present when little movement exists toward progressive goals.

The presence in neoinstitutional economics of these three amorphous groupings, radical or neosocialist, intermediate, and liberal reformist complicates the explanation and development of a neoinstitutional view of democracy.[4] It presents problems of interpretation not only for ideological taxonomists, but for analysts in search of a viable neoinstitutional theory. One should not be dismayed, however, by the fact that evolutionary economists are not of one mind regarding the nature of the existing political economy, the directions in which it should be changed, or the prospects for changing it into a more democratic system. Indeed, the two volumes of which this article is a small part may serve a doctrinal unification and reorientation function for the entire neoinstitutional movement. A neoinstitutional political perspective does exist, but it must be further developed through an elaboration of trends in the politically-oriented literature of instrumentalism. But before this synthesis is attempted, let us briefly consider the present state of democratic theory among English-speaking scholars.

Types of Democratic Theory

The kinds of democratic theory prevalent since about 1960 differ

Table 1. *Types of (Democratic) Political Theory*

Neubauer - Cnudde[a]	*Pennock*[e]	
	Any Form of Constitutional Government	
A. Empirical	A. Descriptive	Motivational
B. Analytical-Conceptual	B. Prescriptive	and Power
C. Normative	C. Ideal-Type	Theories
Riemer[b]	*Edelman*[f]	
A. Empirical	A. Natural Rights	
B. Prudential	B. Contract	
C. Normative	C. Competitive	
	(1) Realist	
	(2) Optimalist	
Dahl[c]	*Mayo*[g]	
A. Madisonian	A. Descriptive	
B. Populistic	B. Empirical	
C. Polyarchal	C. Moral	
Lively[d]		
A. Classifications (ideal types)		
B. Empirical Generalizations		
C. Deductive Models		
D. Utopian Schemes		

SOURCES: *a.* Deane Neubauer and Charles Cnudde, *Empirical Democratic Theory* (Chicago: Markham Publishing Co., 1969); *b.* Neal Riemer, *The Revival of Democratic Theory* (New York: Appleton-Century Crofts, 1962); *c.* Robert Dahl, *Preface to Democratic Theory* (Chicago: Univeristy of Chicago Press, 1964); *d.* Jack Lively, *Democracy* (New York: St. Martin's Press, 1975); *e.* J.R. Pennock, *Democratic Theory* (Princeton, N.J.: Princeton University Press, 1979); *f.* Martin Edelman, *Democratic Theories and the Constitution* (Albany: S.U.N.Y. Press, 1984); *g.* Henry Mayo, *Introduction to Democratic Theory* (New York: Oxford University Press, 1960).

greatly because scholars lack a common focus. (See Table 1). Characteristically they tend to concentrate on one or more of the following: (1) epistemology, (2) methodology, (3) politico-moral content, and (4) linkage between theory and practice. Existing disagreement as to the nature of democratic theory may be attributed to differences of opinion over the nature of democracy itself, lack of consensus as to how to analyze it, and interest in different facets of it. As a result, some democratic theorists adopt an epistemological or methodological approach to the study of democracy based on the distinction between the empirical and the normative; others focus on processes and traits such as power and motivation; still others use democratic theory as a vehicle for linking theory and practice. Together, these different orientations account for much of the diversity in recent theorizing about democracy. As a matter of definition, however, J. Fagg Foster, in typical neoinstitutional fashion, argues that democracy is not a particular institution but a kind of process that brings popular consent to fruition.[5] Following Foster's lead, evolutionary economists have employed a functional definition of democracy that views it as a process of decision-making not locked into a specific set of institutional configurations. As Foster also points out, this is a very important qualification or amendment to those definitions that mistakenly classify democracy as synonomous with capitalism in the West or with Communist rule in Eastern Europe. In neoinstitutional theory, most problems have no final, total, or absolute solution—only partial and relative ones. However, the problem with most utopias is that, by definition, their limits are difficult to specify and their potential costs unmeasurable. But this does not appear to hold true in the instrumentalist utopia of self-correction where the stress is on method rather than on adherence to a rigid blueprint for social reconstruction. Indeed, it is this commitment to a common method that unites the three designated groupings in the contemporary neoinstitutional movement. Experimentalism, science as method, democracy as method, the test of consequences—all these are ideas of instrumentalist derivation that are now part of the doctrinal weaponry of evolutionary economics.

The Neoinstitutional Democratic Perspective

The neoinstitutional democratic perspective is thoroughly instrumentalist in origins and outlook. Indeed, to explain it is to recapitulate John Dewey's political philosophy and the literature produced by his disciples who have developed his approach in ways useful to evolutionary economists.[6] Explicating the political philosophy of instrumentalism in its Deweyan and post-Deweyan forms must begin, however, with an examination of its basic assumptions. First, the neoinstitutional approach separates purposes from status conceived as hierarchy. As Holton Odegaard put it: "It is the situation, the problem, the conflict, the transaction that should provide the material and milieu for the rounding of purposes, not the extraneous authority of independently assumed status. A challenge to the authority of the democratic method by a pretending authority of static status, cannot be admitted."[7] Also, as a point of differentiation, the neoinstitutional theory of democracy involves acceptance of the virtue of change in the interest of progress. Indeed, it is primarily a process and a method for improving unsatisfactory situations. At its most sensitive, it is a form of experimentalism through which alternative ways of thinking and acting are tested.[8] In the eyes of the instrumentalist, democracy is not a formalistic ideology sanctioning certain institutions and election procedures; nor is it a rationale that legitimates a particular system of property relations. Rather, the essence of democracy consists of the view that there are few, if any, social structures that cannot be abandoned or altered, for all social institutions are subject both to the collective will and to the test of usage.[9]

As an approach to valuation, instrumentalism is a naturalistic theory that employs self-correction through judgment of consequences and effects. It is seriously at odds with those ethical and evaluative stances that are either anarchically relativistic or absolutist in nature. For example, the belief in the subjectivity of values that permeates conventional economics assumes an inaccessibility or isolation that privatizes all value criteria. The conclusion all too often drawn is that value is so subjective that when moral goods conflict, there are no standards by which they may be judged better or worse than one another. By contrast, in the neoinstitutional view, a method exists by which to demonstrate that some value criterion and choices are superior to others. Of course, this is the method of self-adjustment or self-correction that makes ends congruent with means and means congruent with ends along a means-ends continuum oriented toward human growth. The relevant consequences to be judged are those upon which successful growth is contingent. As Francis Myers once put it: "The instrumentalist assumption is itself one such theory which is tested by its consequences when acted upon. It is a program of action for which the evidence is not conclusive. Yet it is different in kind from other assumptions, since, as a plan of action, it seeks a conscious control of consequences by which it may be progressively tested and modified."[10]

What is perhaps unique about the neoinstitutional approach is its claim that there are not merely analogies to be drawn between democracy and science but that "the parallel breaks down because, if there is an experimental social science, it is democracy itself."[11] The instrumentalist aim is thus a "politics of truth"—a self-governing, self-correcting, experimental laboratory organized for the creation of truth—a merging of the social reformer with the social scientist.[12] Ultimately, the authority of method and adherence to a method of knowing, can occur only to the extent that individuals are part of a self-correcting method and only if they take part in controlling and extending the method.[13] Those using the method of self-correction recognize that the aim of knowledge is to locate and define the significant problem, in a given time and place, and to develop the solution for it. As Odegaard put it: "appreciation of the hard and unique facts in any situation and of how they are brought into being thus grows from 'authority of the situation' to responsibility to a perfecting method."[14]

John Dewey made his case for the development of democratic institutions and practices, from constitutionalism to frequent elections, by arguing that this kind of polity is analogous to a scientific community's means for productively exchanging ideas. Said Dewey: "The strongest point to be made in behalf of even such rudimentary political forms as democracy has already attended, popular voting, majority rule and so on, is that to some extent they involve a consultation and discussion which uncover social needs and troubles."[15] Or, in another formulation of the same idea, it is only "by extending the application of democratic methods, methods of consultation, persuasion, negotiation, communication, [and] co-operative intelligence" that we can guarantee the sort of social results that an understanding of natural science leads us to expect.[16]

This raises the issue of the role that compromise between conflicting interests must play if the method of self-correction is to function well. There is no reason to assume that the method can always solve a social problem by a mere readjustment of the existing claims of both sides. The present opposition to redistributionist policies and the extension of deliberate planning are examples of where compromise has failed. In addition, a commitment must also exist to the idea of a public interest based on an adequate conception of the general welfare that it is the function of the political system to seek out and implement. Yet as John Livingstone and Robert Thompson observe:

> the most striking characteristic of our actual politics is that the struggle for power is dominated by special-interest groups, each bent on advancing its own special claims; actual policies tend to be compromises of these partial and self-interested claims. Thus, while our generally accepted normative ideas about democracy require that public policies reflect the considered and public-spirited judgments of individual citizens, the actual policy-making process is more often simply a response to the organized pressures of interest groups. To approach the same issue from a different direction, we may also say that, whereas our inherited ideals call for rule by a majority whose opinions are the result of a rational debate of issues, our actual processes of public policy-making are more often the result of bargains negotiated among organized groups.[17]

It is, of course, the experimental method that makes possible the kind of reciprocal control between theory and practice that will facilitate a new perspective on social control. The important role that deliberate change in experimental science must continue to play is the assertion of social control.[18] Yet it may be perhaps anticipated that as participation within the planning venture becomes more widespread and more thorough, the authority of self-corrective procedure will become less an external restraint and more an organic, intrinsic part of the individuals involved.[19]

However, since democracy as a method is often likened to an experiment, it is well to recognize that in neoinstitutional theory it is not experts or elites alone who conduct the experiments and judge the results. Genuinely scientific experimentation requires all the points of view it can functionally absorb. As Francis Myers observes, "In the social sciences, particularly, it needs the perspectives, ideas and beliefs of all who are affected by the experiment, in addition to those of the experts who may be engaged in its direction."[20] Thus the method of self-correction searches for and adheres to public verification of its processes and consequences. In neoinstitutional theory, reconstruction in democracy involves a parallel reconstruction of social science that will be characterized by its merging of the structures of inquiry and politics.

The self-correction and self-criticism that is so vital to self government has not been part of reaching agreement except to a small degree, and then only for short periods in polities practicing free speech. Consequently, the universal utopia toward which all democratic government must ideally point is a utopia of self-correction. The utopia of self-correction, of course, is one that includes the selection and the continuous adjustment of both ends and means along a continuum of ends-means, oriented toward what Thorstein Veblen called the "generic ends" of the life process. What the neoinstitutional theory of democracy offers to social scientists and citizens alike is an approach that can be used to analyze particular political situations and point the way to policies that will facilitate human growth and development.

The Ends of Democracy: Proper Human Growth and Development

John Dewey popularized use of the term "instrumentalism" to mean a process of self-correcting value judgments in dealing with problematic situations.[21] This open-ended approach has been labeled "implemented aimlessness" or worse, but such criticisms overlook the actual ends that Dewey sought—ends that most neoinstitutionalists share. These ends are essentially those of proper human growth and development that a democratic polity must successfully promote if it is to be judged a success.

Whether human growth and development is understood as Dewey portrayed it,[22] as discussed by C. Wright Mills as "craftsmanship,"[23] or as Veblen's "idle curiosity," "workmanship" and "parental bent,"[24] there can be little doubt of its meaning for neoinstitutionalists. Its meaning, however, is part of a moral stance that is alien to the moral agnosticism of neoclassical economics. Consequently, those claims advanced in favor of a more egalitarian, participatory form of democracy are unlikely to impress critics not sharing the moral values of neoinstitutionalists or their views of what human growth and development should mean. In any case, such ends must be grasped in more detail, the obstacles in the way of their achievement better understood, and an evolving democratic theory developed that points to overcoming these barriers to growth. Fortunately, Dewey's writings on the theory and practice of education contain a detailed exposition of his ideas on human growth and development in a democracy. He tells us that "the educational process has no end beyond itself; it is its own end . . . the educational process is one of continual reorganizing, reconstructing, transforming. . . . Since in reality there is nothing to which growth is relative save more growth, there is nothing to which education is subordinate save more education."[25] Some of the critics of neoinstrumentalism suggest that such statements are so vague as to be virtually meaningless and that, in any case, Dewey's views are compatible with almost any form of social and political organization. At their own peril, they have ignored such comments as these: "The notion of 'organism' is thus used to give a philosophic sanction to class distinctions in social organization—a notion which in its educational application again means external dictation instead of growth."[26] It is evident, especially in Dewey's later writings, that he was opposed both to class distinctions and to any external dictation that had pernicious effects on human growth and development. His biases were implanted in the neoinstitutional theory of democracy that stressed both equality and spontaneity. But equality and spontaneity require legal and political sustenance if they are to assume institutional forms, and these forms have both procedural and substantive meaning that requires explanation.

The Means of Democracy

If democratic procedures consistently result in decisions contrary to those ordinarily thought desirable, how should the democrat react?[27] If, for example, the practice of due process of law thwarts proper human growth and development, what are we warranted in concluding? Perhaps substantive policy outputs are as important in evaluating the quality of government as procedural means. In any case, although they may be temporarily separated for analytic purposes, procedures and substantive policy outputs are part of a means-end relationship. As Henry Mayo put it:

> the means employed can seldom, if ever, be entirely divorced from the results which actually occur, or which are intended. Means and ends frequently, perhaps always, affect one another, and there is a prima facie case that a complex political system like democracy must have important influences upon the kind of substantive results obtained or aimed at. Concern over procedure is frequently concern over substance, because procedures so often determine the outcome.[28]

To illustrate Mayo's point further, how many would remain supporters of democracy for long if the processes of representative government consistently produced mass starvation, genocide or war? Obviously, means cannot be separated from ends, and if a particular means produces undesirable results, such procedures are undeserving of support. Of course, it can be argued that authoritarian means produce even worse results. On the basis of empirical and historical evidence there is much to be said for this view. Nevertheless, it cannot be taken for granted that due process of law and majority rule will necessarily produce satisfactory policy outputs. The answer to the dilemma seems to lie, however, in improvement of the available means, rather than in abandonment of them. It is to Dewey's analysis of how to accomplish this that we now turn.

The Democracy-Science Analog

Dewey's "method of intelligence" aims at making indeterminate situations into determinate ones; his version of the method of science thus focuses on social control through democratic institutions.[29] An integral part of this process is making self-adjusting or self-correcting value judgments in addressing problematic situations. This is not only the essence of scientific method as it is practiced in experimental laboratories by chemists and physicists, according to Dewey, it also is the method of democracy or, at least, it is most compatible with democratic institutions. Thus science and democracy are related to each other in that democratic institutions are most likely, in Dewey's view, to create an environment in which self-correcting value judgments can effectively address problematic situations. But is it true that democratic institutions and societies are more effective than authoritarian ones in addressing such situations when they arise?

It is clear that Dewey (and most neoinstitutionalists) believe that pluralistic political and social institutions possess a fluidity and openness that facilitates the use of the method of intelligence in resolving problematic situations. Charles Sanders Peirce saw clearly that the recognition of human intellectual limitations in itself supplies the maxim that should govern human behavior, and that maxim is "do not block the way of inquiry."[30] Extrapolating from Peirce and from the analysis provided by the democracy-science analog, Western institutions should be more productive of scientific achievement and progress than a less malleable and fluid institutional apparatus. The more pluralistic such institutions become, the more capable they will be of enhancing the process of developing self-correcting valuational systems to meet problematic situations.

If the science-democracy analog is correct, it is a potent argument both for buttressing representative government and for undermining authoritarianism. Of course, it is also true that autocratic and totalitarian regimes can harness science for their own ends. Freedom of inquiry may not flourish in such systems, but there is nothing irrational in the short run in their using science as an instrument to promote their own objectives. Nevertheless, the science-democracy analog is justifiably popular among neoinstitutionalists and is a bulwark of their criticisms of authoritarianism, whether the left or the right. It also provides a basis for rejecting both the moral agnosticism of neoclassical economists and the moral absolutism of fundamentalist Marxists. Its utility both in constructing an adequate theory of social value and in warding off prescriptive elitist attacks on democracy will become evident as we proceed.

The Problem of Democratic Publics:
Analysis and Prescription

A perennial problem facing democrats is that public opinion has difficulty forming and solidifying into politically effective vehicles. Perhaps the best early explanation of this was put forth by John Dewey in *The Public and Its Problems.* Dewey's notion of "public opinion" and "publics" is not always easy to distinguish from the "public" or the "public interest," but it is evident that he thinks the four are closely linked and that they are in a state of "eclipse." His ideas are as penetrating and as relevant today as they were when he wrote them in 1927:

> The ramification of issues before the public is so wide and intricate, the technical matters involved are so specialized, the details are so many and shifting, that the public cannot for any length of time identify and hold itself. It is not that there is no public, no large body of persons having a common interest in the consequences of social transactions. There is too much public, a public too diffused and scattered and too intricate in composition. And there are too many publics, for conjoint actions which have indirect, serious and enduring consequences are multitudinous beyond comparison, and each one of them crosses the others and generates its own group of persons especially affected with little to hold these different publics together in an integrated whole.[31]

Dewey was not as pessimistic about the emergence of publics from their eclipse as were some of his critics, such as C. Wright Mills. Perhaps that was because he did not use as high a standard to measure their performance, nor was he very specific. He did indicate, however, that: "the essential need . . . is the improvement of the methods and conditions of debate, discussion and persuasion. That is the problem of the public. We have asserted that this improvement depends essentially upon freeing and perfecting the processes of inquiry and of dissemination of their conclusions."[32] Unfortunately, Dewey did not provide his readers with a description of the political vehicle or technology by which to bring about such changes. Nor did he adequately discuss the means-ends problem, thus disregarding his usual advice to both utopian visionaries and conservatives. For example, he confidently maintains that "communication of the results of social inquiry is the same thing as the formation of public opinion."[33] He does not fully analyze the difficulties of communicating the findings of social inquiry or, for that matter, the fact that such inquiry itself may be seriously incomplete, scientifically deficient, or ideologically biased. Clearly, we can no longer share Dewey's confidence that social inquiry will soon become a part of public opinion or even that all of it should.

Dewey once stated the problem of publics in a series of interrogatives. He asked:

> What is the public? If there is a public, what are the obstacles in the way of its recognizing and articulating itself? Is the public a myth? . . . What, after all, is the public under present conditions? What are the reasons for its eclipse? What hinders it from finding and identifying itself? By what means shall its inchoate and amorphous estate be organized into effective

political action relevant to present social needs and opportunities? What has happened to the public in the century and a half since the theory of political democracy was urged with such assurance and hope?[34]

Dewey, then, intriguingly, claimed that "the problem of a democratically organized public is primarily and essentially an intellectual problem, in a degree to which the political affairs of prior ages offer no parallel."[35] This is not to suggest, however, that he was blind to considerations such as power and economic interest. Rather, he meant that publics that are functionally effective in performing their tasks must deal primarily with the problem of how to communicate ideas and organize people—a problem that is new insofar as it involves the utilization of abstract ideas and unprecedented numbers of people.

Dewey was aware of the political alienation and apathy that already existed in the United States in the 1920s. To overcome it, he argued that the "need is that the non-political forces organize themselves to transform existing political structures: that the divided and troubled publics integrate."[36] However, and this is important, he also warned that: "an inchoate public is capable of organization only when indirect consequences are perceived, and when it is possible to project agencies which order their occurrence. . . . It goes, then, without saying that agencies are not established which canalize the stream of social action and thereby regulate them. Hence, the publics are amorphous and unarticulated."[37] A contemporary version of Dewey's explanation of the eclipse of the public would stress dwindling participation in political affairs, both formal and informal; the manufacture of public opinion through paid professional public relations experts; the privileged access of corporations to the state apparatus and the media of communication; the spread of oligarchy within the bureaucracy of major political parties; the unparalleled increase in the number and kinds of leisure activities that function as diversions from political matters; and, of course, the increasing status and role of scientific-technical expertise in government planning. Although Dewey did not provide a solution to the problem of inadequately formed and communicatively ineffective publics, he renders a partial explanation requiring an update of why public opinion remains uncongealed and unfocused on many potentially important issues.

Consequently, it is to C. Wright Mills that we must turn for further and more recent insights and prescriptions. Mills dealt with the eclipse of public opinion by distinguishing between public and mass. He contended that while the United States was not altogether a mass society, it had never completely been a community of publics. Mills argued that at least four dimensions of the problem of public opinion must be recognized in order to grasp the difference between public and mass.

> There is first, the ratio of the givers of opinion to the receivers, which is the simplest way to state the social meaning of the formal media of mass communication. . . . The second dimension to which we must pay attention is the possibility of answering back an opinion to its realization in social action, the ease with which opinion is effective in the shaping of decisions of powerful consequence. . . . There is, finally, the degree to which institutional authority, with its sanctions and controls, penetrates the public. Here the problem is the degree to which the public has genuine autonomy from instituted authority.[38]

Mills then describes a genuine public and it is evident that he is endorsing its reemergence and its maturation as a precondition for a progressively evolving democratic society.

> In a public . . . (1) virtually as many people express opinions as receive them (2) public communications are so organized that there is a chance immediately and effectively to answer back any opinion expressed in public. Opinion formed by such discussion (3) readily finds an outlet in effective action, even against—if necessary—the prevailing system of authority. And (4) authoritative institutions do not penetrate the public, which is more or less autonomous in its operations. When these conditions prevail, we have the working model of a community of publics, and this model fits closely the several assumptions of classic democratic theories.[39]

Mills contrasts "mass" with "public" to the disadvantage, of course, of mass and warns that the United States has moved a long way in the direction of massification. As he puts it:

> The public and the mass may be most readily distinguished by their dominant modes of communication: in a community of publics, discussion is the ascendant means of communication, and the mass media, if they exist, simply enlarge and animate discussion, linking one primary public with the discussions of another. In a mass society, the dominant type of communication is the formal media, and the publics become mere media markets.[40]

Although this last sentence was written thirty years ago, it still accurately portrays aspects of the public opinion situation in the United States. Complete massification has not occurred, yet publics remain in a state of eclipse.[41] The conversion into commercialized media markets

of publics concerned with serious issues remains a serious problem for
those committed to the fulfillment of democratic values.

Prescriptive Elitism:
The Impossibility or Undesirability of Democracy

The traditional patterns of antidemocratic thought are not so visible
as they once were—no one, for example, takes facist theory seriously
any longer and orthodox Marxism-Leninism is largely recognized as
elitist when applied to Western industrial settings.[42] Although the attack on democratic theory has subsided in recent years in the English-
speaking world, this is because prescriptive elitism has been
transformed into different ideological structures that are not as easy to
identify as the more conventional patterns of antidemocratic thought.
Elitist critics of democracy rarely attack its main assumptions; instead,
they focus on how it works in "practice."[43]

However, rather than analyze the "revisionist" or "realist" interpretation that has been so popular among American political scientists in
the post-war period, I will focus on a group of prescriptive elitists with
whose work neoinstitutional economists are more familiar, namely,
certain of the public choice theorists who are also libertarians. Gordon
Tullock and James Buchanan, for example, theorize behind the cam-
ouflage of constitutional government, but do not subscribe to majoritarian democracy as that term is understood by democratic thinkers.[44]
In recent years their main ideological function has been to divert attention from issues regarding power and wealth to constitutional changes
requiring unanimity or near-unanimity that would prevent expenditures on social welfare measures. These constitutional changes would,
if implemented, largely vitiate majority rule and political equality
which, of course, is what Tullock and Buchanan wish to accomplish.[45]
Prescriptive elitism of this kind is still veiled by ideological forms that
whether intended or not, have the effect of mystifying social relations
by making them appear as "natural," rather than human contrivances.
All too often theories that claim to be "democratic" are phrased in
models and language subservient to the norms and values of the dominant classes. There are few better examples of this than the public
choice theories that take for granted the existing system of property relations and corporate power, while blaming trade unions, government
spending, and minimum wage policies for the plight of the underprivi-
leged and unemployed. Such theories are based on the view that politically potent publics should be discouraged from emerging since they

will demand interventionist policies of a collectivist nature, or, if they do emerge, they should be hamstrung through constitutional devices that make majority rule impossible.

Conclusion

Much of the previous discussion of neoinstitutional theory will strike the reader as politically unrealistic and as an exhibition of naiveté regarding the nature of American insitutions. It should be kept in mind, however, that the analysis is often cast according to how the system might be made to work under ideal conditions. No one seriously claims that Congress or the president habitually resort to Dewey's method of intelligence to solve the nation's problems. In conclusion, then, it is essential to inquire as to the actual state of democratic theory and practice in the United States. It would be pleasing to report that political scientists have evolved a democratic theory that is morally agreeable, behaviorally viable and supported by a consensus, but such is not the case. Indeed, much recent theorizing pessimistically focuses on the declining availability of natural resources, the dangers of environmental pollution, and the difficulty of attaining adequate degrees of socio-economic equality through sustained economic growth.[46]

While it is hard to identify unifying themes regarding the theory and practice of democracy, the ideological position of most democratic theorists has led them to the conclusion that "the cure for the ills of democracy is more democracy."[47] Consequently, it is commonplace for them to recommend that democracy be extended from the political to the economic realm. This is to be done in order to democratize both the workplace and the system of property relations it reflects, and to change the socio-economic base of the political order so as to enhance its egalitarian tendencies. However, at the present time, it is difficult to identify any existing political vehicle or technology in the United States moving in this direction, although in the European Economic Community, and certainly in the developing countries, social forces can be located that support such structural change.

Neoinstitutionalists have traditionally viewed democracy as both means and ends, that is, both as institutional procedures and as substantive policy outputs. It is no longer sufficient, if it ever was, to simply view it on a "lesser-evil" basis as a "protective" system that limits arbitrary power and prevents oppression, important as these are. It must now be seen as a system that is primarily justifiable on the grounds that (1) it most effectively implements the method-of-intelligence, that is, adjusts means-to-ends through a system of self-correcting valuation, and (2) it most efficiently enhances desirable kinds of human growth and development. The more social institutions are democratized, the more efficiently they will implement the method-of-intelligence and maximize human growth and development. As Marc Tool perceives it, "progressive change provides for the continuity of human life and non-invidious recreation of community life through the instrumental use of knowledge."[48]

The obstacles to further democratization of industrial societies, particularly our own, are many and complex, but neoinstitutionalists have stressed the interaction between vested interests and vested ideas as a key point of blockage.[49] However, the role of a neoinstitutional democratic theory need not be primarily negative; it should also aim at bringing democratic values to fruition. Support of a grounded idealism regarding both politics and culture must be combined with the traditional instrumentalist orientation if neoinstitutionalism is to adequately link theory and practice. In the past, evolutionary economists have stressed their own pragmatic roots so that the normative and prescriptive elements have played an underanalyzed role in their thought, yet this liberating strain also has a significant function to perform.

Even if a theoretical and political impasse exists in the age of Ronald Reagan, this should not inhibit articulation of the standards by which to measure an adequate theory of democracy. Fortunately, Michael Margolis has written that:

> a satisfactory theory of modern democracy would need to (1) devise ways for the elected legislature, the central institution of liberal democracy, to control the huge public bureaucracy; (2) limit the military's control of the budgetary resources and technical information that allow it to manipulate public policy in its favor; (3) limit or control the great concentrations of wealth, income, and employment opportunities found in the large private corporations; (4) devise ways to increase or redistribute society's resources so that traditionally underprivileged groups like racial minorities, women, and those of lower socio-economic status get sufficient shares to allow them opportunities to participate in politics with their compatriots on a substantially equal footing; (5) manage to achieve all of the above within the limits of natural resources available for development at reasonable economic and environmental cost.[50]

To accomplish all that Margolis suggests will be a difficult task, both in the theoretical and practical sense. Obviously, there is as yet no adequate post-liberal democratic theory or its equivalent in practice. However, an example of such a theory was Veblen's critique of political economy that exposed the pseudo-natural character of conventional economic categories by revealing the processes of exploitation and emulatory waste hidden under the ideological veil of the free labor contract and free consumer markets. The emancipatory thrust of such a critical theory can claim a moral and political legitimacy that dominant ideologies cannot, in that the latter represent nongeneralizable, that is, particularistic interests. It has been the traditional claim of democrats that democracy, more than any other kind of governmental system, enhances generalizable interests and ensures their triumph.[51] Unfortunately, the present polity exhibits an unwholesome dominance of corporate institutions and market values over democratic claims. Indeed, at times ideals of citizenship threaten to be reduced simply to those of material consumption, while the false harmony of interests promoted by consumerism goes unquestioned. Russell Hanson was correct when he wrote that even a democratic consumerism "can make no special moral claims for itself."[52]

Much of the democratic theorizing of the 1960s and early 1970s did not foresee the difficulties that lay in the way of achieving a more democratic society in the United States. For a neoinstitutional theory of democracy to become a stronger material force, it must, therefore, provide an adequate analysis of the extent of social domination which, once understood, will lead to the elimination of historically unnecessary forms of domination. In the past, economic growth enabled a consumer-oriented society to defeat rival moralistic interpretations of democracy by appealing to the general interest of all classes in maintaining a system that delivered more goods and services to more people. Nevertheless, even a "democratized consumerism," if such a state of affairs were really possible, faces the permanent challenge of a participatory democracy that strives to achieve generalizable interests by cultivating civic virtue. Unfortunately, the depoliticization process that has occurred in parts of the Western world, and certainly in the United States, has emptied much of the content of political life. This process has led to the ritualization of elections and their prolongation into a state of near-permanency. Also, there is evidence of both the iron law of oligarchy within bureaucratized political parties and the weakening of legislatures as the locus of political decision-making. The activities of security and intelligence-gathering organizations and their clandestine monitoring behavior appears ominous at times. The massive growth of a public opinion industry structured along the lines of corporate advertising provides still another obstacle to the democratization of the American polity.[53] Neoinstitutionalists may take little comfort from the prescription of both means and ends that cannot be implemented in a society where the political right and center are in command. The long-term democratization of American life awaits a political technology and vehicle not yet fully within view. But there are liberating forces at work. These forces include the scholar's development of critical truth claims that lay bare structures of exploitation and domination; they also require the articulation of emancipatory tactics and strategy that extend the boundaries of political argumentation to include new as well as existing oppositional groups. Finally, such discourse and organization must somehow be institutionalized through effective political action.

The problem of distorted and suppressed communication and its dissolution through a theory-guided democratic political action remain. But the development of a communication system linking together genuine publics can only be thwarted by illusions that the demonstrative force of argument alone will engage and convince the elites who presently control major social institutions. The reform of advanced industrial society in the West depends upon weakening the power of state and corporate bureaucracies through the formation and solidification of autonomous publics that can exercise countervailing power. The "colonized" public life criticized by C. Wright Mills is now accompanied by the depoliticization of class relationships and the growing anonymity of class domination.[54] The revival of genuinely democratic publics must therefore aim at exposing the existing relations of power and at the formation of political actions to overcome structures of domination.[55]

Notes

1. See J. Ronald Pennock, *Democratic Political Theory,* (Princeton, N.J.: Princeton University, 1979), xiii–xxii. Pennock breaks democratic theory into two categories, motivational theories and power theories. These theories lead to different conclusions regarding the need for and value of political participation. The motivational theories range from those that stress self-interest almost exclusively at one extreme, to those at the other extreme that stress civic virtue and commitment to the public interest as motives for participation. The power theories range from the constitutional elitist, which vests power in small groups and sanctions apathy and indifference on the part of the electorate, to constitutional populist theory, which assumes a maximum of popular participation so that power is distributed equally. Although Pennock's taxonomy of "democratic" theories is misleading as regards the nature of an authentic democratic theory, it is

nevertheless valuable in showing the great divergency of thinking about democracy by American social scientists.

2. It is unclear at this point whether the liberal position is based on (1) the conviction that no political technology or vehicle exists for a structural transformation, or (2) doubt as to whether a socialist economy could function with adequate efficiency, or (3) misgivings about the social equity of a cooperative commonwealth with different power and property relations.

3. The ideological and political diversity within the neoinstitutionalist camp tends to be ignored by neoinstitutionalists in formal analyses. This makes it even more difficult for a sympathetic and knowledgeable critic like Benjamin Ward to appraise the doctrinal structure of evolutionary economics and the ideological predilections of neoinstitutional economists. Ward writes that: "There is ambivalence in some institutionalist thought that is worthy of mention. The analyst who tends to picture a world of barriers inhibiting more satisfactory behavior may react in either a liberal or radical way. That is, the policy prescription may be either a series of modest changes or one big, revolutionary change. The analysis itself may not require dramatic alteration as a consequence of a shift in advocacy from one to the other policy." Benjamin Ward, *The Ideal Worlds of Economics* (New York: Basic Books, 1979), p. 465. Although Ward believes more institutionalists are political liberals than radicals, he recognizes that evolutionary economics has radical potential and political radicals in its ranks, which is the author's point in the text.

4. The recent inability of the members of the Association for Institutional Thought to agree on a policy statement regarding inflation is further evidence of internal divisions with the neoinstitutional movement. However, whether and how disagreement over inflation is related to the three groupings within evolutionary economics I have identified is another question.

5. Nevertheless, if pushed too far, Foster's definition of democracy as a type of process that incorporates the popular will threatens to sever structure from function. Indeed, it could inhibit adequate recognition of the relationship between particular institutional structures and their democratic or nondemocratic consequences. Clearly, there are types of political and legal institutions that render it impossible for democracy to function as a process that brings popular consent to fruition. Democratic structure and function, although not identical, are nonetheless causally related to each other—a point that Foster does not adequately emphasize. See his "The United States, Russia and Democracy," *Journal of Economic Issues,* 15 (December 1981): 975–80.

6. The most recent critical study of John Dewey's political philosophy is Timothy Vance Kaufman-Osborn, *John Dewey and the Politics of Method,* PhD. diss., (Princeton, 1982). Shorter critiques by Kaufman-Osborn are "Pragmatism, Policy Science and the State," *American Journal of Political Science,* 29 (November, 1985): 827–49, and "John Dewey and the Liberal Science of Community," *Journal of Politics,* 46 (November, 1984): 1142–65. Kaufman-Osborn claims Dewey's understanding of science as method leaves him unable to adequately cope with certain questions regarding the institutionalization of technological power. He also contends that his concept of the politics of social engineering is undemocratic and

that "Dewey's effort to advance a scientific conception of democratic politics involves a radical and largely unwelcome departure from more traditional understandings of the theory and practice of democracy." Kaufman-Osborn's work has important parallels with C. Wright Mills's interpretation of Dewey, but like Mills he exaggerates the deficiencies in Dewey's political philosophy.

7. Holton Odegaard, *The Politics of Truth* (University: University of Alabama Press, 1971), p. 139.
8. Ibid.
9. See Hans Joas, *G.H. Mead: A Contemporary Reexamination of His Thought,* trans. Raymond Meyer (Cambridge: The MIT Press, 1985), pp. 138–39.
10. Francis Myers, *The Warfare of Democratic Ideals* (Yellow Springs: The Antioch Press, 1956), p. 203.
11. Odegaard, *The Politics of Truth,* p. 40.
12. Ibid., p. 14.
13. Ibid., p. 289.
14. Ibid., p. 296.
15. John Dewey, *The Public and Its Problems* (Denver: Alan Swallow, 1954) p. 208.
16. John Dewey, *Freedom and Culture* (New York: G.P. Putnam's Sons, 1963) p. 175.
17. John C. Livingston and Robert G. Thompson, *The Consent of the Governed,* second edition (New York: The Macmillan Company, 1966), p. 10. The authors believe that what is ultimately required by the broker state is a convincing theory of social justice that is presently lacking in conventional pluralist theory.
18. Odegaard, *The Politics of Truth,* p. 76.
19. Ibid., p. 228.
20. Myers, *The Warfare of Democratic Ideals,* p. 224.
21. See John Dewey, *Theory of Valuation* (Chicago: University of Chicago Press, 1967), pp. 40–66.
22. See John Dewey, *Democracy and Education* (New York: The Free Press, 1966) and *Experience and Education* (New York: Collier Books, 1963).
23. C. Wright Mills, "On Intellectual Craftsmanship," in *Symposium on Sociological Theory,* ed. Llewellyn Gross (New York: Harper and Row, 1959) pp. 25–53.
24. See Thorstein Veblen, *The Theory of the Leisure Class* (New York: Mentor Books, 1953), and *The Instinct of Workmanship* (New York: W. W. Norton, 1960).
25. Dewey, *Democracy and Education,* pp. 50–51.
26. Ibid., p. 60.
27. On this issue, see the analysis by William Nelson, *On Justifying Democracy* (London: Routledge-Kegan Paul, 1980.).
28. Henry Mayo, *Introduction to Democratic Theory* (New York: Oxford University Press, 1960), p. 214. Mayo also comments that: "The initial doubt about the virtual neutrality of democracy which arises is this: can any system for political policy-making be strictly neutral or instrumental? In a purely technological sense, we say a tool is merely a tool and may be put

to any use, but even here, since some tools are more specialized than others, all tools cannot be put to all uses; and surely democracy, even if "merely a method," must be put in the category of instruments which can only be put to certain uses."

29. See John Dewey, *Logic: The Science of Inquiry* (New York: Henry Holt, 1938) pp. 104–5.

30. C.S. Peirce, "The Scientific Attitude and Fallibilism," in *Philosophical Writings of Peirce*, ed. Justus Buchler (New York: Dover Publications, 1955) p. 4.

31. John Dewey, *The Public and Its Problems*, p. 137.

32. Ibid., p. 208.

33. Ibid., p. 177.

34. Ibid., p. 123–26.

35. Ibid., p. 106.

36. Ibid., p. 124.

37. Ibid., p. 131. "We have said that consideration of this particular condition of the generation of democratic communities and an articulate democratic public carries us beyond the question of intellectual method into that of practical procedure." Ibid., p. 217.

38. C. Wright Mills, *The Power Elite* (New York: Oxford University Press, 1956) pp. 302–3. Also, see Rick Tilman, *C. Wright Mills: A Native Radical and His American Intellectual Roots* (University Park: Penn State Press, 1984).

39. Ibid., pp. 303–4.

40. Ibid., p. 304.

41. In this regard Mills also wrote that "at the opposite extreme, in a mass, (1) far fewer people express opinions than receive them; for the community of public becomes an abstract collection of individuals who receive impressions from the mass media, (2) the communications that prevail are so organized that it is difficult or impossible for the individual to answer back immediately or with any effect, (3) the realization of opinion in action is controlled by authorities who organize and control the channels of such action, (4) the mass has no autonomy from institutions; on the contrary, agents of authorized institutions penetrate this mass, reducing any autonomy it may have in the formation of opinion by discussion." Ibid.

42. It may be that many of the Marxist-Leninist states will eventually shed their police state trappings and monolithic party systems and evolve into genuinely pluralistic political systems. It is evident that some party-members and theoreticians in Eastern Europe believe such changes to be both necessary and inevitable. However, only the Soviet leadership ultimately can decide what the limits and pace of change in Eastern Europe will be. Until democratization occurs, conventional Marxist-Leninist theory and practice must be regarded as elitist.

43. See Henry Mayo, *Introduction to Democratic Theory*, p. 279.

44. Even so competent a political theorist as J. Roland Pennock includes in his taxonomy of democratic thought the work of Tullock and Buchanan. He fails to see that theories that are not majoritarian cannot legitimately be labeled "democratic" without stripping the term of most of its significance. The constitutional changes proposed by Tullock and Buchanan in

the *Calculus of Consent* are certainly compatible with limited government. But government subject to constitutional constraints requiring near unanimity is not democratic, particularly when these constraints aim at frustrating the enactment of social welfare and regulatory measures favored by the American electorate for the past fifty years. See Pennock, *Democratic Political Theory*, pp. 374–96.

45. See Conrad P. Waligorski, "Conservative Economist Critics of Democracy," *Social Science Journal*, 21 (April 1984): 99–116, and James Buchanan and Warren J. Samuels, "On Some Fundamental Issues in Political Economy: An Exchange of Correspondence," *Journal of Economics* 9 (March 1975): 15–38. "Freedom" for libertarians is of a primarily negative and class-restrictive sort and is focused on the right of property owners to dispose of their wealth and income as they choose. Libertarians are conspicuous by their absence from civil rights and civil liberties organizations. Libertarian use of the word "freedom" is primarily linked with support for those recognizable institutional forms of it which stress the free acquisition and disposal of wealth and income. Martin Edelman understated the case when he wrote that "a political theory which, for all its honorable and ancient linkage, cannot get beyond an essentially atomistic conception of political man is probably inadequate." Edelman, *Democratic Theories and the Constitution*, p. 297.

46. On these points see Michael Margolis, "Democracy: American Style," in *Democratic Theory and Practice*, ed. Graeme Duncan (London: Cambridge University Press, 1983) p. 129.

47. Dewey, *The Public and Its Problems*, p. 146.

48. See Marc Tool, "A Social Value Theory in Neoinstitutional Economics," *Journal of Economic Issues* 11 (December, 1977): 820–46, at p. 841.

49. J.M. Keynes once wrote "But, soon or late, it is ideas, not vested interests which are dangerous for good or evil." *The General Theory of Employment, Interest and Money* (London, 1936) p. 384.

50. Margolis, "Democracy: American Style," p. 130.

51. Presently, there is little market for utopian theories based upon a faith in the inherent goodness of man. Nor is American political life unduly infected with the Kantian categorical imperative. Nevertheless, it must be asked whether ultimately a democratic polity should judge itself successful by the extent to which it succeeds in institutionalizing universal ethical principles? Or should government even attempt to cultivate moral virtue as a deliberate end? It is possible that systematic efforts to do so would greatly strain or even rend the social fabric. Perhaps the most government can do is create an atmosphere where the citizens can cultivate moral virtue if they choose. If so, neoinstitutionalists can hope that the ethical principles the citizen invokes are compatible with the instrumentalist theory of valuation and appropriate forms of human growth and development. Regarding moral aspects of the latter, see Lawrence Kohlberg's *The Philosophy of Moral Development: Moral Stages and the Idea of Justice* (San Francisco: Harper and Row, 1981).

52. Russell L. Hanson, *The Democratic Imagination in America; Conversations with Our Past* (Princeton, N.J.: Princeton University Press, 1985), p. 258.

53. On these points, see the excellent study by John Keane, *Public Life and Late Capitalism* (Cambridge: Cambridge University Press, 1984) p. 248.
54. Ibid. p. 93.
55. Although C. B. MacPherson and Jurgen Habermas theorize in other doctrinal contexts and traditions than neoinstrumentalism, the former's idea of a "counter-extractive" democracy and the latter's theory of "pure communication" might play a fruitful role in further development of the democratic view.

About the Authors

Anne Mayhew is Professor and Chairperson, Department of Economics, University of Tennessee-Knoxville. Her work in economic history includes "A Reappraisal of the Causes of Farm Protest in the U.S., 1870–1900," *Journal of Economic History* (1972); "The First Economic Revolution as Fiction," *The Economic History Review* (1982); and "Ideology and the Great Depression: Monetary History Rewritten," *Journal of Economic Issues* (1983). Other *JEI* articles include "Ayresian Technology, Technological Reasoning, and Doomsday," (1981) and "Dangers in Using the Idea of Property Rights," (1985). She has published on economic anthropology in the *JEI*, in *Contributions to Asian Studies,* and in *Institutional Economics,* ed. John Adams (1980). She was President of the Association for Evolutionary Economics in 1986.

Philip Mirowski is Associate Professor of Economics at Tufts University. During 1987–1988 he was a Visiting Associate Professor at Yale University. He is the author of *The Birth of the Business Cycle* (1985), *Against Mechanism: Why Economics Needs Protection from Science* (1987), and, forthcoming from Cambridge University Press, *More Heat Than Light: Economics as Social Physics.* He is Editor of *The Reconstruction of Economic Theory* (1986) and is on the Editorial Board of *History of Political Economy* and *Social Concept.*

Hans E. Jensen is Professor of Economics at The University of Tennessee, Knoxville. He has served on the Editorial Board of the *Journal of Economic Issues* and on the Board of Directors of the Association for Evolutionary Economics. He has published articles on "The Social Economics of Alfred Marshall," *Review of Social Economy* (1987); "J.A. Schumpeter on Economic Sociology," *Eastern Economic Journal* (1985); "Some Aspects of the Social Economics of John Maynard Keynes," *International Journal of Social Economics* (1984); "J.M.

Keynes as a Marshallian," *Journal of Economic Issues* (1983); "Economics as Social Economics: The Views of the 'Founding Fathers'," *Review of Social Economy* (1977); and "Sources and Contours of Adam Smith's Conceptualized Reality in the *Wealth of Nations," Review of Social Economy* (1976).

Paul D. Bush is Professor of Economics at California State University, Fresno. During the 1950s, he studied under J. Fagg Foster at the University of Denver. His Ph.D. is from Claremont Graduate School in California. Professor Bush is a founding member of both the Association for Evolutionary Economics and the Association for Institutional Thought. He is a past president of the Association for Institutional Thought and was editor of its journal, *The Review of Institutional Thought.* He has also served on the Editorial Board of the *Journal of Economic Issues.* His work in institutional economics has focused on the methodological foundations of institutional analysis and the theory of institutional change. His articles have appeared in the *American Journal of Economics and Sociology, Economic Forum, Journal of Economic Issues,* and the *Review of Institutional Thought.*

Steven R. Hickerson is Associate Professor of Economics at Mankato State University in Minnesota. His other publications dealing with instrumental value theory have appeared in the *American Journal of Economics and Sociology, The International Journal of Social Economics,* and *Review of Social Economy.* Professor Hickerson's other areas of professional interest include law and economics and the history of economic thought.

Milton D. Lower is an economist at the Economic Policy Institute in Washington, D.C., the former Senior Economist of the House Committee on Energy and Commerce, and a former economics professor. His publications include reports for the United Steelworkers of America and for the Joint Economic Committee of the U.S. Congress. He has also published numerous other Congressional reports and academic publications. The major Congressional reports he has authored include, *Industrial Import Shock: Policy Challenge of the 1980s* (1985), and *The Energy Inflation Crisis* (1980). Representative academic publications include "The Industrial Economy and International Price Shocks," *Journal of Economic Issues* (1986); and "Evolution of the Institutionalist Theory of Consumption," in *Institutional Economics,* ed. John Adams (1980). Dr. Lower was a Foreign Area Fellow in 1963–1965, and has been the recipient of numerous academic honors. He was President of The Association for Evolutionary Economics in 1985.

Walter C. Neale, Professor of Economics and Chair, Asian Studies,

University of Tennessee-Knoxville, is the author of *Economic Change in Rural India* (1963); *India: the Search for Unity, Democracy & Progress* (1964 and 1976); *Monies in Societies* (1975); *The British Economy: Toward a Decent Society* (1980); and *Developing Rural India* (1987); and of many articles and chapters. He was president of the Association for Evolutionary Economics (1981), of the Society for Economic Anthropology (1984–1985), and of the South East Regional Conference of the Association for Asian Studies (1985–1986). A member of the MIT Team in India (1955–1956), he was also twice a Fulbright Fellow in India (1960–1961 and 1954–1955).

Vernon M. Briggs, Jr. is Professor of Labor Economics in the New York State School of Labor and Industrial Relations at Cornell University. Among the books he has authored or co-authored are *The Negro and Apprenticeship* (1967); *Chicanos and Rural Poverty* (1973); *The Chicano Worker* (1977); *Employment, Income and Welfare in the Rural South* (1977); *Apprenticeship Research: Emerging Findings and Future Trends* (1981); *Immigration Policy and the American Labor Force* (1984); *Public Service Employment in the Rural South* (1984); *The Internationalization of the U.S. Economy: Its Labor Market Implications,* (1986); and a college textbook entitled *Labor Economics: Employment, Wages, Trade Unionism and Public Policy.* He has been a member of the National Council on Employment Policy since 1977 and Chairman of the Council from 1985–1987.

Thomas R. DeGregori is Professor of Economics at the University of Houston. He has published numerous articles and books, the latest of which is *A Theory of Technology* (1985). He received his M.A. from the University of New Mexico, studying under David Hamilton, and his Ph.D. from the University of Texas at Austin, studying under Clarence Ayres and Wendell Gordon. He is a specialist in Technology and Economic Development, and has considerable experience as a lecturer and consultant in Africa, Asia, and Latin America. His current research interests include computer expert systems for technology transfer and the philosophy of a unified technology and human experience. He is currently editing a book on development and serves on the editorial board of *Technovation.*

Baldwin Ranson was Professor of Economics at Western State College of Colorado. His areas of professional interest extend from the history of economic thought, "Rival Economic Epistemologies: The Logics of Marx, Marshall, and Keynes," *Journal of Economic Issues* (1980), to the economic function of education, "Planning Education for Economic Progress," *Journal of Economic Issues* (1986). One of his achievements was to edit the papers of his former professor, John Fagg Foster, which appeared in the *Journal of Economic Issues* in December ·1981.

F. Gregory Hayden is Professor of Economics at the University of Nebraska-Lincoln. His recent articles in the *Journal of Economic Issues* include "Industrial Policy at the State Level in the United States" (1985); "Family Farmland Reserve: A State Government Program for Restructuring Farm Debt" (1986); and "Defining and Articulating Social Change Through the Social Fabric Matrix and System Digraph" (1986). He received the International Social Science Honor Society's Gold Key Award for his article, "Toward a Welfare Construct for Social Indicators" (1977). He was selected by the International Social Science Council (Paris) to participate in Project IDEA (Interdisciplinary Dimensions of Economic Analysis), a four-year (1984–1987) research effort, to explore the future of economics as an interdisciplinary science. Professor Hayden has held numerous policy research director, consulting, and advisory roles.

William H. Melody is Professor, Simon Fraser University, Canada. From 1985–1988 he is on leave as Director, Programme on Information and Communication Technologies, Economic and Social Research Council, United Kingdom. He is co-author of *Information and Communication Technologies* (1986); and *Culture, Communication and Dependency* (1981). He is author of "Telecommunication: Policy Directions for the Technology and Information Services," *Oxford Surveys in Information Technology* (1986); "Implications of the Information and Communication Technologies," *Policy Studies* (1985); "The Information Society," *Journal of Economic Issues* (1985). He is: Board Member, Confederation of Information Communication Industries, United Kingdom; Chairman, Communications Technology Section, International Association of Mass Communication Research; Past President, Transportation and Public Utilities Group, American Economics Association; advisor to government policy organizations, industry, universities and research centers in several countries; C.E. Ayres Visiting Scholar, Association for Evolutionary Economics, 1984.

Philip A. Klein is Professor of Economics at Pennsylvania State University. He is co-author of *Monitoring Growth Cycles in Market-Oriented Countries,* 1985; and author of *The Management of Market-Oriented Economies,* 1973; "Reinventing the Square Wheel: A Behavioral Assessment of Inflation," 1986; "Leading Indicators of Inflation in Market Economies," *International Journal of Forecasting* (1986); "Institutionalism and the New Classical Economics," *Journal of Economic Issues* (1986); and other publications in business cycles and institutional economics. His professional awards and assignments include: Fulbright Fellowship (France, 1963; Yugoslavia, 1970); Research Associate, Center for International Business Cycle Research, Columbia University; Adjunct Scholar, American Enterprise Institute; Award for Distinction in the Social Sciences (Penn State, 1981); Consultant to the United Nations (New York), the European Economic Commission (Brussels), the Organization for Economic Cooperation and Development (Paris), and the World Bank (Washington, D.C.).

Rick Tilman is Professor of Economics at the University of Nevada, Las Vegas. His two recent books are *C. Wright Mills: A Native Radical and His American Intellectual Roots* (1984) and *Thorstein Veblen: A Reference Guide* (1985). He has been a member of the Editorial Board of the *Journal of Economic Issues* and he has contributed to that Journal, as well as to *History of Political Economy, The Historian, Polity, American Journal of Economics and Sociology* and *Western Political Quarterly*. His paper, "The Intellectual Pedigree of C. Wright Mills: A Reappraisal," won the Pi Sigma Alpha Award, of the Western Political Science Association (1977). He presently teaches Economics and Public Administration.

Marc R. Tool is Emeritus Professor of Economics at California State University, Sacramento. He is the author of *The Discretionary Economy: A Normative Theory of Political Economy* (1979), and *Essays in Social Value Theory: A Neoinstitutionalist Contribution* (1986). He was the editor of *An Institutionalist Guide to Economics and Public Policy* (1984). He is a member of the executive board of the Association for Evolutionary Economics and past president of the Association for Institutional Thought. He has been editor of the *Journal of Economic Issues* since 1981.